THE
HAYMARKET
TRAGEDY

THE
HAYMARKET
TRAGEDY

PAUL AVRICH

PRINCETON UNIVERSITY PRESS, PRINCETON, N. J.

All Rights Reserved
Library of Congress Cataloging in Publication Data
will be found on the last printed page of this book
ISBN 0-691-04711-1
ISBN 0-691-00600-8 (pbk.)

This book has been composed in Linotron Trump
Clothbound editions of Princeton University Press books
are printed on acid-free paper, and binding materials
are chosen for strength and durability.
Paperbacks, although satisfactory for personal collections,
are not usually suitable for library rebinding

Printed in the United States of America by
Princeton University Press
Princeton, New Jersey

CONTENTS

ILLUSTRATIONS
(following page 278)

PREFACE

The Haymarket affair, a pivotal event in the history of both the anarchist and labor movements, began on May 3, 1886, when the Chicago police fired into a crowd of strikers at the McCormick Reaper Works, killing and wounding several men. The following evening, May 4, the anarchists held a protest meeting near Haymarket Square. Towards the end of the meeting, which had proceeded without incident, rain clouds suddenly appeared. The crowd began to disperse. The last speaker, Samuel Fielden, was concluding his address when a contingent of policemen marched in and ordered the meeting to be closed. Fielden objected that the gathering was peaceful; in any case, he was just finishing up. The police captain insisted. At that moment a bomb was thrown into the ranks of the police, inflicting severe injury. The officers responded by opening fire on the crowd, killing and wounding a number of civilians, as well as some of their own men. Sixty-seven policemen were hurt, eight of whom afterwards died.

Although the bombthrower was never apprehended, eight Chicago anarchists were brought to trial and convicted of murder. On November 11, 1887, after unsuccessful appeals to the Illinois Supreme Court and the United States Supreme Court, four of the anarchists were hanged. A fifth, Louis Lingg, committed suicide in his cell the day before the executions, and the others received long terms in prison. Six years later, in 1893, the three survivors were pardoned by Governor John Peter Altgeld, who, assailing the judge for conducting the trial with "malicious ferocity," found that the evidence did not show that any of the eight anarchists had been involved in the bombing.

The trial of the Chicago anarchists has been recognized as one of the most unjust in the annals of American jurisprudence. Like the Sacco-Vanzetti case of the 1920s, in which foreign-born anarchists were once again implicated, the Haymarket affair was the *cause célèbre* of American liberals and radicals of the 1880s, with international repercussions and dimensions. It became the focus for all the raging passions of the day, including radicalism, mass immigration, and labor activism. The culmination of a decade of strikes and agitation, Haymarket demonstrated, in more dramatic form than any other event of the post-Civil War era, both the inequities of American capitalism and the limitations of American justice. In addition, it marked the first "Red Scare" in American history, sparking a campaign of radical-baiting and repression that has rarely if ever been surpassed. Like the Dreyfus case in France, it was one of those episodes that divide a nation, arousing deep-seated emotions, defining loyalties, and spawning a literature of social criticism and protest. No other case of the period attracted more widespread attention. For it had a significance that made it symbolic of its time and place, elevating it to the level of genuine tragedy and revealing an aspect of American society that would not otherwise have been so nakedly and harshly exposed. So many forces were at work, so many issues and principles at stake, that for decades afterwards it continued to haunt the nation's conscience.

A century has now passed since the Haymarket tragedy, and it is time for a fresh appraisal of the case. Surprisingly, in view of the episode's importance in American history, there has been only one previous book-length assessment, Henry David's *History of the Haymarket Affair*, published in 1936. David's book, although a worthy achievement, is now nearly fifty years old. A great deal of new material has become available in the intervening decades, throwing significant light on the incident and its background. Recent monographs have explored the railroad strike of 1877, the activities of the Knights of Labor, and other pertinent aspects of American labor history. Biographies have been devoted to Albert Parsons, Lucy Parsons, Johann Most, and others who figured prominently in the affair. The memoirs of Dr. Ernst Schmidt, secretary of the Defense Committee for the arrested anarchists, have also appeared in print, and Bessie Pierce has published a multi-volume history of Chicago with a wealth of useful information.

Professor David, it might be noted, based his work mainly on printed sources, leaving rich archival materials untapped, notably the small but valuable collection of Albert Parsons, one of the principals in the case; the papers of Governors Oglesby and Altgeld, who held office during the conviction and the pardoning of the anarchists; and the papers of the chief prosecutor, Julius S. Grinnell, which have only recently been made available to interested scholars. My own object has been to provide an up-to-date narrative and analysis of the episode, based on the full range of sources and incorporating the findings of recent scholarship.

One might have thought that, after one hundred years, everything that was ever likely to be known about the case had already been disclosed, every speculation laid to rest, every clue pursued to its inevitable dead end. Such a view, however, would be mistaken. Although we still do not know for certain the actual name of the bombthrower, fresh evidence of a reliable and, I believe, convincing nature points in a quite specific direction, and will receive due attention below. Beyond this, a number of lesser mysteries can be at least partially cleared up. How, for example, did bombs get into Louis Lingg's cell a week before the execution? Did Lingg commit suicide, or was he murdered by the police? What was the precise nature of the casualties suffered by the police at the Haymarket, and who was responsible for them? An examination of sources previously neglected or unavailable will shed important light on these and other aspects of the case, among them the career of Rudolph Schnaubelt, accused by the police of throwing the fatal bomb, and the flight of Albert Parsons after the explosion.

Readers of Professor David's book will note that I have approached the subject of Haymarket from a different angle. As in my previous works on anarchism in the United States, *An American Anarchist* (1978) and *The Modern School Movement* (1980), the emphasis in the present volume is biographical. Although I have made every effort to present the essential facts of the case, my aim has been to relate not only what happened and why, but to whom and with what results—in human as well as historical terms. Focusing on individual men and women in actual situations, I have attempted to reconstruct the story around the lives of the anarchists themselves, their hopes and dreams and passions, their differing temperaments and points of view. Who were the Chicago anarchists? Where did they come from? Why did they become anarchists? What did they want? What did they achieve?

While I have not ignored the social and economic background of the case, I have done my best to prevent the chief personalities from being lost in a maze of tendencies and developments. At the same time, I have sought to evoke the elusive quality of atmosphere, without which no episode of history can be rendered real or plausible to those who have not themselves lived through it. My chief concern, however, has been with the human story—with the interest that adheres to men and women who have the courage to defy conventional standards of behavior and to withstand hardship and abuse for the sake of principles that they believe to be right. Anarchism, with its stress on individual freedom and self-reliance, has attracted more than its share of strong personalities who, in the face of persecution, remain faithful to their ideals.

The present volume centers on two such personalities, Albert Parsons and August Spies, about whom I have included a good deal of fresh biographical material, drawn from many hitherto unexamined sources. While concentrating on Parsons and Spies, however, I have not neglected the other characters in the drama. For one of the principal objects of this book has been to provide a detailed picture of the Chicago anarchist movement as a whole—individuals and groups, women and men, immigrants and natives—at a time when it was a rising and significant force.

Throughout the narrative, I have quoted extensively from the speeches and writings of the participants. I have done this not only because they spoke and wrote with passion, and sometimes with eloquence, but because their words can speak to the present generation, across the gulf of a century, with undiminished relevance. The struggle of the 1880s—the struggle for economic security, social justice, personal liberty, and freedom of expression—remains the struggle of today.

I should like to thank the many friends and colleagues who assisted me during the preparation of this volume. I owe a special debt of gratitude to Abraham Ascher, Richard Drinnon, James Joll, Blaine McKinley, Ahrne Thorne, and George Woodcock, without whose advice and encouragement this work could not have been completed. I am also indebted to John L. Thomas of Brown University and to Gail Filion and Marilyn Campbell of Princeton University Press for their valuable suggestions. In addition, O. William Neebe, William D. Parsons, Franz Joseph Schnaubelt, Henry R. Schnaubelt, Marc Schoenitzer, Mary Schwab, and Dr. Milton W. Thorpe were good enough to place at my disposal documents and information that could not be obtained elsewhere.

My thanks are due also to the staffs of the following libraries and institutions for their courteous and efficient help: the Austin Public

PREFACE

Library, the Bancroft Library of the University of California at Berkeley, the Barker Texas History Center of the University of Texas, the Baylor University Texas Collection, the Chicago Historical Society, the Columbia University Library, the University of Florida Library, the International Institute of Social History, the Knox College Archives, the Labadie Collection of the University of Michigan, the New York Public Library, the Newberry Library, the State Historical Society of Wisconsin, the Tamiment Library of New York University, the Texas State Library, and the Waco-McLennan County Library. I am also indebted to H. P. Kraus Rare Books and Manuscripts of New York for allowing me to examine the collection of Julius S. Grinnell, the prosecutor in the Haymarket case.

Finally, I am deeply grateful to the National Endowment for the Humanities and the American Council of Learned Societies for supporting my research. Needless to add, however, the sole responsibility for this volume is my own.

New York City   P.H.A.
November 11, 1983

Part I ‖ ALBERT PARSONS

1 ‖ AN AMERICAN BOYHOOD

Anarchism in the United States has often been dismissed as an alien phenomenon, a doctrine imported from Europe with few native roots or adherents. There was nothing alien, however, about the protagonist of our story. Of Puritan ancestry and southern upbringing, Albert Richard Parsons could hardly have been more American. The scion of a prominent New England family, he could trace his forebears to the earliest settlers of colonial Massachusetts. Five Parsons brothers, refugees from religious persecution in England, were passengers on the second voyage of the *Mayflower*, which landed in 1632 on the shores of Narragansett Bay. Over the next hundred and fifty years, Albert Parsons proudly noted, they and their descendants took "an active and useful part in all the social, religious, political, and revolutionary movements in America."[1]

The first of Albert Parsons's ancestors to achieve distinction was the Reverend Jonathan Parsons of Massachusetts. A graduate of Yale University and pastor of the Congregational church of Newburyport, he emerged as a kind of national patron saint, after whom Americans were typified abroad as "Brother Jonathan," a forerunner of "Uncle Sam." Jonathan Parsons, like his anarchist descendant, was a passionate and eloquent speaker. Employing the revivalist techniques of George Whitefield, the famous English evangelist, he toured the northeastern colonies, preaching to large and enthusiastic audiences. In June 1775 he created a sensation when he delivered an emotional harangue against British tyranny and raised a company of volunteers in the aisles of his church who fought in the battle of Bunker Hill.[2]

Brother Jonathan was only one of the Parsons clan to distinguish himself in the revolutionary struggle. His son, Samuel Holden Parsons, a graduate of Harvard, was a member of the Committees of Correspondence and one of the first rebel leaders to propose the convening of a Continental Congress. He rose to the rank of major general during the Revolutionary War. After assisting in the capture of Fort Ticonderoga, he fought in the battles of Long Island, Harlem

Heights, and White Plains, and served under General Washington in New Jersey. Then, placed in command of the Connecticut division of the Continental Army, he defeated the British at Norwalk. At the end of the war he became the first judge for the Northwest Territory, where he was drowned in 1789 when his canoe overturned in the rapids of the Big Beaver River.[3]

Another Samuel Parsons, Albert's great-great-granduncle, served as a captain in the revolutionary army and lost an arm at Bunker Hill. But it was after the major general that Albert's father, also Samuel Parsons, was named. Unfortunately, scant information about him has come down to us. That he was a Universalist and temperance reformer indicates that, in some measure at least, he shared his son's nonconformist tendencies. Otherwise little is known of his political beliefs, to say nothing of his background and social position. A native of Portland, Maine, he married into the Tompkins-Broadwell family of New Jersey and, in 1830, moved to Montgomery, Alabama, where he established a shoe and leather factory. It was here, on June 20, 1848, that Albert Parsons was born, the youngest of ten children.[4]

By the time Parsons came into the world, his father was one of the leading citizens of the community, a "public spirited, philanthropic man," who held the highest office in the temperance movement of Alabama.[5] Parsons's mother, the former Elizabeth Tompkins, was a woman of "great spirituality of character," as her son describes her. A devout Methodist, she came, like her husband, of pioneer American stock, her ancestors also having distinguished themselves in the War of Independence. A distant uncle, in fact, had been a trooper in General Washington's bodyguard, serving at Trenton, Brandywine, Monmouth, and Valley Forge.[6]

Parsons was always proud of the role played by his forebears in the Revolution. "My ancestors," he declared during the Haymarket trial, "had a hand in drawing up and maintaining the Declaration of Independence. My great great grand-uncle lost a hand at the battle of Bunker Hill. I had a great great grand-uncle with Washington at Brandywine, Monmouth, and Valley Forge."[7] That he himself had inherited their bravery and reforming passion would be demonstrated on many occasions during his lifetime. Little wonder, then, that he should have been characterized as a "Puritan fanatic in zeal, courage, and enthusiasm, spirituality, and tenacity of principle and purpose."[8]

4

Yet there was little in Parsons's early childhood that betokened his future radical career. His first years were spent in a comfortable and loving environment, and he might have followed in his father's footsteps, becoming a respected businessman, had tragedy not intervened. When he was barely two years old, his mother fell ill and died; and less than three years later his father followed. An orphan at five, Parsons went to live with his eldest brother, William Henry Parsons, a married man nearly twenty years his senior, who, after serving under Zachary Taylor in the Mexican War, had established himself in Tyler, Texas, as an attorney and the proprietor of the *Telegraph*, a local Democratic paper.[9]

Tyler, surrounded by unexplored hills and forests, offered Parsons—described by one resident as a "sprightly lad" and "splendid little fellow"[10]—a playground full of excitement and adventure. His stay was cut short, however, when William, in 1855, gave up the *Telegraph* and moved his family to Johnson County, deeper in the interior of the state. This gently rolling region, with its thick woods and winding streams, sat on the edge of the Texas frontier, where buffalo, antelope, and Indians were still common. The family, occupying a small ranch, remained there about three years before moving to Hill County and taking up a farm in the valley of the Brazos River, so remote from the nearest house that they could not hear the barking of their neighbor's dog or the crowing of his rooster.

Life on the frontier gave full scope to Parsons's venturesome character. In later years he would cherish the memories of his boyhood on the Texas range, where he acquired a love of nature and became an expert horseman and a crack shot with rifle and pistol. Like his years in Alabama, however, this idyllic period ended abruptly. In 1859, when Parsons was eleven, William, restless and tired of the farmer's life, moved his family to the town of Waco, where he resumed the practice of law and dabbled in business and real estate. On arriving in Waco, Parsons left his brother's household and moved in with his sister, Mrs. A. J. Byrd, who saw to it that he got some formal schooling.

A year later, when Parsons was twelve, his brother arranged for his apprenticeship on the *Galveston News*, the largest and most influential daily in the state. Parsons, apart from serving as a "printer's devil," became a carrier for the paper and quickly learned his way about town. In a matter of months, he tells us, he was transformed "from a frontier boy into a city civilian."[11]

Parsons's employer, Willard Richardson, was a leader of the pro-slavery movement in Texas. Born in Massachusetts but educated in South Carolina, Richardson was an unswerving disciple of John C. Calhoun and a strong advocate of states' rights, favoring secession to preserve the South from northern domination. Tall and spare, with a mop of greying hair, "Old Whitey" was as unfailingly courteous in his demeanor as he was forceful in expressing his opinions. He was the idol of every secessionist in the state, including Parsons's brother, for whom, as an owner of slaves, the chief issue between North and South was "the purity of blood and supremacy of a distinct race of Anglo-Saxons upon this continent."[12] William was therefore delighted when Richardson, in addition to accepting Parsons as an apprentice, took the boy into his home and treated him as a member of the family.

Parsons, as both ward and employee of Richardson, gained valuable knowledge of the profession that would occupy him in his adult life. With an alert and eager mind he picked up many of the subtler tricks of the journalist's trade and came to see how the printed word could be used to influence a wide public. In later years, when he edited socialist and anarchist publications, he would put the lessons he learned in Galveston to good use.

Parsons, however, did not remain long with the Richardsons. Barely a year after he started his apprenticeship, the War between the States erupted. The boy was seized by a thirst for adventure. Though small in size and only thirteen years old, he ran off to join a local company of Confederate volunteers known as the Lone Star Grays. That the future champion of freedom and equality should have fought on the side of the South is one of the ironies of history. Yet it is not so strange as it might seem. Although of old New England stock, he had been born in Alabama and raised in Texas, a southerner through and through. Everyone he knew, including his brother and employer, was a partisan of the Confederacy. Beyond this, he was driven by a craving for excitement that remained with him all of his life. Those were stirring times, he remembered, and "my young blood caught the infection."[13]

As a member of the Lone Star Grays, Parsons took part in only one engagement. Together with his company he boarded the steamer *Morgan* in the Gulf of Mexico and assisted in the capture of General David E. Twiggs, whose Union soldiers had evacuated their forts on the Texas frontier and were attempting to escape to the North. The whole episode was very brief—a mere "run-away" adventure, as Parsons described it.[14]

On returning to Galveston he received a "pulled ear" from Willard Richardson for having enlisted without his permission. Parsons, however, was undaunted. Having tasted the excitement of combat, he yearned to travel to Virginia and join the forces of General Robert E. Lee. Richardson admired the boy's courage, but, mindful of his size and age, scoffed at the idea. "It's all bluster anyway," he insisted. "It will be ended in the next sixty days, and I'll hold in my hat all the blood that's shed in this war."[15]

This merely convinced Parsons that he must not hesitate, that he must "go at once, before too late."[16] For a second time, therefore, he took French leave of his employer. He did not, however, make the trek to Virginia. Instead, he joined an artillery unit at nearby Sabine Pass, where he served as a powder monkey for the cannoneers and drilled with a company of infantry commanded by his brother, Captain Richard Parsons, who was to die at his post of yellow fever.

After twelve uneventful months at Sabine Pass, Parsons's term of enlistment expired. Still thirsting for action, he joined his brother William, now a Confederate general, who commanded a Texas cavalry brigade on the west bank of the Mississippi River.[17] Already an expert rider and marksman, Parsons became, in spite of his youth, a member of the McIngley Scouts, a unit of his brother's cavalry, and took part in a number of important engagements, from the defeat of General Curtis on the White River to the defeat of General Banks on the Red River, which ended the fighting west of the Mississippi.

Parsons served under his brother until the end of the war, fighting for the doomed cause of the slaveholding South. After the surrender of the Confederacy, he was mustered out of the army. Barely seventeen years old, he had left his childhood behind him. An "excellent scout," in his brother's estimation,[18] he had seen a good deal of action and matured quickly during his four years of service, acquiring a reputation for resourcefulness and courage that would cling to him for the rest of his life. The war had done its part in strengthening his character and in awakening him to the issues of the day. But, by interrupting his apprenticeship, it had left him at loose ends. What was he to do? What career might he follow? Too old to return to his work as a newsboy, he had neither the training to enter a skilled occupation nor the money to resume his education, his sole possession being an army mule. Finding no better alternative, he decided to return to Waco, where he had lived before the war.

On reaching his destination, young Parsons traded his mule for forty acres of corn standing ready for harvest. To help with the reaping, he hired some former slaves and paid them the first wages they had ever received. Parsons made enough on the sale of the corn to cover six-months' tuition at Waco (now Baylor) University, which was directed by Rufus C. Burleson, a well-known Baptist clergyman and educator. Apart from penmanship, composition, and declamation, he studied moral philosophy and political economy, the only higher education he ever got. At the end of the fall semester, he returned to the trade he knew best and worked at a Waco printing office, taking further courses at the university when time and money allowed. Besides this, being "bright and quick-witted," he was able, while on the job, to pick up "a good deal of general information on current topics."[19]

It is unfortunate that we should know so little of this critical period of Parsons's life. For it was during these postwar years that he set out on the path of social and political reform that would ultimately bring him to the scaffold. At first, he showed little sign of becoming a radical. Owing to his charm and good looks and to his family's prestige and connections, he was a popular figure among Waco's respectable citizens. Though small and slightly built, he was handsome, high-spirited, and impeccable in dress and grooming, with clear-cut features, fine dark eyes, straight black hair, and a dark mustache turned up at the ends. He was "a well-disposed, well-mannered young man," a Waco friend later recollected, "a little wild, as most of us were in those days—in fact, as wild as a buck; but I never heard of his doing anything desperate. He moved in the best society the place afforded, and his pleasant ways made him welcome wherever he went. He was not at all reckless or quarrelsome, but was as clean grit as any man that ever drew breath in Texas."[20]

Before long, however, Parsons struck out in a new direction that put an abrupt end to his popularity. After returning to civilian life, he found himself questioning the values and attitudes on which he had been reared. He could no longer accept the conventions—secession, slavery, white supremacy—which he had formerly taken for granted and for which he had risked his life on the side of the Confederacy. On the contrary, he was soon defending the principle of equal opportunity regardless of race or social background. And in

1867, at the youthful age of nineteen, he started a weekly called *The Spectator*, in which he advocated acceptance of the terms of surrender and supported the new constitutional amendments securing the civil and political rights of colored people.

Why had he adopted this course? According to his own testimony, he was following the example of General James Longstreet, one of the most distinguished officers in the Confederate army, who, at the conclusion of hostilities, had become a supporter of Reconstruction. Still more, he was influenced by his brother William, who himself had shed his secessionist beliefs and become a Radical Republican, espousing the cause of the liberated blacks. In addition, Parsons tells us, he had been moved by the memory of "old Aunt Esther," a former slave and house servant of his brother's family, who had raised him as an orphan "with great kindness and a mother's love."[21] By taking up the cause of her people, he was atoning, in some measure, for his service in behalf of the Confederacy, which he had come to regard as a mere adventure, an escapade of immature youth.

Perhaps, too, his months of study at Waco University, by stimulating him to think more deeply about social issues, had played a role in determining the course on which he was now embarked. To this must be added the injustices that he had witnessed since returning to Texas from the war. In spite of the defeat of the Confederacy, the position of the Negro had scarcely changed. "He was now a 'freeman,' " as Parsons noted, "without an inch of soil, a cent of money, a stitch of clothes or a morsel of food." Negro suffrage, moreover, was everywhere being obstructed, and blacks who demanded their rights were hounded and persecuted by white vigilantes. The Ku Klux Klan, active throughout the state, committed atrocities of every kind against black men and women, including robberies, murders, and lynchings.[22]

It was to speak out against such injustices that Parsons launched his paper, *The Spectator*, during the sharpest period of the Reconstruction struggle in Texas. Like his brother, moreover, he went into politics, joining the Radical Republicans and obtaining a post in the district clerk's office at Waco, the first of a series of political jobs which he would hold in the ensuing years. During election campaigns, he took to the stump and encouraged the freedmen to exercise their newly won franchise. Traveling in the company of "one or two intelligent colored men," he addressed meetings throughout central Texas in an effort to get out the black vote and to persuade the whites to accept blacks as equal citizens. Speaking, for instance, in the community of Marlin, some twenty-five miles southeast of Waco, he told a crowd of a thousand, gathered around the local courthouse, that the Negro was no longer subject to any master and was entitled to work for his own benefit and to vote as he saw fit.[23]

This was the first opportunity for Parsons to develop the oratorical skills that he would so often be called on to display in later life. An intense figure on the platform, with his jet-black hair and flowing mustache, he spoke in a resonant tenor voice and with a manifest sincerity that held the attention even of listeners who thoroughly disagreed with what he was saying. Young as he was, Parsons became widely known as a champion of the Negro cause, a "rank abolitionist," to quote his own description, who felt a moral duty to assist those "powerless to defend themselves." As a result, he afterwards noted, "the enfranchised slaves over a large section of the country came to know and idolize me as a friend and defender."[24]

At the same time, however, he incurred the hatred of conservative whites, who branded him a "scalawag" and traitor. No longer was he welcome in Waco society. Many of his old friends and army comrades stopped speaking to him. His daily life, he tells us, was laden with danger. He was, in separate instances, beaten, shot in the leg, kicked down a flight of stairs, and threatened with horse-whipping and lynching. A Waco newspaper denounced him as a "violent agitator, affiliated with the worst class of negroes" and "ever ready to stir them up to strife."[25]

None of this daunted Parsons. On the contrary, he redoubled his efforts to obtain a just place for the Negro in Texas society. When District Judge J. W. Oliver, a fellow partisan of Reconstruction, was impeached as a lunatic and locked up in a Waco prison, Parsons, in the manner of John Brown, raised a band of blacks to free him, but was forced to retreat when confronted with a heavily-armed group of whites.[26] Actions such as this further alienated Parsons from his neighbors. His paper, *The Spectator*, languished and expired. By then— the year was 1868—the atmosphere in Waco had grown too hostile for his safety. Scorned as an apostate, ostracized as a heretic, he made up his mind to depart.

Parsons, as he had done in the past, turned to his brother for assistance. William, now the publisher of the *Houston Telegraph*, placed him on his staff as traveling correspondent and subscription agent.

In 1869, according to Parsons, his job took him on a long trip on horseback through northwestern Texas, during which he encountered the "charming young Spanish Indian maiden" whom he would make his wife. She was living, says Parsons, on her uncle's ranch in Johnson County, where he himself had lived as a boy with his brother's family. Impressed by her beauty and intelligence, he tells us, he lingered awhile in the neighborhood before continuing his journey. Three years later he returned to marry her.[27]

Such at least is Parsons's account of how he discovered his bride. Yet the truth remains shrouded in mystery. Little is known of Lucy Parsons's ancestry or early life. She herself insisted—a story supported by her husband—that she was of Mexican and Indian extraction, with no Negro blood in her veins. She claimed to be the daughter of Marie del Gather, a Mexican woman, and of John Waller, a "civilized" Creek Indian. Orphaned at the age of three, she said, she was taken in by her mother's brother, Henry del Gather, a Mexican rancher and farmer living near Buffalo Creek in Johnson County, where Parsons met her.[28]

Lucy took special pride in her Indian heritage. "I am one whose ancestors are indigenous to the soil of America," she told an audience of London socialists a year after her husband's death. "When Columbus first came in sight of the Western Continent, my father's ancestors were there to give them a native greeting. When the conquering hosts of Cortez moved upon Mexico, my mother's ancestors were there to repulse the invader; so that I represent the genuine American."[29]

Yet there is reason to question this statement. Newspapers both in Waco and in Chicago, where Lucy was to spend the greater part of her life, describe her as a Negro or mulatto; and photographs of her clearly indicate a black or partly black ancestry. "Mrs. Parsons," noted the *Chicago Tribune* during the trial of her husband, "objects to the term 'colored,' as signifying that she has negro blood in her veins. She says her mother was a Mexican and her father an Indian. But she is decidedly colored, just the same, and any ordinary observer would conclude that at least one of her parents was a negro."[30]

It is possible, of course, that Lucy was of mixed racial origin, with Mexican and Indian as well as African roots. According to William Parsons, she spoke fluent Spanish, and on different occasions she gave her maiden name as "Diaz" and "Gonzalez." Elsewhere, however, it is listed as "Carter" and "Hull." Her middle name, too, is uncertain. Most sources give it as "Eldine," but it appears as "Ella" on her daughter's birth certificate and her own death certificate, further compounding the mystery.[31]

What then is the truth about Lucy's origins? Her biographer, Carolyn Ashbaugh, has concluded that she was born a Negro slave in Texas, and that John Waller, the Creek Indian, and Marie del Gather, his Mexican spouse, are fictitious, as is Lucy's uncle, Henry del Gather. Moreover, before she met Parsons (probably in Waco, where he was known and trusted among blacks) she had been living with a former slave named Oliver Gathings (hence the fictitious name "del Gather") and, like Gathings, was probably a former slave of the wealthy Gathings brothers, James and Philip, of Hill County, who owned sixty-two slaves before the emancipation. Philip Gathings had a daughter named Lucy, born in 1849, and it is possible, as Carolyn Ashbaugh suggests, that a slave girl born four years later, as was Lucy Parsons, would have been named after the master's child.[32]

There is uncertainty, furthermore, about the place and date of Lucy and Albert's marriage. Both bride and groom maintained that they were married in Austin in 1872, as does William Parsons, who insists that the wedding was "a matter of public record in that city," adding that Lucy's claim to Spanish and Indian ancestry was "never questioned," else Texas laws against miscegenation would have prevented the union from taking place.[33] Other sources, however, give the year as 1871,[34] while Lucie C. Price, an Austin historian, could find no record at all of a marriage license being issued to the Parsons couple, or of a notary public named Owsley, who, according to Lucy Parsons, performed the ceremony.[35]

Yet, whether or not Lucy and Albert were legally married, theirs was an inseparable union. Deeply and passionately in love, they remained devoted to each other until the end. Lucy, moreover, became not only Albert's spouse but also his political associate. "In all my labors for the up-lifting and emancipation of the wage-worker," Parsons afterwards asserted, "I have had the earnest, honest, intelligent, unflagging support of that grandest, noblest, bravest of women— my wife."[36] Lucy, apart from assisting her husband in his various endeavors, emerged as an important figure in her own right. Tall, slender, well-built, with high cheekbones, dark eyes, and wavy black hair, she cut an attractive figure at radical meetings, speaking in a melodious, low-pitched voice with an intensity which matched that of her husband.[37]

Whatever their differences in background, Lucy and Albert had much in common. Both were vivid personalities, utterly devoted to their ideals. Both, possessed of physical and moral courage, defended the rights of women and workers as well as of ethnic and racial minorities—blacks among them, despite Lucy's efforts to conceal her own Negro origins.[38] As for Albert, we may assume that his commitment to racial equality, already conspicuous during the immediate postwar years, was reinforced by his marriage to a black woman and former slave. For the rest of his life he continued to uphold the rights of colored people, both in the South and in the North, although his sympathy for blacks would be extended to other disadvantaged elements of American society, above all to labor, immigrants, and the unemployed. His Radical Republicanism, in other words, was but a step on the road to socialism and anarchism.

Parsons, shortly after meeting Lucy, relinquished his job on the *Houston Telegraph* and took up a succession of political posts. In 1870, at twenty-one years of age, he was appointed assistant assessor of United States Revenue under President Grant's administration. Moving to Austin the following year, he was elected secretary of the Republican-dominated Texas senate, of which his brother William was a member. Soon after, while retaining his position in the senate, he was appointed chief deputy collector of United States Revenue, impressing his superior, Walter Cox, as "an excellent clerk and perfectly trustworthy."[39] For several months, moreover, he worked in the Texas Office of Public Instruction and served as an officer in the state militia, protecting black citizens against white persecution and harassment.

Matters altered, however, when the Democrats, in January 1873, regained control of the Texas legislature, restoring power to the old aristocracy and ending the Reconstruction government in the state. Parsons, as a result, lost his secretaryship in the senate. To supplement his income, he became a traveling correspondent for a number of Texas newspapers, and, in August 1873, representing the Austin-based *Texas Agriculturist*, joined a group of editors who, as guests of the Missouri, Kansas & Texas Railway, toured a large section of the country, including parts of Illinois, Ohio, and Pennsylvania. It was Parsons's first journey to the North, and it changed the direction of his life. For it was during this trip that he decided to move to Chicago.

Parsons, apparently, had been contemplating such a step for some time. His outspoken stand for Negro rights, his service with the Radical Republicans, and his liaison with a woman of black extraction had made him an unwelcome figure in Texas. "He was practically a political exile," as his brother remarked. "He had either to fight every day or leave."[40] In the North, Parsons reasoned, a mixed couple of advanced political views might expect to find a more congenial environment. Accordingly, in the midst of his journey, he resigned his position with the revenue service and sent word to Lucy to join him in Philadelphia, from which they would travel together to Chicago.[41]

Parsons was never to return to Texas. Yet he had profited greatly from the years he had spent there. Not only had he gained invaluable experience with which to meet the challenges that lay before him, but the events in which he had participated had gone far to shape his attitudes and values. Already conspicuous, for example, was his tendency to champion the underdog and to embrace unpopular causes and movements. Schooled in the turbulence of Reconstruction politics, Parsons would enter Chicago not as an ignorant country bumpkin but as a seasoned propagandist and reformer. In Chicago, as in Texas, he would find a fertile field for the exercise of his journalistic and oratorical talents. A new chapter in his life was about to open. He had started upon the road to Haymarket.

2 || Labor Agitator

Albert and Lucy Parsons arrived in Chicago around the end of 1873. Only two years before, the city had been sent reeling by the great fire of 1871, leaving tens of thousands homeless and destroying millions of dollars' worth of property. Yet, catastrophe though it was, the fire stimulated a development even more spectacular than the previous decades had witnessed, so that Chicago, within a few years, became the financial and industrial capital of the Middle West and the third largest city in the country. In some branches of industry it already led the nation—in farm machinery and packing plants, in lumberyards and sawmills. More than twenty railroads reached out in every direction, while each week hundreds of steam and sail boats arrived and departed over the Great Lakes, bringing the city a rapidly growing, cosmopolitan population, nearly half a million strong by 1873, of whom a fifth were Germans, and with Irish, Scandinavians, and Bohemians (Czechs) represented in large numbers.

Like every great city, Chicago presented a study in contrasts. Magnificent, throbbing metropolis, exuberant with breakneck growth, it was at the same time the focus of ethnic conflict, labor ferment, and police repression. For its expanding working-class population, the cyclical nature of the economy, combined with the abundance of cheap labor and the seasonal character of many jobs, made destitution and unemployment virtually "a way of life."[1] By 1873 slums and tenements were as conspicuous a feature of the city's landscape as its stately boulevards and mansions. Side by side with luxury and splendor existed poverty and distress.

To more than a few visitors, the great, garish city, with its extremes of wealth and want, embodied all that was hateful and ugly in postbellum capitalist civilization. Not so, however, for Lucy and Albert Parsons. After the abuse that they had suffered in Texas, Chicago seemed a haven of opportunity, and they entered it with "animation and hope."[2] Parsons joined Typographical Union No. 16 and soon found work in his old craft, subbing on the *Inter Ocean* before becoming a regular typesetter for the *Times*. Prospects for the couple appeared bright.

Parsons, in finding steady employment, was more fortunate than many other recent arrivals. For, a few months earlier, the panic of 1873 had struck, plunging the country into the worst depression that it had yet experienced. The next six years were among the most difficult in the history of American labor. Hundreds of thousands of men were thrown out of work, while those who, like Parsons, managed to cling to their jobs were subjected to periodic wage reductions. These reductions provoked a spate of desperate strikes, but nearly all of them failed because there were "ten pairs of hands ready and willing to take the place of every single pair that quit work."[3]

The depression continued until 1879, causing unprecedented hardship throughout the nation. Tens of thousands went hungry. Cities like Chicago recorded a rising number of deaths from starvation, not only of single individuals but of whole families. Homeless men and women wandered the streets, seeking shelter in hallways, sleeping on park benches, and lining up daily before the soup kitchens established in working-class neighborhoods. Year after year the depression worsened. By 1877, according to some accounts, the number of unemployed had risen to nearly three million—in a nation of forty-five million people. As many as fifteen million, moreover, were living at the poverty level. Legions of tramps, for whom the *Chicago Tribune* prescribed "a little strychnine or arsenic,"[4] drifted across the country in search of work and shelter.

The depression of the 1870s marked the birth of a militant labor movement in the United States. Hunger parades and mass meetings took place all over the country. For the first time the "army of the unemployed" appeared in force. In New York a "Committee of Safety"—a name, Samuel Gompers noted, borrowed from "the dreaded specter-conjuring agency of the French Revolution"[5]—was formed in December 1873 to lead demonstrations which culminated, on January 13, 1874, in a great open-air meeting at Tompkins Square. When a young German socialist named Justus Schwab unfurled the red flag of the Commune, the bloody Paris rising of 1871, a body of policemen, mounted and on foot, moved in and arrested him. Schwab was dragged off to prison, singing the "Marseillaise" at the top of his lungs. Then, according to an eyewitness, the police charged into the crowd, "indiscriminately swinging their clubs and hitting out at everyone within reach," including women and children, who were "ridden down as they fled in panic."[6] Caught in the melee, Gompers, the future leader of the American Federation of Labor, escaped harm by jumping down a cellarway, but many were injured and arrested before the crowd was dispersed. Newspapers denounced the "rabble" who brandished the red flag in public places, and praised the police for breaking up the "American Commune."[7]

In Chicago, meanwhile, similar developments were unfolding. The city had barely recovered from the great fire when the depression plunged it into renewed turmoil. Thousands of men who had poured in to help rebuild the city were suddenly thrown out of work. Of the 25,000 arrests made by the Chicago police during 1874, the bulk were of jobless laborers and artisans.[8] Detectives were placed at the depots to turn away additional job-hunters and "vagrants." Newspapers issued a warning: mobs of unemployed workers, thrown together by the crisis, could ignite a conflagration more terrible than that of 1871.

In December 1873, about the time that Parsons and his wife arrived from Texas, Chicago witnessed the first of a series of demonstrations by the unemployed—"bread riots," the papers called them—in which throngs of workers paraded through the streets. On December 21 labor organizations in the city arranged a mass meeting in which some five thousand persons took part. It was the largest such assembly Chicago had ever seen. Speeches were delivered in five languages, and a committee was formed to appeal to the city for relief. The next day, at the head of nearly twenty thousand unemployed workers, the committee marched on city hall to demand "bread for the needy, clothing for the naked, and houses for the homeless." Placards bore such messages as "Workers of All Lands, Unite!" "Unity Gives Strength," "Work or Bread," and "Death to Destitution."[9]

Although the city council refused to act, the mayor persuaded the Chicago Relief and Aid Society to release part of a fund that had been collected for victims of the 1871 fire. But the amount provided was inadequate to meet the need—fewer than ten thousand families received assistance, only a fraction of those in desperate straits— and the Relief and Aid Society itself became a target of the protesters, who accused its executive board, on which sat George Pullman, Marshall Field, and other leading businessmen, of investing the relief money in their own enterprises instead of distributing it to the poor.

Protests against the Relief and Aid Society continued sporadically for several years, in the teeth of severe repression. Demonstration after demonstration witnessed attacks by the police upon the elementary rights of workers to assemble and protest. Protesters, on one occasion, were trapped in the LaSalle Street Tunnel and savagely beaten with clubs.[10] Meanwhile the rhetoric of violence mounted. In June 1875 a mass meeting in the Bohemian Turner Hall heard John Simmens, a socialist militant, warn that a "proletarian revolution" would erupt if the "ruling classes" continued to "suffocate the labor movement."[11] In November of that year, according to the *Chicago Tribune*, there was talk in radical circles of burning down the city. The *Tribune*, blaming the trouble on foreign-born agitators, issued a prophetic warning: "If the communists in this country are counting on the looseness of our police system and the tendency to proceed against criminals by due process of law, and hope on that account to receive more leniency than in Europe, they have ignored some of the most significant episodes in American history. There is no people so prone as the American to take the law into their own hands when the sanctity of human life is threatened and the rights of property invaded in a manner that cannot be adequately reached and punished by the tortuous course of the law. Judge Lynch is an American by birth and character. The Vigilance Committee is a peculiarly American institution. . . . Every lamp-post in Chicago will be decorated with a communistic carcass if necessary to prevent wholesale incendiarism or prevent any attempt at it."[12]

It was during this ferment of the 1870s that Parsons, destined to blaze into prominence a few years later, first became interested in the labor question. Freshly arrived from Texas, where he had witnessed the persecution of the blacks, he now was moved by the sufferings of the unemployed. He observed the effects of the depression on the workers: the misery, the hunger, the protests, the police clubbings, the denial of free speech and assembly. His rebellious spirit was aroused; and when the protestors charged that relief funds were being diverted for private gain, he decided to look into the matter. The complaints, he soon discovered, were justified. He was incensed that the Chicago newspapers, dominated by business interests, should label the demonstrators "communists" and "loafers." Recalling his experience in Texas, he found "a great similarity between the abuse heaped upon these poor people by the organs of the rich and the actions of the late Southern slave holders . . . toward the newly enfranchised slaves, whom they accused of wanting to make their former masters 'divide' by giving them 'forty acres and a mule.' "[13]

Parsons carried the analogy a step further. The Civil War, he reasoned, had destroyed Negro slavery and the slaveholding class only to see industrial capitalism create a new kind of slavery and a new set of masters, as arrogant and brutal as any southern planters. Chattel slavery had been replaced by wage slavery, and the difference was merely "one of form." "The substance," wrote Parsons, "remains the same: the capitalist in the former system owned the laborer, and hence his product, while under the latter he owns his labor product, and hence the person of the wage-laborer." For Parsons the parallel between chattel and wage slavery was too compelling to be ignored. He returned to it again and again. The workers, he said, no longer had a bankrupt cotton aristocracy lording it over them, but a new class of industrial robber barons, who tied them to machines in the factories and smothered them to death in the mines. There was, Parsons concluded, "a great fundamental wrong at work in society, in existing social and industrial arrangements."[14]

The comparison between chattel and wage slavery was by no means original with Parsons. It had been a component of labor rhetoric as far back as the 1830s and 1840s. Yet it came to him as something of a revelation, illuminating the role of economics in human relationships. As he remarked, referring to his postwar years in Texas: "I then believed that the colored people were truly free men, and that they needed only courage to assert it. But I did not then understand or know that economic dependence—*i.e.*, industrial servitude—made political liberty impossible. I did not know, nor did the blacks, that they had been merely emancipated from chattel to wage servitude. I did not then know that economic freedom must be the basis for political liberty, and that the wage labor system created classes, antagonisms, and class servitude. And now, as the helots of old, the so-called 'free' blacks, in common with their white brethren, work and die like beasts in the unceasing treadmill of wage slavery."[15]

Parsons, without yet being aware of it, had become a socialist. Aroused by the plight of the workers following the panic of 1873, he had extended his radicalism from the race issue to the "social question" as a whole. Slavery, he had come to believe, was no matter

19

of mere color. It had an economic basis and demanded an economic solution. From this point on, he focused his attention on the working class, of which he himself, as a printer, was now a member. The labor question came to dominate his thoughts. Before long, moreover, it brought him into contact with local socialists. Though few in number, Parsons tells us, they were "the only people who at that time had made any protest against, or offered any remedy for, the enforced poverty of the wealth producers and its collateral evils of ignorance, intemperance, crime and misery."[16] Eager to learn more, he read what little socialist literature he could lay his hands on, including *The Communist Manifesto* of Marx and Engels. The more he studied, the more engrossed he became with socialist doctrines, and the more he yearned to involve himself in the movement they had inspired.

His opportunity to do so came in March 1876. At that time he attended a meeting arranged by the Social Democratic Working-Men's Party of North America, founded two years before in response to the deepening depression. The principal speaker was Peter J. McGuire, an articulate young agitator from New York and a member of the now defunct Committee of Safety which had organized the Tompkins Square protest. A wood-joiner by trade and a member of the Social Democratic executive board, McGuire would achieve distinction as a founder of the United Brotherhood of Carpenters and Joiners and, along with Gompers, of the American Federation of Labor. Now addressing his audience at the Vorwaerts Turner Hall on West 12th Street, he outlined the program of his party, which called for the abolition of capitalism and its replacement by a socialist commonwealth. At the end of his speech, McGuire announced his intention of forming an English section of the party in Chicago, and he invited all who were interested in joining to hand in their names and addresses as they left the hall. Parsons, together with George A. Schilling and Thomas J. Morgan, future stalwarts in the Chicago labor movement, was among the first to sign up.[17]

The next day, a Sunday, McGuire addressed another meeting at the old Globe Hall on Desplaines Street. When he finished speaking, he called for questions from the audience. In response, recalled George Schilling, a "well-dressed man with a clear accent" rose and asked whether, in the cooperative society outlined by the speaker, all persons were to receive equal incomes regardless of the amount they produced. The interrogator, needless to mention, was Parsons, and his question, said Schilling, aroused the "liveliest interest," as "we were all anxious to know whether we had struck a Communistic whack-up-all-around institution, in which the parasite was to find a loafer's paradise at the expense of the industrious worker, or whether the law of merit was still to obtain." McGuire replied that the Social Democrats envisioned the nationalization of the land and the means of production, exchange, and transportation, rewarding each worker in proportion to his effort and output. This satisfied Parsons, along with most of the others in the hall, and from that time onward the newly-formed English section of the Social Democratic Party, of which both Parsons and Schilling were charter members, became a "permanent factor" on the Chicago labor scene.[18]

From that time, too, Parsons devoted his considerable energies and talents to the cause of the working class. Bringing to the movement all the enthusiasm of a convert, he took part in a broad range of socialist and labor activities. His life, as a result, acquired new direction and purpose, and he made new friends and comrades on every side. Most notable among them was Schilling, a cooper by trade and a decent, sympathetic man, with "a heart big enough for all Chicago."[19] In spite of growing disagreement on matters of both doctrine and tactics, Parsons was to remain on intimate terms with Schilling for the rest of his life.

Parsons, meanwhile, was gaining a reputation as a labor agitator. Now in his late twenties, of slender physique, intelligent face, and neat appearance, he was well versed in working-class matters and patently sincere in his concern for the poor. These qualities, combined with his resonant voice and flair for the dramatic, made him one of the most popular orators in Chicago. According to Schilling, Parsons and a colleague named John McAuliffe were the only socialists in the city "capable of expounding in public the principles of the party in the English language." McAuliffe, however, was an "extremist," unwilling to advocate ameliorative measures. Except on special occasions, therefore, the English section "shelved" him, so that Parsons, then still a moderate in his social views, was "practically the only public English speaker we had."[20]

Parsons availed himself of every opportunity to preach the socialist gospel before the workers. Combining rhetoric, humor, and statistical data, he spoke whenever and wherever the occasion afforded—in parks and on street corners, in hired halls and private houses. He echoed Lassalle's position on the "iron law of wages" and Marx on class struggle and historical materialism. So eloquent were his speeches that, in spite of the language barrier, he was able to overcome the distrust with which foreign-born socialists in his audience normally regarded their English-speaking counterparts. One can imagine a typical gathering during these pioneer days of the movement: the small audience of twenty or thirty scattered among the chairs or huddled, at Parsons's request, in the front rows; the speaker pouring out statistics, economic theory, satire, information; and the committee on arrangements, intent upon the question of the rent, hurriedly passing the hat at the end of the speech, before the listeners can get away. "Oft-times," recalled George Schilling, "after posting bills and paying for advertising, we were also compelled to contribute our last nickel for hall rent, and walk home instead of ride."[21]

Parsons's growing prominence as a socialist agitator soon brought him to the attention of Chicago's conservative element, and he found himself as roundly condemned as he had been in Texas. In May 1876 the *Chicago Tribune* branded him and his associates "a parcel of blatant Communist demagogues," acting in behalf of "the Commune." This, Parsons relates, had "an exasperating effect upon me." But its main result was "to renew my zeal all the more in the great work of social redemption."[22]

Nevertheless, it was an uphill struggle. In 1876 the Social Democratic Party contained a mere 1,500 members throughout the country, of whom not more than a fifth were native-born. Many of the others did not speak English. The English-speaking members not only suffered from the prejudice of the general public against radicals, but were viewed with suspicion by their own German-speaking comrades, who believed that the Yankees "needed watching." The party was hampered, in addition, by a lack of literature in English on social and economic subjects. Apart from a few pamphlets, noted Schilling, *The Socialist*, the weekly party organ in New York, was "the only food we had."[23] Other socialist groups, such as the International Working Men's Association (the famous First International) and the Labor Party of Illinois, faced a comparable situation, and the movement as a whole was deeply divided.

What then was to be done? As a first step, consolidation of the disparate socialist factions seemed essential. The Social Democrats had initiated a movement for unification at their Philadelphia convention in 1875. This was followed by a series of conferences in Pittsburgh, New York, and other cities, with the result that, coinciding with the nation's centennial, a general unity convention assembled in Philadelphia in July 1876. At this gathering, delegates from the International Working Men's Association dissolved their own organization and fused with the Social Democrats, the Labor Party of Illinois, and the Socio-Political Labor Union of Cincinnati to form a single body known as the Working-Men's Party of the United States.

Although Germans and other immigrants formed the backbone of the Working-Men's Party, two of its ablest spokesmen came of old American stock: Philip Van Patten, the national secretary, and Parsons himself, a leader of the English section in Chicago. The English section, of which Parsons served as organizer and Thomas Morgan as corresponding secretary, met every Monday evening to discuss the burning issues of the day and map out a program of agitation. Between the fall of 1876 and the spring of 1877, public meetings were held in all parts of the city, at which Parsons was the principal English speaker.

Yet, for all this activity, both in Chicago and throughout the country, the Working-Men's Party failed to achieve its intended objective. From the outset it was torn by dissension. Disputes occurred between reformers and revolutionaries. Tensions between the English-speaking minority and the German-speaking majority persisted. And, as in all radical organizations, differences of personality and temperament created additional friction. But the underlying problem, as Schilling pointed out, was that the merger at the Philadelphia convention had brought together two irreconcilable tendencies, the Marxist and the Lassallean, within the same organization, thereby ruling out concerted activity.[24] The Marxists, many of whom had belonged to the International Working Men's Association, called on party members to join trade unions and achieve emancipation through economic organization and action. The Lassalleans, who had dominated both the Social Democratic Party and the Labor Party of Illinois, focused their energies on political action, pinning their hopes on the ballot to solve the labor question. Because of the "iron law of wages," they argued, every effort of the workers to improve their economic condition through trade unions was doomed to disappointment. Only by gaining control of the state and creating a network of producers' cooperatives, to which all industry would ultimately pass, could the workers secure the final overthrow of capitalism.

In an effort to accommodate both positions, the platform of the Working-Men's Party called for a combination of economic and political action to bring about the emancipation of labor. Parsons was content with this compromise. He saw value in both political and economic methods to better the lot of the workers. He himself, in addition to his labors for the party, was an active member of Typographical Union No. 16, which he had joined in 1874. Furthermore, on July 4, 1876, while speaking in Indianapolis, he was initiated into the Knights of Labor by its Indiana organizer, Calvin A. Light. A few months later, together with Thomas Morgan and George Schilling, Parsons founded "old 400," the first local assembly of the Knights in Chicago. Beyond this, he served as a delegate to District Assembly 24 for two terms, was its Master Workman for one term, and, before Haymarket intervened, was active as a speaker and organizer for the Order throughout the Middle West. When "old 400" disbanded in 1885, Parsons transferred to Local Assembly 1307, of which he remained a member until his death.[25]

By 1877, however, politics was absorbing more and more of Parsons's attention. When the Working-Men's Party entered the Chicago electoral race in the spring of that year, he was nominated as its candidate for alderman in the Fifteenth Ward, running on a platform of municipal ownership of public utilities, fair hours and wages for city employees, and similar measures. George Schilling and other party activists worked "like beavers" for his election. Parsons lost, but he made a respectable showing, polling one-sixth of the total ballot. Equally important, says Schilling, the good impression that he and other socialist candidates made on thoughtful citizens was regarded as "a great moral victory."[26]

This was Parsons's first venture into the political arena. But it was not his last. Over a five-year period, starting in 1877, he was nominated for alderman three times, for state assemblyman twice, and once each for sheriff and county clerk—losing on all occasions.[27] He was even, as we shall see, nominated for President of the United States, but had to decline because he was underage. Before that, however, an event took place that was critical in his ideological development. In July 1877, three months after his first political defeat, a railroad strike erupted in Chicago and around the country. The Working-Men's Party found itself catapulted into national prominence. And Parsons, gaining a foretaste of 1886, had his first serious encounter with the authorities.

3 ‖ The Great Strike

The railroad strike of the summer of 1877 was a manifestation of deep-seated discontent. For four years, as the depression worsened, the fuel had been accumulating for a conflagration. It now burst forth with fury and spread like wildfire across the country. Never before had America witnessed a nationwide uprising of workers, an uprising so obstinate and bitter that it was crushed only after much bloodshed. Local police and state militias alone could not restore order. For the first time federal troops had to be called out during peacetime to suppress a domestic disturbance. In the process, more than a hundred workmen were killed and several hundred wounded. For a full week the strike dominated the front pages of American newspapers. A new reality had entered American economic life. The first great collision between capital and labor, it was a harbinger of things to come.

The trouble began on July 16, when the Baltimore & Ohio Railroad announced a 10 percent cut in wages. This action, coming in the worst year of the depression, precipitated a walkout which, spreading quickly to other lines, soon paralyzed the transportation system throughout the East. Then, from the Baltimore & Ohio, the Pennsylvania, the Erie, and the New York Central, the storm moved rapidly westward. Within a week after the first walkout, stoppages had occurred throughout the Midwest. Rail service was disrupted from Baltimore to St. Louis, equipment was destroyed, and disturbances in a dozen cities resulted in hundreds of deaths and injuries and extensive property damage.

By July 25 the movement had grown into a virtual general strike that reached all the way to the Pacific. "The country was in a feverish state of excitement from Boston to San Francisco, from the Lakes to the Gulf," wrote a newspaper editor in St. Louis.[1] Nor was the strike confined to the railroads. In communities all over the country it was joined by discontented elements of every type: farmers from the surrounding countryside, miners from nearby coal fields, quarrymen, mill hands, stevedores, and unemployed workers. The entire country, as George Schilling remarked, was enveloped in a "social and industrial mutiny that overwhelmed and surprised in its spontaneity and extent the closest observers of economic development."[2]

Everywhere the pattern was the same. A walkout was called, and the railroad brought in scab labor. In the conflict that inevitably ensued, police and militia intervened on the side of the employer. Pitched battles between the strikers and the authorities were frequent and bloody. In Baltimore, militiamen fired into a group of demonstrators, killing a dozen people. In Pittsburgh, where more than twenty were killed in a similar encounter, the militia was besieged by an angry crowd and forced to retreat under fire. With the strike raging out of control, President Hayes called up federal units in order to prevent a "national insurrection."[3]

The strike continued for two weeks before it was suppressed. No previous labor conflict in American history had been so extensive in scope or so bitterly fought. Spreading to seventeen states, it encompassed the widest geographical area and involved the largest number of participants of any industrial strike of the nineteenth century. It was the first large-scale protest against the new conditions brought about by the industrial revolution following the Civil War, "alarming evidence," as George Schilling noted, "of the concentration of wealth and the rapid changes of our economic life." The fires of burning roundhouses, said Schilling, "illumined the skies of our social and industrial life" and revealed "the pinched faces of the workers and the opulence, arrogance, and unscrupulousness of the rich."[4]

For Schilling and other labor activists, the strike was an encouraging development. Samuel Gompers called it "the tocsin that sounded a ringing message of hope to us all."[5] For many Americans, however, it raised the specter of an unmanageable insurrectionary power. Seized by hysteria, well-to-do citizens feared "the appearance of the Commune, bold, audacious, apparently organized."[6] Newspapers and magazines, startled by a strike that so quickly assumed the proportions of a rebellion, printed wild, blood-curdling headlines and clamored for its ruthless suppression. In a single issue, at the height of the troubles, the *New York Times* referred to the strikers in the following terms: disaffected elements, roughs, hoodlums, rioters, mobs, suspicious-looking individuals, bad characters, thieves, looters, communists, rabble, labor-reform agitators, dangerous class of people, gangs, tramps, drunken section-men, law-breakers, bummers, ruffians, loafers, bullies, vagabonds, cowardly mob, bands of worthless fellows, incendiaries, enemies of society, malcontents, wretched people, loud-mouthed orators, rapscallions, brigands, robber mob, riffraff, terrible fellows, felons, and idiots. In a similar spirit, Thomas A. Scott, president of the Pennsylvania Central, called on the militia to give the strikers, who complained of hunger and deprivation, a "rifle diet for a few days and see how they like that kind of bread."[7]

In Chicago, with its widespread unemployment and hunger, the situation was extremely tense. As the strike rolled westward, prosperous citizens grew increasingly alarmed, not only because of the city's importance as a railroad and business center, but also because the workers were lending an ear to the Working-Men's Party, which emerged now for the first time as a significant force. Although the party neither instigated nor led the strike, which was a spontaneous explosion of discontent, it took advantage of the situation to make propaganda, issuing leaflets and calling meetings, as George Schilling recorded, "for the purpose of presenting to an astonished populace the cause and remedy of this general upheaval."[8]

The first such meeting took place on Saturday, July 21, before the strike had reached the city. At 3 P.M. an eager audience packed Sack's Hall on 20th and Brown Streets to hear Albert Parsons and other speakers for the Working-Men's Party flay the "capitalist press" and "railroad kings" for their callousness towards the workers. Parsons made a forceful presentation of the socialist program. Being "uproariously cheered, showing his popularity," he denounced the daily press as the mouthpiece of "monopolies and tyrants." As an example, he cited an editorial in the *Chicago Tribune* upholding the right of management alone to determine the pay of the workers. "If the proprietor has a right to fix the wages and say what labor is worth," declared Parsons, "then we are bound hand and foot—slaves—and we should be perfectly happy: content with a bowl of rice and a rat a week apiece." To this the crowd shouted "No! No!"[9]

Parsons attributed the high rate of unemployment to the wholesale introduction of machinery into the factories. To maximize their profits, he maintained, the employers were reducing the workers to a condition of vagrancy. Rather than scrap the new machines, however, Parsons called for a reduction of the working day to eight hours,

28

so that labor might be equitably distributed and unemployment eliminated. Parsons counseled against the use of violence. In common with the other speakers, he urged his listeners to remain peaceable, advising them to join the Working-Men's Party and to vote for its candidates in the next election. He told them, according to one account, that they should "form their unions, cement their party, go in on a protective and benevolent basis, with right and justice." If they did not do this, "the first they knew they would find themselves with a sword in one hand and a torch in the other. He implored them in God's name not to allow themselves to come to this desperate pass."[10]

The next day, a Sunday, as the city braced for the strike that all felt was imminent, the Working-Men's Party distributed circulars for a mass meeting to be held the following evening, July 23, at Market Square, an open area in Chicago's industrial district at the intersection of Market and Madison Streets. The circulars called on the workers to present a solid phalanx against their oppressors, the "Money Lords of America," who were conspiring to keep them in subjection: "For the sake of our wives and children, and our own self-respect, LET US WAIT NO LONGER! ORGANIZE AT ONCE!"[11]

Responding to the call, workers from every quarter of the city, marching in torchlight procession, converged on Market Square at the appointed hour. Some ten or fifteen thousand strong, they carried placards and banners, in English, German, and French, proclaiming: "We Want Work, Not Charity," "United We Stand, Divided We Fall," "Why Does Over-Production Cause Starvation?" and "Life by Labor or Death by Fight." George Schilling opened the meeting with a moderately worded speech. John McAuliffe, using stronger language, lashed out at the "glutted greed" of monopoly capital and demanded a program of public works to alleviate poverty and unemployment. If the capitalists should open fire on labor's Fort Sumter, he declared, employing the Civil War imagery so popular at the time, the workingmen must "arm for bloody war!"[12]

Parsons was the principal speaker. Where formerly he had to content himself with groups of twenty or thirty, he now had an audience of thousands; and when he mounted the platform, reported a newspaper the next day, "a shout went up from the multitude." Stirred by the size of the crowd, Parsons delivered a powerful speech. Saluting the "Grand Army of Starvation," he denounced the railroad magnates—the Tom Scotts, the Jay Goulds, the Cornelius Vanderbilts—who compelled their employees to work for ninety cents a day and expected them to feed and clothe their families. He criticized the press for filling its pages with stories of crime but never troubling to go to the factories and workshops "to see how the toiling millions give away their lives to the rich bosses of the country." He hailed the strikers in the East, who "demanded of those who have possession of the means of production that they be permitted to live."

As before, however, Parsons adjured his listeners to refrain from violence and to work for legislative solutions. He called on them to join the Working-Men's Party and to exercise the ballot for the purpose of securing state ownership of the means of production, transportation, and communication. By doing so, he said, we shall "extract the sting from the mouths of Jay Gould and Tom Scott." It rests with you, Parsons told his listeners, "to say whether we shall organize ourselves. Will you organize? [Cries of "We will!"] Well, then enroll your names in the Grand Army of Labor, and if the capitalist engages in warfare against our rights, then we shall resist him with all the means that God has given us."[13]

Following Parsons's lead, Philip Van Patten, the party's national secretary, took the rostrum and introduced resolutions demanding the transfer of all railroads and telegraph lines to the government, the strengthening of labor organizations, the reduction of the hours of labor, and the use of the ballot to obtain economic reforms. Then, amid cheers of approval, the meeting was adjourned.

Later that night the strike reached Chicago "in all its fury"[14] when forty switchmen on the Michigan Central Railroad quit work in response to a cut in wages. On Tuesday morning the strike spread rapidly, and by afternoon the entire midwestern transportation system was paralyzed. From the beginning, however, it was more than just a railroad strike. Workers from all crafts and industries, caught by the fever, laid down their tools. Streetcars stopped running on the South Side, ships sat idle at their moorings, and the furniture workers walked off the job, as did the tailors of the North Side. Schilling was instrumental in calling out his fellow coopers, while other socialists initiated walkouts among the lumber shovers and cabinetmakers. Before the day was over, the strike had spread to the ironworkers, brass finishers, carpenters, brickmakers, stonemasons, glaziers, and painters. Most of the city's industry was tied up.

Panic gripped Chicago's wealthier residents. To many of the businessmen and merchants the strike seemed a premeditated plot to cripple industry and inaugurate "the Commune." Fears of a general insurrection were so widespread that the mayor, Monroe Heath, a man "of the rough and ready type so often found among the western pioneers,"[15] issued a proclamation calling on all citizens to preserve order. By now the Working-Men's Party had captured the attention of the press and police. Parsons, although he had repeatedly cautioned against violence, was denounced as the principal troublemaker. Allan Pinkerton, the head of the famous detective agency, blamed the turbulence on the "ranting of a young American communist named Parsons," while the *Inter Ocean* declared flatly that the riots accompanying the walkouts were "all due to Parsons's speech."[16]

Parsons's speech called down the wrath of the business community upon his head. Tuesday morning, when he reported for work on the *Times*, he found that he had been fired from his job as a typesetter, which he had held since 1874. Even worse, as he later learned, he had been blacklisted, so that for the next few years he was unable to find employment in his craft. Though his fellow printers admired his "pluck," they did not walk off the job or otherwise protest his dismissal. Some were afraid even to talk to him. Leaving the building, Parsons went to the office of the *Arbeiter-Zeitung*, the German organ of the Working-Men's Party. About noontime two men came in and asked him to accompany them to the mayor's office. As they hurried out, a breeze flapped the coattails of his escorts, and Parsons saw that they were armed.[17]

Reaching city hall, Parsons was conducted to the mayor's chambers, which were filled with policemen, officials, and leading citizens. Police Superintendent Hickey, seated opposite Parsons, questioned him in an "officious and insulting manner," demanding to know who he was, where he came from, and whether he had a wife and family. Hickey proceeded to lecture Parsons on the trouble he had brought upon the city, asking if he "didn't know better than to come up here from Texas and incite the working people to insurrection." He had done nothing of the sort, Parsons replied. He had simply been a speaker at the meeting, and that was all. The strike, he insisted, had arisen from causes over which he, as an individual, had no control. As he spoke, Parsons was interrupted by cries of "Hang him!" "Lynch him!" "Lock him up!"

After two hours of browbeating, Hickey escorted Parsons to the door. "Parsons," he said, "your life is in danger. I advise you to leave

31

the city at once. Beware. Everything you say or do is made known to me. I have men on your track who shadow you. Do you know you are liable to be assassinated any moment on the street?" Parsons asked him by whom. "Why," Hickey answered, "those Board of Trade men would as leave hang you to a lamp-post as not."[18] It was an ominous prediction.

That same afternoon Parsons was the subject of an editorial in the *Chicago Times*, the paper which, a few hours earlier, had dismissed him from its staff. "His name is Parsons," it read. "Until very recently he was a 'rat' printer. He joined the Typographical Union while running for alderman in the last election. Now he is leading the Commune. A model workingman, truly!"[19]

Around eight o'clock that night Parsons went to the composing room of the *Chicago Tribune* to try to get some work. He was talking to a friend, the chairman of the Typographical Union's executive board, when two strangers seized him from behind and shoved him out the door. Parsons protested. Cursing between their teeth, they dragged him down five flights of stairs, then, placing a gun at his head, told him that if he ever came back there they would blow his brains out. The incident caused excitement in the composing room, the men threatening to walk out in protest, but the proprietor, Joseph Medill, managed to convince them to go back to work.[20]

While Parsons was being thus harassed, the crowds were collecting again in Market Square, where the Working-Man's Party had called another meeting. Nearly three thousand had assembled when they were charged by a detachment of police, who dispersed them with clubs and smashed the speakers' stand "into kindling wood."[21] Parsons emerged from the *Tribune* just in time to witness the scene.

The next day, July 25, the bloodshed began in earnest. On the "Black Road," a section of Blue Island Avenue leading to the McCormick Reaper Works, policemen clashed with strikers who, a thousand strong, had been heckling a group of scabs. At the Chicago, Burlington & Quincy roundhouse on West 16th Street a crowd of 8,000 destroyed two locomotives before being dispersed by the police, who left three dead and seven wounded. Contingents of police fought with strikers at the Randolph Street bridge and charged a noisy crowd at 16th and Halsted Streets, killing two and injuring many others. In further incidents, workers were beaten and fired upon by police, militiamen, and hired thugs.

For several days, meetings of workmen were broken up by the

police, who again and again interfered with the rights of free speech and assembly. The most notorious case occurred on the afternoon of July 26, when the Furniture Workers' Union met to confer with employers at the Vorwaerts Turner Hall on West 12th Street. The police, without warning, broke down the door and clubbed and fired at the men as they struggled to escape, killing one and wounding many more. The incident was made a test case in the courts, and Judge William K. McAllister issued a decision upholding the right of public assembly that some were to remember at the time of the Haymarket affair.

Alarmed by the mounting violence, Chicago businessmen assembled at the Moody and Sanky Tabernacle to demand additional militiamen and to discuss how to put down what Mayor Heath called the "ragged Commune wretches." Parsons's former employer, the *Chicago Times*, called for the use of hand grenades against the strikers, "an uncombed, unwashed mob of gutter-snipes and loafers." Scores of prominent citizens left town in a hurry, and terror held the others by the throat. Some merchants, J. V. Farwell and Marshall Field among them, armed their employees and lent their delivery wagons and horses to move the police to trouble spots around the city. A "Law and Order League" was quickly established, with the industrialist George Pullman at its head. Sworn in as special deputies, bankers, merchants, and lawyers shouldered rifles and patrolled the residential districts against "stray strikers and tramps." In addition, Civil War veterans, citizens' cavalry companies, private guards, and bands of uniformed vigilantes, like the Boys in Blue and the Ellsworth Zouaves, roamed the streets, attacking and dispersing groups of workers.[22]

Meanwhile additional forces were arriving in the city. By July 26 the streets were patrolled by units of the 9th and 22nd United States Infantry, two regiments of state militia, a battery of artillery, several companies of cavalry, 5,000 special deputies, 500 Civil War veterans, and members of various patriotic organizations, besides the regular police. Two companies of veteran Indian fighters, headed by Lieutenant Colonel Frederick Dent Grant, son of the Civil War general, arrived from Dakota Territory, bronzed and still covered with dust, their repeating rifles slung over their shoulders, and clattered through the streets at a brisk trot, bridles jingling and hoofs clanging against the cobblestones. On Thursday afternoon these troops were sent into action against an unruly crowd at the Halsted Street viaduct, which had beaten back the police with stones and bricks. A pitched battle ensued in which a dozen men were killed and twice as many wounded, all the casualties being civilians.

By Friday the strike had been broken. Men were going back to work, the Board of Trade reopened for business, and the city regained a measure of calm. The hospitals and jails, however, were filled with workers. In two days of fighting, between 25 and 50 civilians had been killed, some 200 seriously injured, and between 300 and 400 arrested. Not a single policeman or soldier had lost his life.

On Saturday, July 28, the first freight trains left the yards, under military protection, and normal schedules were resumed in other industries. In economic terms, the workers had gained nothing. Some, in fact, returned to their jobs at lower wages than before. Unemployment remained rife. Yet the struggle was not a total loss. It won wage concessions in scattered instances, gave pause to would-be wage-cutters, and revealed in a dramatic way the power of the workers to engage in militant action on a national scale.[23] The workers had shown that they could stop the trains from running and tie up vast sections of the country's economic life. At the same time, they had become aware of the need for organization in defense of their interests. Following the strike, trade unions and councils sprang into existence in all the larger industrial centers. Labor parties, above all the Working-Men's Party, gained thousands of members, put forward an increasing number of political candidates, and issued a number of new journals in several languages. The strike, as Schilling noted, had "secured us the public ear."[24] People were becoming aware of the profound changes taking place in American society, above all in the methods of production and the distribution of wealth. More than a few socialists dated their conversion from this period, among them Lizzie May Holmes, a friend of Albert and Lucy Parsons. "The great railroad strike of 1877," she wrote, "brought out the vague lines between classes distinctly, and forced every thinking man and woman to take a stand on one side or the other."[25]

But if the strike had been an inspiration for the workers, it had given American capital its first big scare. An English visitor, on the eve of the upheaval, had already found wealthy Americans "pervaded by an uneasy feeling that they were living over a mine of social and industrial discontent, with which the power of Government, under American institutions, was wholly inadequate to deal: and that some day this mine would explode and blow society into the air."[26] Now such fears were greatly reinforced. Not since the slaveholders had ceased to be haunted by nightmares of slave uprisings had propertied elements been so terrified.[27]

And yet business leaders did not turn their energies to social and economic reforms which might have removed the basic causes of the unrest. Quite the contrary. For them the chief lesson of the strike was the need for a stronger apparatus of repression. Along with press and pulpit, they called for a reorganization of the military forces, so that in the future they might be able to deal more effectively with popular outbursts. The erection of government armories in the centers of American cities dates from this period. State militias were reorganized and strengthened. Special manuals on riot duty and street fighting became prescribed reading for local and federal forces. In Chicago, a Citizens' Association, spurred by Marshall Field, was established "to fight communists." The police began to conduct themselves in the manner of an army, drilling regularly in street maneuvers and learning to "handle themselves like soldiers." To the business community the moral of the whole affair, as Floyd Dell observed, was "the need of a Gatling quick-firing gun which could sweep a street from side to side and mow down a thousand men in a few seconds." The Citizens' Association, in 1878, presented two such weapons to the city.[28]

The strike left deep marks on both sides. For many years Chicago was haunted by memories of 1877 and by the specter of an "American Commune." Between capital and labor a reservoir of bitterness had been formed. The use of state and federal troops at the behest of the employers, the brutality with which the police had attacked the workers, the vitriolic tenor of the press in denouncing all strikers as communists and criminals set a pattern for the future and fueled the hatreds and passions without which the Haymarket tragedy would not have occurred.

The strike, moreover, shattered a number of cherished illusions. A prominent example was the notion, so precious to native Americans, that violence in the American labor movement stemmed from European radicalism and that foreign agitators were responsible for social disorders. The events that made 1877 the bloodiest year in the history of American labor occurred without benefit of "alien" theories or conspiracies. Many immigrants took part in the strike. But they played no distinctive role. They were merely swept along with the tide. Like the native workers, by whom they were greatly outnumbered, they were motivated by no revolutionary doctrine, but by hunger and privation.[29]

The strike, by the same token, challenged what later came to be called American "exceptionalism," the theory that, in contrast to Europe, the United States was a place of unlimited opportunity, and that the high standard of living, the absence of sharp class divisions, the informal and egalitarian tone of American life, not to mention the essentially democratic character of the country, with its constitutional rights and guarantees, rendered it immune from the blandishments of socialism and the dangers of social upheaval. Before 1877, as George Schilling expressed it, the "large mass of our people contented themselves with the belief that in this great and free Republic there was no room for real complaint. The idea that all Americans were on an equal footing seemed to be recognized as an incontrovertible fact in the halls of legislation, in the press, and the pulpit." The great strike, said Schilling, had altered this view. For America had been swept by a general labor insurrection, an outburst of popular fury, showing that, just as in Europe, the workers were an exploited and impoverished class, the victims of rapacious capitalism and repressive government. Thenceforth, concluded Schilling, it was no longer permissible "to thank God—with our former vanity—that we were not like other nations."[30]

In Europe itself the strike made a powerful impression. To Marx the flash fires of resistance across the ocean signalled the awakening of the American working class. "What do you think of the workers of the United States?" he wrote to Engels. "This first explosion against the associated oligarchy of capital which has occurred since the Civil War . . . can very well form the point of origin of an earnest workers' party."[31] To the French anarchist Elisée Reclus the lesson for the American workers was not to stop with partial reforms but to take all property in their hands and use it for their own benefit.[32] Kropotkin, his Russian colleague, exulted in the revolutionary spirit that the strike had exhibited. "Its spontaneity," he wrote, "its simultaneity at distant points connected only by telegraph, the aid given by workers of different trades, the resolute character of the rising since its outbreak, the happy idea of striking the owners at their most sensitive nerve—their property—arouses all our sympathies, excites our admiration, and awakens our hopes."[33]

Among American anarchists, too, the strike gave rise to extravagant expectations. Stephen Pearl Andrews, from his vantage point in New York, saw it as the harbinger of a full-scale revolution involving "the whole laboring population."[34] Ezra Heywood of Massachusetts recognized the strikers as "morally lawful belligerents" engaged in "defensive warfare" against their oppressors. Their rebellion, he believed, was merely the opening round of a prolonged contest, which no amount of repression would succeed in stifling. Especially heartening to Heywood was the refusal, at various times during the strike, of militiamen to obey the orders of their superiors. He rejected the notion that, in contrast to the situation in Europe, there was "no tyranny of capital in America." On the contrary, he insisted, "labor is enslaved and defrauded by devices which capital creates and administers. Through the morally indefensible claim to profits; through the control of land, water-courses, steam, railways, currencies, and governments—capital, by sheer compulsive power, is master of the situation; can bide its time, and starve labor into submission. What whips, revolvers, and blood-hounds were to chattel bondage, usurped control of raw materials and the means of exchange, whereby want and destitution are produced to order, is to the profit system." Heywood pointed out how government and press "fiercely side with injustice against labor" and uphold the "existing financial, commercial, and political power of the strong to plunder the weak." In siding with capital against labor, he concluded, "the government reveals its own despotic, felonious character, and makes plain to all eyes the kind of 'law and order' which good citizens are called upon to support."[35]

By stressing the pernicious role of the press, the alliance of government with capital, and the parallel between chattel and wage slavery, Heywood was articulating ideas that Parsons himself had been evolving since his move to Chicago. For Parsons the strike had been a critical experience. As in Texas, he was cursed, hounded, pushed down stairs, and threatened with lynching. He saw innocent people clubbed and fired on by the police, while the newspapers advocated the use of grenades and Gatling guns against those who agitated for better conditions. He lost his job, was blacklisted, and for several years could get no regular work, so that his family was often in need of the basic necessities of life. It was the opinion of

George Schilling that Parsons's later extremism was rooted in his treatment during the strike. This is an oversimplification, for Parsons's radicalization was a gradual process that took a decade to complete. Yet the strike had pushed him strongly to the left. After 1877, he drifted steadily from socialism to anarchism.

4 ‖ FROM SOCIALISM TO ANARCHISM

The events of 1877 gave a strong impetus to the labor movement all over the country. The open hostility of the federal and local authorities, and the alliance of government and capital in crushing the strike, awakened many workers to the need for organization. Following the strike, the Working-Men's Party gained numerous recruits and rapidly expanded its activities. At its next annual convention, which met at Newark in December 1877, it changed its name to the Socialistic Labor Party of North America and, over the next two years, waged spirited political battles in major industrial centers, winning a number of state and municipal elections.

During this period, Chicago emerged as the undisputed center of party activity and influence. With its English, German, French, Scandinavian, and Bohemian sections, it boasted nearly a thousand activists, issued newspapers in three languages, and enjoyed the support of a growing number of workingmen. In the spring 1878 elections the party gained its first political victory when it sent Frank A. Stauber, a Swiss-born hardware dealer, to the city council as alderman for the Fourteenth Ward. "This gave us a prestige," said George Schilling, "and everything was on the upward boom."[1] In the fall of 1878 the Socialistic Labor Party in Chicago elected three state assemblymen and one state senator, who succeeded in obtaining legislation to establish an Illinois Bureau of Labor Statistics. The following spring the party ran a full city ticket, headed by Ernst Schmidt, the candidate for mayor, a popular and highly respected German physician and friend of the workers. Dr. Schmidt, although defeated by Carter H. Harrison, still the incumbent at the time of the Haymarket episode, polled nearly 12,000 votes out of 58,000, while additional aldermen were elected to the city council. In other elections the party supported liberal judges, such as William K. McAllister and Murray F. Tuley, who won by large majorities.

Throughout these years, Parsons, disregarding the police chief's warning to get out of town, remained a key figure within the party and a force in Chicago public life. In the fall elections of 1877, before the Working-Men's Party changed its name, he polled nearly 8,000 votes for county clerk, running 400 votes ahead of his ticket. In December of that year he was chosen as a delegate to the national convention at Newark, which saw the birth of the Socialistic Labor Party. The following spring he was narrowly defeated as alderman for the Fifteenth Ward (it was rumored that he had been "counted out"), and in December 1879 he was once again a delegate to the annual party convention, held at Allegheny City, Pennsylvania, where he was nominated as candidate for President of the United States. This was, Parsons proudly tells us, the first nomination of a workingman by workingmen for that office.[2] And while he declined the honor, not having reached the constitutional age of thirty-five, the nomination was a clear token of the esteem in which he was held within the party ranks.

In addition to campaigning for political office, Parsons was a regular speaker at Socialistic Labor Party gatherings, alongside George Schilling, Thomas Morgan, John McAuliffe, and Philip Van Patten. From time to time, too, he shared the platform with Paul Grottkau, a recent arrival from Berlin, who was "one of the ablest of the German socialist speakers."[3] Parsons spoke, as in the past, wherever and whenever the occasion demanded, venturing if necessary outside the city, as in August 1878, when he addressed a party rally at Indianapolis.[4] Inflamed by the 1877 strike, his spirit was strong and his rhetoric powerful and eloquent, so that among Chicago's conservative element he acquired the reputation of "a pestilent fellow."[5]

Whether at evening torchlight processions or at open-air meetings on Sunday afternoon, Parsons's message was always the same: the capitalist system was evil and oppressive, causing "crime, ignorance, and poverty" and condemning the vast majority of the population to hereditary servitude. Urging the workers to organize and make themselves felt at the polls, he foresaw the day when the "infamous wage-system" would be overturned and replaced by a cooperative commonwealth. The Socialistic Labor Party, as he told one audience of 4,000, would "ere long call a halt to the increasing power of aggregated wealth, which is surely turning our own fair America into a land of paupers, tramps, and dependent menials."[6]

Beyond his role as a speaker, Parsons published articles and letters in an array of publications, including *The National Socialist* of Cincinnati, a Socialistic Labor Party weekly, and *The Labor Standard* of New York, a paper, according to the slogan on its masthead, "devoted to the organization and emancipation of the working class." Then, in September 1878, following a picnic in Ogden's Grove at which $3,000 was raised for the purpose,[7] the Chicago branch of the SLP launched its own newspaper, an English-language weekly called *The Socialist*, with Frank Hirth, a German carpenter, as editor and Parsons as assistant editor. The two made a capable team. Hirth, having edited a similar journal in Detroit, was well equipped for his new assignment, while Parsons, given his skills as a printer and his experience as a journalist in Texas, was equally up to the mark. Lively and ably edited, *The Socialist* was read and discussed by workingmen throughout the Chicago area. "The Means of Life Belong to Man," proclaimed its motto. The contributors, apart from Parsons himself, included his wife and his colleague John McAuliffe, along with such well-known socialist writers as J. F. Bray of Michigan and Adolf Douai of New York, whose "Catechism of Social Democracy" was a featured serial.

Though busy with party endeavors, Parsons did not neglect his commitment to trade-union affairs. As before, he refrained from choosing between political and economic action, for he saw distinct advantages in each. That the political and trade-union factions within the SLP continued to cooperate with one another was due in large measure to Parsons, who enjoyed the confidence of both. He spoke at both party and union gatherings and wrote for both politically and economically oriented labor papers. In 1878, as representative of Typographical Union No. 16, he helped to found the Chicago Trades and Labor Council, was elected its corresponding secretary, and threw himself into the work of strengthening older unions in and around the city and of organizing new ones, particularly among women and the unskilled. On behalf of the Trades and Labor Council, moreover, he testified (along with Schilling, Morgan, and McAuliffe) before a state legislative commission looking into unsafe labor conditions in the Illinois mining industry, and again before a congressional committee investigating the causes of the 1870s depression.[8]

Parsons, during this period, became a champion of the shorter working day. In 1878 he was chosen as recording secretary of the Chicago Eight-Hour League. The same year, he was elected to the provisional central committee of the International Labor Union of America, an organization that united the forces of the eight-hour movement, under Ira Steward and George McNeill, with former leaders of the now defunct International Working Men's Association, including Otto Weydemeyer and Friedrich Sorge. Influential mainly among New England textile workers, the ILU sought to organize the unskilled and obtain relief for the unemployed, a mission always close to Parsons's heart. Its central committee, on which George Schilling served together with Parsons, included representatives from eighteen states, although the total membership of the organization, which expired in 1881, never exceeded a few thousand.[9]

Over the next few years, various trade unions sent Parsons to different states to preach the gospel of shorter hours. For Parsons, a strong admirer of Ira Steward, the eight-hour day was the starting point from which the labor question as a whole might be resolved. Winning shorter hours, he maintained, was "the most effective immediate remedy" for the plight of the underprivileged and underemployed. He sought to show by statistics—he was fascinated by such data and cited figures in almost every address he made—that in the past a reduction of working hours had invariably been followed by an increase in wages and a rising cultural level for the workers. At the same time, he believed, it would give the workers more leisure in which to prepare for the greater task of emancipating themselves from capitalism. Observing a strike at the Chicago *Inter Ocean* called by Typographical Union No. 16, he saw that every man except one left at the command of union representatives, but that as they went out through the front, hungry scabs came in through the back. "If there were not so many idle men, so many so-called tramps, the union would have won," Parsons concluded. "Labor will continue to suffer defeat until it learns how to take its surplus from off the market by reducing the hours of labor until there are no unemployed men."[10]

As part of the campaign for shorter hours, Parsons helped organize Fourth of July picnics, to which he invited guest speakers on the subject. The picnics, held at Ogden's Grove, the socialists' picnic grounds on the North-West Side, were popular affairs which attracted large and enthusiastic crowds. In 1878 the speaker was George McNeill, president of the ILU. The next year it was Ira Steward, father of the shorter-day movement, who shared the platform with

Dr. Ernst Schmidt, the recent SLP candidate for mayor, George Schilling acting as master of ceremonies. For the procession to Ogden's Grove, organized by the Eight-Hour League, the SLP, and the Trades and Labor Council, the Furniture Workers' Union rigged up a large wagon, drawn by six white horses, called the "Eight-Hour Car." A bell mounted on the wagon pealed forth in groups of eight, while a sign on the back bore the words: "IT WILL STOP OVER-PRODUCTION—IT WILL TAKE AWAY THE TRAMPS—IT WILL GIVE THE IDLE BROTHERS WORK."[11]

Steward, a Boston machinist, had worked tirelessly for shorter hours since the 1860s. But his efforts and those of others had borne meager fruit. In 1867 several states and cities had granted the eight-hour day to public employees, and in 1868 Congress had enacted a law, the first of its kind, extending the eight-hour day to federal workers. These laws, however, were seldom enforced, nor did they affect workingmen in private industry. In January 1880, six months after Steward's visit, the Chicago Eight-Hour League sent Parsons as a delegate to a national conference of labor reformers held in Washington, D.C. At this conference Parsons put forward a strongly worded resolution calling the government to account for neglecting to enforce the eight-hour legislation already on the books, at a time when Congress was pushing through a host of new laws demanded by capitalist interests. The resolution was adopted, and the conference appointed a national eight-hour committee, consisting of Parsons, his future anarchist comrade Dyer Lum, and three veteran labor moderates, Richard Trevellick, John Mills, and Charles Litchman, who remained in Washington to lobby for stronger eight-hour legislation. Parsons, an "indefatigable advocate," as Lum recalls, even stayed on an extra week, but Congress did nothing, and "slowly hope withered in legislation and died out."[12]

Apart from the July Fourth celebration, the most spectacular event of 1879 for the Chicago labor movement was a "monster" rally held on Saturday evening, March 22, in commemoration of the Revolution of 1848 and the Paris Commune of 1871. Billed as the "grand anniversary" of the "dawn of liberty," it took place in the huge Exposition Building on the Lake Front, over protests from the Board of Trade. Weeks of preparation brought out the largest crowd in local labor history. Between twenty-five and forty thousand people packed into the building, while thousands more waited outside for hours, unable to gain admission. Workers' self-defense groups, nearly four hundred men strong, formed on the Milwaukee Avenue viaduct, four abreast, with rifles, cartridge boxes, and bayonets, and marched to the hall to the tune of the "Marseillaise." George Schilling, acting as chairman, introduced Ernst Schmidt and Paul Grottkau, who addressed the throng in German. Parsons was to have given the English address, but the building was so crowded that the arrangements committee could not find him.

The meeting, however, carried over to Sunday, when Parsons delivered his speech. The aim of the Socialistic Labor Party, he declared, was the same as that of the Communards and Forty-Eighters: "All the French and German communists wanted during the dark days of '48 and '71 was to establish a self-governing Republic, wherein the working class—the masses—would partake of the civilization which their industry and skill had created. And for this they received the abuse of the capitalist press of the whole world. The Socialistic Labor Party has the same object in view now that the Paris Commune had then. . . . The vital question is, shall Capital continue to rule Labor or shall Labor govern Capital? We mean to place Labor in power."[13]

Preparations for the Paris Commune celebration coincided with the SLP's campaign for the spring 1879 elections. A week after the festival, Dr. Schmidt made his strong bid for mayor, and three socialist candidates were elected to the city council. But the party had reached the zenith of its power. Soon afterwards its influence began to decline. Recently formed sections disbanded, the newer journals (including *The Socialist*) suspended publication, and even many of the older adherents lost interest and dropped out of the movement. In the fall 1879 elections the SLP vote in Chicago fell by a startling 60 percent, from 12,000 to 4,800. By the end of the year only twenty sections of the party were represented at the Allegheny City convention, and total membership had dwindled to less than one-third of what it had been nine months earlier.[14] Finally, in the 1880 presidential election, the party was eliminated as a serious contender for public office.

What had gone wrong? Why had the party faded so swiftly? A number of factors were responsible, but above all the return of prosperity. A new spurt of industrial growth in 1879 and 1880 revived confidence in the existing system. Factories reopened, new businesses sprang up, the demand for labor increased, and wages rose.

The feeling of discontent which had made so many workers responsive to the appeals of socialism during the preceding years subsided, so that agitators like Parsons now found scant and indifferent audiences where they had once faced clamorous throngs. With the return of good times, moreover, many workers who had voted socialist during the depression resumed their old-line affiliations. The party, as a result, slumped at the polls, and the efforts of its leaders to stem the tide were of no avail. "The plundered toilers," declared a disheartened Philip Van Patten, "are rapidly being drawn back to their old paths, and are closing their ears to the appeals of reason. They are selling their birthright for a mess of pottage by rejecting the prospect of future emancipation in their greed for the trifling gains of the present."[15]

Besides this, the SLP's apparent strength during the preceding years had concealed deep internal divisions. A major source of dissension was the question of self-defense—"die Bewaffnungsfrage," as the Germans called it. As early as 1875, a small group of Chicago socialists, most of them German immigrants, had formed an armed club to protect the workers against police and military assaults, as well as against physical intimidation at the polls. Known as the Lehr-und-Wehr Verein (Education and Defense Society), it was modeled after the Turn Verein, the popular German gymnastic association.[16]

In the eyes of its supporters, who included non-Germans like Parsons, the need for such a group was amply demonstrated by the behavior of the police and militia during the 1877 strike. The breaking up of workers' meetings, the arrest of socialist leaders, the use of club, pistol, and bayonet against strikers and their supporters led to an expansion of the Lehr-und-Wehr Verein and to the formation of similar groups, both in Chicago and in other cities, including New York, Cincinnati, and St. Louis. Workers who joined these groups were resolved never again to be shot and beaten without resistance. Nor would they stand idly by while their meeting places were invaded or their wives and children assaulted. They were determined, as Parsons expressed it, to defend both "their persons and their rights."[17]

Where treatment by the authorities had been the most brutal, as in Chicago, the armed groups multiplied apace. Under a variety of names—Lehr-und-Wehr Verein, Bohemian Sharpshooters, Jaeger Verein, Irish Labor Guards—they drilled with rifles and bayonets and held prize shoots and mock battles at the frequent outings sponsored by the socialist movement. On special occasions, such as the big Paris Commune memorial in 1879, they marched through the streets of the city, weapons and ammunition boxes prominently displayed. The Lehr-und-Wehr Verein wore their distinctive blue blouses, the Bohemian Sharpshooters grey dress uniforms, the Irish Labor Guards green worsted, and the Jaeger Verein grey trimmed with green. Prosperous citizens were acutely alarmed. Rumor had it that the socialists were arming in order to seize the country by force. Public statements by the armed groups professing their peaceful intentions and announcing that their guns were for self-defense and the protection of their constitutional rights fell on deaf ears. In the end, the demonstrations of strength were too much for the Illinois legislature, which in 1879 enacted a law banning all paramilitary groups, unless they affiliated themselves with the state militia, and making it a punishable offense for any body of men to assemble with arms and drill or parade within the state without authorization. The law was upheld by the Illinois Supreme Court. As a result, some of the armed groups disbanded, while others went underground, training in the woods outside of town or across the state line in Indiana or Wisconsin.

The question of self-defense provoked a bitter controversy within the SLP. In June 1878 the National Executive Committee, headed by Van Patten, publicly dissociated itself from armed organizations, on the ground that they were seeking "to accomplish by force what they could not obtain by the ballot."[18] What was worse, declared the committee, they gave the public a false picture of the objectives and policies of the socialist movement. The committee thereupon ordered all party members to withdraw from such groups and to refrain from carrying arms in labor processions. The order had little effect, apart from antagonizing the Chicago militants, especially those in the German section. The *Arbeiter-Zeitung*, edited by Paul Grottkau, and the *Vorbote*, edited by Frank Hirth, denounced Van Patten and his committee for interfering with the local rights of party affiliates. The committee responded by dropping the *Vorbote*, its sharpest critic, as an official party organ. Justifying this action, Van Patten declared: "The question of arming is with us neither a matter of protection nor an assertion of rights, but a matter of policy, as every clear-minded member knows. The capitalist class is most anxious to force us into the position of an armed mob."[19]

The issue came to a head at the Allegheny City convention in December 1879. In the name of the executive committee, Van Patten once again repudiated paramilitary groups and appealed to the delegates for a "final vindication" of this position. Parsons, joined by Moritz Bachmann of New York, led the attack against him, upholding the constitutional right of workers to defend themselves. "The question is," said Parsons, "whether the Executive Committee be censured for meddling in other people's business." After a heated debate, the majority of delegates sustained the party leadership and reelected Van Patten as national secretary. Nevertheless, Parsons managed to put through a vote of censure against the executive committee for demanding that individual party members withdraw from military groups.[20]

Another issue that divided the SLP was that of cooperating with the Greenback movement. The Greenback Party, which had taken shape after the financial crisis of 1873, became in 1878 the Greenback-Labor Party and introduced some labor planks into its platform. In several states and cities it entered into alliances with local branches of the SLP (in Detroit, for example, Joseph A. Labadie, a future anarchist of national reputation, was the candidate for mayor in 1879 in the Greenback-SLP coalition). Trouble arose, however, at the Allegheny City convention, when the SLP National Executive Committee suggested that the party, as an organization, unite behind the Greenback-Labor ticket in the 1880 presidential election. Once again the question of local autonomy was at stake. The convention rejected the proposal and decided to put forward a slate of its own. Parsons, as has been noted, was nominated as the presidential candidate, though being underage had to decline.

Ironically, Parsons himself favored some form of agreement with the Greenbackers, hoping to insert a socialist program into the Greenback-Labor platform. When the Greenback nominating convention met in Chicago during the summer of 1880, Parsons was among the forty-four SLP delegates in attendance, together with his wife, Van Patten, Schilling, and Morgan, all of whom took part in framing the platform. Despite their efforts, the convention accepted only a plank calling for the collective ownership of land, along with some vague socialistic phrases ("the divine right of every laborer to the results of his toil") scattered through the document. Not satisfied, Parsons favored withdrawing from the convention and putting forward an independent ticket. Van Patten, however, supported by

Schilling and Morgan, argued that only by supporting the Greenback candidates, headed by James B. Weaver for President, could the socialists save themselves from eclipse. Much to the disgust of the radical element, a party referendum upheld what the opposition branded as the Greenback "compromise," voting to endorse the Greenback ticket. Although the alliance was severed immediately after the campaign, which ended in disaster for both the Greenbackers and the socialists, the party had already lost the support of many of its most active members, Parsons and his wife among them.[21]

Meanwhile another event occurred which, in the eyes of many socialists, further discredited political action. In the spring 1880 campaign, Frank Stauber, the only socialist alderman to be reelected in Chicago, was cheated of his victory by electoral officials. After a prolonged and costly lawsuit, Stauber was finally seated. But the damage had been done. Many party members, especially those who favored self-defense organizations, concluded that they could win nothing at the polls. Disenchantment with politics was widespread. The unseating of Stauber, said George Schilling, "did more, perhaps, than all the other things combined to destroy the faith of the Socialists in Chicago in the efficiency of the ballot."[22]

A strong spirit developed in favor of direct economic and social action. By the fall 1880 elections two divergent factions, a radical and a moderate, had emerged within the party ranks. The radicals, fed up with what they deemed the compromises, sellouts, and business methods of the party leadership, demanded something more virile than election campaigns. Some favored trade-union work for immediate economic gains. Others spurned both political and economic reform for revolutionary action. But trade-unionists and revolutionaries were agreed that efforts to find political solutions to the labor question were doomed to failure.

Almost from its inception the SLP had contained a militant element whose adherents despaired of accomplishing anything meaningful through political action. Impatient with the slow, reformist methods of the party administration, they had long been tempted to espouse more extreme tactics. Only success at the polls in 1878 and 1879 had kept them in line. But the Stauber case convinced them once and for all of the futility of political methods. And, together with the Greenback disaster, it drove them to launch a secessionist movement.

Parsons was swept along by the tide of disillusionment. Like many others who had become radicalized during the 1870s, he had been gradually losing faith in the ballot as a weapon of social reform. That he himself had been defeated in every race which he had entered—possibly being "counted out" on one occasion—doubtless contributed to his disenchantment with politics. But for him too it was the Stauber affair, followed shortly by the Greenback "compromise," that pushed him into the secessionist camp. "It was then I began to realize the hopeless task of political reformation," he afterwards recalled, and "to lose faith in the potency of the ballot or the protection of the law for the poor."[23]

After the Greenback convention, Parsons parted company with Morgan and Schilling and set out on a different path. He did not yet quit the SLP, nor did he completely abandon political measures. In the fall 1880 elections he was nominated for state assemblyman by the Trades and Labor Assembly, in coalition with the anti-compromise faction of the party, running against the regular Greenback-SLP candidate, who was supported by Morgan and Schilling. The result was a fiasco, with fewer than 500 votes for Parsons and 3,500 for his opponent, both of whom were defeated. The following spring an associate of Parsons named Timothy O'Meara ran for mayor in the Trades Assembly coalition, with Schilling himself as the Greenback-SLP nominee. "The campaign was one of hostility to each other, rather than to the common enemy," wrote Schilling, "and was the most unpleasant experience I ever had in the movement."[24] In 1882 the Trades Assembly again ran a separate ticket with Parsons as a candidate for the assembly. The SLP nominated Schilling, but both men withdrew before the election. It was Parsons's last political campaign.[25]

In the meantime events had moved swiftly. In October 1880 ten leading dissidents within the SLP were summarily expelled from membership for their opposition to the Greenback alliance and their denunciations of the National Executive Committee. Among them were Paul Grottkau, editor of the *Arbeiter-Zeitung*, and Peter Peterson, editor of *Den Nye Tid*, the party's Scandinavian organ, as well as two future defendants in the Haymarket trial, Oscar Neebe and August Spies. The following month an irreparable breach occurred when dissidents within the New York sections bolted the party and formed a Social Revolutionary Club that was anarchistic in tendency.[26] Its leading spirit was Wilhelm Hasselmann, a chemist and former deputy in the German Reichstag, who had only recently arrived in America, a refugee from Bismarck's anti-socialist law. The Jewish socialist Abraham Cahan remembers Hasselmann as a tall figure with long blond hair, fluent in speech and "almost an anarchist."[27] Influenced by Blanqui and Bakunin as well as by Lassalle and Marx, Hasselmann had created a furor when, in a speech in the Reichstag on May 4, 1880, he invoked the example of the Paris Communards and summoned the German socialists to militant action. "The time for parliamentary chatter is past," he exclaimed, "and the time for deeds begins."[28] With that he left the Reichstag and Germany and never returned. After brief sojourns in Belgium and England, where he was associated with Johann Most's *Freiheit*, he emigrated to the United States. In August 1880 both Hasselmann and Most were expelled from the German Social Democratic Party, an act which drove them further along the road to anarchism.

Another key figure in the New York Social Revolutionary Club was Moritz Bachmann, who had joined Parsons at the Allegheny City convention in defending the formation of armed organizations. In after years, Bachmann was to become the German translator of Bakunin's *God and the State*, the sworn enemy of Most, and the author of a work on anarchism and the occult.[29] In addition, there was Justus Schwab, who had been arrested for unfurling a red flag during the Tompkins Square riot, and whose beer-hall on the Lower East Side (advertised as "the gathering-place for all bold, joyful, and freedom-loving spirits") was a rendezvous for revolutionaries from all over the world. Tall and powerfully built, with a mane of thick blond hair, Schwab, the son of a Forty-Eighter, looked "like a Viking," a fellow anarchist recalled, and seemed too big for his tiny saloon. And when his deep voice boomed out it made the glasses rattle on the shelves.[30] During the 1880 national elections, Schwab had vehemently opposed the Greenback coalition, thereby incurring the wrath of the SLP executive committee. Like Grottkau and others in Chicago, he was promptly evicted from the ranks, expelled, as he himself put it, for "disregarding the dictates of the would-be authorities of the party."[31]

Such were the leaders of the breakaway faction in New York. Before the year was out, similar clubs had sprung up in Boston, Philadelphia, St. Louis, Milwaukee, Chicago, and other cities with large working-class and immigrant populations, whose hard experience in the labor struggle and impatience with political methods had made them receptive to anarchistic ideas. A new, more revolutionary movement had been launched. An outgrowth of the SLP, it was composed mostly of Germans, many of them refugees from the anti-socialist law of 1878, by which unions in Germany were disbanded, houses searched, newspapers suppressed, meetings broken up, and radicals arrested. They had broken with the SLP because they could no longer believe in the ballot or accept the dictates of the executive committee. Instead they pinned their hopes on direct action and armed struggle to accomplish social change. Men of a militant temper, they refused to compromise with the existing system, believing that the salvation of the workers could be achieved only by destroying it root and branch. They were convinced that the power of the capitalists rested on force and had to be conquered by force. To rely on political action, they felt, was a fatal trap, tantamount to capitulation. It merely turned the working class away from the sole path to emancipation, the path of revolution. Limited reforms were regarded with intense distrust: they were a delusion and a snare, mere sops to the workers, bribes to put off militant action. The social revolutionaries were impatient for the millennium, which they expected at any moment. Any policy, any action that tended to delay its arrival was one that gave assistance to the enemy and prolonged the enslavement of the poor.

These social revolutionary clubs formed the embryo of a revolutionary anarchist movement in America. In Chicago Parsons was one of the first to affiliate himself with the new organization, which found a wide field for the dissemination and acceptance of its ideas and quickly outstripped its New York counterpart in numbers and influence. Having himself tasted political activity, running for local office and lobbying in Congress for the eight-hour day, Parsons had come to believe that "political liberty without economic (industrial) freedom was an empty phrase,"[32] indeed, that no meaningful reform could be obtained within the framework of the capitalist system, and that the workers would remain oppressed if they did not defend their interests by direct action, including violence if necessary. He had witnessed the rigging of elections, the corruption of politicians, the blacklisting of labor activists, and the brutality of the police. His whole being cried out in protest. That millions of men, women, and children, as he saw it, should be plunged into perpetual poverty so that a few might live in splendor had become unbearable to him.

As a result, he took his stand with the revolutionary socialist movement and became one of its principal spokesmen.

Nor was that all. Parsons had come to believe that government
itself was intrinsically oppressive, that it was "merely the agent of
the owners of capital," whose function was to maintain the "economic subjection of the man of labor to the monopolizer of the
means of labor—of life—to capital." The state in every form, declared
Parsons, was "nothing else than an organized conspiracy of the propertied class to deprive the working class of their natural rights." [33]
Parsons had entered the final phase of his ideological development.
Though he did not yet adopt the label, he had to all intents and
purposes become an anarchist.

PART II ‖ THE ANARCHISTS

5 ‖ Social Revolutionaries

Between November 1880, when the first social revolutionary club was established in New York, and October 1883, when a major social revolutionary congress was held in Pittsburgh, a revolutionary anarchist movement of considerable proportions took shape in the United States. The new movement made deep inroads into the ranks of the Socialistic Labor Party, attracting many disgruntled members, whose disillusionment with the ballot and opposition to party policies led them to reject political action and adopt a revolutionary program. By the end of 1881, as George Schilling observed, the English section of the SLP in Chicago had dwindled to "a corporal's guard,"[1] while such influential papers as the *Vorbote* and *Arbeiter-Zeitung* had shifted their allegiance to the social revolutionary camp.

Anarchism, during these initial years, had not yet crystallized into a coherent doctrine, nor was the anarchist label in wide use. Yet the social revolutionaries—as they persisted in calling themselves until the mid-1880s—emerged as an unmistakably anarchistic organization, with aims and methods that sharply distinguished it from the evolutionary and politically oriented party from which it sprang. While abandoning the principles of the SLP, however, the social revolutionaries continued to regard themselves as socialists—but socialists of a distinctive type, anti-statist, anti-parliamentarian, and anti-reformist, who called on the working class to abjure politics and involve itself in a direct and final confrontation with capital.

So it was that an independent and avowedly revolutionary socialist movement began its career in America. The formative period of its history was marked by three important events: the London Social Revolutionary Congress of July 1881, the Chicago Social Revolutionary Congress of October 1881, and the arrival of Johann Most in America in December 1882.

The initiative for the International Social Revolutionary Congress, which met in London from July 14 to 20, 1881, had been taken the previous autumn by Most and other European militants with the object of reestablishing the old International Working Men's Association on a decentralist and anti-authoritarian basis. Most himself, ironically, did not attend, having been imprisoned a few weeks earlier for applauding in his paper *Freiheit* the assassination of Tsar Alexander II. The delegates, however, included Peter Kropotkin, Errico Malatesta, Louise Michel, and other leading anarchists from many countries. The strictest secrecy was maintained, and the delegates, more than forty in all, were identified by code numbers. Despite these precautions, one of them, a certain Serreaux, was later unmasked as a police spy.[2]

Although none of the newly formed social revolutionary groups in the United States sent its own delegates to the London congress, three were represented by proxy. The mandates of the Social Revolutionary Club of New York and Social Revolutionary Group of Philadelphia were held by a German anarchist named Carl Seelig, while another German anarchist, Johann Neve, represented the German section of the SLP in New York, which had discarded reformism for revolution without having broken with the party. In addition, a prominent French delegate, Gustave Brocher, represented the Icarian community, a French utopian settlement in Iowa.

Beyond this there were two delegates at the congress who came from the United States but did not, strictly speaking, represent social revolutionary groups. The first, Marie Le Compte, carried the mandate of the "Boston Revolutionists," a group of native workers and intellectuals, though she herself was of French origin and styled herself "Miss Le Compte, Prolétaire." An exotic and somewhat mysterious figure, Miss Le Compte, now in her middle years ("nicht ganz junge," as the historian Max Nettlau describes her), had been an associate editor of *The Labor Standard* and an active writer and speaker for the socialist movement, with a special sympathy for outlaws and tramps. To the London congress, on July 15, she delivered what Nettlau calls "a romantic speech about all possible forms of vagabond life in the United States."[3] After the congress, she remained in Britain and Ireland and engaged in revolutionary propaganda. At Stratford, in October 1881, she held forth on "The Rebels of the Sea," a paean to pirates. Some months later she journeyed to Spain, France, and Switzerland, continuing her agitational work. Together with Louise Michel, she took part in a "bread riot" in Paris in March 1883. Soon afterwards, she settled in Berne, translated Bakunin's *God and the State* and Kropotkin's *Appeal to the Young* into English, and then, for reasons which remain obscure, dropped out of the movement.[4]

Even more mysterious was the other American delegate, Dr. Edward Nathan-Ganz, who resembled nothing so much as a character out of Dostoevsky or Joseph Conrad. Although from Boston, like Miss Le Compte, Nathan-Ganz represented the Mexican Confederation of Labor (Confederación de los Trabajadores Mexicanos), which contained both anarchist and non-anarchist members. A facile writer in several languages, he contributed articles to *El Socialista* (organ of the Mexican Confederation), Johann Most's *Freiheit*, and Benjamin Tucker's *Liberty*, published in Boston. Tucker, however, afterwards described him as a "refined and rather fascinating crook."[5]

A shadowy figure whose history is not well known, Nathan-Ganz had traveled widely in Europe, North Africa, and Latin America, come to the United States in the 1870s, and spent several years in Boston, where, in January 1881, he launched an ultrarevolutionary journal called *The An-archist*, the first in America to use that name.[6] Subtitled a "Socialistic Revolutionary Review," only two issues appeared, the second being suppressed by the police because of the violent nature of its contents, in particular a series on "Revolutionary War Science," devoted to street-fighting and explosives ("We desire peace, the enemy wants war. He may have it, absolutely. Killing, burning—all means are justifiable. Use them; then will be peace!"). Johann Most, a contributor to the journal, later used the same title, *Revolutionary War Science*, for his notorious dynamite manual of 1885, which figured prominently in the Haymarket proceeding. The SLP, firmly opposed to insurrectionary methods, called *The An-archist* a "wild revolutionary magazine" filled with "rules for the construction of barricades and other nonsense."[7]

When *The An-archist* was shut down, Nathan-Ganz was taken into custody and spent two months in a Boston jail.[8] After his release, he departed for London, where he attended the Social Revolutionary Congress and impressed Josef Peukert, a leading Austrian delegate, as being "the model of an arrogant, insolent fop" (ein Musterexemplar eines arroganten frechen Geckn).[9] Shortly thereafter he went to the continent, traveling through Holland, Belgium, and France. Returning to England, he was arrested at the request of the Dutch authorities on charges of "obtaining money under false pretenses" in Rotterdam. Extradited to Holland, he spent several years behind bars. His subsequent activities are unknown.[10]

At the London congress it was Nathan-Ganz who spoke the loudest for methods of armed insurrection. He urged every group and individual to take up the study of "chemistry and technical science," a euphemism for dynamite and other weapons of destruction. He even suggested the creation of a military school for social revolutionaries, if the necessary funds could be obtained. Because of these recommendations, which coincided closely with those of Serreaux, Nathan-Ganz was suspected of being yet another *agent provocateur.* There is no evidence, however, to support this. Nor were Nathan-Ganz and Serreaux alone in favoring violent methods in the struggle against capital and government. The assassination of Alexander II, occurring earlier the same year, had made a deep impression on the delegates, who adopted a resolution endorsing "propaganda by the deed" and the study of chemistry to bring about the social revolution.[11]

The chief object of the London congress, however, was to reconstitute the First International on the basis of autonomous federations and groups. The delegates duly approved the formation of such an organization, retaining the old name, International Working Men's Association, but with no central authority save that of a bureau of information. Thus was born the so-called Black International. The new organization became a fearful specter in the eyes of governments throughout the Western Hemisphere, which suspected it of being the directing power behind various acts of assassination and terror committed in the ensuing decades. Such suspicions were utterly without foundation. The International, in fact, never became more than a loose association of independent groups, nor did it ever create a central agency of any type, if only because such a body would have been at odds with the federalist convictions of the participants. Even the information bureau led only a phantom existence and soon faded into oblivion. Nor did a second congress, proposed for the following year, ever meet.

Yet the London congress did have a sequel in the United States. Three months later, in October 1881, a convention of social revolutionary groups assembled in Chicago, the seat of the American movement. It was the first attempt to organize the revolutionary socialists on a national scale, the initiative coming from the New York Social Revolutionary Club and other American groups represented at the London affair. The gathering was not, however, limited to anarchists. Socialists of all shades who were "weary of compromise and desirous of accomplishing the social revolution by other means than political action" were invited to participate. Applications were to be sent to August Spies, business manager of the Chicago *Arbeiter-Zeitung*, who served as secretary of the convention, or "Congress of Socialists of the United States," as it was officially designated.[12]

Though billed as a "congress," the meeting lasted only three days (from October 21 to 23) and only twenty-one delegates attended, most of them German immigrants. Poking fun at the assembly, the SLP described it as "a baker's dozen of Chicago malcontents and six delegates from outside cities." To Philip Van Patten they were merely a bunch of *agents provocateurs*, sent by the capitalists "to shout revolution and clamor for blood."[13] Of the fourteen cities represented, nearly all were in the East and Middle West: Boston, New York, Philadelphia, Paterson, Jersey City, Jersey City Heights, Union Hill, Hoboken, Louisville, St. Louis, Kansas City, Milwaukee, Omaha, and Chicago itself. Chicago, with four representatives, had the largest delegation: Parsons, Spies, Timothy O'Meara, and Jacob Winnen, augmented by representatives of the Lehr-und-Wehr Verein and Jaeger Verein. Two additional Chicagoans, J. P. Dusey and Peter Peterson, carried the mandates of Paterson and Kansas City, which participated by proxy. Dr. Joseph H. Swain of Boston came on behalf of the freshly launched journal *Liberty*, edited by Benjamin Tucker, and Justus Schwab represented the Social Revolutionary Club of New York.[14]

Schwab, Parsons, and Spies played the leading roles at the congress, which assembled in the North Side Turner Hall. After the delegates were seated, Spies, a handsome young German of eloquence and charm, introduced a resolution, approved by acclamation, condemning the British government for its repressive behavior in Ireland. A second resolution, likewise enthusiastically accepted, hailed the populists of Russia for their "unrelenting warfare" against the new tsar, whose father had been killed with bombs earlier that year. The resolution expressed "unqualified support in employing any and all means to extirpate such monsters from among men."[15]

Having adopted a militant stance, the congress went on to denounce private property and "wage slavery" and to endorse the decisions of the London congress, upholding propaganda by the deed and other insurrectionary methods of struggle and declaring itself in favor of "armed organizations of workingmen who stand ready to resist, gun in hand, any encroachments upon their rights."[16] On the question of politics, however, the convention took an equivocal stand. Parsons and Spies, while no longer believing in the efficacy of parliamentary action, continued to regard it as a useful means of agitation. But a resolution to that effect was rejected by a majority of the delegates, who repudiated the "great American superstition" that redress might be obtained through the ballot.[17] At its final session, however, the congress adopted a compromise resolution which recognized the right of each group to determine for itself whether or not to engage in political activity.

As an alternative to the SLP, with its political and evolutionary orientation, the congress founded a new organization, christened the Revolutionary Socialistic Party, with emphasis on "revolutionary" to differentiate it from its reformist rival. The first national anarchistic association in the United States, it was at the same time an American branch of the recently revived International in London and, like its parent body, designed as a loose federation of autonomous groups with an information bureau (in Chicago) as the connecting link. According to the rules of the organization, five members could start a local group, and ten such groups could call a national congress. Each group was to enjoy full discretion in matters of agitation and propaganda, provided its activities remained consistent with the party program. Three papers were selected as official organs of the association, *Vorbote*, *Den Nye Tid*, and *Liberty*, all of which had representatives at the congress (Spies, Peterson, and Swain).

On the last evening, a reception was held to celebrate the establishment of the new organization. Nearly three hundred men, women, and children attended. After a zither performance and singing by the Socialistic Male Chorus and the German Typographical Male Chorus, Justus Schwab recited a poem depicting a contest between the "Money Kings" and "Hunger," in which the latter succeeded in winning the prize—"Liberty." The program closed with the singing of the "Marseillaise," followed by dancing until a late hour.[18]

With the holding of the Chicago congress an important step had been taken in the formation of a revolutionary anarchist movement in America. The militant tone of the gathering was to become more and more characteristic of the socialist left in the ensuing years. On the other hand, a coherent organization failed to materialize. Theoretical and tactical differences remained acute, new social revolutionary groups took shape at a sluggish rate, and, as a national coordinating body, the Revolutionary Socialistic Party proved ineffective. Not even the information bureau could be established for many months. Thus did matters continue until the end of 1882. It was only with the arrival of Johann Most that the movement began to close ranks and become a significant revolutionary force.

Of all the major movements of social reform, anarchism has been subject to the grossest distortions of its nature and objectives; and of all the expositors of the anarchist creed, none has been more abused and misrepresented than Most, the German-born revolutionary firebrand, who spent the last twenty-five years of his life in America. Most, it would be no exaggeration to say, was the most vilified social militant of his time. Portrayed in the daily press as a wild revolutionary fanatic, bent on chaos and destruction, he became the cartoonist's stereotype of the bewhiskered, foreign-looking anarchist, with a bomb in one hand and a dagger or pistol in the other, conspiring against rulers and capitalists and taxing the vigilance of the authorities to keep him in check. Most, having served nearly seven years in European prisons before coming to the United States, was to be imprisoned three times on Blackwell's Island between 1886 and 1902. In an editorial published after his death in 1906, the *New York Times* called him a "mad dog" and an "enemy of the human race."[19]

That Most was an uncompromising agitator, an apostle of revolutionary violence and propaganda by the deed, cannot be denied. In his booklet *Revolutionary War Science*, published a year before the Haymarket incident, he provided detailed instructions on the manufacture of explosives and the uses to which they could be put in the war of the poor against the rich. And yet he was far from being the rabid, maniacal figure of caricature. On the contrary, he possessed considerable dignity, erudition, and charm. To Emma Goldman, whom he helped convert to anarchism, he was a highly sensitive individual whose sympathy for the laboring poor furnished the mainspring of his revolutionary energy. A gifted orator and journalist, he drafted the Pittsburgh Manifesto of 1883, which became the charter of the social revolutionary movement. His celebrated paper, the *Freiheit*, which he edited for twenty-seven years, acquired a place in the front ranks of German revolutionary literature, and decades after his death his powerful "Hymn of the Proletariat" continued to be sung by German workers of every radical denomination, in Europe as in America. An indefatigable propagandist for nearly forty years, Most was an international figure whose influence was felt in Switzerland, Austria, and Germany, as well as in England and the United States. When he arrived in New York in December 1882, his legendary reputation had preceded him.

Most had been born in Augsburg in 1846. From his earliest childhood the world seemed to him a vast conspiracy of cruelty and oppression. To begin with, he was born out of wedlock—"contrary to police regulations," was how he himself sardonically put it.[20] His father, a former actor and singer, had been reduced to scratching out a living as a government clerk. His mother, a well-educated, liberal-minded governess whom he adored, died of cholera when he was still a small child. This was the first of a series of tragedies that embittered Most's life. His father soon remarried, but the relationship between the boy and his stepmother, "bigoted, coarse, greedy," in Most's description, was one of constant and bitter conflict. To make matters worse, an operation performed on his jaw when he was thirteen years old left him permanently disfigured. In later life he managed to conceal the deformity to a great extent beneath his beard. In the meantime, however, it caused him profound anguish, made him an object of ridicule, and shattered his dream of becoming an actor, for which he was otherwise amply gifted. Indeed, his powerful revolutionary oratory of later years was, in part at least, an outlet for his thwarted theatrical ambitions.

Instead, the unhappy youth was apprenticed to a bookbinder, a man of hardness and brutality. Small wonder that Most should have grown up hating authority "with all my soul." His whole childhood had, as he put it, been a horrible nightmare, leaving him "deeply embittered" for life.[21] His illegitimate birth, the deformity that made people shrink from him, the cruel stepmother and still more cruel employer had combined to make Most a rebel; and, in some degree at least, his later glorification of violence was his way of making society pay for the sufferings of his youth.

In 1863 Most completed his apprenticeship. The next five years were spent in perfecting his craft. Equipped with his tools, a meager formal education, a love of reading, and an extreme sensitivity because of his disfigurement, he traveled through Germany, Austria, Switzerland, and northern Italy, the victim of insult and humiliation wherever he went. Everywhere he had difficulty in making friends and finding work. While in Switzerland, however, Most encountered a group of socialist workingmen who showed him the first true sympathy and friendship he had ever known. Embracing their doctrine with all the fervor of a convert, he joined the Zurich section of the International Working Men's Association and began his long career as a socialist agitator. His life had acquired new purpose. "From then on," he wrote in his memoirs, "I began to feel like a real human being. A goal loomed before me which went beyond the mere struggle for existence and the satisfaction of momentary personal needs. I began to live in the realm of ideals. . . . The cause of humanity became my cause. Each step that betokened its progress filled me with the greatest joy."[22]

In the fall of 1868, Most left Switzerland for Vienna. He soon attracted notice and became a popular speaker at workers' gatherings. In the summer of 1869 he was arrested and sentenced to a month in prison for making an inflammatory speech. The following year he was condemned to five years on charges of high treason for taking part in a free-speech demonstration. Released after a few months, he set off on an extended propaganda tour. After the outbreak of the Paris Commune in 1871, however, he was banished from the country. Returning to Germany, Most took a leading part in the unfolding socialist movement. During the next seven years he edited socialist papers, was a tireless organizer and speaker, wrote pamphlets and labor songs, produced a popular digest of Marx's *Capital* (which was harshly criticized by Engels), was twice elected to the Reichstag, and spent three years in prison for revolutionary agitation. After the passage of Bismarck's anti-socialist law, Most was expelled from Berlin. Hounded by the authorities, he left Germany in December 1878, never to return.

In company with many another fugitive radical, Most chose to settle in London, where his anarchistic temperament increasingly asserted itself. In January 1879 he launched his famous journal, the *Freiheit*, whose provocative articles and editorials were couched in a graphic, sardonic language that strongly appealed to its working-class audience. Most was a gifted editor, and his paper carried the stamp of his personality. He made no significant contribution to revolutionary theory. His philosophy, a mélange of socialist, anarchist, and Blanquist ideas, seldom went deep. But as a journalist and pamphleteer he had few equals. A polemicist rather than a thinker, he possessed a Rabelaisian wit that rarely missed the mark. According to Marx, the *Freiheit* contained "no revolutionary content" but only "revolutionary phrases."[23] Calculated to agitate, to stir up, to provoke, it seldom inspired quiet reflection.

During 1879 and 1880, *Freiheit* steadily shifted from a socialist to an anarchist publication. By the summer of 1880 it had become the most uninhibited radical paper of the day, preaching the gospel of revolutionary conspiracy and propaganda by the deed. It was because of his growing extremism that Most, along with Hasselmann, was expelled from the German Social Democratic Party. Yet his impatience with piecemeal reform could no longer be contained. He called for the violent destruction of capitalism, the state, and all repressive institutions. When Alexander II was assassinated in March 1881, Most, under the heading "At Last!" published an article in *Freiheit* not only glorifying the act but urging others to emulate it.[24] For this he was promptly arrested and condemned to sixteen months at hard labor. On his release, in October 1882, he received an invitation from the New York Social Revolutionary Club to undertake a lecture tour of the United States. He not only accepted but decided to resettle in America, transferring the *Freiheit* to New York.

On December 2, 1882, Most boarded the steamship *Wisconsin* at Liverpool, landing in New York on December 18. The Revolutionary Socialistic Party received him with open arms. On the day of his arrival, the New York Social Revolutionary Club arranged a mass meeting in the Great Hall of Cooper Union, where he was greeted as a hero. At thirty-six he was already a legendary figure, martyred by seven years in prison. The hall was packed to overflowing with socialists and radicals of every type. After speeches of introduction by Justus Schwab and Victor Drury, a refugee from the Paris Commune, Most delivered a powerful address. He forecast an imminent social revolution that would be written with "blood and iron." The audience was spellbound.[25]

Most's arrival signalled the opening of an energetic campaign of agitation. Immediately after his reception, he embarked on a tour of the East and Middle West. He spoke in Philadelphia, Baltimore, Louisville, Pittsburgh, Cincinnati, Cleveland, Buffalo, Detroit, Milwaukee, and Chicago. Everywhere he went he was given an enthusiastic welcome. In Chicago, where he spoke on December 28, sharing the platform with August Spies, George Schilling, and Ernst Schmidt, 6,000 eager listeners packed the hall, overflowing the galleries and blocking the aisles. His denunciations of capitalists and officials who "welded iron chains for the workingmen," his call for the arming of the proletariat and a direct assault on the established order, drew thunderous applause.[26]

Most was one of the greatest revolutionary orators of his time. In physical appearance he did not at all resemble the wild cartoonist stereotype. Voltairine de Cleyre, on the contrary, found him "courtly in his manners" and the "personification of grace in his movements."[27] Small and slender, with blue eyes and prematurely greying hair, he dressed for speaking engagements in a formal dark suit. His hair and beard were neatly trimmed. Only when he began to speak, one listener recorded, did his "fiery soul" reveal itself.[28] A brilliant platform orator, endowed with eloquence and wit, he could be emotional or sarcastic, humorous or deadly serious. But he always struck to the core of the matter in language that workers could understand. "He spoke eloquently and picturesquely," wrote Emma Goldman, who heard him for the first time in 1889. "As if by magic, his disfigurement disappeared, his lack of physical distinction was forgotten. He seemed transformed into some primitive power, radiating hatred and love, strength and inspiration. The rapid current of his speech, the music of his voice, and his sparkling wit, all combined to produce an effect almost overwhelming. He stirred me to my depths."[29]

Most's flaming rhetoric and vision of a free society raised his listeners to a high pitch of enthusiasm. He could enthrall with his revolutionary passion even those with an imperfect grasp of the language in which he spoke. Along with Germans and Austrians and Swiss, Bohemians and Jews flocked to hear him lecture. His sharp phrases, noted a Jewish anarchist from the Lower East Side, had the "impact of the bombs and dynamite" of which he so often spoke; and he had only to give the word, so it seemed, and "the audience would rush to build barricades and begin the revolution." "It is an understatement," recalled another Jewish comrade, "to say that Most had the ability to inspire an audience. He electrified, all but bewitched every listener, opponent as well as friend." No wonder the press hated and vilified him, said Voltairine de Cleyre after attending one of his lectures, "for his eloquence is so great that even German policemen against whom he thunders his anathemas, applaud him, using their clubs to pat the wall behind them so as not to be seen."[30]

In Most, then, the social revolutionaries of America had gained a formidable propagandist and agitator. More than any other individual he was responsible for the movement's growth. His tour was a stunning success. In city after city new groups sprang up in its wake. It resembled, as the socialist Morris Hillquit put it, "a triumphal procession."[31] The tour, at the same time, put *Freiheit* back on its feet. Almost at once it took its place as the movement's most influential journal, "shooting flames of ridicule, scorn and defiance."[32] Most was untiring in his work of popularizing revolutionary doctrines. He had a knack for simplifying complex theories in phrases accessible to the ordinary worker. Apart from the *Freiheit*, he issued a series of strikingly entitled pamphlets—*The God Pestilence, The Property Beast, The Social Monster* were among the best known—all of them marked by the same caustic humor and polemical genius that set an inimitable stamp on everything he wrote. Translated into many languages, they sold in tens of thousands of copies and were widely disseminated in both Europe and the United States.

Most, a born revolutionary, had little patience with conciliation or compromise. The depth of his hatred of capitalism made him denounce all partial reforms as mere betrayals. Against the influence of the "money kings, railroad magnates, coal barons, and factory lords," legislation availed nothing. One day, Most declared, the American people would learn "that an end is to be made to the mockery of the ballot, and that the best thing one can do with such fellows as Jay Gould and Vanderbilt is to hang them on the nearest lamp-post." Most's own experience as a lawmaker had convinced him of the futility of political action. A parliament, as he saw it, was nothing but a "puppet show," a game of deception which could never assist in the emancipation of the workers. There must be no temporizing with the existing order, but only relentless war until the "property beast" had been "pursued to its last lurking place and totally destroyed." "Fling aside all patching up and smoothing down, all bargaining and compromising," Most exclaimed. "Extirpate the miserable brood! Extirpate the wretches!"[33]

An ardent proponent of direct action, Most maintained that a war of the poor against the rich was the only means of solving the social question. He urged the workers to arm themselves in order to exterminate the "reptile brood," the "race of parasites," as he branded all capitalists and rulers. If the people did not crush their oppressors, he insisted, then the oppressors "will crush the people, drown the revolution in the blood of the best, and rivet the chains of slavery more firmly than ever. Kill or be killed is the alternative." Most, however, never championed violence for its own sake, but only as a weapon of emancipation. "We are revolutionists not from love of gore," he told an audience in Baltimore, "but because there is no other way to free and redeem mankind. History has taught that. No use of trying reform. The Gordian knot can be cut only by the sword, and within a few years the masses will write the history of the world."[34]

Most's fiery oratory, his trenchant journalism, his fervent advocacy of revolution won him a large and devoted following. Though temperamental, self-centered, and inflexible, intolerant of opposition or even disagreement, he was the living personification of the social struggle, a "rebel above everything else."[35] Since childhood he had learned to hate authority and persecution in every form. Religion, government, and capital, he declared, were "carved out of the same piece of wood: to the devil with them all!"[36] Through his speeches, his newspaper, and his tireless agitational efforts, he transformed the social revolutionaries into a coherent and vigorous movement, with a more sharply defined sense of purpose than it had exhibited before his arrival. At the same time, he employed his talents to drive the SLP to the wall. The exponents of political reform seemed tame and colorless beside this apostle of militant action, who held before the workers the exciting idea of complete emancipation as an immediate possibility.

A man of strong and vivid character, a "new Prometheus," as Nettlau calls him, "everlastingly at war with all Olympus,"[37] Most quickly established his preeminence over the revolutionary left. From 1883 to 1886 virtually the whole social revolutionary movement was the expression of the ideas and vision of this one man. By the same token, he came to symbolize all that terrified and alarmed respectable American society. The daily press made him the target of abuse. He was vilified, persecuted, and thrown into prison. His hatred of capitalism, some maintained, glowed hotter in him than his love of mankind. Yet, with his forceful personality and bitter eloquence, he served the cause of radicalism as well as many a gentler man.

6 ‖ THE PITTSBURGH CONGRESS

In undertaking his lecture tour of America, Most had a larger purpose than the formation of new social revolutionary groups, important though he acknowledged this to be. As a national organization the Revolutionary Socialistic Party had lain virtually dormant since its creation in October 1881. A strong effort would be needed to infuse it with life, or to scrap it for something more effective. Furthermore, the socialist movement as a whole remained bitterly divided. Revolutionary socialists vied with political actionists, trade unionists, and other elements for the allegiance of the working class. It was Most's aim to unite the various socialist currents—at any rate, those that accepted a revolutionary program—under a common banner.

Preparations were made, accordingly, for a unification congress to be held at Pittsburgh in October 1883, exactly two years after the Chicago congress. Through the Information Bureau in Chicago, established belatedly in April 1883, the "Socialists of North America" were invited to send delegates to the new assembly, the goal of which was to achieve "a uniform, practical and effective organization and agitation."[1] Most set great hopes on this gathering. It must not, he wrote to August Spies, secretary of the Information Bureau, be a repeat of the October 1881 congress, which in Most's view had accomplished little. What was needed, rather, was an "imposing" and "demonstrative" assembly of socialists from all over the country, who would lay the groundwork for an "international, federalistic, and revolutionary party, without an executive, without a central agency, without paid officials" (ohne Execution, ohne Central-beitrag, ohne besoldete Beamte).[2]

At the opposite end of the country, meanwhile, another man was seeking to unify the socialist movement. He was Burnette G. Haskell, a twenty-six-year-old non-practicing attorney, Chinese-baiter, and publisher of the San Francisco *Truth*, "A Journal for the Poor," to which Albert Parsons was an occasional contributor. Restless, erratic, Haskell never stayed long with any particular cause or movement. Over a ten-year period he became, in turn, a socialist, a near-anarchist, a single-taxer, and a Bellamyite nationalist. To Benjamin Tucker, a stickler for principle, he was "a consummate scoundrel, with whom it is highly dangerous to have any dealings."[3]

A small, sallow man for whom "controversies were meat and drink," Haskell had a passion for conspiracy and dynamite which rivalled that of Most himself. "*Truth* is five cents a copy and dynamite forty cents a pound," proclaimed the masthead of his journal, which contained instructions on street-fighting and the manufacture of explosives, and which urged workers to procure arms without delay ("We have no moment to wait. Arm, I say, to the death! For revolution is upon you"). "War to the palace, peace to the cottage, death to luxurious idleness!" was the paper's ringing motto. "Our object: the reorganization of society independent of Priest, King, Capitalist, or Loafer. Our principles: every man is entitled to the full product of his own labor, and to his proportionate share of all the natural advantages of the earth."[4]

Haskell, it appears, had been contemplating a revolutionary coup in San Francisco. Among his papers is the following statement in his own writing: "Seize Mint, Armories, Sub-Treasury, Custom House, Government Steamer, Alcatraz, Presidio, newspapers." He was plotting, in addition, to lay waste the Hall of Records. A building was to be rented across the street, a tunnel dug, and dynamite planted. But the plan was never consummated. (Haskell, according to rumor, failed to appear at the appointed hour.)[5]

Haskell's claim to our attention, however, lies in his role as founder of the International Workmen's Association, an organization composed almost entirely of native American workers, which, since its formation in 1881, had gained a significant following in the Far West, where the social revolutionaries had not yet struck root. Known as the Red International, it had two main branches, the Pacific Coast Division, with headquarters in San Francisco, and the Rocky Mountain Division, with headquarters in Denver. (There was also a Mexican Division, centered in Chihuahua.) Haskell, as the driving force behind the Red International and secretary of its Pacific Coast Division, was invited to the Pittsburgh congress. Though unable to attend, he drafted an elaborate program designed to reconcile the contending socialist factions and provide a basis on which to unify the movement. He sent copies of his program to August Spies in

Chicago and Joseph Labadie in Detroit, asking that it be presented to the congress on behalf of his organization.

Far from serving as the basis of reconciliation, Haskell's plan aroused a storm of controversy. Containing a mixture of libertarian and authoritarian elements (a "hodge-podge of sense and nonsense," as *Liberty* characterized it),[6] it called, in Blanquist fashion, for the creation of a tiny elite, "a *few* able, daring, heroic and noble men," as Haskell characterized them, to take the lead at the start of the revolution and "hold the helm *with an iron hand* until the desired results shall be accomplished." With ten such men in each city, Haskell suggested, men who "feared neither life nor death" and were prepared to employ "all the resources of science" to achieve their end, the overthrow of capitalism could be secured, and "the New Era would dawn."[7]

When Haskell's plan was introduced at a secret session of the Pittsburgh congress, which took place from October 14 to 16, it was heatedly debated. According to one source, it precipitated "a fist fight in the convention."[8] In the end, however, it was decisively rejected, though some of its language found its way into the declaration of principles adopted by the delegates. A week before the congress, Benjamin Tucker, to whom Labadie had lent his copy, had already written it off as "perhaps the most foolishly inconsistent piece of work that ever came to our notice." It "does not reconcile in the least," complained Tucker, but "simply places Liberty and Authority side by side and arbitrarily says: 'These twain are of one flesh!' "[9]

Tucker, like Haskell, did not attend the Pittsburgh meeting. Nor did he send a representative, as he had done to the Chicago congress, where *Liberty* became the official English organ of the movement. In the interval, Tucker had shifted ground from revolutionary to evolutionary anarchism, rejecting the use of force except in the strictest cases of self-defense. He had also become an implacable opponent of collective ownership of property, a central plank in the platform of the social revolutionaries, whom he had ceased to regard as his allies. Tucker, in fact, was emerging as the foremost exponent of individualist anarchism in the United States, propagating views that were sharply at odds with those of Most and his associates, who dominated the Pittsburgh proceedings.

Most himself attended the congress, accompanied by three other New York delegates, among them Victor Drury, a French militant who had emigrated to America following the suppression of the Paris Commune and who had welcomed Most at Cooper Union on his arrival ten months before. During the 1870s, according to George Schilling, Drury had been "the major part of the brains" among the socialists in New York. Parsons regarded him as "an eloquent speaker and one of the best informed labor men in this country."[10] Parsons himself was one of the five Chicago delegates, the largest contingent at the congress, the others being Spies, Balthasar Rau, J. P. Meng, and Jacob Mikolanda, a leading Bohemian activist.

Both Parsons and Spies took a prominent part in the proceedings, delivering speeches, introducing resolutions, and helping to frame the declaration of principles. Spies, in addition, acted as secretary of the congress, as he had done in 1881. All told, twenty-six cities were represented, nearly twice as many as at the Chicago gathering, a measure of the movement's growth in the intervening years, especially since the arrival of Most. Delegates attended from Boston in the east to Omaha in the west, from Milwaukee in the north to New Orleans in the south, not to mention proxies from the Pacific Coast, British Columbia, and Mexico. Apart from Most, Spies, and Parsons, they included some of the ablest organizers and propagandists of the movement, such as Joseph Reifgraber of St. Louis, Christ Saam of Cleveland, and Joseph Frick of Pittsburgh, the host city. Also present was Labadie of Detroit, a recent convert from state socialism, who later founded the Labadie Collection of radical literature at the University of Michigan. Messages of greeting ("the eyes of the world are upon *you*, comrades") poured in from every part of the country and from anarchist and socialist groups throughout Europe. Although not without its share of disputation, it was an impressive and surprisingly harmonious assembly. Parsons called it "an epoch in the history of the Labor Movement of the North American Continent."[11]

Though the congress did not officially open until October 14, nearly all of the delegates had arrived by the previous day, a Saturday. That evening a reception was held in the Turner Hall at Allegheny City, a suburb of Pittsburgh, where four years earlier Parsons had been nominated for President of the United States by the SLP national convention. The hall was decorated with red flags, and the delegates, together with some four hundred well-wishers and observers, heard a recital by the Masonic Sextet, which sang revolutionary songs for the occasion, including a few by Most. Joseph Frick, a veteran German socialist and ardent disciple of Most's, delivered the welcoming address, followed by Victor Drury, who spoke in English, then Most himself, who spoke in German, exhorting the workers of America to close ranks and throw off the fetters of capitalism.[12]

The next morning the congress settled down to business. It soon became apparent that two distinct elements were present among the participants, elements divided by their attitude towards trade unions. The delegates from New York and other eastern cities, led by Most, declared their opposition to unions and to the struggle for immediate economic gains, such as shorter hours, higher wages, and better working conditions. Achieving limited improvements, they argued, would only blunt the revolutionary ardor of the workers, weaken their will to resist, and delay the final overthrow of capitalism. Most and his followers disdained any temporizing with the existing order, which had to be destroyed root and branch. What was more, they distrusted any large-scale organizations, like the unions, which might engender a permanent body of officials and harden into bureaucratic form.

The delegates from Chicago and the Midwest adopted a different position. Led by Parsons and Spies, they agreed with Most and his supporters about the futility of the ballot and the need for armed insurrection to overthrow the established order. Nevertheless, they remained devoted to the cause of trade unionism, to which many had been committed for several years, Parsons being a notable example. What they favored was not, however, reformist unionism, permeated, as they saw it, with the spirit of bureaucratism and compromise. Theirs was a militant, a revolutionary unionism, which sought to get at the root of labor's difficulties by changing the very basis of society. The trade union, as they viewed it, was an instrument of social revolution rather than of the amelioration of conditions within the prevailing system. It was not—at least in theory— to contend for partial and superficial benefits, but was to be satisfied with nothing less than the elimination of capitalism and its replacement by a cooperative commonwealth, in which the workers would administer the economy for their own benefit. In the struggle against capitalism, moreover, the union was to shun political action, distrust all central authority, and guard against betrayals by self-important leaders. All its faith was to rest in the direct action of the rank and file.[13]

Nor was this all. For the midwesterners the union was more than a vehicle of class struggle. It was, as Parsons described it, "an autonomous commune in the process of incubation," the "embryonic group of the future 'free society.' "[14] Following the destruction of capitalism, the union would become the nucleus of the new social system that would rise on the ashes of the old. This combination of anarchism and revolutionary unionism came to be known as the "Chicago idea," and during the next two-and-a-half years the Chicago anarchists, and especially Parsons and Spies, used it to penetrate deeply into the labor movement and to attract a large working-class following. In theory, according to the "Chicago idea," the union was not to concern itself with the struggle for piecemeal improvements. In practice, however, Parsons and Spies found themselves ignoring this self-imposed injunction, not just out of sympathy for the plight of the workers, but because they saw that only by working for immediate gains could they hope to gather mass support for their revolutionary program.

The "Chicago idea," in its essential outlines, anticipated by some twenty years the doctrine of anarcho-syndicalism, which, in a similar way, rejected centralized authority, disdained political action, and made the union the center of revolutionary struggle as well as the nucleus of the future society. Only two notable features were lacking, sabotage and the general strike, neither of which was theoretically developed until the turn of the century. This is not to say, however, that anarcho-syndicalism originated with Parsons and his associates. As early as the 1860s and 1870s the followers of Proudhon and Bakunin were proposing the formation of workers' councils designed both as a weapon of class struggle against the capitalists and as the structural basis for the libertarian millennium. A free federation of labor unions, Bakunin had written, would form "the living germs of *the new social order*, which is to replace the bourgeois world." In America, similar views cropped up within the Working-Men's Party of the 1870s, where the trade union was proclaimed "a great lever by which the working class will be economically emancipated."[15]

In the proceedings of the Pittsburgh congress the "Chicago idea" occupied a prominent place. After prolonged discussion, it was endorsed by a majority of the delegates, overriding Most's objections. In a resolution put forward by Spies, the trade unions were recognized as both "the advance guard of the coming revolution" and the

73

foundation of the future social order. Another resolution, introduced by Parsons, expressed support for all "progressive" unions, that is, militant unions bent on the abolition of the capitalist system, as distinct from those which clung to the "reactionary principles" of arbitration and conciliation.[16] But the victory of the Chicago faction was more apparent than real. For the congress proceeded to adopt a declaration of principles that was framed entirely in the spirit of Mostian intransigence and contained no mention of trade-union action. For the sake of unity, it would seem, each side had made concessions, and for the remainder of the convention an atmosphere of harmony prevailed.

The declaration of principles, entitled *To the Workingmen of America*, was the most important piece of work to emerge from the congress. Known as the Pittsburgh Manifesto (or proclamation), it was drafted by a committee composed of five leading delegates: Most, Spies, Reifgraber, Drury, and Parsons. Most was the principal author, the document leaning heavily on his article "Our Fundamentals," published in *Freiheit* on the eve of the congress.[17] Yet Parsons's hand was also visible, especially in the citation of statistics and references to Jefferson and the American Revolution, while the concluding phrases, interestingly enough, were lifted verbatim from Haskell's program for unification, which had earlier been rejected by the delegates.

An amalgam of socialist, anarchist, and other radical ideas, the Pittsburgh Manifesto embodied all the basic principles of the revolutionary socialist movement. Appealing to American as well as European traditions, it opened with a variation on a passage from the Declaration of Independence justifying the ouster of tyrannical government: "when a long train of abuses and usurpations, pursuing invariably the same object, evinces a design to reduce them [the people] under absolute despotism, it is their right, it is their duty, to throw off such government, and to provide new guards for their future security." Had the moment not arrived to heed this advice? demanded the framers of the Pittsburgh Manifesto. Had the American government not become an oppressor? Was it anything but "a conspiracy of the ruling classes" against the people?

Invoking both the theory of surplus value and the iron law of wages, which at the time formed part of the intellectual equipment of every socialist and anarchist, the Pittsburgh Manifesto went on to denounce the capitalist system as "unjust, insane and murderous." It condemned the state, the church, and the educational system as instruments of "class domination" employed by the ruling elite to keep the workers in subjection. Indeed, the whole establishment was oppressive, so that it was necessary "to totally destroy it with and by all means." Political reform was futile, for the capitalists would not surrender their authority without a fight. It was therefore "self-evident" that the "struggle of the proletariat with the bourgeoisie must have a violent revolutionary character"—that the one remedy for the evils of capitalism was "FORCE!" The time had come to repeat the "immemorial example" of the founding fathers: "Agitate for the purpose of organization; organize for the purpose of rebellion."

By way of summation, the manifesto listed six key objectives:

FIRST—Destruction of the existing class rule, by all means, i.e., by energetic, relentless, revolutionary and international action.

SECOND—Establishment of a free society based upon co-operative organization of production.

THIRD—Free exchange of equivalent products by and between the productive organizations without commerce and profit-mongery.

FOURTH—Organization of education on a secular, scientific and equal basis for both sexes.

FIFTH—Equal rights for all without distinction of sex or race.

SIXTH—Regulation of all public affairs by free contracts between the autonomous (independent) communes and associations, resting on a federalistic basis.

Borrowing from Haskell's draft program, the manifesto ended by calling on the workers to unite and throw off the yoke of wage slavery: "The day has come for solidarity. Join our ranks! Let the drum beat defiantly the roll of battle: 'Workmen of all countries unite! You have nothing to lose but your chains; you have a world to win!' Tremble, oppressors of the world! Not far beyond your purblind sight there dawns the scarlet and sable lights of JUDGMENT DAY!"[18]

As the official program of the social revolutionary movement, the Pittsburgh Manifesto was a landmark in the history of American radicalism. Issued simultaneously in English and German, it was translated into a number of languages, including French (by Victor Drury), Czech, Spanish, and Yiddish, and was printed and reprinted in anarchist and socialist publications around the world. Hundreds of thousands of copies were distributed in the United States alone, and long after the congress it continued to be accepted by militant workingmen as a concise statement of their creed.[19]

Of more immediate consequence, the manifesto provided a basis for cooperation among the disparate groups represented at the congress, which proceeded to form themselves into a new national organization designed to replace the stillborn Revolutionary Socialistic Party. Like the London congress of July 1881, the organization adopted the name of the First International, of which it considered itself the legitimate successor. For a time the titles "International Working Men's Association" and "International Working People's Association" were used interchangeably, until the latter came to be the prevalent form. (In German the problem did not exist, as the terms were identical: Internationale Arbeiter-Association.)

Following the scheme laid down at the Chicago congress two years before, the International Working People's Association constituted itself as a loose-knit federation of groups, each of which was to contain five or more members and to enjoy full autonomy, so long as it adhered to the credo of the organization as embodied in the Pittsburgh Manifesto. In cities where there were several groups, it was recommended that a general committee be formed to secure concerted action. Such committees, however, were to have no executive powers. As an agency of record-keeping and communication among the far-flung groups, a Bureau of Information was to be created, also without executive powers, in contrast to the Marxist-dominated General Council of the First International and to the National Executive Committee of the SLP.

Three weeks after the congress, such a bureau was established in Chicago, consisting of a secretary for each of the major languages represented in the association: August Spies for English and Paul Grottkau, William Medow, and Jacob Mikolanda for German, French, and Czech. (Danish was no longer represented, as it had been in the Information Bureau of the Revolutionary Socialistic Party.) For purposes of propaganda, the IWPA was divided into nine agitational districts: Eastern States, Central States, Western States, Rocky Mountain States, Pacific Coast States, Southern States, Canada, British Columbia, and Mexico. A congress of the IWPA, according to the rules of the organization, could be summoned at any time by request of a majority of the groups.[20] None, however, was ever called.

Owing in part to the Haymarket incident, the Pittsburgh congress was the last.

Before concluding their work, the delegates passed two further resolutions. One extended sympathy to their fellow revolutionaries in Europe, engaged in the common struggle for emancipation. The other urged the SLP to join with them on the basis of the principles laid down in the Pittsburgh Manifesto. Two months earlier, the SLP had been invited to send representatives to the congress, but the National Executive Committee had declined, insisting that there could be no common ground between socialists and anarchists, the issues of arms and the ballot posing insurmountable barriers to unification. The SLP, however, had been rapidly losing ground to their militant rivals. Despairing of the slow methods of reform, more and more workers had been heeding the proponents of direct action and defecting to the social revolutionary camp. By 1883 membership in the SLP had shrunk to about 1,500. Even such stalwarts as Thomas Morgan and George Schilling had left for greener pastures, Schilling drifting into the Tuckerite school and Morgan retiring to Woodlawn Park, where he built a house and "raised flowers, potatoes and cabbages while Parsons and his associates raised h—."[21]

Yet another blow came in April 1883, when Philip Van Patten, who had been secretary of the party for more than five years and was one of its most capable and faithful officials, abandoned the fight. Disheartened by the endless bickering and by the deteriorating condition of the party, he suddenly disappeared, leaving behind a letter announcing his intention to commit suicide. This, as it turned out, was merely a ruse. Adopting a fictitious name, Van Patten took a minor post in the federal bureaucracy and afterwards became a merchant in Arkansas.

With Van Patten's abrupt departure, the party was in a shambles. By the time of the Pittsburgh congress, the social revolutionaries had eclipsed it in size and importance. The National Executive Committee, sticking to its decision, refused to take part in the proceedings. But when the Pittsburgh Manifesto was published, it did not seem so far from orthodox socialism as many had expected. Voices for unification were raised; and in December 1883 some of the party's most prominent members, among them Alexander Jonas, editor of the *New Yorker Volks-Zeitung*, took it upon themselves to propose a reconciliation. This was done by means of a letter to the Information Bureau in Chicago. "Reading the Proclamation of the

Internationalists as adopted at the Pittsburgh convention," it asserted, "we can hardly find anything in it with which the SLP has not always agreed, except perhaps some obscure clauses of a reactionary coloring." The answer, drafted by Spies, amounted to a rebuff. Taking the position that the SLP had become an obsolete organization, Spies advised it to dissolve itself into autonomous groups and to affiliate with the IWPA in the same manner as the groups already composing it.[22]

It was in these circumstances, its membership dwindling, its overtures to the social revolutionaries rebuffed, that the SLP's national convention assembled in Baltimore later the same month. It was, according to Morris Hillquit, the most dismal annual meeting in the organization's history. Only sixteen delegates attended, determined to do battle with the International. Denouncing Most as a "demagogue," indeed a demagogue with "an eye for money," they issued a proclamation to the workers of America designed as an answer to the Pittsburgh Manifesto. "We do not share the folly of the men who consider dynamite as the best means of agitation," it declared. "We know full well that a revolution must take place in the heads and in the industrial life of man before the working class can achieve lasting success."[23] The convention drew a sharp line between socialism and anarchism. Thereafter all attempts at reconciliation were abandoned as useless, and there was nothing left but war between the two camps. The breach between political and revolutionary socialism had become permanent.

7 ‖ THE INTERNATIONAL WORKING PEOPLE'S ASSOCIATION

Between the Pittsburgh congress of 1883 and the Haymarket explosion of 1886, the IWPA expanded at a rapid pace. New groups were established throughout the country, old groups increased their membership, the *Freiheit* and the *Arbeiter-Zeitung* gained in circulation, and a number of new journals were started, most notably *The Alarm* in Chicago, edited by Albert Parsons. Parsons, Spies, and others went on speaking tours through many states to enroll new workers into the organization. Out of this burst of activity a vigorous revolutionary movement took shape. Anarchism became a distinct power within American labor, particularly within its German-speaking segment.

What made the ground favorable for anarchist propaganda was a new economic crisis, setting in around the time of the Pittsburgh congress and continuing until the Haymarket incident. The depression of 1883-1886, while neither so acute nor prolonged as the depression of 1873-1878, created severe distress, filling the industrial centers with throngs of idle and destitute men. In Chicago alone, according to *The Alarm*, 34,000 were thrown out of work.[1] It was a time of misery and suffering for many, of homelessness and starvation for some. Immigration remained heavy, compounding the problem of unemployment. New arrivals crowded into the cities, where ostentatious wealth rubbed shoulders with grinding poverty. "Never before," noted the Johns Hopkins economist Richard T. Ely, "had there been seen in America such contrasts between fabulous wealth and absolute penury."[2]

By the winter of 1883-1884 the situation in Chicago was so alarming that the Citizens' Association mounted an investigation of living conditions in working-class neighborhoods. The resulting report told of "the wretched condition of the tenements into which thousands of workingmen are huddled, the wholesale violation of all rules for drainage, plumbing, lighting, ventilation and safety in case of fire or accident, the neglect of all laws of health, the horrible condition of sewers and outhouses, the filthy, dingy rooms into which they are crowded, the unwholesome character of their food, and the equally filthy nature of the neighboring streets, alleys, and back lots filled with decaying matter and stagnant pools."[3]

Joseph Gruenhut, a socialist whom the incumbent mayor, Carter Harrison, had appointed factory and tenement inspector, headed the investigating committee. Paul Grottkau, editor of the *Arbeiter-Zeitung*, went along on the first day but was so appalled by what he saw that he could not bring himself to go again. As a result, Michael Schwab, one of the future Haymarket defendants, had to cover the investigation for the paper. Schwab, too, emerged shaken. "Thousands of laborers in the city of Chicago," he declared, "live in rooms without sufficient protection from the weather, without proper ventilation, in which never a stream of sunlight flows. There are hovels where two, three and four families live in one room. How these conditions influence the health and the morals of these unfortunate sufferers, it is needless to say. And how do they live? From the ash barrels they gather half rotten vegetables; in the butcher shops they buy for a few cents offal of meat, and these precious morsels they carry home to prepare from them their meals. The dilapidated houses in which this class of laborers live need repairs very badly, but the greedy landlord waits in most cases till he is compelled by the city to have them done. Is it a wonder that diseases of all kinds kill men, women and children in such places by wholesale, especially children? Is it not horrible in a so-called civilized land where there is plenty of food and riches?"[4]

Given such circumstances, it is hardly surprising that the depression should have inspired a new wave of social unrest, a spontaneous upsurge like that of the 1870s but more impregnated with radical ideas. Open struggles between labor and capital, in the form of strikes, demonstrations, and boycotts, became more and more frequent. By 1886 the number of strikers had reached 500,000, triple the average figure of the previous five years, and the number of establishments struck had nearly quadrupled.[5] The employers, as before, enjoyed the cooperation of the authorities. Strike after strike witnessed the same police brutality and use of militia, scabs, and private detectives, not to mention the blacklist and lockout, with federal troops in the background if needed.

The anarchists, their task of recruitment facilitated by the deepening crisis, worked tirelessly to win over the discontented. Between 1883 and 1886 the IWPA issued a flood of pamphlets and leaflets and published more than a dozen newspapers and journals through which it disseminated its radical doctrines. Along with the printed word went public meetings and demonstrations. Lectures and discussions threshed over the principles of socialism and anarchism and the evils of government and capital. "Who Are the Criminals?" "The Crisis of the Workers," "The Development of Socialism," and "Authority and Autonomy" were typical subjects. Orators railed against "exploiters" and "oppressors" and foretold the dawning of a new era of brotherhood, freedom, and equality.[6]

Apart from Spies and Parsons in Chicago and Most and Drury in New York, the IWPA could boast a full complement of excellent speakers in half a dozen languages, for whom the railroads provided convenient transportation and the cities eager audiences. The strength of their radical sentiment, the fervor of their agitation, is hard to exaggerate. Thousands who listened to their speeches, as William Holmes of Chicago observed, became "imbued with their revolutionary spirit."[7] Traveling from place to place, they spoke in beerhalls and clubhouses, on the streets and in the parks, denouncing the capitalist system and preaching the virtues of a juster life which could be obtained only through the abolition of "wage slavery." Appealing to the workers to awaken from their misery and recognize the true extent of their enslavement, they condemned the hypocrisy of the rich, their aristocratic pretensions, their amusements and dissipations. Something was fundamentally rotten in the country. The growing financial and industrial power was crushing the workers into poverty and depriving them of their dignity and freedom. Pointing to abuses at every hand, they counseled the workers to distrust politicians and representatives of all kinds and to use their own strength and intelligence, their own initiative and efforts, to achieve emancipation. They sought, above all, to inspire their listeners with the vision of a new society, based on individual sovereignty and mutual cooperation, in which free men and women would work willingly for themselves and each other instead of unwillingly for a capitalist employer. In such a society, they insisted, there would be no need for coercion and therefore no need for the state.

Street parades and mass outdoor demonstrations, with red and black banners and bands playing the "Marseillaise" and other revolutionary airs, were the most dramatic form of advertisement at this stage of the movement. A procession of workingmen, organized by the International in January 1885, marched to Fountain Square in downtown Cincinnati, carrying the "Red Flag of the Commune" and placards reading "Bread or Blood" and "Order and Empty Stomachs Can Never Be Allies," as well as a black flag inscribed "No Quarter."[8] Similar demonstrations were common in Chicago and other cities. By the same token, the International organized picnics, concerts, dances, and entertainments of various kinds, imparting a new revolutionary content to traditional social activities. "Those were momentous times," recollected William Holmes. "Days and nights of agitation in out-of-the-way places under great difficulties, by heroic men and women buoyed up by enthusiastic devotion to a great cause; speeches delivered from piles of salt barrels or dry-goods boxes to great crowds of anxious, hungry, almost homeless men and women; 'Thanksgiving parades' through mud and slush, the march of the have-nots through the streets where the do-naughts dwell; solitary street-corner propaganda away into the midnight hours; meetings held in holes and corners—to avoid rent or to reach the proletaire in their own dens, their homes; great halls filled weekly to overflowing by multitudes who came to hear 'glad tidings.' "[9]

In this way, through their press and meetings, their demonstrations and processions, the anarchists carried their message to the workers. Nor were their efforts unavailing. From 1883 to 1886 the movement picked up momentum. Groups of the International multiplied from year to year, and their membership increased steadily. Nine persons sufficed to form a group (formerly the number had been only five), and each group was autonomous, conducting its work "in its own way," according to guidelines laid down in 1886, provided that it remained faithful to the Pittsburgh Manifesto. Most groups had a secretary and a treasurer (elected as a rule for six-month terms) but no permanent officials. Their primary function was that of propaganda, in addition to "the obtaining of additional members, the spread of economic information, the organization and arming of the working people, both men and women," in their particular localities.[10]

It is not easy to determine how many Internationalists there were during this period. The records of the Bureau of Information have not been preserved, and the sources from which we must gauge the numerical strength of the movement—lists of groups published in anarchist newspapers and estimates made by participants and other contemporaries—are unreliable. To compound the problem, some of the groups were short-lived, surviving barely a few months, while others fused or divided and are consequently difficult to trace. Furthermore, none of the lists that have come down to us is accurate or complete. At the same time, they give an inflated picture by including ephemeral groups as well as armed sections and singing societies whose membership overlapped with that of the regular affiliates. One must distinguish, moreover, between active members, who joined the association and took part in its meetings and demonstrations, and sympathizers, who read anarchist literature and followed the movement's activities without directly participating in them. "It is very, very difficult to arrive at anything like a correct approximation in regard to the strength of our movement," wrote August Spies to Professor Ely in November 1885, when the International stood at its zenith. "Our organization may be compared with an overflowing river. The entire country is submerged and you [can] hardly say where the 'bed' (*Flussbett*) begins and where it ends."[11]

Spies himself estimated the number of active members at between ten and twelve thousand. This was, however, too high, the actual figure being less than half as many. Starting with about two thousand in the fall of 1883, when the IWPA was established, it climbed to perhaps five thousand by the fall of 1885. At that time the Bureau of Information reported the total number of groups to be 115, while *The Alarm* listed 86, all "in flourishing condition."[12] There were, in actual fact, about a hundred groups, with an average membership of forty or fifty, though some had more than a hundred members and others as few as ten (such as the group organized by Dr. Mary Herma Aikin in Grinnell, Iowa). In the fall of 1885, when the economy showed signs of recovery, membership in the International appears to have leveled off, so that in January 1886 the number of groups listed in *The Alarm* was the same as in the previous October. A plateau had evidently been reached and was maintained until the Haymarket incident.

At its height, then, from the fall of 1885 to the spring of 1886, the International had some five thousand members, along with perhaps three times as many sympathizers and supporters. Groups were to be found in nearly fifty cities and towns, concentrated in the Northeast and Midwest but reaching as far south as New Orleans and as far west as Denver and San Francisco, where they competed, in the words of *The Alarm*, with "the so-called International owned by Haskell."[13] The centers of the movement were New York, Philadelphia, Chicago, St. Louis, and other industrial cities with large working-class and immigrant populations. But groups were formed in such small towns as Huron, Dakota Territory, Muskegon, Michigan, and Scammonville, Kansas, and in the mining settlements of Illinois, Ohio, and Pennsylvania, following an evangelical tour by Albert Parsons. In the fall of 1885, moreover, a group of farm laborers was organized at Benton Harbor, Michigan, apparently the only one of its kind.[14]

Immigrants constituted the overwhelming majority of the members. For many recent settlers, the impulse to escape the Old World and start afresh in the New had foundered on the hardships that confronted them. America, the land of opportunity and promise, became the land of disappointment and despair. The sudden crowding into slums, the hard conditions of work, the uprooting from family and village life, the enforced pauperization and proletarianization combined to drive them into the anarchist fold. Some had taken part in the socialist movement in Europe, and they brought with them a greater sense of class struggle and revolutionary tradition than American workers normally possessed. They brought, too, as will be seen, the characteristic disease of every political emigration: sectarianism and factional strife.

Of the immigrants within the International, Germans (including Austrians and German Swiss) comprised the largest segment, though there were many Czechs, Scandinavians, and Britons, to say nothing of other nationalities. At the peak of the movement, in fact, the number of German anarchists in the United States probably exceeded that in Germany itself. Nine of the fourteen newspapers published by the International between 1883 and 1886 were in the German language, one of them, the *Chicagoer Arbeiter-Zeitung*, a daily. Of the rest, two were in English, two in Czech, and one in Danish.

Typically, a large city might have two or three German groups, one Bohemian group, and one American group. (The American groups were actually English-speaking bodies which included, besides native Americans, immigrants from Britain, Ireland, and other countries.) In all, there were eleven Bohemian and eleven American groups in early 1886, as compared with more than seventy German groups.

Here and there, in addition, one might find a Russian group (as in Pittsburgh), an Italian group (in New York), or a French group (in St. Louis).[15] Whatever their country of origin, however, the adherents saw themselves as members of an international movement, and they sought to break down the barriers that divided one nationality from another. Not, one might add, without result. Through combined rallies, demonstrations, and social occasions, contacts between natives and immigrants steadily increased, so that the IWPA was, to a noticeable degree, beginning to live up to its title.

Chicago, throughout this period, remained the principal stronghold of the movement, with the deepest roots, the most active press, and the largest number of members and groups. It was here, in 1881, that the first national gathering had taken place. Chicago, moreover, had sent more delegates to the Pittsburgh congress than any other city. The most capable and intelligent leaders, with the exception of Johann Most, were here, too, above all Parsons and Spies. Sensitive, sincere men, extravagant in everything they said and did, they organized groups, arranged demonstrations, published papers, raised funds, and mingled and talked with workers all over the city. Even more, by conducting lecture tours throughout the East and Middle West, they were able to extend their influence beyond the confines of their own bailiwick. Chicago, as a result, became the Mecca of the anarchist movement, to which adherents from all over the country looked for advice and support. It was the seat of the Bureau of Information, and letters poured in from every corner, some of which were published in *The Alarm* and *Arbeiter-Zeitung*, the International's chief media of communication. Parsons and Spies, as editors of these journals and secretaries of the Information Bureau, answered countless inquiries and dispatched large quantities of literature to members and potential recruits. Only Most himself could claim a comparable role in building up a movement of such vitality. Not without reason did George Schilling refer to the "wonderful activity" of the Chicago Internationalists, in particular of Parsons and Spies.[16]

Chicago, with its crowded immigrant population and long history of labor unrest, was fertile soil for anarchist propaganda and organization. In no other American city was class demarcation sharper or the gap between the rich and poor more conspicuous. In no other city was the reputation for police brutality more notorious or the economic crisis more sorely felt. Nor, it might be added, did the press anywhere else denounce with more vehemence all agitators and subversives or more strenuously uphold the right of property and the exigency of preserving law and order, by force if necessary. Given these circumstances, it is little wonder that the rise of the Chicago IWPA should have occurred with such unparalleled swiftness. By the fall of 1885 the city could boast fifteen active groups with nearly one thousand members, about a fifth of the national total.[17] To this must be added a large number of sympathizers, as many as five or six thousand in all. The majority, as in the country at large, were Germans, but there were also many Czechs and other Europeans, as well as a vigorous American Group, of which Parsons was the driving spirit. Scandinavians, while still in evidence, were rapidly waning. By 1884, for reasons not immediately apparent, they were no longer represented in the Bureau of Information, and by 1886 *Den Nye Tid* had ceased to appear.

Because of the large number of groups in Chicago, it was one of the few cities (St. Louis was another) to have a General Committee to coordinate activities. This committee, in accordance with the rules laid down at the Pittsburgh congress, functioned solely as an advisory body. Its members, it is worth noting, included four of the eight Haymarket defendants, Albert Parsons, August Spies, Michael Schwab, and Oscar Neebe, in addition to Balthasar Rau and Anton Hirschberger, both of whom sat also on the Information Bureau, together with Parsons and Spies. Both the General Committee and the Information Bureau held their meetings at 107 Fifth Avenue, the nerve center of the Chicago movement, where *The Alarm* and *Arbeiter-Zeitung* were published, and where the International maintained a library of works on economic and social subjects, of which Schwab was in charge until 1885.

In Chicago, as elsewhere, the International was almost exclusively a working-class organization, with only an occasional professional in its ranks, such as Dr. James D. Taylor, a member of the American Group. Through its propaganda and other activities, the idea of labor solidarity took on flesh and life, and anarchism assumed the character of a genuine class movement. Its ranks included both skilled and unskilled workers and workers in both large and small enterprises. The leaders, however, were mostly independent artisans and tradesmen. Of the eight Haymarket defendants, Parsons and Fischer were printers, Spies an upholsterer turned editor, Schwab a former bookbinder, Fielden a self-employed teamster, Lingg a carpenter, Engel the owner of a toy store, and Neebe the part owner of a yeast company. Nearly all of them had been reared in a rural and preindustrial culture, Parsons in Texas, the Germans in villages and towns. None were industrial workers in the proper sense, although they championed and helped organize this class, to which some (notably Fielden) had belonged in the past.

Their occupations, it should be noted, were not untypical of the anarchists of this period, especially the leadership element. Skilled artisans and craftsmen, confronted by the emergence of industrial capitalism and the mechanization of labor, formed the vanguard of most anarchist organizations of the late nineteenth century, in Europe as well as America. In the decades following the Civil War, the development of large-scale industry was a dominant feature of the American economy, accompanied by profound changes in the structure of society and in the methods of production and distribution. After the depression of 1873-1878, the introduction of machinery took place at an unprecedented rate. By the mid-1880s the factory system had become general, and the grip of mass production was firmly fastened upon the country.

Anarchism, to a large extent, was a reaction against these developments. For many craftsmen and skilled workers, the transformation of America into an industrial society threatened their accustomed way of life, not to mention their vision of a just social order. Samuel Fielden, who himself had labored as a child in the cotton mills of Lancashire, was sharply critical of the emergent system, and he sought, in countless speeches to working-class audiences, to "call their attention to the fact that by the introduction of labor-saving machinery and the subdivision of labor less men were continually needed, more productions produced, and their chance to work decreased." On one occasion, in March 1886, he went to Pullman, Illinois, a suburb of Chicago created by George Pullman, the inventor of the sleeping car, as a model industrial community. To Fielden, however, it was a "model slave pen," a company town in new dress. Only by removing the yoke of capitalism, he told its residents, might labor benefit from the advantages of modern technology.[18]

For other Chicago anarchists, deeply rooted in the traditional crafts, there was a nostalgia for the vanishing agrarian society of the past, before it was corrupted by the money values of manufacturers and financiers. Thus did Michael Schwab, the former bookbinder from Bavaria, mourn the transformation of the farmer into an industrial laborer: "Instead of the melodious tinkling of the bells of his cows, he now hears the task bell of the factory, that calls him to work. Instead of the splashing or roaring of the creeks and cataracts, the whispering of the air in the dark-green forests, he is treated to the clattering of noisy, busy machines. Stout, big-chested, strong-limbed and with rosy cheeks, he fell into the power of enslaving capital. Alas! it lasts not long till the cheeks lose their color, the limbs their strength and the freeman his independence."[19]

Laments such as this do not mean, however, that anarchism was inherently anti-industrial, or that the anarchists wished to turn the clock back to an age of independent farmers and craftsmen, though some would perhaps have liked nothing better. To say that the anarchists rejected modern society is to put the matter too simply. Their response to the rise of large-scale production was by no means merely to affirm the preindustrial values on which they had been reared. Nor did they reject technical innovation. For all their romantic yearnings, they welcomed new inventions that would relieve men of tedious labor and allow time for cultural and intellectual pursuits. Yet they wished to preserve the advantages of machinery within the context of a smaller and more natural society. What they resisted was the mammoth scale of industrial institutions, the excessive division of labor, and the system by which the machines were owned and administered. Under capitalism, Parsons had argued during the 1877 strike, the new technology was not being applied to benefit the working population but to intensify their exploitation. "We don't fight machinery," he repeated in 1886. "We don't oppose the thing. It is only the manner and methods of employing them that we object to. That is all. It is the manipulations of these things in the interests of a few; it is the monopolization of them that we object to. We desire that all the forces of nature, all the forces of society, of the gigantic strength which has resulted from the combined intellect and labor of the ages of the past shall be turned over to man, and made his servant, his obedient slave forever. This is the object of Socialism."[20]

Fielden expressed it in similar terms: "Improved machinery—I claim now what I have claimed all along in the discussion of this industrial problem—is calculated to benefit all classes of humanity and society. But it is the use to which they are put. If they can be bought by one person, so that he can hire labor cheap, or dispense with labor, they are a benefit to no person save the man who has money enough to purchase a machine."[21]

Equally deplorable, in the eyes of the anarchists, was the growing subdivision of labor, with its corrosive effects on the human spirit. Minute specialization, argued Parsons and his associates, benefited only the employer, while promoting boredom and frustration among the workers, accentuating the master-slave relationship, and reinforcing the invidious distinction between manual and intellectual work. Under the capitalist system, the workers were merely hired hands, cogs in an intricate machine, receiving little satisfaction from the monotonous, repetitive drudgery they performed. "We have lost sight of the pleasure of work," was how *The Alarm* succinctly put it.[22] Pride of workmanship, or even a simple understanding of where one stood in the productive process, had no place in the new scheme of things, so that the workers were increasingly estranged from their labor, from themselves, and from their fellow men.

Anarchism, then, was not a protest against industrialism as much as a demand that it be humanized and organized to public advantage. Determined not to be reduced to paid menials, to machine-tenders assigned to a tiny part of the productive process, the anarchists sought to replace capitalism with an economic system that valued personal autonomy and the creativity of labor. They envisioned a decentralized, egalitarian society based on the voluntary cooperation of free individuals, a society without government or property, without hunger or want, in which men and women would direct their own affairs unimpeded by any authority. In such a society, the worker, without sacrificing the gains of modern technology, would regain the lost joy in his labor and the dignity of being his own master. No longer would he be treated as chattel or as a marketable commodity.

Such an ideology exerted a powerful appeal. Many of the recruits to the IWPA came from handicrafts occupations—metals, woodworking, tailoring, cigarmaking—which were being absorbed into the factory system and, in some cases, replaced by machines. This was especially true of the metal crafts, within which the anarchists won their strongest following. Gustav Belz, a leader of the Chicago metal workers, sat on the International's General Committee, and large numbers of the rank and file joined the anarchist-dominated Federative Union of Metal Workers of America, with headquarters in

St. Louis (Joseph Reifgraber serving as president) and branches in New York and Philadelphia as well as in Chicago itself.[23] The majority of the new adherents seem to have worked in small shops, but a growing number were employed in the big, up-to-date factories, such as the Pullman railroad car works and the McCormick and Deering agricultural machinery plants, where Parsons and his comrades were often called upon to speak.

The International, however, attracted not only skilled workers and craftsmen, but also the semi-skilled, the unskilled, and the unemployed. With the rapid introduction of machinery, these groups had been swelling in numbers, replenished by a shift in population from country to city and by the waves of immigrants from Europe. Combined with the depression, the influx into the factories of semi-skilled and unskilled workers, weak in bargaining power because they were so easily replaced, had a disastrous effect upon wages. In 1884 the average cuts amounted to 15 percent. The following year they went even deeper, arousing a wave of anger and frustration. Terence V. Powderly, the leader of the Knights of Labor, noted in April 1885 that "a deep-rooted feeling of discontent pervades the masses," and that "the army of the discontented is gathering fresh recruits day by day."[24]

Owing to the mounting crisis, the unskilled and unemployed were drawn to the International in increasing numbers. Because their lot was so hard and their poverty so bitter, the agitation of the anarchists spoke directly to their hearts and articulated their deepest grievances. Many were instinctive rebels, ignorant of anarchist theory or ideals, whom misfortune and despair had made susceptible to extreme solutions. They joined the International because the total and immediate revolution that the anarchists promised seemed the only possibility of improving their desperate condition. Others saw anarchism simply as a more radical version of socialism, sanctioning the methods of conspiracy and direct action from which the SLP and other moderate groups recoiled.

The International endeavored to rally these elements—the unskilled and unorganized, the unwanted and unemployed—and to make their voices heard. It sought to fill them with a sense of their grievances and with a consciousness of their own power. It appealed to the poorest of the poor—"Les Misérables," The Alarm called them—living on the margin of society and waging a desperate struggle for survival. Gripped by visions of the despised and rejected—

the tramps, the down-and-out vagrants, the *Lumpenproletariat* of the urban slums—rising from the lower depths to exterminate their oppressors, the anarchists regarded these and other outcasts as allies in the social revolution. "Let every dirty, lousy tramp arm himself with a revolver or knife," the *Chicago Tribune* reported Lucy Parsons as saying, "and lay in wait on the steps of the palaces of the rich and stab or shoot the owners as they come out. Let us kill them without mercy, and let it be a war of extermination and without pity. Let us devastate the avenues where the wealthy live as Sheridan devastated the beautiful valley of the Shenandoah."[25]

Thus, attracted by the rhetoric of violence and by hopes of immediate redemption, a growing segment of the Chicago working class—skilled and unskilled, employed and unemployed—flocked to the International. A climax was reached with the disruption of the Amalgamated Trades and Labor Assembly, the city's politically oriented central labor body, when, in late 1883, a dissident faction of the Cigar Makers' Union withdrew and formed the Progressive Cigar Makers' Union. In February 1884 the Progressive Union held a mass meeting and, under the tutelage of August Spies and Paul Grottkau, proclaimed that "the only means whereby the emancipation of mankind can be brought about is the open rebellion of the robbed class in all parts of the country against the existing economic and political institutions."[26]

Having thus asserted its solidarity with the anarchist tendency, the same union took the initiative in organizing a new central labor council. In June 1884 it called upon all unions in the city to secede from the Trades Assembly and to form a Central Labor Union with a revolutionary policy. Four German unions answered the call—the metal workers, the butchers, the cabinetmakers, and the carpenters and joiners—and the Central Labor Union was duly established. In October 1884 the new body adopted a declaration of principles, asserting that all land is a social heritage, that all wealth is created by labor, that between labor and capital there can be no harmony, and that every worker ought to "cut loose from all capitalist political parties and to devote his energy to his trades or labor union," as well as to "stand ready to resist the encroachment of the ruling class upon our liberties."[27]

The conversion of workers from political to direct actionists, from reformists to revolutionaries, must be credited to several factors, among them police brutality, political corruption, the hard line adopted by employers, and the talents of the IWPA spokesmen. Most important, however, was the worsening economic situation. As the depression deepened, the Central Labor Union went from strength to strength, spearheading the creation of new trade unions and drawing away existing unions from the control of the Trades Assembly. In October 1885 thirteen unions already belonged to the new organization, while nineteen were affiliated with its rival. By the eve of Haymarket, in the spring of 1886, the Central Labor Union had become the dominant force in the Chicago labor movement, boasting twenty-four unions, among which were the eleven largest in the city.[28]

From its inception, the Central Labor Union was closely tied with the IWPA. Not only did it hold its business meetings at Greif's Hall on West Lake Street, a popular IWPA gathering place, but it joined with the International in sponsoring picnics, rallies, and lectures, in which Spies, Parsons, and their colleagues took a leading role. Still more, the membership of the organizations overlapped to a large extent. For example, of the 400-odd members of the International Carpenters and Joiners, a Central Labor Union affiliate, nearly all were anarchists or anarchist sympathizers.[29]

Both organizations, moreover, insisted that the labor movement must be revolutionary in character, that its mission of emancipating the workers could be accomplished only by eliminating the capitalist system and reorganizing society on new foundations. By doing so, they incurred the wrath of the Trades Assembly, which accused them of preaching "arson and murder." The militants lashed back at the Assembly for condoning "wage slavery" and "slow starvation" in an effort to curry favor with the bosses. "The social war has come," cried The Alarm, "and those who are not with us are against us."[30]

As tempers flared on both sides, the International challenged the Assembly to a public debate. Some 1,500 people packed the Aurora Turner Hall to witness the fireworks. Nor were they disappointed. Parsons, who spoke first for the International, did not mince his words as he dismissed reformism as a delusion and proclaimed that the "beast of property" was hounding the workers to death and therefore had to be destroyed and replaced by a free society based on "the co-operative organization of production." Fielden, who followed Parsons, ridiculed the notion, put forward by the Trades Assembly, of a harmony of interests between labor and capital. "When a burglar enters the house," Fielden said, "they tap him on the shoulder and say, 'let's us argue this thing; let's harmonize: take seventy-five per cent of what I have but leave me the rest.' We Socialists say to him, 'lay it down.' We have been arguing long enough with the capitalists, and they won't lay it down. The time is coming when they will be compelled to lay it down."[31]

As these speeches indicate, the International and the Central Labor Union differed from the Trades Assembly in being militant organizations dedicated to overthrowing the established order. They had no truck with legislative solutions. "The Central Labor Union, unlike its rival, the Trades Assembly, steers clear of politics and politicians," declared *The Alarm*.[32] The Assembly, for its own part, clung to its moderate course. Arranging a Labor Day parade for September 7, 1885, it secured Mayor Harrison and Congressman Martin Foran as speakers and prohibited the anarchists from taking part. Denouncing this "contemptible flunkeyism," the International and the Central Labor Union hastily arranged a meeting of their own, which assembled in Market Square on Sunday, September 6. After preliminaries, during which Spies delivered an oration in German and the Socialistic Male Chorus sang the "Red Banner," the participants formed themselves in ranks and, with Neebe as marshal and Parsons at his side, marched through downtown Chicago. First in line came a contingent of women in decorated wagons, which bore the slogans: "Down with Government, God and Gold" and "Our Civilization: The Bullet and Policeman's Club." As usual, they ended up at the Ogden's Grove picnic grounds, where Parsons delivered an impassioned speech. Addressing a crowd of several thousand, he decried "the enslavement of the producers to the things which their labor creates." Shall 5 percent of the population, he asked, be allowed to possess the world's wealth? The capitalist, by appropriating the means of life for his exclusive enjoyment, was "a usurper, a thief, and a murderer." The exploitation of man by man must cease, Parsons exclaimed. "To this we are pledged. We are revolutionists. We fight for the destruction of the system of wage-slavery. To the despised, destitute, disinherited of the earth, anarchy offers love, peace and plenty. Statute law, constitutions and government are at war with nature and the inalienable rights of man, and social revolution is the effort of nature to restore its equilibrium. The claim of capital to profit, interest or rent is a robber claim, enforced by piratical methods. Let robbers and pirates meet the fate they deserve! Against them there is but one recourse, force! Agitate, organize, revolt! Proletarians of the world unite! We have nothing to lose but our chains; we have a world to win! Lead on the Red Flag, the sign of labor's emancipation—the emblem of redeemed humanity; lead on to liberty or death!" With this Parsons shook out the folds of a red silk banner and waved it aloft. The crowd burst forth in cheers, the band struck up the "Marseillaise," and all joined in singing their revolutionary anthem.[33]

To moderate labor leaders, in Chicago and elsewhere, the mounting talk of revolution was deeply disturbing. Within the Central Labor Union, as Samuel Gompers later remarked, "dynamite became a familiar thought. Those of us who were trying to develop a constructive trade-union movement were exceedingly apprehensive of the reckless swing toward force."[34] Yet a rising number of workers were defecting to the radical camp, in response, more than anything else, to the failure of both political action and conventional trade unionism to deal with the worsening depression. More and more workers were coming to regard direct action as the only answer to an ineffectual ballot, corrupt politicians, and the use of police, militia, and hired thugs in the suppression of strikes and demonstrations.

A large proportion of the defectors came from the Socialistic Labor Party, whole sections of which went over to the International. No fewer than seven of the eight Haymarket defendants had been members of the SLP, the sole exception being Lingg, who did not come to America until 1885, after the split had become final. By 1884 the party was barely clinging to life. Johann Most, with his characteristic sarcasm, called it "a cadaver that must be buried so that it might not offend the nose of the public."[35]

As a result of the depression, however, the SLP regained some of its former strength, so that the struggle with the anarchists persisted. Vigorous newspaper controversies and public discussions were the order of the day. The most notable of the latter was a debate between Johann Most and Paul Grottkau, held in Chicago on May 24, 1884. Grottkau, as editor of the *Arbeiter-Zeitung*, had been an articulate figure in the social revolutionary movement and, having attended the Pittsburgh congress, a charter member of the International. At heart, however, he had remained a state socialist and was unable to follow the evolution of the International towards anarchism. Resigning from the *Arbeiter-Zeitung*, he returned to the SLP and moved from Chicago to Milwaukee.

The debate between Grottkau and Most took place in Stein-mueller's Hall, a popular socialist meeting place at 45 North Clark Street. The theme was "Anarchism or Communism?" and Balthasar Rau delivered the opening statement. It was a well-matched contest, both opponents being fluent speakers and thoroughly versed in radical theory. For Grottkau anarchism and communism were "antagonistic principles," the former representing individualism, the latter solidarity. Most countered that, not only were they perfectly compatible, but that true communism implied local autonomy and personal freedom. Ably and intelligently conducted, the debate was transcribed by a stenographer and published in pamphlet form by the General Committee of the Chicago IWPA.[36] Sold by *Arbeiter-Zeitung* carriers at ten cents a copy, it had a wide circulation and helped to sharpen the division between the two schools.

Over the next few years, socialist and anarchist papers were filled with articles on the relative merits of the contending movements. Public debates of the subject were frequent, and feelings ran high on both sides. At a meeting in New York the police were called in after a fistfight erupted, and Justus Schwab was arrested for inciting to riot.[37] As part of the SLP campaign against the rising militant tide, special lecture tours were arranged, and Alexander Jonas and other party spokesmen went around the country visiting industrial centers seeking to expose the weaknesses of anarchist doctrine and to buoy up the discouraged socialists. Leaflets and brochures were printed under the auspices of the National Executive Committee and distributed in thousands of copies. A notable example was *Socialism and Anarchism: Antagonistic Opposites*, in which Jonas proclaimed the members of his party to be "the implacable enemies of all anarchism."[38]

As moderate or politically minded socialists like Grottkau returned to the SLP fold, the IWPA became a more uniformly anarchist organization. Adopting an increasingly militant stance, it became, for a brief period, the most dynamic labor body in America. Its unique achievement lay in creating a working-class movement that was genuinely revolutionary, one that refused to accept capitalism as a permanent feature of American life. It helped the workers to organize their forces and taught them the rudiments of social action. Through its processions and demonstrations it aroused public concern about conditions in the slums and factories, while at the same time imbuing the unskilled and unemployed with a sense of solidarity and of their worth as human beings. When strikes occurred in any section of the country, it gave the participants moral and financial support, organized protests in their behalf, sent speakers and observers into the strike area, and reported on events in its press.

Such was the case in the summer of 1884, when four thousand coal miners in the Hocking Valley of Ohio walked out in protest against a reduction in wages. Scab labor, consisting mostly of recent immigrants, were brought in, along with Pinkertons and militia to protect them. The strike attracted wide attention. August Spies went to the scene for the *Arbeiter-Zeitung*, while *The Alarm* denounced the mine owners as "capitalistic cannibals." After six months of turbulence, the strike was defeated, but two new groups of the International had been organized, one German, the other American.[39]

In the spring of 1885, another big strike occurred, this time among the quarrymen of Lemont, Lockport, and Joliet, Illinois, involving some three thousand workers. Once again the dispute centered on a cut in wages, and once again the employers brought in scabs and detectives to break the strike. When matters threatened to get out of hand, Governor Richard J. Oglesby, who was to preside over the Haymarket executions, sent in four companies of state militia, armed with rifles, revolvers, and a Gatling gun, to maintain order. On May 4, 1885, the militia opened fire on a group of unarmed strikers in Lemont, killing at least two and wounding several more, while men and women were clubbed and bayoneted in the streets.

In Chicago the American Group of the International protested against the massacre, and on May 5 Parsons reported from Lemont on the situation for *The Alarm*. That evening he was asked to address a meeting of strikers. When he advised them to organize to defend their rights, a voice called out: "We can't organize. The bosses would break it up; they did it before. It would not be allowed. They would starve us out and break it up." "Then you are slaves," Parsons replied.[40] As in the Hocking Valley, the strike in the quarries was defeated and the men forced to go back on the owners' terms.

The years from 1884 to 1886 saw a rash of similar strikes—among the switchmen of East St. Louis, Illinois, the timbermen of the Saginaw Valley in Michigan, the cotton spinners of Fall River, Massachusetts, the plumbers and bricklayers of New York City, the carpet weavers and shoemakers of Philadelphia, and the railroad workers of the southwestern lines of Jay Gould, who boasted that he could "hire one half of the working class to kill the other half." Nearly all were directed against reductions in wages and for the right of the workingmen to organize. The employers fought back with every weapon at their command: lockouts, blacklists, scabs, armed guards, local police, and state militia. All of these strikes drew national attention, and all were reported in the anarchist press, for which a special target was the employment of Pinkertons, those "banditti of armed outlaws," *The Alarm* branded them, "under a chief ready to cut throats in the service of monopoly."[41]

In Chicago itself, however, the police remained the principal villain. During a streetcar strike in the summer of 1885, not only were the strikers themselves attacked and beaten, but even nonstriking workers and businessmen who got in the way. The man responsible for this was Captain John Bonfield, commander of the Desplaines Street station, who less than a year later was to shoulder much of the burden for the violence in Haymarket Square. Known as "Black Jack" Bonfield, he had made his reputation and earned his promotions by cracking skulls. A "large, powerful, resolute, ruthless man," in the description of Charles Edward Russell, a Chicago-based reporter for the *New York World*, Bonfield was prone to violent behavior and obviously sadistic. He was "without tact or discretion or sympathy," as Mother Jones recalled him, a "most brutal believer in suppression as the method to settle industrial unrest."[42]

At no time was this more apparent than during the 1885 streetcar strike. Contrary to Mayor Harrison's orders, Bonfield ordered his men into action, and they clubbed and beat everyone in sight, including a number of store owners who had stepped outside to see what was happening. According to *The Alarm*, one of the mayor's sons was among the victims. Charles Edward Russell, who witnessed the attack, saw "the clubs descending right and left like flails, and men falling before them, often frightfully injured."[43] Bonfield himself assaulted a group of bystanders near the corner of Western Avenue and Madison Street, then attacked several other people, including a sixty-five-year-old man, whom Bonfield ordered to "fall back," then clubbed before the man could move.

The next day, July 3, the scene was repeated. A crew of gas company workers was digging up the street when a group of strikers and sympathizers began throwing loose dirt onto the streetcar tracks. Bonfield had the gas workers arrested. They were thrown into a police wagon, and when one man stuck his head out to ask about his tools, Bonfield beat him and the man next to him into unconsciousness. Neither man ever fully recovered, and one died in 1889 from complications resulting from his injuries.[44]

Affidavits, filed not only by workers but by shopkeepers and other bystanders, attested to Bonfield's brutality. The testimony was confirmed, interestingly enough, by a fellow police officer, Captain Michael J. Schaack, who himself was to figure prominently in the Haymarket imbroglio.[45] A petition signed by one thousand citizens was sent to Mayor Harrison and the city council, demanding Bonfield's dismissal from the force. Harrison agreed that Bonfield should be removed, but influential persons intervened in his behalf, so that he was not only retained but was soon promoted to inspector and assigned to central police headquarters at city hall.

Thanks to officers like Bonfield, the Chicago police acquired the worst reputation in the country for savagery against labor. As inspector of police, Bonfield, it might be noted, began a campaign of drilling his men in new techniques of riot control. Lucy Parsons wrote about this in *The Alarm*. What is the purpose of the drill? she wondered. "For whom is it intended? Who is to be shot?"[46] *The Alarm* cautioned the workers that the brutality of a Bonfield was precisely what they might expect "just as soon as you try to exercise your 'rights,' as soon as you attempt to throw off the fetters of slavery! If you don't like this, get a gun, get dynamite!"[47] A growing number, under the leadership of the International, were preparing to defend themselves against future attacks. They were determined to avoid a repetition of 1877. What was more, they aimed to secure social justice. The anarchists had inspired them with extravagant hopes, which were fated to be disappointed.

8 ‖ THE AMERICAN GROUP

The IWPA, throughout its existence, remained predominantly German in composition. Yet a growing number of English-speaking workers were joining its ranks. By the end of 1885 there were a dozen American groups around the country, with nearly a thousand members. The largest and most active of these was the American Group of Chicago, founded by Albert Parsons in November 1883, shortly after the Pittsburgh congress. Starting with only five members, it had a limited impact at first. But with the deepening of the depression and the launching of *The Alarm*, it became the most dynamic group in the city. In October 1884, when *The Alarm* began publication, the group had forty-five members. By April 1885 the figure had climbed to ninety-five, more than doubling in a six-month period. According to William Holmes, the group's recording secretary, 150 members were on its rolls in early 1886, though some of these seem to have been merely sympathizers. A more reliable count would place the total membership at about one hundred.[1]

As the American Group increased in size, threatening to become unwieldy, some of its members tried to start a second group, but abandoned the attempt after only two meetings. Thus, at the time of the Haymarket explosion, the American Group was the only English-speaking unit of the International in the Chicago area. A remarkable band, it included five of the eight Haymarket defendants: Parsons, Spies, Fielden, Fischer, and Neebe. Women played a conspicuous role in its activities, most notably Lucy Parsons, Lizzie May Holmes, and Sarah E. Ames. As in the International at large, nearly all of the members were workers. Apart from the Haymarket defendants, whose occupations have already been noted, John A. Henry and William A. Patterson were printers, J. P. Dusey a stockyard worker, and Lucy Parsons a seamstress, to cite examples where information is available. James D. Taylor, a physician, was among the few exceptions.

The term "American group" was something of a misnomer, for

many of the members were in fact immigrants. A significant number, perhaps a dozen in all, came from Britain and Ireland. Unlike other immigrants, they faced no language barrier and, mingling easily with native Americans, were less conspicuous as foreigners.

The most prominent among them, Samuel Fielden, served as treasurer of the group and, as has already been noted, was one of the defendants at the Haymarket trial. A native of Lancashire, he came from the cotton mills on which Marx and Engels based their analysis of the English working class in the throes of industrial revolution. The youngest of three children, he was born on February 25, 1847, in Todmorden, a manufacturing town typical of the area, nestled in a valley with small farms dotting the hillsides. His father, Abram Fielden, was a weaver by trade who had risen to foreman in his factory, where he was to work till incapacitated by illness and age. A man of fine physique and more than ordinary intelligence, he was an active Chartist who took part in agitating for the ten-hour day. He was also an eloquent talker, and on Sundays the Fielden home was the meeting place of an advanced group of workers who discussed the issues of the day. This gave young Sam his first taste for study of the labor question, which he retained for the rest of his life.[2]

At the age of eight, Fielden, as was usual with children of poor Lancashire families, went to work in the mill where his father was employed. For two years he toiled at the spinning machine, enduring "all its horrors and barbarities."[3] From the age of ten to eighteen he did the heavier work of taking spools from the carding room to the machines, and then, until he was twenty-one, wound warps onto beams. Though he lacked a formal education, Fielden learned to read at an early age and soon displayed the germs of that "philosophical character" which some attributed to him in later years. Raised in a Chartist household, he grew up hating injustice and privilege. On the eve of the American Civil War, a group of Negro lecturers spoke in Todmorden on conditions in the South, arousing Fielden's compassion and making him, to his dying day, the black man's friend.[4] He read *Uncle Tom's Cabin* and the travel books of Harriet Martineau, and when the Civil War broke out, he, along with other members of his family, became an ardent champion of the Union cause. His first public speech, delivered as a teenager in his native town, was in support of the North against slavery. Twenty years later, speaking before the American Group, he praised John Brown as "the greatest character in American history," adding that there was "need of such rebels today."[5]

Aside from the political egalitarianism of his father, Fielden inherited the religious egalitarianism of his mother, who died when he was a boy of ten. A small, hard-working woman with "pleasing and regular features," she had been a devoted adherent of the Primitive Methodist sect, which, having broken away from the Wesleyans in the early nineteenth century, emphasized lay preaching of an evangelistic type. Sam himself went through a prolonged phase of religious enthusiasm, joining the Methodists in 1865 and preaching in Todmorden and neighboring towns, a "perambulating talking machine," as he described himself.[6] In Lancashire, as E. P. Thompson has noted, the Methodist workman was marked by a "special earnestness and vigour of moral concern,"[7] qualities that young Fielden exhibited in ample measure. Articulating the ideas of his sect, he became a well-known figure at revivalist meetings and the director of a village Sunday school. In 1886, while the Haymarket trial was in progress, the *Chicago Tribune* published a letter from a former Lancashire Methodist, vouching for Fielden's good character.[8]

In July 1868, at the age of twenty-one, Fielden, who had long dreamed of coming to the United States, set sail for New York. Arriving with only a few dollars in his pocket, he found employment in a Brooklyn hat factory, but quit after two days, as the wages were low and the work disagreeable, then worked for some weeks in the textile mills of Providence, Rhode Island. Meanwhile, reading Horace Greeley in the *New York Tribune*, he was seized with the idea of going West to reap the "glorious opportunities" awaiting a young man of ability.[9] By way of Niagara Falls, Cleveland, and Beria, he made his way to Chicago, preaching the Methodist gospel and working at odd jobs to earn his keep.

Reaching Chicago in August 1869, Fielden labored at various jobs before sailing down the Mississippi to Vicksburg. He worked in Mississippi, Louisiana, and Arkansas, taking every opportunity to learn about the condition of the Negro, in which he had been interested since his youth. The Negro, he found to his dismay, was "as much a bondsman as ever he was, and in many cases worse."[10] In 1871 Fielden returned to Chicago and spent the next eight years at different jobs, dredging the Sag Canal, working as a farmhand, and driving a team in the quarries. Still an avid reader, he spent most of his free time in the library. He also attended lectures by

Robert G. Ingersoll, Theodore Tilton, Bayard Taylor, and other leading reformers of the day.

In the fall of 1879, having saved his money for the journey, Fielden
went back to England to visit his family, whom he had not seen in
nearly a decade. For the last time, he embraced his aging father, who
was to die a week after the Haymarket trial. He also fulfilled a
matrimonial engagement that he had concluded eleven years before,
on the eve of his departure for America, and it was with his bride
that he returned to his adopted country in February 1880.

Back in Chicago, Fielden used his remaining money to purchase
a team of horses. For the next six years, until his arrest in 1886, he
earned a living by hauling stone. He labored fourteen hours a day,
from sunup to dusk. It was backbreaking work, which took him to
every quarter of Chicago. "You can hardly go through a street in
this city," he told the Haymarket court, "that I have not dropped
my sweat upon, that had been produced by the labor of my hands."[11]

And yet for others, Fielden admitted, conditions were worse. With
its unemployment, low wages, and child labor, the present economic
system, he declared, was profoundly unjust, and the man who would
not try to change it was "no man" at all. The remedy, however,
eluded him until he heard about the doctrine of socialism. Socialism,
a friend explained, meant equal opportunity for all. "That was the
touch," recalled Fielden. "From that time I became a Socialist; I
learned more and more what it was. I knew that I had found the
right thing; I had found the medicine that was calculated to cure
the ills of society."[12]

Fielden poured the whole strength of his religious and idealistic
nature into his new cause. "I was deeply stirred by the condition of
the working classes, and sought to do what I could for their betterment," he wrote on the eve of his scheduled execution.[13] When the
first teamsters' union was formed in Chicago, during the summer
of 1880, he was among the charter members and soon became its
vice-president. By 1883 he was addressing labor gatherings throughout the city. A "thorough libertarian," as William Holmes describes
him,[14] he joined the IWPA in July 1884, becoming the treasurer of
the American Group.

Fielden had meanwhile given up Methodism and become an out-
and-out freethinker. Joining the Chicago Liberal League, a branch
of the American Secular Union, he took frequent part in its discussions and "electrified the audiences by his eloquent outbursts of

revolutionary sentiment."[15] Elected vice-president of the league, he served as its delegate to the national congress held at Milwaukee in 1882, where he helped secure the adoption of a labor plank in the organization's platform.

It was as a speaker that Fielden made his mark in the radical movement. With his warm and generous nature, touched by the misery of the poor, he was always ready to hold forth on their behalf against the injustice of existing conditions. Though occasionally long-winded, his speeches were passionate and moving, which made him a great favorite at rallies and demonstrations. Next to Parsons, in fact, he became the International's most popular English speaker, lecturing all over Chicago and the Middle West. In 1885 he addressed a July Fourth picnic in St. Louis and a Thanksgiving Day rally in Cincinnati. In Canton, Ohio, he spoke on "the cause of the hard times, and how it can be prevented."[16] A stocky, rough-hewn man with broad, slightly stooped shoulders, large hands, and muscular arms, he had a full black beard and closely cropped hair and "the bushiest eyebrows ever seen over human eyes."[17] His rugged appearance and fluent, homespun delivery appealed to his working-class audiences. Despite his conversion to free thought, his speeches, filled with biblical allusions and fired with a religiouslike conviction, showed the influence of his Methodist upbringing.

Fielden, as Ernst Schmidt and others attested, was a good-natured man of a mild and nonviolent disposition, completely devoted to his wife and baby daughter, who was two-and-a-half years old at the time of the Haymarket incident. (A son was born while Fielden was in prison awaiting the outcome of the case.) In private gatherings, as Lizzie May Holmes recalled, he was "whole-souled, humorous, full of quaint touches of tenderness, simple uncultured poetry, and good-heartedness."[18] He was also well-read and clear-headed, noted John Henry, and "while I have the advantage of a little more polished manner, I would be glad to exchange it for what he has in his brain."[19]

Yet Fielden's impact was more emotional than intellectual. "Fielden was a man of the people," Lizzie Holmes once remarked. "He had lived, worked and suffered with them; he understood them and his quick, warm sympathies went out to every human being that ever clanked a chain. His sturdy eloquence, rising from a warmly beating heart rather than from a cultured brain, reached the masses and stirred and welded them together, as few men could. I remember so well the immense crowds of hard-handed, collarless workingmen who used to shout or groan or grit their teeth or laugh or weep under the wonderful spell of his eloquence. Fielden was the workingman's orator, the workingman's friend."[20]

In addition to Fielden, the American Group included several other British-born members. Among them was William T. Holmes, the recording secretary, Archibald H. Simpson, afterwards associated with Benjamin Tucker's circle in Boston, and James D. Taylor, who, born in 1810, was the oldest member of the group, a venerable figure with his long white hair and beard. Taylor, a socialist of long standing, had practiced medicine for forty-four years in the United States, chiefly in Illinois. ("Chronic Disease and Its Cure by the Vacuum Treatment," ran his ad in *The Alarm*.) Of the Irish members, J. P. Dusey, Thomas Brown, and John Keegan were the most conspicuous, Dusey for his advocacy of violence ("the unemployed should attack the lives and property of those who have robbed them of their labor products and now turn them adrift to starve," he told a meeting of the American Group).[21]

In some cases, given our scanty information, it is hard to tell whether a member of the group was a native American or an immigrant from Britain or elsewhere. By the same token, it is hard to differentiate the English from the Irish, Scots, or Welsh, as names are often deceiving and biographical data unavailable. Furthermore, one must distinguish between recent arrivals and residents of long standing. Of the latter, several had been in the country for decades— Dr. Taylor since 1842, Thomas Brown since 1852, William Holmes since 1856.

Holmes, with the exception of Fielden, was the most prominent British-born anarchist in Chicago at the time of the Haymarket affair. Besides being secretary of the American Group, he was one of Parsons's closest friends and would shield him from the police in the aftermath of the explosion. Born in Yorkshire in 1851, he was only five when his parents brought him to the United States and settled in Wisconsin. When his father became an invalid, William left school and worked as a sawyer in planing mills and box factories in Wisconsin and afterwards in Chicago, to which the family moved in 1866. Teaching himself shorthand, he got a job as a stenographer. In 1885, owing to poor health, he moved to Geneva, Illinois, a town thirty-five miles west of Chicago, where he opened a school in shorthand and elocution, from which he eked out a living until the Haymarket incident.[22]

Holmes, like Parsons, whom he met in 1880, had been a member of the SLP, from which he withdrew in the early 1880s. In June 1884 he joined the American Group and, thanks to his knowledge of shorthand, immediately became its secretary. He served in the same capacity as a member of the Chicago Liberal League, being an agnostic in religion, as he told Joseph Labadie, "with leanings towards rational spiritualism."[23] A facile writer, Holmes contributed to numerous left-wing journals, including *The Alarm*, *Truth*, and *The Labor Enquirer*. His most notable work, however, was a seventy-five page pamphlet, *The Historical, Philosophical and Economical Bases of Anarchy*, in which he probed the roots of anarchism in Europe and the United States, quoting many American writers to show that anarchism, far from being an alien doctrine, was deeply anchored in American soil.

While at bottom an adherent of the "Kropotkin-Reclus" persuasion, to quote his own description, Holmes was strongly influenced also by Tucker, Proudhon, and other libertarian thinkers. An eclectic anarchist, he drew on all its schools, individualist and collectivist, American and European, in an effort to reconcile their differences. Throughout his career, both before and after Haymarket, he strove to unite the warring factions within the movement, urging compromise and mutual understanding. He himself was uncompromising only in his opposition to government. The state, he declared, "destroys equality, subverts liberty, prostitutes justice. Abolish the state, and these may be enjoyed without stint."[24]

In his efforts to achieve a measure of unity, Holmes was ably assisted by his wife Lizzie, also a member of the group and, along with Lucy Parsons, one of the most active women anarchists in the country. A year older than her husband, she came of pioneer American stock, her ancestors having fought in the War of Independence. "I am," she once remarked, "as American as a person can be who is not a full-blooded, copper-colored Indian."[25]

Brought up in a family of libertarians, Lizzie came to Chicago from Iowa some years before the Haymarket episode. Her mother, Hannah J. Hunt, brother C. F. Hunt, and sister, Lillie D. White, all wrote for *Lucifer*, one of the leading anarchist journals of the period, and Lillie served briefly as its editor. Lizzie herself was a frequent contributor, having come to anarchism in 1883 by way of the Greenback and socialist movements. As prolific a writer as her husband, she published articles, editorials, and poems in a wide range of radical periodicals, among them *The Alarm*, of which she became the assistant editor. Always lucid, well-informed, and vigorous in expression, her writings sometimes appeared under the pen name of "May Huntley," formed from her middle and maiden names, or under the surname of her first husband, Mr. Swank, who died before her conversion to anarchism.

A small, unpretentious woman with short, dark hair, Mrs. Holmes championed the rights of American Indians (as did Parsons and other members of the group) and was, together with her husband, active in the Chicago Liberal League. "She was a noble and self-sacrificing woman," wrote Joseph R. Buchanan, editor of *The Labor Enquirer*, "and one whose honesty and truthfulness were above suspicion."[26] A feminist as well as an anarchist, she was a keen admirer of Mary Wollstonecraft, about whom she wrote and lectured.[27] As a part-time seamstress, she joined the Working Women's Union of Chicago and helped organize what was perhaps the first strike of the city's sewing girls, who toiled for sixteen hours a day in small basement sweatshops at pitiful wages. She often reported on the conditions of working women in the labor and anarchist press. "It is a fact," she wrote in the San Francisco *Truth*, "that women in all ordinary fields of labor are worse off than men. They are paid less, driven a little harder, have less chance to cry out, are more really slaves of slaves."[28]

It was as a member of the American Group that Lizzie came to know William Holmes, whom she married in November 1885, moving into his house at Geneva. Before that, she had lived near the Parsonses on the North-West Side of Chicago, and their frequent encounters, she tells us, were among the "memorable incidents in my life."[29] Even now, despite their remote location, she and her husband remained active in the group and seldom missed a meeting. Lizzie, a former music teacher, was often called upon to sing and play the piano, while William chaired lectures and discussions and kept a record of the proceedings. Without them the International would have been a less effective organization. To Dyer Lum, Parsons's successor as editor of *The Alarm*, they were "two of Chicago's most able and devoted Anarchists."[30]

Apart from its British members, for whom English was the mother tongue, the American Group included immigrants from other countries who had been in the United States long enough to have mastered the language. Among them were Peter Peterson, editor of *Den Nye Tid*, and Michael D. Malkoff, a Russian émigré who, proficient in German as well as English, worked at the *Arbeiter-Zeitung* and shared rooms with Balthasar Rau on Larrabee Street. In the same category, too, were a number of Germans, including three of the Haymarket defendants, Spies, Fischer, and Neebe.

Oscar Neebe was, in actuality, a native of the United States, having been born of German parents in New York City on July 12, 1850. Soon after his birth, however, the family returned to Germany, and Neebe spent his childhood in Hesse-Cassel, where he attended school. When the Neebes came back to America, settling as before in New York, the Civil War was drawing to a close. "I saw the sun-burned soldiers in their torn garments returning from the South," Neebe later recollected, "where they fought for freedom and liberty, and broke down the slavery of the black race to enter the slavery of the white."[31]

Neebe was now fourteen years old, time for him to learn a trade. For two years, until pains in his lungs forced him to quit, he worked in a gold and silver beating shop on Houston Street, then, heeding the advice of Horace Greeley, went West, like Fielden, to seek his fortune. Reaching Chicago, he had difficulty in getting work. At length he found a job as a waiter in a German saloon and was shortly promoted to bartender. After two happy years, he was seized with wanderlust and signed on as cook aboard a vessel plying the waters of Lake Michigan. Soon afterwards he returned to New York and was apprenticed to a tinsmith, an excellent man who taught him the trade in all its branches, enabling him to secure work making milk cans, oil cans, and tea caddies.

At this point Neebe's older brother Louis moved to Philadelphia, and Oscar decided to follow. It was there that he met his wife, Meta, whom he married in 1873. Four years later he returned with her to Chicago and got work in a metals factory at good wages. When the railroad strike erupted, however, Neebe joined the socialist movement and was dismissed from his job as an agitator. Like Parsons, moreover, he found himself blacklisted and unable to get work in his trade. The next two years were extremely difficult, and his family sometimes went without food. Finally, in 1879, Neebe managed to secure a job as a salesman for a yeast company, where he remained until 1881. Then, with his brother Henry and two other partners, he started a small yeast firm of his own, which earned him a comfortable living until he was arrested.

Neebe has generally been regarded as a marginal figure in the International, a man of limited ability and influence, who was swept up in the wave of hysteria aroused by the 1886 explosion. This is far from an accurate picture. In reality, he possessed remarkable gifts, above all as an organizer, and was connected with virtually every phase of the movement, from founding unions and arranging demonstrations to chairing lectures and even decorating meeting halls, for which he had a special talent. Neebe, an avid reader since childhood, cherished the writings of Paine and Jefferson and was stirred by the German peasant wars and by the Commune of 1871 "and the murder of the workingmen of Paris."[32] As a result, he threw all his energies into the cause of emancipating the workers. Together with Parsons, Spies, and Schwab, he belonged to the General Committee of the International for the Chicago area and, apart from his work in the American Group, was active in the North Side German Group. He also served on the board of directors of the Socialistic Publishing Society, publisher of the *Arbeiter-Zeitung*. As an organizer for the Central Labor Union, moreover, Neebe was instrumental in organizing the bakers, the beer-wagon drivers, and the beer brewers, for whom he secured a raise in wages and a ten-hour working day. Because of this, as he afterwards told the court, he was "well known among the workingmen of the city."[33]

While neither a writer nor a public speaker, Neebe was a prominent figure at rallies, picnics, and street processions, usually in the capacity of chief marshal. In Dyer Lum's apt description, he was the "hustler" of the International in Chicago, who issued the circulars, attended to the arrangements, and performed the "heavy work" towards making each occasion a success. Lizzie Holmes portrayed him in similar terms. "Neebe," she said, "was an organizer pure and simple. An adept at collecting men together and lining them up into workable bodies, he was an able ally for the educators, as innocent of wrong as the others."[34]

Thanks to Neebe and other hardworking members, the American Group exerted an influence on the Chicago labor movement quite out of proportion to its numbers. For a period of two-and-a-half years, until the time of the Haymarket incident, the group met twice every week, on Wednesday night and Sunday afternoon. At the Wednesday night meetings, held in Greif's Hall at 54 West Lake Street,[35] papers were delivered on social and economic subjects, followed invariably by animated discussion. Among the topics were "The Distribution of Wealth," "How the Working People Are Being Robbed," "Evils Resulting from the Private Ownership of Property," "The Poverty of the Masses," "What Is Anarchy?" and "Socialism for All." During the summer of 1885, Professor Leo Miller, a guest speaker, addressed the group on "Land Limitation," followed by criticisms from August Spies, Lucy Parsons, and Lizzie Holmes. A few weeks later, T. B. Barry of Michigan gave an account of the strike of lumber workers in the Saginaw Valley, with Lucy Parsons presiding. In December of the same year Spies chaired a debate between Fielden and Dr. W. H. Hale of Washington, D.C., who defended the view that "Socialism is not the best remedy to alleviate the sufferings of the poor." Following comments by Lucy Parsons, Sarah Ames, William Holmes, Archibald Simpson, and James Taylor, all criticizing the arguments of Dr. Hale, Lizzie Holmes concluded the meeting by playing and singing the "Marseillaise."[36]

Except in winter or inclement weather, when an indoor hall was used, the Sunday afternoon meetings were held on the Lake Front, a large grassy area on the shore of Lake Michigan, at the foot of Van Buren Street. Thousands attended to hear Parsons and other speakers hold forth on such topics as "the origin, growth, and purpose of government and the institution of wage slavery founded on private property."[37] Following the lectures, thousands of copies of newspapers, leaflets, and other literature were sold and distributed and new members and subscribers enrolled. With the worsening of the depression, the audiences grew larger and more receptive. By May 1885 between 1,500 and 2,000 were in attendance, as compared with 1,000 the previous fall. Only three months later the meetings were drawing crowds of more than 3,000, eager to hear "these teachers of a new order."[38]

During one six-month period, from May to November 1885, twenty-six meetings were held at the Lake Front, to say nothing of other gatherings around the city. "Dynamite-eating Parsons and his wife were there," said the *Inter Ocean* of one of these meetings, "and so were a lot of the rag, tag, and bobtail of the Communists, from the Clark and Randolph Street resorts."[39] In addition to Parsons, the regular Lake Front speakers included Spies, Fielden, William Holmes, C. S. Griffin, and William J. Gorsuch. Like Burnette Haskell and

Edward Nathan-Ganz, Griffin and Gorsuch belonged to the fire-breathing school that the Tuckerites characterized as "whoop-her-up" revolutionists, their pronouncements conveying an intense hatred, often violently expressed, of the rich and powerful who reveled at the expense of the poor. Griffin, writing in *The Alarm*, defended the assassination of rulers and officials as "wise, just, humane and brave. For freedom, all things are just." At a Lake Front gathering, in a similar vein, he presented "a scientific treatise on nitro-glycerine as a civilizing agent" and upheld "the value of dynamite as a great moral factor in solving the problem of capital and labor."[40] Griffin, however, got cold feet, and, returning to his home town in Maine, severed his connections with the movement and became a state socialist.

Gorsuch, a native of Baltimore, came of old American stock (Charles Gorsuch, a direct forebear, arrived from England in 1662) and prided himself on his ancestry, to which he frequently alluded. His speeches for the International were directed primarily to native workingmen, dwelling on "the duty of Americans to take a strong position in the van of a movement." "Be men, you young Americans," he exhorted a Chicago audience. "Come out, unite with us, and with your help the tyrant's reign shall end."[41] Gorsuch had a distinct weakness for empty rhetoric: "Men, be ye men! Prepare for the revolution that is upon us! . . . Through every vale strike the fierce Alarm! On every hill-top raise the beacon-pyre. The tocsin must be sounded, 'To arms! To arms! Ye brave!' Let man confront the hour. Too long in silence we have suffered. We can endure no more. Aroused at Duty's call we swear, whate'er to us betide, the toilers shall be Free."[42]

Notwithstanding his meager oratorical gifts, Gorsuch sought an appointment as a paid speaker for the International. Vain, unstable, self-centered, he had a highly inflated opinion of his own abilities. "Why can't arrangements be made to start, and afford a living to an english agitator?" he wrote to Spies. "Why can't I fill the bill; or am I not thought worthy? 'By *God*' if I only could be free to think and talk, as I wish, and know my sustenance was even partially assured, I feel it in me to say and do what would be worth to the world all the cost."[43] Though Spies's reply is not recorded, Gorsuch continued to lecture under the International's aegis until the summer of 1885, when he was arrested in Cleveland for inciting to violence, having urged a crowd of strikers to "arm themselves with rifles, visit the warehouses, and take whatever they wished, shooting down all who opposed them." In the wake of this incident, complaints were lodged with the Bureau of Information, and *The Alarm* announced that Gorsuch had "lost the confidence of the I.W.P.A." Not long afterwards, Gorsuch dropped out of the movement and became a temperance reformer. After Haymarket, noted an acquaintance, he "abandoned his radicalism, struck his colors, and got a kind of religion."[44]

Apart from its regular Wednesday and Sunday gatherings, the American Group engaged in a wide range of activities. Immense street parades were arranged, dotted with placards and banners, at which Neebe and Parsons acted as marshals, Parsons's skill as a horseman being keenly admired.[45] Special meetings were held to discuss the "dreadful condition" of the Hocking Valley miners and to condemn the action of the militia at Lemont during the quarrymen's strike of May 1885 and of the police in Chicago during the streetcar strike of July 1885. In September of the same year the group staged an "indignation meeting" to protest the dispersal of a public meeting by the London police and the arrest of William Morris and J. L. Mahon of the Socialist League. The speakers on this occasion, among them Parsons and Spies, emphasized the international character of the labor movement, asserting that "workers of every country were deprived of the results of their labor by the same class—the property holders."[46]

The group, in addition, sent speakers on agitation trips through many states, during which countless meetings were held and new American groups formed. To raise funds for *The Alarm*, moreover, it sponsored picnics, dances, and a variety of entertainments. Vast quantities of literature were printed and distributed. At one time, 25,000 leaflets containing Victor Hugo's *Address to the Rich and the Poor* were circulated throughout the city. Thousands of cards containing on one side announcements of the group's meetings and on the other quotations from radical authors were also distributed broadcast.[47]

Beyond all this, the group, in January 1885, sent written invitations to leading clergymen, lawyers, newspaper editors, "and other opponents of socialism" to debate the labor question before the public.[48] Among the recipients, ironically, was William Perkins Black, who was to defend the anarchists in court the following year. Black did not respond. The only man to accept the challenge was William

M. Salter, speaker for the Chicago Ethical Culture Society, who appeared at an American Group meeting in May 1885 and threshed out the issues with Parsons and his comrades.[49] Through this he became their friend and later worked for the commutation of their sentences.

On another occasion, the West Side Philosophical Society, a group of upper-class parishioners of Dr. Thomas's church, placed the topic of socialism on its program and asked speakers from various organizations to take part. Parsons, although invited, was already booked for another engagement, but the American Group was ably represented by Spies and Archibald Simpson. The resulting debate aroused such intense interest that it was continued at the next meeting, held on March 5, 1885, at Princeton Hall on West Madison Street. This time Parsons was able to attend, along with a large contingent from the American Group, including Spies, Simpson, Fielden, William Holmes, Lizzie Holmes, and Sarah Ames. The hall was filled to capacity, and what Parsons had to say provoked the audience to a dancing fury. George Schilling, who was present, thought it "one of the most eloquent, cutting, and defiant speeches" he had ever heard.[50]

Parsons spoke as follows: "It very seldom happens that I have a chance to speak before a meeting composed of so many gentlemen with nice white shirts and ladies wearing elegant and costly toilets. I am the notorious Parsons, the fellow with the long horns, as you know him from the daily press. I am in the habit of speaking before meetings composed of people who by their labor supply you with all these nice things while they themselves are forced to dress in coarse and common garments; of such people who build your fine palaces, with all those comfortable fixtures, while they themselves are forced to dwell in miserable hovels or to take shelter in a police station. Are not these charitable people—these *sans culottes*—very generous to you?"

A round of hisses greeted this last remark. But Parsons was only beginning. Owing to the depression, he went on, two million heads of families were unemployed. In Connecticut 700 young women in the cotton factories had been thrown out of work and forced to wander from town to town in search of bread. "These female tramps are native American girls," said Parsons, "the daughters of fathers who gave their lives to perpetuate the institutions of the Republic." In Chicago alone there were 35,000 men, women, and children in a starving condition, driven by unemployment to live on charity or to seek a suicide's grave. In the Desplaines Street station, through the cold winter night, as many as 400 homeless, destitute men had sought shelter and slept on the stone floors of cells, receiving a bowl of soup and slice of bread for breakfast. "Listen now to the voice of hunger," declared Parsons, "when I tell you that unless you heed the cry of the people, unless you hearken to the voice of reason, you will be awakened by the thunders of dynamite!" At this there was an uproar among the audience, ladies wiping their faces with handkerchiefs, men shouting and stamping their feet. Parsons tried to go on, explaining that anarchism meant "a free society, where all would produce and consume freely and without restraint." But the chairman called him to order, at which two young ladies came on and attempted to "restore harmony" with some music.[51]

Similar eruptions occurred at meetings of the Chicago Liberal League, in which anarchists from the American Group constituted an outspoken left-wing faction. Unyielding in their opposition to the church, they pointed to the contradiction between a religion that taught that all men were brothers and an economic system that organized them as masters and slaves. Spies, Fielden, and Gorsuch became so disruptive that the League was obliged in "self-defense" to bar them from its platform.[52] Parsons managed to avoid this penalty, although he was equally vociferous in stating his views. "With the acuteness of a trained intellect," recalls Dr. Joseph H. Greer, a longtime member of the group, "he would pick out the weak points of the lecturer's discourse. He was a forceful speaker, earnest and honest. There was no subterfuge in his language. He did not mince his words. To him the suffering of the masses was a terrible reality."[53]

Until Haymarket put an end to his activities, Parsons, the founder of the American Group, remained its driving spirit and most devoted participant. He seldom missed a Wednesday night meeting at Greif's Hall or a Sunday afternoon rally at the Lake Front. When not himself a speaker, he was often in the chair and always took part in the discussions that followed. He sold anarchist literature, distributed circulars, and involved himself in the smallest details of organizational work. He led processions, carried banners, helped with social evenings, and took part in the singing and dancing. At the same time, he edited *The Alarm*, wrote countless articles and editorials, and served on the Bureau of Information and General Committee.

113

As an agitator, moreover, he went on repeated lecture tours, breaking new ground and consolidating existing groups, in "personal contact," he wrote, "with hundreds of thousands of workingmen from Nebraska in the West to New York in the East, and from Maryland to Wisconsin and Minnesota." Sometimes he spoke as a representative of the Knights of Labor, more often of the IWPA, but always "as an organizer of the workingmen, always as a labor speaker at labor meetings."[54]

Parsons's involvement with the International brought forth all his talents as a revolutionary agitator. He spoke whenever the occasion demanded, "accepting every invitation his time and strength would permit of ," as Lizzie Holmes remarked.[55] Like his ancestor Jonathan Parsons, he traveled from one dusty town to the next, preaching a new gospel, a latter-day circuit-rider in an age of industrial capitalism. He addressed both immigrants and native Americans, often sharing the platform with German speakers. He went through the coal fields of Ohio and Pennsylvania, speaking to the miners, living with them, pleading the cause of revolutionary socialism. He spoke to thousands of workers who knew little of socialism or anarchism but could recognize and appreciate an effort to help when it came their way. "The working people thirst for the truths of Socialism and welcome their utterance with shouts of delight," wrote Parsons from Kansas in July 1885. "It only lacks organization and preparation, and the time for the social revolt is at hand. Their miseries have become unendurable, and their necessities will soon compel them to act, whether they are prepared or not. Let us redouble our efforts and make ready for the inevitable. Let us strain every nerve to awaken the people to the dangers of the coming storm between the propertied and the propertyless classes of America. To this work let our lives be devoted. *Vive la Révolution Sociale!*"[56]

Parsons, now in his mid-thirties, had reached the summit of his oratorical powers. A dramatic and forceful speaker in the tradition of Patrick Henry and Wendell Phillips, earnest and passionate in his attacks on injustice and privilege, he had a clear, lilting tenor voice that could hold an audience spellbound for two or three hours at a stretch as he cited statistics, quoted poetry, and roused his listeners to a fury over working conditions and the exploitation of labor. General Matthew M. Trumbull, who came to Parsons's assistance in 1886, considered him "a man of genius, gracefully eloquent in speech. In literary taste and elegance of diction his addresses were far above the average grade of popular oratory. His voice was musical and of great magnetic power. He was a picturesque specimen of that much-quoted product known as the 'Typical American.' "[57]

Whenever Parsons spoke he delivered essentially the same message. He dilated on the evils of capitalism and the virtues of the cooperative commonwealth that would replace it. He railed against economic exploitation, political oppression, and social injustice. He spoke for the workingmen against the establishment, the poor and deprived against the wealthy and powerful. Each address, said Lizzie Holmes, was a "clear, orderly, truthful array of facts, with conclusions most ably drawn and eloquently presented."[58] Citing figures on wages, housing, unemployment, industrial accidents, gleaned from an assortment of newspapers and official reports, he drew up a powerful indictment of American capitalism, a system, as he described it, of "masters and slaves, rulers and ruled, robbers and robbed." The fruits of the toil of millions, he maintained, were being stolen for the benefit of a few. He declared that "the origin of private property was in fraud, force and murder, and that Governments were instituted, and constitutions adopted, and laws manufactured to uphold and perpetuate the outrage; that Government exists for the sole purpose of depriving men of their natural rights; that authority and force was the weapon of tyrants held over their slaves."[59]

Parsons drew his ideas from both American and European sources. He had read a good deal of advanced literature, and the strains of Jefferson and Paine as well as Bakunin and Marx resounded through his speeches. His language echoed that of the French Revolution, with its Declaration of the Rights of Man and formula of "Liberty, Equality, and Fraternity." At the same time, the imagery of the Civil War ran like a scarlet thread through his pronouncements, and he frequently compared the "wage slaves" of the postbellum North with the chattel slaves of the antebellum South. As before, moreover, he rejected the view that the United States was in any way superior to other countries. "America is *not* a free country," he declared in February 1885. "The economic conditions of the workers here are precisely the same as they are in Europe. A wage slave is a *slave* everywhere, without any regard to the country he may happen to have been born in or may be living in." A few months later he returned to the same theme: "Our American rulers differ not one whit from the despots of all other lands. They all fatten upon the miseries of the people, they all live by despoiling the laborers. The

115

boundary lines, flags, customs and languages of the people of the earth may differ, but the poverty, misery and degradation of the useful class, the producers of the world's wealth, is everywhere the same."[60]

How then might labor be emancipated? Only through a social revolution and the abolition of capitalism. The workers had but one choice, Parsons insisted. They must either organize and rebel or remain slaves. The emancipation of the workers, he echoed Marx, was the duty of the workers themselves, and there was no salvation except in a mass upheaval. He was certain that socialism, because of its righteousness, must triumph, and that capitalism, because of its wickedness, must fall; and, in the future libertarian society that he envisioned, competition and exploitation would give place to cooperation and mutual aid.

Not all of Parsons's listeners were receptive to such radical talk. More than once he was greeted with catcalls and shouts of "communist." At St. Joseph, Missouri, he was branded in the press as "the Chicago Anarchist and Dynamiter." In other towns, he tells us, no hall could be rented "for love or money," and printing offices refused to print the handbills announcing his meetings. At Coal Center, Pennsylvania, he was pelted with eggs and threatened with being thrown into the Monongahela River. At South Bend, Indiana, he was threatened with lynching and his speech interrupted by a policeman.[61]

Frequently, however, Parsons found that hostility melted away soon after he began to speak, and that some who had come to jeer afterwards helped to arrange further meetings. As his reputation grew, invitations poured in from every part of the country. In the spring of 1886 he was asked by a group in San Francisco to undertake a tour of the Pacific Coast, where he had not previously lectured. He intended to accept, and to speak at Sacramento, Portland, Tacoma, and Seattle, in addition to San Francisco,[62] but Haymarket prevented him from making the journey.

After each speaking tour Parsons returned to Chicago with fresh enthusiasm and plunged anew into his busy routine. How he could engage in so many activities and still find time for his family it is hard to understand, yet he managed to do so. By now he and Lucy had two children, a son, Albert Jr., born in 1879, and a daughter, Lulu Eda, born in 1881, "a rare beauty," in the words of William Parsons, "and inheriting the vivacity of her mother."[63] Albert and

Lucy remained a devoted couple. "Probably no married life had ever been less clouded than his," said Dyer Lum, Parsons's successor on *The Alarm*.[64] Lucy worked closely with her husband in all the movement's activities. She wrote for *The Alarm*, marched in processions, spoke at rallies, and played an active role in the American Group. Her whole being, said Albert, was "wrapped up in the progress of the social revolution." Appearing at one Lake Front meeting, she was described by the *Inter Ocean* as "a very determined-looking negress," who put down her "anarchist sucklings" only long enough to address the crowd.[65]

Aside from their work for the movement, Albert and Lucy labored together to earn a living. Until he became editor of *The Alarm* in October 1884, Parsons, having been blacklisted in 1877, was unable to find work in Chicago. At one point, during the summer of 1883, he was desperate enough to accept the editorship of *The Connecticut Farmer* at Hartford. But, missing Lucy and the children, he did not remain long.[66] Appointed editor of *The Alarm*, he earned only eight dollars a week, so that he and Lucy had to supplement their income in order to make ends meet. Beneath their apartment on Grand Avenue, they opened a small ladies' tailor shop, which they operated together, Lucy sewing and Albert soliciting business, though he could take turns at the needle.[67]

In spite of his scanty means, Parsons, as William P. Black noted, had "much to make life bright to him, much to make him happy in life." In addition to his wife and children, to whom he was "as tenderly attached as any father to his young I have ever known," said Black, he enjoyed a circle of devoted comrades "who regarded him with intense affection."[68] Handsome and neatly dressed, with his neck-scarf and polished shoes, he was meticulous, almost vain, about his appearance, keeping his mustache carefully trimmed and his prematurely grey hair black with dye. Of nervous temperament and exuberant spirits, he walked with a "quick, springy tread," and his good nature, candid manner, and manifest sincerity were irresistible. "There was not a sign of grossness in his form, face, or complexion," wrote Matthew Trumbull, "and there was a spirituality in his look that revealed a temperament of poetry and dreams." In private company he was genial, full of humor, and an excellent conversationalist and mimic. He had good taste in literature, recited poetry with deep emotion, and sang songs in a rich tenor voice. He could tell a good story and laugh heartily at a good joke. "Whatever

the subject talked of," recalled Lizzie Holmes, "he was very interesting. I used to believe nothing in life could be more pleasant than
to gather with Mr. Parsons and his wife, Mr. Spies, Mr. Fielden, and
others around a table, or in a small circle, and listen to conversation
that flowed and sparkled on so smoothly."[69]

Parsons, as Lizzie Holmes saw him, possessed all the qualities of
a born leader. Proud, intense, combative, he was at the same time
"alert, intelligent, quick to grasp a situation and deal with it, and
equally quick to answer an argument."[70] For nearly a decade he had
been in the forefront of socialist propaganda in Chicago, bringing
his own special enthusiasm to the movement, expending his energies and talents without stint. Agitator and journalist, editor and
organizer, he gave himself completely to his cause. Anarchism, for
Parsons, was not only right but also good and beautiful, the only
system of society in which men could attain true freedom and dignity; and it was one of his most noteworthy achievements to have
brought workers of different nationalities and backgrounds together
and given them a unity of purpose and goals they had previously
lacked.

Parsons, to be sure, had defects that at times impaired his effec-
tiveness—faults of judgment, impulsiveness, a tendency to extend
himself over too wide a field of activity. But in the estimation of
his comrades and many others these faults weighed little in the scale
against his warmheartedness and self-sacrifice, his generosity and
courage. He showed a strong crusading spirit, a burning zeal to reform society at its roots. He was always the bold humanitarian,
ready to destroy the power and privilege of the few for the greater
good of all. "Oh, that I had the means!" he wrote to his wife in
January 1886. "I would batter down the ramparts of wrong and
oppression and plant the flag of humanity on the ruins."[71] One of
the ablest revolutionary orators of his time, he devoted himself passionately, unflinchingly, to the welfare of the working people, especially of the poor and unemployed. No suffering left him unmoved,
no tyranny escaped his condemnation. "Toward any individual in
danger or distress," wrote Charles Edward Russell, "he had an instinctive sympathy."[72]

It was this devotion to his cause that made Parsons so remarkable
a character. It increased his capacities, cast his energies in the mold
of constancy and firmness, and gave aim and direction to his life.
"To know that little children will no more drudge and wither away

in factories and mines," he declared on the eve of the final tragedy that befell him, "that women will not slowly coin their heart's blood over their needle, while starvation eternally stares in at the door; that strong men will not waste their lives in abject slavery or unwilling vagabondage, and that constant fear of cold and hunger and homelessness that so petrifies and stupefies the heart and soul will be banished forever; that woman will be freed from the black clinging trail of the serpent winding through all ages, the selling of herself for bread or splendor; that genius will, no longer crushed in the narrow, suffering limits of neglect and poverty, rise to heights unknown before—is it not worth working, living and dying for?"[73]

9 ‖ AUGUST SPIES

If Parsons had an equal in the Chicago anarchist movement, it was August Spies—"nature's nobleman," Parsons called him[1]—a man of courage, ability, and intellect. In some ways, indeed, Spies was the ablest of those who rose to leadership within the International during the years prior to the Haymarket incident. As Dyer Lum describes him, he was "handsome and intelligent, with a wide range of reading and of studious nature, with a warm heart controlled by a cold, philosopher's brain." Seven years younger than Parsons, he was only thirty at the time of the bombing. Yet, according to Lum, he was already "head centre" of the movement.[2]

While not quite on Parsons's level as a speaker, Spies was fully his match as an organizer, and even surpassed him as a writer, being more erudite, succinct, and profound. His style, as William Holmes remarked, was "vigorous, terse, logical." He could put a great deal in a short paragraph. His knowledge of history—ancient and modern—and of philosophy and economics gave him "a great fund of information which his excellent memory enabled him to draw from at will."[3] Spies had the further advantage over Parsons of speaking German in addition to English, to say nothing of his knowledge of French. Morris Hillquit, the well-known socialist leader, thought him "by all odds the most cultured intellectual of the defendants."[4]

Whatever their differences, however, Spies and Parsons had much in common. Both were charter members of the social revolutionary group in Chicago. Both attended the Chicago congress of 1881, as well as the Pittsburgh congress of 1883, where both had a hand, along with Most, in drafting the Pittsburgh Manifesto. Both became secretaries of the Bureau of Information and members of the Chicago General Committee. Together, in these roles, they formed a bridge between the native and immigrant wings of the movement, bringing to the International a unity which it would otherwise have lacked. And, besides their organizational work, they shouldered the major

120

journalistic burden of the movement, editing its principal newspapers, the *Arbeiter-Zeitung* and *The Alarm*.

Spies and Parsons were both militant trade-unionists, champions of the "Chicago idea," and their economic and social views coincided on all important points. Furthermore, their ideology had evolved along similar lines: both, having run unsuccessfully for office on the Socialistic Labor Party ticket, had lost faith in political methods and gone over to the direct-actionist camp. On a personal level, both were men of great charm, who, according to their friends, brightened every gathering in which they took part. Each, moreover, entered into an unconventional marriage, Spies with a Chicago woman of high society, Parsons with a black and former slave. For both, finally, anarchism was a way of life as well as a social philosophy, and their days and years were consumed by a passion to work for the downtrodden and oppressed.

The eldest of five children, August Vincent Theodore Spies (pronounced *Shpeece* in German, *Speeze* in English) was born at Landeck in central Germany on December 10, 1855. More than thirty years later, at the darkest moment of his life, he could conjure up out of the past vivid memories of his native district with its beautiful valleys and forests. His childhood had been a happy one, spent mostly in reading and play, and he was educated by private tutors before attending the Polytechnicum in Cassel to be trained as a government forester, the occupation of his father. In 1872, however, his father died and Spies was forced to leave school. Soon afterwards he emigrated to America.[5]

Spies landed in New York towards the end of 1872. The following year he moved to Chicago, where, apart from occasional trips—he traveled through the South, worked on a farm, and went on an expedition to Canada, spending several months among the Chippewa Indians[6]—he remained for the rest of his life. In 1874 he went to work as an upholsterer, a trade he had learned in New York. Being of an "independent disposition," he tells us in his autobiography, he opened his own shop in 1876, when he was only twenty.[7] Before the year was out, he was earning enough money to bring over his entire family—mother, sister, and three brothers—who all moved into his house at 2132 Potomac Avenue, near Wicker Park. For several years he continued to support them, until his brothers had established themselves. All three, like August himself, became small tradesmen, Christian a hardware dealer, Ferdinand a jeweler, and

Henry a small cigar manufacturer. His sister, Gretchen, and mother, Christine, remained with him until the eve of his arrest and imprisonment.

Spies, like Parsons, was drawn to socialism by his sympathy for the needy and disinherited. In common with other immigrants, he had dreamed of America as a haven of opportunity; and for himself, having established a successful business, he had no difficulty, he noted, in "getting along" under the existing system. But he was distressed by the conditions in which so many wage-workers were living. Until now, he relates, he had not read a book, nor even a serious essay, on modern socialism. What he knew of it came from the daily papers, which portrayed it in negative terms. In 1875, however, he attended a meeting of the Working-Men's Party and heard his first lecture on the subject. Delivered by a young mechanic, it was unimpressive from a theoretical point of view, Spies recalls, but its substance provided the key "to many interrogation marks which had worried me for a number of years." After this, Spies procured every piece of literature he could get his hands on, in French as well as German and English. These included Marx's *Capital*, Henry Thomas Buckle's *History of Civilization in England*, and Lewis Henry Morgan's *Ancient Society*, which had the greatest influence on his thinking at this stage. Observing the life of the workers, with its misery and exploitation, he says, "I found my favorite teachers corroborated everywhere."[8]

Spies's acceptance of socialism was given a powerful impetus by the railroad strike of 1877. Outraged by the brutality of the police and the use of state and federal troops against the workers, he joined both the Lehr-und-Wehr Verein and the Socialistic Labor Party and became an active figure in the Chicago radical movement. Like Parsons, he ran for local office on the SLP ticket, although he never regarded political action as a panacea. The final emancipation of labor, he insisted, could be achieved "through an economic struggle only, not through politics." When, in the spring of 1880, Frank Stauber was fraudulently denied his seat in the city council, Spies became convinced of the futility of political methods. Thereafter, he relates, he viewed the ballot "with suspicion."[9]

In October 1880 matters came to a head when Spies, together with Neebe and others, was expelled from the SLP. From this point began his association with anarchism. Young, ardent, sincere, he was a capable writer and speaker with a poise that commanded respect.

He was also strikingly handsome and inspired confidence by his forthright manner. Until his imprisonment, he was a member of the Amerikanische Turner Bund, the German gymnastic society,[10] and kept himself in prime physical condition. Of medium height, sturdy build, and erect carriage, he had blue eyes, fair skin, and attractive features, with a light brown mustache and wavy hair. Always neatly dressed, he enjoyed good food and drink, and to some he seemed as much a "ladies' man" as a social militant.

Nor was his character free of vanity. Yet his devotion to his cause was beyond question. He had "all the instincts of a gentleman," said Dyer Lum, and was "never known to be a liar."[11] Indeed, his integrity impressed itself on all who came into contact with him. What was more, as William Holmes observed, his general air of superior intelligence "characterized him as a leader among men." Lizzie Holmes remembered his sardonic humor, directed against friend and foe alike, "but so keen and fine that we enjoyed it even when turned against us." Spies, she added, "possessed a power few men in any age have wielded. Men came and went at his bidding; thought new thoughts or unlearned old ones under his influence; women worshipped him and commenced to think because he expected it of them."[12]

Given such qualities, it is hardly surprising that Spies should have emerged as a central figure in the movement. He was, like Parsons, an orator of convincing power, his delivery being impassioned, his language incisive and popular. Like Parsons, he was called upon often to address working-class meetings, on tour as well as in Chicago. He spoke, moreover, for both the International and the Knights of Labor, of which he had briefly been a member. Charles Edward Russell found him "fluent and plausible in English as in German, a blue-eyed Saxon, emotional, sentimental, and rash." To Dr. J. H. Greer of the Chicago Liberal League he was "sarcastic and often bitter in his criticisms of existing conditions."[13] Spies claims to have spoken in "most of the industrial cities" of the country. One finds him, like Parsons, as far west as Omaha and as far east as New York, where he shared the podium with Most barely a month before the Haymarket bombing. During the strike in the Hocking Valley of Ohio, where he saw "hundreds of lives in the process of slow destruction," he addressed a series of meetings, notwithstanding threats against his life by Pinkertons with Winchester rifles.[14]

The message of Spies's speeches was not unlike that of Parsons.

Both men lashed out bitterly against government and capital in the name of the dispossessed. Both drew upon American as well as European thinkers, most notably Jefferson and Paine. Both were thoroughgoing radicals who advocated, in William Holmes's words, "a complete change in all the relations of mankind, political, sexual, social, and economic."[15] Both, moreover, were indebted to Marx as much as to Proudhon, Bakunin, and Kropotkin. Spies, in a lecture to the Chicago Liberal League, called Marx a "modern Oedipus," who revealed to the world "the lever that caused all social phenomena." That lever, said Spies, was economics, "the substructure of all social, political, and moral institutions and operations."[16]

Spies, like Parsons, depicted the life of the American workman as being an endless treadmill of misery, ending, as Spies put it, "in one of those charitable or reformatory institutes known as the insane asylum, the penitentiary, or poorhouse."[17] For this reason, both favored the arming of the workers in preparation for an all-out revolution. As Spies declared, the "economic change which we so ardently seek to bring about can only be the result of a class struggle, of a *revolution* of the proletariat against the capitalistic class." For the ruling classes of the day, he insisted, would "no more listen to the voice of reason than their predecessors," but rather "attempt by brute force to stay the wheels of progress."[18]

Spies reiterated these views before an audience of Congregational ministers who, in December 1885, had invited him to lecture on socialism. William Holmes, who accompanied him, thought his remarks, however justified, "too brusque, his criticism of the class to which our hosts belonged being especially severe."[19] At the outset Spies launched into a denunciation of "those Christian hypocrites who have made of the religion of Jesus a cloak for iniquity and of the church an auction-place for the sale of virtue and manly honor." Turning to the sphere of economics, he declared that the means of production were falling into the hands of "an ever decreasing number," while the "actual producers," the workers, were being reduced to unemployment, pauperism, vagabondage, and all the evils "which you, gentlemen, would like to exorcize with your little prayer book." But a revolution was on the horizon, warned Spies. "It will come to a fight," for all changes of economic conditions arise from "the struggle between the dominating and dominated class." As a result, Spies concluded, capitalism would be dethroned, ushering in "the era of Socialism, of universal cooperation."[20]

During the course of his address, Spies was more than once interrupted by outbursts from the audience. His criticisms of Christian
morality, especially, drew expressions of disapproval. At the close,
he was sharply questioned by his listeners. In a remarkable exchange,
the Reverend Dr. Scudder demanded to know "how you are going
to carry out the expropriation of the possessing class." Spies, facing
his questioner, replied: "The key is furnished by the storms raging
through the industrial life of the present. You see how penuriously
the owners of the factories, of the mines, cling to their privileges,
and will not yield the breadth of an inch. On the other hand, you
see the half-starved proletarians driven to the verge of violence."

DR. SCUDDER: So your remedy would be violence?

SPIES: Remedy? Well, I should like it better if it could be done
without violence; but you, gentlemen, and the class you represent, take care that it cannot be accomplished otherwise.

DR. SCUDDER: And then where do you get the armies to do it?

SPIES: Our armies? Did you ever read about the eruption of a
volcano? Do you ask the cyclones what they derive their power
from?

DR. SCUDDER: Don't you shudder at the torrents of blood?

SPIES: Why, let those shudder who bring about the bloodshed. You,
gentlemen, belong to the first rank of them. Besides, what does
it matter if some thousands, or even tens of thousands, of drones
are removed during the coming struggle? These are the very
ones who yearly destroy the lives of hundreds of thousands of
proletarians—a fact which *you* don't seem to know.

DR. SCUDDER: So you are organizing a revolution?

SPIES: Such things are hard to organize. A revolution is a sudden
upswelling—a convulsion of the fevered masses of society. We
are preparing society for it, and insist that the laborers should
arm themselves, and keep themselves ready for action. The better they are armed, the easier the struggle will be ended, and
the less there will be of bloodshed.[21]

Spies, in response to a further question, would not speculate on
the precise nature of the future society, except to say that property
would be held in common and labor organized on a cooperative basis.
This provoked a member of the audience to ask whether socialism
would not "destroy all individuality." Quite the contrary, Spies replied. Socialism would enlarge the scope of the individual. It was

125

capitalism, with its minute division of labor, that was transforming men into faceless robots, into cogs in an impersonal machine. But a lot you care about the workers, exclaimed Spies with his characteristic sarcasm. "You feign anxiety about their individuality; about the individuality of a class that has been degraded to machines—used each day for ten or twelve hours as appendages of the lifeless machines! About their individuality you are anxious!" Only the socialists, Spies insisted, were genuinely concerned about the workers. Then he ended on a defiant note: "We are the birds of the coming storm—the prophets of the revolution."[22]

Spies was not, any more than Parsons, a man to mince his words. Neither his speeches nor his writings were tempered by considerations of diplomacy. Bluntly, forcefully, he said what he had to say, inspiring his opponents with a desire to retaliate. As a muckraking journalist, with a gift for irony and invective, he exposed instance after instance of police brutality and political corruption. In December 1884, to cite an example, he had the desk sergeant of the Chicago Avenue precinct arrested for assaulting a sixteen-year-old girl in the station-house and nearly killing her.[23] In another case, with fateful implications, he accused a Chicago banker, Edward S. Dreyer, of irregular real-estate practices and of offering him $10,000 if he would refrain from criticizing Grover Cleveland, the Democratic candidate for President, in his newspaper.[24] Nothing came of these charges. Two years later, however, Dreyer was to serve on the grand jury that indicted Spies and his comrades for complicity in the Haymarket bombing. The accused would become the accuser.

Another instance where Spies's language gave offense reveals an unexpected side of his character. It involved his attitude towards Jews, who were arriving in the United States in increasing numbers. The socialist movement, for all its egalitarian and internationalist pretensions, was strongly tinged with anti-Semitic prejudice. The stereotype of the Jew as the grasping, extortionate moneylender, the incarnation of rapacious capitalism, the crafty trader who drives a hard bargain and fattens on the labor of the poor, became a staple of socialist literature, disfiguring the pronouncements of Marx as well as Bakunin, of Fourier as well as Proudhon, to say nothing of a host of lesser writers, including some in the American radical press. "What is the fatherland?" asked an article in Most's Freiheit. "Is it the sod on which I was born and which I tilled in my childhood, which the Jew later took away because my father could no longer afford the tax burden?" *The Alarm,* in a similar vein, saw fit to reprint the following passage from *Der Arme Teufel,* an anarchist paper edited by Robert Reitzel in Detroit:

> It has been shown long ago that there is a certain similarity between the Jews and the Americans; the opinions are divided only on the question, whether the Jew is more able to cheat the Yankee than is the Yankee to cheat the Jew. Common to both is the unlimited esteem for money. Moses only had left his people for a short while to hold a conference on social politics with the God of Thunder, and quickly they manufactured a golden calf, which they adored. So the American never loses an opportunity in which he reverently might drag the republican eagle at the feet of God Mammon.[25]

Nor was Spies immune from such prejudice. He not only compared the bankers of the Chicago Board of Trade with the money-changers of ancient Israel, a not uncommon analogy in the anarchist press of that time. He also denounced Jewish labor contractors for bringing Eastern European immigrants into the Hocking Valley to replace the striking miners. Spies encountered a "herd" of these scabs while riding on a train in Ohio. When he tried to talk to one of them, a Jewish contractor intervened. Spies, furious, told the "blackguard" (*Schuft*) to "remove his carcass from the range of my boot." The contractor thereupon summoned an armed Pinkerton, who ordered Spies off the train. Spies appealed to the conductor but to no avail.[26] Spies's anger, perhaps, had less to do with the Jewishness of the contractors than with their role as importers of scab labor. Nor does one find further evidence that might warrant labeling him an out-and-out anti-Semite. At one point, on the contrary, he approvingly quotes Macaulay's *Constitutional History of England* in defense of the rights of the Jews.[27] Nevertheless, an element of anti-Jewish feeling is undeniable.

The incident in the Hocking Valley mentioned above was reported in the *Arbeiter-Zeitung,* with which Spies had been associated since 1880. The paper that year was on the verge of bankruptcy, and the Socialistic Publishing Society called on Spies to take over as manager. He was only twenty-four at the time, yet his energy and ability saved the paper from collapse. Within a few years, in fact, it had the highest circulation of any German paper in the city. And when Paul Grottkau resigned as editor in 1884, Spies was appointed his successor, a position in which he remained up to the day of his arrest. Apart from his editorial duties, he himself wrote many of the articles—socialism, labor, tramps, and Pinkertons were his favorite subjects[28]—and he supervised the paper's Saturday and Sunday editions, the *Vorbote* and the *Fackel*. Spies worked twelve to sixteen hours a day to keep the enterprise humming, and by 1886 readership exceeded 20,000.[29]

Under Spies's capable direction, the *Arbeiter-Zeitung* rivalled Most's *Freiheit* as the leading German anarchist paper in America. Part of the credit, however, must go to Michael Schwab, Spies's associate editor. A man of scholarly appearance, with his bespectacled and intellectual face, Schwab might easily have passed for an accountant or professor. He was gaunt, angular, and sallow, with hollow cheeks, prominent cheekbones, dark hair and beard, and long, thin legs. Though dry and somewhat ponderous, he was a fluent speaker and a lucid if not original writer. The Germans, said Lizzie Holmes, "loved him." William Holmes remembered him as "a reticent man— more a thinker and reader than talker," though he thoroughly enjoyed the movement's social evenings, not to mention its picnics and lectures. Dyer Lum thought him "a student in every sense of the word," mild-mannered, erudite, and gentle. To Lucien S. Oliver, chairman of the Haymarket Amnesty Association, "his revolutionary tendencies were of a mild character; his was not of a nature to get violently aggressive."[30]

Married and the father of two children, Schwab was thirty-two years old at the time of the Haymarket incident, and had been in America for seven years. He had begun life in the Franconia region of northern Bavaria on August 9, 1853, at Kitzingen in the beautiful Main valley. His mother came from a family of peasants, and his father was a small tradesman. Both were loving parents, and Schwab's early childhood was happy. When the boy was eight, however, his mother died, followed by his father four years after. The home was broken up, the house and property sold, and Schwab and his sister went to live with an uncle. The next few years were difficult, although reading provided some consolation: it was during this period that Goethe, Schiller, and other German classics fell into Schwab's hands, along with the treasures of Greek and Roman literature. By the time he was sixteen, Schwab relates, he had shed the Catholi-

cism in which he had been reared for "the belief in a personal God."
A few years later, he adds, "I did not even believe that."[31]

Having reached maturity, Schwab was apprenticed to a bookbinder
in Würzburg, an "enthusiast," Schwab tells us, for whom "priest-
craft was the root of all evil." Although a capable workman, the
master had to struggle to eke out a living, both he and Schwab
laboring thirteen hours a day in summer and fifteen to seventeen
hours a day in winter, as well as working nearly every Sunday. "As
an apprentice," Schwab later recalled, "I lived a very solitary life,
books, books, and nothing but books! I bound them and I read them.
How often did I sit till one o'clock in the morning with my beloved
classics! They were everything to me, and a great deal of my time
I thus mentally spent in Italy and Greece. Religious books and pamphlets I studied, too, but they only tended to strengthen my disbelief
in religious teachings."[32]

Schwab first heard of socialism at the age of nineteen, when August Bebel and Wilhelm Liebknecht were tried and imprisoned for
"high treason." That year, 1872, the journeymen of the bookbinding
trade formed a union, and Schwab at once became a member. Soon
afterwards he joined the Social Democratic Party, to which most of
the union's activists belonged. In 1874, however, Schwab left Würzburg on his *Wanderjahre*, during which young artisans travel from
place to place with the object of perfecting their craft. Over the next
few years he visited such cities as Hamburg, Berlin, and Munich, as
well as Berne, Vienna, and Zurich, "the Mecca of every German
Republican." Yet everywhere he went, in Switzerland as well as
Germany and Austria, he found poverty, hunger, and distress. Concluding that "political liberty without economic freedom is a mocking lie," he decided to emigrate to America.[33]

Schwab arrived in New York in 1879 and went immediately to
Chicago. While working at various jobs and traveling through several
states, going as far west as Colorado, he discovered, to his chagrin,
that American capitalism was no better than its European counterpart. There were workingmen, to be sure, who received higher wages,
but "the state of things in a great number of industries was even
worse," and skilled and unskilled laborers alike were "degenerating
rapidly into mere automatic parts of machinery." On the other hand,
Schwab was convinced, the days of capitalism were numbered. For
just as "the German weavers weave shrouds for old Germany," the

"starving coal miners of Pennsylvania, Ohio, Illinois, and other states dig the grave of old America."[34]

Having been a trade-unionist and socialist in Europe, Schwab joined the Socialistic Labor Party. Its methods, however, seemed too tame to eradicate the evils of capitalism. "Seeing the terrible abuses with my own eyes," he wrote, "seeing how girls became prostitutes before they knew it, observing the slaughter of little ones, the killing of workingmen by slow degrees, corruption, misery, crime, hypocrisy, poverty, dirt, ignorance, brutality and hunger everywhere, and conceiving that all these things are the legitimate children of the capitalistic system, which, by establishing the right for single persons to possess the means of production and the land, makes the mass of people wretched, I became a 'kicker.' For an honest and honorable man only one course was left, and I became an opponent to the order of things, and was soon called an anarchist."[35]

In 1881 Schwab became a reporter for the *Arbeiter-Zeitung*, and soon afterwards its associate editor, which he remained until the time of his arrest. Having abandoned the SLP for the International, he was a founding member of the North Side Group, in company with Neebe and Balthasar Rau. For a time he ran the International's library and was a member of the General Committee. In addition, he acted as distributor for Most's *Freiheit* in the Chicago area and spoke often at meetings and demonstrations. Schwab was a man of smaller caliber than either Spies or Parsons. His influence, as Morris Hillquit noted, was due primarily to his "great earnestness and unbounded devotion to the cause of the working class."[36] Yet his talents were nonetheless considerable. And he gave of them without stint right up to the time of the Haymarket tragedy.

10 ‖ Counterculture

Through the activities of the IWPA, the anarchists sought not only an end to capitalism and government but a total revolution in human relations, cultural as well as political and economic. Their object, in an age of growing centralization and standardization, was to create an alternative society, based on freedom, brotherhood, and equality, as opposed to the authority and privilege of the established order. Nor would they wait for the social revolution before putting their ideals into practice. Anarchism, as they conceived it, was not something to dream of for the future. It was a guide to everyday life, a doctrine to be applied, so far as possible, within the interstices of American capitalism. And the extent to which they succeeded in doing so was quite remarkable. Between 1883 and 1886 they developed a rich libertarian counterculture, deeply rooted in the working classes and totally at odds with the values of the prevailing system.

The IWPA, as an organization, was itself an expression of this counterculture. It provided, in the eyes of its adherents, not only a vehicle for social revolution but also a working model of the future society, decentralist, nonhierarchical, and noncoercive. "It is to be noticed," wrote Richard T. Ely of the anarchists, "that they attempt to realize their political ideal as far as possible in their own plan of organization. The International is composed of independent 'groups,' with no central authority or executive, both of which expressions many of them detest. The only bond of union between them is found in their common ideas, in their press, their congresses and local organizations, and a Bureau of Information, formed by the Chicago Groups, which appears to be the nearest approach to a centre of life and activity."[1]

This was an acute observation. The anarchists, as Ely understood, were aware that the methods used to make the revolution were bound to affect the nature of society after the revolution had been accomplished. Accordingly, any attempt to organize the working-class movement on centralist or authoritarian lines would frustrate the libertarian aims that the movement was intended to serve. This, indeed, had been the position of the Bakuninists in the First International when they opposed Marx's insistence on a centrally directed and disciplined organization. "How can you expect an egalitarian and a free society to emerge from an authoritarian organization?" they demanded. "It is impossible. The International, embryo of future human society, must be from this moment the faithful image of our principles of liberty and federation, and reject from its midst any principle leading to authority and dictatorship."[2]

In accordance with this view, the IWPA, as self-proclaimed heir to the Bakuninist wing of the First International, was organized on a federalist and non-authoritarian basis. Throughout its existence it remained a loose association of autonomous groups, without paid or permanent officials, in which the impetus for action came from below, from the laboring rank and file. As Professor Ely noted, there was no executive body of any kind and little formal coordination of activity. The Bureau of Information did not issue orders or impose policy. Yet there was a broad feeling of unity and a continuous intellectual intercourse among the various groups, encouraged by visits, correspondence, and occasional joint meetings. Newspapers and journals served as a further connecting link, especially those with a national circulation, such as *The Alarm* and the *Arbeiter-Zeitung*.

The newspapers, of course, fulfilled an educational as well as organizational function, promoting libertarian values and beliefs. Such an effort was needed, if only to counter the distortions and misrepresentations of the daily press, which the anarchists regarded as the mouthpiece of the propertied classes, designed, as a speaker for the American Group declared, "to aid in the plunder and enslavement of the people."[3] During the three years prior to Haymarket, as has been noted, the International published no fewer than fourteen journals, daily, weekly, fortnightly, which acquainted a growing number of workers with socialist and anarchist ideas. By far the most important were Most's *Freiheit*, Spies's *Arbeiter-Zeitung* (along with the *Vorbote* and *Fackel*), and Parsons's *Alarm*, which was issued, according to its initial number, "in behalf of the wage slaves of this country."[4] The other publications in German were *Die Parole* of St. Louis, edited by Joseph Reifgraber, *Die Zukunft* of Philadelphia, edited by Moritz Bachmann, the *New England Anzeiger*, published by the New Haven Group of the International, and the *New Jersey*

Arbeiter-Zeitung, issued by disciples of Most in Jersey City Heights. Yet another German journal, to which we shall return in the next chapter, was the Chicago-based *Anarchist,* edited by George Engel and Adolph Fischer.[5]

Throughout this period, *The Alarm* remained the International's most important English periodical, although an ephemeral sheet called *Nemesis* appeared in Baltimore in 1884. For Scandinavian readers *Den Nye Tid* continued to appear until 1885, edited by Peter Peterson with the collaboration of Marcus Thrane, a veteran Norwegian socialist. Finally, there were two journals in Czech, *Proletář* of New York and *Budoucnost* (The Future) of Chicago. The latter, organ of the Bohemian Group, was edited by Norbert Zoula, a silversmith from Prague, who had spent eighteen months in an Austrian prison before emigrating to America in 1883, the year in which *Budoucnost* was launched. Assisting him were Josef Pečka, an iron molder, and Jacob Mikolanda, a baker, who had been a delegate to the Pittsburgh congress and who served as Bohemian secretary of the Bureau of Information.

All these journals, in whatever language they were published, trumpeted revolutionary methods and goals. All, moreover, used the term "anarchist" to characterize their political beliefs. Initially, as Parsons relates, the anarchist label had been fastened upon the Internationalists by their opponents, who had sought to stigmatize them as enemies of "law and order." Before long, however, the Internationalists defiantly adopted it as a badge of esteem. "We began to allude to ourselves as anarchists," writes Parsons, "and that name, which was at first imputed to us as a dishonor, we came to cherish and to defend with pride. What's in a name? But names sometimes express ideas, and ideas are everything."[6] While many Internationalists continued to call themselves socialists as well as anarchists, the latter term soon took precedence over the former. As Fielden later recalled: "In regard to whether the term anarchist is the proper one or socialist, I wish to say that [we] were all anarchists at that time."[7]

It is not surprising, then, that the *Freiheit,* in July 1885, should have changed its subtitle from "Organ of Revolutionary Socialists" to "International Organ of German-Speaking Anarchists," or that *The Alarm* should have scrapped "A Socialistic Weekly" for "A Revolutionary Socialistic Newspaper Devoted to the Propaganda of Anarchy." These and their sister journals, however, were labor as well as anarchist organs. They contained a great deal of strike news and other material of interest to workers, including exposés of child labor, industrial accidents, and hard conditions in the factories and mines. Under such headings as "Les Misérables" and "The Property Beast," their columns were filled with stories of starvation and suicide and the general wretchedness of the working class. Beyond this, they carried articles on the history of the labor movement and the history and philosophy of socialism, as well as translations of European anarchist and socialist writers and of fiction dealing with the laboring poor. A notable example of the latter was Emile Zola's *Germinal*, serialized in the *Vorbote* in 1884 and recommended by *The Alarm* as "a truthful description of the conflict between capitalists and laborers [that] finds its parallel in the social conditions of the masses in America."[8]

Apart from history and fiction, poetry occupied a prominent place, above all the German poetry of 1848, of which Heine's "The Weavers" and Freiligrath's "The Revolution" were particular favorites.[9] Many of the poems, however, were written by ordinary workmen and, with metaphors drawn often from biblical and feudal oppression, depicted scenes of exploitation, with laborers referred to as "slaves" and "vassals," employers as "tyrants" and "kings." Some of these were stiff and rhetorical, others graceful and moving. But most, while far from being literary masterpieces, spoke directly to the hearts of the workers in a language they could easily grasp; and more than a few, containing strong millenarian overtones ("It is coming! It is coming! / Hear that distant, sea-like roar! / 'Tis the threat of tortured millions— / 'Tyrants you shall be no more!' "),[10] inspired hopes of imminent liberation.

The militant tone of the journals was best conveyed by the mottoes adorning their mastheads and editorial pages: "The Tools Belong to the Toilers, the Product to the Producers" (*The Alarm*); "Equal Duties, Equal Rights—No Masters, No slaves" (*Die Parole*); "Agitate! Organize! Educate!" (*Nemesis*); "An Eye for an Eye, A Tooth for a Tooth!" (*Budoucnost*). Catechisms and parables, fantasy and satire, parody and caricature—all performed a similar function, as did proverbs, aphorisms, and slogans, such as those in the first number of *The Alarm*: "The more we are governed, the less we are free," "The true science of government is the science of getting rid of government," "In the name of law, authority and government the human race is enslaved!"[11] Most striking of all, however, was a slogan appearing in several publications, "War to the palace, peace to the cottage, death to luxurious idleness!," a battle cry from the German Peasant War of the sixteenth century, revived during the French Revolution and the Paris Commune.

In addition to their newspapers and journals, the anarchists turned out a vast quantity of books, pamphlets, leaflets, circulars, and brochures, which they hawked at lectures and rallies or sold and distributed by mail. From the office of *The Alarm* and *Arbeiter-Zeitung*, for example, one could procure such works as *God and the State* by Bakunin, *An Appeal to the Young* by Kropotkin, *The Communist Manifesto* by Marx and Engels, *An Anarchist on Anarchy* by Elisée Reclus, *Underground Russia* by Stepniak, *The Historical Basis of Socialism in England* by H. M. Hyndman, *Modern French and German Socialism* by Richard T. Ely, *Woman in the Past, Present and Future* by August Bebel, *Progress and Poverty* by Henry George, and *The Co-operative Commonwealth* by Laurence Gronlund.

The pamphlets of Johann Most sold particularly well, as did the debate between Most and Grottkau, the Pittsburgh Manifesto, and two leaflets reprinted from *The Alarm*, Lucy Parsons's *To Tramps, the Unemployed, the Disinherited and Miserable* and Victor Hugo's *Two Messages: One to the Rich, the Other to the Poor*. A passion to educate and uplift drove the anarchist press at a furious pace. Between May and November 1885, according to a report of the Bureau of Information, 387,527 pieces of literature were sold and distributed, including 6,527 books, 200,000 copies of the Pittsburgh Manifesto (in English, German, French, and Czech), 25,000 copies of *The Communist Manifesto*, 10,000 copies each of the leaflets by Lucy Parsons and Victor Hugo, and 5,000 pamphlets by Johann Most.[12]

If not for a shortage of funds, even more might have been accomplished. The anarchist press, relying entirely on the support of impecunious workers, found itself in chronic financial difficulty. *The Alarm* was particularly hard hit. In January 1885, barely three months after its inception, it was compelled to shift from a weekly to a fortnightly schedule owing to monetary pressures. To alleviate the problem, Parsons organized a cooperative publishing group, The Alarm Press Club, and urged supporters to purchase shares at two dollars apiece. (The German papers, which enjoyed a stronger financial position because of their larger readership, had earlier formed a comparable group, the Socialistic Publishing Society.) A committee, consisting of Parsons, his wife, Lizzie Holmes, Oscar Neebe, and Balthasar

Rau, launched a campaign to attract new subscribers and advertisers. In addition, one of the purposes of Parsons's frequent lecture tours was to secure money and readers for the paper; and further support was obtained through picnics, raffles, dances, and like occasions.

Notwithstanding these expedients, *The Alarm* seemed constantly on the brink of collapse. "We are having a hard time here to keep our little paper—and through it our advanced ideas—before the people," wrote William Holmes to an English colleague in April 1886. "But we have many followers and sympathizers in this country. The worst of it is we are all so poor, that in order to sustain the Alarm we have to make many personal sacrifices, and many are too destitute to do even that."[13] Somehow *The Alarm* managed to cling to life, and only after the Haymarket catastrophe was it compelled to suspend publication.

Beyond their publishing ventures, the anarchists engaged in a broad range of cultural and social activities, which enhanced their feeling of solidarity and greatly enriched their lives. In a relatively short period, they created a network of orchestras, choirs, theatrical groups, debating clubs, literary societies, and gymnastic and shooting clubs, involving thousands of participants. They organized lectures, concerts, picnics, dances, plays, and recitations, in which children as well as adults took part. Saloons and beer-gardens—Greif's Hall, Zepf's Hall, Steinmueller's Hall, Neff's Hall—became bustling centers of radical life. The International, moreover, engaged in mutual aid services, providing assistance to members and their families in times of need.[14]

Life was not easy for these working-class radicals, but there were many moments of happiness and laughter. They had their picnics and outings, their dances and concerts, their pageants and festivals, their raffles and shooting contests. Hardly a week went by when there was not some special activity in which to take part. In Chicago alone, during one six-month interval, there was a concert and ball to commemorate the Paris Commune, a "basket and pic-nic and prize play games" sponsored by the Freiheit Group at Ditman's farm, a "bivouac and prize shooting" organized by the Lehr-und-Wehr Verein at the North Side Sharp Shooters' Park, a "grand masque ball" arranged by the Socialistic Male Chorus at Folz's Hall, and a "picnic and summer-night's festival" arranged by the Central Labor Union at Ogden's Grove. Picnics were especially important occasions, not only to dance and eat and drink, but also to hear lectures and to collect money for the anarchist press. "It was a Bohemian crowd," said William Holmes of these gatherings, "without conventionality or elegance, but with more brightness, wisdom and earnest longing for truth than might be found around any millionaire's table, where sparkling wine flowed instead of the more plebeian beer."[15]

At all of these entertainments music occupied a vital place. There were orchestras and bands, chamber and choral groups, and vocal and instrumental soloists, to say nothing of audience participation. Children joined in the singing and shared the floor with adults, executing waltzes, polkas, schottisches, and other popular dances. Often old songs were given new words to suit the industrial era, such as "Marching to Liberty," sung to the tune of the "Marseillaise." Known also as the "Workers' Marseillaise," it was especially popular at rallies and demonstrations. Another favorite was Johann Most's "Hymn of the proletariat":

> Wer schafft das Gold zu Tage?
> Wer hämmert Erz und Stein?
> Wer webet Tuch und Seide?
> Wer bauet Korn und Wein?
> Wer gibt den Reichen all' ihr Brot—
> Und lebt dabei in bitt'rer Not?
> Das sind die Arbeitsmänner, das Proletariat.

> (Who hammers brass and stone?
> Who raiseth from the mine?
> Who weaveth cloth and silk?
> Who tilleth wheat and vine?
> Who worketh for the rich to feed,
> Yet lives himself in sorest need!—
> It is the men who toil, the Proletariat.)[16]

Also popular were William Morris's "March of the Workers" and the revolutionary songs of Herwegh, Freiligrath, and Heine.

Plays and dramatic recitations were yet another conspicuous feature of the counterculture. Often written by the performers themselves, they were as a rule more notable for their energy than for their artistic merit. Yet they were extremely popular and served an important agitational function, portraying both current labor struggles and heroic episodes from the past, such as the German Peasant War and the French Revolution. One four-act drama, devoted to the Russian populists who had recently assassinated the tsar, exercised a powerful hold on the audience and was staged by German groups in both New Haven and Philadelphia. The anarchists saw the populists—or "nihilists," as they invariably misnamed them—as kindred spirits, with their faith in the working people and their self-sacrificing dedication to freedom. The fascination exerted by their revolutionary heroism was extraordinary. Michael Schwab referred to Sophia Perovskaya, who went to the gallows for her role in the assassination, as "that noble anarchist girl."[17]

Plays and pageants had an important place in anarchist protests and demonstrations. One such occasion was an "indignation meeting" arranged by the Chicago Internationalists to denounce the execution of their German comrade August Reinsdorf, beheaded in February 1885 for plotting against the kaiser and other dignitaries. Apart from speeches by Spies and Albert and Lucy Parsons, the meeting featured a "tableau" depicting "the Revolution," in which a woman, dressed as the Goddess of Liberty, stood on a raised platform holding aloft a red flag, while a worker stood beneath, armed with a flaming sword and carrying a cartridge box inscribed "Dynamite." At the conclusion, the audience rose and sang the "Workers' Marseillaise," adjourning amid cheers for the social revolution.[18]

The most prominent occasion for pageantry, however, was the anniversary of the Paris Commune, an event, said William Holmes, that "thrilled the hearts of all true lovers of equality and justice."[19] The anarchists never tired of defending the Commune and glorifying its memory. To them it had been the greatest insurrection of the century, the highest point yet reached in the workers' struggle for emancipation. It was also a harbinger of the coming social revolution. If the workers of America could seize control of a major city (Chicago, for example) and apply within it the principles of libertarian socialism, the revolution would spread quickly throughout the country, ultimately engulfing the entire world. "Vive la Commune!" proclaimed *The Alarm*, "the battle cry that terrifies kings, priests, capitalists and tyrants. Vive la Commune! is a cry which condemns the state, the state which in all its forms seeks but one object, the oppression of the many by the few. Vive la Commune! is a protest against private property which kills all progress. It is a demand for the abolition of all poverty and crime. It feeds the hungry, shelters the homeless and forsaken; it kindles the fire on the home hearth, and restores happiness and joy to millions of lives—a cry for a free community in a free society."[20]

Every year since 1871, giant rallies were held in many cities to commemorate the Commune, drawing thousands of participants and observers. In 1885 the celebration in Chicago, which took place on March 21, was so large that two auditoriums had to be secured, the Vorwaerts Turner Hall on West 12th Street and the North Side Turner Hall at Clark Street and Chicago Avenue. Both were filled to overflowing. At the Vorwaerts Hall, ceremonies began with the performance of a play entitled "The Rich and the Poor, or Life on the Streets of New York City," followed by music and dancing until the early morning hours. At the North Side Turner Hall, beautifully decorated by Oscar Neebe, festivities opened with singing by the Socialistic Male Chorus, followed by addresses by Samuel Fielden and William Holmes. Holmes declared that the Commune of Paris had been a revolt not only against the French ruling class but against "the iniquitous political, industrial and social systems which then prevailed, and under which we still suffer. It was a complete overthrow, for the time being, of all existing institutions, and an attempt to found a social and industrial republic based upon the inherent rights of man"[21]

The following year, on March 18, the fifteenth anniversary of the Commune's inauguration, the celebration was again held at the Vorwaerts Turner Hall. More than 1,500 people attended, many of them women and children. The full panoply of revolutionary emblems and rituals was in evidence, some of them adapted from those of older organizations and traditions, such as the Turn Verein and the Masons, of which Spies and Parsons, respectively, were members. A scarlet banner, "typifying the red blood, the solidarity of the human race," hung from the gallery and stage. Mottoes, printed in bold letters and displayed around the hall, proclaimed that "Every Government is a Conspiracy of the Rich against the Poor," "Liberty without Equality is a Lie," "The Means of Life Belong to All," "Obedience to Statute Law is Slavery," and "Not to be a Slave is to Dare and Do."

As in previous years, the program consisted of a theatrical performance, speeches, singing, music, and dancing. At 10 P.M. Parsons took the platform and announced that the featured speaker, Mme Delescluze, wife of the famous hero of the Commune, was ill and unable to come. Parsons himself then spoke briefly, describing the Commune as a "revolt of labor against the domination of capital, an attempt by force of arms to secure labor's economic emancipation." Similar conditions, Parsons went on, now prevailed in the United States, hundreds of thousands of workers being "prevented from using the means of life, and kept in compulsory idleness, vagabondage, misery and poverty." It would be necessary, as a result, to "proclaim and maintain the American Commune, and the day draws nigh when the workers of the whole world will rise and forever destroy class rule and the robbery of man's birthright." Parsons concluded by reading a poem by Mary Miller, a member of the American Group. The band then played the "Marseillaise," followed by cheers from the audience of "Vive la Commune!" After this, a message of greeting was read in French from the Société Révolutionnaire, composed of survivors of the Commune residing in New York City. The floor was then cleared, the band took up its position, and "to the strains of soft and enchanting music," *The Alarm* reported, "all entered heartily into the joys of the dance and the festivities of the hour until early morning."[22]

For all the enthusiasm of these celebrations, the International attained its greatest degree of public visibility through street demonstrations and processions, often mounted jointly with the Central Labor Union. Such demonstrations, when held on a Sunday or holiday, frequently combined a parade through downtown Chicago with a picnic at Ogden's Grove. As many as three or four thousand demonstrators participated, many of them decorated with red ribbons or rosettes and carrying red or black flags inscribed with mottoes setting forth "the grievances and hopes of the proletariat."[23]

On Sunday, June 7, 1885, for example, two thousand workmen with their wives and children marched through the center of the city to the music of three bands. Heading the column was the stars and stripes, followed by twenty-three red flags and innumerable banners carried by the organizations comprising the procession. On the banners were such mottoes as "Poverty is a Crime," "Exploitation is Legalized Theft," "Anarchy," "Workingmen of the World Unite," "The Priesthood Subserves the Exploitation of Labor," and "No Rights Without Duties, No Duties Without Rights."

From the city the procession marched to Ogden's Grove for a picnic with speeches and dancing. Fielden was the principal speaker.

As reported in *The Alarm*, he told the audience, by then nearly four thousand strong, that the workers must organize and take their rights by force. He said that "armed resistance was not possible while capital controlled all the elements of military warfare, but dynamite, and those destructive explosives which science has placed within the reach of the oppressed, could be used with effect." It was the duty of the despoiled to familiarize themselves with "these insidious little messengers" which startled tyrants by their shock. General Sheridan had said that "these missives could be carried around in one's pocket with perfect safety" and used in such a manner that "whole armies and cities could be destroyed."

Following Fielden's address, Michael Schwab spoke briefly in German. Then the band played the "Marseillaise," and, with prolonged cheers for the social revolution, the throng dispersed amid the grove. Dancing, conversation, and basket lunches ended a day that would be remembered, in the words of *The Alarm*, as "one of the most pleasant of the year." Let it be recorded, proclaimed *The Alarm*, "that on this day another firm resolve was made by the workers to achieve their economic freedom or die in the attempt."[24]

A similar demonstration took place on Sunday, July 26, with Balthasar Rau in charge of the arrangements. As the sun rose bright in a cloudless sky, the procession, composed of fifteen groups of the International, German, Bohemian, and American, along with eight affiliates of the Central Labor Union and a contingent from the Lehrund-Wehr Verein dressed in blue blouses and black pants and armed with Colt revolvers ("it being unlawful for workingmen in Illinois to parade with rifles," as *The Alarm* pointed out), formed in Market Street between Randolph and Madison. Thousands of spectators lined the streets to witness the formation of the procession, which moved off to the strains of four brass bands. Mounted on horses were Neebe, Fielden, and Spies, who, acting as marshals, guided the columns, which stretched for half a mile, along Madison to Clark, then northwards in the direction of Ogden's Grove, the "crimson banner of solidarity" prominently displayed. Many of the marchers carried flags and placards on which the following slogans were inscribed: "Government is for Slaves—Free Men Govern Themselves," "Workingmen Arise!" "Down with Throne, Altar, and Money-Bags," "Our Civilization: the Bullet and Policeman's Club," and "Millions Labor for the Benefit of a Few—We Want to Labor for Ourselves."

Adorning the line of march were several allegorical displays, the

141

equivalent of modern floats. The most elaborate of these was a long flat wagon drawn by two mules, each covered with a cloth, on one of which was printed "Our Representatives" and on the other "Our Senators." The driver, got up as "Uncle Sam," wore a white plug hat and red, white, and blue pants. In the center of the wagon was a large barrel labeled "Five and Ten Cent Drinks," next to which stood a dummy policeman raising a club with one arm while the other encircled the barrel. Attached to his back was a card inscribed "One of the Finest," and beneath, in large letters, were the words "Liberty Enlightening the World." Surrounding the wagon and covering the wheels was a white cloth inscribed with "Americans, Long Live Your Liberty." This tableau, *The Alarm* noted, excited a great deal of comment, as bystanders were moved to recall the recent streetcar strike, when the police had used their clubs against innocent citizens in the name of "law and order."[25]

Another feature of the parade was the appearance, at the head of the American Group, of a huge red banner with four silken cords, borne aloft by William Crowley, with Lucy Parsons, Lizzie Holmes, Sarah Ames, and Mrs. Poller holding the cords as color guards. The sight elicited applause along the line of march, which was three miles in length by the time Ogden's Grove loomed into view. On reaching the grove, the marchers scattered beneath the shade of trees and booths to begin their picnic. By 2 P.M., said *The Alarm*, fully 10,000 people were in the grove, "enjoying themselves to the utmost." After a basket lunch with lemonade, pop, and beer, the dancing platform filled up with "a happy throng tripping the light fantastic to the strains of an elegant band."[26]

At five o'clock the bugle call sounded, and Neebe introduced Parsons for a speech. Parsons struck a solemn note that contrasted with the gaiety of the occasion. Throughout the Middle West, in Missouri, Kansas, Iowa, and Nebraska, where he had recently lectured, he had found "misery, want and hunger in the midst of the greatest abundance." He spoke of poverty and unemployment, of vagabonds and tramps, and "everywhere the concentration of wealth in the hands of the privileged few," who, under the system of private property, amassed their fortunes by "plundering the workers, the useful classes." The workers, however, were "ripening for revolt." Before long there would be "neither masters nor slaves, neither governors nor governed; no law but the natural law which all must obey in order to live; the 'free society,' where all do as they please, it pleasing each

142

to restrain the other from doing wrong to any one, in other words, Anarchy."

Parsons concluded with three cheers for the social revolution, to which the crowd responded with enthusiasm. The band struck up the "Marseillaise," which was sung by the whole assembly. Fielden then spoke on the need for organization and unity, emphasizing the "active participation of women in the labor movement." He exhorted everyone, male and female, to join the International, attend its meetings, subscribe to its newspapers, read its books, and "prepare mentally and physically for the inevitable conflict of force between capitalists and their laborers." Schwab closed the meeting with a short address in German. "Thus," commented *The Alarm*, "passed one more memorable day of the labor movement in Chicago, and the hands of the people were strengthened, and the conviction deepened, and the preparations increased for a final struggle between the upholders of privilege and the defenders of the equal rights of all."[27]

Demonstrations like these were a peculiar feature of the agitation in Chicago in the years before the Haymarket explosion. They were designed, above all, to display the strength of the movement to its opponents and at the same time to encourage its supporters with a sense of their collective power. Yet, combining entertainment with social protest, they had a festive air which belied their seriousness of purpose. With their flags and banners, their placards and posters, their mottoes and slogans, their speeches and music, they brought all the devices of the counterculture into play and provided a vivid example of how traditional social activities might be used for revolutionary purposes.

The most important of these demonstrations, apart from those already cited, took place on July Fourth, Thanksgiving, Christmas, and "other capitalistic holidays," as William Holmes described them. The International was always ready to take advantage of national festivities to hold counterdemonstrations and celebrations. On such occasions, recalled Holmes, the participants, often reaching into the thousands, would gather in Market Square, then march through the fashionable neighborhoods of the city, "each parade being one long line of red."[28]

The first demonstration of this kind occurred on Thanksgiving Day of 1884. To advertise the event, the International issued a cir-

143

cular with the ironic heading "Thank Our Lords." "Workingmen," it declared. "Next Thursday, November 27th, 1884, when our Lords and Masters are feasting on Turkey and Champagne, and offering prayers of gratitude for the bounties they enjoy, the wage-slaves of Chicago, the unemployed, the enforced idle, the tramps—and the homeless and destitute—will assemble on Market Street, between Randolph and Madison Streets, to mutter their curses loud and deep against the 'Lords' who have deprived them of every blessing during the past year. Every wage-worker, every tramp must be on hand to express their thanks in a befitting manner."[29]

November 27 was a cold, windy day, with a mixture of rain and sleet falling. Yet by 2 P.M. more than three thousand people had assembled in Market Square. Near the makeshift speakers' platform a large black flag had been unfurled. It was the new anarchist emblem—"the fearful symbol of hunger, misery and death," as *The Alarm* described it.[30] Parsons ascended the platform and delivered the opening address. Speaking for "the disinherited class of the earth," he compared the "good dinners the capitalists were enjoying today" to the feast of Belshazzar in ancient Babylon, when the handwriting on the wall foretold the end of his kingdom. The dinners of the capitalists, said Parsons, had been "wrung from the blood of our wives and children, and the champagne thus obtained ought to strangle them." In the churches, he went on, they are preaching the Scriptures to the wealthy, but let them read from the epistle of James: "Go to now, ye rich men, weep and howl for your miseries that shall come upon you. Your riches are corrupted, and your garments are moth-eaten. Your gold and silver is cankered; and the rust of them shall be a witness against you, and shall eat your flesh as it were fire. Ye have reaped treasure together for the last days." Parsons declared, by way of closing, that "we do not intend to leave this matter in the hands of the Lord, or wait for any improved future existence. We intend to do something for ourselves, and do it in this world."[31]

Parsons then introduced C. S. Griffin, who denounced the capitalist system in violent terms. The next speaker, Fielden, emphasized the international character of the movement: "Our motto is liberty, equality and fraternity. We do not believe in robbing or abusing a man because he is colored, or a Chinaman, or was born in this country or that. Our international movement is to unite all countries for the mutual good of all, and do away with the robber class." After Fielden came Spies, who, pointing to the black flag, noted that this was the first occasion on which that emblem of retribution had been unfurled on American soil. Schwab spoke next in German, followed by three cheers for the social revolution.

At this point the audience fell into line, forming a procession of more than three thousand, which moved off down Market Street to the sounds of martial music. The black flag, along with a red one, headed the column, while placards and banners proclaimed the usual messages: "Down with Wage-Slavery!" "Workingmen, Organize! " "Liberty without Equality is a Lie! " As the procession passed the Palmer House on State Street, frequented by businessmen and politicians, the band sounded forth with the "Marseillaise," and the marchers cheered and groaned in alternation. Again, passing a businessmen's club on Dearborn, they hissed and hooted at the members, who crowded at the windows, said *The Alarm*, for a glimpse of "their future executioners."[32]

Winding its way through the fashionable boulevards and avenues, lined with elegant mansions on either side, the procession paused at the residence of Elihu Washburne, U.S. ambassador to France at the time of the Paris Commune. Though a former Radical Republican and abolitionist, Washburne, on returning to America, had traveled about the country denouncing the Communards as a mob of cutthroats and thieves. To the demonstrators his name was synonymous with reaction. One man, leaving the line of march, pointed at Washburne's house and cried, "Three cheers for the Paris Commune!" The whole procession joined in the cry, the band struck up the "Marseillaise," and the marchers began to sing. At one point a break was made to enter the house and sack it, but Parsons intervened and managed to keep the crowd quiet. "This high-toned flunkey," said *The Alarm* of Washburne when reporting the incident, "can begin to change the text of his lecture now, and make it read 'The American Commune.' "[33]

Resuming its parade through the city, the procession at length came to a halt at 107 Fifth Avenue, headquarters of *The Alarm* and *Arbeiter-Zeitung*. From a second-floor window Parsons congratulated the participants on the success of their demonstration. He then introduced Fielden, who urged them to "organize and prepare for the inevitable conflict," which the capitalists were forcing upon them. At the close of Fielden's speech, three cheers were given for the miners of the Hocking Valley, the anarchists of France, the socialists of Germany, the "nihilists" of Russia, and the social democrats of England. Then, amid further cheers for the social revolution, the meeting was declared adjourned.[34]

To the consternation of the authorities, the Thanksgiving demonstration of 1884 was repeated the following year. Once again thousands participated and Parsons was the principal speaker, while William Holmes presented a resolution affirming that "no nation can be prosperous and contented where, in the banquet of life, a small number monopolize the general product, while the many are denied a place at nature's table."[35] The 1st Regiment of the Illinois militia held riot duty that day in an unsuccessful effort to intimidate the marchers. In other respects, however, the demonstration was a replica of its predecessor.

Between the two Thanksgiving demonstrations, the International staged yet another mass procession, and one that, because of its impact, warrants detailed description. Billed specifically as a "counter demonstration,"[36] it was planned to coincide with the opening of an elaborate new building on LaSalle Street by the Chicago Board of Trade. The building, on which two million dollars had been lavished in the midst of an economic depression, was denounced by the anarchists as a veritable temple of Mammon, the crowning symbol of all that was hateful in the private property system. On the night of April 28, 1885, while the building was filling up with guests for the inaugural banquet, a few blocks away, in Market Square, there gathered what William Holmes described as "a motley crowd of radicals, tramps, and curiosity seekers" under the IWPA banner.[37]

At 8 P.M. Parsons called the assembly to order. After hearing some speeches, he announced, they would march around the new headquarters of the "Board of Thieves" singing the "Workers' Marseillaise." [Cheers from the audience and cries of "Vive la Commune!"] As he introduced Fielden, the Internationalists from the North Side arrived, bearing aloft red and black flags, and marched to the speakers' stand amid shouts from the assembled crowd. Fielden, pointing to the flags, said that the red flag represented "the red blood of humanity which flowed alike through the veins of all, the equality of rights, of duties and opportunities to which the veriest tramp and beggar was as much entitled as the highest born aristocrat." The other, the black flag, was "the emblem of starvation and misery," and it was especially fitting that it should be flaunted at the Board

146

of Trade, which stood for "starvation for the masses—privileges and luxury for a few." [Cheers and a voice: "Blow it up with dynamite!"]

The Board of Trade, Fielden went on, was a place where "high toned thieves" plied their work. The profit-makers of the world "toil not, neither do they spin," yet "Solomon in all his glory was not arrayed like them." They owned "all that the world contained, all that labor had been for centuries producing." Yet labor was not invited to their banquet. [Cries: "We are going anyway," "We will invite ourselves."] Fielden denounced the Board of Trade men for toasting their two-million-dollar "Temple of Usury" while two-and-a-half million men were jobless in the nation. "How long are we going to stand the present degrading condition of things? How long are we who create all the wealth to be put off with a 15-cent meal with a piece of pie thrown in, while 'these fellows' sit down to twenty-dollar dishes?" Only the workers, said Fielden, could change this abominable system. They must band together and "destroy from the earth every unproductive member of society." [Cries of "Hear, hear!"][38]

Parsons himself was the next speaker. Assailing the "vampires and parasites" who fattened on the misery of the poor, he declared that not a stone of the new Board of Trade building had not been "carved out of the flesh and blood of labor, and cemented by the sweat and tears of the women and children of toil." If the workers would achieve emancipation, "every man must lay by a part of his wages, buy a Colt's navy revolver [Cheers and "That's what we want!"], a Winchester rifle ["And ten pounds of dynamite—we will make it ourselves!"], and learn how to make and use dynamite." [Cheers and cries of "Vive la Commune!"]

At the conclusion of the speeches, the order was given to fall into line. To the music of the band, the procession moved off on Madison Street, forming a line about two blocks in length. At the head of the line marched Lucy Parsons and Lizzie Holmes, each bearing a flag, one black, the other red. At the center of the line there was another pair of flags, black and red, also carried by women. Spectators had meanwhile been gathering on the sidewalks, and, as the procession moved east on Madison Street, cheer after cheer arose from the crowd, which numbered several thousand. At Clark Street, the procession marched south to Jackson, to find its passage barred by a line of police. Turning aside into Adams Street, the column moved west to LaSalle, then turned down that street towards the Board of

Trade building. As at Jackson, however, a cordon of police was stretched across the road, blocking the procession's approach.

At this point a halt was proclaimed. Neebe, marshal of the parade, stepped out to the police line and demanded to know why the people could not pass. Parsons, joining him, asked for the officer in charge. A captain came forward and said: "The way is completely blocked up with carriages. It is impossible for you to go through by that way." After a moment's consultation, the order was given to move east on Adams. At Fifth Avenue the line turned south and, on reaching Jackson, was blocked by yet another phalanx of police, reaching from sidewalk to sidewalk. Here another halt was made. The Board of Trade building, bathed in a sea of electric light only recently installed for the occasion, was in full view half a block away. The band took up a position on the sidewalk, while the crowd gathered around and sent up "shout after shout of defiance and derision" in the direction of the new structure. The band struck up the "Marseillaise" and thousands of voices joined in. Then cheer after cheer went up for the social revolution.

After five or ten minutes of singing and shouting, the order was given to fall in. Moving down Fifth Avenue to Van Buren Street, the procession made a circuit of the entire block around the Board of Trade building. Every approach was blocked by the police. The marchers proceeded to 107 Fifth Avenue, where a final halt was called. From the windows of *The Alarm* and *Arbeiter-Zeitung* on the second floor, two of the large flags that had been borne in the procession were suspended. Parsons stepped out on a window sill and addressed the crowd, assailing the authorities for blocking the demonstration. Once again, he declared, the workers had been taught that "government exists for the sole purpose of defending private property and the privilege to plunder labor." The military had been held in readiness in the armories, and the workers confronted with the choice of "submission to slavery or death by the bayonet." The workers had no choice but to arm themselves. A final confrontation was inevitable. The "enemies of the people" held all the power. They maintained it by force, "and by force alone could the working people obtain their rights. Agitate, organize, revolt!"

Spies then addressed the audience briefly in German and Fielden in English. Fielden urged his listeners to acquire a knowledge of anarchism, the truths of which would "abolish poverty and transform a world of misery into a paradise of happiness and peace." By now it was eleven o'clock, and the meeting adjourned amid cheers for the social revolution.[39]

Demonstrations of this type continued to be held until the spring of 1886, making a deep impression on the Chicago community. For the supporters of the International, they provided a source of inspiration and promoted a feeling of solidarity and strength, of their own dignity and worth, which many had previously lacked. Within the bosom of a society that they detested, they found a spirit of camaraderie, of warmth, of devotion to a common cause. Moreover, by defying the conventions of the prevailing system, they obtained a foretaste of that freer order which they so deeply craved.

On the other hand, the demonstrations sent shivers of fear through the propertied classes. By dramatizing the gulf between the divisions of Chicago society, between the world of authority and privilege and the world of poverty and despair, they fostered an atmosphere of hatred and suspicion without which the Haymarket tragedy would not have occurred. The extremism of the International's opposition to existing institutions, the totality of its commitment to the overthrow of the established order, could not but alarm the city's prosperous residents. Business leaders feared that within the crowds of sullen, rough-looking men, many of them jobless and homeless, many of them foreign-born, there lurked something menacing and destructive. They felt that their world was being threatened and that, unless decisive action were taken, their way of life might be swept away.

11 ‖ THE INTRANSIGENTS

For all the unity displayed at its public meetings, the IWPA was not immune from the disputes and rivalries that plague every revolutionary organization. Behind the scenes there was considerable disharmony within the movement, which sheltered the most divergent temperaments and types. From the outset, it had been weakened by dissension, not only on important matters of doctrine and tactics, but also on the most trivial questions of personality. By the fall of 1885, this dissent reached a critical point with the emergence of an "autonomist" faction within the German-speaking segment, among whose adherents were two of the Haymarket defendants, George Engel and Adolph Fischer.

Autonomism, as a distinct tendency within the movement, had been germinating for several years, in Europe as well as in America. Under the leadership of Josef Peukert and Otto Rinke, an Autonomy Group was established in London in May 1885, and a journal, *Die Autonomie*, the following year, primarily in opposition to Johann Most, whom the autonomists accused of dictatorial behavior. In the United States, the chief stronghold of the autonomists was Chicago's North-West Side Group, of which both Engel and Fischer were members.[1] Noted for its revolutionary intransigence, the North-West Side Group enjoyed the support of the Anarchist Discussion Club, the South-West Side Group No. 3, the Socialistic Male Chorus of the South-West Side, and the second and third companies of the Lehr-und-Wehr Verein.

Taken together, these groups represented a minority of the movement in the city, containing fewer than one-quarter of the German-speaking members. What they lacked in numbers, however, they made up in revolutionary zeal. Their adherents were anarchists of an implacable and ultra-militant stamp. True believers, they disdained the least hint of moderation and refused to compromise on any issue that divided them from their adversaries within the movement. The latter included August Spies and Michael Schwab, whom

150

the autonomists considered insufficiently radical. Where Spies and Schwab concentrated on building a solid base of support among the workers, Engel and Fischer pinned their hopes on small, independent action groups, devoted to armed insurrection and propaganda by the deed. Impatient for the social revolution, which they expected at any moment, they called for the complete destruction of the established order by force.

The autonomists, as their name suggests, cherished the principle of decentralization as a fundamental tenet. For them one of the main attractions of anarchism was the stress that it laid on spontaneity and independence, on the freedom of the individual and local group from bureaucratic pressure and coercion. All but the most loose-knit organizations, they were convinced, contained the seeds of authority and domination, and they distrusted any central body, whether or not it possessed executive power. Accordingly, they refused to send delegates to the General Committee of the Chicago Groups. Nor did Engel or Fischer serve on the Bureau of Information or engage in any other activity on a level higher than that of the local group. Their hostility towards large-scale organizations, moreover, extended to trade unions, and they rejected the "Chicago idea" championed by Parsons and Spies, although Fischer himself was a member of the German Typographical Union, an affiliate of the Central Labor Union.

Fischer, one of the most impressive of the Haymarket defendants, had been familiar with socialist ideas since his youth in Germany. Born in the northern city of Bremen in 1858, he attended school there for eight and a half years before emigrating to America. One day, during his last year at school, the subject of socialism came up in history class, and the teacher described the socialists as "a lot of drunkards, swindlers, and idlers," who wanted to divide up other people's possessions. Fischer, however, knew that his father attended socialist meetings, and wondered why he would associate with such a wicked class of people. That evening, when he came home from school, he told his father what the teacher had said. The father, laughing loudly, embraced the boy affectionately and explained to him what socialism actually meant. After that, Adolph accompanied his father to socialist gatherings and himself became a convert.[2]

In 1873, at the age of fifteen, Fischer sailed for the United States, where an older brother, William, had preceded him. William was now the publisher of a weekly German journal in Little Rock, Arkansas, and when Fischer arrived he became an apprentice in the composing room. After completing his apprenticeship, he worked at his trade in a number of American cities, among them St. Louis, where he joined the local branch of the German Typographical Union in 1879 and was married in 1881. Two years later he moved with his wife and baby to Chicago and worked as a printer at the *Arbeiter-Zeitung*, being foreman of the composing room at the time of his arrest. Two more children arrived in quick succession, one while Fischer was in prison.

Fischer never discarded the socialism that he had imbibed in his early youth. As he matured, on the contrary, his convictions grew more intense. Nor did he hesitate to expound them when called upon to do so. "When I left my native country," he wrote after his arrest, "my dear father (who died since) advised me to always utter fearlessly what I might hold to be the truth, and I have followed his advice faithfully."[3] In the fall of 1883 he joined the IWPA, associating himself with its most militant group. He also joined the Lehr-und-Wehr Verein and became an active member. A revolutionary zealot, possessed of "quiet, reserved strength," he was convinced that the wealthier classes would never abandon their privileges without a struggle, and that the authorities would always side with them in any conflict. "Would a peaceable solution of the social question be possible," he declared, "the anarchists would be the first ones to rejoice over it. But is it not a fact that on occasion of almost every strike the minions of the institutions of private property—militia, police, deputy sheriffs, yes, even federal troops—are being called to the scenes of conflict between capital and labor in order to protect the interests of capital? Did it ever happen that the interests of labor were guarded by these forces?"[4] Fischer, as William Holmes noted, never swerved from his revolutionary purpose. "He expected and desired to lose his life in the cause of human emancipation, and he had little patience with measures looking to the mere amelioration of the working people's condition. The present system must be destroyed root and branch, and in his opinion all means to that heroic end were justifiable."[5]

Fischer, noted Holmes, was "of a totally different type and temperament" from Spies or Parsons. In particular, he showed "decided leanings" towards individualism, his collectivism being tempered by Proudhonian ideas.[6] Furthermore, as Lizzie Holmes observed, he was "a thinker and worker rather than an orator. One seldom heard him speak, but if there was anything to be done Fischer was there to do it. He kept himself and his little family nearly destitute because he gave the greater part of his wages to the cause. He considered nothing on earth of any consequence compared to the advancement of the Social Revolution. He did not think life worth living as things existed, and cared only for that future time when all should have justice and equal opportunity."[7]

Only twenty-seven at the time of the Haymarket episode, Fischer was a tall, strapping young man with large bones, prominent features, and blond mustache and hair. Good-natured, intelligent, affable, with the tenderest affection for his family, he was yet possessed of a highly nervous temperament and passionate nature, remarked Dyer Lum, who knew him well and loved him dearly. Having come to America nearly thirteen years before, he was, Lum said, "as complete a master of English as of German composition," and, while in prison, both Engel and Lingg entrusted him with the work of translating their autobiographies and other writings.[8]

Fischer was Lum's favorite among the Haymarket defendants, and William Holmes too spoke of him in glowing terms. "Fischer's character," said Holmes, "seems to have been but little understood, even among his closest associates. The fact is that here was one of those rare souls who tower so majestically above their fellows as to belong to another sphere. His whole being was so bound up in the movement that he was literally a part of it. His days were passed in labor so that he might have money to spend for the Cause; his nights in agitating, planning, working for its success. His principal amusements were his preparations for the great conflict which he looked upon as inevitable. For Fischer was a revolutionist, and his most ardent hope was that he might take an active part in the great struggle for oppressed humanity."[9]

George Engel, although his senior by more than two decades, was Fischer's closest associate within the autonomist camp. By far the oldest of the Haymarket anarchists, he was born in the city of Cassel on April 15, 1836, the son of an indigent bricklayer. His father, Conrad Engel, died when the boy was only eighteen months old, leaving the mother and four children to struggle in poverty. A decade later she too passed away, and Engel, aged twelve, was left an orphan. After many hard experiences, including periods of near-starvation, he met with a kindly man, a painter in Frankfurt-am-Main, who took him in and taught him his craft. After completing his apprenticeship, Engel traveled through Germany, mostly on foot, practicing his trade in many cities. Times, however, grew hard. The introduction of machinery, Engel afterwards wrote, all but "ruined the small craftsman," so that the outlook for the future appeared dark. Having married and begun a family, he decided to seek his fortune in America, "praised to me by so many as the land of liberty."[10]

In January 1873 Engel disembarked in Philadelphia. He soon found work in a sugar factory and also, as in Germany, as a painter. His heart, he tells us, "swelled up with joy" at the thought of raising his children in a free country. But joy quickly yielded to disappointment. For, having arrived on the eve of the 1873 depression, he witnessed the same poverty and hardship as in Europe. Here, too, he later proclaimed in court, "there are numerous proletarians for whom no table is set; who, as outcasts of society, stray joblessly through life. I have seen human beings gather their daily food from the garbage heaps of the streets, to quiet therewith their gnawing hunger."[11]

In Philadelphia, furthermore, Engel had his first glimpse of labor troubles when he saw the militia march through the streets after subduing some striking miners. From such observations, he relates, he realized that "the same societary evils exist here that exist in Germany."[12] To add to his disenchantment, his health suddenly broke down, his eyes being severely affected. Medical expenses quickly exhausted his savings, and, with his family at the edge of starvation, he was forced to turn to the German Aid Society for help. It was a full year before he recovered and was able to go back to work. Anxious for a new start, he decided to move to Chicago.

It was in Chicago that Engel became a socialist. Soon after his arrival in 1874, he got a job in a wagon factory. One of his fellow workers was a socialist, and from him Engel took his first lessons in the philosophy which "afterwards became for him a religion."[13] His workmate, Engel tells us, described "the causes that brought about the difficult and fruitless battles of the workingman for the means of existence. He explained to me, by the logic of scientific Socialism, how mistaken I was in believing that I could make an independent living by the toil of my hands, so long as machinery, raw material, etc., were guaranteed to the capitalists as private property by the State."[14]

One day his friend showed him a copy of *Der Vorbote*. Engel found it interesting and saw, he later wrote, "that it contained great truths." He began to study socialist doctrines, reading Marx, Lassalle, and other writers. He also attended socialist meetings and was at once impressed by the idealism of his new comrades. It was astonishing, he says, "that men could without the least compensation work so eagerly for the cause of humanity. It struck me what a gigantic work it was to educate and organize the masses, who created everything, only to be cheated by their exploiters out of the fruits of their labor."[15]

Engel was quickly converted and threw all his energies into the cause. He joined the SLP and worked for the socialist ticket. But he soon became disillusioned with politics. He recoiled from the maneuvering and opportunism, the cynical rigging of elections, the compromise of principle for the sake of limited and often transitory gains. He found that the workingman was "too innocent and unsuspecting," an easy prey for "crafty politicians." Residing in the Fourteenth Ward, he saw how his alderman, Frank Stauber, could be cheated of his seat by unscrupulous officials. To rely on the ballot, he concluded, was a delusion and a snare. "I am of the opinion," he declared, "that as long as workingmen are economically enslaved they cannot be politically free."[16]

Abandoning political methods, Engel joined the IWPA at its first appearance in Chicago and became one of its most fervent devotees. "I labored," he recalled, "to bring about a system of society by which it is impossible for one to hoard millions, through improvements in machinery, while the great masses sink to degradation and misery."[17] Now in his late forties, with a plain round face and thinning hair, Engel had none of the glamour of a Spies or Parsons. Yet he was animated, as Dyer Lum remarked, by the same enthusiastic spirit that stirred the hearts of his more youthful comrades. Calm and reticent in his manner, he was neither a public speaker nor a facile writer, but his "genial, equitable nature" was a marked characteristic, and his attorney, W. P. Black, was impressed by the "absolute sincerity in all that he did and said."[18]

Engel, said Oscar Neebe, was a "brave soldier" in the working-class struggle, an "out and out" rebel for the cause.[19] Yet much of his energy was absorbed in factional squabbles, especially with Schwab and Spies. Spies, addressing the court in October 1886, revealed that he and Engel had not been on speaking terms for more than a year,

155

and that Fischer, although employed at the *Arbeiter-Zeitung*, "used to go around making speeches against me."[20] For intransigents like Engel and Fischer, the views of Spies and Schwab were too moderate; and in January 1886, to provide the movement with what they considered a genuinely revolutionary organ, they started a monthly journal called *Der Anarchist*, the mouthpiece of the autonomist faction.

A short-lived venture, *Der Anarchist* was suppressed following the Haymarket explosion, only four issues having been published.[21] For a brief period, however, it preached the unrestrained brand of anarchism ("We Hate Authority," was its motto) that characterized the autonomist school. Rejecting reformist methods as "useless games" (nutzlose Spielerei), it pledged itself to an all-out struggle against the established order, with propaganda by the deed as the "principal means of agitation." Further, as might be expected, it upheld the principle of autonomy in matters of organization, scorning all central bodies and "party popes."[22] On its masthead, accordingly, it indicated neither editors nor managers of any kind, providing only addresses to which communications might be directed.

One of these addresses, 286 Milwaukee Avenue, was that of the two-story house where Engel and his wife had lived and operated a toy store since 1876. Engel was an affectionate husband and father; and his teenage daughter Mary, who stood by him during his trial and imprisonment, was often to be seen distributing literature at anarchist meetings, particularly of the North-West Side Group. Engel had chosen this group, a hotbed of uncompromising radicalism, because of his belief that the propertied elements had to be conquered by force. "The history of all time," he declared, "teaches us that oppressing classes always maintain their tyranny by force and violence." Hence the only solution to the labor problem was a revolutionary one. "I am not for war," Engel insisted, "but I realize that a violent revolution will come, must come, not brought about by the workingmen, but by the capitalists." To prepare for this war, which he regarded as imminent, Engel urged the workers to provide themselves with the best weapons developed by modern science. "Believe no more in the ballot," he exclaimed, "and use all other means at your command." If they would follow his advice, he was sure, then victory lay in their grasp. "No power on earth," he declared at the Haymarket trial, "can rob the workingman of his knowledge of how to make bombs—and that knowledge he possesses."[23]

Like Engel, the oldest of the Haymarket anarchists, the youngest, Louis Lingg, was an uncompromising believer in violent action; "the forces by which the workers are kept in subjugation must be retaliated by force," he said.[24] A born rebel, Lingg was in many ways the most interesting of the eight defendants and was the only one among them who is definitely known to have manufactured bombs. "If they use cannon against us," he told Captain Schaack after his arrest, "we shall use dynamite against them."[25] In Lingg flowed the blood of martyrs, wrote Frank Harris in *The Bomb*, a novel about the Haymarket tragedy. "He had the martyr's pity for men, the martyr's sympathy with suffering and destitution, the martyr's burning contempt for greed and meanness, the martyr's hope in the future, the martyr's belief in the ultimate perfectibility of man."[26]

Whereas the other defendants had lived in America for many years, Lingg did not arrive from Germany until July 1885, only ten months before the Haymarket incident. He had been born at Schwetzingen in Baden on September 9, 1864, not far from Heidelberg and Mannheim. Life had been happy and pleasant during his early childhood years, until his father, Friedrich Lingg, met with an accident. A lumberman by trade, he was trying to recover a log that had slipped from the banks of the Neckar when suddenly the ice gave way and he was barely saved from drowning. His health, however, was ruined, and his employer reduced his wages and at length discharged him. This callous treatment of his father, and the poverty that the family afterwards experienced, awakened in the boy a "bitter hatred against existing society." Three years after the accident, in 1877, the father died, leaving the mother, a laundress, to provide for Lingg and his younger sister. "Not very seldom," Lingg later recalled, "want and hunger were questions in our family, and only the untiring efforts of my mother prevented their visits from becoming daily ones."[27]

As the years passed Lingg's bitterness grew more intense, turning him in the direction of socialism. Apprenticed to a carpenter at Mannheim, he completed his training in 1882 and went on the traditional tramp, wandering for three years through Germany and Switzerland. In Freiburg (Baden) he joined the Working Men's Educational Society, a Lassallean group, and was indoctrinated with socialist ideas. He also became an ardent freethinker, "a domain in which greater men than I have trod," he wrote in 1886, "and still greater than they will continue to walk."[28] In Berne he joined the General Working Men's Society, another socialist group. In Zurich, however, in 1883, he met the famous German anarchist August Reinsdorf and immediately became his disciple. From this time forward he threw himself heart and soul into the anarchist cause, an apostle of propaganda by the deed.

By now Lingg had reached the age for military service in Germany. Under an agreement between the Swiss and German governments, he was subject to deportation if he did not meet his obligation voluntarily. To avoid this, he ceased to register with the Swiss police, as required by law. Before long he was a wanted man. Rather than risk arrest or betray his anti-militarist principles, he decided to emigrate to America.

Lingg landed in New York in July 1885 and went directly to Chicago. Despite his youth, he was already a confirmed revolutionary, and he joined the International Carpenters' and Joiners' Union, an affiliate of the anarchist-dominated Central Labor Union. He soon found employment in a factory but was dismissed when he refused to fill the place of a worker who had struck for higher wages. At this point he met William Seliger, who was afterwards to betray him to the police. Seliger, a fellow carpenter and anarchist, found Lingg a job in the factory where he himself worked, and he invited Lingg to board with him and his wife. Lingg gratefully accepted and remained with the Seligers until the Haymarket incident. In the meantime, he quit his job and became a paid organizer for his union, which elected him as its delegate to the Central Labor Union.

That a twenty-one-year-old immigrant, only recently arrived in the country, should be entrusted with such responsibility was a measure of Lingg's ability and of the respect he could command in others. According to Captain Schaack, who interrogated him after his arrest, he was "scrupulously honest and conscientious in his dealings with his fellow-men."[29] Though young in years, he was recognized by his associates as a man of unusual capacity. That he had sat at the feet of Reinsdorf further elevated him in their esteem.

As yet Lingg possessed only a limited knowledge of English. But he was bright and energetic, to say nothing of his striking good looks. "Lingg," said William Holmes, "was one of the handsomest men the writer has ever met. His well-shaped head crowned with a wealth of curly chestnut hair; his fine blue eyes; his peach and white complexion and straight, regular features, made him a fit model for a Greek god, while his athletic form and general activity showed him to be possessed of an abundance of physical vigor and health."[30]

Lingg, not surprisingly, was popular with women—the "lion of the ballroom," his brother carpenters called him. Young anarchists of the next generation affected his haircomb and lithe manner of walking and considered it the highest compliment to be called by his name.[31]

Lingg, for all his revolutionary militancy, did not align himself with the autonomists. Together with Neebe and Schwab, he belonged to the North Side Group, and he was active in trade-union work. Nor was he associated with *Der Anarchist*, so far as can be determined, despite Max Nettlau's assertion to the contrary.[32] Yet he was no less passionate than the autonomists in his commitment to physical force. A member of the armed section of his union, he recommended "rude force to combat the ruder force of the police."[33] He had a boundless faith in dynamite and vehemently advocated its use. He believed, with men like Engel and Fischer, that the revolution was close at hand and that the workers needed arms to meet the attacks of their oppressors. "We must fight them with as good weapons, even better, than they possess," he told an audience of workmen in the spring of 1886, "and, therefore, I call you to arms!"[34]

That Lingg was a believer in dynamite he never attempted to deny. To his accusers at the Haymarket trial he openly declared that he had made bombs and would have used them had the opportunity presented itself. In this respect, as in others, he was at one with Engel and Fischer. All three, in contrast to Gorsuch, Griffin, and their ilk, were men of backbone and determination, men of action rather than words. They were among the "few ardent souls," as William Holmes characterized them, who not only proclaimed but were willing to carry out acts of propaganda by the deed.[35] Because of this, they were especially feared and hated at the time of the Haymarket proceedings. Of the eight defendants they were temperamentally the most capable of throwing a bomb at the police. That none of them actually did so not even the prosecutor denied. Yet as enemies of "law and order," a phrase to which they themselves always referred with mocking contempt, they were made to pay the ultimate penalty.

12 || CULT OF DYNAMITE

The most important task of the IWPA, apart from propaganda and agitation, came to be the arming of the workers. It may be recalled that the bloody suppression of the 1877 strike had pushed the issue of arms to the forefront. After the strike, the state militia had been strengthened and reequipped, which had led to calls to bolster the workers' self-defenses. During the years that followed, police and militia had been repeatedly used against the workers, and scores of lives had been lost. The courts, the press, the constitution itself seemed to offer no shield against assaults on workingmen and their families, so that self-defense appeared the only protection. Even among the more moderate Internationalists the question of arms received a favorable hearing, and many joined the Lehr-und-Wehr Verein and other paramilitary groups, which continued to drill regularly in the use of weapons.

By 1886 armed sections of the International existed not only in Chicago but in New York, Philadelphia, Detroit, Cincinnati, St. Louis, Denver, San Francisco, and other cities. In New York, at the beginning of 1885, Wilhelm Hasselmann founded a Natural Science Club, which instructed its members in the mysteries of chemistry. In March 1885 the German Group of that city passed a resolution urging all workers "to acquaint themselves with modern chemistry" and "to procure arms, rifles, pistols, etc., and drill and exercise with the same." In case of a general outbreak, the resolution proclaimed, "the first necessity would be to arrest and imprison all leading officials and officers of the army, navy and police."[1]

Similar resolutions were adopted in other cities. In Chicago itself the Jaeger Verein declared itself in favor of "the immediate arming of the proletariat and the application of all the latest discoveries of science, especially chemistry." In October 1885, by the same token, the Central Labor Union passed a resolution, introduced by Spies, calling on all workers to arm themselves "in order to be in a position of meeting our foe with his own argument, force."[2] By that time

160

two Central Labor Union affiliates, the Metal Workers and the International Carpenters and Joiners, had already organized armed sections, which met regularly for drill and instruction in the use of arms; and the American Group had formed a similar auxiliary which assembled for drill every Monday evening at Greif's Hall on West Lake Street. Although Parsons afterwards insisted that this auxiliary was never armed, that it met only four or five times and was disbanded nearly a year before the Haymarket incident, other sources indicate that it held regular meetings right up to the time of the explosion.[3]

The largest armed group in Chicago, however, was the Lehr-und-Wehr Verein. Estimates of its membership vary from a few hundred to more than two thousand. But, according to Captain Schaack, who would not have been likely to minimize its strength, it never exceeded four hundred, itself not an insignificant number.[4] While not officially part of the International, the Lehr-und-Wehr Verein served for all practical purposes as the armed auxiliary of its more militant German groups, in particular the North Side and North-West Side Groups, whose membership overlapped extensively with that of the first and second companies of the Lehr-und-Wehr Verein. In all, there were four companies, each situated in a different part of the city. The first, commanded by Abraham Hermann, a machinist in his mid-thirties, met in Mueller's Hall at the corner of North Avenue and Sedgwick Street. The second, located on the North-West Side, was led by Gustav Breitenfeld, a brush-maker, assisted by Bernhard Schrade, a carpenter. It met in the Thalia Hall at 636 Milwaukee Avenue. The third, with H. Betzel as captain, used the Vorwaerts Turner Hall on West 12th Street for its meeting place, and the fourth, located in suburban Pullman, met at the Rosenheim Pavilion under the command of Paul Pull.[5]

Each week the individual companies assembled in their respective halls for drill and instruction. Once a month, moreover, general drill for the whole organization was held in Neff's Hall at 58 Clybourn Avenue, the meeting place of the North Side Group. Members, in addition, practiced shooting in the woods and held sham battles during the frequent picnics and outings of the International and Central Labor Union. They armed themselves with rifles, pistols, knives, and daggers, and with bombs and grenades in some cases. In 1885 a quartermaster was appointed by the Chicago Internationalists to take charge of procuring weapons. During one six-month period $1,255 was collected for this purpose.[6] The Lehr-und-Wehr Verein, moreover, sponsored an annual ball and organized raffles and shooting contests to replenish its war chest.

The Internationalists justified these preparations primarily as defensive measures. "I did not advocate the use of force," insisted Parsons after the Haymarket trial. "But I denounced the capitalists for employing it for holding the laborers in subjection to them, and declared that such treatment would of necessity drive the workingmen to employ the same means in self-defense."[7] The law, argued Parsons and his comrades, protected only the rich, leaving the poor defenseless. The police clubbed and beat unarmed strikers, shot them down in the streets, even shot at their women and children with impunity. How long was this to be tolerated? How long must the workers allow the hirelings of capital to do as they pleased with them? Such was the anarchist position. The propertied classes "everywhere and always fall back upon the use of *force*, and coerce when they fail to persuade the wage workers," declared *The Alarm*. "In the midst of such a struggle, to talk of peace and peaceful methods to obtain the rights of the enslaved workers is blasphemous and exasperating to the last degree."[8]

Besides, the anarchists insisted, the capitalists would not surrender their privileges without a fight. Those, said Parsons, who deprived the workers of the wealth which they themselves created would "never heed the logic of anything but force—physical force—the only argument that tyrants ever could or would listen to." Peaceful methods were of no avail, for "the powerful, the privileged are not in the least disturbed by argument, protest or petitions. They have but one answer to all appeals—force. By force and fraud they gained their power; by force and fraud they maintain it." Since reform was useless, Parsons continued, revolution had become necessary. The workers had learned this from bitter experience. "They know that they must take possession of the means of life—transform it into societary property for co-operative use—before the system of wage-robbery, with its poverty, misery and ignorance, can be abolished."[9]

The revolution, as the anarchists saw it, was in any case inevitable. They spoke of it in terms of an approaching tempest, bringing "terror and blessing, destruction and freedom," a natural phenomenon, like hurricanes and tornadoes, beyond the power of anyone to prevent. "Anarchists do not make the social revolution," declared Parsons.

"They prophesy its coming." "It is coming," he reiterated in early 1886, "yes, hastening on. The economic forces are at work incessantly, generating the forces of the social revolution. We can neither retard nor hasten the result, but we can aid and direct its forces."[10]

Spies put it in similar terms. Revolutions, he told the Congregational ministers, were the effects of "certain causes and conditions," not the work of the anarchists and their supporters. "If anyone is to blame for the coming revolution it is the ruling class who steadily refuse to make concessions as reforms become necessary; who maintain that they can call a halt to progress, and dictate a standstill to the eternal forces of which they themselves are but the whimsical creation."[11] Nor was Spies alone in this belief. The economic crisis of the 1880s, following hard upon that of the 1870s, had convinced many Internationalists that the capitalist system was on the verge of collapse. The revolution was on the horizon. Of that they were certain. Nor was it they who would bring it. They were merely preparing the workers for the inevitable; and every new repression, every drubbing by the police, brought the day of reckoning a step closer. It was this belief that accounts for their calls to arms, which, while taken by the authorities as exhortations to violence, were more in the way of warnings to the workers to be ready for the impending upheaval.

Some, it is true, saw the coming revolution as a war of good against evil, in which every weapon would be employed. If the end was sufficiently noble, they reasoned, as noble as the emancipation of the workers itself, then any means used to attain it was justified. There were those, indeed, for whom the slaughter of capitalists and officials was righteous work, and who advocated it with all the passion of religious devotion. Once the rich had been eliminated, they believed, the age of peace and mutual assistance would begin. For anarchists of this stamp every employer, every policeman had forfeited his right to exist. The doctrine that the end justifies the means had come to warrant the liquidation of an enemy class.

No one was more vociferous than Johann Most in defending this position. "Against Tyrants All Means Are Justified!" proclaimed the masthead of the *Freiheit*. "Yes, tremble, ye canaille," Most thundered in 1884, "ye bloodsuckers, ye ravishers of maidens, ye murderers and hangmen; the day of reckoning and revenge is near. The fight has begun along the picket line. A girdle of dynamite encircles the world, not only the *old* but the *new*. The bloody band of tyrants are dancing on the surface of a volcano. There is dynamite in England, France, Germany, Russia, Italy, Spain, New York, and Canada. It will be hot on the day of action, and yet the brood will shudder in the sight of death and gnash their teeth. Set fire to the houses, put poison in all kinds of food, put poisoned nails on the chairs occupied by our enemies, dig mines and fill them with explosives, whet your daggers, load your revolvers, cap them, fill bombs and have them ready. Hurl the priest from the altar; shoot him down! Let each prince find a Brutus by his throne."[12]

For several years Most had been reading textbooks on explosives and studying accounts of chemical experiments. Between 1880 and 1885 he filled the columns of *Freiheit* with detailed instructions on the preparation and use of bombs and other weapons of destruction, as well as with exhortations to the workers to carry out acts of propaganda by the deed. "Our enemies have never been fastidious in their methods against the people," he declared. "Let us therefore have an eye for an eye!" "Comrades of *Freiheit*, we say murder the murderers. Rescue mankind through blood, iron, poison, and dynamite."[13]

In July 1885 Most brought much of this material together and published it as a seventy-four-page booklet. A practical manual of urban guerrilla warfare and propaganda by the deed, it was to be cited both in court proceedings in the United States and by Bismarck in the German Reichstag, contributing greatly to Most's reputation as a prophet of terrorism and to the stereotype of the anarchist as a mad bombthrower—a stereotype with fatal results in the Chicago case. The title of the booklet alone was enough to send shivers up the spines of respectable citizens: *Revolutionary War Science: A Little Handbook of Instruction in the Use and Preparation of Nitroglycerine, Dynamite, Gun-Cotton, Fulminating Mercury, Bombs, Fuses, Poisons, etc., etc.,*[14]

Revolutionary War Science was nothing less than a manual for the extermination of the bourgeoisie. The whole "reptile brood," as Most was wont to call it, was to be extirpated, and science was providing the means. By using bombs and other devices, revolutionaries would destroy bridges, capture arsenals, sabotage telegraph and railway lines, blow up government buildings, and kill capitalists and bureaucrats. Terrorist acts were to be carried out by individuals or small groups, so as not to endanger the whole organization. Most explained precisely where and how to plant bombs for maximum effect: in churches and palaces, banquets and ballrooms. He celebrated the damage that dynamite could do when placed "under the table of an opulent banquet," for "what can tear solid rock into splinters may not have a bad effect at a ball where monopolists are assembled." Nor was it only the rulers, officials, clergy, and capitalists that Most wanted to annihilate. The police too were to be slaughtered like animals. For murder, as Most defined it, was the willful killing of human beings, and, to quote one of his speeches, he had never heard it said that a policeman was a human being.[15]

Instructions on the manufacture and use of explosives were only a part of Most's little handbook. Also included were chapters on inflammable liquid compounds for starting fires; poisons, such as curare, "with which certain South American Indians smear their arrows"; the use of code names, cover addresses, ciphers, invisible ink, and the like, to forestall detection and arrest; the use of knives, pistols, and other weapons; the poisoning of bullets, nails, and daggers; and hints about poisoning delicacies to be served at dinners of the rich. Most, moreover, pioneered a number of innovations, such as the incendiary letter, and fantasized that airships would one day be able to drop dynamite on military parades attended by emperors and kings.

To prepare for the impending conflict, Most urged the workers to arm themselves with the best weapons they could afford: rifles, pistols, knives, poisons—but especially explosives of every type. For explosives would be the "decisive factor" in the social war. "To be sure of success," Most declared, "revolutionaries should always have on hand adequate quantities of nitroglycerine, dynamite, hand grenades, and blasting charges—all of which may be easily concealed in one's clothing." These weapons, said Most, were the "proletariat's artillery" and would make ordinary workers invincible against any army. He concluded with a slogan: "Proletarians of all countries, arm yourselves! Arm yourselves by whatever means you can. The hour of battle is near."[16]

Revolutionary War Science gained a wide circulation during the months preceding the Haymarket incident. At ten cents a copy it was sold at picnics and meetings and at the offices of *The Alarm* and *Arbeiter-Zeitung*. Furthermore, its contents were serialized in the anarchist press under such headings as "Dangerous Explosives," "The Manufacture of Dynamite Made Easy," and "Explosives: A

Practical Lesson in Popular Chemistry." *The Alarm* urged its readers to "study their schoolbooks on chemistry, and read the dictionaries and encyclopedias on the composition of all kinds of explosives, and make themselves too strong to be opposed with deadly weapons. This alone can insure against bloodshed. Every person can get that knowledge inside of a week, and a majority now have one or more books containing this information right in their own homes. And every man who is master of these explosives cannot be even approached by an army of men. Therefore, bloodshed being useless, and injustice being defenseless, people will be forced to deal justly and generously with each other."[17]

Dynamite, in the eyes of the anarchists, had become a panacea for the ills of society. They saw it as a great equalizing force, enabling ordinary workmen to stand up against armies, militias, and police, to say nothing of the hired gunmen of the employers. Cheap in price, easy to carry, not hard to obtain, it was the poor man's natural weapon, a power provided by science against tyranny and oppression. "One man armed with a dynamite bomb is equal to one regiment of militia, when it is used at the right time and place," declared *The Alarm*. "Anarchists are of the opinion that the bayonet and Gatling gun will cut but a sorry part in the social revolution. The whole method of warfare has been revolutionized by the latter-day discoveries of science, and the American people will avail themselves of its advantages in the conflict with the upstarts and contemptible braggarts who expect to continue their rascality under the plea of preserving 'law and order.' "[18]

Just as gunpowder had broken the back of feudalism and made way for the rule of the bourgeoisie, so dynamite would bring down capitalism and usher in the reign of the proletariat. Such was the analogy drawn in the anarchist press. "Gunpowder," asserted *The Alarm*, "brought the world some liberty, and dynamite will bring the world as much more as it is stronger than gunpowder." As the *Nemesis* of Baltimore put it: "The discovery of gunpowder overthrew feudalism. Chemistry will liberate the laborer from modern wage-serfdom." And again: "Dynamite is the emancipator! In the hand of the enslaved it cries aloud: 'Justice or—annihilation!' "[19]

In a movement that stood for the insulted and injured, the mystique of dynamite was bound to exert an appeal. For here was a wonderful new substance that made one workingman the equal of an army. At the conclusion of his trial Parsons continued to trumpet

166

its virtues: "It is the equilibrium. It is the annihilator. It is the disseminator of power. It is the downfall of oppression. It is the abolition of authority; it is the dawn of peace; it is the end of war, because war cannot exist unless there is somebody to make war upon, and dynamite makes that unsafe, undesirable, and absolutely impossible. It is a peace-maker; it is man's best friend; it emancipates the world from the domineering of the few over the many, because all government, in the last resort, is violence; all law, in the last resort, is force."[20]

For anarchists all over the country dynamite became a symbol of retribution, a bugbear with which to frighten the propertied classes. "May tyranny go down forever," wrote the secretary of the American Group in Kansas City, "and may Anarchy and dynamite go hand in hand supreme throughout the land." Lucy Parsons, writing in the *Labor Enquirer*, declared that dynamite could defeat armies and overthrow governments, "and if some tyrants must be put out of the way, it should be looked upon as a blessing, inasmuch as the more oppressors dead, and the fewer alive, the freer will be the world." In *The Alarm*, by the same token, she appealed to tramps to learn the use of explosives and petition the capitalists with bombs instead of words. "Keep the stuff *pure!*" warned *The Alarm*. "Beware of sand. . . . It is necessary that the revolutionist should experiment for himself; especially should he practice the knack of throwing bombs."[21]

Up till the time of the Haymarket explosion the powers of dynamite were regularly extolled in the anarchist press. Week after week its virtues were glorified in articles, editorials, and even verse. "Hurrah for science! Hurrah for dynamite!—the power which in our hands shall make an end of tyranny," was the sentiment of a poem in the *Vorbote*. A jingle with a similar message appeared in *The Alarm*:

> The slave that hath no other weapon
> But the dagger, or dynamite,
> Is justified in using both,
> To snap the chain that binds him tight.

In Most's *Freiheit* songs were sung in dynamite's praise:

> At last a toast to science,
> To dynamite, the force,

> The force in our own hands;
> The world gets better day by day.

Or again:

> Dynamite today, dynamite tonight,
> Most tells us how, he shows where,
> He says all in *Freiheit*
> And his good little book on warfare.[22]

Dynamite, it might be noted, had been used in labor conflicts before Haymarket. In February 1885, for example, a dynamite explosion occurred during a strike at a dry-goods firm in New York City. Two weeks later it appeared during a land dispute in Washington Territory, where it blew up the residence of a man who had foreclosed mortgages and evicted tenants from their farms. In July of the same year it was used again by striking workers on the Rio Grande Railroad in Colorado. No lives were lost in any of these incidents, though there was considerable damage to property. In Chicago, in December 1885, an "infernal machine" was discovered by a maid on the porch of a North Side mansion, while another was sent to the offices of the Chicago, Burlington & Quincy Railroad on Adams Street, neither of which went off.[23]

Dynamite, at about the same time, made a dramatic appearance in a work of fiction. In 1885 Emile Zola published his celebrated novel *Germinal*, in which the anarchist Souvarine blows up the coal mine in which he has worked. Then, writes Zola, he "threw away his last cigarette and walked off into the darkness, without so much as a glance behind. His shadowy form dwindled and merged with the night. He was bound for the unknown, calmly going to deal destruction wherever dynamite could be found to blow up cities and men. Doubtless on the day when the last dying bourgeois hear the very stones of the streets exploding under their feet he will be there."[24]

One of the main advantages of dynamite, as the anarchists never tired of pointing out, was the ease with which it might be carried about on one's person. In *Revolutionary War Science* Most, as we have seen, urged all revolutionaries to have on hand a supply of explosive missiles which might be easily concealed in one's clothing. *The Alarm*, by the same token, was fond of quoting Philip Sheridan, commander-in-chief of the U.S. Army, who, in his annual report to Congress in November 1884, warned that "destructive explosives are easily made, and that banks, United States sub-treasuries, public buildings and large mercantile houses can be readily demolished, and the commerce of entire cities destroyed, by an infuriated people with means carried with perfect safety to themselves in the pockets of their clothing." *The Alarm* agreed. "One dynamite bomb, properly placed," it noted in an article entitled "Dynamite: The Protection of the Poor Against the Armies of the Rich," "will destroy a regiment of soldiers, a weapon easily made, and carried with perfect safety in the pockets of one's clothing." Fielden, quoting Sheridan's remark at a picnic in June 1885, exhorted the workers to familiarize themselves with "dynamite and those destructive explosives which science has placed within the reach of the oppressed."[25]

That same month, June 1885, *The Alarm* published a letter from a Professor Mezzeroff of New York, who himself regularly carried a bomb in his pocket and urged all rebels to do the same. Professor Mezzeroff, it is interesting to note, appears to have been the original of the anarchist professor in Joseph Conrad's novel *The Secret Agent*, who walks the streets of London with a bomb in his pocket to discourage the police from approaching. Mezzeroff, in his letter, vowed to educate the people in the techniques of chemistry, "and I won't stop until every workingman in Europe and America knows how to use explosives against autocratic government and grasping monopolies." Mezzeroff's habit of always carrying an explosive on his person ("I take it through the street in my pocket; I carry it about in the horse cars") was his most striking characteristic, as was that of Conrad's professor. "You can learn to make tri-nitro-glycerine," Mezzeroff told the workers, "and if you carry two or three pounds with you people will respect you much more than if you carried a pistol."[26]

The most startling paean to dynamite, however, came from the pen of Gerhard Lizius, secretary of the Indianapolis Group of the International. Fluent in both English and German, Lizius was a prolific contributor to a whole range of anarchist papers, including *The Alarm* and the *Arbeiter-Zeitung*, of which he became city editor after moving to Chicago in early 1886. A former member of the SLP who had abandoned political methods, he advised the workers to leave "the paper knife or ballot severely alone, and use steel knives and bullets to better their condition."[27] "Nothing short of brute force will accomplish our tasks," he insisted. Convinced of the purifying value of explosives, he urged the workers to master the "science of the manufacture and use of dynamite." "Already," he declared, "the rumbling of the social revolution is heard from all quarters of the globe, and the last grand battle for universal liberty and justice may break in on us at any moment."[28]

Lizius wrote of dynamite with an almost mystical intensity. In a remarkable letter to *The Alarm*, quoted at the Haymarket trial, he called for its bold and uninhibited use:

Dynamite! of all the good stuff, this is the stuff. Stuff several pounds of this sublime stuff into an inch pipe, gas or water pipe, plug up both ends, insert a cap with fuse attached, place this in the immediate neighborhood of a lot of rich loafers, who live by the sweat of other people's brows, and light the fuse. A most cheerful and gratifying result will follow. In giving dynamite to the downtrodden millions of the globe, science has done its best work. The dear stuff can be carried around in the pocket without danger, while it is a formidable weapon against any force of militia, police or detectives that may want to stifle the cry for justice that goes forth from the plundered slaves. It is something not very ornamental, but exceedingly useful. It can be used against persons and things; it is better to use it against the former than against bricks and masonry. It is a genuine boon for the disinherited, while it brings terror and fear to the robbers. It brings terror only to the guilty, and consequently the Senator who introduced a bill in congress to stop its manufacture and use, must be guilty of something. He fears the wrath of an outraged people that has been duped and swindled by him and his like. The same must be the case with the 'servant' of the people who introduced a like measure in the senate of the Indiana Legislature. All the good this will do. Like everything else, the more you prohibit it, the more will it be done. Dynamite is like Banquo's ghost, it keeps on fooling around somewhere or other in spite of his satanic majesty. A pound of this good stuff beats a bushel of ballots all hollow, and don't you forget it. Our law makers might as well try to sit down on the crater of a volcano or a bayonet as to endeavor to stop the manufacture and use of dynamite. It takes more justice and right than is contained in laws to quiet the spirit of unrest. If workingmen would be truly free, they must learn to know why they are slaves. They must rise above petty prejudice and learn to think. From thought to action is not far, and when the worker has seen the chains, he need but look a little closer to find near at hand the sledge with which to shatter every link. The sledge is dynamite.[29]

What sort of person might best respond to such an appeal? For many anarchists the answer was to be sought in Bakunin and Nechaev's *Catechism of a Revolutionary*, which portrayed the ideal rebel as a complete immoralist for whom expediency overrode all ethical considerations and for whom decency, honor, and integrity must be cast aside in the name of the revolutionary cause. The *Catechism of a Revolutionary*, excerpts from which were published in *Freiheit* and *The Alarm*, lay down all the qualities to be expected of a revolutionary conspirator, above all the renunciation of every personal gratification for the sake of the revolution. "The revolutionary is a doomed man," the *Catechism* began. "He has no personal interests, no affairs, no sentiments, attachments, property, not even a name of his own. Everything in him is absorbed by one exclusive interest, one thought, one passion—the revolution." He studies chemistry and other sciences for the purpose of destroying his enemies. He has severed all connections with the existing social order and with conventional morality. "To him whatever aids the triumph of the revolution is ethical; all that hinders it is unethical and criminal. . . . Day and night he must have one thought, one aim—inexorable destruction. Striving coldly and unfalteringly towards this aim, he must be ready to perish himself and to destroy with his own hands everything that hinders its realization."[30]

As model revolutionaries the International held up before its members the European anarchists and socialists who, during the 1870s and 1880s, sacrificed their lives in acts of propaganda by the deed. In 1878 alone there were two attempts on the life of the kaiser, one on the king of Spain, and one on the king of Italy. In 1880 another attempt was made on the king of Spain. In 1881 President Garfield was assassinated by a disappointed office-seeker, and Tsar Alexander II of Russia was killed by a dynamite bomb after many attempts. In 1882 the Phoenix Park murders were committed in Dublin, Lord Cavendish, Secretary for Ireland, and Undersecretary Thomas Burke being killed by Irish revolutionaries. Further assassinations were attempted and carried out in the succeeding years.

The Alarm, the *Arbeiter-Zeitung*, and their sister papers showered praise on every terrorist act that occurred during this period and glorified the perpetrators as revolutionary heroes and martyrs. When they were executed for their deeds, anarchist papers appeared with heavy black borders and published eulogies to the "fallen warriors" in the social struggle. Such was the case with August Reinsdorf, the foremost German anarchist of this early phase of the movement, beheaded in 1885 for plotting against Wilhelm I. "One of our noblest and best is no more," lamented Most in the *Freiheit*. "In the prison yard at Halle under the murderous sword of the criminal Hohenzollern band, on the 7th of February, August Reinsdorf ended a life full of battle and self-sacrificing courage, as a martyr to the great revolution."[31]

Similar tributes appeared on the deaths of Anton Kammerer and Hermann Stellmacher, hanged in 1884 for killing Austrian policemen, and of Julius Lieske, beheaded in 1885 for assassinating the police chief of Frankfurt-am-Main. Most, in the *Freiheit*, said that if he had a thousand Stellmachers the revolution would be accomplished in three months. When Lieske was executed, Engel and Fischer's *Anarchist* swore "to take revenge for him—and for all starving humanity." *The Alarm* expressed the same sentiment: "Lieske is a young man, only twenty-two years old, and a shoemaker. He will go to the scaffold as a hero. He dies because he is an Anarchist. But he will be avenged!"[32]

The occasions of these executions were marked by mass demonstrations, rallies, and "indignation meetings" in Chicago and other cities. After the execution of Lieske, for example, Spies presented a resolution before a protest meeting of the International hailing him as a martyr and applauding his "noble act" in eliminating one of the "dirtiest dogs" of German officialdom. Spies spoke again at a memorial meeting for Reinsdorf, sharing the platform with Parsons and Schwab. "He sowed the seed of hope in the heart of the proletariat," said Spies, "by setting an example of self-sacrificing devotion and of marvelous bravery and courage before his persecutors." The St. Louis Groups of the International protested against Reinsdorf's execution with the slogans "Agitate, Organize, Resist!" and "Long Live the Social Revolution!" The biggest demonstration, however, took place in Philadelphia, where Most delivered the principal eulogy. "Reinsdorf's words," Most declared, "spoken to his judges, were a gospel of the social revolution, worth more than a thousand addresses of agitators. The halter for the traitor, the dagger for the jailer, poison for the priest, bullets for the insolent, and bombs for the princes." The revolution, said Most, was near at hand, and dynamite would be its principal asset. "War to the throne, war to the altar, war to the money bags," he proclaimed by way of conclusion. "I prophesy that sooner or later the red flag of the revolution will wave over Independence Hall."[33]

Most himself, as far as is known, never engaged in violent action. For all his inflammatory exhortations, he remained primarily a talker and writer. In 1884, however, unbeknownst to all but his closest comrades, he took up residence in Jersey City Heights, across the Hudson River from New York, and found a job in a dynamite factory under an assumed name. There, at first hand, he learned the techniques of producing explosives, which he incorporated into his manual of revolution. He also succeeded in purloining quantities of dynamite, which he intended to dispatch to Europe.[34] But, encountering difficulties in shipping it, he offered to send twenty-five pounds of the "stuff" to the Hocking Valley, where the miners, as we have seen, were engaged in a prolonged and bitter strike. His go-between was to be August Spies, who had been reporting on the strike for the *Arbeiter-Zeitung* and was acquainted with the militants in the area. "I am in a position to furnish 'medicine,' " Most wrote to Spies in October 1884, "and the 'genuine' article at that." Directions for its use, he said, were probably not necessary with miners, who were accustomed to handling explosives. Such directions, in any case, had been recently published in the *Freiheit*.[35]

Whether anything resulted from this proposal is not known. After the Haymarket bombing, however, the police raided Spies's office at the *Arbeiter-Zeitung* and claimed to have found a package of dynamite in a closet. Spies himself, in January 1886, gave a reporter from the *Chicago Daily News* the casing of a bomb. "Take it to your boss," he said, "and tell him we have nine thousand more like it—only loaded."[36] It was an unwise action on Spies's part, a piece of bravado he was later to regret. After his arrest he maintained that he had had only four such shells in his office, which he had occasionally shown to reporters, but that none of them was loaded. Benjamin Tucker, however, in a private communication to Joseph Labadie, claimed to have incontrovertible knowledge that Spies had kept dynamite in his office, and that the package seized by the police had been sent there long before the Haymarket explosion.[37] The source of this information appears to have been Moritz Bachmann, a founding member of the International; and it seems entirely possible that Most had sent dynamite to Spies, to be used, if not in the Hocking Valley, then for the anticipated social revolution. For lack of conclusive evidence, however, the question must remain open.

Apart from his letter to Labadie, Tucker kept quiet about the dynamite. On the eve of Haymarket, however, he became embroiled in a bitter controversy with Most over the use of violent methods. Under the heading "The Beast of Communism," a parody of Most's "Beast of Property," Tucker, in his magazine *Liberty*, alleged that a number of Most's followers in New York, German and Bohemian Internationalists, had collected large sums of money by insuring their dwellings, removing the contents, setting fire to the premises, and swearing to heavy losses.[38] On May 3, 1886, the day before the Haymarket explosion, the *New York Sun* picked up the story, carrying a long article that repeated the charges in *Liberty* with additional details.

Tucker's source was again Moritz Bachmann, apparently privy to inside information. Tucker denounced the arsonists as "cold-blooded villains parading in the mask of reform." In one of the fires, set in 1885, a woman and two children were burned to death. In another case, in 1886, a man, woman, and baby lost their lives. Tucker was outraged that this should have been the work of professed anarchists. It was one thing to assassinate the tsar of Russia, he remarked, but quite another "to set fire to a tenement house containing hundreds of human beings."[39]

Tucker's article created a sensation. To Most it was a stab in the back. Replying in an article headed "A Stinkbomb," he attacked Tucker as a slanderer and informer, as an auxiliary of the police. Tucker, in turn, repudiated Most, "man, principles, and methods," denying him "even the name of Anarchist."[40] Each ended by excommunicating the other from the movement. Most, who detested Tucker as a bourgeois and defender of property, went so far as to forbid his adherents to subscribe to *Liberty*, which he said was read only by a few old ladies in Boston. Justus Schwab, however, broke with Most over the incident and drove the defenders of arson from his saloon.

No evidence was ever brought forth to connect Most directly with the arsonists or with any other instances of violence. For all his loud talk, he remained a man of words rather than deeds. Nor was he alone in this respect. The gap between the advocacy of terrorism and its actual practice was very wide. Although, according to William Holmes, "there were not wanting those who waited but the opportunity to carry out desperate projects already conceived," the great majority were "content, for the time being, to speak and write in prophetic warning of the wrath to come, and to urge their hearers and readers to make thorough preparations for the revolution."[41]

Of the eight Haymarket defendants most were in the latter category. At one time or another, it is true, all had spoken out in favor of dynamite. All, moreover, believed in retaliatory violence and rejected docile submission to the forces of capital and government. For most, however, their humanitarian outlook shrank from the methods that in theory they justified and professed. Fielden, in all probability, never touched a pistol or saw a bomb in his life. As for Parsons, Spies, and Schwab, they were men of ideals who, especially in time of economic distress, made rash and provocative statements, but themselves did nothing more violent than to assist in the arming of the workers in preparation for what they regarded as the inevitable confrontation with capital.

There were some, however, for whom the impulse to violence was strong, and who were ready to immolate others as well as themselves in the service of what they believed to be just. Lingg, for example, is known to have made and accumulated bombs, and possibly Engel and Fischer as well. According to Captain Schaack, moreover, Neebe lost all five fingers of his right hand by the premature explosion of a bomb with which he was experimenting.[42] It was to men of their stamp, and especially to Engel and Fischer, that William Holmes was alluding when he conceded that there were "those who waited but the opportunity to carry out desperate projects already conceived." At the Board of Trade demonstration, Holmes reveals, "several of our comrades were armed and prepared to defend themselves to the death against any onslaught by the police." According to the *Arbeiter-Zeitung*, "nitroglycerine pills were not missing" among the demonstrators' arsenal, and, had a collision occurred, "there would have been pieces," as the cordons of police "could have been quite excellently adapted for experiments with explosives." Holmes "surely thought that something terrible would happen that night," but the police, under a sensible commanding officer, acted with restraint, and the demonstration dispersed without incident.[43] Had Captain Bonfield or his like been in charge, matters might have turned out differently.

By 1886, at any rate, the Internationalists in Chicago, both talkers and doers, had convinced themselves that the revolution was just around the corner. *The Alarm* and *Arbeiter-Zeitung* spoke more and more of barricades and street-fighting and putting dynamite into the hands of the workers. Spurning all talk of conciliation, they poured out torrents of invective upon the propertied classes and issued trumpet calls for action to bring about the destruction of the existing order. "Nothing but an uprising of the people and a bursting open of all stores and storehouses to the free access of the public, and a free application of dynamite to every one who opposes, will relieve the world of this infernal nightmare of property and wages," declared *The Alarm*. "A dynamite bomb costs 15 cents; a box of matches one cent; and a rope for the taking in any back yard." Likewise the *Arbeiter-Zeitung*: "Arms are more necessary in our time than anything else. Whoever has no money should sell his watch, if he has one, and buy firearms. Stones and sticks will not avail against the hired assassins of the extortionists. It is time to arm yourselves!"[44]

Given such exhortations, it is small wonder that prosperous citizens should have become alarmed. By its incessant agitation the International aroused deep fears within the business community. And the Chicago papers, always ready to capitalize on the sensational, never failed to give the wildest utterances of the anarchists conspicuous display. The *Times*, the *Tribune*, the *News* played up the radical threat and reported each harangue or demonstration as if it were the first blow of the social revolution. By 1886, as a result, the International had been magnified into a horrific bugbear, menacing all that established society held dear. Panic seized the city's wealthier elements. People talked of "another 1877," "another Paris Commune." General Sherman of the U.S. Army issued the following warning: "There will soon come an armed contest between Capital and Labor. They will oppose each other not with words and arguments and ballots, but with shot and shell, gunpowder and cannon. The better classes are tired of the insane howlings of the lower strata, and they mean to stop them."[45]

The growth of the Lehr-und-Wehr Verein and other armed groups heightened the feeling that a conflict was imminent. Business leaders not only came to fear the anarchists; from fear they grew to hate them and to wish for their destruction. In press and pulpit a propaganda campaign was launched against them in which every accusation, smear, and innuendo was employed. They were accused of every kind of immorality and debauchery. They were branded as bombthrowers, arsonists, assassins. That most of them were foreigners, moreover, tended to intensify the prejudice against them. They were painted as aliens, madmen, fanatics, bent on desecrating law and order and uprooting the economic system responsible for America's prosperity and freedom. Police and Pinkertons were used to penetrate their organizations, filing wild, fantastic reports of dynamite conspiracies, if only to show how vigilant they were in carrying out their assignments. According to one informer, Fielden advocated blowing up the new Board of Trade building. Another claimed that Parsons exhibited incendiary devices and urged his comrades to arm themselves with explosives.[46]

The fear of an anarchist conspiracy gripped not only capitalists and the authorities but public opinion in general. For a large segment of the population the anarchists had ceased to be human beings. They had become the incarnation of evil, monsters endowed with infernal powers, onto whom businessmen and ordinary citizens alike projected all that they dreaded and detested. The anarchists responded in kind. Stripping their opponents of their humanity, they reduced them to animals and insects. Policemen were "bloodhounds," the equivalent of "pigs" as used by radical demonstrators during the Vietnam era. Capitalists, by the same token, were "reptiles" and "leeches"—and thus worthy of extermination. Each side had become convinced of the depravity and diabolism of the other. The language of both was full of hate.

As tensions mounted, the authorities vowed to stamp out the rising anarchist menace. The anarchists, for their part, warned that they would answer violence with violence, if only as a matter of self-defense. By the spring of 1886 conditions were ripe for a confrontation. The stage was set for the Haymarket tragedy.

PART III ‖ HAYMARKET

13 ‖ On the Eve

What took place in Chicago on May 4, 1886, was the culmination of passions and prejudices that had been accumulating for several years. The depression of 1883-1886 had witnessed an upsurge of the radical labor movement, and especially of the IWPA, whose incessant agitation heralded the approach of what some believed might be an upheaval worse than that of 1877. A climax was reached during the early months of 1886 with a nationwide crusade for the eight-hour day, one of the most intense labor struggles in American history.

The eight-hour movement, the revival of an old battle dating back to the 1860s, got its present impetus from the Federation of Organized Trades and Labor Unions of the United States and Canada, the immediate forerunner of the American Federation of Labor. At its 1884 national convention, held in Chicago, the federation, whose leaders included Samuel Gompers and Peter McGuire, proclaimed that "eight hours shall constitute a legal day's labor from and after May 1, 1886." The following year the federation repeated its declaration: On May 1, 1886, an eight-hour system was to go into effect throughout the country. It would be supported, moreover, by strikes and demonstrations to persuade recalcitrant employers to yield.

The IWPA at first turned a deaf ear to the eight-hour campaign, regarding it as a reformist maneuver. Only a few years before, Parsons had himself been active in its behalf, a fervent disciple of Ira Steward. But now he and his fellow anarchists, with their dream of social revolution and a totally new society, saw the shorter day as a mere palliative, a compromise with the system that they were struggling to abolish. Even if attained, they argued, it would not fundamentally alter the workers' position, but only serve to delay the decisive battle with capitalism. "Hours of labor, wages, or any other conditions of employment cannot be controlled by those who are in economic bondage and wage-slavery," wrote Parsons in August 1885. "Comrades, for pity's sake do not longer waste your precious time in vain endeavors, but combine to remove the *cause* which makes labor the slave to capital."[1]

Spies was equally emphatic. "We can get no real relief without striking at the root of the evil," he declared in September 1885. Though he did not oppose the eight-hour movement, he saw it as a "lost battle" from which the workers would emerge as before, still "slaves to their capitalist masters." The same attitude was expressed by Fielden. "We do not object to it," he asserted, "but we do not believe in it. As to whether a man works eight hours a day or ten hours a day, he is still a slave." The only solution to the labor problem, said Fielden, was "to abolish private property, and so destroy competition."[2]

Until the end of 1885, then, the leading spirits of the International held themselves aloof from the eight-hour struggle. According to George Schilling, a strong supporter of shorter hours, they regarded it as "a sort of soothing syrup for babies, but of no consequence to grown men." At one point he and Spies almost came to blows when the latter reproached him for bamboozling the workers with the "eight-hour rot."[3] Under the slogan of "No Compromise," Spies and Parsons dismissed the campaign as a mere sop to the workers, diverting them from the real issue: the struggle against capitalism and for a cooperative society. "We of the International are frequently asked why we do not give our active support to the proposed eight-hour movement," *The Alarm* editorialized in December 1885. "Let us take what we can get, say our eight-hour friends, else by asking too much we may get nothing. We answer: Because we will not compromise. Either our position that capitalists have no right to exclusive ownership of the means of life is a true one, or it is not. If we are correct, then to accede the point that capitalists have the right to eight hours of our labor, is more than a compromise, it is a virtual concession that the wage-system is right."[4]

Meanwhile, however, the campaign for shorter hours had caught the imagination of the American workers. By the early weeks of 1886 it had become the all-absorbing topic in labor circles. Notwithstanding the opposition of the anarchists, the movement burgeoned across the country. Thousands of wage earners, skilled and unskilled, men and women, native and immigrant, organized and unorganized, were drawn into the struggle. "There is an eight-hour agitation everywhere," reported *John Swinton's Paper*, a leading labor journal, in April 1886.[5] By that time almost a quarter of a million workers were involved in the crusade. In Chicago, for example, a new Eight-Hour Association had been formed in November 1885, which drew together such disparate groups as the Trades and Labor Assembly, the Socialistic Labor Party, and the local Knights of Labor, as well as such diverse individuals as George Schilling, Joseph Gruenhut, and William Salter. Even Carter Harrison, now in his fourth term as mayor, supported the eight-hour cause.

As the movement picked up momentum, the anarchists began to have second thoughts. Seeing how deeply the workers were everywhere stirred, and how bitterly the employers resisted their efforts, they found it increasingly difficult to play the role of critical onlookers. Besides, it was a class movement, and they did not want to isolate themselves from it. Thus, while the intransigents within the International remained opposed to the eight-hour campaign, men like Parsons and Spies allied themselves with it. They did so, as Parsons later explained, because it was a movement "against class domination, therefore historical and revolutionary and necessary," and because "we did not choose to stand aloof and be misunderstood by our fellow workers."[6] Fielden, Schwab, and Holmes soon climbed on the bandwagon. To oppose the movement, Holmes remarked, would be akin to King Canute's commanding the waters to recede, for "the tide of opinion and determination of most wage-workers has set in this direction, and whether for good or evil it is bound to come."[7]

In changing their position, the anarchists were prompted not only by loyalty to labor in a fight with the class enemy. They had come to view the eight-hour movement as an opportunity rather than as an obstacle to their own program. At the very least, it would serve as a vehicle for agitation and organization, a means of disseminating their ideas and of stressing the value of direct action. At the same time, they hoped, it might grow in size and militancy and become an entering wedge for the social revolution, a lever with which to overthrow the capitalist system. In joining the campaign, therefore, they were reaching beyond the mere attainment of shorter hours. Their motives, in this respect, differed from those of their moderate allies, such as Schilling and Salter, for whom the immediate object remained paramount. The anarchists, by contrast, saw the rising tide of protest as the harbinger of a great upheaval destined to inaugurate the social millennium. "Let there be no halt," declared Spies, addressing the workers in April 1886. When the eight-hour day has been won, press onward "until the last stone of the robber bastille is removed and enslaved humanity is free."[8]

While campaigning for shorter hours, therefore, the anarchists continued to urge the workers to arm themselves. Only dynamite, they insisted, could guarantee success. Resistance by the manufacturers was growing. In due course, Pinkertons would be brought in, and the police and militia would follow. "Say, workingmen," asked *The Alarm*, "are you prepared to meet the latter; are you armed?"[9] A similar position was taken by the Central Labor Union, which endorsed the eight-hour cause. In a resolution put forward by Spies, its members vowed not to slacken their revolutionary efforts and urged "upon all wage-workers the necessity of procuring arms before the inauguration of the proposed eight-hour strike, in order to be in a position of meeting our foe with his own argument, force."[10]

By early 1886 Spies and Parsons had thrown their energies wholeheartedly into the eight-hour struggle. Before long, thanks to their ability as agitators and organizers, they assumed the leadership of the local movement. Together with Fielden and Schwab, they became the most popular speakers at eight-hour rallies and imbued the movement with a revolutionary spirit which it had not formerly possessed. Largely as a result of their efforts, Chicago emerged as the most dynamic center of the eight-hour crusade. Every week, throughout the early spring of 1886, meetings were held, leaflets distributed, and speeches made demanding shorter hours and lashing out at the capitalist system. On April 25, the Sunday preceding May 1, the Central Labor Union staged an immense eight-hour demonstration on the Lake Front at which an estimated 25,000 persons were addressed by Parsons, Spies, Fielden, and Schwab. Banners in English and German contained both reformist and revolutionary slogans: "Eight Hours—Working Time, May 1, 1886," "Private Capital Represents Stolen Labor," "Workingmen Arm," "Down with Throne, Altar and Money-Bags." Parsons delivered a warning: "If the capitalists, by the lockout, raise the black flag of starvation against the producers of wealth, then the producers will raise the banner of liberty, equality, and fraternity."[11]

The demonstration was a resounding success. Businessmen were alarmed by the unity displayed by the workers and by their susceptibility to radical propaganda. Among the Internationalists there was a growing impatience for the social revolution, for the inauguration of a Chicago Commune. Not a few were convinced that the final crisis of capitalism had begun and that the existing order was about to collapse. They talked interminably of the coming upheaval and of the free society that would follow. *The Alarm*, in its last issue before May 1, contained the following proclamation by Gerhard Lizius:

> WORKINGMEN TO ARMS!
> WAR TO THE PALACE, PEACE TO THE COTTAGE, AND DEATH TO LUXURIOUS IDLENESS.
> The wage system is the only cause of the world's misery. It is supported by the rich classes, and to destroy it, they must be either made to work or DIE.
> One pound of DYNAMITE is better than a bushel of BALLOTS!
> MAKE YOUR DEMAND FOR EIGHT HOURS with weapons in your hands to meet the capitalistic bloodhounds—police and militia—in proper manner.[12]

With the approach of May 1, the entire city was in a state of nervous excitement. Both sides anticipated an incident. The anarchists expected it to touch off the long-awaited insurrection. The authorities looked to it as a signal to suppress the radical movement once and for all. Police precautions of the most elaborate sort were taken against a popular outbreak. All reserve forces were mobilized. Special deputies were appointed. The state militia prepared for action, and there were rumors that federal troops stood in readiness to march on the city.[13] Encounters between workers and the police grew frequent, heightening the bitterness and tension.

For many, May 1st acquired an apocalyptic significance. On April 26 William Holmes wrote as follows to the secretary of the Socialist League in London: "The first of May will be very soon here—the day on which will be made the great test between organized labor and the money power for shorter hours. At this writing it is difficult to predict or even to guess at the result." It was probable, thought Holmes, that "there will be a lively time for a while." He then sounded a prophetic note: "These are stirring times, but it is my humble opinion there are still more desperate days to come *very soon*. I hope the revolution will not come too soon—or rather the revolt—of course the revolution cannot become a reality before its time. But what I fear sometimes is that we may grow too impatient and endeavor to hasten it; which would only result in disastrous failure. The next time the Commune is established it must be all over the world at once—and there must be no more failures or partial failures."[14]

May 1 marked the climax of the eight-hour agitation. More than 300,000 workers laid down their tools in 13,000 establishments throughout the country. In Chicago, the center of the movement, 40,000 went out on strike. Lumber shovers, metal workers, freight-handlers, brewers, packers, carpenters, upholsterers, tailors, bakers, and even salesmen and clerks moved into the streets. It was an impressive turnout. "No smoke curled up from the tall chimneys of the factories and mills," reported a Chicago paper, and the city assumed "a Sabbath-like appearance."[15] Spies penned a rousing editorial for the occasion: "Bravely forward! The conflict has begun. An army of wage-laborers are idle. Capitalism conceals its tiger claws behind the ramparts of order. Workmen, let your watchword be: No compromise! Cowards to the rear! Men to the front! The die is cast. The first of May, whose historic significance will be understood and appreciated only in later years, has come."[16]

Throughout the day processions and meetings took place in different parts of the city, with speakers addressing large crowds in English, Czech, and German. The most imposing demonstration was mounted by the IWPA and Central Labor Union. In what was one of the earliest May Day parades, Parsons and his wife, accompanied by their two children, led 80,000 workers up Michigan Avenue, singing and marching arm in arm. On rooftops along the route policemen, Pinkertons, and deputized civilians crouched behind Winchester rifles, while out of sight in the city's armories the militia stood by with Gatling guns awaiting orders.

By now the anarchists were in the forefront of the movement, and the names of Parsons and Spies were household words among Chicago's citizens, idolized by the workers, hated by businessmen and police. In an editorial headed "Brand the Curs," the *Chicago Mail* labeled them as troublemakers and called for appropriate punishment. In the light of subsequent events, the editorial bears quoting in full:

> There are two dangerous ruffians at large in this city; two sneaking cowards who are trying to create trouble. One of them is named Parsons. The other is named Spies. Should trouble come they would be the first to skulk away from the scene of danger, the

first to attempt to shield their worthless carcasses from harm, the first to shirk responsibility.

These two fellows have been at work fomenting disorder for the last ten years. They should have been driven out of the city long ago. They would not be tolerated in any other community on earth.

Parsons and Spies have been engaged for the past six months in perfecting arrangements for precipitating a riot today. They have taken advantage of the excitement attending the eight-hour movement to bring about a series of strikes and to work injury to capital and honest labor in every possible way. They have no love for the eight-hour movement, and are doing all they can to hamper it and prevent its success. These fellows do not want any reasonable concessions. They are looking for riot and plunder. They haven't got one honest aim nor one honorable end in view.

Mark them for today. Keep them in view. Hold them personally responsible for any trouble that occurs. Make an example of them if trouble does occur![17]

In spite of the predictions of the press, May 1 passed without incident. Although large numbers of workers took part in the day's demonstrations, there was no rioting or disorder. Chicago seemed to relax a little. That evening Parsons left for Cincinnati to speak at an eight-hour rally. The next day, a Sunday, was equally calm. The militants in the International began to express concern lest the moment for a rising should be lost. "Now or NEVER," proclaimed *Die Fackel*, the Sunday edition of the *Arbeiter-Zeitung*. "Everything depends upon quick and immediate action. The tactics of the bosses are to gain time; the tactics of the strikers must be to grant them no time. By Monday or Tuesday the conflict must have reached its highest intensity, else success will be doubtful. Within a week the fire, the enthusiasm will be gone, and the bosses will celebrate victory."[18]

Trouble came, however, on Monday, May 3, taking the anarchists unawares and setting in motion a chain of events which were to put Parsons and Spies exactly where the *Chicago Mail* wanted them ("Hold them personally responsible for any trouble that occurs. Make an example of them if trouble does occur!"). The day began quietly enough. Additional workers walked off the job, and further demonstrations were held in support of the eight-hour day, but at first

187

there was no violence. In the afternoon, however, a bloody encounter took place at the McCormick Reaper Works on Blue Island Avenue, a plant with a history of labor disputes dating back to the great strike of 1877, when skirmishes occurred between the workers and police.

Only a year before, in April 1885, Cyrus H. McCormick, Jr., had been forced by a strike to restore a 15 percent wage cut in what has been described as "the bitterest labor-management struggle in the company's history."[19] McCormick, since that time, had been determined to break the union. "The right to hire any man, white or black, union or non-union, Protestant or Catholic, is something I will not surrender," he told the press.[20] Over the next several months he introduced new machinery and did away with the jobs of the skilled iron molders, who had led the 1885 walkout. Finally, in February 1886, he declared a general lockout and replaced his remaining employees with non-union labor. A bitter conflict ensued which was intensified when McCormick brought in three hundred armed Pinkertons to protect the scabs. He enjoyed, in addition, the full cooperation of the Chicago police, under the orders of Inspector Bonfield. Nearly every day during the spring months angry pickets clashed with Pinkertons and policemen along the so-called Black Road, the section of Blue Island Avenue near the McCormick plant. According to the *Centennial History of Illinois*, "it became a pastime for a squad of mounted police, or a detachment in close formation, to disperse with the billy any gathering of workingmen. . . . It was the police, aided by the 'Pinkertons,' who added the great leaven of bitterness to the contest."[21]

The workers, however, fought back. Many joined the anarchist-dominated Metal Workers' Union, whose leader, Gustav Belz, had been employed at the plant. Both the Central Labor Union and the IWPA were active in behalf of the pickets, for the strike involved issues that deeply concerned the anarchists, above all the replacement of men by machines. During March and April, meetings of the locked-out workers were addressed by Parsons, Spies, and Schwab, Parsons dubbing the factory "Fort McCormick" and protesting against the role of the Pinkertons and police, "all armed to the teeth" and "menacing your lives and liberties."[22]

On the afternoon of May 3 serious trouble erupted. Spies had gone to Blue Island Avenue and 22nd Street, a few blocks from the McCormick works, to address an open-air meeting. This meeting had no connection with the dispute at McCormick's. It was held by the Lumber Shovers' Union, whose members were on strike for shorter hours. Spies was there at the behest of the Central Labor Union. Worn-out from the exertions of the past weeks, he had not intended to go, but a committee of workmen had called on him and persuaded him to change his mind.

It was a large gathering, several thousand strong. A number of speeches, in English, German, and Czech, had already been made when Spies arrived, accompanied by Balthasar Rau. Spies addressed the meeting. He called on his listeners to stand firmly together and they would carry the day. He did not mention the McCormick lock-out, nor did he counsel violence. As he was finishing up a bell rang at McCormick's, signalling the end of the workday. At this, some two hundred men detached themselves from Spies's audience and rushed towards the plant to join the pickets in heckling the scabs. Spies pleaded with them not to leave, but his words fell on deaf ears. Spies resumed his speech. Moments later, sounds of a struggle could be heard, but Spies urged his listeners to remain where they were. Soon afterwards, a patrol wagon rattled by, followed by about seventy-five policemen on foot, who rushed towards the McCormick works. They in turn were followed by three or four more patrol wagons. The crowd began to break up. Concluding his speech, Spies hastened to the scene.

A clash had taken place between the strikers and the scabs. From heckling, the pickets had moved to physical attack, driving the strikebreakers back into the factory, which the pickets now pelted with stones. Windows were broken. The patrol wagons came clanging up and a pitched battle ensued, the police wielding their clubs freely. Greeted with a shower of stones, the policemen drew their revolvers and began to fire into the crowd. After a brief stand the strikers broke and fled. Many had been wounded, at least two fatally; the precise casualties were never established. None of the policemen was seriously injured, though the assistant superintendent of the factory was hit in the face by a stone and badly hurt.[23]

Spies arrived in time to witness the bloodshed. The sight of the police beating and shooting unarmed workmen sickened and infuriated him. He ran back to the lumbermen's meeting, which had meanwhile adjourned. People were leaving in small knots, going home. Spies exhorted them to aid the strikers but got no response. Beside himself with anger, he hurried to the office of the *Arbeiter-Zeitung*. There he drafted a fiery leaflet, in English and German,

189

calling on the workers to take up arms and avenge the brutal murder of their brothers. Spies had heard that two men had been killed, apparently the correct number, but when he picked up the *Daily News* the paper reported six deaths. Spies believed this figure and repeated it in his leaflet. The leaflet began, "Workingmen to Arms!" But, without consulting Spies, a compositor, Hermann Pudewa by name, added the word "Revenge" in bold type, thinking it "made a good heading." The document thus became known as the "Revenge Circular."

The English version, appearing at the top of the leaflet, read as follows:

> REVENGE! Workingmen to Arms!!! Your masters sent out their bloodhounds—the police; they killed six of your brothers at McCormicks this afternoon. They killed the poor wretches, because they, like you, had the courage to disobey the supreme will of your bosses. They killed them, because they dared ask for the shortening of the hours of toil. They killed them to show you, 'Free American Citizens,' that you *must* be satisfied and contented with whatever your bosses condescend to allow you, or you will get killed!
>
> You have for years endured the most abject humiliations; you have for years suffered unmeasurable iniquities; you have worked yourself to death; you have endured the pangs of want and hunger; your Children you have sacrificed to the factory-lords—in short: You have been miserable and obedient slaves all these years. Why? To satisfy the insatiable greed, to fill the coffers of your lazy thieving master? When you ask them now to lessen your burden, he sends his bloodhounds out to shoot you, kill you!
>
> If you are men, if you are the sons of your grand sires, who have shed their blood to free you, then you will rise in your might, Hercules, and destroy the hideous monster that seeks to destroy you. To arms we call you, to arms! YOUR BROTHERS.[24]

The German text, also written by Spies, was even more violently phrased ("Slaves, we ask and conjure you, by all that is sacred and dear to you, avenge the atrocious murder that has been committed upon your brothers today and which will likely be committed upon you tomorrow. . . . Annihilate the beasts in human form who call themselves rulers! Uncompromising annihilation to them!").[25] With or without the word "Revenge," the entire tone of the circular was inflammatory. It appealed, in no uncertain terms, for retaliation.

During the next twenty-four hours events moved swiftly towards a climax. On the evening of May 3 a horseman galloped through the city carrying bundles of Spies's circular and dropping them off where workingmen gathered. (All told, 2,500 copies had been printed, of which about half were distributed.) Among the messenger's rounds was the basement of Greif's saloon on West Lake Street, where a meeting of German anarchists was in progress. At the Haymarket trial this meeting would be labeled by the prosecution as the "Monday night conspiracy" and painted in the darkest hues. What went on there, however, was never clearly established. Even the number of participants was in dispute, estimates ranging from thirty to eighty, though the latter figure seems grossly inflated. It is known, however, that those who attended came from the armed auxiliaries of the International and belonged to the most radical groups. Particularly well represented was the North-West Side Group, stronghold of the ultramilitant autonomist faction. Both Engel and Fischer were present, as were Gustav Breitenfeld and Bernhard Schrade, the commanders of the second company of the Lehr-und-Wehr Verein. Apart from Engel and Fischer, however, no other Haymarket defendants were in attendance.

Contrary to the prevailing impression, the Monday night meeting had not been occasioned by the McCormick imbroglio. It stemmed, rather, from an earlier meeting of the North-West Side Group and the second company of the Lehr-und-Wehr Verein, held the previous morning in Liberty Hall on Emma Street. The purpose of this first meeting had been to work out a plan of action should a collision occur between workers and police as a result of the eight-hour struggle. Engel, it seems, came forward with such a plan, though what it entailed was never conclusively established. According to witnesses at the Haymarket trial, it called for seizing the city's arsenals, destroying telegraph lines and other means of communication, and throwing bombs into the police stations and shooting the officers as they came out. These tactics, as the prosecution pointed out, conformed in nearly every detail to those outlined in Most's *Revolutionary War Science*.

One point that the militants had agreed upon, even before the Emma Street conclave, was that the appearance of the letter "Y" in the "Letter-Box" column of the *Arbeiter-Zeitung* would be a signal for the armed sections to meet at Greif's Hall. The signal was to be used only in circumstances of the greatest urgency. It appeared, however, in the afternoon edition of May 3, before the clash at McCormick's or any other incident had occurred. The notice handed to the printer—"Y—Come Monday Night"—was in the handwriting of Balthasar Rau.[26] Why it was inserted, however, remains a mystery.

Equally obscure is what took place at the meeting called as a result of the notice. Our main source is the testimony of Gottfried Waller, the chairman of the meeting, who turned state's evidence at the trial. Waller, a Swiss cabinetmaker, was a member of the North-West Side Group and of the second company of the Lehr-und-Wehr Verein. He had attended the Emma Street meeting the previous day and supported Engel's plan for armed resistance. Engel, according to Waller, now repeated his plan, and it was unanimously approved. A committee was to be appointed to keep watch of unfolding developments; if conflict erupted, the militants would go into action. At Fischer's suggestion, the word "Ruhe" (quiet, rest) was to be printed in the "Letter-Box" column of the *Arbeiter-Zeitung* as a signal to assemble with arms at prearranged points (the North-West Side Group in Wicker Park, the North Side Group in Lincoln Park, and so on) from which to carry out the plan of assault. As Waller made clear, however, the signal was to appear only in an extreme situation— indeed, only if a "downright revolution" had erupted.[27]

By the time the Monday night meeting assembled, the McCormick incident had taken place. As might be expected, it was the subject of intense discussion. Copies of the "Revenge Circular" were distributed. Waller then moved to hold a protest meeting the following morning in Market Square, the site of many rallies in the past. Fischer objected that the square was too small and would box in the workers like a "mouse trap" in the event of a police attack. Besides, he added, the meeting should be held in the evening when more workers would be able to attend. It was decided, therefore, to hold it at 7:30 P.M., and the site was to be the Haymarket, a widening of Randolph Street between Desplaines and Halsted, extending the length of two blocks and with enough space to hold 20,000 people. Nothing was said, however, with reference to any armed action to be taken at the meeting.

Before the Monday night meeting adjourned, Fischer was appointed to see to the printing of handbills and the securing of speakers for the Haymarket rally. Fischer performed these duties the next morning. First he went to the shop of Wehrer & Klein and ordered 25,000 handbills to be printed. The text, in English and German, called in resounding tones for a mass meeting that evening at the Haymarket: "Attention Workingmen! Great MASS-MEETING To-Night, at 7:30 o'clock, HAYMARKET, Randolph St., Bet. Desplaines and Halsted. Good speakers will be present to denounce the latest atrocious act of the police, the shooting of our fellow-workmen yesterday afternoon. *Workingmen Arm Yourselves and Appear in Full Force!* THE EXECUTIVE COMMITTEE."

Having carried out the first part of his assignment, Fischer proceeded to his job at the *Arbeiter-Zeitung*, where he invited Spies to speak at the meeting. It was then about 9 A.M. Still suffering from fatigue, Spies hesitated to accept. But if Fischer could find no one to take his place he would come. At about eleven o'clock Johann Grueneberg, a member of the North-West Side Group and an intimate of Fischer's, arrived with a copy of the printed handbill. He asked Spies to run it in the *Arbeiter-Zeitung* that afternoon as an announcement. Spies read the handbill. When he got to the last line—"*Workingmen Arm Yourselves and Appear in Full Force*"— he became angry. "This is ridiculous," he exclaimed. Summoning Fischer, he told him that he would not speak if this was the circular with which the meeting was to be called. (It was Fischer himself who had inserted the line. Who drafted the remainder of the handbill is not clear.) The reason, he later told the court, was that "I didn't want the workingmen to be shot down in that meeting as on other occasions."[28] At this point Grueneberg intervened. He said that the leaflet had not yet been distributed and that the words could be taken out. Fischer concurred. In that case, said Spies, it would be all right. Spies himself struck out the offending line before handing the leaflet to his compositor to be printed in the *Arbeiter-Zeitung*. Grueneberg, meanwhile, went back to Wehrer & Klein and gave the order to make the deletion. He also ordered the copies already printed to be suppressed. A few hundred, however, managed to avoid destruction and were distributed along with the rest—a circumstance that would weigh heavily at the trial.

As Spies later explained, he had objected to the last line of the handbill because "I thought it was ridiculous to put a phrase in which would prevent people from attending the meeting." Another reason, he added, was that "there was some excitement at that time and a call for arms like that might have caused trouble between the police and the attendants of the meeting."[29] Spies was right. The calm of the first days of May had been shattered by the McCormick encounter. No event could have been better calculated to set the smoldering passions of both sides ablaze. On the morning of May 4 the workers as well as the police were in an ugly mood. Skirmishes occurred throughout the day. In the morning policemen attacked a column of strikers on the South Side, and a crowd destroyed a drugstore from which the police had telephoned messages to headquarters. In the afternoon another clash occurred on the West Side, not far from the McCormick plant.

Spies himself added fuel to the flames. In the *Arbeiter-Zeitung* that afternoon he published a bitter account of the McCormick incident. He reminded the workers that when the eight-hour campaign began the International had warned them to arm themselves. Well, what do you think now? he asked. Were we wrong? Would yesterday's massacre have been possible if our advice had been taken? If the strikers, who defended themselves with stones, had been provided "with good weapons and one single dynamite bomb, not one of the murderers would have escaped his well-deserved fate." Spies's reference to "one single dynamite bomb" drove another nail into his own coffin. What was more, he called again for revenge—revenge without delay: "Whose blood does not course more swiftly through his veins when he hears of this outrage? Whoever is a man must show it today. Men to the front!"[30]

The same issue of the *Arbeiter-Zeitung* carried a similar article by Schwab. "The war of the classes is at hand," it declared. "Yesterday workingmen were shot down in front of McCormick's factory, whose blood cries out for revenge!" The business leaders applauded this action of their "bloodhounds" as necessary to enforce law and order. "In palaces they still fill goblets with costly wines, and pledge the health of the bloody banditti of Order. Dry your tears, ye poor and suffering! Take heart, ye slaves! Rise in your might and level the existing robber rule in the dust."[31]

More consequential, however, than either of these articles was the appearance of a single word in the "Letter-Box" column. The word was "Ruhe," the signal for the armed groups to assemble in force and implement their plan of attack. No major incident had occurred that day, much less the "downright revolution" which, according to Waller, alone would warrant the signal. Waller later testified that he himself did not understand why the word had been published. Nor did he know who had inserted it. The copy handed to the printer and later seized by the police was in Spies's writing. Spies, however, insisted that he had received a note in German which read, "Mr. Editor, please insert in the letter box the word 'Ruhe' in prominent letters," and, believing it a sort of "personal advertisement," copied it in his customary manner for the printer, without knowing its significance.[32]

Yet someone had sent in the notice. Who was it? And why had he done so? Was there in fact a conspiracy to commit violence, as the authorities maintained? Was the publication of the word "Ruhe" meant to trigger an uprising? What were the militants up to? That they had been making bombs and stockpiling weapons and ammunition is beyond dispute. Nor was it ever denied that they had met on May 2 and 3 or that Engel had proposed the use of force. We have it, moreover, from Dyer Lum that Fischer had "cordially adopted" Engel's plan.[33] But what did the plan entail? What "desperate projects," as William Holmes termed them, had the radicals been evolving? Was force to be resorted to only in case of an unprovoked attack by the police? Or were the militants contemplating an insurrection? These are questions for which there may never be satisfactory answers. According to Lum, Fischer, while in prison, told him the "unwritten history" of the whole affair. What it was, however, remains unknown. Lum, at any rate, did not reveal it, though Holmes afterwards conceded that "there was a movement on foot to precipitate the social revolution."[34]

If there was a conspiracy, however, Spies does not seem to have been a party to it. He was never among the inner circle of extremists who might have been planning an insurrection. Nor did he attend the meetings of May 2 and 3. His denial that he had known the import of the word "Ruhe" appears to have been genuine. Not till the afternoon of May 4 did Balthasar Rau, advertising agent of the *Arbeiter-Zeitung*, come in and explain it to him. By then the paper had been printed and distributed. Spies sent for Fischer and asked him if the word had any reference to the meeting to be held at the Haymarket. Fischer assured him that it did not. Spies thereupon instructed Rau to go around at once and tell all his acquaintances in the armed organizations that the word had appeared by mistake.[35] By 5 P.M. Spies was informed that this had been done. Spies had had a busy day. Tired and out of sorts, he went home to get some rest. There was a busier evening yet to come.

14 ‖ The Bomb

On the afternoon of May 4, Mayor Harrison was informed of the circular announcing the Haymarket meeting. Harrison, a Democrat, was now serving his fourth consecutive term in office. Born a Kentucky gentleman and educated at Yale, he had made a fortune in real estate, wore silk underwear, and hobnobbed with the city's aristocracy. Yet he was more liberal than most of his associates, especially in his attitude towards the workers. Neither a boss nor a demagogue, he did not, like so many urban leaders of his time, partake of the spoils system or appeal to the prejudice or ignorance of his constituents. In sympathy with union labor and with the struggle for the eight-hour day, he appointed socialists to the city administration (Joseph Gruenhut was a prominent example) who became, according to Willis J. Abbot, editor of the *Chicago Times*, "without exception creditable and efficient public servants."[1]

Harrison did his utmost to ease the tensions that gripped the city during the eight-hour agitation. Justly regarded as a friend of labor, he vowed never to allow troops to be brought in to shoot down striking workers. He insisted, moreover, on the right of all citizens to free speech and assembly. To interfere with radical propaganda, he felt, would be a violation of the constitution. Accordingly, when word reached him of the planned meeting at the Haymarket, he refused to intervene. Not that he was unaware of the rising tempers within the city. On the contrary, he instructed Frederick K. Ebersold, the general superintendent of police, that "if anything should be aired at that meeting that was likely to call out a recurrence of such proceedings as at McCormick's factory the meeting should be immediately dispersed."[2] For this purpose, a large contingent of officers, consisting of Captain William Ward, 7 lieutenants, and 176 men, under the direction of Inspector Bonfield, was concentrated at the Desplaines Street station, half a block south of Haymarket Square, while additional reserves were assigned to the central station and to various precincts around the city. Beyond this, plainclothes de-

The Haymarket and Vicinity

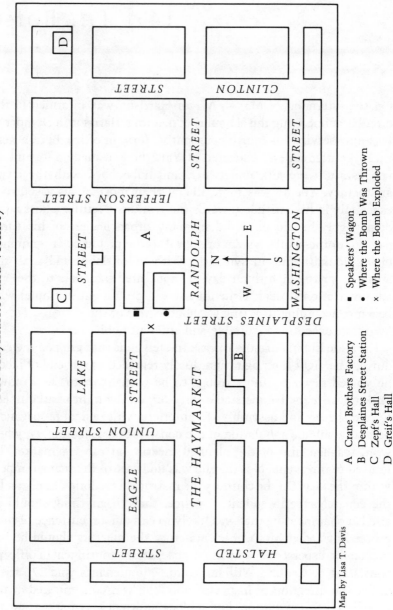

Map by Lisa T. Davis

A Crane Brothers Factory
B Desplaines Street Station
C Zepf's Hall
D Greif's Hall

■ Speakers' Wagon
• Where the Bomb Was Thrown
× Where the Bomb Exploded

tectives were detailed to mingle with the crowd at the Haymarket, and the mayor himself decided to attend to see that order was maintained.

While the mayor's instructions were being carried out, Spies was resting at home in anticipation of the meeting. He had just eaten dinner when his brother Henry dropped by. Spies told him about the meeting and asked him to come along. Henry agreed. It was about 7:45 P.M. when they left for the Haymarket. Although the meeting was scheduled to open at 7:30, they were not in any hurry, for Spies had been asked to speak in German, and it was customary for the German speakers to follow the English speakers at such gatherings. Thus there seemed to be plenty of time. Walking down Milwaukee Avenue, they stopped at the hardware store of Frank Stauber. Before leaving his house Spies had changed his clothes, and the revolver he habitually carried now proved too big to fit comfortably in his pocket. He left it for safekeeping with Stauber.

It was around 8:15 P.M. when Spies and his brother arrived at the Haymarket. To their surprise, the meeting had not yet begun. Here and there knots of men were standing around. The Haymarket, as has been noted, could accommodate 20,000 people, and a large crowd had been expected. The turnout was disappointing. No more than two or three thousand had gathered on the square, and some had already left because the meeting was so late in getting started. With an audience so small, Spies thought it best to move the meeting about half a block north on Desplaines Street near the mouth of Crane's Alley, a driveway behind the Crane Brothers metal-products factory (see map). For a rostrum he chose an empty truck wagon parked on the east side of the street a few feet above the alley. Mounting the wagon, he called the meeting to order. "Is Parsons here? Is Parsons here?" he shouted. Parsons, he had expected, would be the English speaker. A voice replied that Parsons was addressing another meeting a few blocks away. Spies asked the crowd to be patient a moment longer while he went to look for Parsons. Not finding him, he returned to the wagon. He was now informed that Parsons was at a meeting of the American Group in the offices of *The Alarm* and *Arbeiter-Zeitung*. Spies sent Balthasar Rau to fetch him. Meanwhile he himself began to speak.

Being the first speaker, Spies addressed the crowd in English. "There seems to prevail the opinion in certain quarters," he began, "that this meeting has been called for the purpose of inaugurating a riot, hence these warlike preparations on the part of so-called 'law and order' " (a reference to the police detachment at the nearby Desplaines Street station). "However, let me tell you at the beginning that this meeting has not been called for any such purpose. The object of this meeting is to explain the general situation of the eight-hour movement and to throw light upon various incidents in connection with it." Chief among these incidents was yesterday's massacre at McCormick's. Cyrus McCormick, Jr., had charged Spies himself with being the main instigator of the violence. This Spies categorically denied, insisting that McCormick and the police had caused the trouble. McCormick, said Spies, was an "infamous liar" [Cries of "Hang him!"]. "No," said Spies, "make no idle threats. There will be a time, and we are rapidly approaching it, when such men as McCormick will be hanged; there will be a time when monsters who destroy the lives and happiness of the citizens will be dealt with like wild beasts. But that time has not yet come. When it has come you will no longer make threats, but you will go and 'do it.' "[3]

Mayor Harrison, in the audience, listened attentively to these remarks. For a moment he thought he might have to intervene. But the rest of the speech was peaceful and gave no cause for alarm. The mayor relaxed. Mingling with the crowd, he endeavored to make his presence as conspicuous as possible, as a deterrent to would-be troublemakers. Nor was this a difficult task. At sixty-one, he was a big, imposing man of 225 pounds, "straight as an arrow," in Willis Abbot's description, "gray-bearded, square-shouldered and with a genial face which at once compelled respect and liking."[4] With his broad beard and black slouch hat he would have been noticeable in any event, but to make sure that he would be seen he struck match after match as if to relight his cigar. A friend urged him to stop lest he attract violence to himself. He replied: "I want the people to know their mayor is here."[5]

While Spies was addressing the crowd, Rau went to fetch Parsons. Parsons, it will be recalled, had gone to Cincinnati on the evening of May 1, after leading the eight-hour procession. In Cincinnati he spoke on May 2 at a big eight-hour rally and picnic.[6] Departing on the night of May 3, he arrived in Chicago early the next morning, the day of the Haymarket meeting. Once home he took a nap on the couch, and at 10 A.M. his wife awakened him. Together with Sarah Ames and Lizzie Holmes, she had been working among the

sewing girls to organize them for the eight-hour campaign. To pro-
mote these efforts, she suggested to her husband that a meeting of
the American Group be called for that evening. Parsons agreed. At
about 11 A.M. he left his home to make the necessary arrangements.
Unable to find a hall on such short notice, he placed an announcement in the *Chicago Daily News* that a meeting of the group would
be held at 107 Fifth Avenue, the offices of *The Alarm* and *Arbeiter-
Zeitung*. The rest of the day Parsons spent in the office, working at
his usual tasks. Late in the afternoon he learned for the first time
that a meeting had been called at the Haymarket for that evening.
Invited to speak, he was compelled to decline because he had to
attend the meeting of the American Group. At the end of the day
he went home for supper, accompanied by Lizzie Holmes.[7]

Shortly before 8 P.M. Parsons set out, in company with his wife,
their two children, and Lizzie Holmes, to attend the American Group
meeting. Parsons was in a buoyant mood. He spoke of the eight-
hour meeting in Cincinnati, which had been an immense success.
"He was pleasant and talkative," recalls Lizzie Holmes, "giving us
incidents of his journey, and speaking hopefully of the future of our
cause."[8] For the benefit of the ladies, he did a takeoff on a pompous
union official he had met on his trip. He was a good mimic, and
they were all laughing as they reached the corner of Randolph and
Halsted Streets, where they were to take a streetcar downtown. Here
they met two reporters, Edgar Owen of the *Times* and Henry Hei-
nemann of the *Tribune*. Owen asked Parsons if he was to speak at
the Haymarket, which lay close by. No, he replied, he had to attend
another meeting. A streetcar came up. Before boarding it, Parsons
slapped Owen familiarly on the back and asked him if he was armed.
Owen said, "No, have you any dynamite about you?" Parsons laughed,
and Mrs. Parsons said: "He is a very dangerous looking man, isn't
he?" Then they got on the car and went east.[9]

It was 8:30 P.M. when Parsons and his party reached 107 Fifth
Avenue, and the meeting of the American Group was at once called
to order. About fifteen members were present, Fielden among them.
Fielden had worked all day hauling a load of stone to the Waldheim
Cemetery, several miles outside the city, returning home about 5:30
P.M. He had promised to address a meeting of the Central Labor Union
that evening at a hall on West 12th Street. But, looking over the
announcements column of the *Chicago Daily News*, he saw the call
inserted by Parsons for the meeting of the American Group. As

treasurer he felt he ought to attend, in spite of his prior commitment to the Central Labor Union. A replacement could surely be found. Leaving his home after dinner, he reached 107 Fifth Avenue around eight o'clock and waited for Parsons to arrive.

It was fortunate that Fielden attended. When organizing the sewing women came up for discussion, it was decided to hold meetings, hire halls, and print circulars, for which money had to be appropriated. Fielden paid out the necessary funds, and the group named Lizzie Holmes to lead the drive. At this point—it was shortly before 9 P.M.—Rau arrived from the Haymarket with his urgent request for speakers. Parsons and Fielden answered the call. The group, adjourning its meeting, walked in a body to the Haymarket, a distance of half a mile. Spies was still speaking. Word was passed up from the crowd that Parsons had arrived. Spies brought his remarks to a close and introduced Parsons as the next speaker.

Parsons spoke for almost an hour. Given the passions of the moment, his speech was suprisingly temperate. Largely statistical in nature, it reviewed the disturbed condition of American labor, dwelling on the workers' small share of income. Parsons denounced the capitalist system, together with its "hireling press." He spoke of his recent travels in Pennsylvania and Ohio and of the plight of the miners there. There was "something radically wrong in the existing order of things, in our social affairs," he said. He spoke in favor of the shorter work day. "There is nothing in the eight-hour movement to excite the capitalists," he declared. "Do you know that the military are under arms, and a Gatling gun is ready to mow you down? Is this Germany or Russia or Spain?" [Voice: "It looks like it."] Whenever labor demanded better conditions the police and militia were called out and the workers clubbed and murdered. "In the light of these facts and your inalienable right to life, liberty, and the pursuit of happiness, it behooves you, as you love your wives and children, if you would not see them perish with want and hunger, yourselves killed or cut down like dogs in the streets—Americans, as you love liberty and independence, arm, arm yourselves!" [Applause and cries of "We will do it," "We are ready now."]

Parsons concluded by declaring that the only hope of the workers lay in socialism—in "the free association of the people for the purposes of production and consumption." As he had done so often in recent weeks, he called on his listeners to make every effort to secure the eight-hour day, to defend their rights and liberties, and above all "to combine, to unite, for in union there is strength!"[10]

This was standard Parsons fare, served up in countless speeches in the past. There was nothing particularly inflammatory in it. Even the occasional intemperate remark failed to arouse the crowd unduly. At one point he mentioned the name of Jay Gould, the railroad speculator, who had just smashed a strike on his southwestern lines, and someone in the audience cried "Hang him!" Parsons dismissed such ejaculations: "This is not a conflict between individuals, but for a change of system, and socialism is designed to remove the causes which produce the pauper and the millionaire, but does not aim at the life of the individual." He said further: "Kill Jay Gould, and like a jack-in-a-box another or a hundred others like him will come up in his place under the existing social conditions."

As for Parsons's use of the expression "arm, arm yourselves," G. P. English, a reporter for the *Chicago Tribune*, who attended the meeting with instructions to report only the most inflammatory utterances, testified that Parsons pronounced the words in the ordinary tone of voice in which he had been speaking. The words, moreover, came shortly after another statement by Parsons as follows: "I am not here for the purpose of inciting anybody, but to speak out, to tell the facts as they exist, even though it should cost me my life before morning." To English, a veteran reporter, Parsons's speech was milder in character than many others he had heard him deliver on previous occasions.

Mayor Harrison, who attended the meeting with the intention of suppressing it if necessary, came away with a similar impression of Parsons's speech. According to his own testimony, he had heard nothing in it that required any action on his part, and while he would describe it as a "violent political harangue against capital," it was nevertheless quite moderate compared with what was habitual on such occasions. Throughout the speech, noted Harrison, the crowd remained calm and orderly. There were occasional cries of "shoot him" or "hang him," but they evoked a mild response. Several times the cry of "hang him" came from a boy at the edge of the crowd, and the audience would laugh. A few of the ejaculations were bitter, but there was no unusual excitement. Above all, said Harrison, "there was no suggestion made by either of the speakers for the immediate use of force or violence toward any person that night; if there had been I should have dispersed them at once."[11]

Convinced of the harmless character of the meeting, the mayor decided to leave. When Parsons seemed to be concluding his speech, Harrison separated himself from the crowd and went to the Desplaines Street station. Summoning Inspector Bonfield, he told him that the meeting was "tame," and that "nothing had occurred yet or was likely to occur to require interference." He suggested, accordingly, that Bonfield dismiss his reserves, or at least those being held at the other precincts. To this Bonfield replied that he had already issued such an order, since the detectives who were bringing him reports of the meeting had arrived at a similar estimation. Bonfield thought, however, that he should retain his forces at the Desplaines Street station until the meeting had broken up. He had heard rumors, he told the mayor, that part of the crowd might go over to the freight yards of the Milwaukee & St. Paul Railroad, whose workers were out on strike, and attempt to blow them up. Mayor Harrison concurred. For rumors were flying thick and fast. He himself had heard that the Haymarket meeting might be merely a ruse to draw attention away from the real attack, which was to be at McCormick's. Having concluded his discussion with Bonfield, he went back to the meeting to hear a bit more. Then he mounted his white horse and rode home to his mansion on Ashland Avenue.

When the mayor departed Parsons was just finishing up. It was shortly after 10 P.M. After concluding his remarks, he introduced Fielden, the last speaker. Stepping down from the speakers' wagon, Parsons went to another wagon a few paces north of it, on which sat his wife and children and Lizzie Holmes with some friends, and took a place beside them. Fielden began his address. "He talked in a plain, straightforward way, using strong, homely words and illustrations, and seemed to hold the attention of the crowd quite easily," a member of the audience recorded.[12] Fielden had spoken about ten minutes when a dark cloud rolled in from the north, accompanied by a gust of wind. Signs creaked violently, and bits of paper flew in the air. It looked like rain. People began to leave. Parsons called out that the meeting had better adjourn to Zepf's Hall, a tavern half a block north, at the corner of Lake and Desplaines. Someone in the crowd responded that the hall was already occupied by a meeting of the Furniture Workers' Union. Fielden thereupon announced that he would be finished in a few minutes, and then they could all go home.

Fielden proceeded with his remarks. But the suggestion made by

Parsons, combined with the threatening aspect of the sky and the lateness of the hour, caused a large segment of the audience to disperse, including all the women and children. Getting down from their wagon, Parsons and his group went over to Zepf's to await the adjournment of the meeting and the company of friends on their walk home. Fischer, who had been in the audience, took the same course. Not more than three hundred persons still remained for the balance of Fielden's address.

Fielden began to draw his remarks to a close. "There is no security for the working classes under the present social system," he declared. "A few individuals control the means of living, and hold the workingmen in a vise. Everybody does not know that. Those who know it are tired of it, and will end it, and there is no power in the land that will prevent them." The workers had nothing to hope from legislation. "The law is only framed for those who are your enslavers. [Voice: "That's true."] Men in their blind rage attacked Mc-Cormick's factory and were shot down by the law in cold blood, in the city of Chicago, in the protection of property. . . . A million men hold all the property in this country. The law has no use for the other fifty-four millions. [Voice: "Right enough."] You have nothing more to do with the law except to lay hands on it and throttle it until it makes its last kick. It turns your brothers out on the wayside and has degraded them until they have lost the last vestige of humanity, and they are mere things and animals. Keep your eye upon it, throttle it, kill it, stab it, do everything you can to wound it—to impede its progress."[13]

At these words two detectives left the crowd and hurried to the Desplaines Street station. They reported to Inspector Bonfield that the speaker was using inflammatory language, saying that the law must be throttled and killed. Bonfield went into action. Calling out his men, he hastily formed them up in an alley adjoining the station and marched them on the meeting. They marched at quick time, almost at a run, their ranks filling Desplaines Street from curb to curb. As they crossed Randolph Street they hurried forward, compelling the crowd to fall back up Desplaines and to spill onto the sidewalks.

Fielden was winding up his speech: "He that has to obey the will of another is a slave. Can we do anything except by the strong arm of resistance? The Socialists are not going to declare war; but I tell you war has been declared on us; and I ask you to get hold of anything that will help you to resist the onslaught of the enemy and the usurper. The skirmish lines have met. People have been shot. Men, women, and children have not been spared by the capitalists and minions of private capital. It has no mercy—so ought you. You are called upon to defend yourselves, your lives, your future. What matters it whether you kill yourselves with work to get a little relief, or die on the battlefield resisting the enemy? What is the difference? Any animal, however loathsome, will resist when stepped upon. Are men less than snails or worms? I have some resistance in me; I know that you have, too; you have been robbed and you will be starved into a worse condition."[14]

At this point the police marched in. Led by Inspector Bonfield and Captain Ward, they halted a few feet from the speakers' wagon. For a few seconds the crowd stood frozen. They were amazed to see the police appear at such a time, when they were all getting ready to leave anyway. Captain Ward, in a loud voice, called out: "I command you, in the name of the people of the state of Illinois, immediately and peaceably to disperse!" Fielden was astonished. He did not know what to do. "The meeting had been a more than ordinarily peaceable one," he later recalled, "and had been getting smaller and more quiet up to that time, so that there was not more than two or three hundred at the most, in my opinion, when the police arrived."[15] Fielden stopped talking and stared at Captain Ward. "But we are peaceable," he protested. A moment of silence followed. The captain then repeated his command and added, pointing to bystanders, "and I call upon you to assist." The crowd wondered what was happening. "All right, we will go," said Fielden, and began to step down from the wagon.

At this instant something sputtered over the heads of the audience and fell into the midst of the police. A terrific explosion shook the street, shattering windows for blocks around. The Haymarket bomb had been thrown. It exploded with a deafening roar between the second and third ranks of the police. A number of officers fell wounded. For a moment there was a stunned silence. Then the policemen drew their revolvers and began to fire into the crowd. An incessant fire was kept up for several minutes. The crowd scattered in all directions. Men ran up the streets and alleys, pursued by an infuriated police. The air was filled with groans, as on a battlefield ("O God, I'm shot," "Please take me home," "Take me to the hospital"). Men trampled each other, shouting and swearing as they tried to escape the fusillade. The wounded limped into drugstores and saloons or crawled on their hands and feet. Others dragged themselves into doorways and behind walls and empty barrels. "Goaded to madness," reported the *Chicago Tribune*, "the police were in the condition of mind which permitted of no resistance, and in a measure they were as dangerous as any mob, for they were blinded by passion and unable to distinguish between the peaceable citizen and the Nihilist assassin."[16]

Fielden had just stepped onto the sidewalk when he saw the flash in the street and heard the bomb explode. He began to run but was immediately struck in the knee by a bullet, which, after grazing the bone, traveled upward and slightly across and then came out. Fielden felt the blow but did not at first know what it was. He got to the corner of Randolph and Desplaines, running as fast as he could, and then turned east. As soon as he thought himself safe, he paused and felt his knee. Only then, finding it wet with blood, did he realize he had been shot. After looking in vain for his comrades, he went to a drugstore and had his wound dressed.[17]

Spies had been just behind Fielden on the speakers' wagon when Captain Ward gave the order to disperse. He was climbing down from the wagon at the time the bomb exploded. The noise was so great that he thought the police had opened up on the crowd with artillery. "What's that?" asked his brother Henry. "A cannon, I believe," was Spies's reply. Henry, turning around, beheld the barrel of a revolver aimed directly at his brother's back. He grasped the weapon just as it went off, and the bullet struck him in the groin. Unaware of what had happened, Spies lost his brother in the throng and was carried along up the street. Bullets whistled about him. Men were falling left and right. Once or twice he stumbled over others, but succeeded in escaping to Zepf's saloon.[18]

Mayor Harrison had left the meeting shortly after 10 P.M. and reached home about fifteen minutes later. He had just undressed and was about to go to bed when he heard the sound of the explosion. At first he thought it might be thunder, as the weather had been threatening rain. Raising the window, he heard the rattling of pistol shots. They were coming from the direction of the Haymarket. He quickly got dressed and rode back to the square.

The firing continued for two or three minutes. When it finally stopped, the streets were littered with bodies, both of civilians and police. A bell in the Desplaines Street station tolled out a riot alarm.

From all over the city patrol wagons rushed to the scene. Officers, nearly a thousand strong, cleared all the streets within a three-block radius, and "mercilessly clubbed at all who demurred at the order to go."[19] Injured policemen and civilians were taken to the Desplaines Street station, from which the more serious cases were removed to the County Hospital.

Within less than five minutes the Haymarket "riot" was over. Seven policemen and an unknown number of civilians had been fatally wounded. One of the officers, Mathias J. Degan, had suffered a cut from a bomb fragment through a main artery in his left thigh. He died moments later in the Desplaines Street station from loss of blood. He was thirty-four years old, a widower with a thirteen-year-old son.[20] Six other officers died from their wounds during the next few weeks. They were George Mueller (May 6), John J. Barrett (May 6), Timothy Flavin (May 8), Michael Sheehan (May 9), Thomas Redden (May 16), and Nils Hansen (June 14). In addition, sixty policemen had been injured, one of whom, Timothy Sullivan, died two years later, apparently as a result of his wounds.

Sixty-seven casualties was a heavy toll. In most instances, however, they had not been inflicted by the bomb, a fact inadequately brought out at the trial or by historians of the case. Contrary to the general impression, most of the injuries had been caused by bullets rather than by bomb fragments. In fact, of the seven policemen who died before the trial, only Degan can be accounted an indisputable victim of the bomb.[21] As for the other fatalities, a careful examination of the evidence (medical reports, police casualty lists, newspaper accounts, testimony at the trial) reveals that at least three (Mueller, Barrett, and Sheehan) had been shot to death, while the remainder apparently succumbed to a combination of bullet and bomb wounds, though the evidence here is inconclusive. The eighth fatality, Timothy Sullivan, died from the effects of a bullet wound. By the same token, a majority of the officers who survived their injuries had been wounded by pistol rather than bomb. Although reports vary, more than twenty had been wounded by bullets, around twenty by bomb fragments, and perhaps ten by both. The rest had been bruised, trampled upon, and the like.[22]

Another fact is equally noteworthy. All or nearly all of the policemen who had suffered bullet wounds had been shot by their fellow officers and not by civilians in the crowd. There is no question that some of the civilians were armed. Indeed, Spies himself would have been carrying his revolver had it fit more securely in his pocket. Furthermore, at least one member of the audience was seen to be waving a pistol during the speeches. But the number of armed civilians seems to have been small. Mayor Harrison, for one, saw no weapons at all in the crowd.

Be that as it may, nearly all sources agree that it was the police who opened fire; and while it is possible that some civilians fired back, reliable witnesses testified that all the pistol flashes came from the center of the street, where the police were standing, and none from the crowd. Moreover, initial newspaper reports made no mention of firing by civilians.[23] A telegraph pole at the scene was filled with bullet holes, all coming from the direction of the police. The pole was removed the next day and never recovered. Captain Schaack's explanation that it had been "very prosaically, and in the common course of business, removed by the telegraph company," is unconvincing.[24]

There can be little doubt, therefore, that most if not all of the officers had been wounded by their own comrades, who fired indiscriminately in the panic that followed the explosion. Inspector Bonfield, in his official report of the incident, noted that he gave the order to cease fire for fear that "some of our own men in the darkness might fire into each other." Another high police official (who preferred to remain anonymous) told the *Chicago Tribune* that "a very large number of the police were wounded by each other's revolvers. . . . It was every man for himself, and while some got two or three squares away, the rest emptied their revolvers, mainly into each other."[25]

At the same time, of course, a large number of civilians were also killed and wounded. The precise toll has never been determined, though Captain Schaack believed that it was "largely in excess of that on the side of the police."[26] Once again it was the officers who were responsible, firing wildly in the darkness and confusion. "Fire and kill all you can!" shouted Lieutenant James Bowler to his men. He himself got off nine quick shots, then reloaded and fired again. Inspector Bonfield reacted in a similar manner. According to a source well disposed to the police, he "seized a revolver from the hand of a fallen officer, at the same time drawing his own revolver, and from both hands he rained a shower of lead into the ranks of the enemy."[27]

It was a scene of "wild carnage," wrote a reporter for the *Chicago*

Herald, who estimated that fifty or more civilians lay dead or wounded in the streets.[28] B. Le Plant, of Earl Park, Indiana, said: "I bought some peanuts and was eating them when the bomb went off, then a shot broke my leg and I fell. In a second a shot went through my shoulder and a policeman kicked me." Fielden, as we have seen, caught a bullet in the knee, and Henry Spies was wounded in the groin as he fought off a detective who attempted to kill his brother. The *Tribune* reported, moreover, that several shots were fired at a civilian who resembled Parsons, "whom the police were very anxious to make a target of."[29] Drugstores in the vicinity were crowded with wounded men getting their injuries dressed before being carried home by friends. Others were treated on the sidewalk. Streetcars leaving the area contained men who had been wounded but who were still strong enough to help themselves away.

Not many among the dead and injured were publicly identified, however. Few newspapers troubled to make an accounting of civilian casualties, and no complete list was ever published. Four civilians, all of them workers, are definitely known to have been killed: Emil Lutz, a shoemaker, Carl Kiester, a laborer, Mathias Lewis, a shoemaker, and Charles Schumacher, a tailor.[30] But the actual toll was probably higher. More than one source lists Reinhold Krueger, a member of the International, among the civilians shot dead by the police, while some name Frank Lewis, Peter Lay, John Edlund, and Franz Wroch as probable fatalities. The *Chicago Tribune*, in addition, mentions an unidentified Bohemian, about thirty-five years old, who was killed in the affray.[31] Rumor had it that "the anarchists stole their dead away and buried their bodies secretly."[32] While this seems fanciful, a few may have been buried quietly and not turned up in official records; and there were unquestionably some wounded civilians who did not go to the hospital or report their injuries for fear of being arrested. All things considered, a reasonable estimate of civilian casualties would be seven or eight dead and thirty to forty wounded.

It is clear then that, leaving aside the unidentified bombthrower, it was the police and not the anarchists who were the perpetrators of the violence at the Haymarket. What makes this fact particularly disturbing is that no convincing reason was ever provided for their interference. All accounts agree that the meeting had been peaceful. There had been some excitement, as on all such occasions, but no disorder had taken place. The speeches were if anything of a more conservative character than those at similar gatherings in the past. Numerous witnesses at the trial, including some for the prosecution, testified that such was the case. "It was a peaceable and quiet meeting for an out-door meeting," said G. P. English of the *Tribune*. "I didn't see any turbulence. I was there all the time. I thought the speeches they made that night were a little milder than I heard them make for years. . . . I didn't hear any of them say or advise that they were going to use force that night."[33]

Mayor Harrison was equally emphatic on this point. Not only had the meeting been orderly, but it was breaking up of its own accord. Only two or three hundred people remained, and the final speaker was winding up his remarks. A few minutes more and the Haymarket would have been deserted. Had Bonfield remained quiet, the incident would not have occurred. No bomb would have been thrown, no policemen or civilians injured, and the meeting would have passed into history as merely another in a series of labor rallies to which Chicago had long been accustomed. Bonfield's decision to march, after the mayor reported no danger, must be seen as a direct cause of the tragedy. "No one will ever know the exact truth, perhaps," wrote Lizzie Holmes, "but it is certain that had the police remained away the meeting would have dispersed quietly and peaceably." As an anonymous police official put it: "There was a blunder on the part of the man who commanded the police on the night of the Haymarket murders, or this fearful slaughter would not have occurred. Bonfield made the blunder, and he is held responsible for its effects by every man injured there."[34]

Why then did Bonfield intervene? According to his own testimony, he acted because the peaceful character of the meeting changed when Fielden took the platform and urged the audience to "throttle" the law. In his report to Police Superintendent Ebersold, Bonfield maintained that the crowd was "getting excited and the speaker growing more incendiary in his language. I then felt to hesitate any longer would be criminal on my part."[35] Fielden, on his side, insisted that he had used the word "throttle" only in a figurative sense. "If you take the metaphors from the English language, you have no language at all," he told the court. "It's not necessary, your honor, that because a man says 'throttle the law' he means 'kill the policemen.' "[36]

A mere glance at Fielden's speech amply supports this claim. It was no more inflammatory than the harangues he had delivered in the past. Nor, despite Bonfield's testimony, did it unduly agitate his listeners, who remained orderly throughout. There was, in fact, not the slightest reason to descend upon the meeting other than Bonfield's determination to have his way with the participants. For some days Bonfield had been chafing under the policy of restraint urged by Mayor Harrison. His impatience was evident at a meeting of high police officials—a "council of war," the press called it—on the afternoon of May 4. Superintendent Ebersold and nearly every other commanding officer favored a strategy of watchful waiting. But "Inspector Bonfield thought that vigorous measures should be adopted and was willing to be on hand to see that they were carried out at all times," reported the *Chicago Daily News*.[37]

When Bonfield learned of the plans for the Haymarket meeting, he at once "resolved to disperse it," the *Chicago Times* of May 5 quoted him as saying. At the Desplaines Street station, shortly before the meeting, he spoke with Barton Simonson, an acquaintance of Captain Ward's. According to Simonson, who was not a socialist and had no apparent axe to grind, Bonfield "said that the greatest trouble the police had in dealing with the Socialists was that they had their women and children with them at the meetings so that the police could not get at them. He said he wished he could get a crowd of about three thousand of them together, without their women and children, and he would make short work of them."[38] Lieutenant Edward J. Steele, detailed to the Desplaines Street station that evening, was informed that "an unlawful meeting" was about to take place and that the police were under orders to disperse it. At the trial, moreover, two other officers were prepared to testify that they had been told at the station that blood would flow before midnight. The judge, however, would not permit them to do so.

Bonfield, then, at least in a general way, had contemplated in advance the action that he took at the Haymarket. By all accounts, he had been itching for an opportunity to break up the meeting. Fielden's violent-sounding rhetoric gave him the excuse he was waiting for. The mayor had gone home. The women and children had departed. Bonfield's way was clear. His detectives no doubt had reported that Fielden's speech would soon be finished and that the crowd was already beginning to disperse. Unless he acted quickly he would miss his chance. The haste with which he assembled his men and marched them out of the station is a token of his anxiety to get to the meeting before it adjourned. Testimony at the trial showed that the order to fall in was given urgently and that the head of the column was marched out so quickly that those who emerged later had to proceed to their positions on the double. Lieutenant George W. Hubbard testified that he did not have time to form his men into line, but that they had to run down the street after the officers who had already marched out. A civilian witness, John Ferguson, saw the police rush out of the station at top speed. Bonfield was waving his arm and shouting for them to hurry up, so that "they whirled into the street and came down very rapidly towards us." As Fielden described it, "there was a great bustle and hurry on the part of the police to get to the meeting before it ended." And a ranking police official stated: "The whole thing was hasty and ill-advised, arising out of Bonfield's desire to distinguish himself."[39]

Since Bonfield had plainly interfered with a peaceful gathering, he was widely blamed for the ensuing bloodshed, in particular by the anarchists and their defenders. "Has it come to pass," asked W. P. Black at the trial, "that under the constitution of the United States and of this state, our meetings for the discussion of grievances are subject to be scattered to the winds at the breath of a petty police officer?" Black then added: "I ask you again, charging no legal responsibility here, but looking at the man who is morally at fault for the death harvest of that night, who brought it on? Would it have been but for the act of Bonfield?"[40] Some went even further. Since the police, without due provocation, had assaulted the right of public assembly, was not the throwing of the bomb justified? Are citizens to stand idly by while their most cherished liberties are being flouted? As Ezra Heywood put it, "the right or duty of the invaded meeting, in its own defense, to use bombs cannot be questioned on accepted principles of law and order."[41]

There were those, however, who did question whether the throwing of a bomb was a legitimate act of self-defense, given the circumstances in which it occurred. That there had been interference with the right of free speech and assembly was not at issue. But was such extreme retaliation warranted? Despite allegations to the contrary,[42] the police had not attacked the crowd before the explosion occurred. Nor had they marched in with clubs and revolvers drawn, which might have been construed as a provocation. They had stood quietly in formation while Captain Ward ordered the gathering to disperse. Had the bomb not been thrown, the meeting, barring unforeseen developments, would have ended without bloodshed. Benjamin Tucker, while defending his comrades against the charges of murder and conspiracy, questioned how much "wanton violence" the police had actually employed in interfering with the meeting. It seemed unlikely, he suggested, "that their conduct could have been of such a character as to warrant the throwing of the bomb. It seems much more likely, inasmuch as men of ordinary prudence are not in the habit of carrying dynamite bombs in their coat-tail pockets, that the individual who thew it was seeking an opportunity to throw it."[43]

Yet it is possible to condemn the police without at the same time condoning the bombing. It was the police, after all, who initiated the trouble by descending upon a peaceful meeting. Without their interference, the bomb would not have been thrown. The ultimate blame must therefore rest on their shoulders, most of all on the shoulders of Bonfield. There were some who believed that Bonfield was not merely intent upon a head-bashing party, but that he was acting on orders from businessmen "determined to have a blood bath on the Haymarket."[44] Parsons, for one, maintained that Bonfield was "only a willing agent, not the dastardly principal in this outrage. He held plenary power and obeyed what he knew to be the express desire of his masters—the money-kings—who want to suppress free speech, free press, and the right of workingmen to assemble to discuss their grievances." Fielden likewise charged that the entire incident had been prearranged by the industrialists and police to eliminate the International's most troublesome agitators.[45]

Thus both sides were prisoners of conspiracy theories. The police accused the anarchists of conspiring to kill policemen, while the International accused the police of conspiring to get rid of the anarchists. There is no proof to sustain either view. Bonfield, to be sure, defended business interests and had resolved to rid the city of radicals. But it is doubtful that he had any well-conceived plan at the Haymarket. He saw his chance and took it. The same perhaps was true of the bombthrower.

15 ∥ RED SCARE

The Haymarket explosion, as Henry David has noted, brought on the first major "Red Scare" in American history.[1] News of the incident provoked a nationwide convulsion of deep-rooted and violent prejudice. A blind passion seized a great part of the population, whose forebodings about the anarchists seemed confirmed. Violent speech had resulted in violent deeds. Here at last was the dynamite that had been threatened. For the first time in America the deadly substance had been used for the destruction of human life.

Public opinion was deeply aroused. A fear of subversion seized the country, triggering a campaign of radical-baiting rarely if ever surpassed. It was the first great American inquisition since the Salem witch trials of the seventeenth century. For weeks and months the country remained in the grip of hysteria. Nor was it confined to any particular class of citizens. All conditions of men, wage earners and businessmen alike, vied with each other in demanding the prompt suppression of sedition. Popular indignation, moreover, flared out not only against anarchists but against the entire radical movement as well as anyone who had ever expressed the faintest sympathy with it. The radical menace, observed Benjamin Tucker, "filled the public mind."[2]

The panic ran deepest in Chicago. The city was seized with a fear and hatred unprecedented in its history. People gathered on street corners, excited and feverish, talking about the awful event. Wild rumors filled the air: The anarchists were planning to wipe out the police, blow up public buildings, plunder stores and warehouses; there was a deeply laid conspiracy to destroy the whole city; the Haymarket bomb was the signal for a general uprising; the anarchists were scheming to seize control of the entire country. Accumulated tensions were suddenly released in a wave of mob spirit. It was, in the words of Brand Whitlock, the future reform mayor of Toledo, "one of the strangest frenzies of fear that ever distracted a whole community."[3]

Both press and pulpit, the leading molders of public opinion, fanned the terror aroused by the explosion. Clergymen in Sunday sermons denounced the killing of the policemen, condemned the evils of anarchism, and exhorted their parishioners to combat subversion with every means at their command. Even the liberal David Swing, pastor of the independent Central Church, declared: "We need a careful definition of what freedom is. If it means the license to proclaim the gospel of disorder, to preach destruction, and scatter the seeds of anarchy and death, the sooner we exchange the Republic for an iron-handed monarchy the better it will be for all of us."[4] Newspaper editors adopted a similar note, letting loose a stream of vituperation and incitement never before equalled in an industrial struggle in America. "NOW IT IS BLOOD!" was a characteristic headline on the day after the explosion. "The city went insane," recalled Mother Jones, "and the newspapers did everything to keep it like a madhouse. The workers' cry for justice was drowned in the shriek for revenge."[5]

Editors needed no urging to intensify their campaign against the anarchists. Every journalistic device was used to arouse the public against them. Headlines screamed against the "Bloody Brutes," "Red Ruffians," "Dynamarchists," "Bloody Monsters," and "Bomb Throwers." They were maligned as "cowards," "cutthroats," "thieves," "assassins," and "fiends." To the *Chicago Times* they were "arch counselors of riot, pillage, incendiarism and murder," fanatics who threatened every convention on which a civilized society depended. For months and years, editorials complained, these "pestiferous fellows" had been allowed to utter their seditious doctrines with impunity. They had been warmed in "the sunshine of toleration" until "emboldened to strike at society, law, order, and government." It was high time to teach them a lesson.[6]

Newspapers and magazines throughout the nation joined in the clamor. Headlines shrieked and howled, whipping readers into a frenzy of excitement. On May 5 the *New York Times* headed its front-page story "Anarchy's Red Hand." It began: "The villainous teachings of the Anarchists bore bloody fruit in Chicago tonight, and before daylight at least a dozen stalwart policemen will have laid down their lives as a tribute to the doctrine of Herr Johann Most." And again the following day: "No disturbance of the peace that has occurred in the United States since the war of the rebellion has excited public sentiment throughout the Union as it is excited by the Anarchists' murder of policemen in Chicago on Tuesday night. We say murder with the fullest consciousness of what the word means. It is silly to speak of the crime as a riot. All the evidence goes to show that it was a concerted, deliberately planned, and coolly executed murder."

The press, as these extracts indicate, was bitterly one-sided in its reporting of the incident. Accounts were grossly inaccurate, the bomb being invariably laid at the door of Parsons and his associates. The typical headline announced: "Chicago Anarchists Throw Bomb in Midst of Police." Civilian casualties and the role of the police in the violence were seldom mentioned. "The mob appeared crazed with a frantic desire for blood," reported the *New York Tribune*, "and, holding its ground, poured volley after volley into the midst of the officers." A lurid double-page drawing of the incident, published in *Harper's Weekly*, showed a wild-eyed Fielden on the platform and a mob of sinister-looking workmen firing directly into the ranks of the police.[7]

Throughout the country newspapers and journals called for severe reprisals. The *New York Times* offered the following prescription: "In the early stages of an acute outbreak of anarchy a Gatling gun, or if the case be severe, two, is the sovereign remedy. Later on hemp, in judicious doses, has an admirable effect in preventing the spread of the disease." The *Philadelphia Inquirer* recommended a "mailed hand" to teach the anarchists that America was not a shelter for "cutthroats and thieves," while the *Louisville Courier-Journal* insisted that the "blatant cattle" be "strung up," the sooner the better. "Judge Lynch," echoed the *American Israelite* of Cincinnati, "is a tremendous expounder of the law." "It is no time for half measures," agreed the *Springfield Republican*, urging the authorities to make an example of the ringleaders. "There are no good anarchists except dead anarchists," the *St. Louis Globe-Democrat* chimed in.[8]

In Chicago, as elsewhere, the press clamored for revenge, insisting that the bomb was the work of an organized conspiracy to destroy the city. "No time for parleying," proclaimed the *Chicago Daily News*. "The anarchists are amenable to no reason except that taught by the club and rifle." The *Chicago Times* demanded immediate and merciless reprisals: "Let the police, and the militia if called into action, deal with these miscreants in vigorous fashion. 'Fire low' and 'fire quick' should be the command, and it should be remorselessly carried out." The *Chicago Tribune* envisioned a sequence of events for the anarchist leaders illustrated in a four-part cartoon: 1) a wild-eyed radical speaker, 2) Spies, Parsons, Fielden, and Schwab behind bars, 3) four waiting nooses, and 4) four graves marked "August Spies," "Albert R. Parsons," "Samuel Fielden," and "Michael Schwab."[9]

Goaded by an hysterical press, public indignation was roused to fever pitch. Theodore Roosevelt wrote from his ranch in Dakota Territory that his cowboys would like "a chance with rifles" at the unruly Chicago mobs. "I wish I had them with me and a fair show at ten times our number of rioters; my men shoot well and fear very little."[10] From the epithets hurled at the anarchists and from the distorted accounts of the incident, the impression was created that Parsons and his friends had themselves flung the deadly explosive, and so it was believed by a considerable segment of the population. Indignation quickly ignited into a blind desire for vengeance. Few stopped to think of justice, no one of mercy. "Hang them first and try them afterwards!" was the prevailing sentiment, not only among the wealthy and respectable but also among workers and employees. The anarchists must be stamped out at all costs. They were radicals, they were troublemakers, they were advocates of dynamite and arson—that was sufficient for a thoroughly enraged and terrified public. Chicagoans in particular wanted blood. Hate spread to every corner of the city, and with it swelled the cry for retribution. Had the public been allowed to act on its impulse, the anarchists would have been hanged at once from the nearest lamppost. Even Charles C. Bonney, a respected Chicago attorney, held that the throwing of the bomb constituted "a waiver of trial and a plea of guilty."[11]

That a majority of anarchists were foreigners further inflamed public opinion against them. The charge that immigrants carried the seeds of social unrest had become common during the 1870s, but the Haymarket affair raised xenophobia to a new level of intensity, provoking the worst outburst of nativist sentiment in the entire post-Civil War period. "To be a German," wrote Benjamin Tucker, "is to be looked upon with suspicion, and to be a Pole or a Bohemian is to be afraid to show one's head." Journals and newspapers, bristling with contempt for foreign-sounding names and unfamiliar speech and habits, indulged in the crudest forms of immigrant-baiting and abuse. One Chicago daily mocked the accent of Michael Schwab, whom it interviewed shortly after his arrest. Was he part of a conspiracy? the reporter asked. "Gonspeeracy?" Schwab was made to reply. "You vait a vhile und I vill pring thirteen hundred peoples to brove dat dat vas a lie."[12]

In a similar spirit, the *Chicago Herald* complained of the European-born workman that "he cannot understand English," that "he calls himself by names which are very wearing on the American tongue," and that "he has a disposition to raise the devil on the slightest provocation." The "enemy forces" were not American, declared the *Chicago Times*, but "rag-tag and bob-tail cutthroats of Beelzebub from the Rhine, the Danube, the Vistula and the Elbe." Anarchists, other papers joined in, were the "scum and offal" of the Old World, "human and inhuman rubbish," the "lowest stratum found in humanity's formation," the "offscourings of Europe" who had "sought these shores to abuse the hospitality and defy the authority of the country." They did not come here "to secure that freedom of which they are deprived at their homes, but to indulge in that license which, in the places of their breeding, is forbidden them, or if indulged in is swiftly punished with rope, bullet, or axe."[13]

In the popular mind, accordingly, anarchism became identified with foreigners and subversion. It was everywhere execrated as an alien doctrine which aimed to undermine American values, and the stereotype of the anarchist as a foreign-looking, black-cloaked, bomb-wielding fanatic, dedicated to chaos and destruction, became firmly established during this period. The *Chicago Tribune* recommended that patriotism be "inculcated in the public schools" to counter anarchistic subversion. Congress was enjoined to deport the rabble-rousers and to restrict immigration so as to keep out the "foreign savages, with their dynamite bombs and anarchic purposes."[14]

The anti-radical abuse which poured from the daily press lashed the public into a frenzy. All radicals, socialists as well as anarchists, were denounced as subverters of law and order. Even such a moderate as George Schilling was reviled in the *Chicago Tribune*, which demanded that he be hanged with the others.[15] The voices of reason were few. The Chicago Liberal League, of which Fielden and other anarchists were members, hastened to disavow them. Even labor joined the hue and cry. Typographical Union No. 16, notwithstanding Parsons's membership, adopted a resolution denouncing "the heinous acts of the mob at the Haymarket" and offered a reward of $100 for the capture of the bombthrower.[16]

The Knights of Labor took a similar stand. It too ignored Parsons's longstanding affiliation. Terence V. Powderly, Grand Master Work-man of the Order, made frantic efforts to dissociate his organization from the anarchists. "Honest labor," he declared on the day after the bombing, "is not to be found in the ranks of those who march under the red flag of anarchy, which is the emblem of blood and destruction. . . . It is the duty of every organization of working men in America to condemn the outrage committed in Chicago in the name of labor."[17]

Local and state assemblies of the Order were quick to follow Pow-derly's lead. Over Schilling's objections, the Illinois Assembly passed a resolution of sympathy for the families of the dead and injured policemen. At the same time, the Michigan Assembly voted to con-demn "anarchy and revolutionary schemes" and to recognize the stars and stripes as "the only emblem of American workingmen."[18] The most vehement denunciation of the anarchists appeared in the Chicago organ of the Knights. No shriller outburst was to be found in the rantings of the conservative press:

> Let it be understood by all the world that the Knights of Labor have no affiliation, association, sympathy or respect for the band of cowardly murderers, cut-throats and robbers, known as an-archists, who sneak through the country like midnight assassins, stirring up the passions of ignorant foreigners, unfurling the red flag of anarchy and causing riot and bloodshed. Parsons, Spies, Fielding [sic], Most and all their followers, sympathizers, aiders and abettors should be summarily dealt with. They are entitled to no more consideration than wild beasts. The leaders are cowards and their followers are fools.
>
> Knights of Labor, boycott them; if one of the gang of scoundrels should by any mistake get access to our organization, expel them at once, brand them as outlawed monsters. Do not even permit yourselves to hold conversation with one of them; treat them as they deserve to be treated, as human monstrosities not entitled to the sympathy or consideration of any person in the world.
>
> We are sure we voice the sentiment of the entire organization when we say we hope that Parsons, Spies, Most, Fielding and the whole gang of outlaws will be blotted from the surface of the earth.[19]

Among the few labor papers to resist the tide of hysteria were the *Workmen's Advocate* of New Haven, *John Swinton's Paper* of New

York, the *Labor Enquirer* of Denver, and the *Labor Leaf* of Detroit, which blamed the police for the violence and upheld the right of workers to free assembly. The *Chicago Express*, a labor paper that supported the eight-hour movement, branded Inspector Bonfield as the "real author of the Haymarket slaughter."[20]

The police, in the meantime, were busy. Infuriated by the killing of their comrades and excited by the cry for revenge that was every-where being raised, they launched a reign of terror against known and suspected revolutionaries throughout the city. On the morning after the bombing, Inspector Bonfield declared: "We will take active measures to catch the leaders in this business. The action of last night will show that their bombshell and dynamite talk has not been mere vaporings."[21] That very day, under the direction of Bonfield and Captain Schaack, commander of the Chicago Avenue station on the North Side, there began a general roundup of radicals and labor activists. Meeting halls, newspaper offices, and even private homes were invaded and ransacked for evidence. In two days more than fifty gathering places of anarchists and socialists were raided and persons under the slightest suspicion of radical affiliation ar-rested, in most cases without warrant and with no specific charges lodged against them. "Make the raids first and look up the law afterward!" counseled Julius S. Grinnell, the state's attorney for Cook County, who was to prosecute the anarchists' case.[22]

The police cast their dragnet far and wide. The next few weeks saw the detention of hundreds of men and women, most of them foreigners, who were put through the "third degree" to extract in-formation and confessions. Radicals were hunted "like wolves," wrote William Holmes, himself expecting arrest at any moment. Anyone suspected of the remotest connection with the IWPA was held for interrogation. Police headquarters and local precincts bulged with radicals of every type and with men and women who merely "looked like communists," reported the *Chicago Times*, including one "be-cause he spoke of Spies as a gentleman."[23]

Detectives at the central station, in conjunction with Assistant State's Attorney Edmund Furthmann, conducted a "sweating shop" without precedent in Chicago history, employing methods, in Lucy Parsons's words, that "would put to shame the most zealous Russian blood-hound." Prisoners were beaten, sworn at, threatened, and sub-jected to "indignities that must be seen to be believed."[24] On the

221

night of May 7, police without a search warrant burst into the home of Vaclav Djemek, a member of the Bohemian Group, and rummaged through the premises, rousing the children, pulling apart the beds, and confiscating the pillowcases "because they were red." Though Djemek offered no resistance, he was roughed up on the way to the station, then locked away in a cell and refused a preliminary hearing. For many days he was alternately threatened and offered money and immunity from prosecution if he would agree to turn state's evidence. Protesting that he had nothing to say, he was kicked, cursed, and threatened with hanging. The police abused his wife when she tried to see him.[25]

Jacob Mikolanda, another Bohemian activist, was subjected to similar treatment. On May 8 police dragged him from a saloon and forced him to accompany them to his home, which they ransacked without a warrant, "not even permitting the baby's crib, with its sleeping occupant, to escape their unlawful and fruitless search," in the words of Mikolanda's affidavit.[26] Taken to the central station, Mikolanda was promised a job and money if he would testify in court as instructed by the police. When he refused, he was put behind bars for a prolonged period before being released for lack of evidence. Other anarchists were made to suffer in the same manner. Most, however, refused to cooperate and were ultimately turned loose.

For nearly eight weeks Chicago lived under what amounted to a system of martial law. Richard T. Ely, the Johns Hopkins economist, called it "the period of police terrorism" in the city.[27] All constitutional rights were set aside. Mail was intercepted and opened. Anarchist papers were suppressed and their editors arrested. Trade-union meetings were banned or dispersed, halls closed, files of organizations opened, and personal belongings confiscated—all without a shadow of legal process. On May 5 Mayor Harrison, who had previously insisted on the right of all citizens to free speech and assembly, issued a proclamation forbidding public gatherings and street processions under penalty of incarceration. The color red, the symbol of revolution, was banished from public advertising. Freedom of speech and association seemed in danger of annihilation. "Our last, lingering faith in the supremacy of 'American institutions' has been, I fear, forever shattered," wrote Lizzie Holmes in the midst of the repressions. "Real freedom of speech does not exist under the stars and stripes any more than it does under the shadows of imperial thrones in Europe."[28]

In waging their campaign of repression the police received the moral and financial support of the Chicago business community. Immediately after the bombing some three hundred citizens, including Marshall Field, Philip D. Armour, and George M. Pullman, met in secret and subscribed more than $100,000 to help stamp out anarchy and sedition. A share of the money went to the families of the officers who had been killed and wounded at the Haymarket. The remainder was put at the disposal of the police and the prosecution in the anarchist trial. It was this "blood-money," critics maintained, that secured the conviction of the defendants, for, as one Chicago anarchist put it, it encouraged witnesses for the state "to see things they otherwise never would have seen."[29] Following the trial, a comparable sum was raised every year until 1891 for the use of the police in combating subversion. Among the biggest contributors was Cyrus McCormick, Jr., whose stand against labor earned him the gratitude of business interests throughout the country.[30]

Spurred on by the business community, Inspector Bonfield and Captain Schaack redoubled their efforts to root out sedition. Schaack, a man "of restless and unregulated energy and, let us say, of small discretion," in the description of Charles Edward Russell,[31] emerged as the leading spirit of the inquisition. Schaack was a Luxemburger by birth, fluent in German as well as English. Corpulent, pompous, and inordinately vain, he "hugely enjoyed being in the limelight," remarked Sigmund Zeisler, an attorney for the defense.[32] Ambitious and "not overscrupulous," he fed the public with the most shocking tales of conspiracy and subversion. Hardly a day went by without the announcement of a dynamite plot or cache of weapons uncovered by Schaack's men. Each new "find" was assiduously played up in the press. Swiftly the police conception of a desperate conspiracy was unfolded, heightening the sense of panic among the people. The Haymarket bomb loomed as the work of a clandestine anarchist organization that had manufactured hundreds of similar bombs and drilled and armed a body of men for a murderous uprising.

It was not difficult to convince a terror-stricken population of the existence of a gigantic revolutionary conspiracy, aiming at nothing less than the complete destruction of the city. No rumor of additional outrages in the offing, no report of wholesale plotting was too fantastic to be given immediate credence by an hysterical public. It was said, for instance, that Johann Most himself was coming from New York to take charge of further assassinations and disorder.

Detectives were sent to the railroad station, but Most failed to appear. The rumor, of course, was unfounded. Most, in fact, had been indicted on April 28 for delivering an inflammatory speech. Arrested on May 11, he was tried, convicted, and sentenced to a year on Blackwell's Island, his first of three terms in that prison. "Were he in Chicago," observed the historian Max Nettlau, "he would have been hanged."[33]

Thus a vicious circle had taken shape. The terrorized city whipped the police to greater effort, while the police, in turn, kept public fear at a high pitch. "From what the papers said," wrote the novelist Robert Herrick, "you might think there was an anarchist or two skulking in every alley in Chicago with a basket of bombs under his arm."[34] Schaack did everything he could to sustain the ferment. "I have often wondered," wrote Charles Edward Russell, "whether his delusions resulted from a kind of self-hypnotism or from mere mania, but certainly he saw more anarchists than vast hell could hold. Bombs, dynamite, daggers, guns, and pistols danced ever across his excited vision; in the end there was among the foreign-born population no society or association, however innocent or even laudable, that was not to his mind engaged in deviltry. The labor unions, he knew, were composed solely of anarchists; the Turner societies met to plan treason, stratagems, and spoils; the literary guilds contrived murder; the Sunday schools taught destruction. Every man that spoke broken English and went out o'nights was a fearsome creature whose secret purpose was to blow up the Board of Trade or loot Marshall Field's store."[35]

So relentlessly did Schaack conduct his repressions that he disgusted even his superior, Police Chief Ebersold. "Captain Schaack wanted to keep things stirring," Ebersold later admitted. "He wanted bombs to be found here, there, all around, everywhere." And after the anarchist groups had been broken up, he wanted to send out agents to organize new ones, in order to "keep himself prominent before the public." Ebersold refused to authorize the venture. Reviewing the situation, he arrived at the conclusion that "there was perhaps not so much to all this anarchist business as they claimed, and I believe I was right."[36]

But the repressions were taking their toll. On May 5, the day after the bombing, Spies, Schwab, and Fischer arrived at work at their customary hour in the office of the *Arbeiter-Zeitung*. About 9 A.M.

a group of detectives appeared, headed by James Bonfield, a younger brother of the inspector. Detective Bonfield, by his own admission, searched Spies without legal authority. "I took Spies's keys out of his pocket, everything I found, little slips of paper, etc.," said Bonfield. "I literally went through him. I had no warrant for anything of that kind." The detectives arrested Spies and Schwab, as well as Spies's brother Christ, who had come to the office to find out what had happened at the Haymarket. "The fact that his name was Spies," remarked his brother with his customary sarcasm, "sufficed to arrest him and charge him with having committed murder."[37]

Schwab had been at the Haymarket, but had left before the meeting began. Having taken a call at the *Arbeiter-Zeitung*, asking Spies to speak at the Deering Reaper Works, a factory on the far North-West Side, he had gone to the Haymarket to deliver the message. But Spies had not yet arrived, and Schwab, after waiting a few minutes, went himself to Deering's to speak in his place. He was there when the explosion occurred, returning home about 11 P.M. The next morning he read about the incident in the papers and hurried to the *Arbeiter-Zeitung*, where he was placed under arrest. Lucy Parsons and Lizzie Holmes were also in the office, working on the next issue of *The Alarm*, but for the moment they were left unmolested. Albert Parsons was nowhere to be found.

Schwab, Spies, and Spies's brother were taken to the central police station at city hall. There, according to Schwab, they were greeted by Superintendent Ebersold with "choice words from the dictionary of police politeness, dogs, curs, scoundrels, etc." Detective Bonfield later confirmed this. Ebersold, he said, was highly excited "and talked to Spies and Schwab in German and made motions, and I got between them, and I told him this was not the time or place to act that way. I took the liberty to quiet him down a little. He used a word which I understood to compare a man to a dog or something lower."[38]

Word of the arrests spread quickly through the city. Oscar Neebe was peddling his yeast on the South Side when he heard the news. He had not been present at the Haymarket and knew nothing of what had taken place. After finishing his rounds, he stopped at the *Arbeiter-Zeitung* to inquire about his comrades. He was there only a few minutes when the police returned, accompanied by Mayor Harrison and State's Attorney Grinnell. The mayor demanded to know who was in charge. Neebe asked him what was the matter. "I want to have this thing stopped," said Harrison. "There won't be any more inflammable articles allowed in this paper." Neebe promised to read everything in the day's issue and to see that nothing incendiary was included. The mayor appeared satisfied, and he and his retinue left.

Shortly afterwards, however, yet another group of officers arrived. Someone had decided to shut down the enterprise and arrest everyone connected with it. The premises were searched without a warrant; every drawer and closet, every chest and box was broken into and cleaned out. Spies's locked desk was broken open and emptied of its contents. Copies of the "Revenge Circular" were found, as well as of the circular summoning the Haymarket meeting. Together with these documents the police seized Spies's manuscript of the "Revenge Circular," his note with the word "Ruhe," and the manuscript of "Y—Come Monday Night." In addition, some of Schwab's manuscripts were taken, along with galley proofs of the *Arbeiter-Zeitung*, letters to Spies, including some from Most, and a large quantity of flags and banners used at demonstrations of the International.

When the police entered, Lucy Parsons and Lizzie Holmes were seated at a desk writing. "What are you doing there?" said a detective to Lizzie Holmes. "I am corresponding with my brother," she replied. "He is the editor of a labor paper." The detective placed her under arrest. She protested, and he said, "Shut up, you bitch, or I'll knock you down." When Lucy attempted to intervene another detective called her a "black bitch" and threatened to knock her down also. Lizzie was taken to police headquarters and held incommunicado for four days. After her release she returned home to Geneva to join her husband, who had himself managed to avoid arrest. Their house, in the meantime, had been raided, their desks broken open, and their mail intercepted and read, all without proper warrant. In addition, they were denounced in the local papers as "rioters," "bombthrowers," and "murderers." Lizzie bitterly remarked: "I have written my honest thoughts, given to the world the best ideas I could in a simple way garner, and did what seemed to me the best in my power for human freedom. I have never seen or handled dynamite, never possessed arms, and never have been able to kill anything bigger than a mosquito in my life. Yet I am liable to re-arrest any day." This is "practically Russia now," wrote her husband to H. H. Sparling, secretary of the Socialist League in London, "and to be known as a Socialist is to be a marked man or woman."[39]

Apart from Lizzie Holmes, the entire staff of the *Arbeiter-Zeitung*, from printer's devil to foreman, was taken in charge. Among them were Fischer, supervisor of the composing room, Gerhard Lizius, who had recently moved from Indianapolis to become city editor, and Hermann Pudewa, the compositor who had inserted the word "Revenge" in Spies's circular. Lucy Parsons, however, was not arrested, although the police, she said, "questioned me insolently, accusingly."[40] Setting her loose, the authorities hoped she would lead them to her missing husband. Accordingly, she was followed wherever she went. About 4:30 that afternoon, when she entered the house of a friend on West Lake Street, detectives burst in and searched the premises, but Parsons was not there. Lucy was briefly taken into custody. "You still wear the red ribbon, do you?" said Detective Palmer when he saw the red handkerchief around her neck. "Yes," was her defiant reply, "and I'll wear it until I die."[41]

Later the same day Lucy was again briefly arrested, along with her friend Sarah Ames. After her release, she was kept under continuous surveillance. Every house she visited became an object of suspicion and was watched around the clock. For the next six weeks this cat-and-mouse game persisted. Lucy was arrested four times during this interval and "subjected to indignities that should bring the tinge of shame to the calloused cheek of a hardened barbarian," she remarked. On one occasion the police raided her home, ransacked its contents, tore open mattresses, and threatened six-year-old Albert Jr., wrapping him in a rug and spinning him around on the floor. "Where's your daddy?" they demanded. "We're going to string him up when we get him!"[42]

When the police returned to close down the *Arbeiter-Zeitung*, Neebe was still in the office. He was questioned but not arrested. While not a member of the paper's staff, he did everything he could to get it back into operation. The paper did not appear on May 5 or 6. On the 7th, however, a leaflet was issued appealing to the workers of Chicago to continue their support.[43] Before the month was out, the *Arbeiter-Zeitung* succeeded in obtaining a new editor in the person of Albert Currlin, an active Internationalist from St. Louis. Moving its offices to 274 West 12th Street, the paper resumed publication, along with the *Vorbote* and *Fackel*. The *Alarm*, however, also suppressed on May 5, was not revived until November 6, 1887, five days before the executions. *Budoucnost*, the Czech organ of the

International, and *Der Anarchist* of Engel and Fischer were shut down and never reappeared.

Fischer, as has been noted, was arrested on May 5 with the staff of the *Arbeiter-Zeitung*. He had, unlike Schwab and Neebe, attended the Haymarket meeting, but was at Zepf's Hall when the bomb was thrown. The following morning he bought a newspaper on his way to work and read the details of the tragedy. It was about half past ten when he was arrested. Searched, he was found to be carrying a revolver and wearing a belt with "L. & W.V." on the buckle and containing a dagger. When these weapons were discovered the police became so excited, Fischer afterwards recalled, that "it is still a matter of wonder to me that I was not assassinated on the spot." One detective, Reuben Slayton, pointed the revolver at his head and another was about to drive the dagger into him when a lieutenant ordered them to stop.[44]

Fischer was taken to the central station and subjected to prolonged interrogation. After a few days he was ushered into an office and confronted by a large group of men, including State's Attorney Grinnell, Assistant State's Attorney Furthmann, and Lieutenants John Shea and Joseph Kipley, chiefs of the detective squad. Furthmann asked him who threw the bomb. Fischer said he did not know.

FURTHMANN: Spies told us, however, that he had commissioned you to throw one.

FISCHER: If Spies has really told you that, then he has lied. Either you lie or Spies does. That Spies has told an untruth I do not believe. Therefore you are the liar.

FURTHMANN (springing from his seat): What! How! You despicable fellow![45]

Between his arrest and the trial Fischer was questioned again and again. More than once he was offered immunity from prosecution if he would turn state's evidence. Fischer, however, refused. One time, according to Fischer, the following exchange took place:

GRINNELL: Then you persist in your obstinacy?

FISCHER: O, leave me alone.

GRINNELL: You are a coward.

FISCHER: Why?

GRINNELL: Because you won't tell the truth. A brave man does not lie.

FISCHER: Is that so? Then you must be the greatest coward in the world, for you are a lawyer, which signifies a liar by profession. I'll tell you one thing, if you spoke to me like this if I were outside I'd soon show you, hands up, if I am a coward or not.[46]

Fischer's comrades, meanwhile, were undergoing similar treatment. Fielden, one of the speakers at the Haymarket meeting, was arrested at his home the next morning. He had made no attempt to flee. Rising early, he went for a walk around the block, then came home and waited for the police. He was sitting in his room when Detective Slayton arrived with a group of officers and arrested him without a warrant. While Slayton took him out to the street, the officers went through his house, turning it upside down, but found nothing incriminating. Afterwards, when Fielden was in jail, the police came back and searched again, without presenting a warrant to his wife.[47]

Taken to the central station, Fielden was conducted to a room in which Lieutenant Shea was seated on a table, surrounded by detectives. "You___Dutchman," said the lieutenant, "before you came to this country, people were getting good wages." Fielden protested, only to be cursed some more, then taken to the lockup in the basement. On the way downstairs he was met by Police Chief Ebersold, who, having been told that Fielden was wounded, ordered him to take off the bandage and show him. Fielden complied. "Damn your soul," said Ebersold, "it ought to have gone in here," pointing to Fielden's forehead between the eyes. Afterwards, when Fielden asked for someone to dress his wound, a detective told him that they "ought to put strychnine in it."[48]

In addition to Fielden, a dozen members of the American Group were taken into custody and held for varying periods, ranging from a few days to many months. On May 6 William Snyder left a note under Lucy Parsons's door, which was found by the police. He was thereupon arrested and confined until shortly before the trial, which opened in late June. Thomas Brown, who happened to be with Snyder when the detectives came to arrest him, was also taken in, and both men were subjected to intense questioning and pressured in vain to testify against their comrades. John Henry, a printer, was arrested on May 18 while distributing a leaflet demanding the restoration of free speech. Henry's wife intervened, insisting that he was insane, and secured his release by promising to take him out of Chicago.[49]

Several Germans prominent in the movement were arrested but not brought to trial. Among them was Anton Hirschberger, a native of Bavaria, who worked as a compositor for the *Arbeiter-Zeitung*, although he was not on duty when the raids of May 5 took place. A secretary of the Bureau of Information and a member of the General Committee, he had attended the Haymarket meeting and narrowly escaped injury when a bullet passed through his coat.[50] Arrested at his home, he was detained for several weeks before being released. Why he was not tried with the others is not apparent.

The same might be said of Balthasar Rau, advertising agent of the *Arbeiter-Zeitung* and an intimate of Spies. One recalls that it was Rau who accompanied Spies to the meeting near McCormick's, who handed Spies the message "Y—Come Monday Night," who explained to Spies the meaning of "Ruhe," and whom Spies sent to summon Parsons to the Haymarket. Rau, like Hirschberger, was a secretary of the Bureau of Information and a member of the General Committee. He was also a member of the North Side Group, together with Neebe, Schwab, and Lingg. Rau fled Chicago immediately after the explosion. Pursued by Edmund Furthmann, he was captured in Omaha and brought back on charges of murder. Yet he was never tried, apparently because he cooperated with the police during his interrogation.

It remains to describe the arrest of Neebe, Engel, and Lingg. Neebe, it may be recalled, was discharged after questioning on May 5. The police, however, became interested in him as their case against the anarchists developed. On May 9, while he was at work, officers searched his house, where they found a .38-caliber revolver, a sword, a breech-loading rifle, and a red flag, all of which were seized as evidence. According to Neebe's wife, the police returned to their wagon and "waved the red flag and hollered and hurrahed just like a lot of wild Indians." Neebe was not arrested, however, until May 27. The case against him being weak, he was released on bail and, as Dyer Lum remarked, "not having a knowledge of the future—remained!"[51]

On the evening of the Haymarket meeting, George Engel was at home playing cards with friends when Gottfried Waller came in and told them what had happened. Waller, greatly agitated, said that 300 men had been shot by the police, and urged that "we ought to go down there and do something." Engel tried to calm him down. Whoever threw the bomb had done a foolish thing, he said. He did

230

not sympathize with wanton butchery; in any case, the revolution must come from the masses, not from a single individual.[52] On May 6, despite his alibi, Engel was arrested at his home. With him the police brought in "a queer-shaped portable furnace, made of galvanized iron," as the *Chicago Times* described it the following day.[53] About six months earlier, Engel told Superintendent Ebersold, a stranger had left the device with his wife, saying that it was an apparatus for the manufacture of dynamite and that he would call for it in a few days. The stranger, however, never returned. This story seems highly improbable. Indeed, Engel himself later changed it, insisting that the furnace was intended for use in metal work and had nothing to do with making explosives. It was shown, in any case, never to have been used.[54]

Notwithstanding the peculiar "blasting machine," as the police afterwards labeled it, Engel was set free on the good word of Coroner Herz, who attested to having known him for years as "a quiet and well-behaved citizen."[55] Twelve days later, however, Engel disappeared. Unbeknownst to his family and friends, he had been taken into custody. For a week they remained ignorant of his whereabouts. No information could be obtained from the police. Day after day his teenage daughter Mary visited the Chicago Avenue station, where he was rumored to have been locked up on Captain Schaack's orders, but to no avail. Meanwhile the "sweat-box" was brought into play in a vain effort to break Engel's spirit. On the eighth day, Mary again went to the station and insisted on knowing the truth. While there, she heard a voice singing the "Marseillaise" in one of the lower cells. She recognized it as her father's and, raising a fuss, was allowed to see him.[56]

Of the numerous anarchists who were arrested, none offered resistance save one: Louis Lingg. Lingg, it may be recalled, had been boarding at the home of his comrade William Seliger, at 442 Sedgwick Street on the North Side. Although he did not attend the Haymarket meeting, he had spent the afternoon of May 4 making bombs. Seliger and three others helped. All told, they made between thirty and fifty bombs. In the evening, Lingg and Seliger placed the bombs in a small trunk and, assisted by another comrade, carried it to Neff's Hall at 58 Clybourn Avenue, a meeting place of both the North Side Group (of which Lingg and Seliger were members) and the Lehr-und-Wehr Verein, for whom its contents were apparently intended. On the way home, according to Seliger, he and Lingg passed the Larrabee

231

Street police station, and Lingg, becoming excited, said it would be a good thing to blow it up. The men, however, proceeded on their way, arriving home after 11 P.M.

On Thursday, May 6, the police, in the course of their general roundup, went to Seliger's house and inquired after Lingg. Lingg was not at home. Seliger said that he had not seen him since the previous morning and did not know where he was. Seliger himself was thereupon arrested and the house searched. In Lingg's trunk were found a bomb, a pistol, and a quantity of anarchist literature. An alarm went out for his arrest.

Lingg had meanwhile found sanctuary at 80 Ambrose Street on the South-West Side. To change his appearance, he cropped his hair and shaved off his mustache and whiskers. But the police, apparently through informers, got word of his hiding place. On the morning of May 14 a detail was sent to carry out his arrest. The officer in charge was Hermann Schuettler, a rising young detective with a reputation for physical prowess. Yet Schuettler admitted to reporters that he had never before faced such a struggle as in his capture of Lingg.[57]

Schuettler gained entry by a simple ruse. To the woman who answered the door he identified himself as Franz Lorenz, a carpenter acquainted with Lingg. Once inside, he quickly found his way to Lingg's room and opened the door. Lingg was seated at a table, writing. Instantly recognizing his visitor as an officer, he grabbed a revolver which lay on the table. Schuettler sprang on him before he could fire. Both men were strongly built, and they grappled fiercely with each other, rolling on the floor, first one on top and then the other, until Lingg grasped the officer by the throat. Schuettler was choking when he got Lingg's thumb in his mouth and almost bit it off. In spite of the pain, Lingg hung on, and in a moment Schuettler would have been unconscious. But the landlady began to scream, and Schuettler's assistant, Officer Jacob Loewenstein, rushed in and struck Lingg on the head with his club, stunning him. Lingg was overpowered and placed in handcuffs. A knife was found strapped to his waist. He was taken to the Chicago Avenue station to be questioned by Captain Schaack.[58]

Meanwhile the legal process had been taking its course. On May 5 a coroner's inquest was held over the body of Officer Degan, the first policeman to die from his wounds. It found that death had been caused by "a piece of bomb, thrown by an unknown person, aided, and abetted, and encouraged by August Spies, Christ Spies, Michael Schwab, A. R. Parsons, Samuel Fielden, and other unknown persons." The inquest, setting the pattern for the proceedings to follow, recommended that the individuals named should be held without bail to the grand jury on charges of murder.[59]

During the next few weeks six more policemen succumbed to their wounds, and this served to keep the public in a state of indignation against the anarchists. The press called for a swift trial, with speedy executions to follow. No more pussyfooting, exclaimed the *Chicago Times*. No more coddling of vicious criminals.

> Public justice demands that the European assassins, August Spies, Christopher [*sic*] Spies, Michael Schwab, and Sam Fielden, shall be held, tried, and hanged for murder. Public justice demands that the assassin A. R. Parsons, who is said to disgrace this country by having been born in it, shall be seized, tried, and hanged for murder. Public justice demands that the negro woman who passes as the wife of the assassin Parsons, and has been his assistant in the work of organized assassination, shall be seized, tried, and hanged for murder. Public justice demands that every ringleader of the association of assassins called Socialists, Central Union of workingmen, or by whatever name, shall be arrested, convicted, and hanged as a participant murderer. Public justice demands that every assembly-room of the European assassins composing the society or following the red flag shall be immediately and permanently closed, and that no gathering of those criminal conspirators and public enemies shall hereafter be permitted in Chicago. Public justice demands that every organization, society, or combination of the assassins calling themselves Socialists, or preaching the criminal doctrines of the red flag under any name, shall be absolutely and permanently suppressed. Public justice demands that no citizen shall employ or keep in his service any person who is a member of such unlawful organization or association of conspirators and assassins.[60]

On May 17 a grand jury was empaneled in the case. It sat under Judge John G. Rogers, a "dignified, elderly gentleman of excellent reputation," as Sigmund Zeisler describes him.[61] In his instructions to the jury, however, Judge Rogers exhibited a strong bias against radicals, maintaining, for instance, that the red flag constituted a provocation and ought not be permitted in street processions. Judge

Rogers, furthermore, instructed the panel to look not only to the man who actually threw the bomb but also to those who stood behind him, who advised or incited him. This advice implied the existence of a conspiracy, which had yet to be established.

On May 18 the grand jury began the examination of witnesses, Judge Rogers having charged it that "anarchism should be suppressed."[62] Among the members of the jury was the banker E. S. Dreyer, whom Spies had accused of corruption in the *Arbeiter-Zeitung*. Spies protested that Dreyer might therefore be biased against him, but to no avail. Lingg, who appeared in ragged clothing, one sleeve of his jacket torn from wrist to elbow, the result of his scuffle with Detective Schuettler, refused to answer questions.

The most defiant witness, however, was Gerhard Lizius. When asked if he appreciated the solemnity of an oath, reported a Chicago newspaper the following day, "he said he gave it all the appreciation it was worth—which was none." Lizius went on to declare that he did not believe in God and that, with reference to the Haymarket meeting, "the only mistake the Anarchists made was in not using enough bombs." "Do you believe," asked State's Attorney Grinnell, "that the man who threw the bomb over there did right?" "Yes, sir," Lizius replied. "And that it was a righteous act in shooting down the policemen?" "Yes, sir," repeated Lizius, calling it an act of self-defense. "The jury," noted a reporter, "looked upon him as a fanatic, and as he is evidently in the last stages of consumption it is not probable that he will be arrested." This prediction proved correct. Lizius was never brought to trial.[63]

On May 27 the grand jury returned indictments against Albert Parsons, August Spies, Michael Schwab, Samuel Fielden, George Engel, Adolph Fischer, Oscar Neebe, Louis Lingg, William Seliger, and Rudolph Schnaubelt, who were charged with the murder of Officer Degan. In addition, they, along with twenty-one others, were indicted for conspiracy, riot, and unlawful assembly. The indictment of Neebe came as a surprise. Some believed, though no proof was brought forward, that the brewery owners, whose workmen he had organized, had demanded the indictment to get him out of the way.[64]

Yet another feature of the indictments might also have elicited surprise. Since five additional policemen had by now succumbed to their wounds, why were the accused cited only for the murder of Degan? Would not a charge of six murders have strengthened the case for the prosecution and more easily have secured conviction?

No explanation was forthcoming, though the reason, it would appear, was that Degan's death alone had unquestionably been caused by the bomb, and that some if not all of his comrades had fallen victim to the bullets of their fellow policemen, a fact which the state's attorney was not eager to bring to light.

On June 5 the grand jury issued its report to Judge Rogers. It found that the bombthrowing was the result of a "deliberate conspiracy," and that the conspirators were in most cases connected with *The Alarm* and *Arbeiter-Zeitung*. In its concluding remarks, the jury acknowledged a debt to "the officers and men of the police force of Chicago. By their heroic bravery and their conscientious devotion to duty we believe that they have saved this city from a scene of bloodshed and devastation equal to, or perhaps greater than that witnessed by the Commune of Paris."[65]

Of the ten men indicted for Degan's murder, William Seliger avoided prosecution by turning state's evidence, while Rudolph Schnaubelt, about whom more will be said in a moment, fled the city and was never apprehended. The remaining eight were the backbone of the local anarchist movement—its most effective organizers, the editors of its journals, its ablest speakers and writers. The police had long been awaiting an opportunity to silence them.[66]

Where did Rudolph Schnaubelt fit into this company? Until now he has not figured even briefly in our story. Yet when the indictments were handed down he was included among the alleged ringleaders—indeed, was charged with being the actual bombthrower. For the first time the perpetrator had been given a name. Who then was Schnaubelt, and what was his connection with the Haymarket?

Schnaubelt was a machinist by occupation, the brother-in-law of Michael Schwab and a fellow member of the North Side Group. Born in Bohemia in 1863, the son of a forester, he had lived in Vienna before emigrating to the United States in 1884. Already an anarchist when he arrived in Chicago, he at once joined the IWPA, in which the entire Schnaubelt clan played a conspicuous role, including his brother Edward, a distributor of *Freiheit* in Chicago, another brother Henry, who distributed *The Alarm* in San Francisco, his sisters Ida and Maria (the wife of Michael Schwab), and perhaps even his mother Rebecca.[67]

Besides joining the North Side Group, in which he developed a reputation for revolutionary militancy, Schnaubelt took part in mass meetings and demonstrations and donated money to *The Alarm* as well as to the *Arbeiter-Zeitung* and other German papers of the International.[68] A big, powerfully built young man, Schnaubelt was six feet two or three inches tall, had sandy hair and whiskers, and weighed more than two hundred pounds. He attended the Haymarket meeting and was reported to have been seated on the speakers' wagon shortly before the bomb exploded. According to some accounts, he had also attended the Monday night meeting at Greif's Hall, but the evidence for this is uncertain.

Schnaubelt was at work on May 5, the day after the explosion, when he learned that his brother-in-law had been arrested. He went at once to police headquarters to try to bail him out. His efforts, however, were unsuccessful, and he sought the advice of Sigmund Zeisler, attorney for the Central Labor Union and a future defense counsel at the Haymarket trial. Zeisler remembered his visitor as a tall, strapping fellow with a full blond beard and mustache. Speaking in German—he knew little English, having been in the country only two years—Schnaubelt told him that, while Schwab and Spies talked and wrote a lot of incendiary stuff, neither had "the courage to handle a bomb." The police, whom Schnaubelt referred to as "beasts" and "bloodhounds," had come to the Haymarket "to precipitate a row," so that the bombthrowing "served them right."[69]

Two days later Schnaubelt was arrested. The police, having been informed by Schnaubelt himself that he was Schwab's brother-in-law, afterwards learned that he had been seen on the speakers' wagon during the Haymarket meeting. Detective Palmer was sent to the machine shop at 224 East Washington Street, where Schnaubelt had been employed for several weeks, and placed him under arrest. Schnaubelt no longer had his beard, and his mustache was closely trimmed. Questioned by Lieutenant Shea at the central station, he admitted that he had been on the speakers' wagon Tuesday night, but insisted that he had left the meeting before the bomb was thrown. According to Schnaubelt's statement, he could see from his position on the wagon the police leave the Desplaines Street station and form their ranks. Just after the line passed Randolph Street, he slipped off the wagon, elbowed his way out of the crowd, and "put as much distance between himself and the scene of the meeting as he could."[70] Two of Schnaubelt's comrades who were with him during the meeting later testified that he had left around 10 P.M., some twenty minutes before the police arrived, because there were no German speakers and he could not follow the speeches in English. But, according to Detective Palmer, Schnaubelt told him that he departed barely half a minute before the bomb was thrown and was only fifty feet from the wagon when the explosion occurred.[71] This discrepancy has never been resolved, but Schnaubelt himself later repeated that he had left the wagon "when the police came to break up the meeting."[72]

Schnaubelt's account of his movements apparently satisfied his interrogators, for he was shortly allowed to go. After his release, he went again to the office of Sigmund Zeisler, who did not at first recognize him, as he was no longer wearing a beard. He told Zeisler how he had been arrested and "quizzed and sweated" by the police. "I don't see that I can do any good to my friends here," he said before taking his leave, "and the way things are going I believe it would be better for me to get out of Chicago for a time." Zeisler never saw him again.[73]

After leaving Zeisler's office, Schnaubelt returned to his place of work. That evening, however, he informed his boss, Fred P. Rosbeck, that he might not be back the next day, as he feared another visit from the police. He never returned to the shop. His tools and work clothes remained there, along with his unpaid wages, until a friend picked them up a week later. Rosbeck, when questioned by the police, stated that Schnaubelt had been in his employ for about five weeks previous to the Haymarket incident. He was a good machinist, said Rosbeck, although a pronounced anarchist who tried to convert the other workers to his ideas.[74]

Schnaubelt had meanwhile fled Chicago and was nowhere to be found. Various rumors circulated regarding his whereabouts. According to one account, he had made his way to California and lived quietly with his brother Henry before moving to Portland, Oregon, then sailing around the world to Europe.[75] This story acquired a certain credence when Chief Ebersold received a pseudonymous letter from Portland, believed to be in Schnaubelt's hand, taunting him with arresting the wrong men and allowing the real perpetrators, namely the writer and his confederates, to escape. The writer accused the police of seeking glory by invading the Haymarket, so we decided to "give them something to remember." Our act, the letter continued, has demonstrated that there are still "a few determined men willing to risk their lives for their ideas." "See you at the next carnival," it concluded.[76]

The letter turned out to be a false lead. Schnaubelt had nothing to do with it, and the identity of the author, who was never apprehended, remains a mystery. Not long afterwards, the body of a man, said to match Schnaubelt's description, was found in a canal at Erie, Pennsylvania, and it was suggested that, having left Chicago as a stowaway on a boat, he had drowned while trying to come ashore. The body, however, turned out not to be Schnaubelt's. Then, in August 1886, a conductor on the Mexican Central Railroad sent word to Chief Ebersold that he had identified the fugitive in the person of a jeweler in Mexico City, but this too proved to be erroneous.[77]

What had actually become of Schnaubelt? After his arrest on May 7 he had given up any thought of remaining in Chicago. "I knew only too well the hatred and rascality of these 'heroes of order' to be able to foresee that nothing would deter them from satisfying their blood lust," he wrote afterwards. "The farce of the trial had proven how right I was."[78] Leaving Chicago that very night, he stayed on a farm outside the city before heading for the Canadian border, which he crossed on foot. After wandering in the woods, he was given food and shelter by friendly Indians. Soon afterwards he found work on a farm in Quebec, earning enough for his passage to England.

Schnaubelt arrived in England in late September or early October 1886. He inquired after Josef Peukert, whom he had met in Vienna before emigrating to the United States. Peukert, a leader of the autonomist wing of the movement, now resided in London, where he published a weekly paper, *Die Autonomie*. According to Peukert's account, two associates told him that a "mysterious stranger" had come to their club and asked to speak to him. The stranger, of course, was Schnaubelt, who was seeking his help. Peukert found him a room with a comrade at Primrose Hill and also got him work as a machinist. For the next few weeks he visited Schnaubelt often, bringing him mail from Austria and America. Schnaubelt was lonely and restless. He feared capture at any moment. To throw pursuers off his scent, he published a letter in *Die Autonomie* and headed it Christiania (Oslo) instead of London. Reading the letter in his Chicago cell, Schwab, who knew his brother-in-law's true whereabouts and was apparently misled by the dateline, declared it a forgery. Schnaubelt, increasingly fearful of his safety, decided to leave the country. On the advice of the well-known Italian anarchist Errico Malatesta, who was then living in Argentina, Schnaubelt's comrades bought him a ticket on a steamer bound for Buenos Aires. He embarked, under an assumed name, in May 1887. Soon afterwards, he sent Peukert a second letter for publication in *Die Autonomie*. Again headed Christiania, it appeared on June 18. It was the last public message from Schnaubelt's pen.[79]

Schnaubelt passed the remainder of his life in anonymity. Never apprehended, he was the only one of the indicted men to get away. Because of his disappearance, however, the odium of having thrown the Haymarket bomb became inseparably attached to his name. To this day, one hundred years after, there are those who are convinced of his guilt. The basis for such a belief will be examined in a later chapter. Meanwhile, a more important figure in our story remains to be accounted for.

16 ‖ THE FUGITIVE

On May 6, 1886, two days after the Haymarket incident, the *Chicago Times* commended the police for the swift arrest of Spies, Schwab, Fielden, and their fellow leaders of the International Working People's Association. "But one other man comprising this galaxy of blood-preaching anarchists is at large," the paper complained. "This fiend, who for months past has advocated the torch and dagger, the husband of a negress, and a most arrant coward withal, is named A. R. Parsons." Parsons had disappeared on the night of the explosion. The following morning, when the police raided the offices of *The Alarm* and *Arbeiter-Zeitung*, he was nowhere to be found. An intensive search of Chicago and the surrounding country was at once instituted, and a $5,000 reward offered for his apprehension. Newspapers reported him as being in Ohio, Pennsylvania, Missouri, Kansas, Arkansas, Florida, and even Cuba. He was said to have been recognized in Texas and heading for safety in Mexico. "BEAST PARSONS," shrieked the *Waco Daily Examiner* after its old adversary. "Miscegenationist, Murderer, Moral Outlaw, for Whom the Gallows Wait."[1]

What had become of Parsons? Detectives followed every clue, visited his known haunts, but were unable to find him. He had last been seen in public at the Haymarket meeting, in company with his family and Lizzie Holmes. When rain threatened, they had gone to Zepf's saloon, a half-block away, to wait for the meeting to adjourn. Parsons had been in the hall about five minutes and was looking out the window towards the meeting, expecting it to end at any moment, when he saw a "white sheet of light," followed instantly by a deafening roar. A volley of shots rang out. Bullets hit the front of the saloon. "What is it?" cried Lizzie Holmes. "I don't know," said Parsons. "Maybe the Illinois regiments have brought up their Gatling gun." Bullets whistled past them through the open door. Men rushed in seeking shelter. The doors of the saloon were quickly locked, and Parsons and the rest took sanctuary in a room at the rear.[2]

For fifteen or twenty minutes they were shut up in total darkness, ignorant of what was happening outside. Finally they opened the doors and ventured into the street. Everything was quiet. No policemen were in sight. Together with Thomas Brown, a fellow member of the American Group, they started up Desplaines Street on the way home. Lizzie Holmes, however, suggested that Parsons should leave the city for a few days. He was a marked man. His life might be in danger. Parsons hesitated, but Mrs. Holmes managed to convince him. He would take the midnight train to Geneva, where she lived with her husband, and remain there until matters became clarified. Parsons, having little money with him, borrowed a five-dollar gold piece from Brown. Then, on the Desplaines Street viaduct, the group separated, Brown going one way, Lucy and the children another, and Parsons and Lizzie Holmes towards the depot of the Chicago & Northwestern Railroad. Just before turning to leave, Parsons said to his wife: "Kiss me, Lucy. We do not know when we will meet again." There seemed a "sad, almost prophetic, tone in his voice," Lizzie Holmes later recalled.[3]

After walking Parsons to the depot, Lizzie purchased a ticket for Turner Junction (now West Chicago), the nearest point to Geneva that he could reach at night. Parsons's mood was quiet, subdued. Again he asked Lizzie if she really thought it best for him to go. She replied in the affirmative. Before he boarded the train, he made her take part of the change from the ticket to give to his wife and children. He shook her hand warmly, and the train began to move.

Parsons left the train at Turner Junction and stayed in a hotel until morning. He then proceeded to Geneva, arriving about 9:30 A.M. William Holmes was reading the morning papers, filled with accounts of the Haymarket catastrophe, when Parsons reached his house. Deeply absorbed in the news, Holmes did not hear the door open. "Good morning! How do you do?" said the familiar voice. Holmes sprang to his feet and grasped Parsons's outstretched hand. For a few moments the friends stood clasped in an embrace. Finally Holmes said, "You are a fugitive." Parsons nodded. Then, recalls Holmes, came "the recital of the terrible events of the Haymarket meeting; the rush of the invading bluecoats; the throwing of the bomb; the fusillade of pistol shots; and the midnight ride to my Geneva home."[4]

Holmes and his guest spent most of the morning discussing the events of the previous night. Shortly after noon, Holmes went to the village to learn what he could of the situation in Chicago. Wild rumors abounded: The city had been set ablaze and was already half consumed; the anarchists had destroyed city hall; anarchists and socialists were being massacred. Everywhere Holmes went he was met with scowls and looks of disapproval, for his radical connections were well known. Even those who had been his friends avoided him or muttered curses against the anarchists. Holmes hastened back and told Parsons what he had seen and heard. Parsons had meantime been busy writing an editorial for the next issue of *The Alarm*—an issue that would never appear. It denounced the unprovoked invasion of the Haymarket meeting by Inspector Bonfield and his "uniformed ruffians." Parsons did not dream, nor did Holmes, that both *The Alarm* and *Arbeiter-Zeitung* had already been suppressed and their staffs (including Mrs. Holmes) arrested.

The rumors of the massacre and destruction convinced Parsons that the social revolution had begun. His first impulse was to rush back to Chicago and join his comrades on the barricades. He wanted, says Holmes, to be "on the field of action, and in the thickest of the fray." Ten years later Holmes could vividly recall "the pale set face, the flashing eyes and the impatient gestures" of his comrade as he pleaded the necessity of his immediate return to take part in the long-awaited insurrection.[5]

In the middle of the afternoon Holmes went again to the village in quest of information. The first man he encountered told him that a terrible conflict had taken place between the police and the workers, that more than a score of dynamite bombs had been thrown, destroying much property and many lives. In the excitement of the moment Holmes fully believed the report to be true. By a great effort, however, he succeeded in calming himself before reaching home. He told Parsons that there was as yet no reliable news, suppressing any mention of his informant's story. Holmes thought it prudent to wait for the next morning's papers before taking any action. If the worst should prove to be true, he reasoned, nothing would be lost but a few hours' delay, while the time spent in waiting might be used in constructing an appropriate plan.

It was far from easy, however, to persuade Parsons to go along. "Like the true revolutionist he was," remarks Holmes, "he longed for the final conflict, and was ready to face any danger, to do any deed of daring, in order to strengthen the side of the right. He fully expected soon to fight and die for the cause he loved so dearly. He chafed and grew impatient at what seemed to him unnecessary delay." By evening, however, Parsons had been won over. It was mutually agreed that, if the morning's news confirmed the current rumors, they would both immediately return to the city.[6]

The next day, as early as possible, Holmes procured copies of the morning papers. For the first time he and Parsons learned the true state of affairs in Chicago, "of the arrest of our comrades, of the search for Parsons, of the demand for victims to appease capitalistic hate."[7] Their first concern now was for Parsons's safety. With Lizzie Holmes in custody, it was imperative that a more secure retreat be found, for surely it was only a matter of time before the police would be searching her home. Parsons, as it happens, had already been seen, though not recognized, by one of Holmes's neighbors. Early that morning, while Holmes was working in his garden, Parsons had surprised him by boldly walking out of the house and insisting on helping him with his work. While they were thus engaged, the occupant of the next house came to his back door and accosted them, making some remark about the weather.[8]

Nothing resulted from this encounter. But the evening papers announced that detectives were already scouring the country in every direction in an effort to run Parsons to earth. To delay any longer was dangerous. Holmes suggested that Parsons head for Kansas, where he had lectured on several occasions. Parsons, however, decided upon Waukesha, Wisconsin, a resort twenty miles west of Milwaukee, where he knew a man who might protect him.

Before making his departure, Parsons wrote a letter to Melville E. Stone, editor of the *Chicago Daily News*. "Dear Sir," it began, "I want to speak a word through you to my fellow workers, just to let them know that I am still in the land of the living and looking out for their interests." Parsons was in a defiant mood. "I will in due time turn up and answer for myself and for anything I may have said or done," he wrote, "but I have no regrets for past conduct and no pledges for the future if there is to be nothing but blood and death for the toilers of America. Whenever the public decide to use reason and justice in dealing with the producing class, just at that time you will see me. But, should the decision be to continue the present course of death and slavery, just so long will I wage relentless war on all organized force, and all endeavor to find me will be fruitless."

It was useless, said Parsons, to watch his wife and friends in the hope of discovering his whereabouts. "I am dead to them already. I count my life already sacrificed for daring to stand between tyrants and slaves." Instead, advised Parsons, "grant every fair demand of labor. Give these poor creatures enough to satisfy their hunger and I will guarantee a quiet period in which all the great questions of land and wages and rights can be put in operation without further bloodshed. But if not, I am already sacrificed as a martyr for the cause. I have thousands of brethren who will sell their lives just as dearly as I will mine, and at just as great cost to our enemies." Parsons concluded on a melodramatic note: "It must be LIBERTY for the people or DEATH for the CAPITALISTS. I am not choosing more. It is your choice and your last. I love humanity, and therefore die for it. No one could do more. Every drop of my blood shall count an avenger, and woe to America when these are in arms."9

Having drafted this communication, Parsons made ready to leave. As a precaution against capture, he had already shaved off his mustache, which "altered his appearance amazingly," said Holmes. He now took off his collar and neck-scarf, tucked his trousers into his boots, and donned an old slouch hat, drawing it low over his forehead. At first he had determined to carry a pistol and, if arrested, take a few policemen with him. In the end, however, he decided that it would be better to go unarmed. Thus disguised, he set off for Elgin, from which he would take the train to Wisconsin. "He entered my house trim, neat," said Holmes, "a city gentleman. He left it looking like a respectable tramp." Holmes, standing at the gate, watched his friend walk along the dusty road until he was out of sight. The next time he would see him it would be behind bars, "a martyr to his convictions of duty—a victim of those who knew neither mercy nor justice."10

Parsons had left just in time. The next day, May 9, Holmes was visited by the county sheriff, whom Holmes thought a "fine old gentleman." The sheriff, however, was accompanied by his deputy, an "ignorant, burly brute of giant size and strength," and by a "keen, wiry, foxy-looking Pinkerton man." While Holmes sat in the kitchen with the sheriff, explaining his social and economic theories, the other two went methodically through the house in search of Parsons, insisting that he was hiding on the premises. Holmes's mother, who was living with him at the time and was a pious Englishwoman for whom a lie was the most heinous sin, remained loyal to her son and his cause. "Never will I forget the vehemence with which she met the deputy's ferocity and threats," writes Holmes. "Dear soul, she knew nothing and could tell nothing except that Parsons had not been to our house."[11]

Again and again the trio left the house to confer in the front yard. Each time, despite the protests of the sheriff, the deputy and Pinkerton returned to renew the search. The deputy insisted that he had personally seen Parsons enter that morning with a straw hat on his head. He said that he had carefully watched and would swear that no man had since left the house. This positive statement puzzled Holmes at the time, as he was equally certain that Parsons was gone and that no man had entered the house that day. He said nothing, however, except to urge his visitors to still greater diligence in their search, which in the end proved fruitless.

It was not until after dinner, when Holmes was narrating the circumstances to his sister, who lived in the neighborhood, that the mystery was solved. It was she who had come to the house that morning, with an old straw hat of her brother's on her head, which she left when she returned home; and it was she whom the deputy had mistaken for Parsons. Holmes remarks with obvious relish: "The joke on the deputy was so good that his chief soon heard of it and for a time his friends made life miserable for him."[12]

Parsons had meanwhile arrived at Elgin. He stayed there two days, whether with a friend or in a hotel (probably the latter) is not known. On Monday, May 10, he proceeded to Waukesha, where he sought refuge with Daniel Hoan, the proprietor of a small pump factory. Hoan, a socialist, was a subscriber to *The Alarm*, with whom Parsons had corresponded but whom he had never met. An "earnest, whole-souled man," as Lizzie Holmes describes him, he did not understand precisely what it was the anarchists wanted, but his heart went out to them, and he was certain that they had "a great part to play in the redemption of the world."[13]

Hoan did not know that Parsons was coming. Like Holmes, he was taken by surprise. Parsons, having arrived in Waukesha, walked into his shop and engaged him in conversation. Inevitably the Haymarket incident came up, and Hoan "expressed himself so decidedly" that Parsons revealed his identity and was at once welcomed and given shelter. Taking Parsons to his house, Hoan got out some old clothes, including a big grey coat and wide-brimmed hat. Parsons put these on, and Hoan introduced him to his family as "Mr. Jackson," saying that he would stay and work with him for a while.[14]

For the next six weeks Parsons remained secluded in Waukesha. To complete his disguise, he stopped dying his hair, as he had done for ten years, and let his beard and mustache grow in their natural color. With his ill-fitting clothes and with his hair, beard, and mustache nearly white, only his closest associates would have recognized him. To occupy his time, Parsons assisted in Hoan's factory and did the carpentry and painting in the alterations of Hoan's house. Whatever work he undertook—the latticework, turret, and porch— was "well done, though he had previously known nothing of the technical details."[15]

Sometimes, when at work near the eaves, he would talk to the children sitting on the porch beneath, telling stories of his boyhood, "scenes of slavery days," and giving vivid pictures of "the lives and poverty and toil the people in the great cities endured." One girl, Miss Annie, who lived with the Hoans, said she always remembered one remark of "Mr. Jackson's," which impressed her deeply: men and women were "always as good as their conditions allowed them to be."[16]

Waukesha, one of the favorite resorts of Milwaukians, was noted for its green hills and its sparkling springs, whose health-giving waters were shipped all over the United States. Here Parsons passed the last free days of his life. Allowing himself to relax, he got a badly needed rest, remote from the tumult and repressions of Chicago. His favorite spot was Spence's Hill, with the valley and village, nestled in soft spring foliage, spread in a panorama before him. Every morning he would hasten, with that "quick, springy tread of his," to the Acme Spring, sample its waters, then on up through the woods for an hour's solitary ramble, coming in at breakfast with his hands full of wild flowers and ferns and his face bright with animation and health. It was his first vacation in years, and he enjoyed it.[17]

One morning, on a Sunday in June, the Hoans took Parsons for an outing at Pewaukee Lake. "Do you remember that bright and sunny Sabbath morning," Parsons wrote to his hosts from prison a few months later. ". . . The trip, oh, that glorious ride over hill, through valley, amid winding dell, and across gurgling brooks and green fields; the singing birds, the shady groves, the air laden with nature's sweet breath, the perfume of wild roses, clover, cherry, apple, and many beautiful flowers in fragrant bloom lining the roadside all the way; and our hearts, yielding to the pure, the noble influences which nature inspires, gave response in merry laugh and joyous songs—oh, that blessed day! It is treasured in my memory as a bright oasis on life's dreary way."[18]

Only once was this idyl interrupted. One day, while Parsons was at his desk writing, Miss Annie came in quite suddenly and said: "Say—they say you are Mr. Parsons." Parsons did not move, but he said afterwards that he could feel his face grow white. "Is that so? Who says so?" "Oh, a Mr. _____ and Mr. _____, and they say Mr. _____ told them." In a few minutes Daniel Hoan came in. Parsons took him aside and said quietly: "I'll have to get out of this—right away, too. They have it about town that I am Parsons. I am no longer safe here." "Just you keep quiet," said Hoan. "I believe I can fix this all right yet. They know nothing yet—they are only surmising." Hoan went out, tracked down the rumor-mongers, and called them a "pack of fools," asking if Jackson looked anything like the pictures of Parsons in the newspspers, and more to that effect. The rumors were quieted, and if anyone in Waukesha still suspected Jackson's identity, nothing further was said.[19]

The town, indeed, took Parsons to its bosom. The children, the young boys in the shop, the neighbors, the congregants of Reverend Needham's church all came to admire "Mr. Jackson" and were eager to converse with him, as he had much of interest to relate. On one or two occasions he entertained the congregration with a talk or lecture. One of the ladies of the village, noting his intelligent conversation, said: "What a nice man Mr. Jackson seems to be. What a pity he cannot dress better!" Another woman remarked: "But how neatly his shoes are always kept. He must have dressed well at some time in his life. Suppose we club together and buy him a nice coat, that old one is so shabby and big for him."[20]

Up to this time only two persons in the world knew where Parsons was hiding, Daniel Hoan and William Holmes. On May 22 Parsons wrote to the latter, whose house he had been forced to abandon two weeks before. The letter, which had to be forwarded in a roundabout way, as Holmes's mail was still being monitored, was a characteristic product of Parsons's pen, "full of noble sentiment," as its recipient noted, "and written in a spirit of self-sacrifice."[21] "What a howl of rage is going up from the wounded Property Beast!" wrote Parsons. "What shrieks of despair and cries for blood! This is music to all who strive for liberty. The Property Beast is in the last days of its power, its bloodthirstiness, its cruelty. Private capital with its pack of bloodhounds—the police and militia—will ere long be powerless in the presence of an aroused and fearless people. As for the Haymarket tragedy—not upon our heads is their guilty blood. They fell ignobly, striving to suppress free speech and to smother the manifestations of the discontent of enslaved and oppressed labor. From the echo of that Tuesday night the tyrants of the earth may take warning that the reign of brute force and bloody violence is nearing its end all over the world."[22]

Cautioning Holmes against revealing his whereabouts, not even to family and friends, Parsons sent greetings to his wife and inquired after his arrested comrades. Poor Fielden, was his wound serious? And how were his wife and child? The prisoners, Parsons was confident, would prove a match "more than equal to all the lies and arts of liberty's foes." As for himself, he added in a postscript, "my present seclusion is perfect. I am resting and I need it. My health was never better." He was troubled, however, by the suppression of *The Alarm*. Could not a reduced number be issued in his absence? "It would do great good. This is seed time. The harvest is near. We are sowers now, but we will reap very soon."[23]

On the day that Parsons composed this letter, a Defense Committee was organized in Chicago. Four days earlier, on May 18, the grand jury had begun its deliberations, so that it was necessary to secure counsel and collect funds for legal expenses. In charge of these efforts was Ernst Schmidt, a Forty-Eighter who had settled in Chicago during the 1850s and fought in the Northern army during the Civil War. Intelligent and well-educated, he was one of the leading physicians in the city, having served as the first coroner of Cook County and established a reputation for honesty, professional competence, and sympathy for the laboring poor. In 1879, as we have seen, Schmidt had been the SLP candidate for mayor and made a respectable showing. An avowed socialist, Schmidt was convinced, as Sigmund Zeisler put it, that there was "something radically wrong in our social conditions and that the workingmen, generally speaking, were heartlessly exploited by their employers."[24] Yet he was opposed to the use of force as a means of altering the existing system. Dismayed by the violent rhetoric employed by the anarchists, he had often expressed his views on the subject to Spies, with whom he was intimately acquainted. At the same time, he believed implicitly in the lofty motives and good character of Spies and his associates; and, while he deplored the Haymarket bombing, he was convinced that the accused men had had no hand in it. "Immediately after hearing that the labor agitators had been taken into custody," wrote Schmidt in his memoirs, "... I decided to do what I could to give [them] a fair trial."[25]

To raise money for the defense, Schmidt called on as many friends as he could contact. Their response, he tells us, was "magnificent," but not a single hall could be rented at which a defense association might be established. Schmidt, accordingly, summoned a meeting in his own office at 95 Fifth Avenue, the building of the Chicago *Staats-Zeitung*. On the afternoon of May 22, more than a hundred men, mostly anarchists and socialists, crowded into the room, donated money, and organized a Defense Committee of which Ferdinand Spies and George Schilling were members, with Schmidt himself as treasurer and actual head. Given the inflamed state of public opinion, noted Sigmund Zeisler, who himself attended the meeting and became an attorney for the defense, it required "moral courage of the highest order" for Schmidt to undertake the assignment. Aside from Schmidt, Schilling became the most active figure in the defense movement, sparing no labor or hardship in behalf of his former associates. "No effort on my part," acknowledged Schmidt, "would have succeeded without the constant support and encouragement of George Schilling," whose many friends among the labor leaders "donated handsomely to our fund."[26]

During its existence, the Defense Committee was able to collect a considerable sum to meet its mounting expenses. Apart from workers' organizations, Dr. Schmidt issued an appeal to "liberally minded humanitarians of all creeds," inviting their contributions to aid the prisoners. The appeal was widely reproduced in the liberal and labor press, and, says Schmidt, "had its intended effect."[27] Contributions, however, came mostly from the workers, above all from the International itself, some groups making weekly donations throughout the long process of trial and appeals. Nearly all were in small amounts, ranging from one to five dollars. Money poured in from every state and territory in the Union, many contributions being accompanied by letters of sympathy and encouragement. Articles of jewelry were sent, as well as other valuables. About $8,000 was raised in Chicago, of which nearly half was collected at picnics, dances, and raffles. The largest donation—$1,000—came from a Detroit businessman, who made it clear that he was not a socialist but wanted to see fair play. In a short time donations began to trickle in from such distant places as Uppsala, Bombay, and Tokyo. A total of $40,000 was collected, sufficient to pay the heavy expenses of investigation, court reporting, and printing, as well as "moderate fees" for the lawyers.[28]

On May 27 the grand jury handed down its indictments, and the prisoners were transferred from the central police station to Cook County Jail to await trial. By that time the Central Labor Union had retained its regular attorney, Moses Salomon, and his associate, Sigmund Zeisler, to represent them. Both were capable and intelligent men, but Salomon, the senior partner, was only twenty-eight, while Zeisler, two years his junior, had been in America only three years and had just been admitted to the bar. Both were relatively inexperienced, especially in criminal cases, and "neither had a decided personality," in the opinion of Samuel McConnell, a member of the Chicago bar.[29]

But finding an older, more experienced attorney to head the staff proved a difficult task. For, in the prevailing atmosphere of hysteria, no lawyer of any standing was eager to take the job. After consulting with Salomon and Zeisler, Dr. Schmidt sought to retain Luther Laflin Mills, a former state's attorney for Cook County, and then William S. Forrest, a "very able man, versed in all the technicalities of criminal law," as Zeisler describes him. Mills, however, declined outright, while Forrest asked for a fee which went far beyond the means at the disposal of the Defense Committee. Schmidt thought that both men feared the consequences of undertaking the defense of so unpopular a cause, and he was probably right.[30]

After these initial rebuffs, however, the Defense Committee succeeded in persuading William Perkins Black, a prominent corporation lawyer, to take the case. Black was forty-four years old, a tall, handsome man of military bearing, "very dignified and possessing a powerful, mellifluous voice."[31] In 1886 few lawyers in Chicago had achieved greater success or had such glowing prospects for the future. A Civil War hero who had been awarded the Congressional Medal of Honor when he was nineteen, Captain Black (as he was invariably addressed) was alert, articulate, and popular, a charter member of the Chicago bar and a partner in a law firm that numbered among its clients many of the city's leading financiers and manufacturers.[32]

Small wonder that, when Schilling approached him to take charge

250

of the defense, Black was cool to the idea. It was equivalent to asking, as Mrs. Black remarked: "Are you willing to sacrifice all life's prospects to serve justice? Will you lay down all life's ambition rather than sacrifice eight men. . .?"[33] Black, on the other hand, was a man of social conscience and deep faith in humanity, widely respected for his integrity and adherence to principle. His courage, moreover, had been demonstrated in the Civil War. Born in Kentucky, the son of a Presbyterian minister who supported the Confederacy, he nevertheless left college when Fort Sumter was bombarded to join the Union forces as a private. His distinction on the battlefield has been noted. Vaguely liberal in outlook, he defended the Russian populists in a public lecture delivered in 1882, for which the labor editor John Swinton commended "the elevation of his spirit, the charm of his love for truth, justice and man, and the generosity of his sympathy."[34] He had also become interested in socialism—"the cry of the people," he called it—and had heard Schilling and McAuliffe speak on the subject. More than this, he had met Spies and Parsons on several occasions, though he was far from being a "deep student" of their ideas, as William Holmes maintained.[35]

When Schilling approached him, therefore, Black did not reject him out of hand, but asked for a few days in which to secure someone else with more experience in defending men accused of serious crimes. His quest, however, was fruitless. "All such lawyers," his wife observed, "shrank from that case as from the leprosy." The harder Black looked, the more indignant he became. Fearing that the defendants might go to trial without adequate counsel, he solicited the advice of Judge Murray F. Tuley, a former corporation counsel and alderman, who was respected as one of the city's most learned and impartial jurists. Black told Judge Tuley that the anarchists had asked him to undertake their defense and had offered him a retainer—very little money, but all that they could afford. To accept, he added, might mean social ostracism and the loss of his clients and possibly his career. Tuley responded that it was Black's decision to make, but since he had asked he would answer that it was his duty to himself and his profession to accept. Black thanked Tuley for confirming what he himself knew was right.[36]

When Black informed his wife of his decision to accept the case, she vehemently protested, suggesting that he help the defendants in other ways. "I *must* take it," he replied, echoing Martin Luther's celebrated pronouncement. "I can do no otherwise, God helping me.

A great wrong has been done. I must do all I can to right it." He at once plunged into the fight to save the accused men. For the next year and a half everything else was subordinated to this effort. It was a brave undertaking, wrote Zeisler years later, "nothing short of an act of heroism."[37]

Black, however, was not a criminal lawyer. He had established his reputation in corporation law and was neither versed nor experienced in criminal cases. Nor were the youthful Salomon and Zeisler equal to the task. After an intensive search, Black managed to obtain William A. Foster, a recent arrival in Chicago from Davenport, Iowa, as his chief aide. A no-nonsense, down-to-earth criminal lawyer, Foster was about forty years old, of medium height and build, with wavy red hair and long mustache. He chewed tobacco incessantly, even in the courtroom during the trial, and "his aim at the cuspidor was unfailing," Zeisler recalled. He was a "likeable, level-headed fellow," thought Zeisler, "who, however, relied more upon his native wit and talent than upon application or close study."[38] On balance, however, he proved a valuable addition to the defense.

One of Captain Black's first actions as chief attorney for the defense was to ask for a change of venue from the court of Judge Rogers, who had presided over the grand jury and appeared to be biased against the prisoners. According to Zeisler, this step was taken at the insistence of the defendants, who feared that Rogers would not give them a fair trial. Black requested that the case be transferred to the court of Murray Tuley, "than whom," noted Zeisler, "the country has never had an abler or fairer judge."[39] But the prosecutor, State's Attorney Grinnell, would not consent. Instead they agreed upon Tuley's old law partner, Joseph Easton Gary, who was widely held to be a discriminating and impartial judicial officer.

This proved to be a fatal error. Perhaps it would have been impossible under the circumstances to secure a fair trial in any Illinois court, but in the hands of Judge Gary the doom of the defendants was sealed. Even Judge Rogers was to criticize the proceedings under Gary as an unmitigated travesty of justice. And yet the error could not have been foreseen. Gary, who was a few weeks short of his sixty-fifth birthday, had served on the bench for more than twenty years, presiding in many important civil and criminal cases and acquiring the reputation, in the words of one authority, of a "learned, wise and upright judge." Even Zeisler thought him "a very able, keen lawyer and a fine judge."[40]

Gary, however, was to emerge as the most bitterly reviled of all the participants in the case. His bias showed itself almost immediately. On June 10, at the first appearance of the defendants in his chambers, Captain Black made a powerful appeal for a postponement of the trial until fevered passions had cooled. Black's words fell on deaf ears. Yielding to Grinnell's request for a speedy hearing of the case, Gary set the trial for June 21, in Cook County criminal court. It was a foretaste of what was to come.

While the attorneys for the defense were busy with their preparations for the trial, the question arose as to whether Parsons should return to Chicago and stand trial with the others. The matter was brought before Captain Black by Lucy Parsons, to whom her husband had written on May 22. His letter was sent through William Holmes, whom Parsons asked to deliver it in person. "It is the first word she has received from me," he said, "and it contains matters of importance." In it Parsons expressed his willingness to surrender. He asked his wife to consult with the attorneys for the defense and to obtain their views in the matter. If it was judged that his presence at the trial would be likely to be helpful to his comrades, he was ready to come to the bar.[41]

In a separate letter to Holmes, Parsons posed the identical question. He himself was confident that he would be acquitted, as he had been in no way responsible for the Haymarket bombing and had had no knowledge of the meeting itself until shortly before it began. Conspiracy, too, could be easily disproved. "Schwab's absence, as well as the presence, unarmed, of myself, my wife, and my two children shows as much," Parsons wrote. "As for inciting to riot, well, if what I said moved the people to resist the oppressions and throw off the yoke of the capitalist loafers and labor robbers, then I would be happy even in a prison cell to await the dawn of the day when emancipated Labor would proclaim and set me free." "Now comrade," asked Parsons, "what is your advice? Shall I put myself into the hands of the bloodhounds? Shall I stand trial? Confer with Lucy E. and Lizzie M. and other comrades. I am ready now as ever to do my best in the cause against the foul system that keeps labor in bondage to capital."[42]

In keeping with her husband's instructions, Mrs. Parsons went to Captain Black and told him of Parsons's communication. Black, having faith in the judicial system, responded with enthusiasm. He felt sure that the defense could demonstrate "to any dispassionate mind," as he put it, that Parsons had never abetted or counseled the throwing of the bomb. But he realized that, given the inflamed condition of public opinion, "the full rancor of which . . . was not appreciated by any of us," there was danger in the return even of a demonstrably innocent man, especially a man who had been for years a leading labor agitator in the city as well as an apostle of anarchy. We knew, said Black, that Parsons was in "a place of absolute safety," and that every effort of the police to find him had proved unavailing. Should he then come into court? Was the possible advantage of such a step sufficient to justify the hazard?[43]

Captain Black wrote Parsons a letter in which, says Black, "I tried to set before him fully the danger which confronted him in the event of his return, and the possibility of awful consequences, but in which I expressed the personal belief that we could satisfactorily establish his innocence, and therefore could secure his acquittal; that I believed the effect of his return and presence in the trial could not but be advantageous to his co-defendants. But I told him in effect that the responsibility of advising his return was one that I could not and would not take—I could only lay the case fully before him, and leave it to him to determine what action he would take."[44]

So matters stood until June 18, three days before the trial was scheduled to open. On this date Lucy Parsons went again to Captain Black to discuss the advisability of her husband's surrender. Black brought her with him to the daily afternoon conference of the defense attorneys, where the question received prolonged consideration. Black himself remained unshakeably in favor. He had a "strongly developed dramatic instinct," remarked Zeisler, and greatly valued the heroic gesture. In glowing colors he portrayed to the others what a sensation it would create if Parsons should walk into the courtroom on the first day of the trial and take his place beside his comrades. Such a fine, magnanimous act would immediately turn public opinion in favor of the accused.[45]

Foster, however, was skeptical. A hardheaded, practical-minded trial lawyer, he did not believe in risking a client's life for the sake of a beautiful gesture. Having none of Black's sentimental idealism, he thought it folly to submit Parsons to a trial at a time when loathing and prejudice against the anarchists was still at fever heat. Parsons, he argued, had better wait until public reason had reasserted itself before emerging from his retreat. As his legal advisors, they had no right to bring him from a place of safety to a situation of extreme jeopardy. "It has been urged," he later wrote to Lucy Parsons, "that it was the duty of A. R. Parsons to stand by his friends in adversity, and that it was manly for him to return to the trial. I do not believe that manhood demands of any one that he submit himself to a decision warped by prejudice and wrought by passion. Rather should he bide his time, and when the clouds of excitement and anger have rolled by, and then only, true bravery requires that an investigation of the charges against him be invited by the accused. Under the circumstances surrounding the trial, for a free man to voluntarily place himself in the prisoners' dock was equivalent to saying, 'I am willing to die for Anarchy,' and, not being an Anarchist myself, I cannot but consider such an act an inexcusable mistake."[46]

Of the two junior attorneys, Salomon sided with Captain Black, being "highly optimistic," writes his partner, "with unbounded confidence in the strength of the theory of defense we had worked out." Zeisler himself begged to be excused from expressing an opinion, on the ground that he had been in his adopted country only a short time and "was not sufficiently familiar with the operation of the American mind." As for Lucy Parsons, she would only say that her husband should do what he thought wise and right, although, according to Zeisler, she hoped that he would turn himself in.[47]

The decision thus rested with Parsons. When the results of the consultation were made known to him, he felt a sense of relief, as if a weight had been lifted from his conscience. For two of the attorneys, one of them the chief counsel, told him what he had wanted to hear; and his wife appeared to go along. Parsons knew of the dangers awaiting him. He knew that he could remain in hiding until a jury had been empaneled, thereby securing a separate trial under calmer circumstances. Or he might, like Rudolph Schnaubelt, flee farther afield and live out his life in anonymity. Nothing would have been easier than for him to leave the country until the storm had passed. From the editorials in the Chicago papers, he noted, "I could see that the ruling class were wild with rage and fear against labor organizations. Ample means were offered me to carry me safely to distant parts of the earth, if I chose to go. I knew that the beastly howls against the Anarchists, the demand for their bloody extermination, made by the press and pulpit, were merely a pretext of the ruling class to intimidate the growing power of organized labor

255

in the United States. I also perfectly understood the relentless hate and power of the ruling class."[48]

Why then did he choose to surrender? Did he believe the social revolution was imminent? Did he feel a moral duty to be with his comrades? Did he fear that his continued absence might be construed as a confession of guilt and prejudice the jury against them? Did he think that his verbal ability could help save them and himself? Did he have hopes of being vindicated? All of these considerations, it would seem, played a part in his decision. Like Captain Black, he possessed a keen sense of the dramatic and believed that his voluntary surrender would have the effect of demonstrating his integrity, thereby helping himself and the other accused men in their defense. Above all, however, it was his sense of honor and his consciousness of innocence that impelled him to return. His comrades were in danger. The cause he loved needed him. Whatever his qualms or misgivings, he had to be with them and share their fate.

Parsons felt confident of proving his innocence. He did not believe that the state of Illinois would strangle him and his comrades in defiance of all the evidence in their favor. His love of humanity and justice, his faith in the ultimate honesty of mankind, a faith that he shared with Captain Black, led him to walk into the jaws of death. "Knowing myself innocent of crime," he wrote in September 1887, "I came forward and gave myself up for trial. I felt that it was my duty to take my chances with the rest of my comrades. I sought a fair and impartial trial before a jury of my peers, and knew that before any fair-minded jury I could with little difficulty be cleared. I preferred to be tried and take the chances of an acquittal with my friends to being hunted as a felon."[49]

Parsons's decision to return displayed courage and unselfishness of a high order. "That he should, in the retirement and seclusion of his retreat," wrote Captain Black, "after weeks of consideration, during which his own personal safety was demonstrated, have reached and acted upon the fixed resolve to offer his own life in what he believed to be the cause of the wage class, and for the possible advantage of his fellow agitators, was heroic." Nor, once the step had been taken, did he ever have any regrets, though Spies wryly assured him that he had run his neck into a noose. William Holmes, visiting Parsons in prison the day after his surrender, gently upbraided him for "delivering himself to the Philistines," to which Parsons replied: "I could not remain in security knowing that my equally innocent comrades were in danger. I decided to share their fate, whatever it might be."[50]

On June 19, two days before the trial, Parsons notified his friends of his decision, in a letter that Daniel Hoan personally carried to the city. Hoan contrived to "make himself known to the right parties, consult with them, obtain their instructions, and depart for home," without attracting the notice of the police.[51] On the morning of June 20, it was decided that Parsons should start for Chicago that night. That afternoon, he and his hosts made a last visit to Spence's Hill. Parsons talked cheerfully with the others and, in a boyish mood, lay at full length on the ground and rolled down the hill, then climbed up flushed and laughing.

Late that evening a wagon stood ready to convey Parsons to Milwaukee, from which a train left for Chicago at 4:30 A.M. A young son of Hoan's, who would later become the socialist mayor of Milwaukee, drove the twenty miles through the still summer night. As they entered the city they were stopped by a policeman, who wanted to know what they were doing at that late hour. The boy answered: "I am going to take this gentleman to the train." The officer peered curiously into the wagon. "You seem to have come a good distance," he said, putting his hand on the horse's neck. "She's pretty warm." Parsons, to divert attention, said laughingly, "It's not a 'she,' it's a 'he.' " The man laughed and turned away. He had looked quite sharply at a basket in the wagon that contained Parsons's clothes, as though he would like to explore the contents. But he let them go on their way, saying that he was "looking for a man who had stolen something in the city." The boy, wholly ignorant of whom he was carrying, said: "What was the officer looking for, I wonder. Did he think we had bombs in our basket?"[52]

Another incident occurred close to home. About 7:30 A.M., as the train neared Kinzie Street in Chicago, slowing up as usual at that point, Parsons decided to alight rather than go on to the depot. Morning was mistily dawning, and the great city lay shrouded in silence. Parsons leaped from the train, which, however, was gliding along at a swifter rate than he had calculated upon. He fell, rolling over once or twice before he caught himself. A policeman who was standing nearby came over and helped him to his feet, asking him if he was hurt. No, said Parsons, only shaken up a bit. "I'll be all right in a minute or two." The policeman cautioned him not to jump off moving trains and asked him if he knew where he was going.

"Oh, yes," answered Parsons. "I've been there before, and only jumped off because 'twas nearer. I'll bid you good day, sir."[53]

From this adventure Parsons went on his way undisturbed, reaching the house of Sarah Ames on South Morgan Street. In spite of his altered appearance, Mrs. Ames knew him at once. She quickly drew him in, shut the door, and "in the fulness of her heart and her joy that he was thus far safe from the hands of the detectives, she embraced, kissed, and cried over him, so she says, as any good sister comrade would have done."[54] A note was at once sent to his wife. Lucy, though burning with impatience and anxiety, responded with deliberation. Knowing that detectives were likely to be dogging her steps, she sauntered carelessly along the street. In a few minutes, for a brief time, she was reunited with her husband.

In the meantime, word of Parsons's arrival had been conveyed to Captain Black. Swiftly and carefully Parsons's comrades worked through the morning and into the afternoon to complete the arrangements for his surrender. Parsons changed into neat clothes, shaved off his grey beard, and dyed his hair and mustache their customary black. Around 2 P.M. he bid goodbye to his wife and several friends who were present. A. H. Simpson got a cab, picked up Parsons and Mrs. Ames, and told the driver to go to the Criminal Court building.

Captain Black was pacing up and down on the sidewalk in front of the Michigan Street entrance when the cab pulled up. Black shook hands silently and intensely with Parsons, gave him his arm, and they proceeded up the stairs and into the building. As they passed the first landing, on their way to Judge Gary's courtroom, Detective James Bonfield turned, looked after them, and said: "Who was that fellow with Black?" A reporter said: "I believe it was Parsons." "Not much!" exclaimed a detective nearby. "Say, we've been looking for Parsons, and don't you forget it." But Bonfield said: "I'll be damned if it ain't," and started up the stairs after them.[55]

Meanwhile Parsons and Black had entered Judge Gary's courtroom and were advancing towards the bench. Parsons was quickly recognized, and there was a stir and craning of necks. Some in the room rose to their feet to get a better look. Captain Black was about to address the court to announce Parsons's surrender when State's Attorney Grinnell, alerted by his assistant Furthmann, jumped to his feet and said in a loud voice: "Your honor, I see Albert Parsons in the courtroom. I move that he be placed in the custody of the sheriff."

Captain Black, quivering with anger and indignation, said: "Your motion, Mr. Grinnell, is not only most ungracious and cruel, it is also gratuitous. You see that Mr. Parsons is here to surrender himself." They now stood before the judge. Parsons said: "I present myself for trial with my comrades, your honor." Parsons entered a plea of not guilty. "You will take a seat with the prisoners, Mr. Parsons," said the judge. Parsons walked over to the dock and shook hands with Spies and the others, all of whom greeted him warmly. He seemed in the best of spirits and bowed politely to reporters whom he knew. An eighth chair was added, and Parsons took his place among the defendants. He never again emerged as a free man.[56]

The whole episode had lasted a few minutes. When it was over the reporters dashed out to communicate the exciting news. Before long word had flown over the city and across the country that Parsons had given himself up. According to Zeisler, however, the scene that Captain Black had envisaged had "died abornin'." Zeisler says that he deeply felt the humiliation of Captain Black and the disappointment of Mrs. Parsons, who was in the courtroom. They had expected something quite different.[57] Yet the effect was not completely spoiled. It was a "carefully arranged surprise, dramatically carried out," reported one newspaper the following day. In the opinion of William H. Parsons, who had come to Chicago for the trial, his brother's act seemed to disarm the hostility of "disinterested men who believed in fair play." Captain Black himself, whatever else he might have felt, regarded Parsons's surrender as "admirable, having in it a certain touch of the heroic."[58] Yet, in advising Parsons to return, Black's judgment had been colored by emotion. It was to haunt him for the rest of his days.

17 ‖ THE TRIAL

The trial of the Chicago anarchists was unsurpassed in dramatic intensity in the city's legal history. It was the most celebrated trial of the late nineteenth century, involving fundamental social as well as juridical issues. William Holmes saw it as nothing less than "a conflict between the bourgeoisie and proletariat, the robbers and the robbed, a corrupt and festering government and a portion of its victims," as he wrote to H. H. Sparling shortly after the proceedings began. "It is a trial in which freedom of speech and press is at stake, and where bourgeois law—in short the whole damnable system—is arrayed against the rights of the people."[1]

Nor was Holmes alone in recognizing its importance. No case previously brought before the Chicago courts had excited so much interest or attracted a greater crowd. Spectators came from all over the country to observe the anarchists at first hand. Many reporters from out-of-town newspapers were in attendance, and all the Chicago papers were represented. The courtroom was always crowded, and many who applied for admission had to be turned away.

The families of the defendants, including the children, attended regularly throughout the trial. While the selection of the jury was in progress, Mary Engel presented each of the men with a bouquet of red roses. Lulu and Albert Parsons, Jr., ran to greet their father before the day's proceedings began. Parsons embraced and kissed them, putting one on each knee. "Only a faint suggestion of the darkness of their maternal origin could be noticed in either of the children," wrote a reporter for the *Inter Ocean*, "the skin of the little boy being somewhat darker than that of his father." As for the children's mother, "she looked fresh and amiable, walked with a quick, light step, and carried herself with all the assurance of an empress."[2]

William H. Parsons, who had not seen his brother in a dozen years, came to Chicago to lend him moral support, taking a keen interest in the case and working for the defense until the end. General Parsons, a lawyer, had himself sat on the Texas Supreme Court, had been a member of the United States Centennial Commission, and now held the post of inspector of customs at Newport News, Virginia. He had also become a reformer in his own right, though he did not share his brother's extreme views. A member of the Knights of Labor, he described himself as "an old time, original Jeffersonian democrat, believing that all power, where not expressly delegated to the state, is inherently in the people and not in corporations, and that the ballot is the sole and final arbiter of any existing grievances." Of Albert he said that "his voluntary surrender to confront the scaffold proves his sincerity and demonstrates that he has the courage of his convictions."[3]

While General Parsons was optimistic regarding the outcome, William Holmes, who sent reports of the trial to William Morris's paper *The Commonweal*, predicted the worst. "Many of our comrades, and our lawyers, are sanguine of an acquittal," he wrote before the jury had been seated, "but I confess I have great fears for the result. If it was simply a case of justice and law our comrades would certainly be acquitted, as there is not the least evidence against one of the men now awaiting trial; but the whole course of the press and the authorities during the past few weeks proves that they are determined upon *vengeance*, and that no stone will be left unturned to force a verdict of murder and sentence of death upon at least one of the prisoners."[4]

Holmes's forebodings were amply justified. The trial took place in an atmosphere of unparalleled prejudice. The newspapers, which had convicted the anarchists of murder before the proceedings had even begun, demanded that the noose come quickly and with little ado. Public opinion, inflamed by the press, was at fever pitch against the defendants. It was said that neither person nor property would be safe until they were hanged. "I wish I could convey to you some idea of the feeling here in regard to this trial," wrote Holmes to Sparling in London. "One of the theatre managers in Chicago wrote a letter to Judge Gary—which was published in the *Chicago Tribune*—offering to take the eight prisoners and hang them free of charge in his theatre as part of a play, one each night. What do you think of *that* for nineteenth-century civilization? Another man wrote to the *Inter Ocean* recommending that our comrades be placed on a sliding board under a guillotine and sliced up in thin slices, beginning with their feet. What do you think of *that* for Christian toleration and civilization?"[5]

Carl Sandburg, the American writer and poet, was eight years old and growing up in Galena, Illinois, when the trial took place. "We heard about it, read about it, and talked about it, from May 5 through every day of that year of 1886," he later wrote of the case. "Then came the murder trial of the eight men and we saw in the Chicago papers black-and-white drawings of their faces and they looked exactly like what we expected, hard, mean, slimy faces. We saw pictures of the twelve men on the jury and they looked like what we expected, nice, honest, decent faces. We learned the word for the men on trial, anarchists, and they hated the rich and called policemen 'bloodhounds.' They were not regular people and they didn't belong to the human race, for they seemed more like slimy animals who prowl, sneak, and kill in the dark. This I believed along with millions of other people reading and talking about the trial. I didn't meet or hear of anyone in our town who didn't so believe then, at that time."[6]

In such circumstances it would have been difficult, maybe impossible, to secure a fair trial for the defendants. What took place, however, exceeded even Holmes's worst fears. For the trial, reflecting as it did the popular mood of alarm and vengefulness, was one of the most unjust in the annals of American jurisprudence. It has been called a farce and an abomination by many impartial observers: indeed, it is hard to read the record of the proceedings without sharing Morris Hillquit's conclusion that it was "the grossest travesty of justice ever perpetrated in an American court."[7]

For this Judge Gary must bear the major burden of responsibility. Whatever his prior reputation for impartiality, his conduct of the Haymarket case was flagrantly partisan. From the outset he flaunted his bias against the defendants. Not only did he rule virtually every contested point in favor of the prosecution, but he repeatedly made remarks during the trial that bristled with hostility towards the accused and could not but have influenced the jury against them. Perhaps even more damaging to the defendants was the latitude that Gary allowed the prosecution, both in its opening and closing statements and in its presentation of evidence. While he confined the defense in its cross-examinations to specific points touched on by the state, he permitted the state to wander to matters entirely foreign to those in which the witnesses had been questioned. During the closing arguments, moreover, he gave State's Attorney Grinnell an utterly free hand in heaping abuse upon the defendants. Nor did he take any action as the audience applauded Grinnell's remarks.

Even some of Gary's conservative colleagues were shocked by his behavior during the trial. Judge Rogers and his son-in-law Samuel McConnell, himself later a judge in Chicago, agreed that Gary was "ignoring every rule of law which was designed to assure a fair trial for a defendant on trial for his life." Gary "manufactured the law," said McConnell, and "disdained precedent in order that a frightened public might be made to feel secure."[8]

In other ways, too, Gary revealed his contempt for the defendants. Day after day he surrounded himself with well-dressed, attractive young women, "looking for all the world," noted one reporter, "like the principal of a female seminary." They came there as though to the theater, whispering to each other, giggling, and eating candy. Gary, remarked Samuel McConnell, "seemed to treat the affair as a Roman holiday, and so did the women, and the thumbs were all down from the start."[9] One day McConnell's wife, the daughter of Judge Rogers, sat on the bench, and Gary showed her a puzzle while argument was in progress before him. Another young lady afterwards stated that Gary had joked with her and spent most of the time drawing pictures instead of paying attention to the testimony.

Gary himself later admitted that it had been unwise of him to permit the bench to be "filled with spectators, mostly ladies."[10] Yet, largely because of his cavalier deportment, the trial at times resembled a comic opera. During one session, for example, an artist in the courtroom created a sensation by circulating a drawing of the reporter from the *Arbeiter-Zeitung*, with a jug of beer in one hand and a dynamite bomb in the other. Among the spectators on Gary's bench that day, noted the reporter who described the incident, was "a pretty young woman wearing a monstrous big hat trimmed à la facade."[11]

The trial was a long one, lasting from June 21, when selection of the jury began, to August 20, when the jury delivered its verdict. Judge Gary showed his bias from the start. On the first day, William A. Foster, on behalf of the defense, moved that each of his clients be tried separately, fearing that evidence against any one of the accused men might be construed as evidence against all eight, so that Fielden and Schwab, for example, might be tainted with the extremism of Engel and Fischer, or, worse, with the bombs of Lingg.

263

After presenting an affidavit in support of this motion, however, Foster added quite unexpectedly: "While the defense sincerely believes that the court ought to grant this motion in the interest of justice, I hardly expect that it will." To this Judge Gary retorted: "Well, I shall not disappoint you, Mr. Foster." Gary uttered these words, according to Sigmund Zeisler, "in his most sarcastic manner and tone." A titter went around the courtroom. Captain Black and his colleagues were dismayed. Spies was furious. He handed Zeisler the following note: "What in hell does Foster mean? I thought our motion was meant seriously. What was the sense of making it appear perfunctory?" The motion was brusquely overruled, although, as Samuel McConnell noted, there was seldom a case that so plainly demanded separate trials for the defendants.[12]

Gary's prejudice became still more apparent during the selection of the jury, which began the same day. This proved an exceedingly difficult business. Twenty-one days were consumed in the effort, and 981 candidates were examined before the twelve men who tried the case were finally seated. The problem was that, with few exceptions, the candidates admitted to being biased against the defendants or to having already formed an opinion as to their guilt. No court record in the United States reveals a deeper or more widespread prejudice than that disclosed by the veniremen in this case. Day after day passed without the discovery of even one candidate fitted for dispassionate service, and panel after panel of prospective jurors was exhausted with like result.

After eight days of fruitless examination, an unusual expedient was adopted. The candidates for the jury were not to be selected in the customary manner, by drawing names at random from a box. Instead, they would be handpicked by a special bailiff, nominated by the state's attorney and appointed by the court. While this procedure was sanctioned by the defense, it soon became apparent that the bailiff, Henry L. Ryce, was exercising his powers in a grossly unfair manner, weeding out prospective jurors who might be sympathetic to the defendants. Otis S. Favor, a Chicago businessman who was examined for jury duty, later made an affidavit that Ryce had told him, in the presence of witnesses: "I am managing this case, and know what I am about. These fellows are going to be hanged as certain as death. I am calling such men as the prosecution wants."[13]

This plan required the cooperation of Judge Gary, and he gave it. Most of the veniremen called by the bailiff admitted to having a prejudice against the defendants or a preconceived opinion that they were guilty. To Judge Gary, however, this was insufficient reason to exclude them from the jury. Gary, as Samuel McConnell pointed out, was very rigid in his rulings as to cause, holding that even if a venireman acknowledged that he had formed an opinion regarding the guilt of the accused, he was acceptable if he said he could change it if the testimony warranted. This ruling, noted McConnell, was quite out of the ordinary and went "against human experience."[14]

Time and again Gary refused to disqualify a prospective juror who had openly admitted his prejudice against the defendants. Much the same happened in each instance. First the man said that he was biased and could not render a fair verdict. The defense then challenged for cause. Gary, denying the motion, took the man in hand and wheedled him into admitting that his prejudice might be overcome by strong proof of innocence. He was then ruled competent to serve, and the defense was forced to challenge peremptorily. William Neil, a manufacturer, declared: "It would take pretty strong evidence to remove the impression that I now have. I could not dismiss it from my mind, could not lay it altogether aside during the trial. I believe my present opinion, based upon what I have heard and read, would accompany me through the trial, and would influence me in determining and getting at a verdict." Neil was challenged by the defendants on the ground of prejudice. But Judge Gary, after much lecturing and coaxing, got him to say that he could give a fair verdict on whatever evidence he should hear, and thereupon the challenge was overruled.[15]

Similarly, H. F. Chandler, in the stationery business, said that his mind was pretty well made up and that it might be hard for him to change it. He too was challenged for cause, but the court, examining him at some length, got him to say that he believed he could judge the case fairly. In the same manner challenge was overruled in the case of F. L. Wilson, a manufacturer, George N. Porter, a grocer ("I believe what I have read in the papers—believe that the parties are guilty. I would try to go by the evidence, but in this case it would be awful hard work for me to do it"), H. N. Smith, a hardware merchant, and others, all of whom admitted to being prejudiced against the defendants and having an opinion concerning their guilt.

Nor was this all. Gary went so far as to pronounce fit for service M. D. Flavin, a relative of one of the slain policemen (Timothy Flavin), and this after the man had acknowledged that he was deeply biased. Gary failed to disqualify another prospective juror who was a friend of one of the deceased officers and acquainted with top police officials of the city. He had no objection, moreover, to a man who strongly doubted if anything could change his opinion regarding the guilt of the accused. Parsons, after two days of listening to such rulings, handed the following note to Zeisler: "In taking a change of venue from Judge Rogers to Lord Jeffreys [the notorious "hanging judge" under Charles II and James II], did not the defendants jump from the frying pan into the fire?"[16]

By law, each defendant was entitled to twenty peremptory challenges, totalling 160 for the defendants as a group. So frequently, however, were they compelled to invoke this measure during the first few days that they feared all their peremptory challenges might be exhausted long before the jury had been completed. "We realized it was idle to make the effort to get a truly impartial jury," records Zeisler. "Therefore, when, what happened rarely enough, there came a man who, though admittedly prejudiced, showed some degree of fairness and candor, we reluctantly accepted him after unsuccessfully challenging for cause and saved a peremptory challenge."[17]

Even so, the defendants were at length obliged to use all their peremptory challenges, just as Bailiff Ryce had anticipated, and to accept a jury of which every member had confessed to a prejudice against them or to having already formed an opinion concerning their guilt. The jury, as finally chosen, consisted of the following: Frank S. Osborn, thirty-nine, foreman, salesman for Marshall Field & Company; James H. Cole, fifty-three, bookkeeper and former infantry major in the Civil War; James H. Brayton, forty, principal of the Webster School in Chicago; Alanson H. Reed, forty-nine, partner in a music store; Andrew Hamilton, forty-one, hardware dealer; Charles B. Todd, forty-seven, clothing salesman; Harry T. Sandford, twenty-five, voucher clerk for the Chicago & Northwestern Railroad and former pertroleum broker in New York; Scott G. Randall, twenty-three, salesman for a seed company; Theodore E. Denker, twenty-seven, shipping clerk; Charles H. Ludwig, twenty-seven, bookkeeper in a wood-mantel shop; John B. Greiner, twenty-five, clerk in the freight department of the Chicago & Northwestern; and George W. Adams, twenty-seven, paint salesman.

It was far from being an impartial body. Juryman Denker had said before the trial that "the whole damn crowd ought to be hanged." Juryman Adams had expressed a similar opinion, while Andrew

Hamilton had said that someone had to be made an example of because of the bombing. Juryman Greiner believed that being indicted by a grand jury was itself a token of guilt. All the rest had acknowledged a prejudice against the defendants, in Sandford's case a "decided prejudice."[18]

The jury, moreover, was thoroughly middle class in composition, consisting of men, in Benjamin Tucker's words, "whose sympathies and interests range them on the side of capital and privilege."[19] Not one of the twelve was an industrial worker. Nor were any of them of German birth, and only one, Andrew Hamilton (born in Scotland) was not a native American. Not a man had been accepted by the prosecution who had shown the slightest leaning towards the prisoners. To every one of the candidates examined the state's attorney had put these questions: Are you a member of a trade or labor union? Are you a member of the Knights of Labor? Have you any sympathy with communists, anarchists, socialists? Anyone who had answered in the affirmative had been summarily excused.[20] Given these circumstances, Captain Black and his associates could only hope that they had secured, if not an impartial jury, at least a few men who were a bit less prejudiced than the candidates they had rejected.

On July 15 the jurors were sworn in, and State's Attorney Grinnell opened the case for the prosecution, aided by his special assistant, George C. Ingham, and his two regular assistant state attorneys, Francis W. Walker and Edmund Furthmann. Ingham, a veteran lawyer, had the reputation of a skillful prosecutor. Walker, though only thirty, was, in Sigmund Zeisler's estimation, "very talented and well educated, with a very high-pitched voice and a genial expression of face which, however, often changed suddenly into a sneer." Furthmann, whom we have already encountered during the pre-trial investigations, was a thick-set man of about thirty-five with "coarse features, a sinister expression, and a hoarse voice." A former bookkeeper who had only recently come to the bar, he never opened his mouth during the trial, although he frequently prompted his associates. He was, said Zeisler, "more a detective than a lawyer."[21]

Grinnell himself was an astute and forceful prosecutor and, according to Samuel McConnell, "an absolutely honest man." The same age as Captain Black, his counterpart for the defense, he had been born in upstate New York in 1842, graduated with honors from Middlebury College in Vermont, and come to Chicago in 1870 to practice law. Appointed state's attorney in 1884, he was basking in the fame of his recent conviction of a ring of thieving Cook County commissioners and of Joseph ("Chesterfield Joe") Macklin, a powerful Democratic politician, for vote stealing.[22] Grinnell himself was known to aspire to high political office—to the governor's seat, some believed. Thus the opportunity of his life was now before him, and he was bent on conviction at any cost. The question of guilt or innocence meant nothing to him. Driven by ambition, he went into the trial with a determination to hang.

Notwithstanding his reputation for honesty, Grinnell conducted a highly unscrupulous prosecution. His arguments were not only riddled with false and distorted statements, but he relied on hearsay, innuendo, and perjured testimony, twisting both fact and law in his determination to convict. Throughout the trial he played upon the fears and emotions of the jury. Making frequent use of inflammatory language, he referred to the defendants as "loathsome murderers," "organized assassins," "rats to be driven back into their holes." He called them "traitors," "godless foreigners," "infamous scoundrels," "the biggest cowards that I have ever seen in the course of my life." Fielden, at the conclusion of the proceedings, was moved to remind Grinnell that "it is the duty of the prosecuting attorney, as much as it is of the defendants' attorney, to see to it that no innocent man should suffer for any crime." "I am afraid," added Fielden, "there are lawyers to be found who care little as to whether their suit is right or in the interest of justice and truth, so long as they can gain their case and make a reputation for themselves."[23]

Grinnell, however, faced a formidable obstacle. Since the identity of the bombthrower had not been established, how could his act be connected with the defendants? Was it possible to convict men of murder when the actual perpetrator had not been found? Can there, to put it another way, be accessories without a principal? Was it not necessary to identify the party who committed the offense and to establish his association with the men on trial?

In an effort to do so, the state produced two witnesses. The first, M. M. Thompson, was an employee of Marshall Field & Company. Thompson swore that he attended the Haymarket meeting and saw Spies and Schwab go into Crane's Alley. He followed them and overheard snatches of conversation, including the words "pistols" and "police." Spies said: "Do you think one is enough, or hadn't we better go and get more?" Schwab said: "Now, if they come, we will give it to them." Then Spies and Schwab and a third man—whom Thompson did not see in the courtroom—huddled together in the alley, and something was passed to the third man, who put it in his coat pocket. Thompson, shown a photograph of Rudolph Schnaubelt, identified him as the unknown man.

Thompson's story, however, was demolished by the testimony of other witnesses and by many facts in evidence which showed it to be a pure fabrication. The defense was able to establish that Schwab was at the Haymarket for only a few minutes, that he left for Deering's before the meeting got started, and that he at no time that night saw Spies or entered Crane's Alley for any purpose. On cross-examination, moreover, Thompson confessed that he did not understand a word of German, insisting that the conversation between Spies and Schwab had been in English. It was shown by the defense, however, that German, not English, was the language in which they habitually spoke to each other. Thompson further admitted that he had seen the picture of Schnaubelt before the trial ("I think Mr. Furthmann showed it to me"). Thompson's testimony appears to have won little credence. Few were likely to believe, as Dyer Lum pointed out, that he had followed two total strangers into an alley, men he had never seen before, who proceeded to discuss a conspiracy in a language which they were not in the habit of using in ordinary conversation.[24]

Harry L. Gilmer, the other witness, told an even more improbable story. Gilmer, a painter by trade, testified that Spies slipped from the speakers' wagon, met Fischer and a man Gilmer did not know in Crane's Alley, and spoke to them in hushed tones. Gilmer swore that he saw Spies light a match and touch it to the fuse of a bomb, which the man he did not know tossed into the ranks of the police. Gilmer identified the photograph of Schnaubelt as that of the bombthrower. He judged him to be about 5'10" tall, weighing about 180 pounds, and wearing a sandy beard, not very long, and a dark hat.

Gilmer, in short, had seen everything—who lit the bomb, who threw it, and who was with them. And yet, as the defense pointed out, he had made no outcry. Nor had he said anything of all this for days after. He had not been called to testify at the coroner's inquest, nor before the grand jury, despite the vital nature of his information. His testimony in court, moreover, differed essentially from the statement he had earlier made to the police in the presence of reporters.

In this version he did not mention Spies at all and gave a different description of the bombthrower. At one point, in fact, he had identified Fischer as the culprit, rather than Schnaubelt.

Gilmer's story was directly contradicted by a large number of witnesses. Several of these testified that Fischer was in Zepf's Hall at the time of the explosion, others that Spies remained on the speakers' wagon throughout the meeting and did not leave it to go into the alley. It was established, in any case, by the testimony of reporters, policemen, and other witnesses, that the bomb was thrown not from the alley but from a point on the sidewalk of Desplaines Street a considerable distance to the south of it. A number of these witnesses got a glimpse of the bombthrower, who was standing behind a pile of boxes, and he did not in fact resemble Rudolph Schnaubelt. John Bernett, a candymaker by trade, who was not a socialist or anarchist, was standing directly behind him, some thirty-five or forty feet south of the alley. He wore a mustache, Bernett thought, but no beard, and was Bernett's own height, 5'9", or a bit taller. On being shown Schnaubelt's picture, Bernett promptly said he was not the man. Unlike Gilmer, significantly, he had told the same story to Assistant State's Attorney Furthmann immediately after the occurrence.[25]

Gilmer's story was not supported by a single other witness in the trial. On the contrary, ten prominent Chicago citizens, some of them large property-owners, testified that Gilmer was an inveterate liar whom they would not believe even under oath. Gilmer, it might also be mentioned, had ties with the police. He had served as a special policeman in Des Moines, Iowa, and in Chicago he was a member of the Veteran Police Patrol and employed as a deputy during strikes.[26] Moreover he admitted, under cross-examination, to having received money from Detective Bonfield, almost certainly in return for his testimony against the defendants, although Judge Gary prohibited further questioning on this subject.

So completely and overwhelmingly were Thompson and Gilmer discredited that more than a few observers at the trial felt that Grinnell had deliberately offered perjured testimony in his anxiety to connect the defendants with the bombthrower. Be that as it may, not a scrap of credible testimony was offered to prove that Schnaubelt threw the bomb, still less that Spies or any of the others had helped him. On the contrary, Captain Black was able to show that six of the defendants were not even present when the explosion occurred: Fischer and Parsons were at Zepf's, Engel and Neebe were home, Lingg was at Neff's on the North Side, and Schwab was at Deering's five miles away. Three of the men, Engel, Neebe, and Lingg, were never at the Haymarket at all that night. As for Fielden and Spies, both were on the speakers' wagon, in full view of the crowd and the police, when the bomb was thrown.

Thus all eight of the defendants had airtight alibis which the prosecution was unable to crack. Not a shred of reliable evidence was produced to show even the slightest connection between any of them and the bombthrower, or that any of them had ever seen or heard of him. If these were the facts, argued counsel for the defense, how could any of the men in the dock be said to be guilty of murder?

An effort by the prosecution to prove that Fielden, in his speech, had called for the killing of policemen, indeed that he himself had fired on them from the speakers' wagon, proved similarly abortive. A number of policemen testified that Fielden, when Bonfield and the detachment marched up, declared: "Here come the bloodhounds now. Now, men, you do your duty and I'll do mine." According to one officer, Fielden drew a revolver and fired at the police while he was standing on the wagon and before the bomb was thrown; others swore that he first climbed down from the wagon and fired while taking cover behind it.

All this, however, was contradicted by witnesses for both the defense and prosecution. A reporter, William H. Freeman, who was standing near the wagon, swore that he did not hear Fielden say, "Here come the bloodhounds; you do your duty and I'll do mine," or anything else of that import, nor did he see him fire a pistol at the police. Freeman's testimony was corroborated by another reporter, G. P. English, as well as by other witnesses, including policemen. On cross-examination, Detective Louis Haas, who had sworn that Fielden did indeed make the "bloodhounds" statement, admitted that he had appeared before the coroner's jury on May 5 and "did not say in my testimony there anything about this alleged remark of Fielden's."[27]

Fielden himself denied making any such statement. He swore, in addition, that he had never been armed or handled a gun: "I had no revolver with me on the night of May 4. I never had a revolver in my life. I never fired at any person in my life."[28] Other witnesses stated that Fielden was not armed and had not called out for resistance. According to Captain Ward, who gave the order for the meeting to disperse, "There was no pistol firing of any kind by anybody before the explosion of the bomb," a statement confirmed by Lieutenant James P. Stanton and others. It was never proved, moreover, that anybody on the speakers' wagon or in the crowd ever shot at the police. Many witnesses, on the contrary, maintained that it was the police themselves who began the firing, and that all the firing came from them.

How then was the prosecution to make its case? No proof had been offered, apart from the tainted evidence of Thompson and Gilmer, that any of the defendants had had a hand in throwing the bomb. Nor was it proved that Fielden or any of the others had fired on the police or sought to injure them in any way. Nor again was there convincing testimony that any of the speakers had incited violence. Mayor Harrison himself described their speeches as "tame," and G. P. English thought they were "a little milder than I heard them make for years."[29]

What was the state's attorney to do if he hoped to secure a conviction? For one thing, he dropped the pretense that any of the men on trial were involved in the actual bombthrowing. At the same time, the question of who in fact threw the bomb was thrust aside as irrelevant. It was not necessary to bring the bombthrower into court, Grinnell insisted. "Although perhaps none of these men personally threw the bomb, they each and all abetted, encouraged and advised the throwing of it and are therefore as guilty as the individual who in fact threw it."[30]

Having failed to prove actual murder on the part of the prisoners, Grinnell fell back on the charge of conspiracy. By means of the testimony of Gottfried Waller and Bernhard Schrade, who had turned state's evidence, he attempted to establish the existence of a terrorist plot, hatched at the Greif's Hall meeting on May 3, the general object of which was the overthrow of the prevailing order by force. "The armed men were there," Grinnell told the jury. "Fischer was there; Lingg was there; Engel was there." Somebody had to provide the bombs, and Lingg volunteered. "He was the bomb-maker of the Anarchists, and we have found and traced to him at least twenty-two of these infernal machines, one of which passed from his hands to the man who threw it at the Haymarket Square."[31] The death of Officer Degan, Grinnell contended, was a direct result of this plot, and all of the conspirators were accessories to his murder whether the actual perpetrator was found or not.

The case thus constructed against the defendants had an undeniable plausibility. Engel and Fischer were indeed extremists. Lingg did make and distribute bombs. All three were armed and believed in physical force. Everything they and their comrades had allegedly done or said was fitted by the prosecution into a coherent and seemingly malevolent pattern. And all of this, without a doubt, weighed heavily in the minds of the jurors.

At closer look, however, one finds glaring distortions and misstatements on the part of the state's attorney, without which his whole case would have collapsed. In the first place, as both Waller and Schrade admitted, nothing was said at the Greif's Hall meeting about any action to be taken at the Haymarket. If a conspiracy had indeed been set afoot, the incident of May 4 was in no way connected with it. Furthermore, as the defense pointed out, only two of the eight defendants, Engel and Fischer, had been present at the Monday night meeting. Lingg, despite Grinnell's allegation, did not attend. Apart from Captain Schaack, not a single witness, not even Waller or Schrade, testified that he was there. Lingg himself flatly denied it, insisting that he had been at a meeting of the carpenters' union in Zepf's Hall that night. This was corroborated by a fellow member of the union, who swore that Lingg presented a report at 9 P.M. and remained until the close two hours later.

Lingg, moreover, did not attend the Haymarket meeting on May 4 and was not within two miles of it the entire evening. And while he had in fact made bombs that afternoon, it was never proved that the Haymarket bomb was among them. Experts for the state could testify only that the bomb which killed Officer Degan was similar in composition to bombs made by Lingg. Even so, Grinnell's special assistant, Mr. Ingham, was forced to admit that there was a noticeable difference in the thickness of their shells. What was more, as Sigmund Zeisler indicated, the testimony of all witnesses regarding Lingg's actions showed that "whatever he did, whatever he may have attempted, intended or proposed on the North Side that night, he had no knowledge or suspicion that a bomb would be thrown at the Haymarket meeting."[32] Not even William Seliger, the principal witness against Lingg, sought to connect him with the Haymarket incident. Seliger, it is worth noting, admitted under cross-examination that he had been given money by Captain Schaack to testify in behalf of the prosecution. The same admission was made by

Gottfried Waller, and, after the trial, both Seliger and Waller were sent to Germany with their families at police expense.

Lingg was not alone in his ignorance about the Haymarket explosion. It was never shown that any of the defendants had known that a bomb would be thrown at the police, much less that they had engineered the incident. Parsons, in fact, brought his wife and children to the meeting, something he would scarcely have done if violence had been planned or even anticipated. "Is it sensible to suppose that he would have exposed his entire family to the danger of an explosion," asked Dr. Schmidt of the Defense Committee, "if he had known that such a thing was going to happen?" Parsons, in addition, called for the meeting to adjourn to Zepf's, "indicating to any sane person that he knew nothing of the bomb to be thrown."[33] Would Fischer, if he were involved in a conspiracy to throw bombs at the police, have gone, like Parsons, to a beer-hall while the meeting was in progress? Would Engel, the alleged mastermind of the plot, have been at home playing cards? Would Schwab and Neebe have been miles away from the scene?

Such were the questions posed by the attorneys for the defendants. Besides, how could the accused have known that Bonfield would march on the meeting? And why, if there had been a conspiracy to murder policemen, was only a single bomb thrown? "It was just as easy for them to throw a dozen, or fifty," Mayor Harrison remarked, "and to throw them in all parts of the city, as it was to have thrown one."[34] The bomb, moreover, as Lucy Parsons pointed out, "had been thrown with such suddenness and deadly effect that it had thoroughly disorganized and demoralized the police, and they became an easy prey for an enemy to attack and completely annihilate if there had been any conspiracy or concerted understanding."[35]

How, finally, asked Captain Black and his associates, could their clients be shown to be in a conspiracy with an unknown person? To hold them as accessories on the ground of conspiracy, it must be demonstrated by credible evidence that the man who committed the offense was one of the conspirators, and that his act was within the purview of the conspiracy, both of which the prosecution had failed to do. In any case, as Sigmund Zeisler pointed out, the charge of conspiracy when leveled against individuals who had publicly and repeatedly proclaimed their views was patently absurd. Nor, indeed, added Zeisler, could a social revolution be brought about through a conspiracy. It was a phenomenon that developed of itself, and "no single man, nor a dozen of men," could engineer it. Zeisler's words were echoed by Schwab in his final appearance before the court: "A movement is not a conspiracy. All we did was done in open daylight. There were no secrets. We prophesied in word and writing the coming of a great revolution, a change in the system of production in all industrial countries of the globe. And the change will come, and must come." So it was also for Parsons. A reporter, M. E. Dickson, testified to having conversed with him on the subject. "Parsons," he said, "never expressed any distinct proposal to inaugurate the revolution at any particular time, or by the use of any particular force. He simply spoke of the social revolution as the inevitable future."[36]

Thus the case for a conspiracy was shown to be deficient. Grinnell, however, had yet another strategy in reserve. Before the trial, he had discussed with friends and associates the difficulty of proceeding against accessories when the principal had not been identified or apprehended. Among those with whom he had consulted was Melville E. Stone, editor of the *Chicago Daily News*. "I at once took the ground," Stone writes in his memoirs, "that the identity of the bombthrower was of no consequence, and that, inasmuch as Spies and Parsons and Fielden had advocated over and over again the use of violence against the police, and had urged the manufacture and throwing of bombs, their culpability was clear."[37]

It was on this view of the law that the state's attorney now proceeded. The core of his case became the allegation that the bombthrower, whoever he was, had been impelled to commit his act by the inflammatory writings and speeches of the defendants. *The Alarm* and *Arbeiter-Zeitung* were carefully sifted for violent passages which, over the objections of the defense, were presented verbatim to the jury. Days were spent in reading articles, editorials, speeches, notices, and letters advocating violence and insurrection. Every utterance by the defendants that contained or seemed to contain a threat against established society was repeated before the court. In addition, excerpts from Most's *Revolutionary War Science*, the Pittsburgh Manifesto, Lucy Parsons's *Appeal to Tramps*, and Bakunin and Nechaev's *Catechism of a Revolutionary* were introduced, along with Spies's "Revenge Circular" and testimony of a policeman and a Pinkerton, both of whom had infiltrated the International, to the effect that Parsons and his colleagues had repeatedly called for the use of dynamite.

The purpose of this evidence, it quickly became clear, was not only to show that the prisoners had advocated violence, but also to arouse the passions of the jury against them. When the defense rose to protest, Judge Gary said: "Sit down, and don't make scenes!" Gary further admitted in evidence the torn and bloodstained uniforms of the dead and wounded policemen, which were spread out on a table before the jury. It was, as Dyer Lum called it, "a disgusting and vulgar appeal to passions and fears."[38] Surgeons were called to the stand who described the injuries in all their gory detail. "Where," wrote Parsons in his notes made at the trial, "are the crushed and mangled, the dead and dying victims of Monopoly? Countless millions in the tread-mills of Slavery and death under the lash and bayonets of the privileged class?"[39]

In a further effort to inflame the emotions of the jury, the state exhibited bombs, fulminating caps, shells, melting-ladles, and other paraphernalia of the dynamiter's craft, although they had not been traced to any of the defendants and had nothing to do with the death of Officer Degan. Engel's "furnace," or "blasting machine," was similarly introduced, even though it was shown never to have been used for any purpose, let alone to make explosives. In addition, banners with revolutionary mottoes were waved before the jury that for years had been openly displayed in the streets of Chicago during the rallies and processions of the International. Time and again the defense objected to the presentation of such material, only to be overruled by the court. "The enemies of liberty," jotted Parsons in his notebook, "strive to create the belief that an Anarchist is a dynamiter. I deny it. I say that is a villainous slander—a malicious, premeditated falsehood. I'll tell you what an Anarchist is. Anarchists are people who know their rights and dare to maintain them. If this makes me an Anarchist then put me down as such, and if this makes me a dynamiter then count me as one."[40]

The defense made no effort to deny that the Pittsburgh Manifesto, which had been frequently reprinted in the columns of both *The Alarm* and the *Arbeiter-Zeitung*, declared the object of the International to be the "destruction of the existing class rule by all means, i.e., by energetic, relentless, revolutionary and international action," nor that both papers in their articles and editorials, and Spies, Schwab,

Fielden, and Parsons in their speeches, had repeatedly advocated these doctrines and urged the workers to arm themselves against the inevitable conflict with capital, nor yet that Most's *Revolutionary War Science* had been quoted and serialized in these papers and copies of the booklet sold at picnics and meetings of the International and kept in the library of its General Committee. Nevertheless, replied the defense, the prosecution had failed to establish the most vital point of its theory: that the person who threw the bomb had done so at the urging, directly or indirectly, of the prisoners or had in any way been influenced by their written or spoken pronouncements. The mere general advice to commit revolutionary or violent acts, without evidence connecting that advice with the bombthrower, was insufficient to warrant the conviction of any of the defendants as accessories; and since the bombthrower had not been apprehended, it was impossible to determine his motives or to show that he had known the defendants or read any of their writings or heard any of their speeches. For all anyone could tell, he may not have been an anarchist at all, but perhaps an *agent provocateur*, or a madman, or an individual driven to his deed by a desire for revenge for some act of police brutality.

Here lay the ultimate weakness of the prosecution's case. Judge Gary disposed of it, however, in his instructions to the jury, delivered on the last day of the proceedings. At no other point in the trial, except during the selection of the jury, were Gary's rulings more injurious to the defendants. If, he now declared, they conspired to overthrow the law by force, and if, in the pursuance of such a conspiracy, a bomb was thrown by a member of the conspiracy, resulting in the death of Officer Degan, then the defendants were accessories to the murder whether or not the identity of the bombthrower had been established. Further, and even more damaging, if the defendants "by print or speech advised, or encouraged the commission of murder, without designating time, place or occasion at which it should be done, and in pursuance of, and induced by such advice and encouragement, murder was committed, then all of such conspirators are guilty of such murder, whether the person who perpetrated such murder can be identified or not."[41]

Gary, with these words, presented a new, unheard-of charge to the jury. It was, by his own later admission, contrary to all legal precedent. By way of defending his action, he argued that the case itself was of an unprecedented nature, so that it required an unprecedented ruling from the bench. If he had "strained the law" a bit, he was to be commended, not criticized, for doing so.[42] Gary's interpretation of the law proved decisive in leading the jury to its verdict. It was everything the prosecution could have hoped for.

Lucy E. Parsons

2. Lucy Parsons (New York Public Library)

1. The young Albert Parsons (Chicago Historical Society)

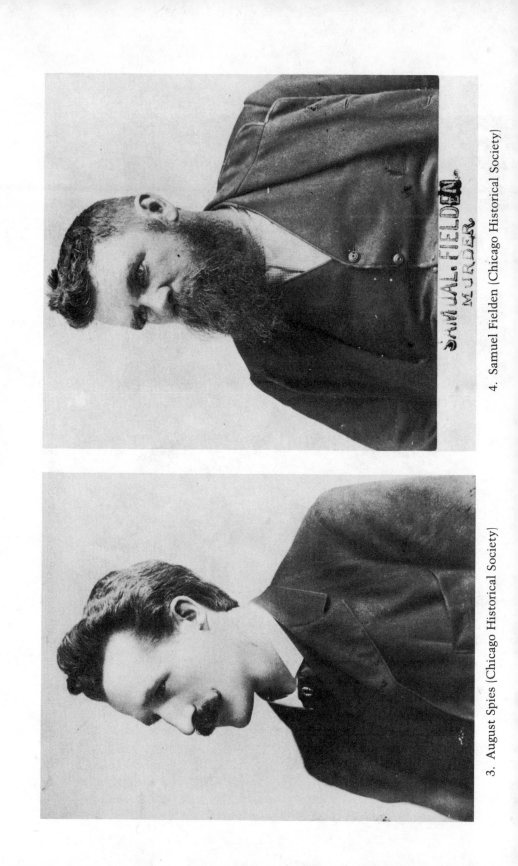

3. August Spies (Chicago Historical Society)

4. Samuel Fielden (Chicago Historical Society)

MICHAEL SCHWAB.
Sentenced to Death.

5. Michael Schwab (Chicago Historical Society)

6. Oscar Neebe (Labadie Collection)

7. George Engel (Chicago
   Historical Society)

8. Adolph Fischer (Chicago
   Historical Society)

9. Louis Lingg (courtesy of H. P. Kraus)

March. 1890.   INTERNATIONALE BIBLIOTHEK.   No. 16 A.

THE SOCIAL MONSTER

BY JOHN MOST.

Entered at the New York Post Office as Second Class Mail Matter. Published Monthly
John Müller, 167 William Street, New York, P. O. Box 3135.

SUBSCRIPTION PRICE, 50 CENTS PER YEAR.

10. *The Social Monster* by Johann Most
(Columbia University Library)

REVENGE!

Workingmen, to Arms!!!

Your masters sent out their bloodhounds — the police –; they killed six of your brothers at McCormicks this afternoon. They killed the poor wretches, because they, like you, had the courage to disobey the supreme will of your bosses. They killed them, because they dared ask for the shortenin of the hours of toil. They killed them to show you, "Free American Citizens!", that you must be satisfied and contended with whatever your bosses condescend to allow you, or you will get killed!

You have for years endured the most abject humiliations; you have for years suffered unmeasurable iniquities; you have worked yourself to death; you have endured the pangs of want and hunger; your Children you have sacrificed to the factory-lords — in short: You have been miserable and obedient slave all these years: Why? To satisfy the insatiable greed, to fill the coffers of your lazy thieving master? When you ask them now to lessen your burden, he sends his bloodhounds out to shoot you, kill you!

If you are men, if you are the sons of your grand sires, who have shed their blood to free you, then you will rise in your might, Hercules, and destroy the hideous monster that seeks to destroy you. To arms we call you, to arms!

Your Brothers.

Rache! Rache!

Arbeiter, zu den Waffen!

Arbeitendes Volk, heute Nachmittag mordeten die Bluthunde Eurer Ausbeuter 6 Eurer Brüder draußen bei McCormick's. Warum mordeten sie dieselben? Weil sie den Muth hatten, mit dem Loos unzufrieden zu sein, welches Eure Ausbeuter ihnen beschieden haben. Sie forderten Brod, man antwortete ihnen mit Blei, eingedenk der Thatsache, daß man damit das Volk am wirksamsten zum Schweigen bringen kann! Viele, viele Jahre habt Ihr alle Demüthigungen ohne Widerspruch ertragen, habt Euch vom frühen Morgen bis zum späten Abend geschunden, habt Entbehrungen jeder Art ertragen, habt Eure Kinder selbst geopfert — Alles, um die Schatzkammern Euer Herren zu füllen, Alles für sie! Und jetzt, wo Ihr vor sie hintretet, und sie ersucht, Eure Bürde etwas zu erleichtern, da hetzen sie zum Dank für Eure Opfer ihre Bluthunde, die Polizei, auf Euch, um Euch mit Bleikugeln von der Unzufriedenheit zu kuriren Sklaven, wir fragen und beschwören Euch bei Allem, was Euch heilig und werth ist, rächt diesen scheußlichen Mord, den man heute an Euren Brüdern begeng, und vielleicht morgen schon an Euch begehen wird. Arbeitendes Volk, Herkules, Du bist am Scheideweg angelangt. Wofür entscheidest Du Dich? Für Sklaverei und Hunger, oder für Freiheit und Brod? Entscheidest Du Dich für das Letztere, dann säume keinen Augenblick; dann, Volk, zu den Waffen! Vernichtung den menschlichen Bestien, die sich Deine Herrscher nennen! Rücksichtslose Vernichtung ihnen — das muß Deine Losung sein! Denk' der Helden, deren Blut den Weg zum Fortschritt, zur Freiheit und zur Menschlichkeit gedüngt — und strebe, ihre würdig zu werden!

Eure Brüder.

11. Spies's "Revenge Circular" (Chicago Historical Society)

12. Announcement of Haymarket meeting (Chicago Historical Society)

13. Haymarket Square, 1890 (Chicago Historical Society)

14. The Haymarket bombing as portrayed in *Harper's Weekly*, 1886 (Chicago Historical Society)

15. Judge Joseph E. Gary (Chicago Historical Society)

16. State's Attorney Julius S. Grinnell (Chicago Historical Society)

17. William P. Black and his wife Hortensia (New York Public Library)

Entered according to Act of Congress in the year 1887 by PAUL J. MORAND, in the Office of the Librarian of Congress, at Washington.

SURRENDER OF PARSONS.

Chicago, June 21, 1886.

18. "Surrender of Parsons," halftone by Paul J. Morand, 1887
(Chicago Historical Society)

19. Mayor Carter H. Harrison, 1893 (Columbia University Library)

20. George A. Schilling, 1888 (Labadie Collection)

21. William Holmes, 1888 (Labadie Collection)

22. Dyer D. Lum (Tamiment Library)

POLICE HEADQUARTERS

CITY OF CHICAGO
INCORPORATED 4TH MARCH 1837

CHICAGO, *June 14th* 188 *6*

Arrest For Murder

and

Inciting Riot,

Rudolph Schnaubelt about 30 years of age, 6 feet high, 190 lbs weight, slightly stooped shouldered, light brown hair, usually wears full light beard, but was shaved off when he left here, and wore light mustache.

Depend more on photograph than above description. Works at making matchmakers tools.

Schnaubelt was one of the leading Anarchists who caused the riot and massacre in Chicago, May 4th

If found arrest him and wire me,

Fredrick Ebersold,
Gen'l Superintendent of Police.

23. Police report on Rudolph Schnaubelt, 1886 (Chicago Historical Society)

24. Schnaubelt and family in Buenos Aires, around 1896 (courtesy of Henry R. Schnaubelt)

FRANK LESLIE'S ILLUSTRATED NEWSPAPER

No. 1,672.—VOL. LXV.]   NEW YORK—FOR THE WEEK ENDING OCTOBER 1, 1887.   [PRICE, 10 CENTS. $4.00 YEARLY. 12 WEEKS, $1.00

NO. 1. MRS. NINA VAN ZANDT SPIES.   NO. 2. AUGUST SPIES.

ILLINOIS.—"MURDERERS' ROW," IN COOK COUNTY JAIL, CHICAGO, SHOWING THE CELLS OF THE CONDEMNED ANARCHISTS, THE "DEATH WATCH," AND THE PRISONERS RECEIVING VISITORS.
FROM A SKETCH BY WILL E. CHAPIN.—SEE PAGE 102.

25. The prisoners receiving visitors, Cook County Jail, 1887
    (State Historical Society of Wisconsin)

26. Albert Parsons, 1887 (courtesy of H. P. Kraus)

AN APPEAL

TO THE PEOPLE OF AMERICA.

TO THE AMERICAN PEOPLE—*Fellow Citizens:* As all the world knows I have been convicted and sentenced to die for the crime of murder—the most heinous offense that can be committed. Under the forms of law two courts—viz., the criminal and supreme courts of the state of Illinois—have sentenced me to death as an accessory before the fact to the murder of Officer Degan on May 4, 1886. Nevertheless I am innocent of the crime charged, and to a candid and unprejudiced world I submit the proof.

In the decision affirming the sentence of death upon me, the supreme court of the state of Illinois says: "It is undisputed that the bomb was thrown that caused the death of Degan. It is conceded that no one of the defendants threw the bomb with his own hands. Plaintiffs in error are charged with being accessories before the fact."

If I did not throw the bomb myself it becomes necessary to prove that I aided, encouraged, and advised the person who did throw it. Is that fact proven? The supreme court says it is. The record says it is not. I appeal to the American people to judge between them.

The supreme court quotes articles from *The Alarm*, the paper edited by me, and from my speeches running back three years before the Haymarket tragedy of May 4, 1886. Upon said articles and speeches the court affirms my sentence of death as an accessory. The court says: "The articles in *The Alarm* were most of them written by the defendant Parsons, and some of them by the defendant Spies," and then proceeds to quote these articles. I refer to the record to prove that of all the articles quoted only one was shown to have been written by me. I wrote, of course, a great many articles for my paper *The Alarm*, but the record will show that only one of these many quoted by the supreme court to prove my guilt as an accessory was written by me, and this article appeared in *The Alarm* Dec. 6, 1884, one year and a half before the Haymarket meeting.

As to Mr. Spies, the record will show that during the three years I was editor of *The Alarm* he did not write for the paper half a dozen articles. For proof as to this I appeal to the record.

The Alarm was a labor paper, and, as is well known, a labor paper is conducted as a medium through which working people can make known their grievances. *The Alarm* was no exception to this rule. I not only did not write "most of the articles," but wrote comparatively few of them. This the record will also show.

In referring to my Haymarket speech the court says: "To the men then listening to him he had addressed the incendiary appeals that had been appearing in *The Alarm* for two years." The court then quotes the "incendiary" article which I did write, and

which is as follows: "One dynamite bomb properly placed will destroy a regiment of soldiers; a weapon easily made and carried with perfect safety in the pockets of one's clothing."

The record will show by referring to *The Alarm* that this is a garbled extract taken from a statement made by General Philip Sheridan in his annual report to congress. It was simply a reiteration of Gen. Sheridan's statement that dynamite was easily made, perfectly safe to handle, and a very destructive

WEAPON OF WARFARE.

The article in full as it appeared in *The Alarm* is as follows:

"Dynamite. The protection of the poor against the armies of the rich. In submitting his annual report Nov. 10, 1884. Gen. Philip Sheridan, commander of the United States army, says: "This nation is growing so rapidly that there are signs of other troubles which I hope will not occur, and which will probably not come upon us if both capital and labor will only be conservative. Still it should be remembered destructive explosives are easily made, and that banks, United States sub-treasuries, public buildings, and large mercantile houses can be readily demolished, and the commerce of entire cities destroyed by an infuriated people with means carried with perfect safety to themselves in the pockets of their clothing."

The editorial comment upon the above, as it appeared in *The Alarm*, is as follows: "A hint to the wise is sufficient. Of course Gen. Sheridan is too modest to tell us this himself. The army will be powerless in the coming revolution between the propertied and propertyless classes. Only in foreign wars can the usual weapons of warfare be used to any advantage. One dynamite bomb properly placed will destroy a regiment of soldiers; a weapon easily made and carried with perfect safety in the pockets of one's clothing. The 1st regiment may as well disband, for if it should ever level its guns upon the workingmen of Chicago it can be totally annihilated."

Again the court says: "He [Parsons] had said to them [referring to the people assembled at the Haymarket] Saturday, April 24, 1886, just ten days before May 4, in the last issue of *The Alarm* that had appeared: "Workingmen, to arms! War to the palace, peace to the cottage, and death to luxurious idleness! The wage system is the only cause of the world's misery. It is supported by the rich classes, and to destroy it they must be either made to work or die. One pound of dynamite is better than a bushel of ballots! Make your demand for eight hours with weapons in your hands to meet the capitalist bloodhounds—police and militia—in a proper manner.'"

The record will show that this article was not written by me, but was published as a

news item. By referring to the columns of *The Alarm*, the following comment appears attached to the above article—viz.: "The above handbill was sent to us from Indianapolis, Ind., as having been posted all over that city last week. Our correspondent says that the police tore them down wherever they found them."

The court, continuing, says: "At the close of another article in the same issue he said: 'The social war has come, and whoever is not with us is against us.'" Asst. State's Atty. Walker read this article to the jury, and at its conclusion stated that it bore my initials and was my article. It is a matter within the knowledge of everyone then present, that I interrupted him and called his attention to the fact that the article did not bear my initials and that I was not its author. Mr. Walker corrected his mistake to the jury.

Now these are the three articles quoted by the supreme court as proof of my guilt as an accessory in a conspiracy to murder Officer Degan. The record will

PROVE WHAT I SAY.

Now as to my speeches. All of them with one exception purporting to be my utterances at the Haymarket are given from the excited imagination and perverted memories of newspaper reporters. Mr. English, who alone took shorthand notes and swore to their correctness, reports me as saying: "It is time to raise a note of warning. There is nothing in the eight-hour movement to excite the capitalist. Don't you know that the militia are under arms and a Gatling gun is ready to mow you down? Was this Germany, or Russia, or Spain? [A voice: 'It looks like it.'] Whenever you make a demand for eight hours' pay, or increase of pay, the militia and deputy sheriffs and the Pinkerton men are called out, and you are shot and clubbed and murdered in the streets. I am not here for the purpose of inciting anybody, but to speak out—to tell the facts as they exist, even though it shall cost me my life before morning!"

Mr. English, continuing, said: "There is another part of it [the speech] right here. 'It behooves you, as you love your wife and children, if you don't want to see them perish with hunger, killed, or cut down like dogs on the street—Americans, in the interest of your liberty and your independence, to arm, arm yourselves!'"

This, be it remembered, is a garbled extract, and it is a matter of record that Reporter English testified that he was instructed by the proprietor of his paper to report only the inflammatory portions of the speeches made at that meeting. Mayor Harrison, who was present and heard this speech, testified before the jury that it was simply "a violent and political harangue," and did not call for his interference as a peace officer.

The speech delivered by me at the Hay-

27. An Appeal to the People of America by Albert Parsons, 1887
(Columbia University Library)

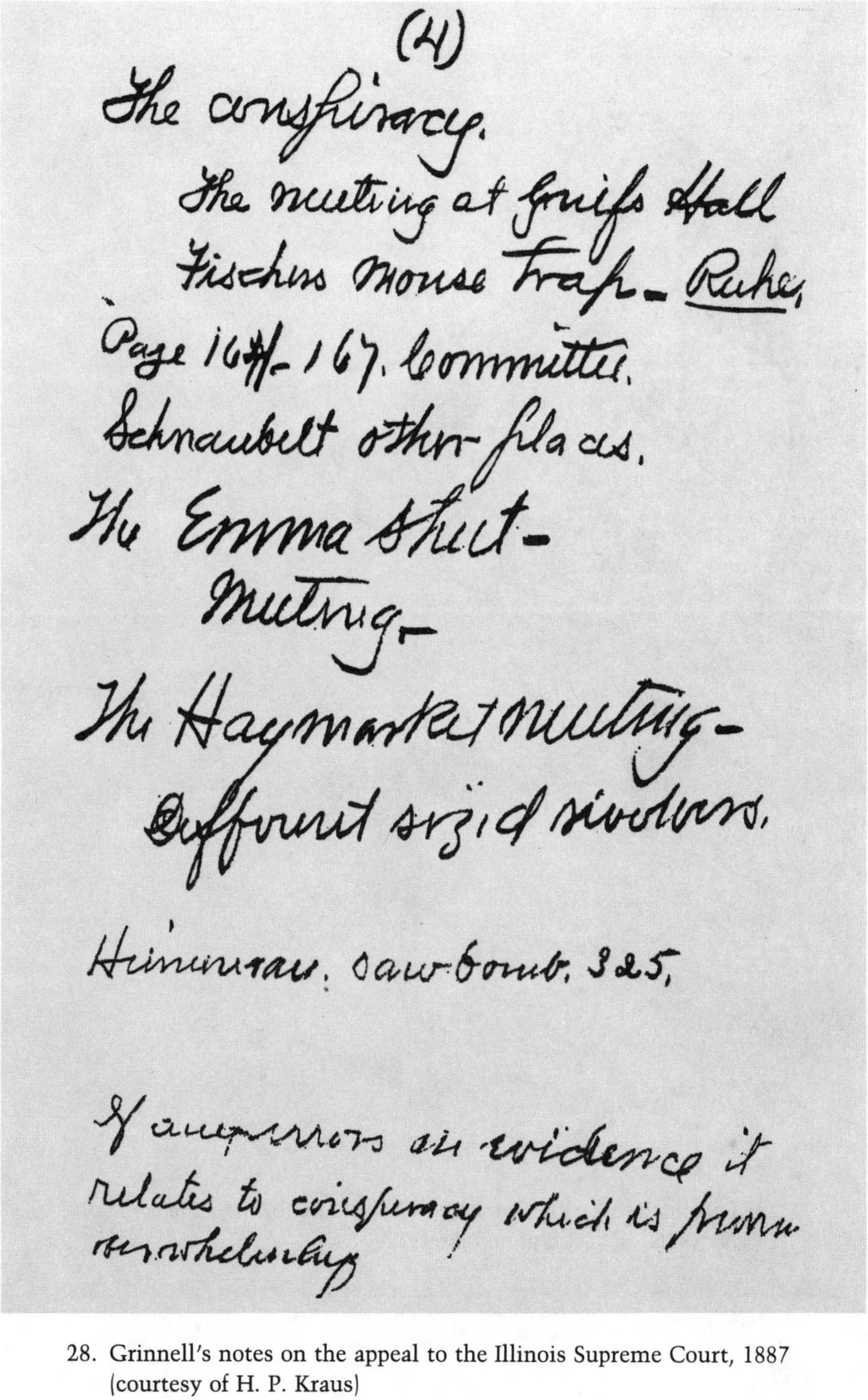

(4)

The conspiracy.

The meeting at Grief's Hall

Fischer Mouse Trap – <u>Ruhe</u>

Page 164 - 167. Committee.

Schnaubelt other places.

The Emma Street—

meeting—

The Haymarket meeting—

Different arg'd vivelars.

Himmraw. saw bomb. 325,

If any errors in evidence it
relates to conspiracy which is proven
overwhelming

28. Grinnell's notes on the appeal to the Illinois Supreme Court, 1887
(courtesy of H. P. Kraus)

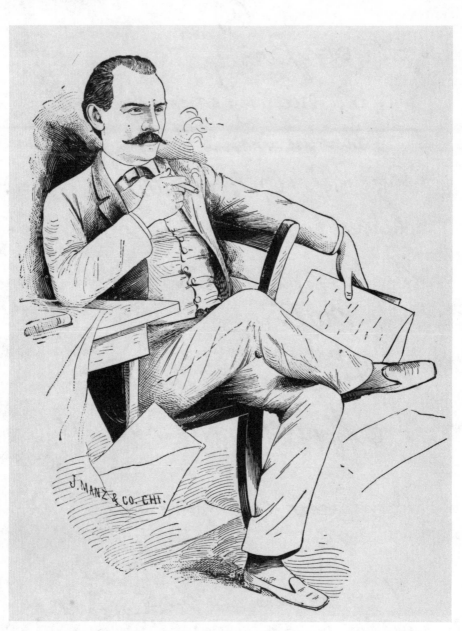

29. Parsons in his cell, sketched by Art Young for the *Chicago Daily News* (New York Public Library)

30. The hanging, November 11, 1887 (Chicago Historical Society)

31. Governor John Peter Altgeld (New York Public Library)

32. The Haymarket monument (Chicago Historical Society)

33. "The Anarchists of Chicago," memorial drawing by Walter Crane,
1894 (Columbia University Library)

18 ‖ THE VERDICT

It was late in the afternoon of August 19, two months after the opening of the trial, when the jurors retired for their deliberations. Only a few hours later it was rumored that they had reached an agreement and would render a verdict the next morning. When the court opened on August 20, special precautions had been taken to prevent any disturbance. No spectators were admitted except for relatives and friends of the defendants. A contingent of police, under the direction of Captain Schaack, was detailed to the courtroom, while additional men guarded the entrances and patrolled the corridors and lobbies. One officer, armed with club and revolver, was assigned to watch each prisoner. Outside the courthouse a crowd gathered to hear the verdict.

The defendants were led in shortly before 10 A.M. Soon afterwards the jurors took their places. Under Illinois law the jurors were required not only to decide on the guilt or innocence of the accused, but also to prescribe the penalty in case of conviction. Judge Gary asked if they had reached a verdict. The foreman, Mr. Osborn, replied, "We have," and handed the clerk a paper. "We, the jury," read the clerk, "find the defendants August Spies, Michael Schwab, Samuel Fielden, Albert R. Parsons, Adolph Fischer, George Engel, and Louis Lingg guilty of murder in manner and form as charged in the indictment, and fix the penalty at death. We find the defendant Oscar Neebe guilty of murder in manner and form as charged in the indictment, and fix the penalty at imprisonment in the penitentiary for fifteen years."[1]

As the clerk finished reading, Maria Schwab, the wife of Michael Schwab and sister of Rudolph Schnaubelt, a "tall and graceful woman of a pure pink-and-white complexion," as Judge Gary describes her, fainted into the arms of Lucy Parsons and Sarah Ames, who had been sitting beside her. Although she quickly revived, she was at once overcome by hysteria, and "sharp, shrill, agonizing screams rent the air of the court-room," wrote a reporter in the audience, "causing the stoutest heart to shudder at the manifest anguish of the sufferer." This occurred just as the prisoners were being led out. Schwab turned for an instant at the door, recognizing the voice of his wife, but was not allowed to go to her relief. Christine Spies, August's mother, clung to her daughter for support. Tears filled the eyes of all the others. Mrs. Engel was "the picture of sadness." General Parsons went over and comforted his sister-in-law, who was sobbing quietly.[2]

The defendants themselves received the verdict with composure. "Not a face blanched," said Captain Black, "not an eye quailed, not a hand trembled."[3] Parsons, a born actor, drew a bright red handkerchief from his pocket and waved it through an open window to the crowd below. The officer assigned to watch him ordered him to stop. Parsons complied, but first took the cords hanging from the blinds and, making a loop, formed them into a noose to apprise the crowd of the decision. A wild cheer went up. Then he was led out of the courtroom with the other prisoners.[4]

The verdict was greeted with approval by an overwhelming majority of the population. Not only in Chicago but across the nation people rejoiced that law and order had triumphed over anarchy and subversion. To voice the smallest doubt regarding the trial, the validity of the verdict, or the propriety of the sentences might be construed as a token of anarchist sympathies. Messages of congratulation poured in upon the state's attorney. "I am proud of our Government," wrote J. V. Farwell, president of the YMCA and a Chicago multimillionaire. "Its beauty and power over all other Governments is demonstrated by the conviction of the Anarchist fiends. . . . Why, even Russia is left behind, for while she sends them to Siberian mines, or to the execution block, it is only as individuals. It was left for our glorious America to teach them a lesson in how to exterminate this social vermin by chopping off its head, and thus kill the body of the movement."[5]

Newspapers throughout the country hailed the verdict in similar terms: it would not only smash anarchism in Chicago but serve as a warning to radicals all over the world that they could not come to America and abuse the precious right of free speech. "The Scaffold Waits," exulted the *Chicago Tribune*. "Seven Dangling Nooses for the Dynamite Fiends." "The socialist malefactors will be hanged," declared the *Chicago Times*, "and if their disciples continue their propaganda of crime, even in whispers, it is only a question of time when they will mount the golden stairs of the same road."[6]

In the entire United States not one important daily paper was critical of the trial or the way in which Judge Gary had conducted it. Gary, for his own part, complimented the jurors. When discharging them after reading the verdict, he remarked that they deserved "some recognition of the service you have performed besides the meager compensation you are to receive." A letter, echoing Gary's sentiments, appeared in the *Chicago Tribune*: "The long agony is over. Law has triumphed. Anarchy is defeated. The conspirators have been promptly convicted. Let them be as promptly punished. The 'twelve good men and true' whose honesty and fearlessness made a conviction possible should not be forgotten. They have performed their unpleasant duty without flinching. Let them be generously remembered. Raise a fund—say $100,000—to be presented with the thanks of a grateful people."[7]

To others, however, it seemed that the jurors had reached their decision with inordinate speed, taking as they had less than three hours to condemn seven men to the gallows and one to fifteen years in prison. "Think of the mass of testimony that the jury would have had to go over in order to give them even a semblance of a fair trial," Lucy Parsons remarked.[8] Captain Black was appalled. For, while the verdict did not come as a complete surprise, he had not expected the seven death sentences, nor the conviction of Neebe, against whom, as even Grinnell admitted, there was only the slenderest evidence of guilt. Indeed, the charges against Neebe would probably have been dismissed halfway through the trial had the state's attorney not feared the influence such a step might have in favor of the other defendants. It was known, furthermore, that the prosecution had had no expectation of securing the death penalty for more than four of the accused: Spies, Fischer, Engel, and Lingg. When Grinnell delivered his closing address, almost his last words to the jury were that there were gradations in the guilt of the men, implying that there should be gradations in the severity of their sentences: "Spies, Fischer, Lingg, Engel, Fielden, Parsons, Schwab, Neebe, in my opinion, based on the proof, is the order of the punishments."[9]

That the penalties should have exceeded even the wishes of the prosecutor was a measure of the jurors' hostility towards the defendants. "Never get tried by the other fellow's hired man," said Colonel Robert G. Ingersoll, America's leading freethinker, to George

Schilling. "If you do you will get left every time. When I die and appear before the bar of Heaven for judgment, if God will come forward himself and listen to my story I'll stand a show. But if he will turn me over to one of his clerks I will be gone."[10]

Nor did the verdict result from any inadequacies on the part of Captain Black and his associates. On the whole, the prisoners had been ably defended, and one is hard put to imagine what might have been done differently that would have significantly altered the outcome. The case was beyond remedy. "Any jury," noted Samuel McConnell, "considering the state of public opinion and Judge Gary's rulings and instructions, would have convicted the defendants."[11] McConnell was right. Indeed, even if the actual bombthrower had given himself up, the eight men, it seems likely, would still have been tried as accessories, found guilty, and made to suffer the extreme penalty. As it was, the environment in the courtroom was implacably hostile to justice. In an atmosphere of hatred, before a packed jury and a blatantly prejudiced judge, the defendants never had a chance. The verdict, as Parsons rightly noted, was "a verdict of passion, born in passion, nurtured in passion"; it was "the sum total of the organized passion of the city of Chicago."[12] As Spies and Fischer interpreted it, seven policemen had died, and therefore seven anarchists had to pay the penalty. Guilt or innocence was of no consequence. The state wanted blood—and got it.

It was for this reason, one suspects, that no careful investigation had been made to discover the actual bombthrower. What difference did it make who had flung the deadly missile? The anarchists were to blame. They had spoken and written of dynamite. They had urged resistance to the police. They belonged to an organization—the International—dedicated to the overthrow of the existing order. Lingg had made bombs, and Engel had had in his home a contraption that could have been used for a similar purpose. Hence, whether or not they were responsible for this particular murder, society would be well rid of them; and society had the right, indeed the duty, to protect itself against bombthrowers and assassins, even if this should mean stretching the law for the purpose.

Such was the logic of the prosecution, as well as of the judge and jury. The necessity of establishing a solid judicial case of guilt, the legal obligation of proceeding in an atmosphere conducive to a fair trial—these things were dismissed as hairsplitting or as reflecting sympathy for the elements that threatened the safety and well-being of the city.[13] To a community rendered mad from indignation and fear, such an attitude seemed entirely proper. It had the approval, for one, of George Emery, a member of the Citizens' Association. "Well," he told Hortensia Black, the wife of the chief counsel for the defense, "your husband's clients are going to be hung." "Not lawfully," she replied. "Law! I care nothing for law!" exclaimed Emery. "They shall be hung whether it is lawful or not!" "Stay," said Mrs. Black, "you do admit then there's no law by which they can be convicted?" "Oh, yes," replied Emery. "I'll admit that, but will say that it won't affect the issue; they must be hung anyhow."[14]

Emery's was the voice of public opinion, inflamed by the throwing of the bomb. Judge, jury, and prosecution were merely reflectors of this opinion. To them, as to the public at large, the eight defendants personified a doctrine that inspired the most passionate and deep-seated hatred. The popular cry was for retribution, for a merciless example that would silence the anarchists once and for all. And the machinery of law and order performed its required task.[15]

The defendants, in effect, had not been tried for murder, as charged in the indictment, but for their social and economic beliefs. The state had failed utterly to connect them with the bombing. What had been demonstrated, rather, was that they were anarchists who had denounced capitalism and government, agitators who had spoken and written against the prevailing order. As Parsons put it: "The only fact established by proof, as well as by our own admission, cheerfully given before the jury, was that we held opinions and preached a doctrine that is considered dangerous to the rascality and infamies of the privileged, law-creating class, known as monopolists." "There is no evidence," he wrote to a friend, "that I or any of us killed, or had anything to do with the killing of, policemen at the Haymarket. None at all. But it was proven clearly that we were, all of us, anarchists, socialists, communists, Knights of Labor, unionists. It was proven that three of us were editors of labor papers; that five of us were labor organizers and speakers at workingmen's mass meetings. They, this class court, jury, law and verdict, have decided that we must be put to death because, as they say, we are 'leaders' of men who denounce and battle against the oppression, slaveries, robbery and influences of the monopolists. Of these crimes against the capitalist class they found us guilty beyond any reasonable doubt, and, so finding, they have sentenced us."[16]

That this was the real issue had been made clear from the very outset. "Gentlemen," declared Grinnell in his opening address to the jury, "for the first time in the history of our country are people on trial for their lives for endeavoring to make Anarchy the rule, and in that attempt for ruthlessly and awfully destroying life." He warned that "the strength of our institutions may depend upon this case, because there is only one step beyond republicanism—that is Anarchy. See that we never take that step, and let us stand today as we have stood for years, firmly planted on the laws of our country." At the end of the proceedings Grinnell struck a similar note. "Law is on trial," he exclaimed. "Anarchy is on trial. These men have been selected, picked out by the grand jury and indicted because they were leaders. They are no more guilty than the thousands who follow them. Gentlemen of the jury, convict these men, make examples of them, hang them and you save our institutions, our society."[17]

In vain did counsel for the defendants argue that their clients must not be judged for their beliefs but only on whether or not they had committed murder. "If these men are to be tried on general principles," declared William Foster, "for advocating doctrines opposed to our ideas of propriety, there is no use for me to argue this case. Let the sheriff go and erect the scaffold. . . . Let us stop this farce now if the verdict is to be upon prejudice and general principles." Moses Salomon, in the same vein, pleaded with the jurors not to allow themselves "to convict any of the defendants either because he may be an Anarchist or a Socialist." The prisoners, he stressed, "are not charged with Anarchy; they are not charged with Socialism." They had been indicted for the murder of Officer Degan, and on that count alone they had to be judged. "Now these defendants," he insisted, "are not criminals; they are not robbers; they are not burglars; they are not common thieves; they descend to no small criminal act. On the contrary, the evidence shows conclusively that they are men of broad feelings of humanity, that their one desire has been and their lives have been consecrated to the betterment of their fellow-men"[18]

These appeals, however, fell on deaf ears. The jury proceeded inexorably to its verdict. For the accused, accordingly, American justice had shown its limitations. They had been convicted, they maintained, not because they had committed murder but because they had protested against a social system which they considered unjust; they had been condemned to death because they were champions of the poor and oppressed, because they had dared to explain to the workers the causes of their misery and enslavement. "A class jury, class law, class hate, and a court blinded with prejudice against our opinions has done its work," said Parsons. "We are its victims."[19] In a letter to his wife, written on the day of the verdict, he expressed the same sentiment: "Our verdict this morning cheers the hearts of tyrants throughout the world, and the result will be celebrated by King Capital in its drunken feast of flowing wine from Chicago to St. Petersburg. . . . There was *no evidence* that any one of the eight doomed men knew of, or advised, or abetted the Haymarket tragedy. But what does that matter? The privileged class *demands a victim*, and we are offered as a sacrifice to appease the hungry yells of an infuriated mob of millionaires, who will be contented with nothing less than our lives. Monopoly triumphs! Labor in chains ascends the scaffold for having dared to cry out for liberty and right!"[20]

Lucy had arrived at the same conclusion. Her husband and his comrades were being "sacrificed on the altar of class hatred," railroaded to the gallows for preaching against injustice and exploitation. To Lizzie Holmes it was "the most infamously unjust verdict that was ever reached by a jury." Capitalist "justice" had thrown off the mask. "After this," she wrote, "what possible claim can America have to being freer and better than other nations?"[21]

Following the delivery of the verdict, Captain Black asked for a new trial, on the ground that the defendants had not been proved guilty of the charges against them. On October 7 Judge Gary denied the request. No one had seriously thought he would do otherwise. Before passing sentence, however, he permitted the convicted men to address the court. All eight prisoners availed themselves of this opportunity and, in the traditional manner of revolutionaries, used the court as a forum for their ideas. (When there is no hope of escape, Most had written in his *Revolutionary War Science*, the revolutionist has "a different duty, the highest duty, to fulfil: he must defend his actions from the revolutionary-anarchist standpoint and convert the prisoners' dock into a tribune.")[22]

The speeches lasted three days, from October 7 to 9. One by one the condemned men rose from their seats: Spies, Schwab, Neebe, Fischer, Lingg, Engel, Fielden, Parsons. In words charged with defiance and indignation, they denounced the court and the whole system of "wage-slavery" that supported it, declaring themselves ready to die for the principles which they loved and which, they were certain, would one day liberate mankind and make life a pleasure and a joy worth living. This, for the prisoners, was their supreme hour. They felt that what they said would go far beyond the confines of the courtroom, that the whole world would judge them and the cause for which they pleaded by their present utterances.

Without exception they delivered powerful, deeply felt speeches, addressing themselves to workingmen everywhere. The style varied with the character and background of each speaker: autobiographical and impersonal, succinct and wordy, eloquent and plain. Some spoke for hours, some for only a few minutes. The addresses of Spies, Fielden, and Parsons were in the classic oratorical vein; the others were shorter and less philosophical but had an unadorned sincerity that was impressive. Unshakeable in anarchist principle and throbbing with the consciousness of martyrdom, the eight speeches echoed far and wide. They were printed and reprinted, translated into many languages, made into pamphlets, serialized in the anarchist press, and circulated by anarchist groups throughout the world. In no time they became classics of anarchist propaganda, cherished as gospels of the workers' cause. All of them defiant, some tinged with irony or pathos, they threw light on the personalities and aims of the defendants and scathingly exposed the unfairness of their trial.

The first man to speak was Spies. Addressing the court as "the representative of one class to the representative of another," he denounced the judicial system that had sentenced himself and his comrades to death, charging the state with deliberately plotting to use the Haymarket incident as a pretext to eliminate the leaders of the working class. "You may pronounce the sentence upon me, honorable judge," Spies declared, "but let the world know that in A.D. 1886, in the State of Illinois, eight men were sentenced to death because they believed in a better future, because they had not lost their faith in the ultimate victory of liberty and justice!"[23]

Spies drew a scathing picture of the capitalist "order"—he spoke the word with bitter irony—which the court was so determined to uphold: "Go with me to the half-starved miners of the Hocking Valley. Look at the pariahs in the Monongahela Valley, and many other mining districts in this country, or pass along the railroads of that most orderly and law-abiding citizen, Jay Gould. And then tell me whether this order has in it any moral principle for which it should be preserved."[24]

Seven policemen had died, Spies continued, and you, demanding a life for a life, sentence to the gallows an equal number of men, though they had nothing to do with the killings. "But if you think that by hanging us you can stamp out the labor movement—the movement from which the downtrodden millions, the millions who toil and live in want and misery, the wage slaves, expect salvation—if this is your opinion, then hang us! Here you will tread upon a spark, but here, and there, and behind you, and in front of you, and everywhere, the flames will blaze up. It is a subterranean fire. You cannot put it out. The ground is on fire upon which you stand."[25]

"Now," concluded Spies, "these are my ideas. They constitute a part of myself. I cannot divest myself of them, nor would I, if I could. And if you think that you can crush them out by sending us to the gallows, if you would once more have people suffer the penalty of death because they dared to tell the truth—and I defy you to show us where we have told a lie—I say, if death is the penalty for proclaiming the truth, then I will proudly and defiantly pay the costly price! Call your hangman! Truth crucified in Socrates, in Christ, in Giordano Bruno, in Huss, in Galileo, still lives—they and others whose number is legion have preceded us on this path. We are ready to follow!"[26]

Schwab, Spies's associate, was the second speaker. In a brief address he underscored the irregularities of the trial. Justice had not prevailed, he insisted, nor could it have under the circumstances, for "if one class is arrayed against the other, it is idle and hypocritical to think about justice." Anarchy had been on trial, as the state's attorney admitted. It mattered little who threw the bomb. "It was the movement the blow was aimed at." Grinnell had depicted anarchism as "something horrible—arson, rapine, murder." How then could it be that such eminent scholars as Peter Kropotkin and Elisée Reclus were avowed anarchists, even editors of anarchist newspapers? Anarchism, Schwab insisted, was far from being a synonym for violence. "Violence is one thing and Anarchy another. In the present state of society violence is used on all sides, and, therefore, we advocated the use of violence against violence, but against violence only, as a necessary means of defense. I never read Mr. Most's book, simply because I did not find time to read it. And if I had, what of it? I am an agnostic, but I like to read the Bible nevertheless. I have not the slightest idea who threw the bomb on the Haymarket, and had no knowledge of any conspiracy to use violence on that or any other night."[27]

Next came Neebe, whom at least one observer thought the most impressive speaker ("His voice is clear and resonant, and he has a better presence than any of the other defendants").[28] Echoing Schwab and Spies, Neebe showed how flimsy was the case against him, whereas the police themselves, by contrast, had violated the law at every turn: "They searched hundreds of houses, and money was stolen and watches were stolen, and nobody knew whether they were stolen by the police or not. Nobody but Captain Schaack; he knows it. His gang was one of the worst in this city." Schaack, seated in the audience, laughed. "You need not laugh about it, Captain Schaack. You are one of them. You are an Anarchist, as you understand it. You are all Anarchists, in this sense of the word, I must say." Neebe concluded by asking that he be hanged with his comrades, "for I think it is more honorable to die suddenly than to be killed by inches. I have a family and children; and if they know their father is dead, they will bury him. They can go to the grave, and kneel down by the side of it; but they can't go to the penitentiary and see their father, who was convicted for a crime that he hadn't anything to do with. That is all I have got to say. Your honor, I am sorry I am not to be hung with the rest of the men."[29]

Fischer, who followed Neebe, delivered the shortest speech. He was calm, powerful, even majestic in his look and bearing, wrote William Holmes, his tall form stretched to its full height. Like the others, he denied any complicity in the Haymarket episode, calling the verdict "a death-blow against free speech, free press, and free thought in this country." Fischer summed up the injustice of the trial when he exclaimed: "I was tried here in this room for murder, and I was convicted of Anarchy. I protest against being sentenced to death, because I have not been found guilty of murder. However, if I am to die on account of being an Anarchist, on account of my love for liberty, fraternity and equality, I will not remonstrate. If death is the penalty for our love of freedom of the human race, then I say openly I have forfeited my life; but a murderer I am not."[30]

The day was drawing to a close when Lingg took the floor. His whole being was taut, intense, his manner "that of a caged tiger."[31] Throughout the trial he had contemptuously ignored the proceedings, spending most of his time reading. But now he was concentrated, alert, and his brief but powerful speech commanded the attention of the courtroom. Lingg spoke in German, with bitter irony, pausing as his words were translated into English. "You have charged me with despising 'law and order,' " he exclaimed. "What does your 'law and order' amount to? Its representatives are the police, and they have thieves in their ranks. Here sits Captain Schaack. He has himself admitted to me that my hat and books have been stolen from him in his office—stolen by policemen. These are your defenders of property rights!"[32]

Lingg laughed at the court and its laws. With the same defiance that he had shown during the trial he said: "I do not recognize your law, jumbled together as it is by the nobodies of by-gone centuries, and I do not recognize the decision of the court." His concluding words evoked his whole rebellious, uncompromising character: "I repeat that I am the enemy of the 'order' of today, and I repeat that, with all my powers, so long as breath remains in me, I shall combat it. I declare again, frankly and openly, that I am in favor of using force. I have told Captain Schaack, and I stand by it, 'If you cannonade us, we shall dynamite you.' [Laughter in the courtroom.] You laugh! Perhaps you think, 'You'll throw no more bombs'; but let me assure you that I die happy on the gallows, so confident am I that the hundreds and thousands to whom I have spoken will remember my words; and when you shall have hanged us, then, mark my words, they will do the bomb throwing! In this hope I say to you: I despise you. I despise your order, your laws, your force-propped authority. Hang me for it!"[33]

Following Lingg's address, the court adjourned until the next day, October 8, when Engel was the opening speaker. Like Lingg, he spoke in German, which was translated sentence by sentence by an interpreter. "All that I have to say about my conviction," he declared, "is that I was not at all surprised; for it has ever been that the men who have endeavored to enlighten their fellow men have been thrown into prison or put to death, as was the case with John Brown. I found, long ago, that the workingman had no more rights here than anywhere else in the world." William Holmes thought Engel "stolid, almost phlegmatic" as he addressed the court. Yet there was power in his simple language and steady delivery: "We see from the history of this country that the first colonists won their liberty only through force; that through force slavery was abolished, and just as the man who agitated against slavery in this country had to ascend the gallows, so also must we. He who speaks for the workingman today must hang."[34]

Engel, like Lingg and Fischer, spoke briefly. Fielden, who followed him, delivered a long, heartfelt address, "undoubtedly the greatest of his life," thought William Holmes, which went on until late afternoon, interrupted by a recess for lunch. A born orator, Fielden made the most of the opportunity, bringing tears to many eyes and arousing sympathy among all but the most inveterate anarchist-haters in the courtroom. "His honest, straightforward manner," says Holmes, "his moderate language, his telling criticisms of the testimony of the purchased witnesses who testified against him, made a deep and lasting impression upon us all. Even the bloody-minded Grinnell afterwards condescended to remark that if Fielden's speech could have been made to the jury it would have had great weight with them."[35]

Fielden began by reciting Freiligrath's poem "Revolution," a favorite of the Chicago Internationalists and of anarchists and socialists everywhere. Having thus set the mood for his speech, he proceeded to describe his childhood in the cotton mills of Lancashire, the injustices of the capitalist system, his emigration to America, his conversion to socialism and anarchism, his speech before the Haymarket meeting, and the circumstances of his arrest and prosecution. "We are convicted," he declared, echoing the words of the previous speakers, "not because we have committed murder. We are convicted because we were very energetic in advocacy of the rights of labor." Yet, whatever may be our fate, "we feel satisfied that we have not lived in this world for nothing; that we have done some good for our fellow men, and done what we believe to be in the interest of humanity and for the furtherance of justice. . . . If my life is to be taken for advocating the principles of Socialism and Anarchy, as I have understood them and honestly believe them in the interest of humanity, I say to you that I gladly give it up; and the price is very small for the result that is gained." Fielden concluded on a similar note: "I have loved my fellow men as I have loved myself. I have hated treachery, dishonesty, and injustice. The nineteenth century commits the crime of killing its best friend. It will live to repent of it."[36]

It was late in the afternoon when Parsons, the last speaker, stepped forward. His was by far the longest speech, rambling, repetitious, disjointed, but with moments of great passion and eloquence. He spoke for two hours on October 8 and for another six on the 9th. On the second day he became tired and asked several times for an intermission, but this was denied by the impatient judge, so that when he finished he was near collapse. His speech, as Benjamin Tucker noted, "suffered considerably from its extreme length and his exhaustion."[37] Yet, among its many merits, it offered a powerful refutation of the charges against him and his comrades.

Like Fielden, Parsons began by reciting a German revolutionary poem, Herwegh's "Bread Is Freedom." Then, speaking as "one of the people, a common man, a workingman," he surveyed the condition of labor in the United States, presenting, as was his custom, statistics on such matters as the number of women and children employed in industry. Summarizing the basic tenets of anarchism and social- ism, he explained the labor theory of value, the theory of surplus value, and the role of government in upholding the capitalist order. "I am an Anarchist," he declared. "Now strike! But hear me before you strike. What is Socialism, or Anarchism? Briefly stated, it is the right of the toiler to the free and equal use of the tools of production, and the right of the producers to their products." "I am a Socialist," he went on. "I am one of those, although myself a wage slave, who holds that it is wrong, wrong to myself, wrong to my neighbor, and unjust to my fellow men, for me, wage slave that I am, to undertake to make my escape from wage slavery by becoming a master and an owner of slaves myself. I refuse to do it; I refuse equally to be a slave or the owner of slaves. Had I chosen another path in life, I might be upon the avenue of the city of Chicago today, surrounded in my beautiful home with luxury and ease, with slaves to do my bidding. But I chose the other road, and instead I stand here today upon the scaffold."[38]

Reviewing the evidence against him, Parsons insisted that he had broken no laws, that he had never advocated force except in self- defense, and that he had been convicted for his beliefs rather than for any criminal act. To carry out the sentence would therefore be nothing but judicial murder, "and judicial murder is far more infa- mous than lynch law—far worse. Bear in mind, please, that this trial was conducted by a mob, prosecuted by a mob, by the shrieks and howls of a mob, an organized, powerful mob."[39]

As for the bombthrower, Parsons charged that he had been hired by business interests intent on disrupting the campaign for shorter hours and destroying the radical labor movement. The verdict, he said, had been a "class verdict," the expression of "class feelings." "I charge it here and now frankly that in order to bring about this conviction the prosecution, the representatives of the State, the sworn officers of the law, those whose obligation to the people is to obey the laws and preserve order—I charge upon them a willful, a malicious, a purposed violation of every law which guarantees a right to American citizens. They have violated free speech. In the prosecution of this case they have violated a free press. They have violated the right of public assembly. Yea, they have even violated and denounced the right of self-defense. I charge the crime home to them. These great blood-bought rights, for which our forefathers spent centuries of struggle, it is attempted to run them like rats into a hole by the prosecution in this case. Why, gentlemen, law is upon trial; government is upon trial, indeed. Yea, they are themselves guilty of the precise thing of which they accuse me. They say that I am an Anarchist and refuse to respect the law. 'By their works ye shall know them,' and out of their mouths they stand condemned. They are the real Anarchists in this case, while we stand upon the constitution of the United States. I have violated no law of this country. Neither I nor my colleagues have violated any legal right of American citizens. We stand upon the right of free speech, of free press, of public assemblage, unmolested and undisturbed. We stand upon the constitutional right of self-defense, and we defy the prosecution to rob the people of America of these dearly bought rights."[40]

In his closing words, Parsons described how he had left his sanctuary in Wisconsin and voluntarily returned to Chicago. "I sent word to Captain Black that I was here and prepared to surrender. He sent word back to me that he was ready to receive me. I met him at the threshold of this building and we came up here together. I stood in the presence of this court. I have nothing, not even now, to regret." As he spoke, Parsons went to where Captain Black was seated and placed his arm on his shoulders, "as if speaking the words to me," Black later recalled. "He knew that I had carried a certain burden . . . because of the part I had taken in connection with his return. It was of me that he thought in that moment, and for my comfort that he spoke the words."[41]

The speeches were now at an end. In reply, Judge Gary told the defendants that they had received a trial "unexampled in the patience with which an outraged people have extended you every protection and privilege of the law which you have derided and defied."

Gary added: "The people of this country love their institutions. They love their homes. They love their property. They will never consent that by violence and murder their institutions shall be broken down, their homes despoiled, their property destroyed."[42]

Gary then pronounced the sentence, as fixed by the jury, setting the date of the executions for December 3. A fleeting handshake for relatives and friends, and the prisoners were marched to their cells. Then began the tedious process of appeal, which would drag on for more than a year before the issue of life and death was finally settled.

PART IV ‖ THE ORDEAL

19 ‖ THE APPEAL

After the sentence was pronounced, every legal resource was brought into play to save the prisoners. With the date of the hangings set for December 3, 1886, there was not a moment to be lost. On November 2 Captain Black appealed to the Illinois Supreme Court for a writ of error; and on Thanksgiving Day, November 25, Chief Justice John M. Scott granted a stay of execution pending a hearing on the appeal.

The Defense Committee, spurred on by George Schilling and Ernst Schmidt, worked tirelessly to raise funds for the appeal. The treasury had been exhausted by the trial, and money was desperately needed. The committee's first step was to issue a leaflet calling on "All Friends of an Impartial Administration of Justice" to send contributions without delay.[1] Further appeals for funds appeared in the anarchist press, in Europe as well as in America. The London *Freedom*, founded by Kropotkin and his circle, called on its readers to help reverse "the infamous death sentence passed upon our comrades for their opinions." Similar appeals were published in the London *Anarchist*, edited by Henry Seymour, as well as in Most's *Freiheit*, the Chicago *Arbeiter-Zeitung*, and their sister American journals.[2]

Beyond soliciting contributions, the Defense Committee carried on a range of activities. It sponsored protest meetings, circulated petitions for a new trial, and sought to win public sympathy for the condemned men. But its chief concern remained financial. Money was urgently needed for the appeal to the state court. To help defray expenses, Parsons's speech at the Haymarket was printed in pamphlet form and sold for ten cents a copy, the proceeds going to the defense fund. This, however, was hardly enough. In order to raise additional funds, Lucy Parsons, in October 1886, set out on an extended lecture tour, intent, as she said, on "saving the lives of seven innocent men, one of whom I love dearer than life itself." "There is work to be done," she declared, "and although nearly exhausted, I must be up and at it. The world must hear from me now. The voice of my husband has been silenced, for the present at any rate, and perhaps forever in this world, but his life will speak in eloquent terms in the cause of suffering humanity until the emancipation of wage-slavery comes. We are weak, tired, oppressed, but not discouraged or disheartened. It is a day of struggle. Our cause is worth fighting for and worth dying for."[3]

Over the next few months, Lucy moved back and forth across the country, addressing more than 200,000 people in sixteen states. Leaving Chicago on October 9, immediately after sentence was pronounced by Judge Gary, she spoke in Cincinnati, New York, Philadelphia, and New Haven, where students of Yale University attended her lecture in spite of a driving rain. Speaking at night and traveling by day, she appeared before IWPA groups, Knights of Labor assemblies, and other radical and labor organizations. She spoke about anarchism and socialism, about the plight of the workers, about her husband and his comrades and the travesty of "capitalist justice." She mocked the stereotype of anarchism promoted by the daily papers. In New Haven she said: "You may have expected me to belch forth great flames of dynamite and stand before you with bombs in my hands. If you are disappointed, you have only the capitalist press to thank for it."[4]

On her return to Chicago in November 1886, she was invited to speak in St. Louis by Joseph Reifgraber, who congratulated her on her "most energetic and successful agitation" in the East. "We are whit you," wrote Reifgraber in his imperfect English, ". . . Our hards are bleeding for our brothers in Chicago."[5] Lucy decided to accept. Not yet rested from her previous journey, she embarked on a tour of the Middle West, speaking on the injustice of the trial. Later, between January and March 1887, she was again on the road, lecturing and selling literature, carrying the case of her husband before the American people. Often harassed and insulted, always closely watched by the police, she drove herself from one city to the next, finding it difficult in many places to obtain a hall in which to speak. Sometimes her meetings were broken up, as in Columbus, Ohio, where she was arrested and jailed. Incensed at her illegal detention, Parsons, from his own cell in Chicago, fired off a message to the press: "Lucy E. Parsons, in prison: the poor have no rights which the law respects. The constitution is a dead letter to the people of the United States."[6]

Lucy was not the only figure to lecture on behalf of the Defense Committee, although she was undoubtedly the most effective. William Holmes, who had moved to Chicago from Geneva to be closer to his comrades in their hour of need, was called on to perform a similar function. On November 15, 1886, he began a prolonged tour of the Middle and Far West, speaking in such cities as St. Louis, Denver, and San Francisco. The day before his departure, he visited Cook County Jail to bid farewell to his comrades. The stay of execution had not yet been granted, and the men were scheduled to hang on December 3. With heavy heart he went to the prison to say what he thought might be a last goodbye. Fischer took Holmes aside and, with his face close to the wire mesh of the visitors' cage, talked to him of his former home in St. Louis and gave him a parting message to the comrades there. "Tell them," he said, "that I gladly die for my principles. Tell them that I shall not falter or hesitate; that they must not weep for me or mourn me dead, but that they must carry on the good work and be prepared, if necessary, also to give up their lives for our great cause." Holmes broke down, stirred by Fischer's words. In vain he tried to hide his emotion. But Fischer only smiled and added: "I would not change places with the richest man in America."[7]

On November 25, eight days before the date set for the hangings, the stay of execution was granted by Justice Scott. Captain Black, relieved by the news, now cast about for a new associate—a replacement for William Foster, who had left the case—to assist him in handling the appeal. His initial choice fell on Robert G. Ingersoll, the noted lawyer and orator, known as "the great agnostic" because of his powerful attacks on religion. Black invited Ingersoll to enter the case. Ingersoll, according to George Schilling, who consulted him on behalf of the Defense Committee, showed "the warmest possible interest in the case and his sympathies were with these men and their friends." Not that he expressed himself in favor of anarchism; but he believed that the defendants were entitled to a fair trial, and that "as social agitators and political revolutionists, however mistaken in thought or in method, they were actuated by humanitarian considerations." Ingersoll, however, declined on the ground that, as the foremost infidel in the country, he would only jeopardize the chances of the accused. Were he to associate himself with the case, he told Schilling, press and pulpit would at once raise the cry, "We have got the whole brood together now, Atheists and Anarchists," and would create such a storm that nothing on earth could withstand it.[8]

Ingersoll advised the defense to secure a counselor whose political and religious orthodoxy was beyond question. "Schilling," he said, "you must get a lawyer of national reputation who is a pillar of the church and who can cover these men in his conservative life and character." Following this advice, the Defense Committee approached Leonard Swett, erstwhile law associate of Abraham Lincoln at the Illinois bar. Swett, an attorney of unblemished character and high professional standing, agreed to join the defense.

The appeal was argued before the Illinois Supreme Court in March 1887, with Grinnell, his assistant Ingham, and the Illinois attorney general representing the state. Speaking for the defense, Black and Swett scathingly exposed the deficiencies of the trial, from the "grave, persistent and inexcusable errors" in the selection of the jury to the many improprieties on the part of the prosecution and the erroneous instructions of the judge in laying down the law. Thoroughly impugning the testimony of Thompson and Gilmer, they demonstrated that the state's case had been built in large part on perjured evidence and on evidence obtained by unlawful means.[9]

It was Black who presented the closing argument. He insisted that the throwing of the bomb was neither the work nor the desire of the defendants. Quite the contrary: "It brought to an end their efforts. It disappointed their hopes. It was not of their devising. The record shows it." The question before the court, Black concluded, was "whether upon the barbaric *lex talionis* [law of retaliation], that whenever a man was slain a man of the opposing faction must be slain, these seven men shall die, because seven policemen, whom they did not like as a class, and who certainly did not love them, have died. You know the barbarians never stopped to fix individual responsibility for the crime. They simply said: 'One of ours is dead, and we cannot rest until one of theirs dies for him!' It has been done so here."[10]

Fully six months elapsed before the Illinois court handed down its decision. In the meantime, public sentiment underwent a perceptible shift. The conviction of men for murder who had not even been present when the bomb was thrown, the packed jury, the perjured testimony, the twisted interpretation of the law by a judge plainly determined to hang the defendants, the open avowal of the prosecution that the men were being tried for their opinions rather than deeds—these things and others had their effect. As time passed,

300

moreover, tempers cooled and hysteria died away. A growing number of observers, most of whom abhorred anarchism and had no sympathy with radical propaganda of any sort, concluded that the condemned men had not received impartial justice.

While a majority continued to clamor for retribution, a substantial segment of the public called for a review of the case. Liberals, labor leaders, and other concerned citizens spoke out against the verdict. The Reverend Hugh O. Pentecost of Newark and Rabbi Isaac M. Wise of Cincinnati were among the clergymen who protested. Rabbi Wise, who had previously excoriated the anarchists and even threatened them with lynching, now declared himself against the death sentence because the defendants "had acted for the benefit of their fellow-men, from convictions which are undoubtedly false and unreasonable, but not criminal *per se.*"[11]

By the time the state court acted, a full-scale movement of protest had taken shape. Meetings were held and petitions circulated in behalf of the prisoners. Support came from many and diverse quarters. Men and women throughout the country, who shared no common political label or social position but whose sense of justice had been outraged, demanded a new trial. Such protests called for courage, since critics of the trial and verdict risked being smeared with defending anarchy and terror. It was an occasion to test one's mettle, a time, as Benjamin Tucker put it, "when every individual, especially every individual of prominence, had to choose between the path of shame and the path of glory."[12] By seeking justice for the condemned men, William Dean Howells, Henry Demarest Lloyd, and William Mackintire Salter chose the path of glory.

Howells, then America's leading man of letters, was deeply affected by the case. For months, he wrote to a friend, "it has not been for one hour out of my waking thoughts; it is the last thing when I lie down, and the first thing when I rise up; it blackens my life."[13] More than any other event, Haymarket awakened his concern with the social ills of America, to which he would devote some of his most notable works, above all *A Hazard of New Fortunes*. Through his involvement in the affair, through his sympathy and support for the defendants, "my horizons have been indefinitely widened," he afterwards said.[14]

Howells, from the earliest stages, was convinced of the innocence of the defendants. As he wrote to George William Curtis, editor of *Harper's Weekly*, "it was not a fair trial, either as to the selection of the jury or the rulings of the judge. The evidence shows that neither Parsons nor Spies was concerned in promoting riot and disorder, and their speeches show them to have been active friends of a peaceful solution of the labor troubles. They are condemned to death upon a principle that would have sent every ardent antislavery man to the gallows."[15]

A reading of *August Spies' Auto-Biography* and of Dyer Lum's *Concise History of the Great Trial of the Chicago Anarchists*, containing copious extracts from the court record, reinforced Howells's belief that the proceedings, as he told Curtis, had been "hysterical and unjust," and that the defendants were "doomed to suffer for their opinions' sake." Justice, he declared, had been perverted: "Look how the case was worked up beforehand by the press and the police; how the jury was impaneled regardless of the acknowledged prejudices of eight or nine of the jurors; how partial the court's rulings seem to be; how inflammatory the prosecuting attorney's appeals; how purely circumstantial and conjectural the evidence, and how distinctly and squarely met; how that 'reasonable doubt' which should have been made to favor the accused was tormented throughout into proof against them." "I will own," Howells added, "that this case has taken a deep hold of me, and that I feel strongly the calamity which error in it must embody. Civilization cannot afford to give martyrs to a bad cause; and if the cause of these men is good, what an awful mistake to put them to death!"[16]

But Curtis, who had already committed *Harper's* against the anarchists, remained unconvinced. "They are not condemned for their opinions," he replied, "but for deliberately inciting, without any pretense of reason, to a horrible crime which was committed with disastrous results."[17] Howells could not agree. In the course of the trial, he insisted, they had "proved themselves absolutely guiltless of the murder charged upon them." He himself held no brief for their doctrines, which "must always remain, to plain common sense, unthinkable." But he deplored the savagery with which they were being treated, the "fear and hatred that seem to have debauched this nation."[18] As events moved swiftly towards a climax, he watched with deepening alarm. Finally, although he feared for his livelihood and reputation, he threw himself into the struggle to save the condemned men.

Howells stood virtually alone among American literary figures in his protest. His stand for justice brought him much abuse. But it also won him admiration. "However brilliant the literary fame that he may leave behind," wrote Tucker of Howells a decade later, "his fame as a man, resting chiefly on the brave and simple appeal that he then made for justice, will far outshine it, and I am sure that to him this act is the most precious of his career."[19]

There were some individuals, moreover, with whom Howells found a common bond in the case. Of these none worked harder to save the defendants than Henry Demarest Lloyd, a former financial editor of the *Chicago Tribune*. Lloyd, no less than Howells, disapproved of extremism and violence. He would "take out the rotten planks in the ship of state and replace them with new ones," he said, "rather than sink the ship itself."[20] Like Howells, he employed both pen and purse in the cause of the doomed men. So strongly did he speak out in their behalf that his father-in-law, William Bross, a part owner of the *Tribune*, angrily changed his will, leaving his estate to his grandchildren and cutting Lloyd off from the guardianship.

Yet Lloyd had no regrets. An early critic of business monopoly, he had always sided with the workers against the "lords of industry," as he called them. He was repelled by the greed, the hypocrisy, the corruption of the business community, untempered by any concern for the poor, by any social feeling or compassion. In a series of widely-read articles, he had warned against the rise of monopoly capitalism, with its pools and trusts and price fixing, its rebates and manipulations. In so doing, Lloyd blazed a trail for the muckrakers of succeeding generations. He was a reformer, in the words of Ernst Schmidt, "who never fail[ed] to espouse the causes of the poor."[21]

Lloyd, deeply touched by the plight of the anarchists, labored without rest to arouse public sentiment in their favor. He had taken up their cause, he told his father, because they were "connected with the agitation of the great social question of our day." What was more, he was convinced that they were innocent. Judge Gary's conduct of the trial had aroused in him a "seething wrath" which, in view of his normally mild disposition, greatly surprised those who knew him. Gary, he maintained, had acted "as prosecuting attorney on the bench." By the same token, Grinnell and his staff had flouted constitutional guarantees in obtaining evidence against the defendants. Such shameless violations of civil rights, Lloyd feared, might lead to "continental methods of government by police." "Shall we be safe in setting—by the State—the precedent of arrest without warrant, search without warrant, and condemnation to death for being 'leaders'?" he asked. "The country is perfectly safe; these men, caged, are entirely at our mercy, a poor miserable handful. No need for panic or passion—we can loosen the tension of a false fright, created by flaring fools, by detectives exaggerating their own importance, by police most of whom have brought to this country the notions of Mitchelstown."[22]

For defending the rights of the accused, Lloyd faced social ostracism. Acquaintances cut him in his club and on the street. "I met an old friend yesterday," he told his sister, "and he gave me a look of the most intense hatred possible from one human being to another." For a long time the antagonism persisted. Some years later Lloyd was dining in Boston when the host asked him to relate the story of the anarchists. As the party broke up, a member of one of New England's leading families, taking his leave of the others, turned his back on Lloyd and left without speaking to him. Very few, and greatly treasured, were the friendly words which he received, as when the wife of the French consul in Chicago thanked him for his work in the anarchists' behalf, or when William Clarke, a Fabian socialist, wrote from London to congratulate him: "You will never regret having said a word for justice and mercy while the whole press of America was howling for these men's blood."[23]

Another who said a word for justice and mercy was William M. Salter, lecturer for the Chicago branch of the Ethical Culture Society, who also worked privately and publicly to secure leniency for the anarchists. A graduate of Knox College in Galesburg, Illinois, Salter had attended both Yale and Harvard Divinity Schools, taking additional work at Göttingen and Columbia, before accumulating doubts drove him from a religious career. Appointed lecturer of the Ethical Culture Society in 1883, he was the only Chicagoan of note to accept the invitation of the American Group to debate the question of socialism at its meetings. He quickly developed an interest in the subject, without, however, becoming a convert. Above all, he came to admire the sincerity of Parsons and Spies in their concern for the poor and oppressed. In January 1886 he himself began to write for the The Alarm, his first contribution being an editorial on Russian populism; and in May, when the anarchists were arrested, he took up the cudgel in their defense.

Appalled by the trial and conviction, Salter spoke out for a reprieve. In a public lecture delivered at the Grand Opera House he argued that the defendants, although charged with murder, had in fact been condemned for their opinions, and that, while having used "seditious and treasonable language" which might warrant legal punishment, had been unjustly sentenced to death. Salter's lecture created a sensation and brought upon him a storm of abuse, both from those who felt he had gone too far in defending the anarchists and from those who felt he had not gone far enough ("I have yet to learn," complained Lizzie Holmes, "that under this government there can be such a thing as 'treasonable language' ").[24]

Published both as an article and as a pamphlet, Salter's lecture was one of a growing number of writings directed at the unfairness of the trial. Others of the same genre included *A Common-Sense View of the Anarchist Case* by an anonymous "Home-Spun Western Lawyer," in which the Chicago police, and especially Inspector Bonfield, were accused of being the "rioters"; *The Facts Concerning the Eight Condemned Leaders* and *The Ides of November: An Appeal for the Seven Condemned Leaders and a Protest Against Their Judicial Assassination*, both by Leon Lewis of Greenpoint, New York; and, most notable of all, two pamphlets by General Matthew M. Trumbull, *Was It a Fair Trial?* and *The Trial of the Judgment: A Review of the Anarchist Case.*

These pamphlets, sold and distributed by the Defense Committee at protest meetings around the country, played a distinct role in shifting opinion in favor of the defendants. Lucy Parsons, it was said, was able to sell 5,000 copies of Trumbull's *Was It a Fair Trial?* in a single day on the streets of Chicago.[25] Trumbull, a sixty-year-old Chicago lawyer, was neither an anarchist nor a supporter of revolution. He had, however, been a Chartist in his native England, from which he had emigrated in 1847. A staunch opponent of slavery, he had fought in the Civil War, rising to the rank of general. Since the war he had practiced law in obscure respectability, from which he suddenly emerged to fight the case of the anarchists in the court of public opinion.[26]

Convinced that the anarchists were innocent, Trumbull demanded a review of the case. "The record," he declared in his first pamphlet, "shows that none of the condemned men were fairly proven guilty, while some of them were fairly proven innocent; not innocent of sedition, and inflammatory speech"—here Trumbull was echoing Salter—"but innocent of murder." In order to secure conviction, said Trumbull, the law had been "bent and strained to the breaking point." Furthermore, the scales of justice were not poised evenly between the accused and the state: "They were poor; the prosecution was rich. The whole machinery of the city and county government was at the service of the prosecution. The treasury was reckless of cost. The police force, the detective force, and every official influence were active against the prisoners. They were beaten from the start." Loosing a barrage of closely reasoned arguments, Trumbull demonstrated the utter failure of the prosecution to prove its case. With an "unerring hand," as an admirer wrote, he revealed "the incredible chicanery, the absolute unscrupulousness, and the consummate perfidy of the constituted authorities." At a time when most men remained silent, "his powerful words rang out clearly and brought some light where before all had been darkness."[27]

But criticism was far from being limited to isolated voices like Trumbull's. In the weeks and months following the trial, a flurry of mass meetings took place in Chicago and other cities to protest against the verdict ("All who believe in the American Liberty of 1776 are urged to be present," ran one announcement). In Baltimore and Boston, William Gorsuch and C. S. Griffin—erstwhile "whoop-her-up" anarchists—returned to the platform to speak out against the death sentence. Johann Most and Victor Drury were among the protesters in New York, where the verdict, noted Abraham Cahan, produced a "militant spirit" among the radicals.[28]

Reformists and revolutionaries temporarily buried their differences in a show of solidarity for the prisoners. (On one such occasion Thomas Morgan and Lucy Parsons shared the podium in Sheffield, Indiana, across the Illinois border, where the Chicago police could not disrupt the meeting.) At public rallies Herwegh's "Bread Is Freedom," recited by Parsons in court, was sung by the audience, as was "A Shout of Protest" by Arthur Cheesewright, a socialist from Denver:

> In Chicago stand convicted
> Seven of nature's noblest men,
> Jailed because they have predicted
> What was truth and clear to them;
> Giving to the rich a warning
> That their end is drawing near,
> Telling of a coming dawning,
> Of a future bright and clear.

Let us save our noble brothers!
Raise your voices loud and high!
Noble men who lived for others,
Cannot, will not, must not die![29]

As time passed, the protest movement gathered strength. Far from stifling radical sentiment, the conviction of the anarchists produced the opposite effect. It "is helping us in one way," wrote William Holmes to H. H. Sparling. "*It is making socialists.* Notwithstanding what the press and public may say about socialism and anarchism being dead in this country, the fact remains that we were never so strong before, never so enthusiastic, determined and united."[30] Spies made a similar observation in a letter to Josef Peukert: "The international character of the anarchist movement and anarchist idea has never been so strikingly illustrated as in our late so-called 'trial.' Americans, Englishmen, and Germans—all accused of treason against villainy, all proclaiming the gospel of humanity as against that of nationalism, patriotism, and other curses of the human race! Our trial has been a greater propaganda of the principles we contend for than oral agitation of years and years." "The direct result of our persecution," wrote Spies on another occasion, "has been—general activity in labor circles; great progress in organization and, particularly, in ideas. The radical elements have come to the front everywhere, while the conservatives [have been] pushed to the wall. The *Arbeiter-Zeitung* has tripled its subscription list since Grinnell's agitation began. At that time it had 4,000 subscribers; it has now over 10,000."[31]

Among workers, both native and immigrant, the change of sentiment was indeed striking. When the bombthrowing occurred, most labor leaders had tried to dissociate themselves from the anarchists. But opinion began to shift during the trial, when to many it appeared that the enemies of labor were using the anarchists as a club against the workers as a whole. The conduct of Grinnell and Gary in particular reinforced this view. At the conclusion of the proceedings, large numbers were convinced that a gross miscarriage of justice had taken place. "The whole episode," declared one labor paper, was "one of the most disgraceful in the judicial annals of civilized states." The harshness of the sentence shocked additional workmen into opposition. "This verdict is a crime against the workers," exclaimed the *Yidishe Folks-Tsaytung* of New York.[32] A cry of indignation went up in labor circles, and it would have been louder were it believed that so unjust a sentence could be carried out.

Two prominent labor journalists denounced the persecution of the anarchists from the beginning. Joseph R. Buchanan, editor of the Denver *Labor Enquirer* and head of the Rocky Mountain Division of the International Workmen's Association, went so far as to move to Chicago so as to place himself at the prisoners' disposal. John Swinton, his counterpart in the East, had earlier given up his post as managing editor of the *New York Sun* to start a small labor weekly, *John Swinton's Paper*. A champion of reform rather than revolution, he had no use for violent methods. He called the Haymarket bomb "a godsend to the enemies of labor."[33] Yet his heart went out to the arrested anarchists. Like Henry Lloyd, he saw them as spokesmen for the oppressed. "Dear Mr. Lloyd," he wrote in May 1886, "Can't you do something to help secure those accused men a fair trial?" Lloyd, for his part, thought Swinton the "greatest patriot" in New York for coming to the aid of the defendants.[34] When the trial took place, Swinton watched with mounting indignation. The rulings of Judge Gary, he wrote the following year, were "a disgrace to the American bench, and entitle him to a place alongside Scroggs and Jeffreys. The conviction of the accused was an outrage against evidence, law, decency, fair play, reason, justice, freedom, human nature, and the Constitution."[35]

In January 1887 Henry George, author of *Progress and Poverty* and perhaps the most celebrated social reformer of the day, added his voice to those of Swinton and Buchanan, branding the trial a "legal farce." The defendants, declared George's paper, *The Standard*, had been "convicted by a jury chosen in a manner so shamelessly illegal that it would be charity to suspect the judge of incompetency." The state of Illinois, warned *The Standard*, would "sow the dragon's teeth if it executed men, not proven guilty, who hold hateful and foreign ideas."[36]

Prodded by statements of this type, labor organizations joined the campaign for a reprieve. All over the United States demonstrations were mounted against the verdict. Trade unions passed resolutions and issued appeals. The Central Labor Union of New York gathered petitions for a new trial. The Central Labor Union of Boston and the Trades Assembly of Louisville pledged their moral and financial support. Parsons, encouraged, wrote to George Schilling: "The *light* is breaking! The blind to see, the deaf to hear."[37]

The Knights of Labor, however, held back. Powderly, Grand Master Workman of the Order, was an opponent of militant action. As such he had no truck with the anarchists and their doctrine of armed insurrection. He was anxious, on the contrary, to assert the respectability of his organization before the bar of public opinion. To defend the anarchists, he feared, might be construed as implying sympathy with violent methods. Anarchism, he believed, was "un-American, and has no business in this country." "The Anarchist in America," he averred, "is no more to be considered a part of the labor movement than the man who sits up nights to work his way into a bank vault that he may enrich himself from the earnings of others." Anarchists were "cowardly and deceitful." They used the label "socialist" and joined the Knights of Labor merely "to cover up their DIABOLICAL SCHEMES."[38]

For Parsons, a veteran member of the Order, this was a bitter pill to swallow. The "foundation principle" of anarchism he held to be identical with that of the Knights—namely, the "abolition of the wages system" and its replacement by "universal cooperation." Powderly had a different conception: "He is a true Knight of Labor who with one hand clutches anarchy by the throat and with the other strangles monopoly."[39] On July 4, 1886, his tenth anniversary as a Knight, Parsons replied to Powderly from his cell: "Whether we live or whether we die, the social revolution is imminent. The boundaries of human freedom must be enlarged and widened. The seventeenth century was a struggle for religious liberty; the eighteenth for political equality; and in the nineteenth century mankind is demanding economic or industrial freedom. The fruition of this struggle means the social revolution. We see its coming; we predict it; we hail it with joy. Are we criminals for that?"[40]

Powderly remained unmoved. Indeed, he claimed at a private meeting of the Order to have "evidence enough to convict the men of Chicago of murder," although no such evidence was brought forward. Not content to attack the defendants, he lashed out at Parsons's wife. Asked his reasons, he replied: "Because she is not his wife, because they only live together and are not married, and because it is not my business to look after any woman of bad reputation, white or negro, who tramps around the country as she does."[41]

Yet, even as Powderly washed his hands of the anarchists, more than a few local branches espoused their cause, raising money and passing resolutions in their behalf. Joining the protests was District

Assembly 49 of New York, the largest affiliate of the Order, and Local Assembly 1307 of Chicago, known as the "Sons of Liberty" Assembly, of which Parsons had been one of the founders. In an open letter against the death sentence, Local Assembly 1307 noted that, in spite of Powderly's animadversions, Parsons's career as a Knight was "without a blemish." In addition, the local Chicago journal of the Order, which had strongly condemned the anarchists after the bombing, not only came out against the verdict but began to serialize the autobiographies of the defendants.[42]

Even more significant, at the General Assembly of the Knights, held at Richmond in October 1886, representatives of District Assembly 49, Victor Drury among them, put forward a resolution in support of the convicted men. Powderly fought these delegates tooth and nail. After prolonged debate, he finally permitted the adoption of a watered-down version which, while asking mercy for the prisoners, emphasized that "we are not in sympathy with the acts of the anarchists, nor with any attempts of individuals or associated bodies that teach or practice violent infractions of the law, believing that peaceful methods are the surest and best means to secure necessary reforms."[43]

Powderly, however, was not satisfied. In December 1886 he instructed all local assemblies, on pain of expulsion from the Order, to cease collecting money or issuing appeals for the defendants. A large number of Knights disobeyed, in particular the more militant elements. "Powderly's order did not scare 1307 much, did it?" wrote Lizzie Holmes to Parsons, after the maverick local resolved to ignore it. District Assembly 49 was likewise defiant; and Johann Most, suspicious of all labor organizations, was beside himself with fury. "You rat, Powderly," he wrote in *Freiheit*. "You expel locals with anarchist leanings, and you tell your union not to give money and not to express sympathy for the condemned of Haymarket. You are the Grand Master Rat!"[44]

It was from anarchists like Most, needless to say, that the defendants received their strongest support. *Lucifer*, prefiguring the language of the 1960s, spoke of the "contemplated murder of the Chicago Seven." Most himself had greeted the verdict as follows: "On the 20th of August, 1886, twelve carefully selected, bribed scoundrels, directed by the lowly servitors of the ruling monied classes, under pressure from the demonic, degenerate, motley rabble of outcasts of the press of the world, committed a monstrous crime

310

in Chicago, the enormity of which has not been surpassed in the records of judicial murder throughout the annals of crime."[45]

Benjamin Tucker and his circle, for all their disagreements with the International, added their voices to the rest. "I am an individualistic Anarchist," wrote J. William Lloyd, "not a communistic one, and I have very little sympathy with Most, Spies, Parsons, *et al.*, in so far as their methods and precepts are concerned. But when these men are gagged and their pens broken by the strong hands of a tyrannical government, then their cause becomes my cause, and I protest for them as I would protest for myself."[46] Ezra Heywood, who visited the condemned men in prison, regretted that "but one American is elected worthy to suffer with these Lafayettes and Kosciuskos." Heywood compared their approaching martyrdom with the martyrdom of John Brown. "Spies & Co.," he declared, "have a thousand fold more influence today than they would have had if never arrested at all; if released, they will soon become as ordinary men; if hanged, their souls will 'march on' in ever-growing power."[47]

As for Tucker himself, he regarded Spies and his associates as "rash but noble men," who had been condemned for their opinions rather than for the commission of an actual crime. Whatever his reservations concerning their beliefs, he saw them as "victims of outrage and injustice, and everything should be done to aid them that can be done, without endangering or misrepresenting genuine Anarchism." Tucker felt, at the same time, that his opposition to violence had been vindicated—that the use of mere incendiary language, let alone incendiary deeds, would invite the authorities to retaliate. More than ever before he was convinced that peaceful methods alone could bring about the removal of the state: "The monster cannot be reformed; *it must be killed*. But how? Not by dynamite; that will not harm it. How, then? By light. It thrives in the darkness of its victims' ignorance; it and they must be flooded with the light of liberty."[48]

Tucker, like Heywood, compared the defendants with John Brown. "Are the authorities bent on inaugurating another fratricidal war," he asked, "of which Chicago is to be the Harper's Ferry?"[49] J. William Lloyd, too, perceived the parallel. Writing in *Liberty* he foresaw the most fearful consequences should the death sentence be carried out: "Will hanging these men bring safety to the rich or comfort and content to the poor? Will not the drops of their victim-blood become fountains of gore? Will not violence bring forth violence, and murder revenge, till the days of death are fulfilled? They are sowing the wind. Listen! The whirlwind mutters in the distance. They are planting the teeth of the dragon. Hark! The roar of innumerable voices, the sudden tramp of millions, thronging like bloodhounds on the scent! Alas, my country!"[50]

20 ‖ Convicts

All men know that eventually they must die, but only the condemned prisoner must live with the knowledge, barring a postponement or reprieve, of the exact date on which his end will come. That date, for the Chicago anarchists, had been set for December 3, 1886. Ten days before its arrival, however, a stay of execution was obtained to allow them time for an appeal. Since May they had been languishing in prison, their fate hanging precariously in the balance. And there they were to remain for fully eighteen months, hovering, as Kropotkin put it, "between life and death, between hope and despair."[1]

It was an enervating, not to say degrading, existence. The prisoners, confined in the Cook County Jail, lived in individual stone cells, measuring six by eight feet, in the upper tier of the section known as "murderers' row." In front of the cells ran a narrow footway reached by a flight of iron steps at one end. Parsons occupied cell 29, Fischer 30, Fielden 31, Schwab 32, Spies 33, Engel 34, Lingg 35, and Neebe 36. (Neebe, slated to serve his fifteen-year sentence in the Illinois State Prison at Joliet, remained with his comrades pending the outcome of the appeal.)

Prison life was dull and monotonous. Most of the time the men were restricted to their cells, with two armed guards—the death watch—constantly pacing up and down before them. Twice a day, except on Sundays, they were permitted to receive visitors and to exercise in the corridor, but they were never allowed out of doors. In a letter to Dyer Lum, Fischer described the prison routine: "With the precision with which an old-country village herdsman drives his herd out and into town, they let us out of our cells, and then lock us up again. This comparison is not very aesthetical, but, nevertheless, it stands the test. Thus hours become days, days become weeks, and before we are aware of it the hangman may come around and invite us to follow him to the corner—in the name of 'law and order.' "[2]

As the months dragged on, according to Lucy Parsons, the men suffered acutely from want of exercise. She said of her husband's confinement: "he never breathed a breath of pure, fresh air, never looked upon a growing sprig of grass, never beheld either earth or sky." Nothing met his eye but "bare stone walls relieved only by bolts, bars and chains." He was denied the company of family and friends, "excepting the few moments when granted the privilege of conversing with them through a close wire netting," and he "never touched the hand even of his wife, save twice, all the long period of his imprisonment."[3]

Yet the men bore up well under the strain. "We eat, sleep, read, write, think," wrote Parsons to the Hoans after the trial. "We—all of us—are cheerful, and bid our comrades everywhere stand for the right and falter not."[4] A year later the situation was unchanged. "My health and spirits have been good throughout my fifteen months of incarceration," wrote Parsons to Justus Schwab in New York. "So of all the others." A visitor to the jail at this time described the inmates as being "in good health"; and though confinement was "telling somewhat upon them, they none exhibit any signs of weakness."[5]

Nor could the men complain of ill-treatment by their warders. The head jailer, Captain Folz, an elderly man with a grizzled beard, was unfailingly kind and considerate, and his deputies on the whole followed suit. The prisoners reciprocated, comporting themselves with politeness and dignity, a fact to which all their jailers attested. Spies, always aesthetic in his tastes, tried to make his cell as pleasant as possible. A rug covered the stone floor before his bunk, pictures adorned the walls, and flowers stood on a shelf that served as a mantel. In the center, from the ceiling, hung a bird cage in which fluttered a canary. But, commented Dyer Lum, a frequent visitor to the prison, "the poor bird could not stand the double confinement, and weakened and died."[6]

Morning and afternoon visiting hours marked the high points of the prisoners' day. At 10 A.M. and 4 P.M. friends and relatives descended upon the jail, bringing wurst, ham, smoked beef, herring, cheese, cigars, and consolation—"above all, consolation," wrote Spies to Robert Reitzel, a leading German anarchist in Detroit.[7] Insofar as these visits served to lift the prisoners' spirits, Sundays, on which the men were locked in their cells all day, were especially hard on their morale, as were other occasions on which visitors, for one reason or another, were barred, as when President Cleveland came to Chicago in October 1887. (Cleveland, it might be noted, expressed a desire to see the site of the bombthrowing, to which he was conducted by the then mayor, John A. Roche, Carter Harrison's successor in office.)[8]

During their year and a half in confinement, the anarchists received a great number of visitors from different parts of the country, and even a few from abroad. The "cage" into which these visitors were admitted consisted of a large wire network through which they had to converse with the inmates. From Princeton, Massachusetts, came Ezra Heywood, an adherent of the individualist school of anarchism headed by Benjamin Tucker. From Detroit came Joseph A. Labadie, a prominent labor editor and recent convert to anarchism, who shook hands with the men, he recalled nearly fifty years later, by putting his little finger through the iron grating.[9] Joseph R. Buchanan, having moved from Denver to Chicago in February 1887, called at the jail to see "the boys," bringing greetings from their friends in the West. Over the next nine months, Buchanan relates, he passed "many interesting hours in conversation—the iron grating between us—with those intelligent, brave men, who never whimpered nor once showed the pallid flag of fear."[10]

Parsons received many callers, but he was particularly touched by a visit from a Texas friend who had served with him in the administration of the senate at Austin in the early 1870s. Through the grating he gave Parsons a badge with a blue silk ribbon on which was printed "Texas and Freedom." Parsons, reading these words, became emotional. "God bless Texas and you, my good friend," he said.[11]

From Europe came Wilhelm Liebknecht, the German socialist leader, together with the Englishman Edward Aveling and his wife Eleanor Marx Aveling, Karl Marx's youngest daughter, who, in the fall of 1886, were on a fifteen-day tour of the United States under the auspices of the Socialistic Labor Party. During their four days in Chicago, they visited the jail to offer their sympathies to the condemned men, and Fielden, with whom Aveling spoke with fingers interlocked through the wire mesh, clung to him "as a fragment of his own land."[12]

Before coming to Chicago, Eleanor Marx, at a mass meeting in New York, had already pleaded ardently for the defendants. For the remainder of her tour, following her visit to the prison, she made it her business to speak out in favor of a new trial. Before the Chicago Liberal League, for example, she declared that the men had been condemned "not for what they have done, but for what they have said and believe. That cowardly and infamous sentence will *not* be carried out. The vote cast by the working class will put a stop to that, at least so I believe. Should these men be murdered, we may say of the executioners what my father said of those who massacred the people of Paris, 'They are already nailed to that eternal pillory from which all the prayers of their priests will not avail to redeem them.' "[13]

While in Chicago, the Avelings met the chief counsel for the defendants, Captain Black. They thought him dignified and hand-some, "fully six feet in height, and built in perfect proportions, with long, quite white hair, and a darker moustache and imperial, very strong, keen eyes." Black had fought, they were aware, in the Civil War, and he sang the "Battle Hymn of the Republic" in their hotel room "with a swing and a ring in his voice as if he were marching along at the head of a company."[14]

Yet the case had already left its mark on Captain Black. Not only had his hair grown whiter and his face acquired new lines, but his whole demeanor had become suffused with anxiety over the plight of his clients, for whom he had developed an intense admiration, viewing them as martyrs in the struggle for human redemption. During the trial, in his closing address to the jury, he had likened their self-sacrificing idealism to that of Jesus Christ and John Brown ("Jesus, the great socialist of Judea, has preached the socialism taught by Spies and his other apostles. John Brown in his attack on Harper's Ferry may be compared to the socialists' attack on modern evils"). Since their conviction, moreover, he had been impressed by the calm resignation with which they contemplated their approaching exe-cution and the steadfastness with which they refused to recant their principles or abase themselves before the powers in whose hands it was to spare their lives. Such, he was convinced, was the stuff of which martyrs are made. As he later remarked, if the American people could only have known these men as he himself had come to know them, they would have understood "why my whole heart was in the struggle for their deliverance."[15]

Black became obsessed with the case to an extent which alarmed his relatives and friends, however much they might stand by him in his effort to save the defendants. Only his wife gave him unstinting support. A bright, energetic little woman, as the Avelings describe her,[16] possessed of social awareness and religious conviction, she followed the case with deepening interest, attending nearly all the sessions of the trial and often visiting and talking with the prisoners. No less than her husband, she was impressed by their idealism and selfless dedication to the poor. Stunned by the verdict, she poured out her feelings in a letter to the *Chicago Daily News*. She too, like other Chicagoans, had "felt horror" at the events of May 4. She had never seen an anarchist, nor even knew what the term meant, until her husband became counsel for the defense. But gradually she discovered that there were two sides to the story. "When I learned the facts I became assured in my own mind that the wrong men had been arrested, and thrown into cells and subjected to the most horrible treatment. . . . Anarchy is simply a human effort to bring about the millennium. Why do we want to hang men for that, when every pulpit has thundered that the time is near at hand?"[17]

For all their esteem for Mrs. Black, the Avelings viewed her with not a little of the disdain with which they regarded all idealists and reformers who did not embrace the tenets of "scientific socialism." She had, as they saw it, been "bitten with the amiable variety of Anarchism that attacks those by whom neither the history nor the economics of the question has been studied." Nevertheless, they hastened to acknowledge, her visits to the jail with her husband, her "cheerful courage and enthusiastic faith in the ultimate getting of justice done," were of "great solace" to the condemned men.[18]

Aside from the Blacks, Ernst Schmidt, George Schilling, William Salter, and Henry Lloyd were among the Chicagoans who regularly visited the prisoners. Of their anarchist comrades, none was more faithful than William Holmes, who called on them several times a week, entwining a finger with one of theirs through the grating in lieu of a proper handshake. Holmes, no less than Captain Black, was inspired by the courage with which the men contemplated their approaching execution. "They all talked freely to me of the past few weeks, and of their own feelings," he wrote to H. H. Sparling in England. "They will bravely meet whatever may come, and you may be sure none will show the white feather."[19]

Yet another regular visitor was Dyer Lum, who, for reasons soon to become apparent, merits special attention. Lum, like Holmes, came nearly every day, bringing the prisoners gifts and news of the anarchist movement, in which he was a prominent figure. Born in 1839, he was, like Albert Parsons, a native American of Puritan descent. His great-grandfather had been a minuteman in Northampton, Massachusetts, during the Revolutionary War, and his grandfather a brother of the well-known abolitionists Lewis and Arthur Tappan. Lum himself became an abolitionist at an early age, and when the Civil War broke out he enlisted as an infantryman to fight for the emancipation of the slaves. He twice escaped from Confederate prisons, then transferred to the cavalry, rising from private to captain owing to bravery in combat. In later years, however, he was to refer to his army service as a period "when I risked my life to spread cheap labor over the South." For he perceived, as his lover Voltairine de Cleyre put it, that "it had turned out to be a Northern manufacturers' game, with the inevitable commercial result—concentration, centralization, surrender of historical tradition (State sovereignty), the nucleus of a formidable military power," with the net result being "a limited gain for the negro and an unlimited loss for the white man."[20]

For Lum, as for Parsons, the turning point was the depression of the 1870s. In 1876 he entered Massachusetts politics, running unsuccessfully for lieutenant governor with Wendell Phillips, the celebrated abolitionist and reformer, on the Greenback ticket. A solitary photograph taken during this period shows him as a real Yankee, with a long mustache and penetrating eyes, every inch the former cavalry officer. Now a bookbinder by trade, he plunged into the emerging labor movement, served briefly as secretary to Samuel Gompers, and turned to radical agitation in 1877, the year of the great strike, becoming the secretary of a congressional committee to inquire into the "depression of labor."[21]

In 1879 Lum met Parsons and was impressed by his "earnestness and sincerity."[22] In 1880 the two were delegates together at the eight-hour conference in Washington sponsored by the Greenback-Labor Party, and both were appointed to a national committee to press for shorter hours before Congress. By 1883, however, both Lum and Parsons had lost their faith in legislation and discarded state socialism for anarchism; and when Parsons started *The Alarm* in 1884 Lum became a frequent contributor, pouring out articles, editorials, translations, and poems in an unceasing flow. In addition to *The Alarm*, he wrote for a variety of radical journals, among them Tucker's *Liberty*, his pieces including a poetic eulogy to Wendell Phillips, his former running mate and mentor. Covering a wide range of subjects, from money and land reform to ethics and religion, he dabbled in Buddhism and oriental philosophy and praised the cooperative ventures of the Mormons, whom he ably defended against their detractors.

Lum, however, has been one of the most misunderstood figures in the history of the anarchist movement. "In disposition," wrote a friend after his death, "Mr. Lum was most amiable; in the character of his mind, he was philosophical; in mental capacity, he was at once keen and broad." To the historian Henry David, he stood "intellectually head and shoulders above most of the Chicago revolutionaries."[23] But there was another side to Lum's personality which has received little attention. Beneath the calm, academic exterior burned the flame of an uncompromising rebel, for whom violence, including terrorism, was a necessary weapon in the social struggle. Indebted as he was to Garrison and Phillips, he also possessed much of the fire of John Brown, for whom his admiration was boundless and like whom he was willing—indeed yearning—to lay down his life for the cause of human emancipation.[24]

On closer examination of Lum's career, with its dynamite plots and secret codes, he comes to resemble a character out of the subterranean world described by Henry James in *The Princess Casamassima* and Joseph Conrad in *The Secret Agent*. "I am just uncultured and savage enough to confess to *hatred* as *la grande passion* of my contradictory psychological anatomy," he wrote to Voltairine de Cleyre. "I am slow to wrath, but when I get mad it sticks and feeds on everything till it becomes full grown hatred."[25] Lum prided himself on being a social militant, favoring armed resistance to tyranny and exploitation. In his article on "The Social Revolution," in his poems on the French Revolution, in his eulogy of Julius Lieske, hanged for assassinating the police commissioner of Frankfurt, he glorified the heroes who act rather than content themselves with mere propaganda. "There is more education in a single event than in years of agitation by speech and pen," he remarked to William Holmes.[26] Writing in *The Alarm* in June 1885, he appealed to the "wage slaves of America" to arm themselves against their oppressors, arguing that those in power yield only to force, which alone can alter entrenched social conditions and relieve the workers from their misery. Not long before the Haymarket explosion, he prophesied a great popular upheaval: "From the Atlantic to the Mississippi, the air seems charged with an exhilarating ingredient that fills men's thoughts with a new purpose." The social revolution was approaching. "Educate the people to grow up to the issue? Nonsense! Events are the true schoolmasters."[27]

Lum, as Voltairine de Cleyre notes, was "in all of his writings the advocate of resistance, the champion of rebellion," believing in revolution "as he believed in cyclones; when the time comes for the cloud to burst it bursts, and so will burst the pent up storm in the people when it can no longer be contained." "I am glad the 4th of May occurred," he said, referring to the Haymarket incident. Despite the ensuing persecution of his comrades, he could "shed no tears." On the contrary, the explosion was an occasion for celebration, as it heralded the approaching revolution. To Lum the bombthrower was an authentic hero, the latter-day equivalent of John Brown.[28]

Lum was operating a bookbindery in Port Jervis, New York, when the Haymarket bombing occurred. He sold his business and hastened to Chicago to place himself at the service of his comrades. From this point on he becomes a key figure in the drama. With Parsons in prison, his chief object was to revive *The Alarm*. Together with Lizzie Holmes, whom he chose as his associate editor, he issued an appeal for financial support and, putting $1,500 of his own money into the venture, "ran the gauntlet of police, detectives and the crowd haters of Anarchy," as Voltairine de Cleyre recollected, to restore the journal to life.[29]

The task took more than a year to accomplish. But on November 5, 1887, less than a week before the rescheduled executions, *The Alarm* once again sounded forth. The first issue, published at 169 Washington Street, contained a message from Parsons, the former editor, urging his comrades to continue the struggle: "Falter not. Lay bare the iniquities of capitalism; expose the slavery of the law; proclaim the tyranny of government; denounce the greed, cruelty, abominations of the privileged class who riot and revel on the labor of their wage-slaves. Farewell. A. R. Parsons. Prison Cell 29, Chicago, Illinois." Lum, as Parsons's successor, issued a powerful statement of his own: "Today the John Brown of the Haymarket is unknown, and the Garrisons—the prophets of the ages, the assertors of the idea—are awaiting the scaffold, while press, pulpit, and courts congratulate themselves as the wise men of 1859 did when John Brown 'paid the penalty of violated law' and eased their guilty fears of retribution. True, John Brown died, but the idea lived! If Garrison had died with him as an accessory, the same wild howl of delight would have been heard over the vindication of law and order."[30]

Lum, during his sojourn in Chicago, was a constant visitor at the prison, loved and trusted by the men who were doomed to die. Lum returned their love, and never in after years, writes Voltairine de Cleyre, "was he able to speak much of them without tears filling his eyes."[31] Visiting nearly every day, Lum was able also to win the confidence of the jailers, to whom his presence became a familiar sight. In due course, he managed to secure a pass enabling him to enter outside the normal visiting hours, when he could talk and shake hands with the inmates through the bars of their cells, rather than through the close-knit wire mesh of the visitors' cage. At times, moreover, he was allowed into the "lawyers' cage," a separate enclosure in which attorneys consulted with their clients, and he would call down one or two of his comrades and give them an extra hour outside their cells. Such occasions, he tells us, were special treats. Parsons and Fischer in particular enjoyed the opportunity to "throw their arms around their visitor and realize that no bars nor wire screen stood between them."[32]

The most cherished of all the visits, however, were those by the prisoners' families. The wives came almost every day, among them Maria Schwab, a tall, handsome woman of "good presence and commanding behavior," whose small children, Ida and Rudolph, bright and pretty and always neatly dressed, accompanied her to the cage to see their father. Fischer's wife Johanna was also a daily visitor, often bringing their three children, the youngest, Adolph Jr., born the day after the death sentence was passed on his father. Another regular visitor was Engel's daughter Mary, pretty and "an immense favorite." Engel's wife came too, upon whom, recalled Captain Black, had "fallen the frosts of many winters," and they would sit for hours on the opposite sides of the iron grating engaged "in loving conversation, quiet, self-restrained," as the weeks and months wore on between the verdict and the execution. For Black the scene remained forever "one of infinite pathos."[33]

No less pathetic were the visits of Fielden's wife, a small woman with a shy manner, English and "very domestic." She was one of those "home bodies," remarked Lum, who cling to their husbands, and after Fielden's arrest she did not know her way downtown on the streetcars without assistance. Her whole life had been wrapped up in his. Their little daughter Alice was now three years old, and when allowed to go behind the bars, a privilege sometimes accorded to the children, she invariably ran to her father's cell and ransacked his clothes, for Fielden, prior to his imprisonment, had been in the habit, when returning from work, of bringing her candy or fruit and permitting her to hunt for it in his pockets. Fielden, in addition, rejoiced to see his baby boy Sam Jr., born on the day before Judge Gary pronounced sentence.[34]

Towards the end of August 1886, barely a week after the conclusion of the trial, news reached Fielden from England of the death of his father in Lancashire. Another tragedy occurred in March 1887 when Neebe's wife Meta, a woman in her mid-thirties, suddenly died after a brief illness. Her death, so it was said, had been brought on by her husband's tribulations. Badly shaken by the verdict, by which he was sentenced to fifteen years in prison, she sickened, as William Holmes recorded, and "died of a broken heart." The cause assigned to her death was apoplexy. According to Neebe, however, she had succumbed to the "anguish and trouble weighing on her tender heart."[35] A funeral was arranged by the anarchists at Mueller's Hall, the meeting place of the North Side Group, of which Neebe had been a member. The hall was decorated with flowers and emblems of mourning, and speeches were made. Neebe, accompanied by a police escort, was allowed to view his wife's body at their home before it was taken to the cemetery.[36]

Lucy Parsons, when not on the road for the Defense Committee, was another frequent visitor to the jail, often accompanied by her children and on occasion by Lizzie Holmes or William Parsons. The family, since Parsons's surrender, had fallen on hard times. Lucy, having given up her ladies's tailor shop to devote herself to her husband's appeal, could no longer afford their apartment on Indiana Street and was forced to move to a third-floor walkup on Milwaukee Avenue. Parsons himself was reduced to applying to the Defense Committee for a grant to buy underwear and socks. The committee, however, having already paid out $200 for Meta Neebe's funeral, was loath to accede, since its treasury, as Dr. Schmidt indicated, was intended for legal expenses and not for the personal needs of the prisoners.[37]

To Parsons, who apparently had to make do with what clothing he already possessed, this was a trifling matter. He worried, however, about his family, who suffered bitterly from his incarceration. "Well, my poor, dear wife," he wrote to Lucy after the verdict was announced, "I personally feel sorry for you and the helpless little babes of our loins. You I bequeath to the people, a woman of the people. I have one request to make of you: Commit no rash act to yourself when I am gone, but take up the great cause of Socialism where I am compelled to lay it down. My children—well, their father had better die in the endeavor to secure their liberty and happiness than live contented in a society which condemns nine-tenths of the children to a life of wage-slavery and poverty. Bless them; I love them unspeakably, my poor helpless little ones. Ah, my wife, living or dead we are as one. For you my affection is everlasting. For the people—humanity—I cry out again and again in the doomed victim's cell: Liberty—Justice—Equality."[38]

Throughout his term of confinement, Parsons's family was seldom far from his thoughts. During the late summer of 1886, with Parsons behind bars and his wife laboring for the appeal, Lulu and Albert Jr. spent several weeks at Waukesha as guests of the Hoans. "Kiss the little ones for papa and mama," Parsons wrote affectionately from his cell.[39] In mid-December, while Lucy was on tour, Lulu, then five years old, fell suddenly ill. The disease could not be diagnosed. Alarmed, Parsons cabled Dyer Lum: "See Lulu at once and tell me how she is." Parsons asked Lizzie Holmes to do the same, and on December 23 she wrote to assure him that Lulu was out of danger. "My dear comrade," she added, "I can't wish you a merry Christmas, for that would be in vain, but I wish you strength and courage to endure your martyrdom. I would gladly give my freedom for yours, and my life for your life, if I could."[40]

Meanwhile the two unmarried prisoners, Spies and Lingg, did not lack for female visitors. Since the trial, says Dyer Lum, several young ladies had been in love with Spies, and Lum, while visiting the jail, enjoyed winking at him through the cage "between two girls talking to him at once!"[41] The most ardent of Spies's admirers was the twenty-four-year-old Nina Van Zandt, a graduate of Vassar College and the daughter of a Chicago pharmaceuticals manufacturer, "slenderly fashioned, handsome, always exquisitely gowned, and having the deportment of a refined and educated woman," as Charles Edward Russell remembered her.[42]

Nina, like many other young society women, had been a regular attendant at the trial. From the hostile accounts in the press, she had expected, on her initial visit, to see "a fiendish-looking wretch in each of the chairs set for the prisoners," she wrote. To her surprise, however, she could "not detect an ill-looking man amongst them," while several, on the contrary, had "noble faces." She found that Fielden, so far from being cruel and malevolent, as the newspapers portrayed him, was "almost worshipped by his neighbors and associates for his universal kindness and generosity," while his co-defendants too commanded respect.[43]

Nina, as she followed the proceedings, became convinced that the defendants were innocent. "They had committed no crime," she remarked, "except that of agitating the labor question," of telling the worker "that he had a right to the common decencies of life." Yet, innocent or not, the prosecution seemed bent on sending them to the gallows. Animated by a "feeling of horror," she vowed to assist them in every way she could.[44]

Nina found herself drawn especially to Spies and began to visit him in prison. Spies came to look forward to her visits. They began to work together on his autobiography, and at one point Nina brought him a portrait of herself, which he hung on the wall of his cell. Nina, an only child, was of a romantic and headstrong temper. Her parents placed no obstacle in the way of her attachment to Spies, and her infatuation with the handsome anarchist ripened quickly into love. She espoused his cause with her whole impetuous nature. Through her love for him, moreover, she drew the rest of her family into the case.

By December 1886 Nina had become a constant visitor at the jail, frequently accompanied by her mother and sometimes also by her father. That month, however, Canute R. Matson was installed as the sheriff of Cook County, and matters took an unhappy turn. A Norwegian by birth and a disciplinarian by character, Matson quickly won the reputation of an autocrat—the "czar of all the jail," the anarchists dubbed him[45]—at whose orders the pettiest rules were vigorously enforced. Nina, as a mere acquaintance of the prisoners, found her visiting privileges sharply curtailed.

To circumvent these restrictions Nina and Spies decided to marry. Their plans created a sensation. Newspapers "howled and raved," as Nina recorded. Had she been some "obscure, foreign girl," she said, not the least tremor would have occurred, but as an American of old ancestry and standing she drew down a torrent of abuse. "That's unheard of," it was said. "The girl must be silly." She had read too many "trashy novels." But worst of all were the reporters. Had she committed the most horrible crime, Nina noted, they could not have vilified her more. On the other hand, "had I married an old invalid debauché with great riches, those 'moral' gentlemen who assail me now would have lauded me to the skies."[46]

No less appalled by the news, ironically, were the lawyers for the defense, concerned lest the wedding should somehow jeopardize their appeal to the Illinois Supreme Court. "Swett says—the marriage *must* be stopped," wrote Captain Black to George Schilling. "Swett is in close contact with the capitalistic class, and feels their resentment, and is apprehensive of the results of their hate." Black himself was greatly upset, as was his wife, to whom Nina seemed a tool of the prosecution, a "Delilah set to entrap Spies." "Oh, I am deeply concerned," she confided to Schilling. "August Spies' marriage to this woman will ruin him. She is totally unworthy—she talks of the working people as 'scum'—she will cause his death."[47]

Yet Spies could not be dissuaded. Despite the most urgent pleas from his attorneys, he refused even to delay the wedding, which was set for January 29, 1887. When Sheriff Matson would not permit a ceremony in the jail, the couple were married by proxy, Henry Spies taking the vows for his brother. A few days later, a mob attacked the Van Zandt home on East Huron Street, throwing stones and mud and smashing a basement window, as Nina and her mother huddled terrified within. "Some of the young hoodlums were very obscene and profane," wrote Nina soon after the incident, "coupling my own and my husband's names in the most vulgar terms. Virulent attacks were made upon the personal character of my husband and upon his family. They were charged with every crime imaginable, and represented to be coarse, ignorant and uncouth. Nor were my father and mother excepted from their vile attacks, while I was the unhappy subject for every form of abuse known to habitual *roués* and rowdies."[48]

A flurry of rumors followed the wedding. It was said that Spies had acted from selfish motives, that he cared not a whit for Nina but hoped the marriage would secure him a reprieve. "Day after day she longs and pines and sighs for a sight of the fellow who with lordly indifference puffs his clouds of nicotine in her suffering face and lectures to her romantic talk with the carelessness born of his own self-conceit and flatulent oratory," wrote Joseph Howard of the *Boston Globe*. Spies, it was further reported, greedily contemplated his bride's inheritance, which he would share after his release from prison. To this Nina responded with indignation: "Now, when I joined hands with my beloved husband, he well knew that I brought him only myself, with a wealth of affection, trust and reverence."[49]

Of Nina herself it was charged that, far from being in love with Spies, she was a mere notoriety-seeker who hankered to be in the limelight. In reality, she had sacrificed both friends and social position, not to mention a $400,000 legacy of which an aunt, Mrs. John Arthur of Pittsburgh, was said to have deprived her as a result of the marriage.[50] Furthermore, she remained devoted to her husband throughout his ordeal. According to Dyer Lum, her "untiring love was consecrated to his welfare."[51]

Spies, for his part, kept Nina's picture in his cell and spoke of her with affection and respect. When Sheriff Matson, after the wedding, callously barred her from the prison, so that her health broke down from her distress, Spies implored him to allow her to visit.[52] So too did her grieving father, who entreated the sheriff to reconsider. "Dear Mr. Matson," he wrote on February 17, 1887, "It is painful to me to be so importuning—but when I see the distress and anguish of my child there is nothing for me to do but plead with you to turn the key. Looking at the matter seriously, I am satisfied if we cannot do something soon my sorrow will have only begun. May I beg you to let her in today or tomorrow. Very truly yours, James K. Van Zandt."[53] Matson at length relented, allowing Nina to visit from time to time, if not so often as in the past. Nina, when unable to visit her husband, wrote him tender letters of love and encouragement.

Lingg, the only other bachelor among the defendants, likewise received his share of female visitors. He especially enjoyed the company of Elise Friedel, a young immigrant girl who had lived in the same part of Germany where he had been born and raised, and who visited the jail often, sometimes with Mary Engel, with whom she had become friendly during the trial, bringing him food, books, and other gifts.[54] Lingg, moreover, was fond of children, and when those of his comrades visited the jail he would romp and play with them. Otherwise, as Captain Schaack noted, his demeanor throughout his imprisonment was much the same as at the trial—"cool, collected and unconcerned."[55] He held himself aloof from strangers, above all from representatives of the press, for whom, not without reason, he harbored the deepest distrust. Reporters, as they had done since his arrest, continued to treat him as a demon or monster. Joseph Howard of the *Boston Globe* referred to his "caged hyena bearing." To others he was a "wild beast," a "madman," a "dynamite fiend."

No wonder that, when Charles Edward Russell sought to interview him for the *New York World*, Lingg refused to cooperate. "To every question or remark," Russell recalled, "he was wont to respond with a silent stare of malignant and calculating hatred, rather disconcerting; and I think that in those days few strangers observed him without a secret feeling of relief that he was on the other side of the steel bars." Similarly, when Art Young, then a Chicago newspaper illustrator, went to sketch the prisoners in their cells, Lingg "sat proudly in his chair, facing me with unblinking eyes, and silent."[56]

From Lingg's comrades and admirers, however, we get a more sympathetic picture. Dyer Lum spoke of "his personal beauty, his youth, his magnificent head of hair, a leonine mane one might say to see him so proudly shake back his flowing locks."[57] To a German lady who used to bring him food, he seemed, locked up behind bars, a more pitiful than terrifying sight. One day he said to her: "I was dancing in my cell last night. They had a ball over there somewhere, and I heard the music, and oh! I did so want to be there and dance!"[58] The prison officials, as William Holmes noted, spoke of Lingg's conduct "in terms of the highest praise." Jailer Osborne remarked: "Ah, I wish all the young men in town were as pure in their morals and thought as Louis Lingg is. In all the time I have known him in the jail, as thoroughly as I have come to know him, I have never heard him use a profane word or make an indelicate allusion. He is neat and tidy about his person and his cell."[59]

As to Lingg's suspicion of reporters, he was hardly alone in this respect. Indeed, it was a feeling shared by all the defendants, to whom newspapermen seemed a pernicious breed of sensation-mongers who cared less for the truth than for a good story. Even Parsons, while maintaining friendly relations with individual correspondents, branded the press "monopoly's mouthpiece"[60] and was constantly on his guard against sensationalists. With good reason, as one example will show. On December 3, 1886, the date originally set for the executions, a reporter for the *Chicago Mail* scribbled the following to Parsons in his cell: "How are you feeling today? What is your pulse, respiration etc.? Have you a tingling sensation about the neck? Are they feeding you well? Are you gloomy? Are you hopeful of a new trial? Did you dream last night of Sheriff Hanchett [Matson's predecessor] playing 'seven up' today? By the way, what were your dreams? Tell me lots of stuff to make a good reading article as this is 'Dec. 3.' You see the point. I will say nothing mean. Just a pleasant item. Nothing else."[61]

Apart from daily exercise and receiving visitors, the prisoners passed the time in a variety of occupations. Fischer read Dickens and studied history and current events. His chief complaint was that, under the stringent regime of Sheriff Matson, the guards on death row were no longer permitted to play cards with the inmates, so that he was compelled to abjure his beloved pinochle.[62] Parsons, in his spare time, whittled miniature tugboats with his pocketknife, one of which he sent to Justus Schwab in New York to be raffled for the benefit of his family. In the box he enclosed a piece of rope obtained from a deputy sheriff. "My Dear Comrade," he wrote to Schwab, "With this I express to you the tug boat which I made with my pocket knife to while away the lonely hours in my cell. Also I send you a hangman's noose, which is emblematic of our capitalistic, Christian civilization. The knot was tied by myself, and is the regulation style. I give it to you as a memento of our time."[63]

The boat was duly put up for raffle, but doubts arose that so artistic a piece of work could have been fashioned by Parsons with only a pocketknife. A dispatch was wired to him for clarification. Parsons, offended, replied as follows: "It was made in my cell by myself to be raffled for the benefit of my family, but I feel like presenting it to Comrade Schwab." The raffle, however, took place as scheduled and netted nearly $150.[64]

Lingg, too, indulged in whittling, passing the time, says Captain Schaack, "by cutting pretty little carvings out of cigar-boxes with his jack-knife, and in this he displayed considerable ingenuity." Besides this, he and Fischer wrote rhyming letters in German to one another, samples of which were published in the anarchist press.[65] During the long months of confinement, Lingg managed to improve his English somewhat, but he refused to study it in any systematic fashion or, like Fischer, to read seriously in any subject. One evening, while visiting the prisoners, Lum asked Lingg why he did not apply himself to such matters. "What's the use?" he answered, placing his fingers around his throat and giving vent to a choking sound.[66]

For all the prisoners, Lingg not excepted, writing was an important occupation. They worked on their autobiographies, corresponded with comrades and relatives, and wrote letters to newspapers and journals, a task in which Parsons was especially prolific, heading his communications "Cook County Bastille, Cell No. 29." Their letters, both private and public, throbbed with the consciousness of approaching martyrdom. "Is my life at an end?" wrote Parsons to his friends at Waukesha. "Am I already buried in my tomb? The law—man's law—has so decreed it. Nature—or God's law—revolts at the verdict. Which ought to—yea, which shall prevail? I know not. But this I know: that millions of nature's noblest and best have their thoughts to-day with myself and loved comrades in prison, doomed to suffer an unnatural death."[67]

A few weeks later Parsons sounded a similar note. Again addressing his Waukesha friends, he said: "Our crime—our only crime—is that we declare, we defend the right of every human being to life and liberty. We seek the millennium of peace, of joy, of fraternal brotherhood. The penalty, or their punishment, is to put us to an ignominious death. Do we die in vain? No, my friends, not in vain, nor do we suffer in vain. We pay the price, but those who come after us will receive the reward of our efforts, viz.: Liberty. Already the people—not the rulers, but *The People*—are greatly stirred. The day dawns. Hallelujah!"[68]

The prisoners, in turn, received messages of encouragement from all over the country and around the world. One letter, addressed to Parsons from his ancestral state of Maine, declared that his persecution would "forever make the name of the city of Chicago a *by-word*, a *disgrace*, a *stench* in the minds of all noble, true men and women."[69] The others received similar communications. Almost daily, wrote Spies to Robert Reitzel, letters of sympathy poured in from German Christian sectarians in different parts of America, assuring the condemned men that they were "fulfilling the word of the Lord" by sacrificing their lives for the poor.[70]

Spies, it is interesting to note, continued from his cell to write for the *Arbeiter-Zeitung* and to assist in managing its affairs. Schwab, too, remained a frequent contributor, his pieces, like those of Spies, being smuggled out of the prison by visiting relatives and friends. "Until now," confided Spies to a comrade in July 1887, "Schwab and I have been writing the principal editorial material, though of course the fact is not generally known." Ironically, the nominal editor, Albert Currlin, found himself criticized by readers of the paper for "endangering the lives of the prisoners" with his inflammatory editorials—editorials in fact written by Spies.[71]

Some anarchist writers made an effort to tone down their utterances, lest they endanger the appeal of the defendants to the higher court. Fischer indignantly complained about this to Lizzie Holmes during one of her visits to the prison. "You people are not doing anything," he said. "You seem to have stopped working entirely because we fellows are in jail." "We do not wish to hurt your cases or compromise you in any way," she replied. "Bah!" exclaimed Fischer impatiently. "Are you going to cease all work because the capitalists have got a few of us behind the bars? Then you'll never do anything again, for they will have some of us right along from now on. I tell you the battle is right now!"[72]

Fischer himself remained outspoken in proclaiming his anarchist beliefs. "The spirit of the social revolution lives in me as before," he wrote to Dyer Lum, "and gives me courage and endurance." In a letter to Most's *Freiheit* he deprecated reformism of every type, insisting that all governments were essentially evil: "The state is the state, just as a thief is a thief. There is no good or bad state, just as there is no good or bad thief. The state in any form is reprehensible, for it is based upon class domination."[73]

Fischer, accordingly, continued to preach the gospel of armed insurrection. To make an end of capitalism, he insisted, it was necessary to abolish the state. In a letter to Henry Lloyd and William Salter he clarified his position on violence: "As I have told you before, anarchism and force as such are contrary to each other. But we deny that any individual has the right to curtail the liberty or rights of others. The *oppressed* have the natural right to use force against their oppressors; or, to speak with Jefferson, force is justified as a defense of the rights of men. In accordance with this principle, the Constitution of the United States says that the right of citizens to bear arms is inviolable. No *thinking man* will deny that the present condition of society is not bearable much longer. We stand before a radical transformation of society. Will those whom the peculiar state of society gives such enormous advantages give up their privileges peacefully? This is the question. If the anarchists would be convinced of this they would be the happiest of men. But from all observations they conclude that the privileged classes will not give way to reason, but will uphold their privileges by force, and that therefore a general conflict between the diametrical classes is inevitable."[74]

These were also the views of Engel and Lingg, Fischer's fellow intransigents among the defendants. Throughout their confinement they never wavered, never compromised, never yielded an inch. Lingg, for his part, continued to proclaim the virtues of dynamite. One of his letters, written during the summer of 1887, ends with the battle cry: "Long live propaganda by the deed!" Engel, too, as Dyer Lum noted, remained "cool, self-confident, and daring. He has no regrets, and no apologies to make."[75] As for the other prisoners, they too clung to their principles with unyielding tenacity, if not with the same belligerence as their comrades. "Anarchy is the perfection of personal liberty and self-government," wrote Parsons in a letter to the *New York Herald*. "It is the free play of nature's law, the abrogation of the statute. It is the negation of force or the domination of man by man."[76]

It was to counteract the false impression of anarchism conveyed in the daily press that Parsons issued declarations of this type. And it was for the same purpose that he and his co-defendants wrote their autobiographies, which, hastily revised by Lum, were serialized in the Chicago *Knights of Labor* starting in October 1886. The same month an effort was launched to publish their courtroom speeches; and, before the year was out, both German and English editions had appeared in print. In addition, the prisoners asked Lum to produce a summary record of the trial, so that a broader public might be acquainted with their beliefs and alerted to the injustice of their condemnation. "We know of no other man," they told him, "who could undertake this work with the same degree of competency and discriminative capacity as yourself."[77]

Lum set to work without delay and, by early 1887, had completed and published an able condensation of the proceedings, which strongly influenced William Dean Howells and contributed in no small measure to the shift of public opinion in favor of the defendants. About the same time, it might be noted, William H. Parsons began work on a mammoth history of the entire case, to be called *Dawn of the Social Revolution*. Within a few months he had written some 800 pages. The book, however, never saw the light, and the manuscript has unfortunately been lost.[78]

Quite apart from these ventures, Spies and Parsons compiled separate books of their own during the period of their incarceration.

331

The work by Spies, consisting of his autobiography and speech in court along with miscellaneous notes, was published in February 1887 by his wife of a few weeks, who had helped him put it together and contributed a brief preface. Parsons, who also enjoyed the collaboration of his wife, did not begin his book until the fall of 1887 and regretted the lack of time he had to prepare it. He remarked, however, in a note to the reader: "The circumstances under which the work has been performed, in my dungeon, beneath the shadow of the gallows, should, if aught could, lend additional interest and importance to the matters printed therein."[79] In fact, it was a pedestrian compilation, containing an essay by Parsons on the rise of American capitalism that was strongly influenced by Marx and concluded with an extract from the *Communist Manifesto*, excerpts from the speeches of the defendants before Judge Gary, essays on anarchism by Kropotkin, Reclus, Dyer Lum, and C. L. James, and miscellaneous materials pertaining to the case.

The general object of these various publications was to lay before America and the world the ideas for which the defendants had been struggling and were ready, if necessary, to die. Was their death indeed in the offing? The answer, throughout the spring and summer of 1887, rested with the Supreme Court of Illinois. Captain Black, who had argued the case before the court, was hopeful about the outcome, as was William H. Parsons. General Parsons, himself an experienced attorney, felt sure that the verdict would be overturned. "It is a constitutional question of the right of the people to repel attack upon a peaceful and lawful assemblage," he said. It was "not a case of homicide, but constitutional defense."[80] Nor was he alone in holding this view. Few of the defendants' supporters believed that the sentence would be carried out. The general opinion was that somehow the scaffold would be averted.

The prisoners themselves were not optimistic. "Well," wrote Parsons to Justus Schwab on August 30, 1887, "the air is full of rumors as the day for the supreme court draws nigh to render their decision. The capitalist press and combined wealth of this whole country are bulldozing the supreme court into confirming the sentence of Hangman Gary. If they succeed, what a spectacle for 'free America.' Men put to death only because they made speeches that were offensive to the ruling class! That is the whole of it! Russia will be out-Russiad. After the infamy of Gary's court the proletaire may know what to expect from the 'law and order' bourgeoisie."[81]

Fischer was of the same opinion. "There are some sanguine people who believe still that justice, respecting our final acquittal, will be the outcome of our case," he wrote to Dyer Lum on September 5. "But I don't believe it. If a so-called court of justice could convict and sentence seven men to death on no other evidence than the fact that they held certain principles, that they were anarchists, then there must be some purpose to such preconcerted 'verdict,' and it is likely to be executed too."[82] Nine days later, the Illinois Supreme Court gave Fischer further reason for believing that he was right.

21 ‖ Governor Oglesby

On September 14, 1887, after six months of deliberation, the Supreme Court of Illinois rendered its decision. In a unanimous opinion, read by Justice Benjamin D. Magruder, the verdict of the lower court was upheld. Of the seven members of the court, only one, Justice John H. Mulkey, voiced any misgivings. "I do not wish to be understood as holding that the record is free from error, for I do not think it is," he declared. "I am nevertheless of the opinion that none of the errors complained of are of so serious a character as to require a reversal of the judgment."[1] The court, refusing to order a new trial, fixed November 11, 1887, as the date for the execution of the seven men who had been sentenced to hang.

Captain Black was bitterly disappointed. Yet there was still one more legal step open to him, an appeal to the United States Supreme Court, and he at once set about making the necessary preparations. To assist him, the Defense Committee recruited three distinguished attorneys, all of proven ability and national reputation. The first was Roger A. Pryor, a prominent Wall Street lawyer, who had been a brigadier general in the Confederate army. General Pryor, with the approval of the Defense Committee, engaged a second attorney, John Randolph Tucker, who had served as attorney general of Virginia under the Confederacy and who, in the opinion of Captain Black, was "one of the best constitutional lawyers in the country."[2]

Given the background of Pryor and Tucker, it seems odd that the third choice of the Defense Committee should have fallen on General Benjamin F. Butler, the Yankee firebrand who had won the hatred of the South by his tyrannical administration of New Orleans. Yet Butler, a former congressman and governor of Massachusetts, was a capable lawyer of wide experience and contacts; and, having been the Greenback candidate for President in 1884, his political views were more sympathetic to labor than those of his two associates.

Butler, although persuaded by Justus Schwab and Johann Most to

334

enter the case, questioned the efficacy of an appeal. As he pointed out to Most, the defendants had been convicted of murder under the laws of the state of Illinois, and he doubted whether any federal issue was involved that might justify the intervention of the United States Surpeme Court. Nor was he alone in this opinion. In Chicago, too, as Spies told Schilling, "local lawyers claim that the case cannot be taken to the federal court." "Most likely they are right," Spies himself concluded.[3]

General Pryor, however, thought otherwise. "On examination of the papers left with me," he wrote to Schilling, "I am of opinion, 1st That the case is reviewable by the United States Supreme Court; 2d That a stay of execution may be obtained; 3rd That there is a reasonable probability of reversing the conviction."[4] For his services, however, Pryor demanded an immediate retainer of $1,000 plus an additional $1,500 after filing the appeal. Tucker and Butler requested similar compensation. The Defense Committee worked desperately to obtain the necessary funds, and within weeks all three attorneys were paid in full.[5]

On October 27, 1887, counsel for the defense appeared before the United States Supreme Court and petitioned for a writ of error to review the judgment of the Supreme Court of Illinois. The arguments occupied two days, and the court reserved decision until November 2, when Chief Justice Morrison R. Waite gave the unanimous verdict. The court, as Benjamin Butler had foreseen, ruled that it lacked jurisdiction in the case because no federal issue was involved. Critics, however, hastened to point out that, during the arrests and trial, fundamental constitutional rights had been violated, including freedom of speech and assembly, protection from illegal search and seizure, and due process of law.[6]

Thus the long, wearying months of legal maneuvering had brought no result. That very evening, Neebe was quietly removed from the Cook County Jail and taken to the Illinois State Prison at Joliet to begin his fifteen-year sentence. As for the others, only nine days remained before the date set for their execution. Following the announcement by the Supreme Court, Lucy Parsons brought Lulu and Albert Jr. to the jail to see their father. The jailers heard the children shouting "Papa! Papa!" before they had reached the cell block. Lucy had just learned the bad news from Washington. She was deeply upset. But she managed a wan smile as she put her lips to the wire mesh of the visitors' cage and attempted to kiss her husband. The children were wild with excitement. The warders let them out of the cage, and they ran to their father, who hugged and kissed them. "Give me a ride!" cried Lulu. Parsons hoisted her onto his shoulders and ran back and forth in the corridor while Albert Jr. followed at his heels shouting with delight. Then, thoroughly exhausted, Parsons put Lulu down and turned to have a talk with his wife.[7]

With the refusal of the United States Supreme Court to review the case, the last legal remedy had been exhausted. Now the only hope of averting the hangings was the exercise of executive clemency. The power of life and death rested with a single man, the governor of Illinois.

The incumbent was Richard J. Oglesby, a sixty-three-year-old Republican and former abolitionist, who was credited with dubbing Lincoln the "railsplitter" and had worked hard for his election in 1860. Resigning from Congress in 1861 to enlist in the Union army, Oglesby distinguished himself in battle and retired as a major general after suffering a near-fatal wound. Returning to politics, he served a term in the United States Senate before being elected to the governorship. Oglesby was a popular figure, regarded with esteem by men of widely disparate political and social views. Even Robert G. Ingersoll, America's most outspoken agnostic, was able to write of him to Schilling: "Governor Oglesby has as much physical courage as any man in the world. He has a good heart. His instincts are noble and all his tendencies are towards the right. I have the greatest respect for him."[8]

For Schilling, who had been toiling night and day to save the prisoners, these were indeed heartening words. Still more, there was evidence that Oglesby disapproved of the manner in which the case had been conducted. To State Senator Richard Burke, a supporter of clemency for the defendants, he had remarked after the verdict was delivered: "If that had been the law during the anti-slavery agitation, all of us Abolitionists could have been hanged long ago."[9] But Oglesby, for all his reputed bravery and fair-mindedness, lacked the courage of his convictions. He was not given to independent judgment. On the contrary, he tended to follow the opinions of big business and was easily swayed by the passions of the moment. No one understood this better than Ingersoll. "The only fear I have," he confided to Schilling, "is that he will be over-awed by the general feeling—by the demand of the 'upper classes.' "[10]

Nevertheless, a vigorous attempt was made to induce the governor to commute the death sentences to life imprisonment. Even before the United States Supreme Court denied the defendants a writ of error, Schilling and his associates on the Defense Committee had initiated a movement for clemency. To supplement their efforts, a more broadly based Amnesty Association was established, with Lucien S. Oliver as president, its main functions being to raise funds, arrange meetings, circulate petitions, and swing public sentiment in favor of a reprieve.

The Amnesty Association set to work with astonishing energy. Time was of the essence. Spurred by such ardent supporters of leniency as Henry Lloyd, William Salter, and Samuel McConnell, the work of distributing petitions and obtaining signatures was taken up by hundreds of men and women from all walks of life. Lloyd himself, apart from contributing to the amnesty fund, printed petitions at his own expense that were circulated in clubs and businesses throughout the city.[11] More than a dozen tables, laden with circulars and petitions, were set up in different neighborhoods and, on November 6, the Sunday before the scheduled hangings, at the doors of the principal churches. One stand was placed at the entrance to city hall, where the central police station was quartered, only to be kicked over and demolished and the attendants assaulted by detectives who swarmed in and out.[12]

Lucy Parsons was one of those who worked to collect signatures and funds. Day after day she appeared on street corners and in public parks, beside her a small wooden stand piled high with petitions and pamphlets. She would not give up the fight to save her husband from the gallows. Her efforts, noted a contemporary, "have excited the pity and admiration of the whole country."[13] More than once she was compelled to pack up and move along by the policeman on the beat, and one day she was arrested for distributing circulars without a permit, in violation of a city regulation. Appearing in court, she sat quietly by the window reading the paper. She looked weary and depressed. The troubles of the past months had brought new lines to her face. The matron sat down beside her, and they began to talk about Lulu, who, for reasons not yet apparent, had once again fallen ill. Suddenly the judge interrupted the case in progress and called Mrs. Parsons. In a sympathetic voice he said: "Mrs. Parsons, there has been a technical violation of an ordinance on your part. There is not the slightest desire on my part to deal harshly with you, as I know the depth of your sorrow. I will fine you five dollars and suspend the fine. You may go." Silently she left the court.[14]

In spite of occasional setbacks, the work of the Amnesty Association was producing results. In a short time a vast quantity of literature was distributed. Petitions were signed "like wildfire" in restaurants, offices, and clubs. To William Holmes, treasurer of the association, it seemed that a "revolution of public feeling" was taking place.[15] Captain Schaack viewed these developments with consternation. "It was surprising," he later recorded, "to note how many, who had hitherto clamored for blood in atonement for the Haymarket massacre, now exert themselves in the effort to secure executive clemency. With my own eyes I saw people who had made the most fuss shouting 'Hang the Anarchists! Don't give them a chance for their lives. Destroy them at once. They must be roasted out; the balance of them must leave the country,' the first to weaken. They began calling the doomed Anarchists 'poor innocent men; it is too bad to hang them' "[16] A notable example was Melville E. Stone, editor of the *Chicago Daily News*. Few men had done more to whip up feeling against the anarchists, yet he was now among the most active in the effort to save their lives. Potter Palmer, the wealthy merchant, was another prominent Chicagoan who shifted ground after the trial, sending a check to the Amnesty Association and signing a petition for a commutation of sentence.[17]

As November 11 approached, Oglesby was swamped with petitions in favor of clemency. They came from every part of the country, from famous men and obscure, from people stirred as by no comparable event of the century. Leaders of business and the professions joined with heads of labor organizations in pleading for mercy. In less than a week more than 40,000 signatures were collected in Chicago alone from citizens of all classes and beliefs. Many of the city's most respected inhabitants added their names to the appeal: judges like Murray F. Tuley, William K. McAllister, Frank Baker, and Thomas Moran; lawyers like Edward Osgood Brown, Benjamin F. Ayer, William C. Goudy (head of Chicago's bar), and Stephen S. Gregory (future president of the American Bar Association); businessmen like Marvin Hughitt, president of the Chicago & Northwestern Railroad, and Lyman J. Gage, executive officer of the First National Bank of Chicago and future secretary of the treasury under William McKinley; and political leaders like State Senators Richard

Burke and Alson J. Streeter, State Representative Charles G. Dixon, and Alderman William Manierre. In addition, there were Rabbi Emil Hirsch of Sinai Temple; Paul Carus, editor of *The Open Court*; and Lyman Trumbull, Lincoln's old law partner, who had been a justice of the Illinois Supreme Court and for eighteen years a United States senator. Trumbull, when approached by Samuel McConnell on behalf of the Amnesty Association, read the petition, then buried his face in his hands and said: "I will sign. Those men did not have a fair trial."[18]

Outside Chicago support came from such diverse figures as Moncure D. Conway, biographer of Paine and Carlyle; B. F. Underwood, editor and freethinker; Thomas Davidson, author and philosopher; and Steele MacKaye, a leading actor of the day, who denounced the impending executions as "a national folly and a national disgrace."[19] The Reverend J. C. Kimball of Hartford raised his voice against the executions, as did Rabbi Sabato Morais of Philadelphia and Professor Felix Adler of New York, leader of the Ethical Culture Society. Such prominent New York clergymen as Dr. Lyman Abbott, R. Heber Newton, and Father Edward McGlynn signed petitions for leniency, while Father James Huntington, prior of the Order of the Holy Cross, called for a meeting of religious leaders of all denominations at the Calvary Church on East 23rd Street, at which a resolution was adopted petitioning Oglesby to commute the death sentences.[20]

Persons of standing in the intellectual world—writers, lecturers, poets—joined the number asking for clemency. Of these William Dean Howells remained the most important. Following the decision of the Illinois Supreme Court, Howells plunged himself into the campaign to save the defendants from the gallows. "I have never believed them guilty of murder," he wrote to Roger Pryor, "or of anything else but their opinions, and I do not think they were justly convicted."[21] Exerting himself in their behalf, he signed a petition for clemency, sent money to the amnesty fund, and wrote to Governor Oglesby appealing for a commutation.

More than that, Howells worked hard to induce others to follow his example, among them John Greenleaf Whittier, the celebrated Quaker poet. "The fact is," he wrote to Whittier, "that those men were sentenced for murder when they ought to have been indicted for conspiracy." (Howells afterwards went farther, telling William Salter that they should not have had "any sentence at all under that *bouffe* trial, with its cock-and-bull pretence of a conspiracy.") Howells asked Whittier to write a letter to Governor Oglesby appealing for mercy, just as he himself had done. "I urge you to write it," he implored, "and do what one great and blameless man may do to arrest the greatest wrong that ever threatened our fame as a nation." Whittier in the end refused, answering that, although opposed to capital punishment, he had "never interfered with the law" and could "see no reason for making the case of the anarchists an exception."[22]

Howells continued his efforts to the end. When the United States Supreme Court denied a writ of error, he wrote an open letter to the *New York Tribune* urging its readers to petition Governor Oglesby for a commutation of sentence. Published on November 6, the letter expressed Howells's dismay that the nation's highest tribunal had refused to review the case, as the Illinois Supreme Court had "simply affirmed the legality of the forms under which the Chicago court proceeded; it did not affirm the propriety of trying for murder men fairly indictable for conspiracy alone; and it by no means approved the principle of punishing them because of their frantic opinions for a crime which they were not shown to have committed." For these reasons it was lamentable that "the justice or injustice of their sentences" was not to be determined by the United States Supreme Court. "That question," concluded Howells, "must remain for history, which judges the judgment of courts, to deal with; and I, for one, cannot doubt what the decision of history will be."[23]

It took great courage for Howells to speak out as he did. For publishing his letter he was castigated in newspapers throughout the country, some of which, he remarked, "abused me as heartily as if I had proclaimed myself a dynamiter."[24] An editor in Maine wrote that he could "hardly believe these words embody the sentiments of the greatest of American novelists. What—after they have been judged guilty of murder: after the Supreme Court has affirmed the legality of the lower court proceedings which convicted them? . . . They are murderers, bomb throwers, enemies of our civilization, destroyers of homes, villains and cut-throats. Why should they not suffer for their wrong-doing like other convicted murderers? The position which you have taken, Mr. Howells, must sever you from the loyal friendship of thousands of your readers and admirers."[25]

From those who favored leniency, by contrast, Howells's action brought expressions of gratitude. Eleanor Marx called him a "brave poet and just man" for what he had done. "Great as your work is," said Harriet Prescott Spofford, "you never wrote more immortal words than those in behalf of these men who are dying for free speech." Many people, Brand Whitlock afterwards remarked, had sent letters and signed petitions to Governor Oglesby, but there was "no appeal stronger, and no protest braver" than that expressed by Howells in his letter.[26]

Together with Howells, Robert Ingersoll was another of the prominent writers and speakers who supported the clemency movement. In a remarkable prophecy, uttered on November 3, he foretold the consequences that executing the anarchists might bring: "After these six or seven men have been, in accordance with the forms of the law, strangled to death, there will be a few pieces of clay, and about them will gather a few friends, a few admirers—and these pieces will be buried, and over the grave will be erected a monument, and those who were executed as criminals will be remembered by thousands as saints. It is far better for society to have a little mercy. The effect upon the community will be good. If these men are imprisoned, people will examine their teachings without prejudice. If they are executed, seen through the tears of pity their virtues, their sufferings, their heroism will be exaggerated, others may emulate their deeds, and the gulf between the rich and the poor will be widened— a gulf that may not close until it has devoured the noblest and the best."[27]

In contrast to Howells, however, Ingersoll chose to remain in the background, believing that his public advocacy of the anarchists might harm whatever chances still remained to them. Yet, a few days before the scheduled hangings, he did sign a petition in New York, along with such other noted freethinkers as Thaddeus B. Wakeman and Courtlandt Palmer, appealing for a commutation of the death sentence. Moreover, in response to the urging of George Schilling, he promised to write Oglesby "the best letter I can," though Schilling was to say nothing about it until after the governor had announced his decision, lest the resultant hue and cry nullify any positive effect that it might have.[28]

George Francis Train, another leading orator of the period, was more outspoken in his defense of the prisoners. Perennial eccentric and flouter of convention, Train declared that America could better afford to hang the seven justices of the Illinois Supreme Court than the seven men "assigned for the gallows by them."[29] Breaking a long period of silence, he wired the prisoners that he would go out on a lecture tour in their behalf if they thought it might help their cause.[30] When they replied in the affirmative, he came to Chicago and, dressed in a black cutaway, white vest, and lavender kid gloves, cautioned an audience at the Princess Skating Rink against executing men as "accessories to a crime for which there is no principal." "You hang these men," he exclaimed , "and I will head twenty million workingmen to cut the throats of everybody in Chicago."[31]

Following this outburst, Train was barred by the authorities from delivering further speeches in the city. Parsons thereupon wrote him a note. Addressed to "Citizen George Francis Train, Champion of Free Speech, Free Press and Public Assemblage," it read: "Despotism of America's money-mongers again demonstrated. They deny the right of the people to assemble to hear you speak to them. Free speech! They will not allow the people to buy or read the *Psycho-Anarchist*. Free press! They interdict the right of the people to assemble and petition for redress of grievances. Right of assembly! . . . America's plutocrats of 1887 sneer at these things. Police censorship over press, speech and assemblage! Russia, Spain, Italy, France—abashed!"[32]

While Train was in Chicago, he sent a basket of fruit to each of the prisoners. In return, he received a letter from Fischer: "Citizen George Francis Train: I thank you for the basket of fruit you were kind enough to send. I noticed that the daily papers refer to you as the 'champion crank.' Don't mind that! What is a crank, anyway? As much as I know there is not a specific definition of the word, but I do know that all men who are in advance of their age go under the category 'crank.' Socrates, Christ, Huss, Luther, Galileo, Rousseau, Paine, Jefferson, Franklin, Phillips, and last but not least, old John Brown, and many other more or less known apostles of progress have been considered 'cranks' by their contemporaries because they held ideas which were contrary to and in advance of the customary social, political, religious, or scientific arrangements of things. But for these 'cranks' civilization would be in its infancy yet. Therefore, long live the 'cranks.' With hearty greetings, sir, I subscribe myself, Adolph Fischer."[33]

Train was not alone in sending fruit to the condemned prisoners. On November 7, John Brown, Jr., eldest of John Brown's children, sent each a box of Catawba grapes, accompanied by a message of support. "Brother," it read, accept these grapes "as a slight token of my sympathy for you, and for the cause which you represent. Four days before his execution, my Father wrote to a friend the following: 'It is a great comfort to feel assured that I am permitted to die for a cause—not merely to pay the debt of nature, as all must.' That a like assurance may be a comfort to you, is the earnest desire of: Ever yours for the cause of the faithful, honest laborer, John Brown, Jr."[34]

In a letter to Franklin Sanborn, his father's friend and the biographer of Emerson and Thoreau, Brown told of his gift to the condemned men and added an interesting comment: "Father's favorite theme was that of the *Community plan of cooperative industry,* in which all should labor for the Common good; 'having all things in common' as did the disciples of Jesus in his day. This also has been, and still is, my Communistic or Socialistic faith." Brown expected to lose "many friends in consequence of my small token of sympathy for those men, who have, according to the measure of their light and honest convictions, been *faithful to their highest ideas.* It will make no difference with me if such should be the result; for I have in this matter been faithful to my highest sense of duty."[35]

The prisoners took special comfort from Brown's gift, as they all, without exception, revered the memory of his martyred father, whom Fielden, at a meeting of the American Group in 1885, had called "the greatest character in American history."[36] But if Brown's gesture provided an unexpected boost to their morale, their greatest disappointment came from Henry George, who, having publicly embraced their cause in his journal and privately written to them in prison pledging his sympathy and support, reversed himself after the Illinois Supreme Court sustained the decision against them. George no longer believed that "the anarchists were condemned on insufficient evidence," as he had formerly stated, but that, although it was not proved that any of them threw the bomb, it was "proved beyond a doubt that these men were engaged in a conspiracy, as a result of which the bomb was thrown, and were therefore under the laws of Illinois as guilty as though they themselves had done the act."[37]

George, accordingly, found "no ground for asking executive clemency" in their behalf. They had been tried and convicted in a Chicago court, and the Supreme Court of Illinois, "after an elaborate examination of the evidence and the law," had unanimously confirmed the verdict. "It may be said," George remarked, "that these men had worked themselves up to the belief that it is only by acts of violence and bloodshed that social reform can be attained, but that does not affect the justice of their sentence. No matter how honest or how intense may have been their conviction on this point, organized society is none the less justified in protecting itself against such acts."[38]

George's reversal could not have come at a worse time for the condemned men. Only the intervention of Governor Oglesby might now save them from the gallows, and they needed all the support that they could get. Partisans of clemency were outraged. By shifting his ground at such a critical moment, declared the London *Freedom*, George had himself become an accessory—"in the crime of Bonfield, Gary & Co." William Morris found nothing less than capital letters adequate to the branding of George's action: "Henry George approves of this murder; do not let anybody waste many words to qualify this wretch's conduct. One word will include all the rest—TRAITOR!!"[39]

Why had George shifted his ground? Some saw political ambition as the cause. Less than a year before, he had astonished the nation by rolling up a vote of 68,000 as an independent candidate for mayor of New York City, nearly winning the election. In the summer of 1887 he was nominated for the office of secretary of state of New York. His remarkable showing of 1886 had, according to Benjamin Tucker, inspired him with "insane hopes of speedy political victory." The month of September 1887 found him in the thick of his campaign; and it was at this moment that the Illinois Supreme Court upheld the verdict against the anarchists. For some weeks George remained silent. But the demand that he take a stand became too loud for him to ignore, and in *The Standard* of October 8 appeared, over his signature, the editorial that, said Tucker, "at once damned Henry George forever in the eyes of every decent and unbiased man." Emma Goldman held the same view. The facts, she later wrote, demonstrate that "Henry George, the social iconoclast, the lover of freedom and justice, had been slain by Henry George, the politician, the candidate for the position of Secretary of State of New York."[40]

If indeed George changed his position for political reasons, he had seriously miscalculated. Because of his turnabout, workers and radicals deserted him in droves, and he ran a poor third in the election. As he had nearly won the mayoralty of New York the year before with socialist and labor help, his defeat was particularly humiliating. A number of his partisans had foreseen the debacle, but George had refused to listen. To a Scottish disciple he had written: "I got your note about the Anarchists. It is a subject that I hate to have to handle, but I cannot take the same view that you men on the other side seem to take. We have a thoroughly bad element here who are constantly preaching dynamite and who are really a great difficulty."[41]

George cleaved to this view until the end, refusing to sign petitions for executive clemency. On November 5, however, six days before the scheduled executions, he wrote a private letter to Governor Oglesby asking for a commutation of the death sentences. He did so from considerations of expediency rather than of morality or law. There existed, he told the governor, "through all parts of the country and among great bodies of men a deep and bitter consciousness of social injustice" with regard to the case, coupled with a belief, even among men who had no sympathy for acts of violence, "that in the excited state of public opinion in Chicago the anarchists did not get a fair trial." Under these circumstances, said George, echoing the prophecy of Robert Ingersoll quoted earlier, "their tragic death upon the scaffold will most powerfully tend to excite sympathy for them and their families, and to condone their acts and to throw something of the halo of martyrdom around their teachings. Men who bitterly feel the injustice of social conditions which condemn them to want in the midst of plenty will be told, 'These men died in your cause,' and the result will at least be to familiarize their minds with the idea of violence."[42]

George concluded his letter with the following words: "I am one of a large number of citizens who, aiming at the redressing of social and political grievances by constitutional means, are most keenly alive to the dangers involved in the growth of a spirit of violence. For this reason and because I know that the feeling that these men ought not to suffer death is widespread and deep, I now venture to urge upon you as a matter of wise discretion, based upon consid- erations of public policy relating not only to the state of Illinois but to the whole country, that you so mitigate the sentences of the Chicago anarchists as to avoid giving to the advocates of violence a most powerful means of appealing to the sympathies of well inten- tioned men."[43]

By the time George had written his letter, a mountain of paper had accumulated in the governor's office at Springfield containing ap- peals for executive clemency. Day after day, petitions, letters, tel- egrams, resolutions flowed in from all parts of America and the world. Laid end to end, one newspaper noted, the petitions would form a line at least a dozen miles long. Some of the communications contained "vile, silly, and malignant threats," as Oglesby remarked,[44] but most were pleas from the heart, earnest entreaties for mercy. One writer sent Oglesby the following lines by James Russell Lowell:

> Right forever on the scaffold,
> Wrong forever on the throne.
> Yet that scaffold sways the future
> And behind the dim unknown
> God is standing in the shadow,
> Keeping watch above his own.[45]

Among the letters was one from Clara Shuntz, aged eight years, who named the guilty party, hoping that Oglesby would spare the prisoners. "Dear Dear Govenor," it began, "I hope you will not let them [be] hanged. They are not guilty." The actual culprit was Fritz Bentz, "an offle Bad Man," wrote Clara. "He told my Pappa last night his Watch had not kept such a time as it did the day he thrown that Dinamont."[46]

Apart from the written appeals that poured in upon the governor in increasing volume, meetings of indignation and protest were mounted in support of the condemned men. On September 18, 1887, four days after the Illinois Supreme Court affirmed the death sentence, a coalition of German anarchists and socialists in New York called on the American workers to "arise in your imposing might and let your righteous wrath fall in an unmistakable protest upon those interpreters of the law who have basely betrayed their trust." Only the workers could prevent "the consummation on November 11 of this horrible deed to which the deeds of cannibals are as nothing."[47]

As the day of execution drew near, labor organizations throughout the country took an increasingly forthright stand in defense of the doomed anarchists. From far and wide came calls for a commutation or at least a postponement of the sentence. Even the Socialistic Labor Party, in spite of its longstanding feud with the International, went on record in favor of clemency, declaring the confirmation of the judgment by the higher court "to be unjust, to be dictated by prejudice and hatred, and to be an act of class justice."[48]

In a similar spirit, the American Federation of Labor adopted a resolution appealing for leniency, while at the same time repudiating the use of violence to better the lot of the workers. It was a difficult decision for the young organization, founded in 1886, yet its leadership disdained expediency in favor of justice and mercy. "We stand for a fair trial for the underdog whether called anarchist or any other name," declared its president, Samuel Gompers, who felt that the labor movement could not safely abandon its radical wing to the "vengeance of the common enemy." Labor, Gompers insisted, "must do its best to maintain justice for radicals or find itself denied the rights of free men."[49]

Gompers elucidated his position in a letter to James W. Smith, a member of the Federation's Executive Council, who had questioned the wisdom of endorsing the clemency movement. "I abhor anarchy," wrote Gompers, "but I also abhor injustice when meted out even to the most despicable being on earth. . . . No person seems to know who threw the fatal bomb. Consequently, no connection was or could be proven between the party who threw it and the seven condemned men who are charged with inciting some 'person unknown' to throw it. So long as capital punishment is part of the laws of our State and Country, if it could be enforced, no discrimination should be indulged in favor of one nor the law strained to shield another class."[50]

Gompers believed that it would not only be a gross miscarriage of justice to execute the anarchists, but that their execution, as he told Smith, "would place a halo of martyrdom around them which would lead many to the violent agitation we so much deplore. In the interest of the cause of labor and peaceful methods of improving the conditions of achieving the final emancipation of labor, I am opposed to this execution. It would be a blot on the escutcheon of our country." Smith warned Gompers that his espousal of clemency was bringing him and the American Federation of Labor severe criticism and that many labor men did not support his efforts in behalf of the anarchists. Gompers replied that he was "trying to keep a cool head and to view matters as they exist, to maintain the dignity and honor of our organization, and withal to be manly and uncringing."[51]

On November 7, 1887, four days before the execution date, Gompers wrote a letter to Governor Oglesby begging him, in the name of mercy and humanity, to exercise his prerogative and commute the death sentences to life imprisonment. "Grant this prayer," the letter concluded, "and you will be blessed by the living and the countless thousands yet unborn and incur the everlasting gratitude of, Yours most Respectfully, Samuel Gompers, President American Federation of Labor."[52] As a representative of the Central Labor Union of New York, Gompers, together with James E. Quinn of District Assembly 49 of the Knights of Labor and twelve other labor leaders, signed a public appeal to the workers of America, urging them to do all in their power to secure a commutation. "Liberty, free speech and justice, impartially meted out to friend and foe," it proclaimed, "are the only safeguards and the primary conditions of a peaceable social development in this country." Insisting that the condemned men were victims of prejudice and class hatred, and that their execution would be "a disgrace to the honor of our nation, and would strengthen the doctrines that it is ostensibly directed against," the appeal called on all labor organizations to hold meetings and demonstrations in favor of executive clemency.[53]

In response, hundreds of gatherings took place to denounce the approaching executions. Rallies and processions were mounted in every part of the country. On October 8 a huge crowd packed the Great Hall of Cooper Union in New York to hear Gompers, Peter McGuire, and Daniel De Leon, and to pass resolutions that disavowed sympathy with anarchism but protested against the denial of impartial justice. "I come here deliberately and for the grand name of our beloved country," proclaimed De Leon, then a lecturer at Columbia University, "that its proud record shall not be bloodstained by a judicial crime as the one contemplated in Chicago."[54] A workers' meeting in St. Paul, Minnesota, appealed for a commutation of sentence on grounds that the trial had been "unduly influenced by an inflamed public sentiment brought about by the capitalistic clamor for the blood of some leaders of the labor movement, having as its object the checking of its rapid and peaceful growth." At a rally in Union Hill, New Jersey, the 1,500 people assembled at the local skating rink were, without warning or provocation, set upon and clubbed by the police; and a similar incident occurred in New York's Union Square during a rally sponsored by the SLP.[55]

Among the major working-class organizations involved in the protests, the Knights of Labor remained sharply divided in its attitude towards the defendants. Powderly, ever fearful lest the general public accuse the Order of abetting violence, threatened to expel any affiliate that supported the clemency movement. "Better that seven times seven men hang," he declared, "than to hang a millstone of odium around the standard of the Order by affiliating in any way with this element of destruction."[56] To this Spies reacted with bitter irony. "Powderly," he wrote to Schilling, "is opposed to 'Anarchy'— the man who swore that *only* by force could Ireland be liberated, and that he would help to liberate it. Contemptible hypocrite!"[57]

Powderly's order, however, was flouted by local assemblies throughout the country. In New York, as we have seen, the large District Assembly 49 joined forces with the Central Labor Union to mount a campaign of petitions and demonstrations. In Chicago, too, Local Assembly 1307 took part in the movement to secure executive clemency, as did Women's Assembly 1789 (led by Sarah Ames) and the local journal of the Order, *The Knights of Labor*.[58]

The climax of this opposition was reached at the Minneapolis General Assembly in October 1887, barely a month before the scheduled executions. On October 10 James E. Quinn of District Assembly 49 introduced the following resolution: "Considering that the development of the human mind in the nineteenth century has reached a point expressed almost universally against capital punishment, or taking human life by judicial process, as a relic of barbarism, therefore be it resolved, That this convention express sorrow that the men in Chicago were doomed to death, and that it use every endeavor to secure the commutation of the sentence of death passed upon them."[59]

The moment this was read there was an uproar. Quinn begged, in the name of humanity, that the resolution be adopted. But Powderly, who presided, declared it out of order. An appeal was entered, and half a day was taken up discussing the issue, Schilling of Chicago and Labadie of Detroit speaking in favor of the resolution. Powderly, leaving the chair, made what Labadie termed an "illogical, cowardly, brutal and violent" speech, in which he threatened, as reported by Labadie, that if the resolution passed there would never be another session of the General Assembly, and that no matter what action the Assembly took he would not be bound by it. He warned the convention that if it passed the resolution he would "go out on the public platform and denounce the men under sentence of death." "I hate the name of anarchy," Powderly told the Assembly. "Through its encroachments it has tarnished the name of socialism and caused men to believe that socialism and anarchism were one." The anarchists, Powderly continued, "drive men from the labor movement by their wild and foolish mouthings wherever they congregate, and they usually congregate where beer flows freely." For anarchism, he repeated, "I have nothing but hatred, and if I could I would forever wipe from the face of the earth the last vestige of its double-damned presence, and in doing so would feel that the best act of my life, in the interest of labor, had been performed."[60]

The struggle was bitter. Indeed, the verbal thrusts nearly broke up the convention and left deep scars on the unity of the organization. When the resolution was put to a vote, the Grand Master Workman was sustained by a two-to-one margin. Powderly felt vindicated. "I did not hate the condemned men," he afterwards insisted. "I did not oppose every man doing what he could to cause the governor to deal leniently with them, and I did not desire their execution, as has been said. What I opposed was committing the Order of the Knights of Labor to the teachings of anarchy. That was all that I did, and that would I do again."[61]

But the resolution, as Labadie pointed out, in no way committed the Order "to any system of social philosophy nor to any particular line of method." It appealed, rather, to "the broadest principles of humanity," and yet only one-third of the delegates "dared to raise their voices in behalf of the men unjustly tried and convicted." So disgusted was Spies by the result that he wrote to Schilling in Minneapolis not to ask any of the delegates who had opposed the resolution to sign a petition for clemency. "I don't," said Spies, "or we don't, treasure our lives higher than our honor!"[62] After the convention, a number of local assemblies withdrew from the Order, among them the Sons of Liberty of Chicago. Powderly's behavior had greatly exacerbated the frictions within the organization and contributed to its subsequent decline.

Meanwhile, the flood of appeals to Governor Oglesby showed no sign of abating. Stacks of petitions and letters continued to pile up, many of which came from abroad, particularly from England, where a vigorous campaign had been launched against the approaching executions. In London a petition for clemency was signed by more than 16,000 members of workingmen's clubs on a single Sunday. Kropotkin, in a letter to the *New York Herald*, spoke of a "great contest between labor and capital—which constitutes the very essence of modern history." Owing to the death sentence in Chicago, he warned, "the contest is going to take in America a turn even more acute and brutal than it ever took in Europe."[63]

The case from the very outset had aroused international excitement. Meetings of indignation took place in nearly every country of Europe, where the trial and verdict were widely denounced in the anarchist and socialist press. Henry Seymour, editor of *The Anarchist* of London, asked how men could be made to suffer the extreme penalty as accessories to an unknown perpetrator. Such an outrage, he wrote, would be without precedent in the history of civilized communities. A meeting of London anarchists organized by Seymour and his associates affirmed "the right of the Anarchists of America to avenge, by any means, this bloody and brutal murder of innocent men by the State of Illinois."[64]

In a similar vein the London *Freedom*, founded in October 1886 by Kropotkin and his disciples, denounced "this atrocious attempt by the common enemy to terrorise the proletariat into submission to property rule." The United States, noted *Freedom*, prided itself on its republican institutions, and yet there was no country in the world where "the toiling masses are met by more arbitrary and brutal ferocity when they show any decided intention to free themselves from the control of the possessors of wealth." Seven men had been condemned to death because they had proclaimed the right and duty of the workers to resist oppression. "The property owners are terrified at the energy of the protest against their authority, and clamour for some vengeance which may strike terror into the rebels. Hence the mock trial of the eight Anarchists before a packed jury and a prejudiced judge, and their condemnation to death in defiance of the evidence."[65]

Socialists joined hands with the anarchists in protesting against the execution of sentence. Three days before the scheduled hangings, the *Pall Mall Gazette* published an interview with Eleanor Marx, stating the facts of the case for the first time in a middle-class paper. "There really was not enough evidence to hang a dog upon," she declared. The jury was "admittedly prejudiced" and the judge "unblushingly partisan." In the socialist paper *To-Day*, she and her husband Edward Aveling wrote that their antagonism to the teachings of anarchism "strengthens our position in asking justice for the condemned men." The sentence, they said, "is a class-sentence; the execution will be a class execution."[66]

Echoing these sentiments, Henry M. Hyndman, England's leading disciple of Marx, declared: "Personally, I am perhaps as strongly opposed to Anarchist tactics as many of the capitalist class themselves, regarding as I do such individual outrages and unorganized outbursts as aids to reaction, rather than helps to the great organized Social Revolution which Social Democrats strive for." Yet Hyndman added his voice to the protests. Despite America's lack of an aristocracy and an established church, he said, despite its possession of universal manhood suffrage and free education, "all are now driven to admit that the same class struggle is going on under the guise of nominal peace and freedom."[67]

Thus socialists and anarchists were agreed that the image of freedom, opportunity, and equality long associated with America by enlightened Europeans had shown itself to be fraudulent. To William Morris, the greatest socialist of his day, the Haymarket affair had demonstrated that any hope of social betterment founded on existing American models was a "pernicious fallacy." The case exhibited to the full what Morris called "that spirit of cold cruelty, heartless and careless at once, which is one of the most noticeable characteristics of American commercialism." In the view of its citizens, America was "a country with universal suffrage, no king, no House of Lords, no privilege as you fondly think; only a little standing army chiefly used for the murder of red-skins; a democracy after your model." With all that, said Morris, it was "a society corrupt to the core, and at this moment engaged in suppressing freedom with just the same reckless brutality and blind ignorance as the Czar of All the Russias uses."[68]

Morris, despite all the efforts to save the defendants, feared the worst. "A friend told me this morning," he wrote in October 1887, "that speaking to some American acquaintances on this subject they answered his expostulations by saying something like this: 'Ah, but you forget that Most has published a most atrocious book against society.' This is exactly the spirit of the Chicago trial. One man has written a book, so seven others are to be hanged for it."[69]

Yet Morris did his utmost to prevent the tragedy from taking place. Like Howells in America, he sent letters to colleagues in the literary world begging them to petition for clemency. To Robert Browning he wrote that he was "much troubled by this horror," urging that Browning sign an appeal to Governor Oglesby, "and so to do what you can to save the lives of seven men who have been condemned to death for a deed of which they were not guilty after a mere mockery of a trial."[70] On October 6, moreover, Morris spoke at a meeting called by London socialists and anarchists to protest against "the outrageous sentence passed upon the Chicago Anarchists" and the decision of the Illinois Supreme Court to refuse a new trial. Among the other speakers at the meeting, held at the Communist Club on Tottenham Street, were H. H. Sparling, secretary of the Socialist League, and Henry Seymour, editor of *The Anarchist*.[71]

This was but one of a series of such gatherings in which Morris took a prominent part, uttering vehement denunciations of the savagery to which the Chicago anarchists were being subjected. At the largest, held in the South Place Institute on October 14, he shared the platform with Annie Besant of the National Secular Society, George Bernard Shaw of the Fabian Society, and Kropotkin, Stepniak, and Charlotte Wilson of the Freedom Group. Kropotkin described Haymarket as "a retaliation upon prisoners taken in the virtual civil war that was going on between the two great classes." Shaw, who disclaimed any sympathy with anarchism, supported the view that "this was a question alone of freedom of speech and opinion." A resolution, moved by Charlotte Wilson and seconded by Morris, was passed by acclamation. It read in part: "We cannot admit that the political views of the seven condemned men have anything to do with the principle involved; and we protest against this sentence, which, if carried out, will practically make the holding of meetings of working men in their own interest a capital offence throughout the United States of America, since it is always possible for the authorities to provoke a crowd to reprisals involving danger to life."[72]

When the United States Supreme Court denied a writ of error on November 2, it provoked through Europe a "widespread outburst of fresh indignation and horror," in the words of the London *Freedom*.[73] Urgent meetings were held and resolutions passed against the execution of the sentence. A telegram petitioning Governor Oglesby for a commutation was signed by artists, writers, and a whole galaxy of British radicals and reformers, from Edward Carpenter and William Morris to Olive Schreiner and Eleanor Marx. Among the other signatories were Oscar Wilde, George Bernard Shaw, Walter Crane, William Rossetti, Henry Hyndman, Edward Aveling, E. Belfort Bax, E. Nesbit, Friedrich Engels, Stopford Brooke, Annie Besant, Walter Besant, Stepniak, Richard Heath, and R. B. Cunninghame Graham, "the one M.P. who dared put humanity before political ambition." Many organizations were also represented, including liberal and radical clubs and branches of the Socialist League, the Social Democratic Federation, and the Labour Emancipation League.[74]

On the continent, meanwhile, meetings were held in Paris, Brussels, Zurich, Rome, Madrid, and other cities, and workers sent contributions to the defense fund.[75] In France a group from the Chamber of Deputies telegraphed an appeal to Governor Oglesby, as did the Municipal Council of Paris and the Council of the Department of the Seine, while as far away as Sydney and Melbourne crowds gathered to protest against the impending executions.[76] Oglesby was beleaguered from all directions. The time was quickly approaching when he would have to render a decision.

22 ∥ SPRINGFIELD

For the governor of Illinois to commute a sentence of death, the laws of the state required that the condemned submit a formal appeal for clemency. As the execution date drew near, counsel for the defense, members of the Defense Committee and the Amnesty Association, and friends and relatives of the doomed anarchists descended on the jail and urged the prisoners to petition Oglesby to spare their lives. Henry Lloyd and William Salter were especially importunate. They prevailed on the men to issue a statement expressing regret over the Haymarket incident and renouncing the doctrine of violence. Unless they did this, the pair insisted, clemency would be impossible and the hangings would take place as scheduled. As Fielden afterwards wrote, "the situation appeared to them to be that if we could conscientiously admit even that we had made mistakes in our propaganda, that might assist." Both Lloyd and Salter were aware, said Fielden, that the sentences were unjust, and they "did not for a moment ask us to say anything that would imply our guilt." But they knew that public opinion had been inflamed by falsehoods and that the governor would therefore be "hard to move."[1]

At length the entreaties of Lloyd and Salter bore fruit. Fielden, Schwab, and, more reluctantly, Spies agreed to petition for a commutation. Spies had reservations. "I am, as a matter of course, sorry for the poor devils who lost their lives at the Haymarket," he confided to Salter, "but I am more so for the lives of the poor devils who perished on the previous day [at the McCormick factory]. Who cares for their wretched families? Nobody. Now, for me to express condolence over the killing of the policemen, and not at the same time over that of the poor fellows at McCormick's or at East St. Louis, would be an act of hypocrisy such as I would not be guilty of under any circumstances. Suffice it to say that I abhor murder in *every* form. If I did not I would never have become a socialist!"[2]

Spies's objections were incorporated into the letter sent by the three men to Governor Oglesby. Written on November 3, the day after the United States Supreme Court declined to review the conviction, it insisted that "we never advocated the use of force, excepting in the case of self-defense," and that, "while we attacked the present social arrangements, in writing and speeches, and exposed their iniquities, we have never consciously broken any laws." The prisoners then added: "If, in the excitement of propagating our views, we were led into expressions which caused workingmen to think that aggressive force was a proper instrument of reform, we regret it. We deplore the loss of life at the Haymarket, at McCormick's factory, at East St. Louis, and at the Chicago Stock Yards."[3]

During the next few days, the men also wrote individual letters to the governor. Fielden, while again protesting his innocence, admitted that he had been indiscreet in his utterances:

> It is true that I have said things in such heat that in calmer moments I should not have said. I made violent speeches. I supported the use of force as a means of righting the wrongs which seemed to me to be apparent.
>
> I cannot admit that I used all the words imputed to me by the State, nor can I pretend to remember the actual phrases that I did utter. I am conscious, however, as I have said, that I was frequently aroused to a pitch of excitement which made me in a sense irresponsible. I was intoxicated with the applause of my hearers, and the more violent my language, the more applause I received. My audience and myself mutually excited each other. I think, however, it is true that, for sensational or other purposes, words were put into my mouth and charged to me which I never uttered; but, whether this be true or not, I say now that I no longer believe it proper that any class of society should attempt to right its own wrongs by violence. I can now see that much that I said under excitement was unwise, and all this I regret. It is not true, however, that I ever consciously attempted to incite any man to the commission of crime. Although I do admit that I belonged to an organization which was engaged at one time in preparing for a social revolution, I was not engaged in any conspiracy to manufacture or throw bombs. I never owned or carried a revolver in my life and did not fire one at the Haymarket. I had not the slightest idea that the meeting at the Haymarket would be other than a peaceable and orderly one, such as I had often addressed in the city,

and was utterly astounded at its bloody outcome, and have always felt keenly the loss of life and suffering there occasioned.

In view of these facts, I respectfully submit that, while I confess with regret the use of extravagant and unjustifiable words, I am not a murderer. I never had any murderous intent, and I humbly pray relief from the murderer's doom. That these statements are true I do again solemnly affirm by every tie that I hold sacred, and I hope that your Excellency will give a considerate hearing to the merits of my case, and also to those of my imprisoned companions who have been sentenced with me.[4]

Schwab's letter, though briefer, contained a similar message: "I realize that many utterances of mine in connection with the labor agitation of the past, expressions made under intense excitement, and often without any deliberation, were injudicious. These I regret, believing that they must have had a tendency to incite unnecessary violence oftentimes. I protest again that I had no thought or purpose of violence in connection with the Haymarket meeting, which I did not even attend, and that I have always deplored the results of that meeting."[5]

Spies's letter was of a quite different character. He had signed the joint letter to Oglesby under pressure from counsel and friends. He had done it against his own better judgment, and almost immediately he regretted his action. Besides, as soon as it became known that he had begged for clemency, a cry went up among the German militants that he had disgraced the movement and shown himself a coward. When Spies learned what was being said about him, he resolved to undo, so far as possible, what had been done. On November 6, three days after signing the earlier letter, he wrote to the governor withdrawing his request for mercy and asking that he be allowed to pay the penalty for all the condemned men. "If a sacrifice of life there must be," he said, "will not my life suffice? The State's attorney of Cook county asked for no more. Take this, then! Take my life! I offer it to you so that you may satisfy the fury of a semi-barbaric mob, and save that of my comrades! . . . In the name of the traditions of our country, I beg you to prevent a seven-fold murder upon men whose only crime is that they are idealists, that they long for a better future for all. If legal murder there must be, let one, let mine, suffice."[6] The letter was placed in the hands of Joseph Buchanan, who was shortly to visit Oglesby at the state capital. It was

357

Spies's atonement for having petitioned for clemency. Buchanan promised that he would not leave the governor until he had acquainted him with "every syllable of its contents."[7]

In contrast to Fielden, Schwab, and Spies, the three intransigents among the prisoners, Engel, Fischer, and Lingg, refused absolutely to make any appeal for mercy. As they viewed the situation, a single choice lay before them: honor and death or dishonor and a miserable existence, if indeed clemency was forthcoming. To men of their mold there could be no hesitation. Repeatedly they proclaimed their defiance and their willingness to die. In letters to Governor Oglesby, full of pride and contempt, they rejected a commutation of sentence for a crime of which they were innocent. Unless he could obtain real justice, wrote Fischer, "I prefer that the verdict should be carried out as it stands." Engel insisted that he had violated no laws but merely exercised his right of "free speech, free press, free thought, and free assemblage as guaranteed by the constitution." The authorities, he said, "may *murder* me, but they cannot *legally punish* me. I protest against a commutation of my sentence and demand either liberty or death. I renounce any kind of mercy." And Lingg, in nearly identical words, declared: "I demand either liberty or death. If you are really a servant of the people, according to the constitution, then you will, by virtue of your office, unconditionally release me."[8]

All three, of course, loved life as well as any vigorous, full-blooded men could. But they were ready, every one of them, to make the supreme sacrifice. "I love my family as much as any father is capable of loving his family," wrote Fischer to the members of his union, Typographical No. 9, but to beg for leniency "would be contrary to my sense of human dignity. No scintilla of proof has been forthcoming, and, having done nothing wrong, I cannot sign an appeal for mercy. So let them proceed to murder me!"[9] All of Fischer's letters breathed the same defiant spirit. "The social revolution must have its impetus," he wrote to Johann Most, "and our noble anarchist cause its martyrs. So be it. I am ready to lay down my life on the altar of our ideal."[10]

Fischer never courted death, said Dyer Lum of his comrade, but he preferred it to dishonor, and "such he deemed a cowardly cringing to the authorities for permission to escape a legal condemnation for an alleged offense of which he knew nothing." As Fischer told Lum during one of his visits to the prison, "I heartily wish the 11th of November was to be tomorrow. You know, Dyer, I am a revolutionist and also a husband and a father. Alone I am calm and self-possessed and ready for the sacrifice; before my family other ties pull upon my heart-strings. But dearly as I love them I cannot dishonor them by my cowardice."[11] To Captain Black he said the same: "I do not care a particle if they take me out of here and hang me tomorrow. I am ready to die for the cause of the people." Fischer's words, Black recalled, were spoken with the utmost sincerity and with a smile that lit up his face. His whole countenance showed an exaltation of spirit that made death "not only a matter without terror to him, but an event of gladness. The only regret he expressed was for his wife and babes."[12]

To the end Fischer never swerved from his position, insisting on liberty or death. "This was his shibboleth," wrote William Holmes, "and no influence could prevail to shake him." Possessed of health, vitality, and abundant animal spirit, with a host of warm friends and a family for whom he felt the tenderest affection, he was "well equipped for happiness and to make others happy." Yet he deemed it "a glorious privilege to sacrifice his life for the cause which he loved better than all else besides." It was with a clearsighted passion, then, that Fischer embraced his martyrdom. "He was a tower of strength, firm as a rock, looking his coming doom in the face with an unfaltering eye, awaiting it with a calmness, a cheerfulness and even a gladness that was born of real heroism."[13]

Engel, no less than Fischer, gloried in his approaching martyrdom. He too had a powerful appetite for life, yet he reveled in the prospect of dying for the cause, the ideal, which he loved. "I willingly sacrifice my life," he declared in an open letter to the citizens of Chicago and the United States, "if in any manner it will teach the working people who are their true friends and who are their enemies." Captain Black was deeply impressed by Engel's readiness to meet death, by his "steadfast and unfaltering conviction of the righteousness of his position."[14]

Lingg showed the same unflinching courage in the face of death. "His will," Black remarked, "was indomitable; his spirit mocked at adversities." From the first day in his cell he calmly awaited the end. He had no illusions. He knew that he was the most hated and feared of all the defendants and that the authorities would not release him alive. "He is a genuine revolutionist," said Lum, who knew and understood him well. "He believes his time has come, and accepts the 'logic of events.' His only regret is that the charges against him are not more weighty!"[15]

Lingg, as might be expected, disdained all petitions and appeals. His signature on the appeal to the Illinois Supreme Court had been obtained "with difficulty," noted Lum, and then only out of regard for the wishes of his comrades. His signature on the appeal to the United States Supreme Court was never obtained, for he had renounced any further recourse to "capitalist justice." He believed, in any case, that anarchism would be better served by his death than by a reprieve. "I am firmly convinced," he wrote the day after the Illinois Supreme Court denied the appeal, "that the sacrifice of our lives, if it should occur now, will further the decline of capitalism infinitely more than if it should take place three or four years hence, when the federal court will have decided." The immediate execution of sentence, he was certain, would bring about "the final terror and annihilation of all tyrants."[16]

Where did Parsons stand in the matter of executive clemency? Of all the condemned men, he enjoyed the largest measure of public sympathy. His American origins, his voluntary surrender in court, his conduct during the trial and the obvious sincerity of his motives had made a favorable impression. Governor Oglesby was inclined to spare him, and it was made known to Captain Black that if Parsons would sign a petition for a commutation the governor would grant it. Yet Parsons refused to sign. He refused to ask for mercy. Such a request, he felt, would be tantamount to an admission of guilt. As an innocent man, he insisted, he was entitled not to a commutation but to complete and unconditional freedom. Schwab and Fielden may have been willing to accept imprisonment instead of death. "For my own self," he wrote to Justus Schwab, "I count suffering and even death both a pleasure and honor, when oppressed humanity requires it, and the economic emancipation of labor is thereby promoted."[17]

Not that Parsons wished to be a martyr. He was loved by his family and friends, and he loved them in return. "Am I tired of life?" he wrote to Schwab. "Ah, no; I am still a young man (thirty-eight years). I have a wife and two children (a boy of eight years, and a girl of six years). I worship my family and they idolize papa." Yet he would not grovel, he said, before the authorities, nor flinch if the fatal moment should come. "Well, let it come," he wrote to another

New York comrade. "We are ready to meet it like men—like anarchists. If by our death at the hands of the executioner 'liberty, fraternity, equality' can be made to triumph, then we welcome death in such a cause. To die for man, the rights of man, while I do not seek yet I do not shun it. Death for liberty's sake is better than to die in uncomplaining slavery. If we must die, then we can die."[18]

On September 21, 1887, a week after the Illinois Supreme Court upheld the verdict, Parsons issued *An Appeal to the People of America*, in which he steadfastly refused executive clemency and reasserted his willingness to die:

> I am prepared to die. I am ready, if need be, to lay down my life for my rights and the rights of my fellow men. But I object to being killed on false or unproved accusations. Therefore I cannot countenance or accept the effort of those who would endeavor to procure a commutation of my sentence to imprisonment in the penitentiary. Neither do I approve of any further appeals to the courts of law. I believe them to be all alike—the agency of the privileged class to perpetuate their power, to oppress and plunder the toiling masses. As between capital and its legal rights and labor and its natural rights, the courts of law must side with the capitalist class. To appeal to them is vain. It is the appeal of the wage slave to his capitalistic master for liberty. The answer is curses, blows, imprisonment, and death.

Reviewing the events that had brought him face to face with death, Parsons reaffirmed his innocence, condemned the trial, denounced the decision of the higher court, and rejected a commutation of sentence. "I appeal not for mercy, but for justice," he insisted. "As for me, the utterance of Patrick Henry is so apropos that I can do no better than let him speak: 'Is life so dear and peace so sweet as to be purchased at the price of chains and slavery? Forbid it, Almighty God! I know not what course others may pursue, but as for me, give me liberty or give me death!' "[19]

Three weeks later, on October 13, Parsons repeated these sentiments in an open letter to Governor Oglesby: Either he was guilty or he was innocent of the charges for which he stood condemned; if guilty, he preferred death to imprisonment; if innocent, he was entitled to nothing less than freedom. "I am innocent," Parsons reiterated, "and I say to you that under no circumstances will I accept a commutation to imprisonment. In the name of the American people I demand my right, my lawful, constitutional, natural, inalienable right to liberty."[20]

The governor, as has been noted, was prepared to exercise clemency if Parsons would but request it. The Defense Committee and men of influence urged Parsons to file the necessary petition. They pleaded with him. They implored him to beg for his life. George Schilling spent hours with his old friend trying to persuade him to sign. But Parsons's mind was made up, and nothing could alter it. To every argument and appeal he had but one answer: "I must be honest with myself."[21]

From that resolution nothing could move him. On Sunday, November 6, Melville E. Stone, editor of the *Chicago Daily News*, visited Parsons in his cell and spent more than two hours urging him to sign a petition, assuring him that he would have the influence of his paper in favor of commutation. In vain. Parsons dismissed him with the following words: "You, Mr. Stone, are responsible for my fate. No one has done more than you to compass the iniquity under which I stand here awaiting Friday's deliverance. I courted trial, knowing my innocence; your venomous attacks condemned us in advance. I shall die with less fear and less regret than you will feel in living, for my blood is upon your head."[22]

The most forceful plea, however, came from his attorney, Captain Black. Black felt a deep sense of guilt for having advised Parsons to come out of hiding and surrender himself in court. But he had been informed, on reliable authority, that a special effort would be made to secure a commutation for Parsons, owing to the peculiar circumstances of his case. On November 8 Black went to Parsons and had a long talk with him, the last of many such conversations, urging him to sign a petition which Black had prepared on his behalf. Black begged him, for the sake of his wife and children, to sign. He told him that Oglesby was favorably disposed in his case, and that he should sign so that the governor might have his technical compliance with the law. If he refused, the chances were that he would be executed. Black argued that at least he should leave no legal excuse for the governor's refusal to extend him clemency.

Parsons listened patiently to all that Black said. But he refused to put his signature on the document. "My mind is firmly and irrevocably made up," he told his counselor, "and I beg you to urge me no further upon the subject. I am an innocent man—innocent of this offense of which I have been found guilty by the jury, and the world

knows my innocence. If I am to be executed at all it is because I am
an Anarchist, not because I am a murderer; it is because of what I
have taught and spoken and written in the past, and not because of
the throwing of the Haymarket bomb."[23]

Black remained silent, at a loss for what to reply. He knew, however, that his face showed something of the pain that he felt, for
suddenly Parsons's manner softened. There was another reason, he
confided, for his refusal to sign the appeal. Such an action on his
part would irrevocably seal the doom of his comrades, for whom he
had already given himself up when in safe hiding. Certainly this was
true in the case of Fischer, Engel, and Lingg. To abandon them now
was something of which he would not be guilty. If they could be
saved at all, and he knew that their chances were slim, it was only
by his standing with them, so that "whatever action is taken in my
case might with equal propriety be taken in theirs." If, however, he
should separate his fate from theirs and sign a petition on which
the governor could commute his sentence alone, he was certain that
they would be hanged. For this reason, said Parsons, "I have determined to make their cause and their fate my own."[24]

Black again remained silent. He could make no reply to such an
argument, nor did he try. He knew that what Parsons had said was
true. He knew that if anything in the world could save the three
who, like Parsons himself, had refused to appeal for executive clemency, it would be that Parsons would stand with them and share
their fate. He knew, too, that the chances were that they would all
perish together, "but as against a man calmly facing death, and
putting his determination upon such exalted grounds of self-sacrifice
and of faithfulness to the obligations of comradeship, I had no reply
to make. I took him by the hand, looked into his face, and said to
him: 'Your action is worthy of you!' and came away."[25]

Among Parsons's most intimate comrades there were two, William Holmes and Dyer Lum, who counseled him not to yield. Holmes,
convinced that all the defendants had been "marked for sacrifice,"
was anxious for them to maintain their dignity and not to pose as
repentant criminals.[26] Years later, he recalled a conversation he had
had with Parsons through the visitors' cage of the jail: "With his
face close to mine, only the steel mesh between us, with those
piercing black eyes searching my very soul, even as they had searched
me on that memorable morning at my house at Geneva when he
gave his life and liberty into my keeping, he asked me what he should

363

do, what I would do under similar circumstances. It was a dreadful moment; a fearful responsibility rested upon me. I believed in my inmost soul that his acquiescence to the wishes of his friends would simply rob him of his glory of martyrdom. I believed then and I believe now that if he had weakened, the monsters of capitalism would have mercilessly and scornfully put him to death. They were not content to merely murder him; they sought also to disgrace him. This I told him and, with the sweat of agony upon my face, I said to him that I would not sue."[27]

Lum advised the same. Though he did not want his comrades to die if they could be saved without abasing themselves before the authorities ("I am anxious to do anything to save their lives," he had told George Schilling in June 1887),[28] yet he wanted them to remain firm. By appealing for clemency, he feared, they would surrender their revolutionary integrity, and this Lum cherished above everything else. He was, as Voltairine de Cleyre put it, "the jealous guardian of their highest honor." As such, he considered Schwab and Fielden "cowards" because they had pleaded for mercy. As to the others, he later expressed his feelings in verse:

Ye did not humble, noble Five, though press and pulpit sought
To have you sign recanting words, and then as cowards die.[29]

One day, while Lum was visiting the prisoners, Parsons drew him aside and asked whether or not he should sign a petition to the governor. "I cannot advise you," said Lum. Pressed, however, he said: "Die, Parsons." Parsons replied: "I am glad you said it. It is what I wished."[30] Lum never regretted his words. He saw Parsons not only as a man, a friend, but as an emblem of the revolutionary struggle. To spare his life would be to spoil a martyr. Parsons, Lum was proud to say, "rose to the height of manhood and coolly laughed death in the face rather than submit to a cowardly alternative."[31]

Lum exulted, moreover, over the decision of the other intransigents. "*The four will not sign* or compromise their position," he wrote to Joseph Labadie five days before the scheduled executions. "I saw them yesterday and they are firm. Spies is now de-Spies (I beg pardon). Only terrorism—I honestly believe—will now save them."[32]

Lum's seemingly heartless attitude cost him more than a few friends within the movement. "I was taunted everywhere with 'wishing their death,'" he afterwards told Voltairine de Cleyre. "That

skinful of sentiment Nina Van Zandt repeated it to Spies. I did and
I didn't: I wanted their honor to the cause and they saved it, to hell
with life without that, and they agreed with me! Most and Lucy
Parsons believed me a cold 'hair splitter.' So be it." Yes, he did want
their death, echoed Voltairine de Cleyre. He wanted it because "he
loved liberty, and honor, and pride, and the future, and their true
glory—more than his own life and more than theirs."[33] He would
gladly have joined them on the scaffold, had the state demanded it.
Indeed, he was yearning for a martyr's death, after the example of
John Brown. George Schilling, in a letter to Lum, laid bare this
hidden obsession: "It is impossible to eradicate the infatuation from
which you suffer. The trouble is you want to be with Engel, with
Spies and Parsons, stand a crown upon your forehead and a bomb
within your hand; you want to be a martyr and fill a martyr's grave."[34]

By now the campaign for executive clemency had reached its final
phase. During the last days before November 11, thousands of appeals for commutation deluged the governor's office. On the other
hand, a large number urged the full execution of the law. One letter
warned Oglesby that "the people are talking hard if you let up on
the anarchists. Of course, do as you please. But it will cost you and
the Republicans thousands of votes if you do." Lieutenant Governor
J. C. Smith similarly counseled against leniency. "I think I know
the public pulse," he said, "and it is that the law take its course."[35]
Others who opposed clemency argued that the anarchists had received every benefit of the legal process, that the country must be
protected against assassins, that nothing less than Christian morality and American values was at stake. They urged the governor to
remember the widows and orphans of the dead policemen and to
act accordingly.

Despite Melville Stone's defection, the press remained overwhelmingly in favor of carrying out the sentence. *The Nation* accused the defendants of being "chicken-hearted" and deplored the
"disgusting spectacle" of their attempts to save themselves from
the hangman. "The frantic exertions they are making just now to
escape the gallows," exclaimed the editor, E. L. Godkin, "and the
joy with which they would welcome a 'life sentence,' shows clearly
that the gallows is the punishment the case calls for."[36] Among the
strongest opponents of clemency were such powerful entrepreneurs

as George M. Pullman, Cyrus H. McCormick, Jr., Philip D. Armour, and Marshall Field, who held fast to the idea that the men must die.

Governor Oglesby was thus besieged on both sides. The ultimate division was between those who thought that the anarchists posed a challenge to society which could be answered only by their death and those who thought that the test of a nation's civilization lay in the scrupulousness with which it protected the rights of dissenters. During the last week, Oglesby sent word to Lyman Gage of the First National Bank, indicating that he was prepared to commute the sentences of Parsons, Spies, Fielden, and Schwab if the business community should request it. Gage, a supporter of clemency, immediately called together some fifty leading patrons of his bank, informed them of the governor's offer, and urged that they submit the request. Gage argued that the inviolability of the law had been amply vindicated and that to execute the men would only make martyrs of them and embitter the workers and upset labor relations for years to come.

It looked at first as though a request for the commutations would be made. But Julius Grinnell, who was present, rose to oppose any such action, at least in behalf of Parsons and Spies. Marshall Field also stood against it. That settled the matter. After Field spoke, the meeting broke up. None cared to take issue with him. "It was terribly mortifying to me," said Gage. "Afterwards many of the men present came around to me singly, and said they had agreed with me in my views and would have been glad to join in such an appeal, but that in the face of the opposition of powerful men like Marshall Field they did not like to do so, as it might injure them in business, or socially, etc."[37]

In spite of this setback, public sentiment continued to shift in favor of the prisoners. Even Judge Gary wrote to Oglesby in Fielden's behalf: "There is in the nature and private character of the man a love of justice, and impatience at undeserved sufferings. . . . In his own private life he was the honest, industrious, and peaceful laboring man. In what he said in court before sentence he was respectful and decorous. His language and conduct since have been irreproachable. As there is no evidence that he knew of any preparation to do the specific act of throwing the bomb that killed Degan, he does not understand even now that general advice to large masses to do violence makes him responsible for the violence done by reason of that advice. . . . In short, he was more a misguided enthusiast than a criminal conscious of the horrible nature and effect of his teachings and of his responsibility therefor."[38]

In making this concession, Gary gave the lie to the principal charges against Fielden, namely, that he had been party to a conspiracy and had engaged in violent behavior at the Haymarket. What then was left of the case against him? Grinnell, by the same token, largely exculpated Schwab when, penning an endorsement to Gary's letter, he called him merely the "pliant, weak tool of a stronger will and more designing person," a reference to Spies, towards whom the state's attorney had developed a powerful animosity as the case unfolded. Grinnell added, moreover, that Schwab's conduct during and since the trial had been, like Fielden's, "decorous, respectful to the law and commendable."[39]

With the accelerating shift of public opinion, the hopes of the Amnesty Association mounted. At this moment, however, there was an occurrence that turned the tide in the other direction. On Sunday morning, November 6, four bombs were discovered in Lingg's cell. They were found under his cot, enclosed in a wooden box covered with papers and odds and ends. The bombs were of the narrow pipe variety, seven inches long and less than one inch in diameter, with an inch-long fuse at one end. The discovery caused a sensation. At once there was wild speculation: the prisoners had meant to destroy the jail, or to force an escape, or to go down fighting rather than submit to the executioner (Lingg had "made up his mind to die and intended to take as many on board the train going to eternity as one engine could haul," wrote George Schilling to Joseph Labadie).[40]

But the bombs were hardly adequate for these purposes. For one thing, they were too small; for another, the fuses were so short that explosion would occur only a second or two after lighting. Clearly they were fit only for self-destruction, as a means of escaping the gallows. Nevertheless, rumors of bloody plans involving the destruction of the jail, of the whole city, persisted, and had the effect of intimidation. The wave of sympathy receded. Panic once again banished reason and humanity.

The effect on the clemency movement was disastrous. Men "cursed and hissed" at Nina Van Zandt's mother as she tried to sell literature in the streets. "From this time on," observed William Holmes, "it was virtually impossible to get any more signatures to petitions. Loud and clamorous grew the demand for death, and even the most sanguine of our friends ceased to hope."[41]

This led to the charge that the bombs had been planted for this very purpose by the police. The authorities, asserted Mrs. Van Zandt, felt that "something must be done to counteract this tide of sympathy and justice" in favor of the condemned men. "It's a mare's nest, a canard," cried Parsons, "a fake, a put-up job to create a sensation and manufacture public prejudice." Bombs in Lingg's cell? questioned William Morris. Indeed! Who put them there? "Does it not make certain that there was no case against the men when authority is forced to resort to such base and clumsy shifts as this to justify its murder?"[42]

But the bombs were not the work of the police. They had been smuggled in by Dyer Lum. Lum, as we have seen, was a regular visitor to the prison. He came often and was well known to the guards. Not only did he have access to the lawyers' cage, where he could talk to his comrades without the interference of a wire screen, but he had a pass from the sheriff which enabled him, on certain occasions, to go directly to the cells, where he could reach his arm through the bars.[43] It was thus that manuscripts (including Lingg's last letter) were smuggled out of the jail for publication in *The Alarm* and other journals.[44] And by the same means, as Lum confided to Voltairine de Cleyre, were the bombs passed into Lingg's cell, concealed within the casings of cigars.[45] (Nearly all the prisoners, Lingg included, smoked cigars and often received boxes of cigars as gifts, which Lingg afterwards used for his carvings.) It is known that Lum visited the men on November 5, the day before the explosives were discovered,[46] and the delivery may have been made on this occasion. Lum, interestingly enough, even before acquiring his special pass, had managed to smuggle a pair of one-pound dumbbells to Parsons, who wanted to use them for exercise. The weights were concealed in Parsons's cell for several months and went undetected until a thorough search was made following the discovery of the bombs on November 6.[47]

Immediately after the discovery, security at the prison was tightened. Unfamiliar visitors were turned away and visits from friends and relatives sharply curtailed. Lingg was removed to a cell in the lower corridor, which opened onto the examination cage occupied by a deputy day and night. As Mrs. Van Zandt put it, he was "jerked out of bed and down stairs to the office and searched, treated as if a wild beast and then thrust into a ground-floor dungeon heavily guarded."[48] The others, with the exception of Fielden and Schwab, were also moved to different cells, Parsons, Fischer, and Engel downstairs.

The discovery of the bombs, in the midst of the concerted drive for clemency, could not but harm the men's chances. The Amnesty Association was thrown into a panic. William Salter, for one, feared the worst. On November 7 he wrote a frantic letter to Spies demanding that he disavow in writing any connection with the explosives and "emphatically condemn the use of violence at this time." Do so immediately, urged Salter, and have Parsons sign too, so that it can appear in the afternoon papers and thereby minimize damage to the commutation efforts. "The wave of feeling in your favor is set back," Salter warned. "You must say this or all our labor is in vain. Put it as strongly as you can. After his course, I feel that you have no obligation to Lingg. If you and Fielden and Schwab and Parsons are hung, it will be due to Lingg."[49]

Spies responded at once, drafting a letter to the Chicago press. He was furious that Lingg should have taken it upon himself to sacrifice not only his own life but the lives of the other prisoners. Calling Lingg a "monomaniac" with a martyr complex, he denied that he and the others had any knowledge of the bombs:

The first intimation I received of the matter came from Sheriff Matson, last evening. I could not believe it at first, and can hardly believe it now! I haven't spoken to Lingg for—I think—nine months. I don't know much of him, but I think that he is a monomaniac. I had only seen him once or twice before we were put together and charged with "conspiracy." I don't believe that a single one of the other prisoners had even so much as a suspicion; for, otherwise, they would undoubtedly have reasoned the man out of his folly. What use was he going to make of the shells? Throw them into the jail? What intention, what object could there have been in such an undertaking? I repeat, no sane man would be capable of such a thing!

Lingg, as far as I can judge him, seeks to be martyred. And to be candid, would like the rest of us to go with him. Did he put those instruments into his cell so that they might be *found?*— This is the question I have been asking myself. If he had them there for any *purpose*, this is the only one that looks plausible to me. He wants to die, thinking thereby to help the cause of labor. But he wanted us to die also. Perhaps he thought that the best and surest way to bring this about was to place a few bombs in his cell. I have never met as peculiar a man as he is before in my life, and for almost a year I have considered him a monomaniac, and have had nothing to do with him.

It is useless to condemn the action of an *irresponsible* man! If any one holds us, or any one of us, responsible for Lingg's deeds, then I can't see why we shouldn't be held responsible for any mischief whatsoever, committed in this world. And it has actually come to that. We are being made the scapegoats for everything. Let it be so.[50]

When this letter was published, Lum, incensed by what he considered Spies's cowardice, denounced him as a "son of a bitch."[51] Fielden and Schwab added their names to Spies's letter, but not Parsons, as Salter had hoped. Fischer wrote Salter a separate note, which also appeared in the press. "I don't know what to think of it," he wrote. "I cannot comprehend that Lingg intended to take the life of the jail officials who in every respect have treated us very kindly. Neither do I believe that Lingg wanted to commit suicide, because he possesses too much courage. The whole story is a puzzle to me. May my fate be what it may, I will be grateful to the jail officials for their kind treatment to the last."[52]

In a private letter to Salter, accompanying his letter for the press, Spies once more questioned Lingg's mental competence. "Lingg has often expressed his satisfaction over *our* conviction," Spies wrote. "That he would be hung a dozen times if we were hung with him. I am confident that he placed those bombs there, when he saw the public sentiment was changing in our favor. He ought to be examined by a commission *lunatico inquisitio.* I feel extremely sorry for him—even now!"[53]

Spies was by no means alone in this opinion. Indeed, on November 9, without Lingg's knowledge or consent, a delegation went before Judge Richard J. Prendergast of the County Court in Chicago and filed a petition to test the young man's sanity. Among the witnesses was Dr. James G. Kiernan, an expert for the defense at the trial of Charles Guiteau, the assassin of President Garfield, who maintained that Lingg's was a "case of paranoia." Having heard the arguments, Judge Prendergast ruled that he had no jurisdiction in the matter. The next day the same petition was presented to Judge Frank Baker of the Court of Appeals, once again without result.[54]

Although the bombs in Lingg's cell put a damper on the clemency campaign, the impact of the news on Governor Oglesby is difficult to gauge. When the discovery was made, Melville Stone cabled his reporter at Springfield, Robert B. Peattie: "Four iron gas pipe bombs seven inches long by three quarters of an inch thick loaded and fitted with percussion caps were found in Lingg's cell today. See Oglesby. Plumb the information at him and ask if it will have any effect upon his decision."[55] Unable to get in to see the governor, Peattie sent him a note with Stone's telegram enclosed. Oglesby's reply was noncommital: "Mr. Peattie, the telegram rec'd. You must be aware as I am sure Mr. Stone is I can have no opinion at present to express on such a subject."[56]

With the execution date less than a week away, however, the governor's decision could not be long in coming. On November 7 Oglesby announced that he would devote Wednesday, the 9th, to receiving at the State House all who desired to present appeals for clemency. To those who had been working for a reprieve, a new ray of hope began to show itself. From all over the country they descended upon the Illinois capital in hopes of persuading the governor to exercise leniency. Among the friends and relatives of the condemned men who made the journey were Captain Black, Mrs. Black, Maria Schwab, Johanna Fischer, Christine Spies, Gretchen Spies, Mary Engel, and Elise Friedel. The Amnesty Association was represented by its president, Lucien S. Oliver, and by Cora L. V. Richmond, a noted spiritualist and reformer. From New York there was Samuel Gompers, president of the American Federation of Labor. On November 8 Gompers had been working in his office when Edward King and James Quinn of District Assembly 49 came in and asked him to go with them to Springfield. "They presented to me," Gompers afterwards wrote, "the idea that because of my being well and favorably known and that I was regarded as a conservative man, my plea would help." Gompers left immediately for the train with nothing but what he was wearing at the time.[57]

Some of those who went to Springfield were men who had borne the weight of the clemency movement from the outset: Henry Lloyd, William Salter, Samuel McConnell, Matthew Trumbull, George Schilling, Joseph Buchanan. Governor Oglesby being a friend of Mrs. Lloyd's father, she decided to go with her husband. Before they left, she happened to bump into Joseph Medill, editor of the *Chicago Tribune*, of which her father was an owner. Medill asked her whether

what he had heard was true: that her husband was going to Springfield to plead for the anarchists. When she assured him that this not
only was true but that she was accompanying him, Medill warned
her against such a course. "Do you realize what you are doing?" he
asked. "Have you and Mr. Lloyd considered how this will influence
your future?" Medill pictured the extreme displeasure of her father,
who felt strongly that the anarchists should hang. He even predicted
(accurately) that it would result in her disinheritance and urged her
to persuade her husband to reconsider. "Do you suppose that any
such consideration will stop Henry Lloyd from doing what he believes right?" she replied.[58]

On November 9 the Lloyds, together with William Salter and
Samuel McConnell, were among the first to arrive at the State House.
At 9:40 A.M. the doors were opened. By eleven o'clock several hundred
petitioners had assembled in one of the larger rooms, where the
hearing was scheduled to take place. Most of them were from Chicago, but a hundred or more had come from other cities and states,
every part of the country being represented. There were trade-unionists, farmers, and members of the Illinois legislature, women's organizations, and "nearly every social group."[59] Since Lloyd and his
associates represented neither the Amnesty Association nor any other
organization, they requested that their petition be considered separately and were promised a private audience with the governor at
the conclusion of the proceedings.

When the hearing began, George Schilling acted as a sort of master
of ceremonies, introducing to the governor the representatives of
the Amnesty Association, labor organizations, and other groups who
had come to plead for the condemned men. Among those who spoke
were Captain Black, General Trumbull, Cora Richmond, State Senator Alson Streeter, State Representative Charles Dixon, Samuel
Gompers, and labor representatives from a dozen eastern and midwestern cities. Lucien Oliver, in the name of the Amnesty Association, brought forward the petition containing the names of 41,000
Chicago residents. The petition of the 16,000 London workers was
also presented.

The first speaker was Captain Black, who set forth in detail the
grounds on which the power of commutation might be invoked to
save his clients. He was followed by General Trumbull, who addressed the governor as an "old soldier, who has fought with you
on the battlefield of the Republic." Then came Mrs. Richmond, who

argued that the defendants "did not intend a murder, and the fact cannot be shown that they had any direct connection with the throwing of the bomb which caused the death of Officer Degan." Should the sentences be carried out, she warned, "the shock upon the rising generation will be such that it will take fifty or one hundred years to wipe it out." Senator Streeter expressed the belief that "this case marks an epoch in our history" and pleaded for clemency on the ground of the "common good of society."[60]

The most effective appeal, however, in the opinion of the *Chicago Tribune* and of Oglesby himself, was that of Samuel Gompers. Gompers told the governor that, while he and the anarchists were "fighting for labor upon different sides of the house," he did not like to see injustice done to any individuals, regardless of their beliefs, and suggested that the Chicago police were themselves "in some measure" responsible for the tragedy. What good could come to the country by putting the anarchists to death? he asked. "If these men are executed it would simply be an impetus to this so-called revolutionary movement which no other thing on earth can give. These men would, apart from any consideration of mercy or humanity, be looked upon as martyrs. Thousands and hundreds of thousands of labor men all over the world would consider that these men had been executed because they were standing up for free speech and free assemblage. We ask you, sir, to interpose your great power to prevent so dire a calamity. If this great country could be great and magnanimous enough to grant amnesty to Jefferson Davis, it ought to be great and magnanimous enough to grant clemency to these men."[61]

As the public hearings were drawing to a close, Joseph Buchanan approached Governor Oglesby and asked for an interview at which only a small number would be present. The governor hesitated, but when Buchanan explained that he had a letter from Spies to present, Oglesby granted the request and fixed the time he would allow at twenty minutes. Buchanan then asked George Schilling to choose a few of the most radical Germans present and bring them to the governor's rooms at the appointed hour. Buchanan's object was to show the men who had denounced him that Spies was not the coward he had been branded. Schilling returned with five men selected as witnesses, along with Lloyd, Salter, and McConnell, who, though themselves promised a private meeting with the governor after the hearing, asked to join Buchanan's party. As they were about to enter

Oglesby's office, Captain Black came up and handed Buchanan a folded sheet of paper. "Read this also to the governor," he said. "It is from Parsons."[62]

Standing before the governor, Buchanan proceeded to read the letter from Spies, requesting that Oglesby spare the lives of his comrades and let him alone be executed to placate the wrath of the public. Oglesby was visibly affected. When Buchanan finished reading, he saw on the governor's face a "look of deep sorrow, and his eyes were filled with tears." Yet the irony of the letter totally escaped him. "My opinion at the time," Oglesby afterwards wrote, "was that it was intended for publication at some time by friends of the anarchists. It was of course not expected to have any impression upon my mind in deciding the cases. Its suggestions are too absurd for serious consideration by me upon whom would fall the duty of deciding the cases in the light alone of the exercise of clemency."[63]

"Governor," resumed Buchanan, "here is something else I have been requested to read to you." Buchanan read the letter from Parsons. It too was drenched with irony, stating that, since he was to be hanged merely because he had attended the Haymarket meeting, the governor ought to know that Mrs. Parsons, their two children, and Lizzie Holmes had also been present. Parsons, with a Swiftian thrust, suggested that his own execution be delayed until they too could be "arrested, tried and condemned to die upon the scaffold in company with their equally guilty husband, father, and friend." "My God, this is terrible!" exclaimed the governor, hiding his face in his hands. "I do not believe," remarked Samuel McConnell, "that in all my life I ever saw so sad a face as that of Governor Oglesby." Yet Oglesby was afterwards capable of writing of Parsons's letter that it contained "neither law nor decency" and did not constitute a "genuine petition for clemency."[64]

Before taking his leave, Buchanan had one more petition to deliver, signed by nearly fifty delegates to the recent Knights of Labor convention in Minneapolis. He did so quickly, then, thanking the governor, withdrew from the room, accompanied by Schilling and the German militants. Salter, Lloyd, and McConnell remained behind, as they had their own appeals to present. By now it was 5 P.M., the end of a full day of public hearings. Yet the governor listened courteously to the three men and asked many questions. Lloyd spoke first. For two days he had hardly eaten or rested, and the fatigue showed. But he made a powerful plea for commutation, calling it "the greatest question of State since the pardoning of Jefferson Davis and Robert E. Lee." Although the law demanded punishment, Lloyd conceded, "justice demands that the punishment should be less than death."[65]

Salter followed, pleading mercy as a wise policy and presenting a petition bearing the signatures of more then one hundred prominent citizens of Chicago and a dozen states. Last came Samuel McConnell. That morning he had met Captain Black, who had asked him to put in a good word for Parsons. "If he is hanged," Black had pleaded, "I shall be responsible for his death. He was safely away and I advised him to come back and enter his appearance. I thought that would save him, and I thought it would help the others. It was a great blunder. I have blundered, McConnell, clear through."[66] McConnell had promised to do what he could, and when he addressed the governor he made a special plea in Parsons's behalf. He also said that Lyman Trumball, Murray Tuley, and others who had signed the petition for clemency constituted a worthier tribunal than that of the court and jury which had condemned the men "in a time of terror and excitement." The governor, McConnell observed, gave his "profound attention," and the men came away with the feeling that they had made a strong impression.[67] Late that night they returned to Chicago. It was understood that Oglesby would render his decision the next day.

On November 10, just before nine o'clock in the morning, a sharp explosion occurred in Lingg's cell. Rushing in, the guards beheld a horrible sight. Lingg was slumped on his cot in a pool of blood, pieces of flesh and bone scattered in every direction. His face was drenched in blood. The base of his mouth and part of the tongue had been blown away, the upper lip and nose torn to shreds, the cheeks badly lacerated. He was bleeding profusely as jailers carried him to the office, where emergency surgery was performed. Suffering untold agony, with his features frightfully mangled, he remained conscious, unable to speak, while three physicians worked on him. He never uttered a groan or an expression of pain. For nearly six hours he clung to life, then sank fast. His last words, written in pencil and stained with his own blood, were: "Please support my back. When I lie down I can't breathe." He died at 2:50 P.M. Then, according to Mrs. Van Zandt, his body was "thrown into a filthy bath tub to await the death of the others."[68]

There were some, Mrs. Van Zandt among them, who maintained that Lingg had been murdered by the police with an explosive cigar. "Lingg ought not to hang," Captain Schaack was quoted as saying. "He should have his own physic!"[69] But there is not the least evidence to support this charge. As Alexander Berkman later wrote to Emma Goldman, "About that story re Lingg, I don't think it plausible. They knew well enough that Lingg would have to hang. Why then should they want to kill him before that? On the other hand Lingg was probably the kind of man who'd prefer to die by his own hand."[70]

Berkman's analysis was well founded. Lingg had resented the idea of being pinioned and led to slaughter like a sheep. During the trial he had proclaimed to Judge Gary that he did not recognize capitalist justice. He did not recognize its right to take his life. And he would not permit it to do so. His death was an act of self-immolation whereby he eluded the ignominy of the hangman's noose and of a public execution. As the London *Freedom* put it, he "died, as he had lived, defying the law and its valets." A few days before his suicide, his mother had written to him, her only son: "I shall be as proud of you after your death as I have been during your life." "Dear Louis," wrote his aunt, "whatever happens—even the worst—show no weakness before those wretches."[71]

In selecting the instrument for his destruction, Lingg chose the material with which his name had become associated: dynamite. Accustomed to lie on his bed and smoke a cigar, on the morning of the 10th, after smoking a good cigar, he placed a dynamite cartridge in his mouth, calmly lit the fuse, and awaited results. "Devoted and fearless," wrote Dyer Lum of his friend, "never for an instant allowing false hope to swerve him from the path of principle, he died as he had lived—a child of nature."[72]

Lum was in a position to know. For it was he who had given Lingg the explosive cigar with which he cheated the hangman. The popular story, recorded by Charles Edward Russell and repeated by Frank Harris in *The Bomb*, was that Lingg's girlfriend had conveyed the deadly instrument to her lover. Voltairine de Cleyre, who knew otherwise, alluded to this in a speech on the Haymarket affair: "the public may believe that Lingg's sweetheart gave him a bomb to kill himself with, if it likes. I do not." In another speech she referred to the "dynamite cartridge given him in a cigar by a friend." The friend was Dyer Lum, as she told her son, who afterwards relayed the information to Agnes Inglis, curator of the Labadie Collection.[73] Lum had smuggled it to Lingg along with the other four bombs of the same type that were discovered on November 6. Lingg, planning to use it on himself, kept it in a separate hiding place in his cell, where it went undetected when the search was made and Lingg moved to the floor below. How did he manage to retrieve it? Lum, in a previously overlooked passage, gives us part of the answer: "One fact hitherto unpublished is amusing. Lingg had two men constantly before his cell, with instructions to carefully watch any motion. The cigar containing the dynamite cartridge had been left in his former cell. He had to adopt a ruse to obtain it. He succeeded, and the officials themselves presented him, unknowingly, with the cartridge which cheated them out of the pleasure of choking him to death."[74] Unfortunately Lum does not tell us what the ruse was, but we may guess that Lingg persuaded the guards to fetch from upstairs some seemingly innocent object in which the fatal device was concealed.

Lingg's death made headlines around the globe. "Miserable Lingg!" wrote William Dean Howells on hearing the news. "I'm glad he's out of the story; but even with his death, it seems to me that humanity's judgment of the law begins. All over the world people must be asking themselves, What cause is this really, for which men die so gladly, so inexorably?"[75] To Spies and Schwab, Lingg remained a "monomaniac," but Engel, who had grown to love him, was heartbroken over his death; and when a roadshow offered several thousand dollars for the body, in order to display it on tour, the Engel family, to whom it had been entrusted, brusquely refused.[76]

Lingg, thought Lizzie Holmes, would have made himself felt had he lived. He "utterly defied the law, the institutions, the system which ground humanity down, and hounded him, an innocent man, to his death, because he worshipped liberty. The saddest of all the tragedies of that tragic time was the cutting off of that bright young life."[77] To Emma Goldman and Alexander Berkman, leaders of the next generation of American anarchists, Lingg stood out as "the sublime hero among the eight. His unbending spirit, his utter contempt for his accusers and judges, his will-power, which made him rob his enemies of their prey and die by his own hand—everything about that boy of twenty-two lent romance and beauty to his personality. He became the beacon of our lives." Berkman, indeed, vowed that he too would die by his own hand, "like Lingg."[78] And he did.

At 5:20 P.M. on November 10, about two hours after the news of Lingg's suicide had reached Springfield, Governor Oglesby announced that he was commuting the sentences of Fielden and Schwab to life imprisonment. Parsons, Spies, Engel, and Fischer were to die on the gallows as scheduled. How much Lingg's act had affected the governor's decision is not known, but probably very little, if at all. In a public statement Oglesby said he had been prevented from considering a commutation for the other prisoners because they had not requested one, as the law required. Fielden and Schwab, by contrast, had asked for mercy, and, satisfied though he was that they were guilty along with the rest, he felt that their sentences could be reduced "in the interest of humanity, and without doing violence to public justice."[79]

That evening Ernst Schmidt called at Captain Black's office to learn what the governor had decided. Reaching the second floor of the building, he heard "a shriek, high-pitched and agonizing." He realized that the "hoped for miracle" had not occurred. A door opened, Schmidt later recorded, and "I saw the unfortunate wives and mothers of the men whose fate the governor's telegram had sealed. . . . I have had to look upon many terrifying and horrible scenes in my life but nothing worse than the one in Black's office. The moans and cries of those women who had been reduced almost to unconsciousness by eighteen months of anguish have never ceased to echo in my heart."[80]

Meanwhile Oglesby, having rendered his decision, handed the commutation papers to George Schilling and State Senator Richard Burke, who, in recognition of his efforts in behalf of clemency, accorded Henry Lloyd the privilege of delivering them. Lloyd carried the documents to the Cook County Jail and presented them to Fielden and Schwab. Those who heard him tell the story of Haymarket in later years remembered the intense feeling with which he mentioned this fact, saying, "I shall always think more of this right arm for that service."[81]

It was to Oglesby's credit, thought many observers, that he spared the lives of the two men. Yet some felt he should have done more. According to Benjamin Tucker, he had listened to the petitioners "with ears of stone," the commutations being "the only crumb of comfort flung to an enlightened minority hungering for justice." "To you, Sir," wrote one lifelong Republican to the governor, "in free and civilized America belongs the distinction of having first used the halter as a mode of punishment" for political offenders. But there were those, on the other hand, who believed that Oglesby should have done nothing at all and left all six prisoners to their fate—who disapproved, as one critic put it, of his "opening the door away from the gallows to two enemies of good government, fireside safety, and supremacy of the law."[82]

Yet efforts to save the other four anarchists continued up to the last. On the afternoon of November 10, shortly before Oglesby commuted the sentences of Fielden and Schwab, Captain Black received the following telegram from New York: "I have proof showing Anarchists to be innocent. Guilty man in New York—located. Have telegraphed to Governor Oglesby. Proof is under oath. How shall I communicate it? August P. Wagener, Counselor-at-law, 59 Second Avenue."[83] Summoning Joseph Buchanan to his office, Black read him the telegram, then introduced him to William Fleron, a New York newspaperman, who knew the sender and believed the meaning of the message was that the man who threw the Haymarket bomb was in the hands of the anarchists in New York. Black asked Buchanan to accompany them to Springfield and place the matter before the governor. Buchanan agreed, and Black sent a telegram to George Schilling, who had remained in Springfield after the hearings: "Arrange for immediate interview with Governor. Don't delay. Take all responsibilities. William P. Black."[84]

Late that night the three men boarded a train for the state capital, arriving at seven o'clock the following morning, barely five hours before the executions were set to take place. It was 8:35 when they presented themselves at the executive mansion. A company of militia stood guard on the grounds, but a few words from Captain Black carried them past the sentries and into the library of Oglesby's residence, where the governor was waiting to receive them. They apprised him of the new developments. Oglesby said that he too had received the telegram and asked if they placed any credence in it. Captain Black replied: "From what Mr. Fleron has told us and what we have learned from other sources, we feel justified in saying we believe that there is a strong probability that the telegram states the truth." "Admitting for the moment that you are right," said the governor, "what do you propose in the matter?" Black answered: "We thought of asking you for a reprieve of sixty or ninety days, to allow time to bring the alleged bomb-thrower back to the state, so that his testimony—which certainly is important—could be taken.

We know that you are willing to give the men in jail, sentenced to be executed today, every just and legal chance for their lives, and we assume that you desire the apprehension of the bomb-thrower. Surely there is sufficient ground to justify the request we make of you, Governor." Without asking any questions of Fleron, the governor withdrew to consider the matter. After twenty minutes he returned and refused the request. The last decision had been made, noted Buchanan. The hangman would do his terrible work.[85]

23 ‖ The Scaffold

The news that Governor Oglesby would not commute the sentences of Parsons, Spies, Engel, and Fischer was received by the four men with composure. They had long been prepared for the worst. A deputy sheriff who was with Parsons on the night of November 10 reported that he was in good spirits, indeed "very cheerful and hopeful." Parsons, in a garrulous mood, talked almost incessantly for several hours. He spoke about socialism and anarchism, about Haymarket, about his wife and children. It was not until he reached the last subject that he manifested any regret, and "the more he talked about it, the more sorrowful he became." He said that Lucy was "a brave woman, a true wife and a good mother."[1]

After the lights had been turned out and the prisoners settled down for the night, the silence of death row was broken by Parsons's voice, reciting Whittier's poem "The Reformer":

> Whether on the gallows high,
> Or in the battle van,
> The noblest place for man to die
> Is where he dies for man.

Later in the night, Parsons broke the silence once again, this time with the melancholy strains of "Annie Laurie" ("And for bonnie Annie Laurie, I'd lay me doon and dee"). In Parsons's clear tenor voice, verse after verse of the Scottish ballad rang through the gloomy corridor, while the other inmates listened "as if to the death-song of a dying hero."[2] Deputy Hawkins suggested that Parsons ought to get some sleep. "How can a fellow go to sleep with the music made by putting up the gallows?" Parsons joked. The sound of sawing and hammering could be heard late into the night as the scaffold was erected in the north corridor. By two o'clock, however, Parsons was sleeping "as soundly as he ever did in his life."[3]

Spies too did not fall asleep until the small hours. Like Parsons, he chatted with the deputies, smoked cigars, and seemed on the whole in cheerful spirits. Earlier that evening he had been allowed a brief visit from Ernst Schmidt, treasurer of the Defense Committee. The old friends embraced for the last time. "Well," said Spies, "if we should not see each other again, live long and happily—and don't forget me!"[4] A few days before, Spies already had said farewell to his mother. "Mein Sohn, mein Liebling," she pleaded, "muss ich dich denn so verlieren?" (My son, my dearest, must I then lose you like this?) In vain Spies tried to console her. It was, as even the jailers acknowledged, a heart-rending scene.[5]

Fischer, remarked one of the deputies on the death watch, was "the jolliest of the lot" that final night. When asked if he had a last wish, he replied, "A bottle of champagne!" Though the youngest of the doomed men, he talked "with the coolness and sangfroid of a veteran." Only once did his spirits falter, when he spoke of his wife and three children. But then, with a shrug of his shoulders, he said: "It is far more easy for me to die than for my enemies to bear the burden of it."[6]

Engel, like his comrades, conversed pleasantly with the guards, smoked a good cigar and enjoyed it. To a clergyman who came to console him he said: "In the shadow of the gallows, as I stand, I have done nothing wrong. I have not done everything right during my life, but I have endeavored to live so that I need not fear to die. Monopoly has crushed competition and the poor man has no show, but the revolution will surely come, and the working man will get his rights. Socialism and Christianity can walk hand in hand together as brothers, for both are laboring in the interest of the amel-ioration of mankind. I have no religion but to wrong no man and to do good to everybody."[7]

Later that night Engel recited Heine's poem "The Weavers," with its intimations of popular vengeance:

> With tearless eyes, in despair and gloom,
> Gnashing their teeth, they sit at the loom.
> Thy shroud we weave, Germany of old,
> We weave into it the curse three-fold.
> We are weaving, weaving, weaving.

At 1:30 A.M. the death watch was changed. Deputy Charles W. Pe-ters, who was now with Engel, said: "He is perfectly resigned to his fate, and expresses no sorrow for anything. On the contrary, he says he would repeat his actions if he had the opportunity." Engel spoke of his family with tenderness and affection. He had always tried to comfort his wife and daughter during their visits. "From the very first," he told the deputy, "I have prepared them gradually for what is now to happen. I told them not to indulge in false hopes. I have always believed that we would die. I was not in favor of appealing the case to higher courts. I knew it was useless. But our death will do more for socialism than our lives could. It has grown stronger and faster since our arrest than ever before. The time is coming when we will be vindicated. Socialism is too great, too grand, too good to die."[8]

On the morning of November 11—"Black Friday," as the anarchists called it—Chicago was in a virtual state of siege. Three hundred policemen, equipped with rifles, shotguns, and pistols, guarded Cook County Jail and its environs. A block away in each direction ropes were stretched across the streets, and all traffic was suspended. Behind the ropes stood lines of policemen armed with Winchester rifles. The sidewalks leading from the jail were patrolled by heavily armed police. The jail itself was like a fortress. Cordons of policemen were drawn around it, and from every window an officer looked out, rifle or shotgun in hand. The roof was "black with policemen."[9]

The city had been turned into an armed camp in anticipation of an attempted rescue. Was it possible, wrote Lizzie Holmes, that the people would allow "this awful wrong" to be perpetrated? Victor Yarros, associate editor of Tucker's *Liberty*, asked: "Do the workingmen of this country, for whom the condemned men worked and struggled, and whom they sought to emancipate from the yoke of economic servitude, intend to stand indifferently by while the legal bandits choke their fellows to death upon the gallows?"[10] Spies, for one, had no illusions on this score. "You are incorrigible enthusiasts in your reliance upon the 'people,' as if in reality there were anything occult in this word," he wrote to a friend. "Nonsense! The mob would have lynched us long ago had it the opportunity, not because it had a reason, but to demonstrate to its gods how currish, mean and servile it is. Out upon the people! Faugh!"[11]

But surely their own comrades would endeavor to stop the executions. Such was the widespread assumption. Wild reports circulated of armed and desperate anarchists bent on freeing the doomed men by an assault on the prison. It was rumored that the jail would be bombed and destroyed, along with every public building in the

city. Anarchists from other localities were said to be streaming towards Chicago to join in the rescue effort. One newspaper reported
that the jail had already been mined, great stores of dynamite placed
beneath, and at the moment of the hanging the whole structure and
everyone in it would be blown to smithereens.[12]

Public anxiety was intense. Several regiments of militia were camped
close to city hall with Gatling guns and cannon. Everything was
feared, but above all dynamite and arson, and the fire department
was on the alert. At the hotels new arrivals were carefully scruti-
nized, and every public building was under guard. The homes of
Judge Gary, State's Attorney Grinnell, the jurors, Police Chief Ebersold, Inspector Bonfield, Captain Schaack, and Sheriff Matson were
placed under special protection. The larger factories were closed,
shopkeepers barricaded their stores, and newspapers, banks, business
offices, and the Board of Trade were guarded throughout the day.
More than a few well-to-do residents found it desirable to leave town,
while others did not stir out of doors. "A cloud of apprehension
lowered over the city," noted Melville Stone in his memoirs. "There
was a hush and men spoke in whispers. . . . I have never experienced
quite the like condition."[13]

Was there any substance to the rumors? Some observers dismissed
them out of hand, maintaining that no preparations had been made
either to rescue the prisoners or to carry out reprisals after the execution. William Holmes, however, knew otherwise. There had indeed been "plans of rescue," he revealed years later. "Probably no
other man in the city of Chicago knew better than I what foundation
there was for such rumors," he wrote, intimating that he himself
had been party to the conspiracy.[14]

The masterminds, however, were Robert Reitzel and Dyer Lum.
Reitzel, editor of *Der Arme Teufel* in Detroit, had come to Chicago
shortly before the scheduled executions and, together with Lum,
had begun to organize a plot to blow up the jail in an effort to liberate
the inmates ("Only terrorism will now save them," Lum had written
on November 6). The escape was planned for the 10th, the eve of
the scheduled hangings, "Annie Laurie Day," as Lum later spoke of
it from the song Parsons sang in his cell. Reitzel, who saw in the
death sentences the "lust for blood of monster capitalism," confided
his intentions to Ernst Schmidt. The latter tried to deter him, pointing out that "police were stationed at every downtown corner,"
backed up by militia with "a Gatling gun or two." Reitzel, however,

as Voltairine de Cleyre wrote, was "ready to die" to save his comrades.[15] But he never got the chance.

It was the prisoners themselves who prevented the plan from going forward. " 'The boys,' in the shadow of death, stopped it," wrote Lum to Voltairine de Cleyre. "They said their deaths were better—and they died." As Lingg had told him shortly before his suicide, "Work till we are dead. The time for vengeance will come later."[16] Fischer in particular was opposed to the plan. He knew, as one Chicago anarchist later put it, that "the blood of martyrs is the seed of the church," and he was "happy that his blood was sown as seed to the winds."[17] He felt, moreover, noted William Holmes, that armed retaliation would be counterproductive, "that such reprisals, accompanied as they surely would be by terrible destruction and bloodshed, would have put the movement for liberty and solidarity backward many years. As he was to die in defense of those principles, he felt that he had a right to demand that they should not be jeopardized by foolish, though well-meaning, friends." "Let the fact be known to the world," added Holmes, "that the city of Chicago was saved from destruction only by the intervention of the men awaiting death. They repaid persecution, treachery, imprisonment, torture and murder by forbearance and mercy. Let our silence speak, was the thought of one and all."[18]

Accordingly, the trouble for which the police had so carefully prepared did not materialize. No bombs exploded. No attack occurred. No reprisals were attempted. In vain did militants await the signal for retaliation in order that November 11, as one of them put it, should be "a living inspiration to the toilers of every land, instead of a day of mourning."[19] In New York, on the evening of the 10th, 7,000 workers marched through the streets to protest against the impending executions. "The Gallows versus Liberty," "Citizens Arise!" "Ye Sons of Toil Awake to Glory," "We Protest Against Judicial Murder," proclaimed the placards they carried.[20] But Chicago remained a city of silence.

On the morning of the execution, Nina Van Zandt and her mother rode to the jail to see Spies for the last time. Barred by the cordon of police, they turned their carriage around, returned home, and closed all the curtains on the windows. People heard sobs and cries from the house. There were false reports that Nina had attempted suicide.[21]

Meanwhile a similar incident occurred involving Lucy Parsons and her children. The previous evening, after Governor Oglesby had announced his decision, Lucy, accompanied by Lizzie and William Holmes, had gone to the jail to say a last goodbye to her husband. She was denied admission but was told by a deputy sheriff that she would be allowed in at half-past eight the following morning. At the appointed hour, she and her children and Lizzie Holmes arrived at the barrier a block from the gates. Every street leading to the prison was roped off and guarded by police. At the first corner, Lucy stated her mission and repeated the instructions given her the previous day. The lieutenant said she could not enter at that point, but that she should pass on to the next corner where the officer in charge would let her through. This she did, but with the same result. A captain told her that she must first get an order from the sheriff. On inquiring where he could be found, she was told to go to another corner where a message might be sent to him. At this corner, however, no one knew anything about it. Again she was sent on. "And so," remarked Lizzie Holmes, "for more than an hour we were urged along in a veritable game of 'Pussy Wants a Corner' that would have been ridiculous had it not been so tragical." Not once did an officer say, "You positively cannot see your husband. You are forbidden to enter the premises and bid him farewell." Rather, Lucy was continually offered the inducement that, if she passed quietly along, at some point she would be admitted.[22]

Meanwhile, the minutes were flying. Lulu's face was blue with cold, and her eyes were swimming with tears. Albert too was shivering in the raw air as he followed his mother from street to street. At length Lucy begged the officers to take only the children so that they might receive their father's last blessing, but this request too was refused. In desperation, she crossed the line and defied the police to "kill her as they were murdering her husband." Leading her to yet another corner with the promise of "seeing about it," they hustled her, the children, and Lizzie Holmes into a patrol wagon, rushed them to the Chicago Avenue station, and locked them up in basement cells, Lucy and the children in one, Lizzie in another. Then they were stripped and searched. Even the children, crying with fright, were undressed and carefully gone over. The police were looking for explosives. A matron ran her fingers through Lizzie Holmes's hair, through the hem of her skirt, through her underclothes and stockings. Lizzie asked her what she expected to find. "I don't know," she replied. "This is my duty."[23]

The matron clanged the door behind her, and the prisoners were left alone. Lucy and Lizzie could hear each other's voice but not see each other. In this condition they spent several anxious hours. At a few minutes past noon, the matron came in and said, "It's all over," then left. No one came to offer Lucy any comfort, while Lizzie, the one friend near her, could only sit there shivering with her face pressed to the bars, "listening to her low, despairing moans." Friends who called to inquire after their whereabouts were abruptly turned away, nor were they themselves told that anyone had been to see them. William Holmes came as soon as he heard of their arrest and was not only denied information but was threatened with arrest himself if he "hung around." At three o'clock Captain Schaack, commander of the station, came down and, professing ignorance of their detention, asked how long they had been there. Their cells were then opened and they were allowed to go home.[24]

By eight o'clock that morning all the doomed men were awake. Parsons was calm and collected. He washed his face, greeted his comrades, ate fried oysters for breakfast and seemed to enjoy them. After breakfast he recited Marc Cook's poem "Waiting":

> My ship has gone down in waters unknown,
> And in vain has been my waiting.

Then, conversing with his guard, he said: "I am a Mason and have always tried to help my fellow-man all my life. I am going out of the world with a clear conscience. I die that others may live."[25]

A short while later Parsons was visited by Reverend Dr. H. W. Bolton, pastor of the First Methodist Episcopal Church of Chicago, who had come to assist the men in their preparations for death. Parsons received him courteously. But, having listened to Bolton's sermon, he replied: "Preachers are all Pharisees, and you know what Jesus Christ's opinion of the Pharisees was. He called them a generation of vipers and likened them to whited sepulchres. I don't desire to have anything to do with either." At this the minister rose to leave. Parsons shook his hand. "Thank you," he said. "Don't forget, though, I didn't send for you."[26]

Parsons then sat down with the morning papers and read the latest accumulation of mail. Letters and telegrams had been pouring in.

From New York his brother William sent the following cable: "Another Gethsemane to-night. More than a legion of angels with pitying eyes survey the spectacle of man's inhumanity to man. Millions of hearts in Europe and America are now throbbing with sympathy for the men who are to die for humanity. I am proud of your sublimity, your fortitude, and your hereditary heroism."[27] "Bravo Parsons," wrote four sympathizers in San Francisco. "Your name will live when people will ask each other who was Oglesby." "Not goodbye," wrote Josephine Tilton of Boston, "but hail brothers. From the gallows trap the march will be taken up. I will listen for the beating of the drum."[28]

After answering a few of these messages, Parsons sent a note to Sheriff Matson asking that his body be delivered to his wife at their apartment on Milwaukee Avenue. The reason for this request was that influential citizens had tried to persuade the sheriff to secrete the bodies of the doomed men lest their burial place become a revolutionary shrine. Matson refused to comply and, to prevent the bodies from being removed without his knowledge, advised the prisoners to request that they be turned over to their families after the execution.[29]

Parsons's final letter was reserved for Dyer Lum. "Well, my dear old comrade," he wrote, "the fatal hour draws near. Caesar kept me awake till late at night with the noise (music) of hammer and saw, erecting his throne, my scaffold. Refinement! Civilization! Matson (sheriff) tells me he refused to agree to let Caesar (state) secrete my body, and he has just got my wife's address from me to send her my remains. Magnanimous Caesar! Alas, good-bye! Hail the social revolution! Salutations to all."[30]

Spies occupied himself with similar duties. On a sheet headed "Jail Report" he wrote a last letter to his mother and sister. He urged them to remain firm and "not to give our murderers an opportunity to see weakness on your part." To Nina Van Zandt he wrote as follows: "My Beloved Wife: It has come. Be strong; show no weakness. It is no great task for me to die for the cause of humanity. Bear up bravely, and live to see your husband—not avenged, but his foul murder understood and lamented by those blind and ignorant masses for whose sake he died. Live to see the cause of humanity and progress triumph over the usurpations and plottings against the people. My last thoughts are of you, my love—my best wishes for you. Farewell. August."[31]

At 9:30 A.M. William Salter tried to get in to see Spies but was refused admission. Finally allowed into the vestibule, he hastily wrote a letter which a deputy delivered to Spies:

It is of no use for me to say now what I think of Governor Oglesby's decision. I believe he acted in conscience. Do not charge him, or even Mr. Grinnell or Judge Gary, with a crime. Whatever crime there is in hanging you and Parsons is in the hearts of our people, who have been all along, and are now, as Mr. Lloyd said, nine to one against you. But for the strong public sentiment, Mr. Grinnell would not have prosecuted as he did, nor would Judge Gary have ruled as he did, nor would the Governor have decided as he has.

Do not think it was the Citizens' Ass. or the press even—influential as these may have been, or powerful as they might have been in consoling public sentiment, and leading men to think more discriminately and justly. There is no tyrant like the people, and that you now feel. You know I do not hold you altogether guiltless, tho I hold you are not guilty of the crime for which you are to be hanged. You have made mistakes, and now the Demon has its turn. You called for revenge, and now the public has its revenge.

I wish in my soul that you and Parsons could live—and all the rest for that matter—and could have a chance to clear up your own minds, and help bring the public mind into a juster and nobler temper. But try in the few moments that are left you to purge your mind of bitterness, so that you may leave this life with nought but humanity and the love of justice in your soul. These are a man's only sacraments, good for life, good for death. Do not resent this, for I know what reasons for bitterness you have. Be sure I shall do what I can to see you right in the future. Farewell. William M. Salter.

After half an hour the deputy returned with the following answer from Spies: "Mr. Salter: Accept my thanks for your kindness in our behalf. Oh no! I am not of a revengeful disposition. My fault lies not in that direction. I am too sensitive, too full of feeling—that is my *fault*! I feel pretty much like John Huss, when he said: '*O sancta simplicitas!*' I have nothing to regret! Farewell! As ever yours, A. Spies."[32]

The other men were equally composed. Engel rose at 6 A.M., having

389

had a good night's rest. "I hope we have a nice day and have a good time," he jested. "If another minister comes, let me see him. I hope I will do him more good than he does me." The last words Engel wrote in his diary were:

> Für Freiheit und Recht
> Wir kämpften nicht schlecht.
>
> (For freedom and right
> We made a good fight.)[33]

Fischer too was in a cheerful mood, if somewhat more pensive than his comrade. The night before he had dreamt of Germany, which he had left as a boy of fifteen to seek his fortune in America. His childhood, his father's house, the streets of his native Bremen had all passed again before his eyes. Now he took up pen and paper and wrote a letter to his young children, consoling them that "the noblest men throughout the ages have at one time or another been harbored by prison walls. One need not be a criminal to be in prison. ... As you grow up you will comprehend that you need not be ashamed of my fate, but, on the contrary, that you have reason to be proud of your father."[34]

A few days before, Fischer had written to the members of his union, Typographical No. 9, with instructions regarding his burial, for which they had assumed responsibility. He requested that "all religious humbug" be kept out of the ceremony, but that they should place in his grave "our beloved red emblem, the symbol of equality, freedom, and brotherhood, for which I have lived and now must die. Do not sing any sentimental songs, but instead, when I am lowered into the pit, sing free, brisk words, like those of the 'Marseillaise.' " Fischer, to whom martyrdom for his cause had always seemed the most glorious of fates, concluded on an elevated note: "In view of the great and noble cause for which I am to die, my trek to the gallows becomes easy. In my mind's eye I already see, on the horizon, the dawning of a better day for humanity. The day of the brotherhood of man is no longer distant."[35] Now, on the morning of the execution, Fischer himself began to sing the "Workers' Marseillaise," the hymn of labor struggling for emancipation. Hardly were the first notes heard in the adjoining cells than Spies, Parsons, and Engel caught up the refrain and made the corridors ring with the anthem.

A few minutes before the men were led out to the scaffold, Parsons recited another poem by Marc Cook, "A Farewell":

> Come not to my grave with your mournings,
> With your lamentations and tears,
> With your sad forebodings and fears;
> When my lips are dumb,
> Do not come.
>
> Bring no long train of carriages,
> No hearse crowned with waving plumes,
> Which the gaunt glory of death illumes;
> But with hands on my breast
> Let me rest.
>
> Insult not my dust with your pity,
> Ye who're left on this desolate shore
> Still to suffer and lose and deplore—
> 'Tis I should, as I do,
> Pity you.
>
> For me no more are the hardships,
> The bitterness, heartaches, and strife,
> The sadness and sorrow of life,
> But the glory divine—
> This is mine.
>
> Poor creatures!
> Afraid of the darkness,
> Who groan at the anguish to come.
> How silent I go to my home!
> Cease your sorrowful bell—
> I am well![36]

Parsons talked with the guards about his wife and children, then sang the "Workers' Marseillaise" once more. A deputy offered him a glass of wine. He refused it, saying: "No thanks. I would prefer a cup of coffee." A pot of coffee and a bowl of crackers were brought. He drank the coffee and ate a few of the crackers. "Now I feel all right," he said. "Let's finish the business."[37]

At 11:30 A.M. Sheriff Matson and his assistants entered murderers' row. Not a muscle of the four men quivered as Matson read the death warrants. Fischer looked scornfully about him. Engel stood like a soldier at attention, a slight smile flitting over his face. Parsons's hand played carelessly with his mustache. Spies listened with his arms folded, his face emotionless. When Matson was finished, Spies stepped into the corridor. A thick leather belt was placed around his chest and his arms pinioned just above the elbows. His hands were handcuffed behind his back and his body draped in a white muslin shroud. Fischer and Engel were treated in the same fashion, followed by Parsons. As his arms were being fastened, Parsons looked up to Fielden in the tier of cells above. "Goodbye, Sam," he said. Then he turned to the reporters, who were scrutinizing his every action. "Won't you come inside?" he said to them.[38]

The men then formed a procession and moved along the central corridor. The death march had begun. As they passed through the door leading into the north corridor, the gallows rose before their eyes. On one side of the corridor there were four tiers of cells with barred doors. On the other side· and at either end were the bare whitewashed walls of the building. Seated on rows of benches were 170 witnesses, more than fifty of whom were reporters, including Charles Edward Russell of the *New York World*. Among the rest were doctors, officials, and the jury members at the trial. Governor Oglesby was represented by his son Robert. The witnesses stopped their talking when they heard the sound of feet on the iron stairway. One after another the prisoners appeared, each guarded by a deputy. Spies, at the head, erect and firm, stepped to his place on the scaffold and turned towards the spectators. Close behind him came Fischer, his chest thrust out, his bearing dignified, to all appearances unconcerned. Glaring at the crowd, he planted himself on the spot assigned to him, threw his head back and waited. Engel came next, and then Parsons. Engel looked absolutely happy. His face showed no absence of color, and his eyes twinkled. Parsons, by contrast, wore an abstracted look, as if his mind were on something else quite remote from the business at hand.

The deputies passed a leather strap around each man's ankles, binding them closely together. The ropes were placed about their necks, and the knot fixed under the left ear. As the rope was slipped over Spies's throat, the noose tightened. The deputy quickly loosened it a bit, and Spies smiled his thanks. Fischer, who was taller than his deputy, bent his head to help out. Engel accepted the noose as if it were a wreath of honor. Parsons stood silent, his eyes turned upward. The shrouds, open at the back, were now fastened. Then white caps, gathered by a string at the neck, were put on, completely hiding the head and face. Apart from their bare necks, which showed between the caps and shrouds, the men stood clad from top to toe in white.

There was an instant of silence. Then from beneath Spies's hood came the words: "The time will come when our silence will be more powerful than the voices you strangle today!" "Hurrah for anarchy!" cried Fischer, his voice ringing out strong and clear. "Hurrah for anarchy!" shouted Engel still more loudly. "This is the happiest moment of my life!" exclaimed Fischer. There was a second's pause. Then Parsons's voice was heard: "Will I be allowed to speak, O men of America? Let me speak, Sheriff Matson! Let the voice of the people be heard! O—." Parsons did not have time to finish. The signal had been given, and as the sound of the last word left his lips it was lost in the loud "bang" of the plunging trap. The four men shot downwards together.[39]

Suddenly all eyes were fastened on the body of Spies, which was writhing horribly. The shoulders twitched, the chest heaved, and repeatedly the legs drew up and straightened out. The convulsions continued for a long time. When they finally became less pronounced, the body of Fischer began to move also. Spies grew still, while Fischer was twitching and jerking, and the body of Parsons began to show signs of animation. Beside each man stood a physician, who announced from time to time the pulse of the victim. Fainter and fainter the pulses beat, and finally tapered off to nothing. At 12:06 it was all over. The bodies were completely still. Seven minutes and forty-five seconds after the drop, all four anarchists were pronounced dead.[40]

The audience was perfectly silent. For a few moments the only sound that could be heard was the distant rumble of wagons on the street. The spectators, many of whom had been visibly affected by the scene, remained seated. Finally, a few people in the rear rose. The rest followed suit and began to file out of the corridor, each turning as he reached the exit to look at the four white figures, which appeared at that distance to be hanging against the wall. At 12:15 P.M. the bodies were cut down from the gallows and placed in wooden coffins. The doctors began their final examinations. The necks of none of the men had been broken by the fall. They had all died from slow strangulation.[41]

The grisly work was done. Runners carried the news from the jail to specially prepared bulletin boards in the downtown area and to the newspaper offices lining Dearborn Street south of Madison. On the bulletin board at the Palmer House appeared the laconic notice: "Trap fell. Spies, Parsons, Fischer, and Engle [*sic*] expiate their crime and the law vindicated." Robert Oglesby cabled his father in Springfield: "Condemned men hung at three minutes before twelve. Crowd dispersing and people becoming quiet."[42] November 11, 1887, had become history. Ironically it was Captain Black's birthday. He was forty-five years old. It was the saddest day of his life.

On Saturday morning, November 12, Fielden and Schwab were removed from the jail and sent to Joliet to join Neebe. At the same time, the bodies of their comrades were turned over to their families as requested. By Engel's wish, the remains of Lingg, who had no relatives in America, were taken to his home on Milwaukee Avenue to be prepared for burial along with his own, although Lingg's cuff-buttons and breast-pin, which he had left to Elise Friedel, could not be found among his personal effects. Throughout the day the two corpses rested side by side in the back room of the toy store, which Mrs. Engel had managed since her husband's arrest a year and a half before, and thousands of friends and sympathizers filed past the open caskets to pay their last respects. Similarly, at the home of Christine Spies on Bryson Street, thousands came to view the body of her son. Captain Black made a brief speech over the coffin. "By his death," he said, "August Spies has earned the gratitude of the world, and the time is not far distant when it will be accorded. This thought, this conviction, should suffice to sustain and comfort his sorrowing ones."[43]

For Lucy Parsons, waiting dressed in black for the body of her husband to arrive, such words would have been spoken in vain. Nothing could diminish her grief. She had rested but little the previous night, and her eyes were swollen from crying. Shortly before 11 A.M. the undertaker's wagon drew up. Lucy grew agitated as the casket was brought in and set on two chairs in the sitting room. The top was removed and the calm, pale features exposed. Lucy looked with tear-filled eyes at her husband's corpse, touched the mark of the rope on its neck, and cried: "Oh! Albert, Albert, they have murdered you!" A terrible sound escaped her lips, then she fell to the floor in a faint. Lizzie Holmes and Sarah Ames rushed to her side and tried to revive her. Lulu and Albert Jr. stood, crying and unnoticed, in a corner of the room until Mrs. Fielden went to comfort them. Presently the whole room was in tears. As soon as Lucy recovered, she returned to her husband's body, crying and calling his name. Frank Stauber emerged from the apartment with tears rolling down his cheeks. "I have seen grief-stricken people before," he said, "but never in all my life have I seen such grief as that. I am actually afraid that the woman is dying. And this is the female tiger the papers tell about."[44]

By 11:30 P.M., when the doors to the Parsons apartment were closed, nearly ten thousand people had come to see the body. William Holmes and M. Walters, Master Workman of Local Assembly 1307 of the Knights of Labor, of which Parsons had been a member, stood guard over their dead comrade throughout the night.

Sunday, November 13, dawned bright and sunny, a crisp Chicago autumn day. It was the day of the anarchists' funeral. Special conditions had been laid down by Mayor John A. Roche, Carter Harrison's successor in office, under which the procession was to be conducted. The line of march was delineated in advance. No banners, no placards, no arms would be displayed, no music except dirges played, no revolutionary songs sung, no speeches delivered, no demonstrations made. The instructions were followed to the letter.

At twelve noon the hearse bearing the body of Spies left the house of his mother at 154 Bryson Street. In the carriage which followed rode Mrs. Spies and her daughter Gretchen, together with Nina Van Zandt and her mother. A band played "Die Wacht am Rhein," and several thousand marchers fell in behind. The procession stopped at 1336 Dean Street to pick up the body of Fischer. Fischer's coffin was placed on a hearse, and his wife and three children rode behind. Another band was here, and additional marchers fell into line. At 785 Milwaukee Avenue they met the third burial carriage, and Parsons's remains joined the procession, his widow and children riding behind. Finally, at 286 Milwaukee Avenue a stop was made for the coffins of Engel and Lingg, each covered with a large red flag, and a crowd of two thousand mourners, along with several bands, swelled the procession to a multitude.

With more than 20,000 participants it was the largest funeral ever seen in Chicago. From front to rear "there ran a feeling that the dead men had died for them—that they were martyrs in the cause of the poor against the rich, the weak against the powerful," wrote a reporter who was in attendance.[45] Huge crowds, estimated at more than 200,000, lined the streets of the downtown area as the procession threaded its way towards the Wisconsin Central Station, from which the bodies were to be conveyed to the cemetery. Lizzie Holmes later remembered the long, slowly moving line, with its five black hearses loaded with flowers, the thousands of grieving mourners following steadily, the densely packed streets, "the sorrow on the faces of the work-hardened toilers along the route, the sweet, sad music of the bands, the deep intensity of silent emotion manifest everywhere." Everyone seemed to be in tears, even some of the policemen lining the route. It was an impressive and deeply moving spectacle, "never to be forgotten by anyone who witnessed it."[46]

At the Wisconsin Central depot a special train was waiting to take the families and friends of the anarchists to the Waldheim Cemetery, ten miles west of the city on the banks of the Desplaines River. The train was filled within minutes, and another had to be made available, as more than 10,000 people went out to attend the burial. The sun was a low red ball in the autumn sky when the mourners arrived at their destination. Nearly all wore badges made of flaming red ribbon, the women on their bonnets and the men on their coats. A passage had to be cleared through the dense throng for the procession to pass. Wreaths and flowers were everywhere. The coffins were decorated in scarlet, the color of anarchism and revolution, and even the bodies of the dead men had been wrapped in red sashes. Among Parsons's pallbearers were Joseph Buchanan, Dyer Lum, William Holmes, M. Walters of the Knights of Labor, and Lucien Oliver of the Amnesty Association, bearing a silver plate with the inscription "Albert R. Parsons, Age 39 Years, Executed by the State of Illinois, November 11, 1887." Lucy Parsons walked behind her husband's casket, supported by Lizzie Holmes and Sarah Ames.[47]

The sun was just setting as the bodies were placed in a temporary vault. Following songs by the Aurora Turn Verein and socialist choral groups, there were eulogies by Captain Black, Robert Reitzel, Thomas Morgan, and Albert Currlin. Captain Black spoke first. "The world knows how bravely, how unflinchingly, with what self-sacrifice these men went to their end," he said. "Without a tremor of fear or doubt, without a shudder of regret, they offered up their lives.

We do not stand here by the bodies of felons. There is nothing disgraceful about their death. They died for liberty, for the sacred right of untrammeled speech, and for humanity. We are proud to have been their friends."[48]

Reitzel was next, delivering a fiery speech in German. He excoriated the workers of Chicago for allowing "five of their best men" to be murdered in their midst. "We demand blood for blood," he declared. "We do not grieve for these men who are dead, but we do grieve that in this century murder most foul can be committed under the guise of authority and law. We grieve at ourselves that we did not rise in our might and prevent this crime. ... Night is falling fast, and I shall close. In this darkening hour think of the darkness and sorrow which society has brought over those we love. Let me appeal to you with Herwegh: 'We have loved long enough; now we are going to hate!' " (Wir haben lang' genug geliebt; wir wollen endlich hassen!)[49]

The next speaker, Thomas Morgan, cautioned against retaliation. A socialist and practical trade-unionist, he urged that every effort be made to disabuse the public of its association of anarchism with violence. Currlin, however, echoing Reitzel, castigated the workingmen for having permitted the "five-fold murder" to be accomplished. "So far, you have only shown that you are a people which knows how to bury its dead," he chided. "Oh, workmen of Chicago, be one, be strong. Be one from this day. Vow it in the presence of these dead. Shake off the yoke which Mammon lays upon your shoulders. Be free!"[50]

With these words the ceremony drew to a close. By train, by carriage, and on horseback the mourners returned to the city. But the burial was not yet over. On Sunday, December 18, the five caskets were reinterrred in a permanent vault which had meanwhile been built at Waldheim to receive them. A large group of people assembled to witness these final ceremonies. It was a chill winter day. Snow and ice covered the ground. A cold wind blew through the barren trees as Lucy Parsons led her children to the grave site. She had embroidered a pillow with "Our Papa" in small violets and placed it beside the vault. The remains of the five anarchists were removed from their temporary resting place, the coffins opened, and the bodies viewed for the last time. They were then placed side by

397

side in the vault, and a heavy flagstone was lowered and firmly cemented to protect them.[51]

With the final burial of the dead, the mourners dispersed to their homes. The drawn-out tragedy had come at last to an end. All was over, wrote William Dean Howells, "except the judgment that begins at once for every unjust and evil deed, and goes on forever."[52]

PART V ‖ THE AFTERMATH

24 ‖ REPERCUSSIONS

Although opinion was sharply divided over the executions, a majority of Americans greeted them with approval. One Illinois resident, writing to Governor Oglesby, called him "the grandest and bravest man in the United States" for allowing the machinery of justice to go forward. Sheriff Matson expressed a similar view. "Your decision," he wrote to the governor, "is fully approved by all right thinking people who know anything about the case."[1] Many, including the sheriff, affirmed that society had the duty to protect itself and, while the men who had been executed may themselves have been innocent of the bombthrowing, they had called for the use of force to abolish American institutions and were therefore, as James Russell Lowell declared, "well hanged."[2]

Except for labor and radical journals, the press everywhere exulted. "Law has triumphed over anarchy!" proclaimed the *Chicago Tribune*. "Those who draw the sword against peace and law in this free country will perish by the sword!" The *Illinois Staats-Zeitung* rejoiced that "the bloodshed of May 4, 1886," had been avenged. "Yesterday's executions," the paper declared on November 12, "marked the beginning of the end of anarchy in America."[3] Abroad, the *Times* of London thundered praise for "Chicago justice," noting with approval that juries in America drew no distinction between "incendiaries of the platform" and "the men who do their dirty work." The paper commended the hangings as an example to be followed by the British authorities in dealing with labor unrest and looked enviously across the Atlantic where policemen carried revolvers and used them "without mercy when they see signs of resistance."[4]

The general reaction, then, as Lizzie Holmes summed it up, was that the anarchists, as members of a "wickedly secret, dark and bloody band intent only on violence and murder," had deserved their fate, and that the state had acted properly in executing them.[5] The day after the hanging, Theodore Roosevelt and his cowboys in the Dakota Bad Lands burned the dead men in effigy. In Grinnell, Iowa, founded by a cousin of the Cook County prosecutor, bells were rung and bonfires lit to celebrate the event. In Galesburg, Illinois, where schools were closed early on November 11, the poet Carl Sandburg, then nine years old, was going home when he heard one man, a railroad worker, hail another in words he would never forget: "Well, they hanged 'em!" The man went on his way at a brisk pace. He was "more than happy," said Sandburg, to deliver the news. "You could tell that by his voice, by the way he sang it out with a glad howl. No need to say more. Everybody knew what had gone before. The end of the story was " 'Well, they hanged 'em!' "[6]

Six weeks after the hanging, the Chicago Bar Association held a dinner in honor of Judge Gary. On behalf of the association, Wirt Dexter, attorney for Marshall Field and a recognized spokesman for Chicago's wealthy element, declared that the legal profession had proven itself a "bulwark" of conservatism against radicals and malcontents. "How needful is this bulwark at the present time I need not say," Dexter added, "with the deep unrest that exists about us. When men armed with destructive theories seek their enforcement, which would speedily make for us an earthly hell, other professions will expostulate, but the law—and I say it with Judge Gary sitting in our midst—will hang! I mention his name in obedience to an impulse of the heart too strong to resist, for I don't believe he will ever know how we feel towards him, and how we love him!" Gary himself followed with a slashing attack on organized labor, whose "tyranny," he insisted, far exceeded that of the "monopolies of capital," which was in fact "so light as to be scarcely felt." Condemning the "arrogant assumption" of the unions "to control the acts of every man who lives by manual labor," he asked, "What can we do to break it down?"[7]

Henry Lloyd was incensed by Gary's speech. In a letter to the *Chicago Herald* strongly criticizing it, he upheld the right of labor to organize in its own interests. Clarence Darrow sent Lloyd a message of support: "The cause of organized labor is fortunate in having such a champion." Captain Black, praising Lloyd for his "manly and courageous action," denounced Gary and "the flunkeys who pour out to him their fulsome adulation *ad nauseam.*" "Your own masterly setting forth of the case which you have undertaken to champion," Black wrote, "does equal credit to your head and your heart. May God strengthen you and your splendid work, and redouble your courage."[8]

402

No one was more deeply affected than Lloyd by the hanging of the anarchists, whose lives he had so passionately endeavored to save. On the day of the execution he sat down and wrote a two-stanza hymn, entitled "Voices of the Gallows," prefaced by the last words of Parsons and Spies: "Let the voice of the people be heard!" and "The time will come when our silence will be more powerful than the voices you are strangling today." That evening, at the Lloyd home in suburban Winnetka, the entire family sang the hymn, to the tune of "Annie Laurie," accompanied by Mrs. Lloyd at the piano. Afterwards Lloyd wept bitterly.[9]

William Dean Howells reacted to the deaths with comparable anguish. Pouring out his feelings in letters to relatives and friends, he denounced the execution as a "civic murder," a "thing forever damnable before God and abominable to civilized men," an "atrocious piece of frenzy and cruelty, for which we must stand ashamed forever before history." "The historical perspective," he wrote to his father, "is that this free Republic has killed five men for their opinions." To his sister Annie he recorded his "heartache and horror" over what had taken place and vowed some day to "do justice to these irreparably wronged men."[10]

Howells, as a first step, suggested to William Salter the publication of a book—to which he himself would contribute a letter—containing tributes to the dead anarchists, along with a short history of the case, the profits going to the victims' families. "It still seems impossible," he said, "that those five men should have really been killed two weeks ago. Think of Parsons actually coming back from safety and giving himself up to that incredible death! Was ever a generous man so atrociously dealt with before? I don't understand how you could get through it all, unbroken." "I think of those men every day," he wrote to Salter a few weeks later, "and of the wrong their names are under, and long to have them righted before the world."[11]

Howells, however, did not write at length about the case, although his novel *A Hazard of New Fortunes* shows its impact on his emotions and thoughts. Nor did the volume which he suggested to Salter ever see the light of day. On the other hand, he had written, on the day after the execution, a long and eloquent letter to the *New York Tribune*—a letter that he never sent—expressing his grief at the miscarriage of justice that had taken place. This was the letter, apparently, that he had intended to include in the proposed memorial collection. Entitled "A Word to the Dead," it read in part:

All over the world where civilized men can think and feel, they are even now asking themselves, For what, really, did those four men die so bravely? Why did one other die so miserably? Next week the journalistic theory that they did so because they were desperate murderers will have grown even more insufficient than it is now for the minds and hearts of dispassionate inquirers, and history will make the answer to which she must adhere for all time. *They died, in the prime of the first Republic the world has ever known, for their opinions' sake.*

It is useless to deny this truth, to cover it up, to turn your backs upon it, to frown it down, or sneer it down. We have committed an atrocious and irreparable wrong. We have been undergoing one of those spasms of paroxysmal righteousness to which our Anglo-Saxon race is peculiarly subject, and in which, let us hope, we are not more responsible for our actions than the victims of *petit mal*. Otherwise, we could not forgive ourselves; and I say we, because this deed has apparently been done with the approval of the whole nation. The dead men, who now accuse us of the suicidal violence in which they perished, would be alive today, if one thousandth part of the means employed to compass their death had been used by the people to inquire into the question of their guilt; for, under the forms of law, their trial has not been a trial by justice, but a trial by passion, by terror, by prejudice, by hate, by newspaper.

Except for the hideous result, Howells continued, the convictions might have seemed a colossal piece of American humor. "But perhaps the wildest of our humorists could not have conceived of a joke so monstrous as the conviction of seven men for a murderous conspiracy which they carried into effect while one was at home playing cards with his family, another was addressing a meeting five miles away, another was present with his wife and little children, two others had made pacific speeches, and not one, except on the testimony of a single, notoriously untruthful witness, was proven to have had anything to do with throwing the Haymarket bomb, or to have even remotely instigated the act."[12]

Howells went on to censure State's Attorney Grinnell for having failed in his duty "to seek the truth concerning the accused rather than to seek their destruction." He lashed out at Judge Gary for twisting the law and for his bias against the defendants. We have had, he concluded, a "political execution" in Chicago. "The sooner we realize this, the better for us. By such perversion of law as brought the Anarchists to their doom, William Lloyd Garrison, who published a paper denouncing the Constitution as a compact with hell and a covenant with death, and every week stirred up the blacks and their friends throughout the country to abhor the social system of the South, could have been sentenced to the gallows if a slave had killed his master. Emerson, Parker, Howe, Giddings and Wade, Sumner and Greeley, all who encouraged the fight against slavery in Kansas and the New England philanthropists who supplied the Free State men with Sharp's Rifles could have been held morally responsible and made to pay with their persons, when John Brown took seven Missourians out of their beds and shot them. Wendell Phillips, and Thoreau, and the other literary men whose sympathies influenced Brown to homicidal insurrection at Harper's Ferry could have been put to death with the same justice that consigned the Anarchists to the gallows in Chicago."[13]

It was a powerful indictment, an expression of the "helpless grief and rage," as Howells described his feelings to William Salter, which overwhelmed him as a result of the executions, and which persisted for a number of weeks thereafter. Salter himself was in the thrall of similar emotions. "My mind," he wrote to Howells on November 27, "frequently reverts to that black day, and I shudder to think of it."[14] Indeed, to all the proponents of executive clemency the hangings came as a terrible blow. "My heart was never so full, my pen so halt," wrote Benjamin Tucker after the event. George Schilling, for whom the strain of the last days had been unbearable, had "never had such a bitter experience in my life." Samuel Gompers, after pleading with Governor Oglesby at Springfield, had spent a "night of horrors" brooding over the impending butchery. The following day he wandered aimlessly through the streets of Chicago, his spirits utterly crushed by the tragedy.[15] Joseph Buchanan, another prominent advocate of mercy, described his feelings when the trap was sprung and his friends plummeted to their death: "A woman screams. I can hold up no longer. Grown man though I am, my face is deluged with tears. But an ocean of tears could not wash from my memory the recollections of that week and that hour." Samuel McConnell felt that "a horrible wrong" had been committed, that innocent men had been "slaughtered by the law." According to Captain Black, "enlightened civilization never before witnessed such a sentence and its execution." Benjamin Butler saw it as a repetition of the witch hangings in Puritan Massachusetts. To William H. Parsons it was nothing less than "the crime of this century," to Johann Most "the greatest outrage of modern times."[16]

The prevailing mood among supporters of the strangled men was one of helplessness and frustration, mingled with anger, indignation, and an overwhelming sense of loss. "Heartbroken, we walked for days like mourners," Abraham Cahan recollected. "But our pain struck deeper because of our realization that the American workers had remained indifferent or, in many cases, had even applauded the execution." The hardest task, wrote Lizzie Holmes, was that of "learning how to live without them; of taking up the burden of life again; of trying to carry on their work without their advice and encouragement; of realizing the mighty loss we and the cause had sustained; of knowing that the little personal services, the breathless efforts to save, the intensity of anxiety of the past eighteen months, had ceased forever, and the awful sacrifice was completed. This was the most difficult part. And many a true comrade came through the ordeal changed and broken, never to be again what he had been."[17]

For some the feeling of sorrow was mingled with yearnings for vengeance. "REVENGE, BLOODY REVENGE!" demanded one anarchist journal in bold letters, beneath which loomed the sketch of a bomb.[18] Leaflets called for revolutionary action to avenge the juridical murders. "Grinnell brands us as cowards," read one. "Time will show whether we are cowards or not."[19] Governor Oglesby received threatening letters: "If you believe in God, say your prayers. Your days are numbered. . . . Hurrah for Anarchy!" "I declare you the greatest scoundrel and murderer that has ever dishonored the United States. . . . Be vigilant. You will not escape our revenge. For scoundrels of your calibre we will always be able to find another bomb."[20]

The authorities took such threats seriously. For a long time after the executions they were prepared for retaliatory action. According to Captain Schaack, more than a few Chicago anarchists were ready to commit murder or arson to revenge themselves upon those whom they held responsible for the hanging of their comrades. In July 1888 Inspector Bonfield claimed to have uncovered a "dynamite plot" to assassinate Judge Gary and Prosecutor Grinnell in retribution for November 11. Four Bohemian workmen were arrested, one of whom received twelve years in prison for his part in the alleged conspiracy, although the evidence was far from conclusive that there was indeed a plot. Lucy Parsons, attributing the affair to the "hellish imagination of Bonfield and his minions," was quoted as saying: "They haven't murdered any Anarchists since November last, and they seem to be thirsting for more blood. If Gary and Grinnell are not killed very soon I will kill them myself, and you can rest assured I will not make a botch of it."[21]

Yet threats, some sympathizers cautioned, could only bring further repressions, while at the same time strengthening in the public mind the association of anarchism with violence. "Shall we pursue these men, who have slain our beloved, with the secret awful shadow of our implacable vengeance?" asked J. William Lloyd in *Liberty*. "Shall the bludgeon smite them down in the darkness, the poisoned dagger sting them at midday, the terrible volcanoes of dynamite roar out their doom in the still hours of midnight?" Lloyd begged his Chicago comrades to refrain from any such reprisals. "I tell you," he said, "that your eight martyrs have done more to advance your cause than would the sacking of eight cities like Chicago. But I tell you again that the blood of the first man that you assassinate by way of revenge will wipe out half their work, and when the first dynamite bomb thrown by your revengeful hands enters a drawing-room window and tears the tender flesh of innocent women and babes, the whole of it will be undone."[22]

But there were those—in particular Robert Reitzel and Dyer Lum— who rejected moderate counsel. Their plans to liberate the doomed men had been frustrated and the execution taken place without the least attempt to prevent it. There had been no attack upon the jail. No mines or bombs had exploded. No armed men had appeared to menace the supremacy of the state. This unclouded victory of authority troubled them beyond measure. They seethed with a thirst for revenge. For Reitzel, a comrade remarked, the "dull, sullen, peaceful, inexpressibly saddening picture" of the funeral procession remained the most bitter memory of his life.[23] At the cemetery he demanded "blood for blood." But no avenger came forward. No retaliatory blow was struck. No buildings were demolished or individuals assassinated. Gary, Grinnell, and their confederates remained unmolested. Chicago resumed its normal whirl, and the tragedy passed into history.

Nor did Reitzel himself take up the gauntlet, however much he may have yearned to do so. As for Lum, he did in fact work out a scheme of reprisal, vowing that "the 'resources of civilization' would be called into requisition." Yet he too failed to act. As late as 1892, nearly five years after the hangings, he still harbored vague plans to strike back. From his letters to Voltairine de Cleyre, he seems to have been contemplating a suicide plot, an act of propaganda by the deed, to avenge his fallen comrades. For all the delay, he was determined to make good his "pledge," as he called it, to Engel, Fischer, and the rest. He had never lost sight of "my purpose," he insisted. "I will raise the money and carry out my part of the programme. I am cold, relentless, unflinching. If any fools get in the way, so much the worse for them. In this sentiment cuts no figure. And this time a poster will let the people know the 'police' did not do it—as Mrs. Parsons said before. If done, and I think it will work, as we use chemicals, the responsibility will be assumed in posters on the walls."[24]

In the end, however, Lum failed to execute his plan. Instead, he sank into a deep psychological depression, unable to eat or sleep, his mind in constant turmoil, his life a bitter struggle against poverty. Moving to a flophouse on the Bowery in New York City, he fell to heavy drinking and, his insomnia worsening, took opiates to fall asleep. Late at night, under the influence of alcohol and drugs, he wrote his last letters to his comrades, rambling, agitated, almost incoherent. He was driving himself towards the grave. In this distracted mood he fled to his ancestral home in Massachusetts, but, unable to find respite, returned to his lodgings in New York. There a friend encountered him in September 1892, seven months before his death: "He came trudging along the street, soft felt hat carelessly slung on one side, blue flannel shirt and red necktie, a suit of well worn homespun clothes, a pair of well worn shoes, and a large bundle of papers and writings under his arm; looking at no one, caring for nothing save the propaganda of Anarchism."[25]

Lum, until the end, continued to brood on the Haymarket tragedy. Its memory dominated the final months and years of his life. At length, Voltairine de Cleyre tells us, he "seized the unknown Monster, Death, with a smile on his lips." After a "farewell look into a friend's eyes, he went out into the April night and took his last walk in the roar of the great city." Then, returning to his room, he swallowed a fatal draft of poison. "His genius, his work, his character," wrote Voltairine after his passing, "was one of those rare gems produced in the great mine of suffering and flashing backward with all its changing lights the hopes, the fears, the gaieties, the griefs, the dreams, the doubts, the loves, the hates, the sum of that which is buried, low down there, in the human mine."[26]

Although there were no physical reprisals, the execution of the Chicago anarchists aroused a storm of indignation and protest. From Boston to San Francisco mass meetings were held to mourn the loss of the defendants. Johann Most, the day after the hangings, made an incendiary speech in New York for which he was tried and condemned to a year in prison. In Chicago Lizzie Holmes vowed "eternal warfare against the existing order of society. Hang us, torture us, lock us up as you will, we mean it. We are fulfilling the conscious inner sense of right in our souls when we declare it, and your petty penalties have no power against this living righteous principle."[27]

The executions were branded judicial murder not only by the anarchists but by liberals and moderates who cherished the principles of free speech and assembly and due process of law. The men, it was widely believed, had been hanged merely for holding and voicing opinions, for organizing and encouraging the workers, for championing the cause of the oppressed. They had denounced capitalism and government with a vehemence that aroused the wrath of the propertied classes—it was for this that they were done to death. To Art Young, the newspaper illustrator, they had fallen victim to "the worst mob of all—respectable, legalized vengeance." In the name of "law and order," a fourfold murder had been committed, a legal lynching, American style. General Matthew Trumbull chastised Governor Oglesby for succumbing to the "clamor of an angry populace." A woman in New York wrote to Oglesby: "Even in Russia or Germany the lives of these men would not have been forfeited. That was reserved for this land of 'free speech.' The stain of this murder will not be forgotten in a hundred years."[28]

In Europe, as in America, hundreds of meetings took place to denounce what was regarded as a monstrous miscarriage of justice. All through Italy, according to anarchists in Turin, "peasants and artisans speak the names of Parsons, Spies, Lingg, Fischer, and Engel with even more admiration than our fathers of Young Italy gave to the name of Mazzini or Garibaldi." At a workers' rally in Havana, $955 was collected to aid the families of the martyred anarchists, and the executions were branded as "the most atrocious murder ever committed in any portion of the civilized world."[29]

Both at home and abroad, radical publications appeared with black borders as a token of deep mourning. "GETHSEMANE!" proclaimed the Chicago *Labor Enquirer*. "America Making History. Free Speech and Free Assemblage Dealt a Deadening Blow." "FOULEST MURDER," declared the organ of the Socialistic Labor Party in New Haven. "BRAVE MEN DIE BRAVELY FOR LABOR'S CAUSE." *The People*, a labor paper in San Francisco, regarded the killing as "a million times worse than that committed at the Haymarket, because of its being done in the name of law and justice—worse than the crucifixion of Jesus Christ, for the latter took place nearly two thousand years ago, in a despotic Asiatic country, governed by robber-kings and controlled by religious superstition—worse than the murder of John Brown, for it is supposed to be done by free men, and not slaveholders."[30]

Benjamin Tucker's *Liberty* contained a particularly moving tribute to the executed men. Below the masthead, the entire front page was blank except for a verse, in bold letters, from Byron's "Marino Falerio, Doge of Venice":

> They never fail who die
> In a great cause: the block may soak their gore;
> Their heads may sodden in the sun; their limbs
> Be strung to city gates and castle walls—
> But still their spirit walks abroad. Though years
> Elapse, and others share as dark a doom,
> They but augment the deep and sweeping thoughts
> Which overpower all others, and conduct
> The world at last to freedom.[31]

The London *Freedom*, comparing the hanging with that of the Russian populists in 1881, declared: "November 11th will henceforward be a red-letter day in the Socialist calendar. Red, for it is stained with the blood of some of the most earnest and devoted men who ever championed the cause of the people. Memorable, because that quarter of an hour's legal murder will do more to shake the blind faith of the masses in law and authority than the eloquence of years."[32]

The suicide of Lingg and the hanging of Spies, Parsons, Engel, and Fischer consecrated them with the halo of martyrdom. Friends of the dead men murmured, "They died like John Brown of Osawatomie."[33] And just as Brown had made the scaffold "glorious like the cross," as Emerson had written, the same was now remarked of Parsons and his comrades. Among those who drew the parallel was

410

Benjamin Tucker. "When these men ascended the gallows," he wrote in *Liberty*, "they added to the splendor of the glory with which John Brown had already invested it." Moses Harman, the editor of *Lucifer*, was another: "It has been said of John Brown and his comrades that they made the 'scaffold glorious.' If this be true of the martyrs in the abolition cause, much more is it true now of the martyrs in the cause of Labor vs. Monopoly."[34]

For the anarchists, as these quotations suggest, the scaffold assumed the significance of the cross. Mindful of the parallel, William Holmes put forward a suggestion: "Let us then make gallows of available substances, and wear them upon our persons in commemoration of the murder of our martyrs. Not in a spirit of worship or adoration—those who come after us will require no gods—but as a badge of our fealty to the principles for which they died." In Chicago, Holmes noted, a number had already taken up the practice, and it soon spread to other areas, so that thousands of men and women were wearing miniature gallows of gold and silver with a noose hanging from the crossbeam.[35]

The Chicago Martyrs—as they were thereafter called by their admirers—were also memorialized in other ways. Anarchists named their children in their honor. Their portraits decorated anarchist literature and were displayed in anarchist meeting halls throughout the world. For many years, moreover, the anniversary of November 11, 1887—"an anniversary," as the London *Freedom* put it, "which every worker, every lover of liberty, ought to engrave in fiery letters on his heart"[36]—was observed by anarchists and socialists as a revolutionary memorial. On the first anniversary, in November 1888, mass meetings took place in Boston, New York, Philadelphia, Baltimore, Cleveland, St. Louis, Denver, San Francisco, and other cities, as well as in Chicago itself. At the Waldheim Cemetery a special commemoration was held, attended by more than three thousand people, at which George Schilling read a letter left by Parsons for his son and daughter with instructions that it not be opened until November 11, 1888. "Oh my children," Parsons had written, "how dearly your Papa loves you. We show our love by living *for* our loved ones, we also *prove* our love by dying, when necessary, for them. Of my life and the cause of my unnatural and cruel death, you will learn from others. *Your Father is a self-offered Sacrifice upon the Altar of Liberty and Happiness*. To you I leave the legacy of an honest name and duty done. Preserve it, emulate it. . . . Your mother!

She is the grandest, noblest of women. Love, honor, and obey her. My children, my precious ones, I request you to read this parting message on each recurring anniversary of my Death in remembrance of him who dies not alone for you, but for the children yet unborn. Bless you, my Darlings. Farewell."[37]

Outside the United States, memorial meetings took place in many countries, including England, France, Holland, Spain, and Italy, so that, as *The Alarm* observed, "the cause for which our comrades so exultantly mounted the scaffold-cross of the nineteenth century finds an international echo." In Spain, Kropotkin observed, there was not a city worth naming "where the bloody anniversary was not commemorated by enthusiastic crowds of workers. Not one in Italy. Not one in Germany where the names of Parsons, Spies, Engel, Schwab, Fischer, Lingg, Neebe and Fielden were not invoked by workers who met in small groups, as they were not allowed to hold big meetings. The commemoration of the Chicago martyrs has almost acquired the same importance as the commemoration of the Paris Commune."[38] Year after year, anarchists all over the world gathered together to pay tribute to the martyrs of Chicago and to retell their story, a story, in the words of Moses Harman, "which can never grow old so long as men love liberty, hate tyranny, and honor manly courage in defense of the right, the true, the equitable."[39]

These meetings, however, did not always pass without incident. Thus in Philadelphia, on November 11, 1889, the mayor ordered the Odd Fellows' Temple closed against a scheduled Haymarket commemoration. In Chicago, two years later, the police broke up an orderly meeting at the Vorwaerts Turner Hall and hoisted the stars and stripes above the red flag. The same year, when the English artist and socialist Walter Crane spoke at a Haymarket memorial in Boston, he was threatened with "social ostracism" and with the cancellation of his art exhibition by angry members of the mercantile establishment. In Providence, on November 11, 1892, a memorial gathering was invaded by the police, who prevented Emma Goldman, the guest speaker, from entering the hall, put her on a train, and forced her to leave the city.[40]

More than once, in Chicago, Lucy Parsons was interrupted while addressing anniversary meetings. On November 11, 1895, a police inspector stopped her by roughly grabbing her arm when she said that she "did not want to go to a heaven where there was a Gary." From the audience came cries of "Shame! Shame! We are not in

412

Russia!" The following year she was again interrupted by the police, who hustled her off the stage amid protests from the crowd.[41] Further trouble erupted when the officials of the Waldheim Cemetery placed restrictions on the annual memorial ceremonies and threatened to ban them entirely. As a result, Mrs. Engel and others considered exhuming the bodies and moving them to another resting place. Lucy Parsons, however, was opposed. "Speaking personally," she wrote in a letter to an anarchist paper, "I say, spare me the opening afresh of the wound. I shrink from standing by that mound and seeing my dear one brought forth, hearing the sensational capitalistic press gloat over the whole scene, lay bare the horror."[42] Lucy's wishes prevailed, as the cemetery authorities and the families of the dead men managed to settle their differences.

Meanwhile, an impressive bronze monument had been erected over the grave site, the hooded figure of a woman laying a wreath on the brow of a fallen worker. To Emma Goldman she seemed to express "defiance and revolt, mingled with pity and love." Her face was "beautiful in its great humanity," her gesture one of "infinite tenderness."[43] On the base of the monument were inscribed the year 1887 and the last words of Spies on the scaffold: "The day will come when our silence will be more powerful than the voices you are throttling today." Designed by the sculptor Albert Weinert, it was built with funds raised by the Pioneer Aid and Support Association, an organization founded in December 1887 to assist the families of the executed and imprisoned men.[44]

On Sunday, June 25, 1893, some eight thousand people gathered at Waldheim to witness the dedication of the monument. The Chicago World's Fair was taking place at this time, and visitors from many countries came out to the cemetery, including delegations from England, France, and Belgium, to deposit flowers at the Haymarket tomb. As his mother stood nearby, wearing the small gold gallows that had become a symbol of the anarchist movement, thirteen-year-old Albert Parsons, Jr., drew aside the red curtain that covered the monument. An orchestra played the "Marseillaise," the Humboldt Singing Society sang the hymn "Wachet Auf" (Awake), and there were speeches in English, German, Czech, and Polish. Ernst Schmidt delivered the main address. "When the hatred and passions of our time resound no more," he said, "for you too, who are resting here, the hour of a juster verdict will have come. Until then, may this monument prove to the unbelievers, to the yet doubting and hesitating ones, that those who fell in the struggle for a better social order have left an honorable memory with all friends of justice and liberty."[45]

Waldheim, with its hauntingly beautiful monument, became a revolutionary shrine, a place of pilgrimage for anarchists and socialists from all over the world. In the decades immediately following its unveiling, there were years, according to an authority on Chicago, when "almost as many visitors came to it in the course of twelve months as to the statue of Abraham Lincoln in the park which bears his name."[46] The bronze statue, in the words of Lucy Robins Lang, became "the sacred center" towards which the hearts and thoughts of American radicals turned during the last years of the nineteenth century and the beginning of the twentieth. It meant to them "as much as the Church of the Holy Sepulchre means to the Christian, or Mecca to the Moslem, or the Wailing Wall to the Jew." As for herself, an anarchist of the younger generation, she could never look back on the memorial without "a great surge of conflicting emotions, a deep tenderness and a strong, rebellious resolution." It was "the fountain from which my revolutionary idealism sprang."[47]

25 ‖ THE PARDON

Following the execution of Spies, Parsons, Fischer, and Engel, the anarchist scare in Chicago began to subside. Gradually public hysteria gave way to calmer reflection. And, as fear and anger receded, a movement was set on foot to secure the release of the three survivors, Neebe, Fielden, and Schwab, from Joliet prison. This movement consisted of several more or less distinct components, all in agreement as to purpose but actuated by differing motives. First, although in numbers the fewest, were those who felt that all eight defendants had been wrongfully convicted, and who were bent on obtaining the only reparation now possible for what in their view had been a grievous judicial crime. Another group maintained that, while at least some of the men had been justly convicted, a policy of leniency might better have served the interests of society. Still another, and perhaps the largest, group included those who had applauded the executions but who now believed that the ends of justice had been sufficiently served and that it would be both politic and humane to free the imprisoned survivors as an act of mercy.[1]

The movement to get Fielden, Schwab, and Neebe out of jail was nurtured by a number of circumstances. Most important was the revelation, in January 1889, that Inspector Bonfield and Captain Schaack had for some time been receiving payments from saloonkeepers, prostitutes, and thieves, and had been trafficking in stolen goods, a large quantity of which was unearthed in the residence of Detective Jacob Loewenstein, an officer from Schaack's precinct. Loewenstein, it may be recalled, had assisted in the capture of Lingg after the bombthrowing, and among the articles discovered in Loewenstein's apartment were the breast-pin and cuff-buttons which Lingg had bequeathed to Elise Friedel but which were missing when Lingg's personal effects were turned over to his friends.[2]

When the story was printed in the *Chicago Times*, Bonfield had the editors arrested and tried to shut the paper down. This proved too much for the public to swallow, and Bonfield and Schaack were suspended from the force pending an investigation. "The end of the official career of Bonfield is drawing near," gloated an editorial in the *Times*. "His official days are numbered. His brutal assumption of authority, his clubbing exploits, his reception of presents from courtesans, gamblers, and saloon-keepers, his protection to disreputables, will soon be a thing of the past. When the time comes it will be a glorious result for the city of Chicago. People do not want to be terrorized; they want to be protected in their lives and liberty and property. Bonfield may well prepare to retire to private life. Chicago has had enough of him and his methods."[3]

Following the investigation, Bonfield and Schaack were both cashiered in disgrace. Bonfield subsequently established a private detective agency, while Schaack retired to a farm in Wisconsin. It was a signal victory for the anarchists and their supporters, who had accused the police of corruption all along. More than that, the character of the men who had pursued them and sent their comrades to the gallows was exposed for all to see. Conscience rode hard upon Chicago's inhabitants, and more than a few felt shame and remorse.

In the wake of these developments, an Amnesty Committee was formed to campaign for the release of the prisoners. Headed by William Penn Nixon, editor of the Chicago *Inter Ocean*, with Henry Lloyd as vice-president, its members included such prominent businessmen and professionals as Lyman Gage, Lyman Trumbull, Samuel McConnell, Murray F. Tuley, Edward Osgood Brown, Clarence Darrow, Matthew Trumbull, Edward F. Dunne, and William C. Goudy, some of whom had been conspicuous in the commutation efforts of 1887. Also active on the committee was Edward S. Dreyer, who had served on the grand jury that indicted the anarchists and whom Spies, one may recall, had accused of wanting to settle personal scores with him. After the executions, Dreyer demonstrated a complete change of heart, becoming one of the most ardent supporters of a pardon for the survivors. "He frequently discussed the case with me," Sigmund Zeisler later recalled, "and several times manifested great emotion in expressing his sorrow over the outcome and his participation in the work of the grand jury." John N. Hills, foreman of the grand jury, was likewise repentant. "I have never worried so much about any one thing as I have your unjust confinement," he wrote to Neebe, "and daily . . . I have argued your case to everyone."[4]

Through the Amnesty Committee strong pressure in behalf of Neebe, Schwab, and Fielden was brought to bear on Governor Joseph

W. Fifer, who in 1889 had succeeded Oglesby as the chief executive of Illinois. But Fifer, a "shrewd political nonentity," in the description of Ernst Schmidt, proved obdurate, and the amnesty workers had to await the advent of a new administration for action to be taken.[5]

This came in January 1893, with the inauguration of John Peter Altgeld as governor. Altgeld, a man of more liberal views than his predecessor, had earned the reputation of being a thoroughly honest public servant, and one who was unafraid to voice his convictions or to act upon them. Born in Germany and brought to the United States as an infant, he had grown up on a farm in Ohio, enlisted in the Union army at sixteen, studied law after the Civil War, and made his way to high office by sheer ability and strength of character, becoming a state's attorney, then judge of the Superior Court in Chicago, where he had made a fortune in real estate. Altgeld was a complex, introverted figure, whose career epitomized the rags-to-riches legend so prominent in postbellum America. At the same time he was a genuine humanitarian, who despised injustice and recoiled at seeing the law made into a tool of the rich against the poor. His outspoken stand in behalf of penal reform won him the image of a "man of the people" with which he was catapulted into the state house, where a band of young reformers, Brand Whitlock and Clarence Darrow among them, gathered about him.

With Altgeld's election, the fate of the Haymarket survivors entered a sunnier phase. Although he had taken no part in earlier moves in the anarchists' behalf, not even signing a petition for clemency before the executions, his utterances in public life breathed a spirit of fairness and of sympathy for the downtrodden and oppressed. In 1891, for example, he had sharply protested against police brutality during raids on workingmen's meetings. To R. W. McClaughry, the then chief of the Chicago police, he wrote: "The American people are not prepared to substitute government by police ruffians for government by law. . . . We can not for a moment admit that by simply applying an unpopular and obloquious name to men, whether that name be anarchist or socialist, capitalist or vagabond, republican or democrat, an officer can be justified in depriving men of rights guaranteed by the fundamental law, and can break up their meeting, can club, search and imprison them, not for what they have done, but for what he, in his wisdom, or his prejudice, or his caprice, fears they might do."[6]

In view of Altgeld's subsequent action as governor, this declaration and others like it take on added significance. "In the spring of 1886," he wrote in the same letter to Chief McClaughry, "we had some extensive strikes and labor troubles on the West Side. At that time there were meetings of labor people, and the Police Department then pursued the course which your officers have just been pursuing; when there was no trouble meetings were broken up, men were clubbed to the right and to the left without any provocation, and this was kept up for weeks, until finally some wretch, whose name, if they knew it, the police have never been willing to make public, threw a bomb at a squad of police who were in the act of dispersing another peaceable meeting—a meeting which the Mayor had attended and pronounced peaceable—and the result was the killing and maiming of a large number of policemen, most of them officers who were simply obeying the orders of their superiors, and were not responsible for the brutal killing done by other officers. If the course which your force has started in to pursue shall long continue, can you, in all reason, expect any other result to follow than bloodshed?"[7]

Altgeld concluded as follows: "I will say to you that it will be an evil day for our country when the poor and ignorant, misguided though they may be, shall feel that a bullet is the only minister of justice which can right their wrongs, and the conduct of your officers now, like the conduct of certain officers in the spring of '86, will certainly tend to create that feeling and to accelerate its growth."[8]

Little wonder, therefore, that Altgeld's election brought fresh hope to the champions of amnesty and spurred them to redouble their efforts. Besides, there was another encouraging development. In January 1893, only days after the governor took office, the Illinois Supreme Court, reversing its stand in the Haymarket case, ruled in *The People vs. Coughlin* that a prospective juror who had read about a case in the press and had formed an opinion as to the defendant's guilt was ineligible to serve. Justice Magruder, who had delivered the unanimous opinion in *Spies vs. Illinois*, now conceded that, if the court was right in the Coughlin case, then it had erred in regard to the anarchists.[9]

The case of *The People vs. Coughlin* gave the new governor a strong legal basis for a pardon. But Altgeld's way was to do things circumspectly. He was determined not to act before making a thorough analysis of the trial and the circumstances surrounding it.

Shortly after his inauguration, he asked the sheriff of Cook County to send him the files on the Haymarket case. At the same time, he procured a transcript of the trial from the state supreme court, and he asked George Schilling, whom he had appointed secretary of the Illinois Bureau of Labor Statistics, to collect pertinent affidavits. If affidavits were wanted, said Schilling, gesturing with his hand, he could get a stack "this high!" And, setting to work with his customary energy, he brought in a huge pile of material—on the selection of the jury and on police brutality, among other matters—which proved critical in shaping Altgeld's decision.

As he studied the various aspects of the case, Altgeld was deluged with petitions for the release of the imprisoned anarchists. Public sentiment, noted Willis J. Abbot, editor of the *Chicago Times*, was by now "undoubtedly in favor of their pardon," and a petition bearing the signatures of some 60,000 persons, among them many of Chicago's most respected business and professional men, was presented to the governor. In March 1893, moreover, the Trades and Labor Assembly of Chicago, now the local affiliate of the American Federation of Labor, issued an open letter to Altgeld pleading for clemency.[10]

But the governor still did not act. As time slipped by, the supporters of amnesty grew impatient. Some, wondering whether they had been deceived in Altgeld, began to reproach him for the delay. Altgeld, wrote Benjamin Tucker, was "fast losing the confidence of those who had supposed him to be an honest man."[11]

Clarence Darrow, on behalf of the Amnesty Committee, went to Springfield to see the governor. For Darrow, the rising lawyer from Ohio who had come to Chicago shortly before the executions, one of the deepest regrets of his life was that he had not been on hand to participate in the defense of the anarchists. He had, however, plunged into the efforts to obtain a commutation, and now he played an important role in the movement to pardon the survivors. Securing an audience with Altgeld, he told him that his friends were growing restless and disappointed. They could see no excuse for the delay. Three months was surely enough time. The men should be released at once. Altgeld answered calmly and precisely. "Go tell your friends," he said, "that when I am ready I will act. I do not know how I will act, but I will do what I think is right."[12]

Not long after Darrow's visit, Samuel McConnell, now a judge as well as a friend of Altgeld's, appeared in Springfield on a similar mission. McConnell pleaded with the governor to pardon the men forthwith, even though it might wreck his political career. Altgeld bristled at the suggestion that personal ambition might stay his hand: "By God! If I decide that they are innocent, I will pardon them if I never hold office another day!"[13]

In April 1893, while Altgeld was studying the records of the case, Judge Gary, long silent on the matter, defended his conduct of the trial in a long article in *The Century Magazine*. His chief purpose in doing so was to answer the charge, lately repeated by the champions of amnesty, that the anarchists had been convicted for their opinions. Quite the contrary, Gary insisted. They had been punished "not for opinions, but for horrible deeds," and what had moved them was "envy and hatred of all people whose condition in life was better than their own." The greater portion of the article, however, was given over to lurid quotations from the speeches and writings of the anarchists, especially from those of Parsons and Spies. In short, as Harry Barnard has pointed out, Gary's emphasis was on their opinions and not their acts, despite his assertion to the contrary. The article, moreover, contained gross factual distortions regarding both the McCormick and Haymarket incidents; and Gary, while insisting that the verdict fully accorded with established law, admitted that it was on the basis of new law that the anarchists had been hanged ("This case is without precedent; there is no example in the law books of a case of this sort").[14]

Gary's article provoked a bitter reaction. Benjamin Tucker called it the work of "a murderer in defense of his own crime," Matthew Trumbull and Sarah Ames published devastating replies, and Clarence Darrow attacked it in a speech before the Law Club of Chicago while Gary himself sat in the audience.[15] Altgeld meanwhile remained silent. April and May passed, and June was winding its days, and still he kept his own counsel. On June 3 he condemned the lynching of a black in Decatur in an official proclamation that made a stir across the nation. Four days later he delivered a notable address to the graduating class of the University of Illinois in which he told the students to think of justice as "a struggling towards the right." He pointed out—clearly he was thinking of Haymarket—that "the wrongs done in the courts of justice themselves are so great that they cry to heaven." On June 9, when a labor dispute erupted in Lemont during which several workers were killed and wounded by rifle fire, Altgeld hurried to the scene to make a personal investi-

420

gation. In a detailed report he censured the local authorities for their failure to prevent the violence and charged the "wanton killing" to the employers.[16]

Yet still no word on the imprisoned anarchists. Not that Altgeld had been neglecting the case. For several months, as time permitted, he had been scrutinizing the trial record and the material which Schilling had accumulated. He had been brooding over the entire episode. Gradually, as he read and studied, the conviction was borne upon him that a monstrous legal wrong had been committed, a wrong which had sent five men to their death and kept three behind bars for seven years. And yet to release anarchists judged guilty of murder and conspiracy was not an easy decision. To take such a step, Altgeld was fully aware, would not only open old wounds but might spell his own political demise. If he granted the pardon, he told Clarence Darrow, "from that day I will be a dead man."[17]

On the other hand, as Henry Lloyd remarked, Altgeld's training as a lawyer, and his respect for the forms of law, "revolted against the sentences imposed on these men, and he felt that he must undo, so far as he could, the wrong committed against them."[18] Towards the end of June, Samuel McConnell was again in Springfield and had dinner with the governor in his mansion. After the meal, Altgeld took him to his library. Pointing to a stack of papers, he said: "There is the record of the anarchist case. I have read every word of it and I have decided to pardon all three of the men."[19] His decision, as Altgeld himself realized, marked the greatest turning point of his life.

On the morning of June 26, 1893, the day after the unveiling of the Haymarket monument, William H. Hinrichsen, the Illinois secretary of state, was summoned to Altgeld's private office. "I am going to pardon Fielden, Schwab, and Neebe this morning," said the governor, "and I thought you might like to sign the papers in person rather than have your signature affixed by your chief clerk." "Do you think it a good policy to pardon them?" asked Hinrichsen, who then added, "I do not." "It is right!" said Altgeld emphatically, striking the desk with his fist.[20]

Brand Whitlock, then a young official in Hinrichsen's department, was instructed to make out the pardons. Whitlock, a supporter of amnesty, was happy to comply. "I cannot tell in what surprise, in what a haze, or with what emotions I went about that task," he later recalled. He secured the necessary forms and "made out those three pardons in the largest, roundest hand I could command," bringing them to Hinrichsen to sign. He then took them to the governor's office and handed them to Altgeld. The only other person in the room was E. S. Dreyer, who had labored tirelessly to have the men released. Dreyer was exceedingly nervous. The moment, says Whitlock, meant much to him. The governor signed the pardons and handed them to Dreyer. The banker took them and began to say something. But he got only as far as, "Governor, I hardly—" when he broke down and wept. Altgeld gestured impatiently, concealing his own emotion. He was gazing out the window at the elm trees in the yard. He took out his watch and said that Dreyer must hurry or he would miss his train to Joliet, where he was to deliver the pardons to the men in prison and go on to Chicago with them that night. Dreyer nervously rolled up the papers, shook hands, and left.[21]

In conjunction with his unconditional pardon of Fielden, Schwab, and Neebe, Altgeld issued a lengthy statement reviewing the essential features of the case and setting forth his reasons for releasing the three men. It was a "bold and scathing" document, as Benjamin Tucker aptly described it, "probably the most merciless message of mercy ever penned." The historian Allan Nevins has called it "one of the best state papers ever written in America."[22]

Altgeld did not mince his words. He denounced the trial in all its aspects—from the selection of the jurors and the testimony of the witnesses to the behavior of the judge and the prosecutor—as a shameless travesty of justice. He showed, with ample documentation, that the defendants had been convicted by a packed and prejudiced jury, that they had not been proven guilty of the charges against them, and that no reliable evidence had been produced to link them with the bombthrower or to indicate that he had acted on their advice. Altgeld stated his own belief that the bomb had been thrown by someone "seeking personal revenge" for having been clubbed during the labor troubles of that period, so that "Captain Bonfield is the man who is really responsible for the death of the police officers." He declared further that "much of the evidence given at the trial was a pure fabrication; that some of the prominent police officials, in their zeal, not only terrorized ignorant men by throwing them into prison and threatening them with torture if they refused to swear to anything desired, but that they offered money and employment to those who would consent to do this; further, that they deliberately planned to have fictitious conspiracies formed in order that they might get the glory of discovering them."[23]

Above all, Altgeld made plain the extreme bias of Judge Gary against the defendants. The record, he said, revealed that Gary had conducted the trial with "malicious ferocity," that he had compelled all eight men to be tried together, that he had permitted the state's attorney to go into matters "entirely foreign" to the case, that "every ruling throughout the long trial on any contested point was in favor of the state; and further, that page after page in the record contains insinuating remarks of the judge, made in the hearing of the jury, and with the evident intent of bringing the jury to his way of thinking." Perhaps most important, Altgeld found no precedent to sustain the ruling of Judge Gary that it had not been necessary for the state to identify the actual perpetrator or to prove that he had acted under the influence of the accused. "In all the centuries during which government has been maintained among men, and crime has been punished," declared the governor, "no judge in a civilized country has ever laid down such a rule."[24]

The governor had said it all. While exposing the enormity of the judicial outrage, his message echoed all the important criticisms that the anarchists and their defenders had made at the time, amply confirming their contention that the trial had been a farce and the judge a rabid partisan incapable of fairness to the men before him. He made it clear, moreover, that he was freeing Fielden, Schwab, and Neebe not as an act of simple mercy, not because they had suffered enough, but because they had been wrongfully convicted and were innocent of the crime for which they had been imprisoned. What was more, his statement exonerated not only the three survivors but also the men who had gone to their deaths. He showed that the court, the prosecution, and the jury had yielded to the hysteria promoted by the press and the police, and that the entire machinery of justice had been perverted to grossly unjust ends. By implication at least, he was charging the community at large with judicial murder. No matter what the defendants had been accused of, he insisted, "they were entitled to a fair trial, and no greater damage could possibly threaten our institutions than to have the courts of justice run wild or give way to popular clamor."[25]

No one foresaw more clearly than Altgeld himself the consequences of his action. He knew that his political fortunes might hang on the release of the three men. The morning after the pardon,

Brand Whitlock met the governor near the state house as he was walking to work. Altgeld was on horseback and drew up for a word of greeting, smiling that "faint, wan smile" of his. "Well," said Whitlock, "the storm will break now." "Oh, yes," replied the governor. "I was prepared for that. It was merely doing right."[26]

The expected happened. The storm broke, and with a fury that never completely abated in Altgeld's lifetime. Newspapers throughout the country united in heaping abuse on the man who had "opened the gates" to anarchy. He was called everything from "a wild-haired demagogue" to "the Nero of the last decade of the nineteenth century," from an "enemy of society" to the "destroyer of American values." The *Toledo Blade* declared that he had "encouraged anarchy, rapine and the overthrow of civilization." The *Milwaukee Sentinel* feared that his pardon message would breed more anarchists "than all the speeches and writings of the men he has released." The *New York Sun* concluded a poem "To Anarchy" with the following lines:

> O wild Chicago, when the time
> Is ripe for ruin's deeds,
> When constitutions, courts, and laws
> Go down midst crashing creeds,
> Lift up your weak and guilty hands
> From out of the wreck of States,
> And as the crumbling towers fall down
> Write ALTGELD on your gates!

Suddenly Altgeld, who had spent all but the first three months of his life in the United States, was labeled a "foreigner," who, in the words of the *Washington Post*, had "little or no stake in the problem of American social evolution." To the *Chicago Tribune* he had not "a drop of true American blood in his veins. He does not reason like an American, does not feel like one, and consequently does not behave like one." Other papers called him a "socialist," an "anarchist," a "fomentor of lawlessness," an "apologist for murder."[27]

And so it went day after day, both in newspapers and in magazines. The pardon made Altgeld for a long time one of the most reviled men in America. Not since Lincoln had so much concentrated hate been focused on a public figure. The attack came from all sides and in every conceivable form. He was burned in effigy, denounced from the pulpit, and there was talk of starting a movement for his im-

424

peachment. Cartoonists portrayed him as a depraved terrorist, an instigator of bloodshed and evil. Dr. Lyman Abbott, who had supported the clemency movement in 1887 but opposed a pardon, branded him "the crowned hero and worshipped deity of the Anarchists of the Northwest." To Theodore Roosevelt he was "a friend of the lawless classes," a man who "condones and encourages the most infamous of murderers."[28]

What offended most of Altgeld's critics was not the pardon itself as much as the attack on the court and the police in his accompanying statement, still more the uncompromising bluntness with which it was phrased. Had he freed the anarchists merely as an act of mercy, had he composed a short note to the effect that the men were repentant and had suffered enough, and that justice had been adequately served, he would have been widely praised and little criticized. Instead, however, he had called the sanctity of the judicial process into question, and with a body of evidence so overwhelming that it could not be easily refuted. Many, including even Brand Whitlock and Clarence Darrow, while warmly applauding the pardon, were dismayed by the language in which Altgeld's message was couched, particularly in his attack on Judge Gary. The tone was wrong, said Samuel McConnell. It was too personal. There was "too much Altgeld and not enough Governor in it."[29]

Altgeld, however, stood his ground. To a reporter from the *Chicago Tribune* he declared: "I have done what I thought was right, and if my action was right, it will stand in the judgment of the people." When a New York correspondent asked him how he was enduring the criticism, he laughed and said: "Let them pitch in and give me the devil if they want to; they could not cut through my hide in three weeks with an axe."[30]

Altgeld, at the same time, took comfort in the praise which the pardon drew from radical and liberal elements. By setting the men free, wrote Benjamin Tucker, the governor had performed "an act of magnificent, if somewhat tardy, justice. It is the bravest act standing to the credit of a politician since Horace Greeley bailed Jefferson Davis."[31] Labor organizations, including the A F of L, passed acclamatory resolutions, and Samuel Gompers and John Swinton were among those who wrote to Altgeld to congratulate him for his action. Another was Matthew Trumbull, who, writing for the Amnesty Committee, said that the pardon was "an act of magnanimity and justice worthy of a brave and upright magistrate, fearless of popular clamor, actuated by a sense of duty and right, and a regard for the supremacy of the Constitution and the laws of Illinois." Dr. J. H. Greer, vice-president of the American Secular Union, rejoiced that "Illinois at last has a governor with backbone," ready to carry out the dictates of his conscience. The workers, he told Altgeld, would never forget him, and "as citizens, we are proud of you."[32]

Henry Lloyd, who "never ceased to feel deep reverence" for the man who issued the pardon, published a glowing tribute to Altgeld in the *Chicago Herald*:

> In overruling the injustice done by the—as to criminal matters— lower tribunals, including the Supreme Court, the Governor did a much greater thing than an act of justice or mercy to individuals, no matter how greatly wronged. As far as in him lay, he broke the wheels of a judge-made revolution which would deprive the people of trial by juries of their peers, would put upon the accused the burden in the Russian style of proving themselves to be innocent, would establish a precedent of introducing class distinction in the administration of justice, and in clear defiance of the Constitution would take away the rights of "speaking freely" and meeting in public, and place them at the mercy of the police, who are to tell "by ear" when the people shall speak or keep silence.[33]

Lloyd and his wife invited the Altgelds to "run away and hide" at their summer home, "The Wayside," until the storm had passed. The governor declined, but Mrs. Altgeld thanked the Lloyds for their "cheery message of sympathy, for just now kind words go a long way." Her husband, she added, said that, judging from the political climate, "it may not be long until the Altgelds take up their abode by the wayside."[34]

Most gratifying of all, perhaps, was the letter that Altgeld received from the pardoned men themselves, who had meanwhile returned to Chicago and resumed their interrupted lives. "Your Excellency," it read, has "given us back wife and children, home and liberty. You did this after having carefully considered the facts which could be known. Having weighed evidence against evidence you pursued the course dictated by your conscience, regardless of the torrent of abuse which you knew would be the consequence of your courage. This was the deed of a brave heart, and it will live as such in history."[35]

How much the pardon affected Altgeld's subsequent career is difficult to measure. Although he failed to be reelected as governor, it would be a mistake to write him off as a political cipher. For in the councils of his party he remained a powerful influence. During his term in office, he succeeded in enacting a program of reform that attracted nationwide attention. He wrote the Democratic platform for the national elections of 1896, and, according to one authority, "only the constitutional technicality of his German birth prevented his nomination for President."[36] For all the vilification in the press, moreover, a large body of citizens recognized him as their champion. "The newspapers, the profiteers, the money-mongers, and the pharisees fought him bitterly," observed Clarence Darrow, "but in the humble dwelling-places of the poor, in the factories and mills, among the failures, the misfits and despised, he was worshipped almost as a god. For the maimed and beaten, the sightless and voiceless, he was eyes and ears, and a flaming tongue crying in the wilderness for kindness and humanity and understanding."[37]

Altgeld's pardon of the anarchists, so bitterly resented at the time, came to be regarded as a wise and noble decision, one of the most courageous acts of justice performed by any man in American public life. Altgeld himself considered it the most noteworthy achievement of his entire career. Near the end of his life, when asked if he had ever regretted what he had done, he replied emphatically: "Never! Never! If I had the matter to act upon again tomorrow, I'd do it over again. . . . I knew that in every civilized land, and especially in the United States, would ring out curses loud and bitter against me for what I did. I saw my duty and I did it."[38] When Altgeld died in 1902 and his body lay in state in the Chicago Public Library, thousands of people lined up on Michigan Avenue in a cold March wind to pay their respects. "He was a man before he was a politician," said Lucy Parsons. "He was one of those rare characters who could remain true to his high ideals in spite of politics." Lizzie Holmes held a similar view. He was a wise and dauntless figure, she wrote of Altgeld, who "would have justice though the heavens fall."[39]

26 ‖ The Legacy

Following the pardon of the survivors, the Haymarket affair passed into history. But it had left an imprint on America that was never completely eradicated. Thereafter anarchism, in the public mind, was inseparably linked with terrorism and destruction. The image of the anarchist as a wild-eyed, foreign-looking maniac with a dynamite bomb in one hand and a pistol or dagger in the other became so firmly embedded in the popular consciousness that the passage of one hundred years has failed to alter it.

This image was reinforced by a series of crude psychological and anthropological treatises equating anarchism with depravity and violence. In 1891, for example, the well-known Italian criminologist, Cesare Lombroso, published a two-part article in the Chicago journal *The Monist* placing the anarchists among an hereditary "criminal type" distinguished by facial asymmetry, cranial deformities, skin discoloration, anomalies of the ears and nose, and the like. Karl Marx, by contrast, had "a very fine physiognomy," with his "very full forehead, bushy hair and beard, and soft eyes."[1]

It was left for Michael Schwab, then still confined in Joliet prison, to expose the absurdities of Lombroso's argument, pointing out, for instance, that Most's asymmetrical face was the result of an operation and not of heredity; that crime was to a great extent the product of environmental conditions; that in studying physiognomies one's judgment is colored by prejudice and emotion; that evidence may be easily and unconsciously selected to fit the desired conclusion; and that "anarchist" is an imprecise category that does not lend itself to scientific analysis.[2]

While Alexander Berkman called Lombroso a "learned donkey" and Kropotkin dismissed him as a "make-believe" savant,[3] his theories soon filtered down to the more popular journals and newspapers and furnished support for public hostility towards the anarchists. To Brand Whitlock this showed how labels can transform ordinary mortals into satanic monsters, into demons in human form. It taught him "the power of words, the force of phrases, the obdurate and terrible tyranny of a term. The men who had been hanged were called anarchists, when, as it happened, they were men, just men. And out of that original error in terminology there was evolved that overmastering fear which raved and slew in a frenzy of passion that decades hence will puzzle the psychologist who studies the mind of the crowd."[4]

Yet the anarchists were not the only object of persecution. The hysteria aroused by the bombthrowing, while it focused primarily on the more radical elements, was directed against workers of every ideology and affiliation. Not for nothing did John Swinton call the bomb "a godsend to all enemies of the labor movement." According to Terence Powderly, it "did more injury to the good name of labor than all the strikes of that year." To Samuel Gompers it "struck at the foundations of the organized labor movement." In particular, said Gompers, it "demolished the eight-hour movement." "The effect of that bomb," he wrote, "was that it not only killed the policeman, but it killed our eight-hour movement for that year and for a few years later, notwithstanding we had no connection with these people."[5]

On the other hand, the effect of the explosion on American labor must not be exaggerated. It did not in fact destroy the eight-hour movement, which soon revived, as Gompers himself noted, under the aegis of the A F of L. Labor, moreover, had made other gains during the months preceding the incident and by no means lost all of them in the reaction that followed. Yet Haymarket, it must be conceded, drove the fear of labor militancy deep into the nation's mentality; and though the tendency to blame industrial conflict on "foreign agitators" had already been evident for some time, it received a powerful impetus from the affair, so that, over the succeeding decades, the tensions generated by mass immigration and breakneck urban and industrial growth found release in retaliation against radicals. Anarchists and socialists in particular, and especially those of foreign birth, were made the scapegoat for mounting economic and social ills. "For years," as John Higham has noted, "the memory of Haymarket and the dread of imported anarchy haunted the American consciousness. No nativist image prevailed more widely than that of the immigrant as a lawless creature, given over to violence and disorder."[6]

Small wonder, then, that efforts to exclude foreign radicals from the country should have originated in the wake of the case. In 1888 a resolution was proposed in the House of Representatives calling for "the removal of dangerous aliens from the United States," but it failed to carry. The following year a bill was introduced in the Senate making it unlawful for "an avowed anarchist or nihilist or one who is personally hostile to the principles of the Constitution of the United States or to the forms of Government" to enter the country. It, too, however, failed to pass. In 1894, following a wave of assassinations in Europe, further bills were introduced in both houses to regulate the admission of undesirable aliens. The assassination of President McKinley in 1901 revived these efforts, and in 1903 Congress finally enacted an immigration law excluding anarchists from America's shores.[7]

Immediately after Haymarket, moreover, businessmen throughout the country closed ranks for the purpose of dealing more effectively with industrial unrest. Repressive measures against labor increased, and employers took advantage of the atmosphere of reaction to disrupt trade-union activity. "Since May last," wrote John Swinton in September 1886, "many corporations and employers' associations have been resorting to all sorts of unusual expedients to break up the labor organizations, whose strength has become so great within the past two or three years."[8] The use of Pinkertons, lockouts, blacklists, and anti-union oaths intensified. The courts convicted a growing number of union activists of incitement, intimidation, and rioting. State legislatures (Illinois's among them) adopted stronger conspiracy laws and other measures to curb labor activity. Beyond all this, efforts were begun to strengthen local police, state militias, and federal armed forces, supplemented by a host of vigilante groups, known usually as "Law and Order Leagues," armed with rusty rifles of the Grand Army of the Republic. Wealthy citizens in Chicago donated land and money to establish Fort Sheridan and the Great Lakes Naval Training Station, while elsewhere private subscriptions built and equipped new city armories.[9]

Symbolic of the mood was the erection in Haymarket Square of a memorial to the policemen killed in the May 4 encounter. Funds for this purpose were raised by a group of Chicago businessmen headed by Richard T. Crane, next to whose factory the melee had occurred. Dedicated on Memorial Day 1889, the imposing bronze statue, designed by Charles F. Batchelder, showed a policeman with his right arm upraised commanding peace in the name of the people.

The sixteen-year-old son of Officer Degan performed the unveiling before a crowd of 2,000 onlookers.[10] During the Chicago World's Fair of 1893, the model for the statue, Patrolman Thomas J. Birmingham, was stationed in the Haymarket and described the episode to thousands of visitors. A few years later, however, he was dismissed from the force for consorting with known criminals and trafficking in stolen goods. He died a pauper in Cook County Hospital in 1912, having been a drunk on skid row for many years.[11]

Over the years the statue itself was plagued with troubles. In 1903 the crest of the city and state was stolen from its base. In 1925 it was knocked over by a streetcar that had jumped the tracks. Restored, it was moved to Union Park and years later to a special platform built for it during the construction of the John F. Kennedy Expressway. At the time of the Vietnam War, the statue drew nationwide attention as the focus of numerous protests, especially during the conspiracy trial of the so-called Chicago Seven stemming from disorders at the Democratic National Convention. On May 4, 1968, the eighty-second anniversary of Haymarket, the statue was defaced with black paint after a clash between anti-war demonstrators and the police. On October 6, 1969, during the "Days of Rage" protests against the war, the monument was shattered by an explosive charge placed between the legs of the figure. Nearly a hundred windows in the area were broken, and pieces of the statue were showered onto the Kennedy Expressway, the Weatherman faction of the Students for a Democratic Society claiming credit for the deed. The statue was quickly restored, only to be blown up a year later, once again by the Weathermen. After the second bombing, Mayor Richard J. Daley denounced the perpetrators as "evil creatures who work in the dark," and he ordered the statue to be rebuilt.[12] At the rededication ceremony, Daley vowed that the monument "will always remain as a testimonial of the people's gratitude to the police," and he placed it under twenty-four-hour protection. This, however, proved too costly, and in February 1972 the statue found a permanent haven in the lobby of Chicago police headquarters.[13]

With the labor movement everywhere under attack, more than a few workingmen, anxious to escape the onus of dynamite, severed their radical connections. In November 1887, for instance, a member of the Boston Anarchists' Club requested that his name be stricken from the rolls. "I cannot afford to be known as an *Anarchist*," he wrote to A. H. Simpson, now the secretary of the group. "It seems to me little short of madness to use the term."[14] Other workmen took a similar course, some turning to the "pure and simple" unionism of the A F of L, which was to dominate the labor scene for the next half-century.

Particularly hard hit by desertions were the Knights of Labor, although Haymarket was not the sole cause. The return of economic prosperity, friction between leadership and rank and file, Powderly's opposition to strikes and to the eight-hour crusade, to say nothing of his stand with regard to the convicted anarchists, all went far to undermine the organization's strength. After 1886, in any event, membership in the Knights declined sharply, and the Order soon ceased to exist as a significant force. Not surprisingly, popular revulsion against labor militancy extended to the IWPA. After Haymarket, its influence dwindled rapidly, and, although it clung to life until the eve of the First World War, it never again played an important role in the labor movement.

It would be wrong, however, to conclude that Haymarket precipitated the downfall of American anarchism. On the contrary, the incident and its sequel, so prominently reported in the press, kindled widespread interest in anarchist personalities and ideas and did more to disseminate the anarchist message than all the speeches of the Internationalists, all their rallies and demonstrations, of the preceding years. As John Henry of the American Group put it, "the bomb which exploded in Chicago spread more knowledge of the Anarchistic doctrine than endless harangues would have done."[15] Adolph Fischer, after the trial, underscored this point: "Thousands of workingmen have been led by our 'conviction' to study anarchism, and if we are executed, we can ascend the scaffold with the satisfaction that by our death we have advanced our noble cause more than we could have possibly done had we grown as old as Methuselah."[16]

In some places, to be sure, the movement had received a setback. This was especially true of Chicago, where, having been deprived of its principal leaders, it did not regain its former influence. Faced with continuous police harassment, the Chicago anarchists toned down their revolutionary propaganda and in general became more circumspect and subdued, so that the center of activity shifted to New York and other locations. Yet even in Chicago itself the movement remained strong for many years, with the appearance of new groups and publications and the founding of Anarchist Sunday Schools in different parts of the city, directly inspired by the Haymarket executions. And if the IWPA faded after 1886, this was less the result of Haymarket than of shifting patterns of immigration, which saw a decline of Germans, Bohemians, and Britons, who had formed the backbone of the organization, and a rise of southern and eastern Europeans, in particular Italians, Russians, and Jews, who provided the anarchist movement with a new generation of recruits. In terms of both membership and activity, it is safe to say, anarchism in America reached its zenith only after the Haymarket episode, i.e., between the late 1880s and the First World War, when new groups and periodicals proliferated and the movement attained its fullest flowering.

Haymarket itself, to a notable extent, was responsible for this resurgence. The unfairness of the trial, the savagery of the sentences, the character and bearing of the defendants fired the imagination of young idealists and won numerous converts to the anarchist cause. "Many of our most intelligent and earnest workers," noted William Holmes in 1897, "were brought to us as a result of the Chicago judicial murder. Who that reads these lines has not gained a near friend and comrade by that crime?" "It was the 11th of November, 1887," declared one convert at a Haymarket commemoration, "that made me an anarchist." "And us, too!" the audience responded.[17]

It is impossible to know the number of individuals whose political awakening stemmed from the Haymarket episode. But they included many well-known figures, among them Emma Goldman. Deeply affected by the case, she read everything about it that she could lay her hands on. "I devoured every line on anarchism I could get, every word about the men, their lives, their work," she writes in her memoirs. "I read about their heroic stand while on trial and their marvellous defense. I saw a new world opening before me." When the executions came her spirits were crushed, and yet she felt that "something new and wonderful had been born in my soul. A great ideal, a burning faith, a determination to dedicate myself to the memory of my martyred comrades, to make their cause my own, to make known to the world their beautiful lives and heroic deaths." For the rest of her life she would remember November 11, 1887, as the day of her "spiritual birth" and the death of her comrades as "the most decisive influence in my existence." "As to myself," she wrote in 1930, "I wish to say that the trial and death of the Chicago Anarchists decided my life and activities. In fact, the Chicago tragedy

433

was the awakening of my social consciousness. I may also say that it had the same effect on hundreds, perhaps thousands, of people. I myself know a great many persons whose lives were moulded by the judicial murder of the martyrs."[18]

One of these was Alexander Berkman, her closest companion in the movement, who had immigrated to America barely three months after the hanging. He too was deeply stirred by the case, still the subject of heated discussion when he arrived. "I immediately became interested in it," he later recalled. "I carefully studied all its angles. I became convinced that a great injustice had been committed, that innocent men had been hanged because they had championed the cause of labor." For Berkman, as for Emma Goldman, the life and death of the Chicago anarchists remained "a potent and vital inspiration." He too was seized with a determination to dedicate himself to their cause, to devote his life to the ideals for which they had so heroically perished.[19]

Nor were Goldman and Berkman isolated examples. Another notable convert was Voltairine de Cleyre, whom Goldman called "the greatest woman Anarchist of America."[20] As with Goldman and Berkman, Haymarket remained permanently embedded in her consciousness and runs like a scarlet thread through her writings. She dedicated a poem to Governor Altgeld when he pardoned Fielden, Neebe, and Schwab, and yet another after his death in 1902. She wrote a poem to Matthew Trumbull, whose pamphlets had aroused public attention to the injustices of the case. For the epigraph of her poem "The Hurricane" she quoted the prophecy of Spies: "We are the birds of the coming storm." And nearly every year she took part in memorial meetings for her comrades, delivering moving and deeply felt orations, the most powerful of her career.[21]

Similarly for William D. Haywood, leader of the Industrial Workers of the World, Haymarket was the decisive event in shaping his radical convictions. He talked about the case incessantly and thought about it every day. Who threw the bomb? he wondered. Why did the police march on the meeting? Why were the authorities "so anxious to hang these men called anarchists?" The last words of Spies, Haywood afterwards remembered, "kept running through my mind: 'There will come a time when our silence will be more powerful than the voices you are strangling today.' It was a turning point in my life."[22]

Such examples could be easily multiplied, in Europe as well as in

America. For, since the Paris Commune of 1871, no event had exercised a more powerful influence on the international anarchist movement. As the London *Freedom* phrased it, "no event in the world-wide evolution of the struggle between Socialism and the existing order of society has been so important, so significant, as the tragedy of Chicago."[23] Pamphlets and articles about the case appeared in every language, as did the speeches and autobiographies of the victims. Moreover, May First, the day of international working-class solidarity, became inextricably linked with the Haymarket episode, having grown out of the eight-hour struggle that centered in Chicago on May 1, 1886.[24]

As a result, in the words of the London *Freedom*, "thousands and tens of thousands" of workingmen flocked to the anarchist banner, and the names of the Chicago martyrs were "engraved on the hearts of all those who struggle for freedom."[25] Samuel Gompers provided interesting confirmation. Visiting a number of European cities in 1895, he noticed that "in nearly every labor hall there were pictures of Parsons, Spies, Lingg, etc., and with an inscription: 'Labor's Martyrs to American Capitalism.' " On later visits, added Gompers, "I have seen the same pictures still there."[26]

Nor was the impact of Haymarket limited to Europe. It was felt as well in other parts of the world, from South America to the Far East. By 1912, as an associate of Emma Goldman noted, the speeches of the Chicago anarchists were being read by the youth of China, Japan, Egypt, and Persia; and in 1926 the Chinese writer Pa Chin produced a concise history of the case, illustrated with portraits of the executed men.[27]

In Latin America the tragedy struck deep roots. Enrique Flores Magón, the celebrated Mexican revolutionary, was ten years old when Parsons, Spies, Engel, and Fischer were hanged. His father spoke of them as martyrs, who had sacrificed their lives to save the poor. As he listened, Flores Magón later remembered, he wondered "how the bodies of the hanged men must have looked, dangling to and fro from the ends of ropes fastened to the branches of a tall, leafy oak, as men are hanged in Mexico." He thought of them accepting their fate "with manly poise, serene, smiling, conscious of the end, but conscious also of the immortality of their Ideals for which they were made to die."[28]

Many years later, on May 1, 1924, the American poet Witter Bynner, together with D. H. Lawrence and his wife Frieda, was in a town near Mexico City where a cornerstone was laid for a statue to "The Martyrs of Chicago," followed by a parade in the capital. At the ceremony, Bynner recalls, much was said about the "shameless and villainous" murder which, thirty-seven years after, continued to stir "all Mexico" to protest.[29] During a trip to Mexico City in 1939, Oscar Neebe's grandson was shown a mural by Diego Rivera in the Palace of Justice depicting the story of the Haymarket anarchists. Afterwards he attended a May Day celebration and saw, as a relative of his put it, "how the world shows respect to your grandfather."[30]

How can these emotions be explained? Why did the Haymarket episode make such a powerful and lasting impression? Others had died for the people, observed Kropotkin on the first anniversary of the hanging, but none had been "so enthusiastically adopted by the workers as *their* martyrs." Why should this be so? Surely the epic character of their story was partly responsible, with its imagery of self-sacrifice and human redemption. George Schilling thought it nothing less than "the chief tragedy of the closing years of the nine-teenth century."[31] For Kropotkin, however, the answer lay in the moral qualities of the executed men. "The workmen knew that our brethren were thoroughly *honest*," he explained. "Not one single black spot could be detected in their lives, even by their enemies. Not one single black spot!" What was more, "they had no ambition. They were Anarchists and understood when they became Socialists that it was not that they might climb themselves upon the shoulders of their fellow-workers. . . . They sought no power over others, no place in the ranks of the ruling classes." Nor did they cease to uphold the principles for which they had been convicted. They proclaimed them "during the terrible year spent on the threshold of death; they proclaimed them on the scaffold, and they hailed the day on which they died for those principles as the happiest of their lives. Such men *can* inspire the generations to come with the noblest of feelings. And so they do, and will do." Kropotkin often repeated these sentiments. The heroism and integrity of the Haymarket martyrs, he declared a decade later, "remain a lesson for the old, an inspiration for the young."[32]

27 ‖ THE BOMBTHROWER

Who threw the Haymarket bomb? Was it an act of private retaliation or of public protest? To this day, one hundred years after the event, the matter has not been resolved. Both the identity and the motive of the assailant have remained a mystery, and the likelihood of clearing it up beyond any shadow of doubt has faded with the passage of time. Yet, if the whole truth may never be known, we are by no means completely in the dark. For, as will be seen in a moment, important evidence previously unknown or overlooked points strongly in a single direction.

There have been many theories about the bombthrower and his motive. Governor Altgeld in his pardon message suggested that the perpetrator was a disgruntled workman who had been beaten by the police and was bent on settling accounts.[1] This, however, was mere conjecture, without the least proof being offered to substantiate it. Another theory, likewise unsupported by concrete evidence yet widely credited in labor and radical circles, was that the act had been committed by an *agent provocateur* in order to destroy the eight-hour movement. "We believe firmly," proclaimed the *Workmen's Advocate*, "that the bomb was thrown by a Pinkerton."[2]

Parsons also adhered to this view. In his speech before Judge Gary he declared that the deed had been "instigated by eastern monopolists to produce public sentiment against popular movements, especially the eight-hour movement then pending, and that some of the Pinkertons were their tools to execute the plan." Captain Black was of the same opinion. For "reasons which are cogent with me," he wrote to Henry Lloyd in 1893, "I have always had great doubt as to whether that bomb was thrown by an anarchist at all; as to whether it was not thrown by a police minion, for the purpose of breaking up the eight-hour movement."[3]

Parsons, citing the testimony of one John Philip Deluse, alleged that the bombthrower had been sent from New York City to carry out his deadly mission. Deluse, a saloonkeeper in Indianapolis, had made an affidavit, supported by two witnesses, that on May 1, 1886, a stranger came into his place carrying a satchel, which he set on the bar while he ordered a drink. The stranger said that he came from New York and was on his way to Chicago, and he spoke of the labor troubles there. Pointing to his satchel he said: "I have got something in here that will work. You will hear of it." The man finished his drink. Then, turning at the door as he went out, he held up the satchel and said: "You will hear of it soon."[4] The description of this man tallied with that given by John Bernett, a witness at the Haymarket trial, who had been standing directly behind the bomb-thrower when the missile was flung. Yet, if the stranger and the bombthrower were indeed one and the same person, no proof was offered by Parsons or anyone else that he was acting at the behest of big business.

The police, for their part, insisted that the bomb had been thrown by an anarchist, Rudolph Schnaubelt usually being named. Suspicion had focused on Schnaubelt because of his disappearance from Chicago after the incident. Innocent men do not run when a crime is committed; they stay and face the music. So it was argued by the police. Besides, had Schnaubelt not left the speakers' wagon only moments before the explosion? Did not his height and powerful frame—he was over six feet tall and weighed more than 200 pounds—account for the missile's deadly accuracy? Was he not by temperament and ideology perfectly suited for the role?

Schnaubelt himself, from his place of sanctuary, categorically denied that he was the bombthrower. "Had I in fact thrown the bomb," he wrote in April 1887, "I would surely have no reason to be ashamed. As it was, such an act had never occurred to me."[5] The police, however, insisted that he was the guilty party. "There is no doubt," declared Captain Schaack, "that he threw the fatal bomb." According to Schaack, moreover, Balthasar Rau, under questioning, had admitted that Schnaubelt (in company with Engel) had tested bombs at Sheffield, Indiana, across the Illinois border.[6]

Nor were the police alone in pointing the accusing finger at Schnaubelt. George Schilling and Ernst Schmidt held the same view, as did the reporter Charles Edward Russell, although for differing reasons. That Schnaubelt, who had been taken into custody after the bombthrowing, should have been released hours later, at a time when the police were arresting and holding all the anarchists they could get their hands on, raised the suspicion in some quarters that he was a spy. "Could it be," asked Dr. Schmidt, "that he had acted as an *agent provocateur* for certain interests that wanted to get rid of the men who were agitating for eight-hour workdays and better living conditions for the laboring man?"[7]

Yet all this was sheer speculation and utterly without foundation. There is not a shred of evidence that Schnaubelt hurled the explosive or committed any other violent act. Nor did he fit the description of the bombthrower given at the trial by John Bernett, the only impartial witness who claimed to have seen him. Suspicion, we have noted, had fallen on Schnaubelt because he had fled the city. But innocent men also flee—from fear of being unjustly accused. Witness the examples of Parsons and Rau, neither of whom threw the bomb. Might not Schnaubelt's disappearance have been caused by his fear of the kind of justice he would receive amid the hysteria that followed the explosion, a fear soon to be borne out by the fate of his comrades? Further, would Schnaubelt have seated himself on the speakers' wagon if he was carrying a bomb in his pocket? Even more, would he have gone to police headquarters the day after the incident to try to secure Schwab's release? These questions alone would suffice to cast doubt on the accusations against him. But beyond this there is further evidence, to be considered presently, that points to quite another hand than his.

When Schnaubelt left Chicago, it will be recalled, he made his way to England, then to Argentina. Gradually his name sank into oblivion, forgotten even by the authorities. Twenty years later, however, it suddenly reappeared before the public when, in 1908, the English writer Frank Harris published *The Bomb*, a fictionalized treatment of the case. In the opening lines of the book Harris has Schnaubelt confessing on his deathbed to being the bombthrower: "My name is Rudolph Schnaubelt. I threw the bomb which killed eight policemen and wounded sixty in Chicago in 1886. Now I lie here in Reichholz, Bavaria, dying of consumption under a false name, in peace at last."[8]

With the appearance of *The Bomb* old questions came rushing back. Was Schnaubelt's flight not an implicit confession of guilt? Was he not indeed the bombthrower, as the police had all along maintained? But Max Baginski, a well-informed German anarchist and colleague of Emma Goldman, ridiculed Harris's story. "As a matter of fact," he pointed out, "Schnaubelt never lived in Germany, nor is he dead." Nor, Baginski added, did he throw the bomb.[9] Lucy

Parsons, years later, joined in the attack. At the time that Harris had Schnaubelt making his deathbed confession in Bavaria, he was, she insisted, alive and well in California and had a family of grown children. She knew this, she said, because she had personally met him there.[10]

Now it is true, as Lucy Parsons maintained, that Schnaubelt was alive and in good health when Harris's book appeared in print. But she was mistaken that she had met him in California. Apparently she was confusing him with his brother Edward, who had also been an Internationalist in Chicago at the time of the Haymarket affair and who had afterwards moved to California and raised a family. In 1913, it might be mentioned, Edward Schnaubelt was driven off his homestead by land speculators and shot down in cold blood while his two young sons scurried to safety. His tombstone, in the town of Trinidad, reads: "Murdered by Capitalism."[11]

His brother Rudolph, however, never returned to the United States. He spent the rest of his days in Argentina, becoming a manufacturer of machinery and farm equipment. His business prospered, and he married a young German woman, a native of Berlin, with whom he had three children. A photograph taken in Buenos Aires about ten years after his flight from Chicago shows him, surrounded by his family, as the model of bourgeois respectability. About 1915 his sister, Maria Schwab, traveled to Argentina and saw him for the first time in three decades. Following her return to America she corresponded with him regularly until her death in 1927, after which contact between the families was lost.[12]

Two subsequent events are worthy of mention. In 1932 a letter purporting to be from Rudolph Schnaubelt was received by Ray G. Schroeder, a commentator for radio station WIL in St. Louis. The writer, confessing to the Haymarket bombing, claimed to have settled in St. Louis in 1890 and amassed a small fortune in the intervening years. Complaining of failing health, he expressed a desire to leave his money to the state of Illinois or the city of Chicago as restitution for the wrong he had done.[13] The letter, however, savoring of Harris's *The Bomb*, was plainly a fabrication.

The second incident occurred in 1942, when another Rudolph Schnaubelt, some forty years younger than the alleged bombthrower, was questioned by the Federal Bureau of Investigation in connection with the Haymarket explosion. The agents, totally ignorant of the circumstances of the case, suspected him of being the perpetrator, although he had in fact been born fully two decades after the incident.[14] At the time of the questioning, in all probability, both the older Rudolph Schnaubelt and the actual bombthrower were no longer among the living.

But to eliminate Schnaubelt as a suspect is not to say that the bombthrower was not an anarchist. Indeed, not a few anarchists themselves believed—or at any rate hoped—that someone from their ranks was responsible. The police, they maintained, had got what was coming to them, not merely for invading a peaceful meeting, but for past atrocities committed against the workers. For once the brutality had been punished. "The police of Chicago have learned that they may not always have things their own way," as William Holmes expressed it. "They have learned, too late for some of them, that there is virtue in a dynamite-bomb when thrown by a practiced hand."[15]

Holmes was not alone in this opinion. "The bomb in Chicago was legally justified," exulted Johann Most in the *Freiheit*, "and, in a military sense, excellent. All honor to him who produced and made use of it." George Brown, in a similar vein, was impressed by "the dramatic precision with which the bomb was thrown and the exact justice it wrought."[16] Among the Haymarket defendants, Spies and Engel felt that it had saved more lives than it had destroyed. If the bomb had not been thrown, said Engel, "at least 300 workingmen would have been killed or wounded by the police." The police had wanted blood, added Engel, but what they got was a taste of their own medicine. "It came out differently, and that is what the police were so enraged about. They intended to slaughter the workingmen, but were disappointed."[17] There are those, wrote Charles Doering of Portland, who insist that it was the work of a paid hireling, but "let me cherish the belief that it was an anarchist who returned force with force." T. P. Quinn of New York only regretted that "there were not enough such men and such bombs to wipe out of existence every traitor to free speech and human liberty in the advancing column on that night."[18]

Assuming that the perpetrator was in fact an anarchist, as militants like Doering so fervently wished, what had prompted him to act? One theory is that he had read an uncorrected copy of the Haymarket circular, instructing the workers to come to the meeting with arms (*"Workingmen Arm Yourselves and Appear in Full Force"*).

Although the circular with the offending line had been suppressed, a few hundred had nevertheless been distributed, and one of these may have fallen into the hands of the bombthrower. Or perhaps, to cite an alternative hypothesis, he had seen the code-word "Ruhe" in the *Arbeiter-Zeitung*, the signal for the militants to appear with arms, and was not notified by Rau that it had been inserted in error.

William Holmes, according to the historian Max Nettlau, adhered to the latter explanation. In the summer of 1888, says Nettlau, William Morris received a letter from Holmes, who was then in regular correspondence with Morris's Socialist League. Holmes wrote that, shortly before the Haymarket incident, the Chicago militants had decided to answer further police violence in kind, but that on May 4 the decision was rescinded. One of the militants, however, had not been informed of the change of plans, and when the police advanced on the meeting he threw the bomb.[19] It is not known whether this was mere conjecture on Holmes's part or whether it was based on actual knowledge. His letter, unfortunately, has not survived.

There is other evidence, however, that may help to clarify the matter. This evidence consists of statements by Robert Reitzel and Dyer Lum, both of whom were in close touch with the militant wing of movement. When Reitzel returned to Detroit after the funeral, he told a fellow anarchist, Dr. Urban Hartung: "The bombthrower is known, but let us forget about it; even if he had confessed, the lives of our comrades could not have been saved."[20] This statement strongly suggests that the bombthrower was an anarchist; and the suggestion is supported by Lum, who, both in published articles and private correspondence, reveals that he knew the identity of the assailant and that he was an anarchist militant.

Lum's fullest statement to this effect occurs in an essay on Spies which he published in 1891 in the semi-anarchist journal *Twentieth Century*. On the afternoon of May 4, he writes, Spies had dispatched Rau with instructions to notify all militants that no arms were to be brought to the Haymarket. But, Lum goes on, "one man disobeyed that order; always self-determined, he acted upon his own responsibility, preferring to be prepared for resistance to onslaught rather than to quietly imitate the spiritual 'lamb led to slaughter.' " This man, of whose action Lum plainly approved, was the bombthrower. At that time, says Lum, none of the eight defendants knew who threw the bomb, and only two of them would ever find out, "but neither Spies nor Parsons was one of these." (The two, it would appear, were Fischer and Engel.) Lum, "by way of comment upon the perspicacity of the Chicago detectives," adds the following: "the man who did thus resist an unjustifiable invasion of a meeting, which the mayor of the city had fifteen minutes before pronounced 'peaceable and orderly,' was never mentioned in the trial and is today unknown to the public."[21]

Lum does not, of course, name the bombthrower, who would have been liable to prosecution. Yet several conclusions may be drawn from what he does tell us. First, the bombthrower was an anarchist, and probably a German, a member of the armed sections contacted by Rau. Second, he was someone who was known in the movement ("always self-determined," in Lum's description), although, since his name did not come up at the trial, he was not one of the defendants, nor any other figure of prominence in the case, including Schnaubelt. His identity, moreover, remained unknown to all but a tiny circle of militants, among them Lum and Reitzel and probably Engel and Fischer. To this may be added a physical description, if the testimony of John Bernett may be accepted as accurate: he was five feet nine or ten inches tall and wore a mustache but no beard.

Lum rejoiced in his heart that it was an anarchist who had thrown the bomb. He was proud of this fact, believed it to be fitting and just, and was itching to proclaim it before the world. He regretted only that it was an isolated act, and that "there was not proper organization with it."[22] At times he seemed on the verge of telling the whole story. It was "puerile," he wrote on one occasion, to attribute the bomb to a Pinkerton, implying that an anarchist had done the deed.[23] But he shrank in the end from saying more, having already, he doubtless thought, said quite enough.

Nor is there any need to question his statements on the subject. Not only was there no apparent reason for him to invent them, but he was uniquely informed on the inner workings of the movement ("He was the confidant of Parsons in his last hours," noted a reporter for the *Chicago Herald*, "and is probably in possession of more of the secrets of the Anarchists who were executed than any other living Anarchist in Chicago"). Moreover, his reputation for honesty was without blemish. Lum, as Voltairine de Cleyre put it, was "one who never lied." What was more, his public utterances regarding the bombthrower coincided with what he revealed in his private correspondence, in particular with Voltairine de Cleyre.[24]

To Voltairine, with whom he was on intimate terms, Lum told

what he knew about the case, and in after years fragments cropped up in her memorial speeches. Thus, on November 11, 1899, she declared: "the time has gone past when one should stand up and say, as has been said in the past, that 'the Haymarket bomb was a police plot.' The police never plotted anything half so just! The Haymarket bomb was the defense of a man who stood upon the constitutional declaration that the right of free speech, and the right of people peaceably to assemble, shall not be abridged."[25] Emma Goldman, who had known both Lum and de Cleyre as well as Reitzel, echoed these words years later when she confided to her lover, a Chicago osteopath, that the bombthrower had indeed been an anarchist.[26]

While Lum refrained from naming the bombthrower, others suggested Rheinhold Krueger ("Big Krueger," as he was known in the International), although without offering the least supporting evidence. Indeed, where Lum, writing in 1891, intimates that the assailant was still alive, Krueger, a Chicago militant, had been killed by a policeman's bullet in the melee following the Haymarket explosion.[27] Two further candidates may be disposed of for lack of proof: Thomas Owens, a carpenter from Homestead, Pennsylvania, who confessed on his deathbed to the deed; and Klimann Schuetz of New York, the subject of the eleventh-hour telegram with which Captain Black sought to delay the execution.[28]

A likelier possibility, although the evidence is far from satisfactory, was a certain George Schwab (no relation to Michael or Justus), whose name did not come to light until 1933, when someone proposed that the veterans of 1886-1887 hold a reunion in Chicago, where the World's Fair was to take place. Taking up this suggestion, Carl Nold, a well-known German anarchist from Detroit, wrote to a few of his old comrades, one of whom, Claus Timmermann, replied: "The old timers are mostly dead, including the bomb thrower, who died in 1924 in the Poor hospital in Blackwell's Island, without leaving anything behind."[29]

Nold, intrigued by this remark, pressed Timmermann for further information. Timmermann, the former editor of a journal called *Der Anarchist*, the successor of Engel and Fischer's paper of the same name, had long been associated with the autonomist wing of the movement, a champion of dynamite and insurrection. In his answer to Nold he identified the bombthrower as George Schwab, a German shoemaker and ultramilitant, whom he had known for many years, and who had been a member of the Schlüsselbein (Collarbone) Group in New York, to which only "the most desperate" comrades belonged. Although Timmermann himself had no proof that Schwab was the actual bombthrower, he had been so informed by August Lott, another German militant, to whom Schwab had confessed the deed. Schwab, according to Lott's story, had gone to Chicago from New York on May 1, 1886, and left for California the morning after the explosion, remaining there until 1900, when he finally returned to New York.[30]

Schwab, if indeed the bombthrower, held his tongue for a long time ("If a person wants to commit a revolutionary act," wrote Most in *Revolutionary War Science*, "he should not talk to others but go about it in silence").[31] It was only after the legal appeals had been exhausted, and when the lives of his comrades stood in immediate jeopardy, that he informed the inner circle of his role. It was decided, however, not to bring him forward. The defendants, it was felt, could not be saved. It would "only mean one more victim."[32]

It remains, by way of conclusion, to account for the survivors of the Haymarket tragedy, above all Fielden, Neebe, and Schwab. What became of the three men after their pardon by Governor Altgeld? In all the furor aroused by Altgeld's pardon message, their activities after their release were hardly noticed. And this was the way they preferred it. From the moment of their liberation from prison they conducted themselves with circumspection. Indeed, to avoid a scene at their arrival in Chicago, they alighted from the train in the freight yards outside the city and made their way on foot to their homes. Schwab resumed a measure of his former propaganda activity, but not with the same fervor as in the past. He spoke at a memorial meeting at Waldheim Cemetery on November 11, 1893, and wrote again for the *Arbeiter-Zeitung*, of which he had been associate editor before his arrest. But he found it hard to adjust. His six years behind bars had undermined his health. He seemed, noted William Holmes, like a man "broken by much suffering."[1]

In 1895, Schwab resigned from the *Arbeiter-Zeitung* and opened a shoe store on the North-West Side, where he carried a stock of books along with the regular line of wares. The business failed, however, and he became ill. Emma Goldman, while visiting Chicago in the spring of 1898, found Schwab in the hospital with tuberculosis, his body wasted, his cheeks flushed, his eyes "shining with the fatal fever in his blood." Yet he did not complain of his misfortunes. He said hardly anything about himself at all. Rather, "his ideal was uppermost in his mind, and everything bearing upon it was still his sole interest." Goldman felt a "feeling of awe" for the man whose "proud spirit" the authorities had failed to break.[2]

Schwab succumbed to his illness on June 29, 1898, and was buried at Waldheim with his comrades. He was forty-five years old and left a wife and four children, two of whom were born after his release from prison. One of the latter was named Johanna Altgeld Schwab in honor of the governor who had pardoned him. She grew up in San

Francisco and became a doctor and a noted humanitarian, assisting in the rescue of Jews from Europe during Hitler's persecutions.[3]

Neebe, whose wife had died while he was in Cook County Jail, leaving two girls and a boy, married a widow shortly after his pardon, who owned a saloon near the Chicago stockyards, which he operated for a number of years, living a quiet and respectable life. He became interested in the Populist movement and attended the 1907 convention of the Industrial Workers of the World, but on the whole his political activity was slight. He died on April 22, 1916, aged sixty-five, having been ill and half-blind for some time, and was interred, like Schwab before him, beside the Haymarket monument in Waldheim.[4]

Fielden, the last of the Haymarket anarchists to quit the scene, went back to his old job of hauling stone. After a short time, however, he received news that a relative in England had died and left him an inheritance. With the money thus obtained he moved his family to Colorado, purchased a ranch near La Veta, and took up the peaceful occupation of raising cattle and chickens. Finding little difficulty in making friends, he became a respected member of the community. "He is happily in possession of good health and spirits," wrote William Holmes, who had moved to the same locality, "and looks back upon his long years of imprisonment as upon a frightful dream. I have never had the idea that Sam is a hero worshipper, but I do know that his soul is filled with eternal gratitude for his brave deliverer—John P. Altgeld."[5]

Ten years after the pardon, in October 1903, J. William Lloyd was a guest of the Holmeses at La Veta, and they went up India Creek to visit Fielden's ranch. It was a scene of idyllic beauty, Lloyd recorded. Approaching Fielden's log cabin, they were greeted by the aging anarchist, wearing overalls and a cap and with a long white beard, still stocky and powerfully built. Hermit though he was, noted Lloyd, he was "up-to-date on all passing questions." Haymarket, however, continued to dominate his thoughts. Five years before, he had spoken at a memorial meeting in Denver and, according to William Holmes, who had been present, "seemed imbued with much of his old-time spirit and fire." Again, as in the 1880s, his body swayed with emotion, he gesticulated freely, and his voice "rang with indignation against the robbers and oppressors of the poor." Now, too, he reminisced about the tragedy. After dinner they all mounted horses and rode out on the beautiful mesas surrounding the ranch, conversing as they went. Fielden insisted, says Lloyd, that "there was no conspiracy, and that none of the leaders knew of the bombthrower or his intention; and so little did they anticipate violence that they brought their wives and little children to the meeting."[6]

Fielden ended his days in La Veta in quiet obscurity. He died on February 7, 1922, three weeks short of his seventy-fifth birthday, and was laid to rest in Colorado, the only one of the eight defendants not to be buried at Waldheim. He had lived long enough to hear of the arrest and trial of Nicola Sacco and Bartolomeo Vanzetti, who were to suffer the same fate as his comrades.

Among the other key figures in the case, the fate of Carter Harrison is worth noting. In 1887 Harrison withdrew from the mayoral race and embarked on a sixteen-month tour of the globe. He was elected again, for a fifth time, in 1893, but was shot to death on his doorstep by a disappointed office-seeker.[7] Julius Grinnell, the state's attorney, was elected judge of the Circuit Court of Cook County following his successful prosecution of the anarchists. "Tomorrow," warned the London *Anarchist*, "he will be 'bombed' from the Judgeship to a more elevated position still."[8] Grinnell, as it turned out, died peacefully in 1898, having earlier reentered private practice. Inspector Bonfield died the same year—"two infamous men," one anarchist journal called them[9]—and Governor Oglesby the year after. Judge Gary lived a long life, passing away in 1906 at the age of eighty-five. He held court on the day before his death, having occupied the bench for forty-three years.

For the friends and families of the Chicago anarchists, the case left a trail of shattered dreams and broken lives. Children were left orphans, wives widows, for whom to contemplate the agony of their loved ones was still painful many years later. Careers, in some instances, were damaged. Captain Black, who had been a partner in one of Chicago's most sucessful law firms, forfeited his lucrative practice as a result of his participation in the case. Not only was the partnership dissolved, but nearly all of his business clients abandoned him, so that for a number of years after the trial he could earn only a modest income. As Black wrote to Henry Lloyd in 1893, his connection with the defendants "left me in debt, without a business and without a clientage, and in a community all of whose wealthy citizens were in active hostility to me. I have had a somewhat uphill struggle in the years that have elapsed . . . and my time and energies have been taxed to the uttermost to make ends meet."[10]

With the passage of time, however, the hostility towards Black gradually diminished, and he managed to rebuild part of his practice. He even won praise in some quarters for his dignified conduct during the case. "He did what he considered his duty," wrote one Chicago editorialist, "as dauntlessly as he did when a soldier." Black's association with the anarchists had radicalized him to some degree. He spoke before labor groups and at meetings memorializing the defendants. At the same time, he retained his interest in conventional politics, campaigning for William Jennings Bryan in his presidential bids and running unsuccessfully for the office of circuit court judge, once as a Democrat and later on the United Silver ticket. By the time of his death in 1916, he was, however, a long-forgotten figure.[11]

For William and Lizzie Holmes the death of their comrades left a void that could never be filled. When they thought back on Parsons and the others, powerful emotions gripped their hearts. Year after year, as a form of catharsis, they wrote and spoke about the case. "History," said William in 1891, "records scarcely an instance of men so young, so gifted, so devoted, whose short lives were so full of effective work and whose deaths left such a deep impression on humanity."[12] Between 1890 and 1892, he and Lizzie helped get out the Chicago *Freedom*, a magazine edited by Lucy Parsons, and contributed to many other publications of the day. Not long after the pardon, however, they left Chicago for Colorado, where, according to J. William Lloyd, they were "popular and respected members of La Veta society."[13]

From La Veta the Holmeses moved to Denver, where William took up the practice of law. Their home, recalled Emma Goldman, became a haven for visiting anarchists, who found them, as she did, "persons of keen and clear minds," who remained as devoted to their ideal as "in the days when their faith was young and their hopes high."[14] Again and again, over the ensuing decades, their thoughts returned to the events of 1886-1887 and to the tragedy that had crushed their hearts, as Lizzie put it. In their lectures and writings a sad regret mingled with their memories as they looked back on "those stirring, enthusiastic days of fifteen and twenty years ago." Moving to New Mexico, the Holmeses lived to a ripe age, Lizzie dying in 1926 and William two years after.[15]

The fate of Nina Van Zandt was more tragic. Following the executions, she went into deep mourning. She hung a photograph of Spies in the parlor window of her father's house and for a time locked herself in against the outside world. Afterwards, although twice remarried and divorced, she continued to cherish Spies's memory, referring to him always "not only in terms of marked respect but in language of unaffected endearment."[16] After the death of her parents, who themselves had been devastated by the case, Nina was reduced to poverty. She moved to Halsted Street, where she opened a rooming house and eked out a shabby existence. For many years she spoke at Haymarket commemorations and marched in labor and radical demonstrations, often side by side with Lucy Parsons. The two fell out, however, and for a long time did not speak to each other.

In her later years, Nina lived amid "squalor and filth" in a ramshackle house on Morgan Street, surrounded by dozens of cats and dogs which she took in off the street. Towards the end, she and Lucy Parsons managed to patch up their differences and appeared again together at radical meetings. One such occasion was a gathering in her own honor arranged by the anarchists and IWWs of Chicago. Nina, the once glamorous and wealthy socialite, was "almost in rags and wearing men's shoes," noted the Wobbly poet Ralph Chaplin.[17] She died not long afterwards, on April 9, 1936, in her seventy-fifth year. A memorial meeting was held on April 12, at which Lucy Parsons, herself rapidly aging, was the principal speaker. "You and I, Comrade Nina, have passed along these fifty years together," she said. "Now the great curtain of mystery and death has fallen and you are beyond. It is only a matter of days and months or hours before I must render my account with nature. If there be another world, we will join hands and march on together, but I know nothing of that. Comrade Nina, fare thee well."[18]

The following day Nina was buried at Waldheim, not far from the Haymarket monument. It was a big funeral. The long procession of cars trailed past the Crane building and through the Haymarket, where the fateful incident had taken place fifty years before. At the cemetery "the old faithful of the past generation and some of the younger members of the revolutionary cult" gathered around the open grave, wrote Ralph Chaplin, who was one of the speakers. It was a bright spring day "with trees in bud and tulips ankle high around the curbing."[19]

450

With Nina gone, Lucy Parsons was the sole survivor among the many actors in the drama. Her life since the execution had been dogged by misfortune. Lulu, her daughter, "wonderfully bright in mind and amiable in disposition,"[20] did not survive childhood. She died at the age of eight of lymphedema, a disease of the lymph glands from which she had been suffering for many months, and was buried at Waldheim in an unmarked grave near that of her father and his comrades. William Holmes delivered a brief address (time was, he said, when Lulu was "the pride of a fond father's heart"), and Mrs. Kinsella sang "Annie Laurie" in a subdued voice, while Lucy, torn with grief, stood nearby.[21]

As if this were not enough, tragedy was visited also upon her son, Albert Jr., on whom she had set her hopes to avenge her husband's death. "What do you suppose I am raising him for?" she said to a reporter in 1888. "I shall teach him that his father was murdered and by whom! Those red-handed butchers had better look out!" At a memorial meeting some years later she expressed a similar idea: "I am the widow of Albert R. Parsons and the mother of his son. I charge the police and the court with murdering my husband. I live to bring up his son to take up the work which was stricken from his father's hands."[22]

Lucy, however, was doomed to disappointment. Not only did Albert Jr. begin to attend church and to develop an interest in spiritualism, but when he was eighteen, at the time of the Spanish-American War, he enlisted in the army over his mother's fierce opposition. In July 1899 she had him committed to the Illinois Northern Hospital for the Insane, where he spent the remainder of his life, dying there of tuberculosis in August 1919, a month short of his fortieth birthday. His body was cremated and the ashes kept by his mother at her home.[23]

How Lucy survived these blows is far from easy to explain. Possessed, however, of a burning sense of mission, she refused to yield to despair. For more than half a century following the Haymarket episode, she dedicated herself to vindicating her husband's memory, not only by publishing his speeches and writings, but also by ceaseless agitation for the cause for which he had died. She edited newspapers (Freedom, The Liberator, The Alarm), published books and pamphlets, traveled and lectured extensively, and took part in countless meetings and demonstrations in behalf of the working class. As before, she directed her energies to the poorest and most downtrodden elements of society, the unskilled, unemployed, and foreign-born, allying herself with every movement that championed their interests.

In 1905, together with such figures as Bill Haywood, Mother Jones, and Eugene Victor Debs, she took part in the founding convention of the Industrial Workers of the World in Chicago, whose delegates visited Waldheim Cemetery and laid a wreath at the Haymarket tomb. In a speech before the convention—which she attended, she told the audience, because she had "ears to hear the cry of the downcast and miserable of the earth"—she called for a program of "revolutionary socialism" that would usher in a society in which "the land shall belong to the landless, the tools to the toilers, and the product to the producers."[24]

Year after year Lucy traveled about the country, lecturing and selling literature, especially on the Haymarket case. She never ceased to excoriate those who had sent her husband to the scaffold, declaring that governments are "always wielded in the interests of the few and at the expense of the many," and that "men will abuse power when they possess it."[25] Wearing an old-fashioned dress and carrying her bundle of pamphlets wherever she went, she cut an exotic figure, "both frightening and beautiful in her intense earnestness," as Ralph Chaplin remarked. There was, thought Lucy Robins Lang, "something mysterious in her appearance that added to the air of tragedy that surrounded her." One newspaper called her the "Jeanne d'Arc of the Chicago anarchists."[26]

It was a stormy life, throughout which she had to fight that she might be heard. She was continually harassed by the authorities. More than once she was arrested for distributing literature "without a license,"[27] and nearly every time she tried to speak in Chicago she was interrupted, taken to the police station, charged with disorderly conduct, and then released. When she rose, for example, to address an open-air meeting in July 1900, she was struck on the shoulder by a police captain and instructed to "move on." Protesting against this interference with her constitutional rights, she was pushed to the sidewalk and threatened with having her teeth "knocked down her throat." Still resisting, she was thrown into a patrol wagon, and bystanders who protested were set upon and clubbed.[28]

Elsewhere her treatment was not much different. In Philadelphia and Newark, in Los Angeles and San Francisco, she was prevented from speaking and from selling her literature. At the Los Angeles police station a matron made her strip for a body search and tried to pull from her finger a ring given to her by her husband.[29] Beyond all this, she was cursed and maligned by anonymous correspondents. "You are a She renegade," wrote one. "Born of wolfish proclivities. A frequenter of dens of thieves. And murderess. Your parentage was enjendered [sic] in the Jungle along with the Hyena. And kindred carniverous [sic] animals."[30]

Yet Lucy remained undaunted. Until the 1920s, when her eyesight began to deteriorate, she wandered over the country in defense of labor causes. After the Russian Revolution she drifted towards the Communist camp, regarding the Soviet Union as "the land of promise."[31] Her last fifteen years were spent working closely with the Communists, and though she did not become a member of the party, she frequently spoke in its behalf. "While I don't belong to the Communist Party," she wrote to Carl Nold in 1930, "I have been working with them to some extent, as they are the *only* bunch who are making a vigorous protest against the present horrible conditions!" As for her anarchist comrades, they were adept only "at showing the shortcomings of other organizations," while themselves doing nothing to solve society's problems. "Anarchism," she lamented, "is a dead issue in American life today. . . . Despotism is on horseback, riding at high speed."[32]

In her declining years, Lucy was blind and grey, her body bent with the weight of her tragic life. "Well, dear old friend," she wrote to George Schilling in 1935, "how are you standing the racket in the evening of your life? Have things grown better or worse since you and I, fifty years ago, began to watch the human procession?" In her own view, things had gotten worse, what with the rise of Mussolini and Hitler and ruthless "money-mad maniacs" everywhere in command.[33] Yet her spirit never flagged. To the end she remained a steadfast rebel, taking part in left-wing rallies and marches to the extent that her strength permitted. On November 11, 1937, she addressed a fiftieth-anniversary Haymarket meeting at the Amalgamated Center on Ashland Boulevard, attended by an over-flow crowd, and took part in a ceremony at Waldheim Cemetery in which representatives from several countries participated, including a delegation from the CNT of Spain, then in the throes of civil war.

Lucy, at this time, lived in a small frame house on North Troy Street, where she kept the ashes of her son in a small urn and had a library of close to 3,000 volumes, devoted to "sex and socialism and anarchy."[34] On March 7, 1942, the final tragedy struck. Her wood stove accidentally caught fire and Lucy, nearing her ninetieth birthday, was trapped and burned to death. George Markstall, her companion for many years, died in an effort to save her. Lucy was buried a few days later next to the Haymarket monument. Her life, observed one newspaper, had been "one long battle with the established order of society."[35] Only a short time before her death, she had mounted a soapbox and delivered an impassioned speech to the striking workers of the International Harvester Company, the old McCormick Company, where Haymarket had all begun. She had served the cause of labor to the last.

Haymarket, with its manifold effects, was a major event in American history. For the first time it brought anarchism to the attention of the general public, identifying it with terrorist violence and inspiring a horror of its teachings and practices. Equally important, it marked the climax of one of the most bitter industrial struggles in America's experience, interrupting the eight-hour movement and turning labor away from radical doctrines for years to come. Haymarket, on the other hand, forms part of the foundation on which the heritage of American labor rests. For, besides its connection with the eight-hour struggle, it gave to the labor movement its first revolutionary martyrs, whose sense of outrage against economic and social injustice, whose vision of a society in which the resources of production are available for the benefit of all, provided a source of inspiration for workers of every stripe. As a modern libertarian summed it up: "The men of the Haymarket gave backbone to the whole movement of labor to stand up for its rights."[36]

Haymarket, at the same time, revealed the weaknesses of the anarchist movement. The anarchists, for all their dynamic energy, overestimated both the extent of their support and the effect of their propaganda among the workers. Organizationally they were too fragmented to exercise a sustained influence, while in their ideas they were too divided to mount a coherent agitational campaign. What was more, their advocacy of violence, even as a defensive measure, isolated them from the great majority of American citizens, who preferred peaceful reform to armed insurrection. George Schilling, in a remarkable letter to Lucy Parsons, underscored this point: "The open espousal of physical force—especially when advocated by foreigners—as a remedy for social maladjustments can only lead to greater despotism. When you terrorize the public mind and threaten the stability of society with violence, you create the conditions which place the Bonfields and Garys in the saddle, hailed as the saviors of society. Fear is not the mother of progress and liberty, but oft times of reaction and aggression. Your agitation inspires fear; it shocks the public mind and conscience and inevitably calls forth strong and brutal men to meet force with force. By your mistaken methods you have the misfortune of repelling those you should attract, of antagonizing where you should unite in mutual sympathy and cooperation for a common good."

To this Schilling added the following: "At Waldheim sleep five men—among them your beloved husband—who died in the hope that their execution might accelerate the emancipation of the world. Blessed be their memories and may future generations do full justice to their courage and motives, but I do not believe that the time will ever come when the judgment of an enlightened world will say that their methods were wise or correct. They worshipped at the shrine of force; wrote it and preached it; until finally they were overpowered by their own Gods and slain in their own temple. The revenge circular of August Spies was met by the revenge of the public mind, terrorized by fear until it reeled like a drunken man, and in its frenzy swept away the safeguards of the law and turned its officers into pliant tools yielding to its will."[37]

Schilling was by no means alone in his opposition to violent methods. Among the anarchists themselves there were those for whom the apocalyptic fervor of 1883-1886, the belief that the social revolution was imminent and physical force unavoidable, had begun to fade. Thus William Holmes could write in October 1892: "It is hardly necessary that we should refer to certain capitalists as scoundrels, dirty dogs, blood-sucking vampires, hyenas in human form, and, naming certain individuals, denounce them as not fit to live. It is not necessary that we should make threats, darkly hint at conspiracies to overthrow the capitalistic system, enter into details as to contemplated acts of destruction and the manner of conducting the social revolution, shout our defiance of the authorities, make an attempt to justify murder, or extoll the excellence of dynamite as a factor in the coming crisis. Much of this kind of agitation we have had in the past. And what have been its legitimate fruits? The scorn and hatred of the very class (the working people) whom we most desire to win; the bitter enmity and persecution of the authorities; the contempt of the capitalists; and the antagonism of all classes."[38]

Even Johann Most, although he never shed his belief in armed retaliation, came to realize that his was a voice crying in the wilderness, and that America was not to be the center of world revolution, as he had hoped. Most's thoughts turned increasingly across the ocean, back to the land from which he had come. As he wrote to Max Nettlau in October 1890, "I burn with the longing to return once more to action à la Marat, to throw myself anew into the whirlpool of revolution, which is possible only on European soil."[39] Most's yearnings, however, were never fulfilled. For the rest of his life he remained in the United States, subject to continual persecution. He collapsed and died in 1906, at the age of sixty, while on a lecture tour in Cincinnati.

Yet if Haymarket revealed the deficiencies of the anarchist movement, it also revealed the limitations of American justice. For, while the defendants had preached revolution and would have welcomed the forcible overthrow of the existing order, they nevertheless did not receive a fair trial, nor were they proven guilty of any crime. "I am sure," wrote Adolph Fischer to Governor Oglesby shortly before the hanging, "that coming ages will look upon our trial, conviction, and execution as the people of the nineteenth century regard the barbarities of past generations—as the outcome of intolerance and prejudice against advanced ideas."[40]

Although Haymarket was by no means the only instance where American justice has failed, it was nonetheless a black mark on a legal system that professes truth and fairness as its highest principles. The defendants, all dying like men, all protesting their innocence, were put to death with a ferocity that shocked the enlightened world. As a barbarous act of power it was without parallel in American legal history. Naked force, it appeared to many, was to be the final answer of the authorities when the dispossessed insisted on pressing their claims. For Alexander Berkman, deeply disturbed by the hanging, it was a striking illustration of the kind of justice that militant labor could expect from the capitalist system, "a demonstration of its class character and of the means to which capital and government will resort to crush the workers."[41]

But Haymarket was more than a test of the American judicial system. It threw a glaring light on the nation's moral condition, which likewise was found to be wanting. Its impact, moreover, was far reaching, engaging the passions of men and women around the world. To duplicate its repercussions one would have to look forward to the Sacco-Vanzetti case of the 1920s, when anarchists, during a time of anti-radical hysteria, were once again martyred following a tainted and prejudiced trial. Haymarket, for all these reasons, assumed the dimensions of historical tragedy. No one who was touched by it remained the same. It was, as contemporaries noted, the great social drama of the era. The London *Freedom* went even further: "Take all history, search all its pages, you will find nothing like what we saw that time in America!"[42]

NOTES

Chapter 1: An American Boyhood

1. *The Autobiographies of the Haymarket Martyrs*, ed. Philip S. Foner (New York: Humanities Press, 1969), p. 28.
2. *Appleton's Cyclopedia of American Biography*, 6 vols. (New York, 1888-1889), IV, 663; Alan Calmer, *Labor Agitator: The Story of Albert R. Parsons* (New York: International Publishers, 1937), p. 9; "Biographical: Brief Sketches of the Lives of the Chicago Martyrs," *Free Society*, November 6, 1898.
3. William H. Parsons, "Albert R. Parsons' Ancestors," *Life of Albert R. Parsons*, ed. Lucy E. Parsons, rev. ed. [1st ed., 1889] (Chicago: Lucy E. Parsons, 1903), p. 1; *Appleton's Cyclopedia*, IV, 663; C. S. Hall, *Life and Letters of Samuel Holden Parsons: Major General in the Continental Army and Chief Judge of the North-Western Territory, 1787-1789* (Binghamton, N.Y.: Otseningo Publishing Co., 1905).
4. There is some uncertainty about Parsons's date of birth. In some accounts it is given (apparently in error) as June 24, 1848, while the Montgomery County census of 1850 and Texas censuses of 1860 and 1870 list his age as five, fifteen, and twenty-four, respectively, which would put his birth in 1845. He and his brother William, however, always recorded the year as 1848. See Gary Goodman, "Albert R. Parsons in Texas: The Origins of a Radical Agitator," University of New Mexico, typescript, p. 34, a valuable paper with much interesting detail.
5. *Autobiographies of the Haymarket Martyrs*, p. 27; Calmer, *Labor Agitator*, pp. 9-10.
6. *Autobiographies of the Haymarket Martyrs*, p. 27; *Life of Albert R. Parsons*, pp. 1-2.
7. *The Famous Speeches of the Eight Chicago Anarchists in Court*, rev. ed. [1st ed., 1886] (Chicago: Lucy E. Parsons, 1910), p. 109.
8. *Life of Albert R. Parsons*, p. 311.
9. *The Knights of Labor*, November 6, 1886; *The Handbook of Texas*, ed. Walter Prescott Webb et al., 3 vols. (Austin, Texas: State Historical Society, 1952-1976), III, 324.
10. Quoted in Goodman, "Albert R. Parsons in Texas," p. 5.
11. *Autobiographies of the Haymarket Martyrs*, p. 28.

12. *Dictionary of American Biography*, VIII, 576-77; *Handbook of Texas*, II, 470-71; Carolyn Ashbaugh, *Lucy Parsons: American Revolutionary* (Chicago: Charles H. Kerr Publishing Co., 1976), pp. 13-14. During this period William Parsons himself published a secessionist paper in Waco called *The Southwest*.

13. *Autobiographies of the Haymarket Martyrs*, p. 28.

14, Ibid.

15. Ibid.

16. Ibid.

17. A colonel in the Confederate army, William Parsons was appointed acting brigadier general in 1862 and, while never permanently promoted to that rank, was thereafter known as "General Parsons." *Handbook of Texas*, III, 706; Stephen B. Oates, *Confederate Cavalry West of the River* (Austin: University of Texas Press, 1961), pp. 28, 49; John Q. Anderson, ed., *Campaigning with Parsons' Texas Cavalry Brigade, CSA* (Hillsboro, Tex.: Hill Junior College Press, 1967). General Parsons left an account of his unit's campaigns: *Condensed History of Parsons' Texas Cavalry Brigade* (1883).

18. *Workmen's Advocate*, October 29, 1887.

19. *Autobiographies of the Haymarket Martyrs*, p. 29; *Waco Day*, May 6, 1886; Goodman, "Albert R. Parsons in Texas," p. 12. On Burleson see *Dictionary of American Biography*, III, 287-88. *A Register of Baylor University*, III, 9, indicates that Parsons attended Waco University in 1865, 1866, and 1867. I am grateful to Virginia Ming of the Baylor University Texas Collection for this information.

20. *Louisville Courier-Journal*, September 21, 1886, quoted in *Life of Albert R. Parsons*, pp. 211-12.

21. *Autobiographies of the Haymarket Martyrs*, p. 29.

22. Albert R. Parsons, *Anarchism: Its Philosophy and Scientific Basis as Defined by Some of Its Apostles*, ed. Lucy E. Parsons (Chicago: Mrs. A. R. Parsons, 1887), p. 15; Ashbaugh, *Lucy Parsons*, pp. 14-15.

23. Albert R. Parsons to George A. Schilling, November 7, 1887, *Life of Albert R. Parsons*, 1889 ed., pp. 216-18.

24. Ibid., p. 215; *Autobiographies of the Haymarket Martyrs*, p. 29.

25. *Autobiographies of the Haymarket Martyrs*, p. 29; *Waco Day*, May 6, 1886.

26. *Waco Day*, May 6, 1886; William M. Sleeper and Allan D. Sanford, *Waco Bar and Incidents of Waco History*, pp. 36-38, reproduced in Betty Ann McSwain, ed., *The Bench and Bar of Waco and McLennan County, 1849-1976* (Waco: Texian Press, 1976), pp. 38-40. Goodman, "Albert R. Parsons in Texas," p. 38, questions, however, whether Parsons actually took part in the Oliver affair.

27. *Autobiographies of the Haymarket Martyrs*, pp. 29-30.

28. *Chicago Herald*, September 18, 1886; *The Knights of Labor*, November 20, 1886.
29. *The Commonweal*, November 17, 1888.
30. *Chicago Tribune*, August 3, 1886. According to the *Waco Day* (May 6, 1886), she was "a colored woman (rather bright color)."
31. Parsons, *Anarchism*, p. 188; Ashbaugh, *Lucy Parsons*, pp. 267-68; *Dictionary of American Biography*, VII, 265-66. Her daughter was named Lulu Eda Parsons.
32. *Waco Day*, May 6, 1886; *Chicago Herald*, September 18, 1886; Ashbaugh, *Lucy Parsons*, pp. 13, 267. On the other hand, the Rosser family of Houston claimed that she was their former slave Malinda, born of a black mother and a Mexican father, who had left them after the Civil War. *Chicago Inter Ocean*, November 20, 1886.
33. *Autobiographies of the Haymarket Martyrs*, p. 30; *The Knights of Labor*, November 20, 1886; *Workmen's Advocate*, October 29, 1887; Parsons, *Anarchism*, p. 188.
34. Lucy herself fixed the date as June 10, 1871, when providing information on her husband for the *Dictionary of American Biography*.
35. Lucie C. Price, *Travis County, Texas, Marriage Records, 1840-1882* (Austin, 1973), in Ashbaugh, *Lucy Parsons*, p. 268.
36. *Autobiographies of the Haymarket Martyrs*, p. 55.
37. William Parsons thought her a woman of "youth, beauty and genius," while an English comrade called her "the Louise Michel of America," after the well-known French anarchist and feminist. Parsons, *Anarchism*, p. 188; *The Anarchist*, November 1887. William Morris, who met her in 1888, also found her of striking appearance, "Indian with a touch of negro," he wrote, "but she speaks pure Yankee." *The Letters of William Morris to His Family and Friends*, ed. Philip Henderson (London: Longman's, Green, 1950), p. 314.
38. See, for example, Lucy E. Parsons, "The Negro," *The Alarm*, April 3, 1886.
39. *The Knights of Labor*, November 6, 1886.
40. Ibid.
41. *Autobiographies of the Haymarket Martyrs*, p. 30; "A. R. Parsons," *The Labor Enquirer* (Denver), November 19, 1887.

Chapter 2: Labor Agitator

1. William J. Adelman, *Haymarket Revisited* (Chicago: The Illinois Labor History Society, 1976), p. 5.
2. *Proceedings of the First Convention of the Industrial Workers of the World* (New York: Labor News Co., 1905), p. 168.

3. J. Seymour Currey, *Chicago: Its History and Its Builders*, 5 vols. (Chicago: S. J. Clarke Publishing Co., 1912), II, 296.

4. *Chicago Tribune*, July 12, 1877.

5. Samuel Gompers, *Seventy Years of Life and Labor* (New York: Dutton, 1925), p. 92.

6. Quoted in M. B. Schnapper, *American Labor: A Pictorial Social History* (Washington, D.C.: Public Affairs Press, 1972), p. 95.

7. Gompers, *Seventy Years*, p. 96; Lillian Symes and Travers Clement, *Rebel America: The Story of Social Revolt in the United States* (New York: Harper & Row, 1934), pp. 138-39; Herbert Gutman, "The Tompkins Square 'Riot' in New York City on January 13, 1874: A Re-examination of Its Causes and Its Aftermath," *Labor History* 6 (Winter 1965), 44-70.

8. Lloyd Lewis and Henry J. Smith, *Chicago: The History of Its Reputation* (New York: Harcourt, Brace & Co., 1929), p. 150.

9. *Chicago Tribune*, December 23, 1873; Samuel Bernstein, *The First International in America* (New York: A. M. Kelley, 1962), pp. 227-29; Symes and Clement, *Rebel America*, p. 135; Joseph G. Rayback, *A History of American Labor*, rev. ed. (New York: The Free Press, 1966), p. 130.

10. Adelman, *Haymarket Revisited*, p. 54.

11. Bessie L. Pierce, *A History of Chicago*, vol. III: *The Rise of a Modern City, 1871-1893* (New York: Knopf, 1957), p. 243.

12. *Chicago Tribune*, November 23, 1875, quoted in Harry Barnard, *"Eagle Forgotten": The Life of John Peter Altgeld* (Indianapolis: Bobbs-Merrill, 1938), p. 45.

13. *Autobiographies of the Haymarket Martyrs*, p. 30. The state of Illinois ordered an investigation of its own and found that the Relief and Aid Society had indeed used money for private ventures instead of giving it to the poor. Adelman, *Haymarket Revisited*, p. 5.

14. *Life of Albert R. Parsons*, pp. 100-101; *Autobiographies of the Haymarket Martyrs*, pp. 30-31. Cf. Albert R. Parsons, "Chattel and Wage Slavery," *Truth*, October 1884; and Eric Foner, *Politics and Ideology in the Age of the Civil War* (New York: Oxford University Press, 1980), pp. 59-60.

15. *Waco Day*, November 9, 1887; *The Commonweal*, December 24, 1887.

16. *Autobiographies of the Haymarket Martyrs*, p. 31.

17. George A. Schilling, "History of the Labor Movement in Chicago," *Life of Albert R. Parsons*, p. xxii. Parsons himself dates his membership in the Social Democratic Party from 1875. *Autobiographies of the Haymarket Martyrs*, p. 31.

18. *Life of Albert R. Parsons*, pp. xxii-xxiii.

19. Quoted in Voltairine de Cleyre to George Schilling, May 1, 1893, Schilling Papers.
20. *Life of Albert R. Parsons*, p. xxiii.
21. Ibid., p. xxiv; Floyd Dell, "Socialism and Anarchism in Chicago," in Currey, *Chicago*, II, 370.
22. *Chicago Tribune*, May 10, 1876, quoted in Pierce, *History of Chicago*, III, 244; *Autobiographies of the Haymarket Martyrs*, p. 31.
23. *Life of Albert R. Parsons*, p. xxiii.
24. Ibid., pp. xxiii-xxiv.
25. Ibid., p. xxiv; *Autobiographies of the Haymarket Martyrs*, p. 35; *The Labor Enquirer* (Denver), November 19, 1887.
26. *Life of Albert R. Parsons*, pp. xxiv-xxv; *Vorbote*, April 14, 1877.
27. *Life of Albert R. Parsons*, pp. 3-4; *Autobiographies of the Haymarket Martyrs*, p. 35.

Chapter 3: The Great Strike

1. Joseph A. Dacus, *Annals of the Great Strikes in the United States* (St. Louis: Scammell & Co., 1877), p. 205.
2. *Life of Albert R. Parsons*, p. xxv.
3. Quoted in Schnapper, *American Labor*, p. 118.
4. *Life of Albert R. Parsons*, pp. xxv-xxvii.
5. Gompers, *Seventy Years*, p. 140.
6. Dacus, *Annals of the Great Strikes*, p. 88.
7. *New York Times*, July 26, 1877, quoted in Samuel Yellen, *American Labor Struggles, 1877-1934* (New York: Harcourt, Brace & Co., 1936), pp. 21-22; Symes and Clement, *Rebel America*, p. 147.
8. *Life of Albert R. Parsons*, p. xxv.
9. *Chicago Tribune*, July 22, 1877; Pierce, *History of Chicago*, III, 246; Philip S. Foner, *The Great Labor Uprising of 1877* (New York: Monad Press, 1977), p. 141.
10. Dell in Currey, *Chicago*, II, 371-73.
11. Quoted in Pierce, *History of Chicago*, III, 246-47.
12. Ibid.; *Chicago Tribune*, July 24, 1877; Robert V. Bruce, *1877: Year of Violence* (Indianapolis: Bobbs-Merrill, 1959), p. 238; Foner, *Great Labor Uprising*, pp. 142-43. The size of the crowd was variously estimated as between 6,000 and 40,000.
13. *Chicago Tribune*, July 24, 1877; Foner, *Great Labor Uprising*, pp. 143-44; Dell in Currey, *Chicago*, II, 372-73. The *Tribune* conceded that Parsons had advocated "obedience to law and order," counseling the workers "never to attack anyone until they were attacked."
14. *Life of Albert R. Parsons*, p. xxv.
15. Currey, *Chicago*, II, 294.

16. *Autobiographies of the Haymarket Martyrs*, p. 34; *Life of Albert R. Parsons*, p. xxvi; Allan Pinkerton, *Strikers, Communists, Tramps and Detectives* (New York: G. W. Carleton & Co., 1878), pp. 265-66.
17. *Autobiographies of the Haymarket Martyrs*, pp. 31-32.
18. Ibid., pp. 32-33; *Life of Albert R. Parsons*, pp. 18-19.
19. *Chicago Times*, July 24, 1877, quoted in Foner, *Great Labor Uprising*, p. 147.
20. *Autobiographies of the Haymarket Martyrs*, pp. 33-34.
21. Ibid.; *Life of Albert R. Parsons*, p. xxvi.
22. Dell in Currey, *Chicago*, ii, 372-73; Bruce, *1877*, p. 239; Lewis and Smith, *Chicago*, p. 153.
23. Jeremy Brecher, *Strike!* (Greenwich, Conn.: Fawcett, 1974), pp. 46-47.
24. *Life of Albert R. Parsons*, p. xxvii.
25. *The Commonweal*, June 9, 1888.
26. Quoted in Bruce, *1877*, p. 26.
27. Rayback, *History of American Labor*, p. 135.
28. William T. Hutchinson, *Cyrus Hall McCormick* (New York: D. Appleton-Century, 1935), quoted in Barnard, *Eagle Forgotten*, p. 54; Currey, *Chicago*, ii, 304, 376-77; *The Alarm*, April 18, 1885.
29. Symes and Clement, *Rebel America*, pp. 143, 152.
30. *Life of Albert R. Parsons*, p. xxv.
31. Quoted in Bruce, *1877*, p. 276.
32. Elisée Reclus, "La grève d'Amérique," *Le Travailleur*, September 1877. Cf. Reclus, *Evolution and Revolution* (London: W. Reeves, n.d.), p. 5.
33. Peter Kropotkin, "Affaires d'Amérique," *Bulletin de la Fédération Jurassienne*, August 5, 1877.
34. Quoted in James J. Martin, *Men Against the State: The Expositors of Individualist Anarchism in America, 1827-1908*, rev. ed. (Colorado Springs: Ralph Myles Publisher, 1970), p. 164.
35. Ezra H. Heywood, "The Great Strike: Its Relations to Labor, Property, and Government," *The Radical Review*, November 1877.

Chapter 4: From Socialism to Anarchism

1. *Life of Albert R. Parsons*, p. xxvii.
2. *Autobiographies of the Haymarket Martyrs*, p. 35.
3. *Freedom*, August 1898.
4. *The National Socialist*, August 24, 1878.
5. *Life of Albert R. Parsons*, p. 173.
6. *The National Socialist*, June 15, 1878. See also *The Socialist*, October 19 and November 9, 1878.
7. Lucy E. Parsons, "Reminiscences," *The Alarm*, November 1915.

8. Albert R. Parsons, "The Progress of the Labor Movement," *The Labor Standard*, August 18, 1878; Ashbaugh, *Lucy Parsons*, pp. 33, 36.

9. Albert R. Parsons, "Chicago Labor Unions," *The National Socialist*, May 18, 1878. See also *The Labor Standard*, September 7 and October 13, 1878; George E. McNeill, ed., *The Labor Movement* (Boston: A. M. Bridgman & Co., 1887), pp. 161-62; and John R. Commons et al., *History of Labor in the United States*, 4 vols. (New York: Macmillan, 1918-1935), II, 302-306.

10. *The Socialist*, July 5, 1879; *The Labor Standard*, August 18, 1878; Calmer, *Labor Agitator*, pp. 46-47.

11. *The Socialist*, July 12, 1879; Calmer, *Labor Agitator*, p. 37; Ashbaugh, *Lucy Parsons*, p. 35.

12. *Autobiographies of the Haymarket Martyrs*, pp. 37-38; Commons, *History of Labor*, II, 249-50, 285; Dyer D. Lum, "Some Reminiscences," *The Alarm*, December 3, 1887; Lum, *A Concise History of the Great Trial of the Chicago Anarchists in 1886* (Chicago: Socialistic Publishing Co., 1887), p. 13.

13. *Life of Albert R. Parsons*, p. xxvii; "The Rise of the Movement in Chicago," *Freedom*, February 1901; Calmer, *Labor Agitator*, pp. 41-45; Ashbaugh, *Lucy Parsons*, p. 29.

14. Commons, *History of Labor*, II, 284; Morris Hillquit, *History of Socialism in the United States*, rev. ed. (New York: Funk & Wagnalls, 1910), p. 207; Dell in Currey, *Chicago*, II, 381.

15. Quoted in Hillquit, *History of Socialism*, p. 206.

16. August Spies, *Reminiscenzen von Aug. Spies: Seine Rede vor Richter Gary, sozialpolitische Abhandlungen, Briefe, Notizen, u.*, ed. Albert Currlin (Chicago: Christine Spies, 1888), p. 107; Commons, *History of Labor*, II, 280. A copy of the Lehr-und-Wehr Verein constitution and bylaws has been preserved in the Grinnell Papers: *Constitution und Nebengesetze des Lehr-und-Wehr Vereinen von Chicago* (Chicago: Social-Democratic Printing Association, n.d. [1879?]).

17. *Autobiographies of the Haymarket Martyrs*, p. 36.

18. Quoted in Sidney Lens, *Radicalism in America*, 2d ed. (New York: Crowell, 1969), p. 164.

19. Quoted in Nathan Fine, *Labor and Farmer Parties in the United States, 1828-1928* (New York: Rand School, 1928), p. 109.

20. *Report of the Proceedings of the National Convention of the Socialistic Labor Party, 1879-1880*, pp. 25, 43-44, in Howard H. Quint, *The Forging of American Socialism* (Columbia, S.C.: University of South Carolina Press, 1953), p. 17; Calmer, *Labor Agitator*, pp. 56-57; Ashbaugh, *Lucy Parsons*, p. 37.

21. Dell in Currey, *Chicago*, II, 381; Calmer, *Labor Agitator*, p. 51; *Autobiographies of the Haymarket Martyrs*, p. 37.

22. *Life of Albert R. Parsons,* p. xxviii. As Lizzie Holmes put it, "Politics was so corrupt that it contaminated every one that touched it." *Mother Earth,* November 1912.
23. *Autobiographies of the Haymarket Martyrs,* p. 36. See also Albert R. Parsons, "Die Illinoiser Greenbacker und der Sozialismus," *Vorbote,* May 8, 1880.
24. *Life of Albert R. Parsons,* p. xxix.
25. Commons, *History of Labor,* ii, 289-90; Edward B. Mittelman, "Chicago Labor Politics, 1877-96," *The Journal of Political Economy* 28 (May 1920), 416-17; Ashbaugh, *Lucy Parsons,* p. 43. In early 1880 the Trades and Labor Council, of which Parsons was a founder, had changed its name to Trades and Labor Assembly.
26. *Freiheit,* December 11, 1880, January 8, 1881; Max Nettlau, *Anarchisten und Sozialrevolutionäre: Die historische Entwicklung des Anarchismus in den Jahren 1880-1886* (Berlin: "Der Syndikalist," 1931), p. 164. The New York Social Revolutionary Club was established on November 15, 1880.
27. Abraham Cahan, *The Education of Abraham Cahan* (Philadelphia: Jewish Publication Society of America, 1969), pp. 327-28.
28. Vernon L. Lidtke, *The Outlawed Party: Social Democracy in Germany, 1878-1890* (Princeton: Princeton University Press, 1966), pp. 77, 115; Calmer, *Labor Agitator,* p. 191. On Hasselmann see also Günther Bers, *Wilhelm Hasselmann (1844-1916): Sozialrevolutionärer Agitator und Reichstagsabgeordneter* (Cologne: Einhorn Verlag, 1973).
29. Moritz A. Bachmann, *Der Anarchismus im Lichte des Occultismus* (Schweidnitz: Frömsdorf Verlag, 1904).
30. *Sturmvogel,* June 15, 1898; Harry Kelly, "Twenty-Fifth Anniversary of Freie Arbeiter Stimme," manuscript, Modern School Collection, Rutgers University.
31. Quoted in *Liberty,* February 4, 1882. Yet another founder of the New York Social Revolutionary Club was Peter Knauer, a frequent contributor to Most's *Freiheit.* See, for example, "Die Taktik der revolutionären Arbeiter-Partei," July 10, 1881, and his poem "Krieg der Autorität," August 11, 1883.
32. *Autobiographies of the Haymarket Martyrs,* p. 36.
33. Ibid., p. 37.

Chapter 5: Social Revolutionaries

1. *Life of Albert R. Parsons,* p. xxix.
2. *Le Révolté,* July 22, 1882. On the London Congress see ibid., July 23-September 3, 1881; *Freiheit,* July 30-August 13, 1881; and Nettlau,

Anarchisten und Sozialrevolutionäre, pp. 187-231. A report of the congress appeared in the San Francisco Truth of August 4, 1883, based on the account in Le Révolté.

3. Nettlau, Anarchisten und Sozialrevolutionäre, pp. 205-206, 353.

4. For her translations of Bakunin and Kropotkin see Truth, September 8, 1883-January 19, 1884, and January 5-26, 1884. See also her interesting letter in Liberty, August 25, 1883, and her report of a Barcelona revolutionary congress in The Anarchist, September 15, 1885.

5. Max Nettlau to Benjamin R. Tucker, March 22, 1937, Tucker Papers.

6. Nathan-Ganz followed the hyphenated spelling used by Proudhon, who coined the label in 1840 in What Is Property?

7. Quoted in Ashbaugh, Lucy Parsons, p. 42.

8. Freiheit, April 23 and 30, 1881.

9. Josef Peukert, Erinnerungen eines Proletariers aus der revolutionären Arbeiterbewegung (Berlin: Verlag des Sozialistischen Bundes, 1913), p. 72.

10. Nettlau, Anarchisten und Sozialrevolutionäre, p. 313; Nettlau to Benjamin Tucker, July 2, 1937, Tucker Papers; Certamen internacional de "La Protesta" (Buenos Aires: "La Protesta," 1927), pp. 72-89.

11. Le Révolté, July 22, 1881; Nettlau, Anarchisten und Sozialrevolutionäre, p. 221; Max Nomad, "The Anarchist Tradition," in The Revolutionary Internationals, 1864-1943, ed. Milorad M. Drachkovitch (Stanford: Stanford University Press, 1966), pp. 75-76.

12. Liberty, October 15 and November 12, 1881.

13. Calmer, Labor Agitator, p. 59; Ashbaugh, Lucy Parsons, p. 42.

14. Freiheit, October 19, 1881; Vorbote, October 29, 1881; Liberty, November 12, 1881; Chicago Tribune, October 22-24, 1881. A few months earlier, it may be recalled, O'Meara had run for mayor of Chicago on the anti-Greenback socialist ticket.

15. Liberty, November 12, 1881.

16. Ibid.; Vorbote, October 29, 1881.

17. Quoted in Pierce, History of Chicago, III, 256.

18. Liberty, November 12, 1881.

19. Max Nomad, Apostles of Revolution (Boston: Little, Brown & Co., 1939), p. 300.

20. Johann Most, Memoiren: Erlebtes, Erforschtes und Erdachtes, 4 vols. (New York: John Most, 1903), I, 10.

21. Ibid., I, 17; Rudolf Rocker, Johann Most: Das Leben eines Rebellen (Berlin: "Der Syndikalist," 1924), p. 12.

22. Most, Memoiren, I, 52-53.

23. Karl Marx to Friedrich Sorge, September 19, 1879, Karl Marx and Frie-

467

drich Engels, *Letters to Americans, 1848-1895* (New York: International Publishers, 1953), p. 118.

24. *Freiheit*, March 19, 1881.

25. Ibid., December 23, 1882; Rocker, *Johann Most*, p. 136; Frederic Trautmann, *The Voice of Terror: A Biography of Johann Most* (Westport, Conn.: Greenwood Press, 1980), p. 118.

26. Johann Most, "Die Revolution und der Aufbau einer neuen Gesellschaft," *Freiheit*, January 13, 1883; Pierce, *History of Chicago*, iii, 257.

27. Quoted in Paul Avrich, *An American Anarchist: The Life of Voltairine de Cleyre* (Princeton: Princeton University Press, 1978), p. 95.

28. *Discontent*, February 14, 1900.

29. Emma Goldman, *Living My Life* (New York: Knopf, 1931), p. 6.

30. Elias Tcherikower, ed., *The Early Jewish Labor Movement in the United States* (New York: YIVO Institute for Jewish Research, 1961), pp. 220-21; Avrich, *An American Anarchist*, pp. 95-96.

31. Hillquit, *History of Socialism*, p. 215.

32. Goldman, *Living My Life*, p. 9.

33. Johann Most, *Beast and Monster: The Beast of Property and The Social Monster* (Tucson: "The Match!" 1973), pp. 2-16; Richard T. Ely, *The Labor Movement in America* (New York: Crowell, 1886), pp. 262-63.

34. Most, *Beast and Monster*, pp. 6-8; *The Alarm*, October 11, 1884.

35. Alexander Berkman, introduction to Rocker, *Johann Most*, p. 6.

36. Quoted in Ely, *Labor Movement*, p. 243.

37. *Freedom*, June 1924.

Chapter 6: The Pittsburgh Congress

1. Quoted in Henry David, *The History of the Haymarket Affair*, rev. ed. [1st ed., 1936] (New York: Russell & Russell, 1958), p. 90.

2. Johann Most to August Spies, July 11, 1883, Grinnell Papers.

3. *Liberty*, April 28, 1888.

4. Robert V. Hine, *California's Utopian Colonies* (New Haven: Yale University Press, 1966), pp. 79-80; Joseph R. Buchanan, *The Story of a Labor Agitator* (New York: Outlook Co., 1903), pp. 266-70.

5. Frank Roney, *Frank Roney, Irish Rebel and California Labor Leader*, ed. Ira B. Cross (Berkeley: University of California Press, 1931), pp. 473-74; Ira B. Cross, *A History of the Labor Movement in California* (Berkeley: University of California Press, 1935), p. 163.

6. *Liberty*, October 6, 1883.

7. Chester M. Destler, *American Radicalism, 1865-1901* (New London: Connecticut College Press, 1946), pp. 78-104. Joseph Labadie's copy of

Haskell's program, reprinted by Destler, has been preserved in the Labadie Collection at the University of Michigan.

8. *The Knights of Labor*, April 30, 1887.

9. *Liberty*, October 6, 1883. In a private communication to Haskell, Peter
J. McGuire, who had converted Parsons to socialism and was now general secretary of the carpenters' union, cautioned that there must be "a
certain unity of thought, or in its absence, a catholicity of spirit" among
the various socialist tendencies in order for solidarity to be achieved.
For McGuire the exertions of "revolutionary prattlers" like Most ran
counter to that spirit. McGuire to Haskell, February 20, 1884, International Workmen's Association Papers.

10. *Life of Albert R. Parsons*, p. xxiii; *The Alarm*, November 8, 1884.

11. Albert R. Parsons, "The International," *Truth*, November 17, 1883. See
also *Vorbote*, October 20 and 27, 1883; and *Freiheit*, October 20, 1883.

12. *Freiheit*, October 20, 1883; Carl Nold, "Fifty Years Ago," *Man!*, January
1934; Trautmann, *Voice of Terror*, p. 121.

13. Commons, *History of Labor*, II, 290-300; Yellen, *American Labor Struggles*, pp. 46-47.

14. *The Alarm*, April 4, 1885. See also *Life of Albert R. Parsons*, p. 108.

15. Rudolf Rocker, *Anarcho-Syndicalism* (Indore, n.d.), p. 88; Bernstein,
First International in America, p. 291.

16. *Plan of Organization, Method of Propaganda, and Resolutions Adopted
by the Pittsburgh Congress of the International Working-People's Association* (Chicago: I.W.P.A., 1883).

17. Johann Most, "Unsere Grundsätze," *Freiheit*, October 13, 1883.

18. *To the Workingmen of America* (New York: I.W.P.A., Committee of
Agitation, 1883).

19. As William Holmes remarked, "all active members of the International
groups which were then and afterwards organized, based their revolutionary teachings chiefly upon that manifesto." *The Rebel*, November
20, 1895. The Pittsburgh congress authorized an initial printing of 100,000
copies in English, 50,000 in German, and 10,000 in French. Apart from
its frequent publication in *Freiheit*, the *Arbeiter-Zeitung*, and *The Alarm*,
see *Lucha Obrera* (Buenos Aires), June 22, 1884; *Der Arbeter Fraynd*
(London), September 23 and 30, 1887; and *Le Réveil des Mineurs* (Has-
tings, Pa.), May 2, 1891.

20. *Plan of Organization*.

21. *Life of Albert R. Parsons*, p. xxix; Ashbaugh, *Lucy Parsons*, pp. 52-53.
The launching of Tucker's *Liberty*, Schilling observed, had marked "an
epoch in the intellectual progress of the movement."

22. Hillquit, *History of Socialism*, p. 218; Dell in Currey, *Chicago*, II, 392-
93.

23. Hillquit, *History of Socialism*, p. 219; Quint, *Forging of American Socialism*, pp. 24-25.

Chapter 7: The International Working People's Association

1. *The Alarm*, October 4, 1884.
2. Ely, *Labor Movement*, p. 219. See also Samuel Rezneck, "Patterns of Thought and Action in an American Depression, 1882-1886," *American Historical Review*, January 1956, pp. 284-307.
3. *Report of the Committee on Tenement Houses of the Citizens' Association of Chicago*, September 1884, p. 3, quoted in David, *History of the Haymarket Affair*, p. 15.
4. *Famous Speeches*, p. 26.
5. Brecher, *Strike!*, p. 31.
6. Pierce, *History of Chicago*, III, 260-61.
7. *The Rebel*, November 20, 1895.
8. *The Alarm*, January 24, 1885.
9. *Freedom* (Chicago), January 1, 1891.
10. "How to Organize," *The Alarm*, January 23, 1886.
11. August Spies to Richard T. Ely, November 3, 1885, Ely Papers. In Chicago, dues-paying members of the IWPA (ten cents a month) were issued red cards on which they were identified only by number. Four such cards, as well as one from the Chicago Lehr-und-Wehr Verein, have been preserved in the Grinnell Papers.
12. *The Alarm*, September 5, October 17, November 14, 1885.
13. Ibid., April 4, 1885. *The Alarm* of August 8, 1885, made the fantastic claim that the anarchist movement and its sympathizers consisted of "over one hundred thousand people in the United States and Canada, and over one million adherents throughout Europe."
14. Ibid., November 28, 1885. Cities with three or more groups of the International were Chicago, New York, Philadelphia, St. Louis, Cleveland, Cincinnati, Pittsburgh, and Allegheny City.
15. It might be noted that there were as yet few Jews in the International, as Jewish immigration was only just beginning on a large scale. However, the secretary of the New Haven Group, Isidor Stein, was a Jewish immigrant.
16. *Life of Albert R. Parsons*, p. xxx. The Bureau of Information, elected for a six-month term, consisted of the following members (February and November 1885): Albert Parsons and August Spies (English), Joseph Bach and Balthasar Rau (German), and Anton Hirschberger (French). There was also a Bohemian secretary, probably Jacob Mikolanda, though

his name is not recorded with the others. *The Alarm*, February 21 and November 14, 1885.

17. In October 1885 Chicago and its environs had the following IWPA groups: the North Side Group, the North-West Side Group, the South Side Group, the South-West Side Group No. 1, the South-West Side Group No. 3, the Freiheit Group, the Vorwaerts Group, the Jefferson Group, the Brotherhood Group, the American Group, the Bohemian Group, the Revolutionary Cigarmakers' Association Group, the Bridgeport Group, and the Town of Lake Groups No. 1 and 2. At various times, moreover, four additional groups were in existence: the South-West Group No. 2, the Karl Marx Group, the Pullman Group, and the Anarchist Discussion Club. Some sources provide higher estimates for the total membership of all Chicago groups. Thus Nettlau gives a figure of 3,000, as does William Holmes of the American Group. Holmes, however, maintains that some of the German groups had as many as 400 to 600 members, surely an exaggeration. Nettlau, *Anarchisten und Sozialrevolutionäre*, p. 385; *The Rebel*, November 20, 1895. *The Alarm*, April 18, 1885, placed the number of active members at more than 2,000, and claimed an additional 10,000 sympathizers.

18. *The Alarm*, March 20, 1886.

19. *Autobiographies of the Haymarket Martyrs*, p. 109.

20. *Famous Speeches*, p. 72.

21. Ibid., p. 55. Compare the position of Johann Most: "To go back to the small industry of former days is not possible. . . . The advantages of mass production and the organization of labor are too apparent ever to be given up." *Beast and Monster*, p. 10.

22. *The Alarm*, November 1, 1884.

23. Ibid., November 20, 1885; *Die Zukunft*, May 30, 1885; *Die Parole*, February 3, 1886; Commons, *History of Labor*, II, 388-89.

24. Rayback, *History of American Labor*, pp. 159-60; Terence V. Powderly, "The Army of the Discontented," *The North American Review*, April 1885, pp. 369-77.

25. *Chicago Tribune*, May 7, 1885, quoted in Barnard, *Eagle Forgotten*, p. 80.

26. *Vorbote*, February 20, 1884, quoted in Commons, *History of Labor*, II, 387.

27. Quoted in Commons, *History of Labor*, II, 388.

28. The Central Labor Union affiliates were the following: Typographical No. 9, Tassel and Fringe Makers, Fresco Painters, Furniture Workers No. 1, Furniture Workers (Pullman), Bakers No. 10, South Side Bakers, Lumber Workers, Custom Tailors, Hod Carriers, Brewers and Malters, Beer Barrel Coopers, Brickmakers, International Carpenters and Joiners,

International Carpenters (Bohemian), Independent Carpenters and Joiners, Carpenters and Joiners (Lake View), Wagon Workers, Harness Makers, Butchers, Progressive Cigar Makers, Metal Workers No. 1, 2, and 3, and Metal Workers (Pullman). *Vorbote*, April 24, 1886.

29. *Vorbote*, March 4, and May 20, 1885.

30. *The Alarm*, January 24, 1885.

31. Ibid., February 7, 1885.

32. Ibid., March 20, 1886.

33. Ibid., September 19, 1885; Calmer, *Labor Agitator*, p. 75.

34. Gompers, *Seventy Years*, p. 237.

35. Rocker, *Johann Most*, p. 162.

36. *Discussion über das Thema: "Anarchismus oder Communismus!" Geführt von Paul Grottkau und Johann Most, am 24. Mai 1884 in Chicago* (Chicago: Das Central Comite der Chicagoer Gruppen der I.A.A., 1884).

37. *The Alarm*, February 7 and May 30, 1885.

38. Alexander Jonas, *Socialism and Anarchism: Antagonistic Opposites* (New York: Socialistic Labor Party, 1886); Hillquit, *History of Socialism*, p. 220; Dell in Currey, *Chicago*, II, 393-94.

39. *The Alarm*, October 4 and December 6, 1884; McNeill, *Labor Movement*, pp. 261-64.

40. *The Alarm*, May 16, 1885.

41. Ibid., September 19, 1885.

42. Charles Edward Russell, *These Shifting Scenes* (New York: Hodder & Stoughton, 1914), p. 81; Mary Harris Jones, *The Autobiography of Mother Jones*, 3rd ed. [1st ed., 1925] (Chicago: Charles H. Kerr, 1974), p. 21.

43. *The Alarm*, July 11, 1885; Russell, *Shifting Scenes*, p. 81.

44. *Detroit Evening Journal*, July 3, 1885, in Haymarket Scrapbook, Labadie Collection; Ashbaugh, *Lucy Parsons*, pp. 60-61.

45. *The Rights of Labor*, May 4, 1893.

46. *The Alarm*, December 21, 1885, quoted in Adelman, *Haymarket Revisited*, p. 10.

47. *The Alarm*, February 6, 1886.

Chapter 8: The American Group

1. *The Alarm*, May 16, 1885; *The Rebel*, November 20, 1895. Samuel Fielden, at the trial, placed the number at 175. *In the Supreme Court of Illinois, Northern Grand Division. March Term, A.D. 1887. August Spies et al., vs. The People of the State of Illinois. Abstract of Record*, 2 vols. (Chicago: Barnard & Gunthorpe, 1887), II, 270 (hereafter cited as *Abstract of Record*).

2. *Freedom*, November 1891.

3. *Autobiographies of the Haymarket Martyrs*, p. 138.

4. Ibid., p. 142.

5. *Famous Speeches*, pp. 42-43; *The Alarm*, November 28, 1885.

6. *Autobiographies of the Haymarket Martyrs*, p. 134; *Famous Speeches*, p. 43.

7. E. P. Thompson, *The Making of the English Working Class* (New York: Pantheon, 1963), p. 54.

8. *Autobiographies of the Haymarket Martyrs*, p. 147.

9. Ibid., p. 148.

10. Ibid., p. 151.

11. *Famous Speeches*, p. 43.

12. Ibid., pp. 44-46.

13. Samuel Fielden to Richard J. Oglesby, November 5, 1887, in George N. McLean, *The Rise and Fall of Anarchy in America* (Chicago: R. G. Badoux & Co., 1888), p. 220.

14. William Holmes, "Were the Chicago Martyrs Anarchists?" *Free Society*, September 18, 1904.

15. William Holmes, "Reminiscences," *Mother Earth*, November 1912.

16. *The Alarm*, February 21 and December 12, 1885.

17. J. William Lloyd, "A Visit to Sam. Fielden," *The Comrade*, February 1904.

18. Frederick R. Schmidt, ed., *He Chose: The Other Was a Treadmill Thing* (Santa Fe: F. R. Schmidt, 1968), p. 130; William and Lizzie Holmes, "Reminiscences," *Free Society*, November 5, 1899.

19. *Freedom*, November 1890.

20. Lizzie Holmes, "Twenty-Five Years After," *Mother Earth*, November 1912.

21. *The Alarm*, October 11, 1884.

22. William Holmes to Joseph A. Labadie, April 7, 1889, Labadie Collection; *Chicago Herald*, November 27, 1887.

23. William Holmes, "Reminiscences," *Free Society*, November 6, 1898; Holmes to Labadie, April 7, 1889, Labadie Collection.

24. William Holmes, *The Historical, Philosophical and Economical Bases of Anarchy* (Columbus Junction, Ia.: E. H. Fulton, 1896), p. 10.

25. Lizzie M. Swank, "What Are 'American Institutions'?" *The Commonweal*, July 16, 1887.

26. Buchanan, *Story of a Labor Agitator*, p. 422. For her defense of the Indians see *The Alarm*, April 28, 1888; and *Freedom* (Chicago), February 1, 1891.

27. See, for example, *Lucifer*, April 30, 1903.

28. Lizzie M. Swank, "The Working Women of America," *Truth*, June 1884; Ashbaugh, *Lucy Parsons*, pp. 50-51.

29. Lizzie May Holmes, "Personal Reminiscences of Albert R. Parsons," *Life of Albert R. Parsons*, p. 213.
30. *The Alarm*, December 12, 1885.
31. *Autobiographies of the Haymarket Martyrs*, p. 161.
32. Ibid., p. 166.
33. *Famous Speeches*, p. 28.
34. Dyer D. Lum to Benjamin R. Tucker, December 25, 1886, *Liberty*, February 12, 1887; *Mother Earth*, November 1912.
35. In the fall of 1885 the group moved its meeting place to 106 Randolph Street.
36. *The Alarm*, August 8, September 19, and December 26, 1885.
37. Ibid., May 30, 1885.
38. Ibid., August 22, 1885; Mother Jones, *Autobiography*, p. 19.
39. *The Alarm*, November 28, 1885; *Chicago Inter Ocean*, October 12, 1885.
40. *The Alarm*, November 15, 1884, April 18, 1885.
41. Ibid., February 7, 1885.
42. William J. Gorsuch, *Revolt! An American to Americans* (Allegheny City: Group No. 1, I.W.P.A., 1885).
43. William J. Gorsuch to August Spies, August 21, 1884, Grinnell Papers.
44. *The Alarm*, July 25 and October 17, 1885; George E. Macdonald, *Fifty Years of Freethought*, 2 vols. (New York: "The Truth Seeker," 1929-1931), I, 382. See also William J. Gorsuch, *True Reform* (Bridgeport, Conn.: N.P.U., 1891).
45. *Free Society*, November 5, 1899.
46. *The Alarm*, December 6, 1884, July 11 and October 3, 1885. On the incident in London, which occurred on September 20, 1885, see E. P. Thompson, *William Morris: Romantic to Revolutionary*, rev. ed. (New York: Pantheon, 1977), pp. 395-97.
47. *Freedom*, February 1901.
48. *The Alarm*, January 13, 1885.
49. Ibid., May 16, 1885.
50. *Life of Albert R. Parsons*, pp. xxxi.
51. Ibid., pp. 109-11; *The Alarm*, March 21, 1885.
52. Macdonald, *Fifty Years of Freethought*, I, 396.
53. J. H. Greer, "Our Dead," *Mother Earth*, November 1912.
54. *Famous Speeches*, p. 74.
55. *Life of Albert R. Parsons*, p. 212.
56. Ibid., p. 38.
57. Ibid., p. 312.
58. Ibid., p. 213.
59. Ibid., pp. 33, 41.

60. *The Alarm*, February 21 and September 19, 1885.

61. Ibid., October 15, 1884, July 25, 1885, February 4, 1886.

62. Ibid., April 3, 1886.

63. *Life of Albert R. Parsons*, p. 3. Both children were identified as "nigger" on their birth certificates.

64. Ibid., p. 229. "Few such instances of mutual devotion have characterized married life as in this case," wrote Lum on another occasion. *The Alarm*, December 3, 1887.

65. Albert R. Parsons to Lucy E. Parsons, January 26, 1886, *Life of Albert R. Parsons*, p. 95; Ashbaugh, *Lucy Parsons*, p. 60.

66. Albèrt R. Parsons to William H. Brewer, July 26, 1883, Brewer Papers, Yale University. In 1885 Parsons returned to Hartford as a speaker for the International and "made many converts and won a large number of sympathizers." S. Anna Heath To Richard J. Oglesby, December 7, 1887, Oglesby Papers, Illinois State Archives.

67. On his daughter's birth certificate his occupation was listed as "clothier." Ashbaugh, *Lucy Parsons*, p. 269.

68. *Life of Albert R. Parsons*, p. 173. Cf. *The Alarm*, December 3, 1887.

69. *Life of Albert R. Parsons*, pp. 213, 217, 312. Cf. *Free Society*, November 5, 1899.

70. *Mother Earth*, November 1912.

71. Albert R. Parsons to Lucy E. Parsons, January 26, 1886, *Life of Albert R. Parsons*, p. 98.

72. Russell, *Shifting Scenes*, p. 85.

73. Parsons, *Anarchism*, pp. 177-78.

Chapter 9: August Spies

1. Albert R. Parsons to William Holmes, May 22, 1886, *Free Society*, November 5, 1899.

2. *The Alarm*, December 31, 1887; *Liberty*, February 12, 1887. "Head-centre" was a term used by Irish revolutionaries of the Fenian Brotherhood to designate a leader.

3. *Free Society*, November 6, 1898.

4. Hillquit, *History of Socialism*, p. 226. To Michael Schwab, Spies was "undoubtedly the most gifted of all the indicted anarchists." *The Monist*, July 1891, p. 521. Harry Kelly, an associate of Emma Goldman and Alexander Berkman, considered Spies "the most brilliant of the Haymarket Anarchists." Kelly, "Roll Back the Years: Odyssey of a Libertarian," manuscript, Tamiment Library, chap. 17, p. 5.

5. *Autobiographies of the Haymarket Martyrs*, pp. 59-66; *Freedom*, November 1891.

6. *Freiheit*, September 18, 1886.
7. *Autobiographies of the Haymarket Martyrs*, p. 69.
8. Ibid., pp. 66-68.
9. Ibid., p. 69.
10. In 1883 he attended its national convention in Davenport, Iowa, as a delegate from Chicago.
11. Dyer D. Lum, "August Spies," *Twentieth Century*, September 3, 1891.
12. *Free Society*, November 6, 1898, November 5, 1899; *Mother Earth*, November 1912.
13. Russell, *Shifting Scenes*, p. 95; *Mother Earth*, November 1912. Jay Fox, later a well-known Chicago anarchist, thought Spies and Parsons "two of the most convincing speakers it has been my good fortune to hear." *The Demonstrator*, November 7, 1906.
14. *Autobiographies of the Haymarket Martyrs*, p. 71; *Famous Speeches*, p. 18.
15. *Free Society*, November 6, 1898.
16. *The Alarm*, February 7, 1885; *Autobiographies of the Haymarket Martyrs*, p. 69.
17. *Autobiographies of the Haymarket Martyrs*, p. 65.
18. *The Alarm*, February 20, 1886; *Famous Speeches*, p. 14.
19. *Free Society*, November 5, 1899.
20. *The Alarm*, December 31, 1887; *Famous Speeches*, p. 19.
21. *Famous Speeches*, pp. 19-21; *The Alarm*, January 9, 1886.
22. *Famous Speeches*, p. 21; *The Alarm*, December 31, 1887; *The Rebel*, November 20, 1895; *Free Society*, November 6, 1898.
23. *The Alarm*, December 13, 1884, February 21, 1885. The officer was tried and acquitted.
24. *Autobiographies of the Haymarket Martyrs*, p. 70.
25. *Freiheit*, May 1, 1880, quoted in Lidtke, *Outlawed Party*, p. 114; *The Alarm*, July 25, 1885.
26. Spies, *Reminiscenzen*, p. 17.
27. August Spies, *August Spies' Auto-Biography, His Speech in Court, and General Notes* (Chicago: Nina Van Zandt, 1887), p. 69.
28. A selection of Spies's journalism is included in his *Reminiscenzen*, pp. 74-138. He also contributed articles in English to *The Alarm*.
29. August Spies to Richard T. Ely, November 3, 1885, Ely Papers.
30. *Mother Earth*, November 1912; *Free Society*, July 17 and November 6, 1898; *Liberty*, February 12, 1887.
31. *Autobiographies of the Haymarket Martyrs*, p. 104.
32. Ibid., pp. 104-105.
33. Ibid., pp. 108-109.
34. Ibid., p. 112; *Famous Speeches*, p. 26.

35. *Autobiographies of the Haymarket Martyrs*, p. 125.
36. Hillquit, *History of Socialism*, p. 226.

Chapter 10: Counterculture

1. Ely, *Labor Movement*, p. 241.
2. Quoted in James Joll, *The Anarchists* (London: Eyre & Spottiswoode, 1964), p. 105.
3. J. C. Goodden at a Lake Front meeting in November 1884. *The Alarm*, November 22, 1884.
4. Ibid., October 4, 1884.
5. For several months in 1886 there appeared *Die Amerikanische Arbeiter-Zeitung* in New York, to which Wilhelm Hasselmann was the most notable contributor.
6. *Autobiographies of the Haymarket Martyrs*, p. 43.
7. Caroline A. Lloyd, *Henry Demarest Lloyd*, 2 vols. (New York: G. P. Putnam's Sons, 1912), I, 89.
8. *The Alarm*, May 2, 1885.
9. English translations of these and other German poems appeared regularly in *The Alarm* as well as in *Liberty* and the *Workmen's Advocate*.
10. J. William Lloyd, "It is Coming!" *The Alarm*, October 11, 1884. Cf. L. Pfau, "Der Tag wird kommen," *Freiheit*, August 7, 1886.
11. *The Alarm*, October 4, 1884.
12. Ibid., November 28, 1885.
13. William Holmes to H. H. Sparling, April 26, 1886, Socialist League Archive.
14. Cf. Carol Poore, "German-American Socialist Culture," *Cultural Correspondence*, Spring 1978, pp. 13-20.
15. *Free Society*, November 5, 1899.
16. English translation in *The Alarm*, November 28, 1885.
17. *Autobiographies of the Haymarket Martyrs*, p. 126. For announcements of the play, entitled *Die Nihilisten*, see the *New England Anzeiger*, January 24, 1885; and *Die Zukunft*, February 28, 1885.
18. *The Alarm*, February 21, 1885.
19. Ibid., March 20, 1886.
20. Ibid.
21. Ibid., April 4, 1885.
22. Ibid., March 20, 1886.
23. *Freedom*, February 1901.
24. *The Alarm*, June 13, 1885.
25. Ibid., August 8, 1885.
26. Ibid.

27. Ibid.
28. *Mother Earth*, November 1912.
29. *The Alarm*, November 22, 1884.
30. "The Black Flag," ibid., November 29, 1884. See also Mariner J. Kent's poem "The Black Flag of Hunger," ibid., March 21, 1885.
31. Ibid., November 29, 1884.
32. Ibid.
33. Ibid.; *Free Society*, November 6, 1898. During the suppression of the Commune, according to one source, Washburne had intervened in behalf of Elisée Reclus, the anarchist geographer, and prevented his banishment to New Caledonia. Joseph Ishill, ed., *Elisée and Elie Reclus: In Memoriam* (Berkeley Heights, N.J.: The Oriole Press, 1927), p. 18.
34. *The Alarm*, November 29, 1884.
35. Ibid., December 15, 1885.
36. Ibid., May 2, 1885.
37. *Free Society*, November 5, 1899.
38. *The Alarm*, May 2, 1885; Lewis and Smith, *Chicago*, pp. 157-58.
39. *The Alarm*, May 2, 1885; *Arbeiter-Zeitung*, April 29, 1885.

Chapter 11: The Intransigents

1. According to Captain Schaack, August Spies had been a member of the North-West Side Group before joining the American Group.
2. *Autobiographies of the Haymarket Martyrs*, pp. 74-75.
3. Ibid., p. 91.
4. Ibid., p. 85.
5. *Free Society*, November 6, 1898.
6. Ibid.; *Free Society*, September 18, 1904. See also Fischer's letter to Lum, *Liberty*, February 26, 1887. On another occasion, however, Fischer dissociated himself from the "middle-class" anarchists of the Proudhonian school. *Autobiographies of the Haymarket Martyrs*, p. 81.
7. *Mother Earth*, November 1912. Cf. William Holmes: "He is not an orator, but is, in every fibre of his being, the man of action." Introduction to *The Chicago Martyrs: The Famous Speeches of the Eight Anarchists in Judge Gary's Court* (San Francisco: Free Society Publishing Co., 1899).
8. *The Alarm*, January 14, 1888; *Liberty*, February 12, 1887.
9. *Free Society*, November 5, 1899.
10. *Autobiographies of the Haymarket Martyrs*, pp. 93-94; *Famous Speeches*, p. 37. See also *Freiheit*, September 27, 1886; *Freedom*, November 1891; and *Free Society*, December 10, 1899.
11. *Famous Speeches*, p. 37.
12. Ibid.
13. *Free Society*, November 6, 1898.

14. *Famous Speeches*, p. 37.
15. *Autobiographies of the Haymarket Martyrs*, pp. 95-96.
16. Ibid., p. 97; *Famous Speeches*, pp. 37-38.
17. *Famous Speeches*, p. 39.
18. William P. Black, "Characteristics of the Murdered Men," *Free Society*, November 6, 1898.
19. David, *History of the Haymarket Affair*, p. x.
20. *Famous Speeches*, p. 23. See also Paul Bulian to Adolph Fischer, April 30, 1886, Grinnell Papers.
21. Only two issues of the *Anarchist* (Nos. 1 and 4, January 1 and April 1, 1886, "Organ of the Autonomous Groups of the I.W.P.A.") have survived and are to be found in the Grinnell Papers.
22. *Anarchist*, January 1 and April 1, 1886. See also *Der Anarchist* (St. Louis), August 1, 1889; and *Freedom*, February 1901.
23. *Autobiographies of the Haymarket Martyrs*, pp. 97-98; *Famous Speeches*, p. 39.
24. *Autobiographies of the Haymarket Martyrs*, p. 177.
25. *Famous Speeches*, p. 35.
26. Frank Harris, *The Bomb* [1st ed., 1908] (Chicago: University of Chicago Press, 1963), p. 320.
27. *Autobiographies of the Haymarket Martyrs*, pp. 169-70.
28. Ibid., p. 178.
29. Michael J. Schaack, *Anarchy and Anarchists: A History of the Red Terror and the Social Revolution in America and Europe* (Chicago: F. J. Schulte, 1889), p. 655. Lingg, it might be noted, was also a champion of women's rights: "A woman has a right to all positions which she can administer, and in a free (anarchistic) society she will know how to exercise the right, too. She will be no longer the mere servant, the cookmaid of her spouse, but the equal of him. As a consequence of the pulling down of the barriers to a true civilization, the female sex would become absolutely independent of the bearded half of humanity, socially as well as economically, and the result of this would be free and pure love." *The Alarm*, December 17, 1887, translated from the German by Adolph Fischer.
30. *Free Society*, November 6, 1898.
31. *The Alarm*, November 10, 1888; Alexander Berkman, *Prison Memoirs of an Anarchist* (New York: Mother Earth Publishing Association, 1912), p. 9.
32. Nettlau, *Anarchisten und Sozialrevolutionäre*, p. 382.
33. *Famous Speeches*, p. 34.
34. Schaack, *Anarchy and Anarchists*, pp. 121-22.
35. *The Rebel*, November 20, 1895.

479

Chapter 12: Cult of Dynamite

1. *The Alarm*, April 4, 1885.
2. Ibid., October 17, 1885; *Vorbote*, October 4, 1885; *Freiheit*, October 20, 1885.
3. Parsons, *Anarchism*, p. 183. From August 14, 1885, to April 24, 1886, the last issue before its suppression by the police, *The Alarm* carried a standing notice of meetings of the armed section of the American Group.
4. Schaack, *Anarchy and Anarchists*, p. 64.
5. According to some sources, Breitenfeld was commander-in-chief of the whole Chicago Lehr-und-Wehr Verein and Schrade captain of the second company.
6. *The Alarm*, November 14, 1885.
7. Quoted in Albert Fried, ed., *Socialism in America: From the Shakers to the Third International* (Garden City, N.Y.: Anchor Books, 1970), p. 178. Force, wrote Parsons in his autobiography, is justifiable "only when employed to repel force." *Autobiographies of the Haymarket Martyrs*, p. 45.
8. *The Alarm*, December 13, 1884.
9. Ibid., October 18, 1884; *Life of Albert R. Parsons*, pp. 42-43, 63-64.
10. *Autobiographies of the Haymarket Martyrs*, pp. 45-46; *The Alarm*, February 20, 1886; *Life of Albert R. Parsons*, pp. 5, 101.
11. *Famous Speeches*, p. 15.
12. *Freiheit*, August 24, 1884; McLean, *Rise and Fall of Anarchy*, p. 250; Andrew Carlson, *Anarchism in Germany* (Metuchen, N.J.: The Scarecrow Press, 1972), pp. 253-54.
13. *Freiheit*, March 14 and June 7, 1884; Tcherikower, *Early Jewish Labor Movement*, p. 220; Calmer, *Labor Agitator*, p. 254.
14. Johann Most, *Revolutionäre Kreigswissenschaft: Ein Handbüchlein zur Anleitung betreffend Gebrauches und Herstellung von Nitro-Glycerin, Dynamit, Schiessbaumwolle, Knallquicksilber, Bomben, Brandsätzen, Giften u.s.w., u.s.w.* (New York: Verlag des Internationalen Zeitungs-Vereins, 1885).
15. *Freiheit*, August 14, 1884; Ely, *Labor Movement*, p. 362. Most's remark was made in a eulogy to Hermann Stellmacher, hanged for killing an Austrian policeman.
16. Most, *Revolutionäre Kriegswissenschaft*, pp. 3, 51, 58-59.
17. *The Alarm*, October 25, 1884.
18. Ibid., October 18, 1884.
19. Ibid., November 15, 1884; *Nemesis*, May 17, 1884.
20. *Famous Speeches*, p. 82.
21. *The Alarm*, June 27, 1885.

480

22. Ibid., December 13, 1884; Ely, *Labor Movement*, p. 255; Trautmann, *Voice of Terror*, p. 124.

23. *The Alarm*, February 7, February 21, July 25, 1885, January 23, 1886.

24. In America as in Europe anarchists were deeply impressed by this work, the *Vorbote* serializing it in German and *The Alarm* commending it to its readers in glowing terms. *The Alarm*, May 2, 1885.

25. *The Alarm*, November 15 and December 6, 1884, June 13, 1885.

26. Ibid., June 13, 1885. See also Paul Avrich, "Conrad's Anarchist Professor: An Undiscovered Source," *Labor History* 18 (Summer 1977), 397-402.

27. *The Alarm*, November 8, 1884, November 28, 1885.

28. Ibid., January 13 and April 4, 1885, February 20, 1886.

29. Ibid., February 21, 1885.

30. *Freiheit*, September 18, 1880, March 18, 1883; *The Alarm*, December 26, 1885, January 23, 1886. Although *Freiheit* and *The Alarm* attributed the *Catechism* to Bakunin alone, most modern scholars regard Nechaev as the principal and perhaps sole author.

31. *Freiheit*, February 14, 1885; Ely, *Labor Movement*, p. 263. Cf. the poem "August Reinsdorf," *The Alarm*, April 18, 1885.

32. *Freiheit*, August 14, 1884; *Anarchist*, January 1, 1886; *The Alarm*, July 25, 1885.

33. Spies, *Reminiscenzen*, p. 176; *The Alarm*, December 27, 1884, January 24 and February 21, 1885.

34. Nettlau, *Anarchisten und Sozialrevolutionäre*, p. 382.

35. Johann Most to August Spies, October 2, 1884, Grinnell Papers; *Abstract of Record*, II, 312-13.

36. Quoted in Barnard, *Eagle Forgotten*, p. 81. Cf. Melville E. Stone, *Fifty Years a Journalist* (New York: Doubleday, Doran & Co., 1921), p. 169.

37. Benjamin R. Tucker to Joseph A. Labadie, June 5, 1886, Labadie Collection.

38. *Liberty*, March 27, 1886.

39. Ibid.

40. *Freiheit*, April 10, 1886; *Liberty*, September 18, 1886. See also Rocker, *Johann Most*, p. 299.

41. *The Rebel*, November 20, 1895.

42. Schaack, *Anarchy and Anarchists*, p. 169. Neebe told his son, however, that his hand had been crushed by a stone while he was helping to build a house. Interview with O. William Neebe, Chicago, October 11, 1982.

43. *Mother Earth*, November 1912; *Arbeiter-Zeitung*, April 29, 1885.

44. *The Alarm*, November 29, 1884, March 6, 1886; Louis Adamic, *Dynamite: The Story of Class Violence in America* (New York: Harper & Row, 1931), p. 68.

45. Symes and Clement, *Rebel America*, p. 170.

46. Lum, *Concise History*, pp. 87-88; Schaack, *Anarchy and Anarchists*, pp. 445-46. The spies, William Holmes insisted, were "generally known" to the International. *The Rebel*, November 20, 1895.

Chapter 13: On the Eve

1. *The Alarm*, August 8, 1885.
2. Ibid., September 5 and October 17, 1885; Pierce, *History of Chicago*, III, 272.
3. *Life of Albert R. Parsons*, p. xxxii; Barnard, *Eagle Forgotten*, p. 92.
4. *The Alarm*, December 12, 1885.
5. *John Swinton's Paper*, April 18, 1886.
6. *Autobiographies of the Haymarket Martyrs*, p. 47.
7. *The Alarm*, February 20, 1886.
8. *Arbeiter-Zeitung*, April 26, 1886.
9. Ibid., January 22, 1886; *The Alarm*, September 5, 1885.
10. *The Alarm*, October 17, 1885.
11. Ashbaugh, *Lucy Parsons*, pp. 70-71; Schaack, *Anarchy and Anarchists*, p. 108.
12. *The Alarm*, April 24, 1886.
13. Barnard, *Eagle Forgotten*, pp. 96-97.
14. William Holmes to H. H. Sparling, April 26, 1886, Socialist League Archive.
15. Quoted in Calmer, *Labor Agitator*, p. 79.
16. *Arbeiter-Zeitung*, May 1, 1886; Lum, *Concise History*, pp. 20-21.
17. *Chicago Mail*, May 1, 1886, reprinted in *The Alarm*, December 31, 1887.
18. *Die Fackel*, May 2, 1886.
19. Robert Ozanne, *A Century of Labor-Management Relations at McCormick and International Harvester* (Madison: University of Wisconsin Press, 1967), p. 11.
20. Quoted in Art Young, *Art Young: His Life and Times* (New York: Sheridan House, 1939), p. 80.
21. *Centennial History of Illinois*, ed. Clarence W. Alvord, 5 vols. (Springfield: Illinois Centennial Commission, 1918-1920), IV, 167-68.
22. *The Alarm*, March 6, 1886.
23. *Chicago Herald*, May 4, 1886; *Arbeiter-Zeitung*, May 4, 1886.
24. Facsimile in Schaack, *Anarchy and Anarchists*, p. 130. Spies mistakenly linked the McCormick dispute with the fight for the eight-hour day.
25. *Arbeiter-Zeitung*, May 4, 1886.
26. Testimony of Theodore Fricke, business manager of the *Arbeiter-Zeitung*, in Lum, *Concise History*, pp. 78-79.
27. *Abstract of Record*, II, 5.
28. *Famous Speeches*, p. 32.

29. *Abstract of Record*, II, 311.
30. Schaack, *Anarchy and Anarchists*, pp. 130-31; Lum, *Concise History*, pp. 25-26.
31. Quoted in Lewis and Smith, *Chicago*, p. 160. The manuscript of this article, in Schwab's hand, has been preserved in the Grinnell Papers.
32. *Abstract of Record*, II, 306; Lum, *Concise History*, pp. 138-39.
33. *The Alarm*, January 4, 1888. Fischer, indeed, seems to have been coauthor of the plan, which, says Lum, was "nipped in the bud" by the Haymarket explosion. *The Individualist*, November, 2, 1889.
34. Dyer D. Lum to Voltairine de Cleyre, March 1, 1891, Ishill Papers, University of Florida; *The Commonweal*, August 28, 1886.
35. According to Dyer Lum, Spies told Rau to visit every place "where the more excitable men might be found." *The Alarm*, December 31, 1887.

Chapter 14: The Bomb

1. Willis J. Abbot, *Carter Henry Harrison: A Memoir* (New York: Dodd, Mead & Co., 1895), p. 140.
2. *Abstract of Record*, II, 174; Lum, *Concise History*, p. 29.
3. *Abstract of Record*, II, 129; Lum, *Concise History*, pp. 35-38.
4. Willis J. Abbot, *Watching the World Go By* (Boston: Little, Brown & Co., 1933), p. 85.
5. Lewis and Smith, *Chicago*, p. 160.
6. *Cincinnati Enquirer*, May 3, 1886, in James M. Morris, "No Haymarket for Cincinnati," *Ohio History* 83 (Winter 1974), 24.
7. *Autobiographies of the Haymarket Martyrs*, pp. 47-49.
8. *Life of Albert R. Parsons*, p. 213.
9. Ibid., p. 174.
10. Ibid., pp. 116-27; Albert R. Parsons, *The Haymarket Speech* (Chicago: Chicago Labor Press Association, 1886).
11. *Abstract of Record*, II, 175; Lum, *Concise History*, pp. 111-12. Cf. *Chicago Inter Ocean*, May 5, 1886.
12. George Brown, in *Free Society*, November 23, 1902.
13. *Abstract of Record*, II, 132; Lum, *Concise History*, pp. 93-94.
14. *Abstract of Record*, II, 133; Lum, *Concise History*, p. 94.
15. *Autobiographies of the Haymarket Martyrs*, p. 158.
16. *Chicago Tribune*, May 5, 1886. According to the *Chicago Herald* of the same date, the officers were "crazy with fury."
17. *Autobiographies of the Haymarket Martyrs*, pp. 159-60.
18. *Abstract of Record*, II, 242, 303; Lum, *Concise History*, pp. 27-28.
19. *Chicago Tribune*, May 5, 1886.
20. The two bomb fragments removed from Degan's body are preserved in the Grinnell Papers.

21. Even Degan, according to the medical examiner, had also suffered bullet wounds, though how this could have happened if he was instantly felled by the bomb was not explained.

22. See Schaack, *Anarchy and Anarchists*, pp. 150-55; McLean, *Rise and Fall of Anarchy*, pp. 28-30; *Abstract of Record*, II, 152-57; *Chicago Tribune*, May 6, 1886; Haymarket Scrapbook, Columbia University Special Collections; and Michael L. Ahern, *Political History of Chicago, 1837-1887* (Chicago: Donahue, Henneberry Co., 1887), p. 249.

23. According to Ernst Schmidt (*He Chose*, p. 128), Spies told him that he did not hear more than five or six shots that could have been fired from the audience.

24. Schaack, *Anarchy and Anarchists*, p. 490.

25. Ahern, *Political History of Chicago*, p. 242; *Chicago Tribune*, June 27, 1886.

26. Schaack, *Anarchy and Anarchists*, p. 155.

27. McLean, *Rise and Fall of Anarchy*, pp. 18-19.

28. *Chicago Herald*, May 5, 1886.

29. Lum, *Concise History*, p. 34; Ashbaugh, *Lucy Parsons*, p. 80.

30. Adelman, *Haymarket Revisited*, p. 38; *Illinois Labor History Society Reporter*, November 1973; *Chicago Tribune*, May 9, 1886.

31. Haymarket Scrapbook, Columbia University; *Chicago Tribune*, May 5 and June 30, 1886.

32. Barnard, *Eagle Forgotten*, p. 106.

33. *Abstract of Record*, II, 133.

34. *The Commonweal*, June 19, 1886; *Chicago Tribune*, June 27, 1886.

35. John Bonfield to Frederick K. Ebersold, July 1, 1886, Chicago Historical Society; Ahern, *Political History of Chicago*, p. 240.

36. *Abstract of Record*, II, 266.

37. *Chicago Daily News*, May 4, 1886; Barnard, *Eagle Forgotten*, pp. 103-104.

38. *Abstract of Record*, II, 179-80; Lum, *Concise History*, p. 32.

39. *Abstract of Record*, II, 183; Lum, *Concise History*, pp. 115-16; *Free Society*, November 9, 1902; *Chicago Tribune*, June 27, 1886.

40. Lum, *Concise History*, p. 187.

41. *The Word*, December 1887.

42. Lucy E. Parsons, "Eleventh of November, 1887," *Famous Speeches*, 1912 ed.; Voltairine de Cleyre, *The First Mayday: The Haymarket Speeches, 1895-1910*, ed. Paul Avrich (New York: Libertarian Book Club, 1980), p. 6; George Brown, *Free Society*, November 20, 1902.

43. *Liberty*, May 22, 1886.

44. *Mother Earth*, November 1912.

45. *Autobiographies of the Haymarket Martyrs*, pp. 51-52; *Free Society*, November 9, 1902.

Chapter 15: Red Scare

1. David, *History of the Haymarket Affair*, p. 528.
2. *Liberty*, November 1896.
3. Brand Whitlock, *Forty Years of It* (New York: D. Appleton-Century, 1914), p. 73.
4. Quoted in Pierce, *History of Chicago*, III, 280.
5. *Chicago Inter Ocean*, May 5, 1886; Mother Jones, *Autobiography*, p. 21. A New York anarchist, T. P. Quinn, wrote that he would never forget "the howlings of the whore press and the mouthings of the sub-sidized pulpit" that followed the blast. *Free Society*, November 6, 1898.
6. Yellen, *American Labor Struggles*, p. 58; *Chicago Times, Inter Ocean*, and *Tribune*, May 6, 1886.
7. *Harper's Weekly*, May 15, 1886. See also Nhat Hong, *The Anarchist Beast: The Anti-Anarchist Crusade in Periodical Literature (1884-1906)* (Minneapolis: "Soil of Liberty," 1980).
8. *New York Times*, May 6, 1886; *Philadelphia Inquirer*, May 5, 1886; Morris U. Schappes, "Haymarket and the Jews," *Jewish Life*, November 1956, p. 26; John G. Sproat, *"The Best Men": Liberal Reformers in the Gilded Age* (New York: Oxford University Press, 1968), p. 232; Everett Carter, *Howells and the Age of Realism* (Philadelphia: Lippincott, 1954), p. 181.
9. *The Commonweal*, May 29, 1886; *Chicago Journal*, May 7, 1886; Ash-baugh, *Lucy Parsons*, p. 87.
10. Quoted in Henry Pringle, *Theodore Roosevelt: A Biography* (New York: Harcourt, Brace & Co., 1931), pp. 110-11.
11. Sigmund Zeisler, *Reminiscences of the Anarchist Case* (Chicago: Chicago Literary Club, 1927), p. 11; Robert Herrick, *The Memoirs of an American Citizen* (New York: Macmillan, 1905), pp. 66-67; Pierce, *History of Chicago*, III, 280.
12. John Higham, *Strangers in the Land: Patterns of American Nativism, 1860-1925*, rev. ed. (New York: Atheneum, 1971), p. 54; *Liberty*, May 22, 1886; Haymarket Scrapbook, Columbia University.
13. *Chicago Herald*, May 5 and 6, 1886; *Chicago Times*, May 5, 1886; *Chicago Tribune*, May 5, 1886; *The Commonweal*, May 29, 1886; Ernest B. Zeisler, *The Haymarket Riot* (Chicago: A. J. Isaacs, 1956), pp. 20-29; Higham, *Strangers in the Land*, pp. 54-55; Barnard, *Eagle Forgotten*, pp. 132-33.
14. *Chicago Tribune*, May 9, 1886; David, *History of the Haymarket Affair*, p. 213.
15. *Chicago Tribune*, May 7, 1886.
16. *The Truth Seeker*, July 17, 1886; Haymarket Scrapbook, Columbia University. See also *Chicago Tribune*, May 11, 1886.

17. Quoted in Charles A. Madison, *American Labor Leaders* (New York: Harper & Row, 1950), p. 52. See also Vincent J. Falzone, *Terence V. Powderly: Middle-Class Reformer* (Washington, D.C.: University Press of America, 1978), p. 112.

18. Quoted in Ashbaugh, *Lucy Parsons*, pp. 88-89; leaflet, Labadie Collection (Labor Vertical File).

19. *The Knights of Labor*, May 8, 1886.

20. Quoted in Ashbaugh, *Lucy Parsons*, pp. 89-90.

21. *Terre Haute Evening Gazette*, May 5, 1886, quoted in Yellen, *American Labor Struggles*, p. 56.

22. *Chicago Times*, May 6, 1886. On May 5 Bonfield personally went and closed Zepf's and Greif's saloons, where members of the International were wont to congregate. *Chicago Evening Journal*, May 5, 1886.

23. William Holmes to H. H. Sparling, May 7, 1886, Socialist League Archive; *The Commonweal*, May 29, 1886; *Chicago Times*, May 6, 1886; Zeisler, *Haymarket Riot*, p. 23.

24. Zeisler, *Reminiscences of the Anarchist Case*, p. 16; *The Labor Enquirer* (Denver), May 17, 1886.

25. John Peter Altgeld, *Reasons for Pardoning Fielden, Neebe and Schwab* (n.p., n.d. [Chicago, 1893]), pp. 53-54.

26. Ibid.

27. Richard T. Ely, *Under Our Feet: An Autobiography* (New York: Macmillan, 1938), p. 70.

28. Lizzie M. Swank, "Free Speech," *The Labor Enquirer* (Denver), quoted in *The Commonweal*, June 19, 1886.

29. Max Baginski, "Black Friday, 1887," *Mother Earth*, November 1914; Jay Fox, "The Chicago Martyrs," *The Demonstrator*, November 7, 1906.

30. See, for example, Solon L. Goode to Cyrus H. McCormick, Jr., May 19, 1886, McCormick Papers.

31. Russell, *Shifting Scenes*, p. 89.

32. Zeisler, *Reminiscences of the Anarchist Case*, p. 16.

33. Nettlau, *Anarchisten und Sozialrevolutionäre*, p. 380.

34. Herrick, *Memoirs of an American Citizen*, p. 66.

35. Russell, *Shifting Scenes*, pp. 89-90.

36. *Chicago Daily News*, May 10, 1889.

37. Lum, *Concise History*, p. 29.

38. *Autobiographies of the Haymarket Martyrs*, p. 78.

39. *Famous Speeches*, pp. 28-29; *The Commonweal*, July 17, 1886; *Lucifer*, April 13, 1905.

40. John N. Beffel, "Four Radicals," *The American Mercury*, April 1932.

41. *The Labor Enquirer* (Denver), May 15, 1886.

42. Quoted in Ashbaugh, *Lucy Parsons*, p. 84.

43. *Chicago Times*, May 8, 1886.

44. *Freiheit*, December 17, 1887; *The Alarm*, January 14, 1888.
45. Ibid.
46. Ibid.
47. *Autobiographies of the Haymarket Martyrs*, p. 160.
48. *Famous Speeches*, pp. 59-60.
49. Ashbaugh, *Lucy Parsons*, pp. 89-90. A copy of Henry's leaflet, *The Right of Free Speech*, may be found in the Parsons Papers.
50. *Chicago Tribune*, May 9, 1886.
51. *Famous Speeches*, p. 31; *Liberty*, February 12, 1887.
52. Lum, *Concise History*, p. 71; *Autobiographies of the Haymarket Martyrs*, p. 97.
53. *Chicago Times*, May 7, 1886.
54. Lum, *Concise History*, p. 99. See also *The Alarm*, January 28, 1888.
55. *The Monist*, July 1891, p. 521.
56. *The Alarm*, January 28, 1888.
57. Ernst Schmidt called Schuettler, who was later promoted to assistant chief of police, "one of the bravest men I have ever known." *He Chose*, p. 137.
58. *Chicago Daily News*, May 15, 1886; *Abstract of Record*, II, 149-50; Lum, *Concise History*, p. 99.
59. Pierce, *History of Chicago*, III, 282; Lum, *Concise History*, p. 85; *Autobiographies of the Haymarket Martyrs*, p. 160.
60. Quoted in *The Commonweal*, May 29, 1886.
61. Zeisler, *Reminiscences of the Anarchist Case*, p. 15.
62. Lum, *Concise History*, p. 48.
63. Unidentified clipping, May 22, 1886, Haymarket Scrapbook, Columbia University; Schaack, *Anarchy and Anarchists*, pp. 378-82.
64. Ashbaugh, *Lucy Parsons*, p. 87.
65. Quoted in McLean, *Rise and Fall of Anarchy*, pp. 133-35.
66. Cf. Jay Fox, *The Demonstrator*, November 7, 1906.
67. See Schaack, *Anarchy and Anarchists*, p. 694.
68. See the list of contributors in *The Alarm* of September 19, 1885.
69. Zeisler, *Reminiscences of the Anarchist Case*, p. 11.
70. *Chicago Inter Ocean*, May 8, 1886.
71. Schaack, *Anarchy and Anarchists*, p. 384.
72. *Die Autonomie*, April 9, 1887.
73. Zeisler, *Reminiscences of the Anarchist Case*, pp. 12-13.
74. Unidentified clipping, May 22, 1886, Haymarket Scrapbook, Columbia University.
75. *Workmen's Advocate*, May 14, 1887.
76. Letter to Frederick Ebersold, May 20, 1886, Grinnell Papers. There is an excerpt in Schaack, *Anarchy and Anarchists*, p. 228.
77. McLean, *Rise and Fall of Anarchy*, pp. 137-38.

78. *Die Autonomie*, April 9, 1887.

79. Ibid., April 7 and June 18, 1887; Peukert, *Erinnerungen*, pp. 252-56, 268.

Chapter 16: The Fugitive

1. *Chicago Inter Ocean*, May 8, 1886; *Chicago Tribune*, May 9, 1886; *The Knights of Labor*, November 6, 1886; Ashbaugh, *Lucy Parsons*, p. 86.

2. *Autobiographies of the Haymarket Martyrs*, pp. 48-49, 87-88; *Life of Albert R. Parsons*, p. 215; *Abstract of Record*, II, 315; Lum, *Concise History*, pp. 140-43.

3. *Life of Albert R. Parsons*, p. 215.

4. Ibid., pp. 223-27; William Holmes, "The Eleventh of November, 1887," *The Firebrand*, November 15, 1896. See also Holmes to Labadie, April 7, 1889, Labadie Collection.

5. *The Firebrand*, November 15, 1896.

6. Ibid.; *Life of Albert R. Parsons*, pp. 225-26.

7. *The Firebrand*, November 15, 1896.

8. *Life of Albert R. Parsons*, pp. 226-27.

9. *Chicago Daily News*, May 9, 1886; McLean, *Rise and Fall of Anarchy*, pp. 252-54.

10. *The Firebrand*, November 15, 1896; *Life of Albert R. Parsons*, pp. 226-27.

11. *Mother Earth*, November 1912.

12. Ibid.

13. *Life of Albert R. Parsons*, pp. 215-16.

14. Ibid., p. 216; *Famous Speeches*, p. 121; *The Alarm*, November 10, 1888.

15. *Life of Albert R. Parsons*, pp. 216-17.

16. Ibid.; *The Alarm*, August 25, 1888.

17. *Life of Albert R. Parsons*, p. 217; *The Alarm*, August 25, 1888; *Famous Speeches*, p. 121.

18. Parsons letter of August 12 [actually August 21], 1886, *Two Letters of Albert R. Parsons to My Dear Friends at Waukesha*, brochure, December 21, 1886, Parsons Papers. There is a slightly abridged version in *Life of Albert R. Parsons*, pp. 235-36.

19. *Life of Albert R. Parsons*, pp. 218-19.

20. Ibid., p. 216.

21. *The Firebrand*, November 15, 1896.

22. Albert R. Parsons to William Holmes, May 22, 1886, *Free Society*, November 5, 1899.

23. Ibid.

24. Zeisler, *Reminiscences of the Anarchist Case*, p. 17.

25. Schmidt, *He Chose*, p. 147.

26. Ibid.; Zeisler, *Reminiscences of the Anarchist Case*, p. 17; *Chicago Inter*

Ocean, May 31, 1886. On May 8, 1886, the Metal Workers' Union No. 1, an affiliate of the Central Labor Union, had already passed a resolution in support of the arrested anarchists and calling for a defense fund in their behalf. Grinnell Papers.

27. Schmidt, *He Chose*, p. 147.

28. Ibid., pp. 142-48; Zeisler, *Reminiscences of the Anarchist Case*, pp. 16-18. In addition, A. H. Simpson of the American Group started a Fair Trial Fund in June 1886, which sought contributions from reformers and freethinkers as well as anarchists and socialists. See his letter in *The Truth Seeker*, June 26, 1886.

29. Schappes, "Haymarket and the Jews," p. 27; Samuel P. McConnell, "The Chicago Bomb Case: Personal Recollections of an American Tragedy," *Harper's Magazine*, May 1934, p. 734.

30. Zeisler, *Reminiscences of the Anarchist Case*, p. 17; Schmidt, *He Chose*, p. 145.

31. Zeisler, *Reminiscences of the Anarchist Case*, p. 18.

32. Herman Kogan, "William Perkins Black: Haymarket Lawyer," *Chicago History* 5 (Summer 1976), 85-94.

33. Hortensia M. Black, "Capt. William P. Black," *Social Science*, October 12, 1887.

34. *Liberty*, October 14, 1882. Black's address was published in pamphlet form as *Russia and Nihilism* (Chicago, 1882).

35. Black, "Capt. William P. Black"; William Holmes, "The Great Trial," *The Commonweal*, October 2, 1886.

36. Black, "Capt. William P. Black"; Kogan, "William Perkins Black."

37. Black, "Capt. William P. Black"; Zeisler, *Reminiscences of the Anarchist Case*, p. 18.

38. Zeisler, *Reminiscences of the Anarchist Case*, p. 18.

39. Ibid., pp. 15, 19.

40. Ibid., p. 19; Francis X. Busch, "The Haymarket Riot and the Trial of the Anarchists," *Journal of the Illinois State Historical Society* 48 (Autumn 1955), 253.

41. *Free Society*, November 5, 1899.

42. Ibid.

43. *Life of Albert R. Parsons*, pp. 171-72.

44. Ibid., p. 172.

45. Zeisler, *Reminiscences of the Anarchist Case*, pp. 19-20.

46. William A. Foster to Lucy E. Parsons, October 16, 1888, *Life of Albert R. Parsons*, pp. 188-91.

47. Zeisler, *Reminiscences of the Anarchist Case*, p. 20.

48. *Autobiographies of the Haymarket Martyrs*, pp. 49-50.

49. Albert R. Parsons, *An Appeal to the People of America*, Chicago, 1887,

Parsons Papers. The appeal is reprinted in Parsons, *Anarchism*, pp. 183-84.

50. *Life of Albert R. Parsons*, p. 173; *Liberty*, February 12, 1887; *Twentieth Century*, September 3, 1891; *The Firebrand*, November 15, 1896. Cf. William Holmes in *Free Society*, November 6, 1898, and *Mother Earth*, November 1912.

51. *Life of Albert R. Parsons*, p. 219.

52. Ibid., p. 220; *Autobiographies of the Haymarket Martyrs*, p. 50.

53. *Life of Albert R. Parsons*, pp. 220-21.

54. Ibid., p. 221.

55. Ibid., p. 222; *Famous Speeches*, p. 121; Lum, *Concise History*, p. 49.

56. *Life of Albert R. Parsons*, p. 222; *Autobiographies of the Haymarket Martyrs*, p. 50; Zeisler, *Reminiscences of the Anarchist Case*, p. 22; Haymarket Scrapbook, Columbia University.

57. Zeisler, *Reminiscences of the Anarchist Case*, p. 23.

58. *Life of Albert R. Parsons*, pp. 7, 168, 173. Cf. *Lucifer*, June 25, 1886: Parsons's surrender will "challenge the respect and sympathy of every brave and honorable man."

Chapter 17: The Trial

1. William Holmes to H. H. Sparling, July 17, 1886, Socialist League Archive.

2. Unidentified clipping, July 1, 1886, Haymarket Scrapbook, Columbia University; *Chicago Inter Ocean*, June 23 and August 26, 1886.

3. *The Knights of Labor*, November 6, 1886; *Life of Albert R. Parsons*, p. 4; Ashbaugh, *Lucy Parsons*, p. 98.

4. *The Commonweal*, July 17, 1886.

5. William Holmes to H. H. Sparling, August 7, 1886, Socialist League Archive.

6. Carl Sandburg, *Always the Young Strangers* (New York: Harcourt, Brace & Co., 1952), pp. 132-33.

7. Hillquit, *History of Socialism*, p. 227. Among the anarchists, Jay Fox thought the trial "despicable and disgusting," while Gerhard Lizius called it a "legal farce" and Lucy Robins Lang "a trial that remains a disgrace to America." *The Agitator*, November 15, 1910; *Freiheit*, July 31, 1886; Lucy Robins Lang, *Tomorrow is Beautiful* (New York, Macmillan, 1948), p. 27.

8. McConnell, "The Chicago Bomb Case," p. 734.

9. Ibid., p. 733; *Chicago Inter Ocean*, August 3, 1886.

10. Joseph E. Gary, "The Chicago Anarchists of 1886: The Crime, and the Trial, and the Punishment," *The Century Magazine*, April 1893, p. 805.

11. Unidentified clipping, July 1, 1886, Haymarket Scrapbook, Columbia University.
12. Zeisler, *Reminiscences of the Anarchist Case*, pp. 21-22; McConnell, "The Chicago Bomb Case," pp. 732-33.
13. Altgeld, *Reasons*, p. 8. O. J. Smith of the American Press Association knew Bailiff Ryce and thought him "a perfectly unmoral creature." William Dean Howells to William M. Salter, December 1, 1887, Salter Papers.
14. McConnell, "The Chicago Bomb Case," p. 733.
15. *Abstract of Record*, I, 57.
16. Ibid., I, 84-85; Zeisler, *Reminiscences of the Anarchist Case*, p. 24.
17. Zeisler, *Reminiscences of the Anarchist Case*, p. 25.
18. *Life of Albert R. Parsons*, p. 8.
19. *Liberty*, September 18, 1886.
20. *Famous Speeches*, p. 100. One prospective juror who expressed sympathy for the defendants was afterwards fired by his employer. Adelman, *Haymarket Revisited*, p. 47.
21. Zeisler, *Reminiscences of the Anarchist Case*, p. 21.
22. McLean, *Rise and Fall of Anarchy*, pp. 262-63; Ahern, *Political History of Chicago*, pp. 302-303; Kogan, "William Perkins Black."
23. *Famous Speeches*, p. 60.
24. *Abstract of Record*, II, 136-37; Lum, *Concise History*, pp. 95-96.
25. *Abstract of Record*, II, 292-93; Lum, *Concise History*, pp. 133-34. Ernest B. Zeisler, a son of the defense attorney, later theorized that the bomb was thrown from the vestibule of a building at the northeast corner of Randolph and Desplaines Streets (*Haymarket Riot*, pp. 95-101). A large number of witnesses, however, placed the bombthrower half-way up the street, between twenty and forty feet south of Crane's Alley.
26. Lum, *Concise History*, p. 146.
27. *Abstract of Record*, II, 105-108, 127-28; Lum, *Concise History*, p. 93.
28. *Abstract of Record*, II, 164ff.; Lum, *Concise History*, pp. 131-32.
29. *Abstract of Record*, II, 133, 175; Lum, *Concise History*, pp. 93-94.
30. Schaack, *Anarchy and Anarchists*, p. 403.
31. Ibid., pp. 397-98.
32. Zeisler, *Reminiscences of the Anarchist Case*, pp. 28-29.
33. Schmidt, *He Chose*, pp. 136-37. Cf. Parsons in *Famous Speeches*, p. 121.
34. Quoted in *Famous Speeches*, p. 86.
35. *The Labor Enquirer* (Denver), May 17, 1886.
36. *Famous Speeches*, p. 25; *Abstract of Record*, II, 115; Lum, *Concise History*, p. 91.
37. Stone, *Fifty Years a Journalist*, p. 173.
38. Lum, *Concise History*, p. 172.

39. Parsons Papers.
40. Ibid.
41. *Abstract of Record*, I, 7.
42. *Famous Speeches*, pp. 114-15; Gary, "The Chicago Anarchists," p. 809.

Chapter 18: The Verdict

1. *Abstract of Record*, I, 2.
2. Gary, "The Chicago Anarchists," p. 807; unidentified clipping, Haymarket Scrapbook, Columbia University.
3. *Free Society*, November 6, 1898; *Life of Albert R. Parsons*, p. 182.
4. *Chicago Tribune*, August 21, 1886.
5. *Life of Albert R. Parsons*, p. 234.
6. *Chicago Tribune* and *Chicago Times*, August 21, 1886.
7. Lum, *Concise History*, p. 188.
8. Lucy Parsons, "The Eleventh of November, 1887," preface to *Famous Speeches*, 1912 ed.
9. Schaack, *Anarchy and Anarchists*, p. 577.
10. *Lucifer*, May 14, 1903.
11. McConnell, "The Chicago Bomb Case," p. 733.
12. *Famous Speeches*, p. 66.
13. Cf. Barnard, *Eagle Forgotten*, p. 107.
14. *Workmen's Advocate*, September 24, 1887; *The Anarchist*, November 1887. Cf. Parsons: "I am a sacrifice to those who say: 'These men may be innocent. No matter. They are anarchists. We must hang them anyway.' " Parsons, *Anarchism*, p. 184.
15. Cf. Waldo R. Browne, *Altgeld of Illinois: A Record of His Life and Work* (New York: B. W. Huebsch, 1924), pp. 81-82.
16. *Autobiographies of the Haymarket Martyrs*, pp. 56-57; *The Alarm*, August 11, 1888.
17. Schaack, *Anarchy and Anarchists*, p. 390; Parsons, *Anarchism*, pp. 51-53.
18. Lum, *Concise History*, pp. 103-107.
19. *Autobiographies of the Haymarket Martyrs*, pp. 56-57.
20. *Life of Albert R. Parsons*, pp. 234-35.
21. Lucy Parsons, "Publisher's Note," Parsons, *Anarchism*; Lizzie M. Swank, "The Verdict," *The Labor Enquirer* (Denver), September 4, 1886.
22. Most, *Revolutionäre Kriegswissenschaft*, p. 62.
23. *Famous Speeches*, pp. 11, 14. In fact, of course, only seven men had been condemned to death, and Neebe to fifteen years' imprisonment.
24. Ibid., pp. 16-17.
25. Ibid.
26. Ibid., p. 24.

27. Ibid., pp. 25-27.
28. McLean, *Rise and Fall of Anarchy*, p. 49.
29. *Famous Speeches*, p. 31.
30. William Holmes, introduction to *Famous Speeches*, 1899 ed.; *Famous Speeches*, p. 32.
31. *The Alarm*, December 17, 1887; Holmes, introduction to *Famous Speeches*, 1899 ed.
32. *Famous Speeches*, p. 34.
33. Ibid., pp. 35-36.
34. Ibid., p. 38; Holmes, introduction to *Famous Speeches*, 1899 ed.
35. Holmes, introduction to *Famous Speeches*, 1899 ed. Cf. Benjamin Tucker: "His speech will live in history. For plain, straightforward statement of facts, and simple, modest, moving eloquence, but few utterances on record will stand comparison with it." *Liberty*, October 30, 1886.
36. *Famous Speeches*, pp. 61-64.
37. *Liberty*, October 30, 1886.
38. *Famous Speeches*, pp. 67-71.
39. Ibid., p. 67.
40. Ibid., pp. 73, 119.
41. Ibid., p. 121; *Life of Albert R. Parsons*, p. 172.
42. Schaack, *Anarchy and Anarchists*, pp. 606-607.

Chapter 19: The Appeal

1. *To All Friends of an Impartial Administration of Justice!* Chicago, 1886, Parsons Papers, signed by Ernst Schmidt, George Schilling, Frank A. Stauber, Albert Currlin, Peter Peterson, Ferdinand Spies, Frank Bielefeld, Edward Gottge, Julius Leon, Henry Linnemeyer, and Charles F. Seib.
2. *Freedom*, September 1887; *The Anarchist*, May 1887; *Vorbote*, August 25, 1886. See also *Appeal to the Friends of Liberty and Justice In Behalf of the Condemned Chicago Agitators*, San Francisco, California Defense Fund Association, n.d., Parsons Papers.
3. Richard O. Boyer and Herbert M. Morais, *Labor's Untold Story* (New York: Cameron, 1955), p. 101; Ashbaugh, *Lucy Parsons*, p. 104.
4. Ashbaugh, *Lucy Parsons*, pp. 106-108.
5. J. J. Reifgraber to Lucy E. Parsons, November 6, 1886, Grinnell Papers.
6. Ashbaugh, *Lucy Parsons*, p. 113. See also Lucy Parsons to Albert Parsons, March 5, 1887, Parsons Papers.
7. *Free Society*, November 6, 1898. Cf. *The Firebrand*, November 15, 1896.
8. George Schilling in *Lucifer*, May 14, 1903; Robert G. Ingersoll, *Letters*, ed. Eva Ingersoll Wakefield (New York: Philosophical Library, 1951), p. 628. See also O. P. Larson, *American Infidel: The Life of Robert G. Ingersoll* (New York: Citadel Press, 1962), p. 219; and Clarence H. Cra-

mer, *Royal Bob: The Life of Robert G. Ingersoll* (Indianapolis: Bobbs-Merrill, 1952), pp. 226-27.

9. *In the Supreme Court of Illinois. . . . Argument of W. P. Black*, p. 1.
10. Ibid., p. 36.
11. *The American Israelite*, September 3, 1886, quoted in Schappes, "Haymarket and the Jews," p. 27. Pentecost, however, afterwards withdrew his support, concluding that the defendants "had been convicted on evidence sufficient to establish their guilt." See *Liberty*, February 24, 1896.
12. *Liberty*, November 1896.
13. William Dean Howells to Francis Fisher Browne, November 4, 1887, *Chicago Tribune*, November 8, 1887. See also John William Ward, "Another Howells Anarchist Letter," *American Literature* 22 (January 1951), 489-90.
14. Howells to Hamlin Garland, January 15, 1888, *Life in Letters of William Dean Howells*, ed. Mildred Howells, 2 vols. (Garden City, N.Y.: Doubleday, Doran & Co., 1928), I, 407-408. See also Sender Garlin, *William Dean Howells and the Haymarket Era* (New York: The American Institute for Marxist Studies, 1979); and Kenneth S. Lynn, *William Dean Howells: An American Life* (New York: Harcourt, Brace, Jovanovich, 1971), pp. 290-92.
15. Howells to George William Curtis, August 10, 1887, quoted in Clara and Rudolf Kirk, "William Dean Howells, George William Curtis, and the Haymarket Affair," *American Literature* 40 (1969), 489.
16. Howells to Curtis, August 18, 1887, ibid., pp. 490-91.
17. Curtis to Howells, September 23, 1887, ibid., pp. 494-95.
18. Howells to Thomas S. Perry, April 14, 1888, *Life in Letters*, I, 413; Howells, "A Word for the Dead," November 12, 1887, in Cady, *Realist at War*, p. 77; Howells to Edwin D. Mead, November 13, 1887, in Howard A. Wilson, "William Dean Howells' Unpublished Letters About the Haymarket Affair," *Journal of the Illinois State Historical Society* 56 (Spring 1963), 12.
19. *Liberty*, November 1891.
20. Quoted in Chester M. Destler, *Henry Demarest Lloyd and the Empire of Reform* (Philadelphia: University of Pennsylvania Press, 1963), p. 156.
21. Henry D. Lloyd, "Lords of Industry," *The North American Review*, June 1884, pp. 535-53; Schmidt, *He Chose*, p. 153.
22. Lloyd, *Henry Demarest Lloyd*, I, 86, 91, 96-97; Destler, *Henry Demarest Lloyd*, p. 161. At Mitchelstown, Ireland, in September 1887, the police broke up a public meeting with great brutality.
23. Lloyd, *Henry Demarest Lloyd*, I, 101-102; Destler, *Henry Demarest Lloyd*, p. 166. See also John L. Thomas, *Alternative America* (Cambridge, Mass.: Harvard University Press, 1983), pp. 207ff.

24. William M. Salter, "What Shall Be Done with the Anarchists?" *The Open Court*, October 27, 1887; Pierce, *History of Chicago,* III, 285; *The Labor Enquirer* (Denver), October 29, 1887.

25. M. M. Trumbull, *Was It a Fair Trial?* (Chicago: The Author, 1887). A German translation appeared in the *Vorbote* of November 9, 1887.

26. For Trumbull see Wheelbarrow [M. M. Trumbull], *Articles and Discussions on the Labor Question* (Chicago: "Open Court," 1890); G. S. [George Schumm], "General M. M. Trumbull," *Liberty*, June 2, 1894; Rowland T. Berthoff, *British Immigrants in Industrial America, 1790-1950* (Cambridge, Mass.: Harvard University Press, 1953), p. 104; Ray Boston, *British Chartists in America, 1839-1900* (Manchester: Manchester University Press, 1971), pp. 28-29, 70-74, 95-96; and Boston, "General Matthew Trumbull," *Journal of the Illinois State Historical Society* 66 (1973), 3-25.

27. Schumm, "General M. M. Trumbull," *Liberty*, June 2, 1894.

28. *Freiheit*, October 2, 1886; *Liberty*, October 8, 1887; Cahan, *Education*, p. 326. For announcements and reports of protest meetings see also Grinnell and Parsons Papers and *Chicago Times*, August 25, 1886.

29. *The Labor Enquirer* (Denver), October 19, 1887; Philip S. Foner, ed., *American Labor Songs of the Nineteenth Century* (Urbana: University of Illinois Press, 1975), pp. 227-28.

30. William Holmes to H. H. Sparling, August 27, 1886, Socialist League Archive.

31. August Spies to Josef Peukert, October 26, 1886, Peukert Archive.

32. Quoted in *Workmen's Advocate*, July 9, 1887; Schappes, "Haymarket and the Jews," p. 27.

33. *John Swinton's Paper*, May 16, 1886.

34. John Swinton to Henry D. Lloyd, May 26, 1886, Lloyd Papers; Destler, *Henry Demarest Lloyd*, p. 159.

35. Quoted in *Workmen's Advocate*, July 9, 1887.

36. *The Standard*, January 15, 1887. The editorial in which these words appeared was written by George's assistant, Louis F. Post. George, however, acknowledged that "the opinion expressed there was my opinion." George to F. Gutschow, November 25, 1887, George Papers.

37. Parsons to Schilling, September 15, 1886, Schilling Papers; *John Swinton's Paper*, November 21, 1886.

38. Terence V. Powderly, *Thirty Years of Labor, 1859 to 1889* (Columbus, Ohio: Rankin & O'Neal, 1889), pp. 531-57; Ray Ginger, *Altgeld's America* (New York: Funk & Wagnall, 1958), p. 49.

39. *Chicago Daily News*, July 6, 1886; Robert H. Wiebe, *The Search for Order, 1877-1920* (New York: Hill & Wang, 1967), p. 68.

40. Parsons, *Anarchism*, p. 189. See also Parsons's letter in the *Chicago Times*, August 25, 1886.

41. Quoted in Ashbaugh, *Lucy Parsons*, p. 124.
42. *The Commonweal*, December 4, 1886; *The Knights of Labor*, October 16, 1886 ff. The autobiography of Lingg, omitted without explanation, was later published in *The Alarm* (December 29, 1888-January 12, 1889).
43. *Freedom*, November 1886; *Life of Albert R. Parsons*, p. xxxiv; Madison, *American Labor Leaders*, pp. 62-63.
44. Lizzie Holmes to Albert Parsons, December 23, 1886, Parsons Papers; Trautmann, *Voice of Terror*, p. 207.
45. *Lucifer*, October 21, 1887; *Freiheit*, August 28, 1886.
46. *The Truth Seeker*, July 17, 1886.
47. *The Word*, September 1886.
48. *Liberty*, September 18, 1886, September 24, 1887.
49. Ibid., October 30, 1886.
50. Ibid., October 22, 1887.

Chapter 20: Convicts

1. *Freedom*, December 1898.
2. Adolph Fischer to Dyer Lum, September 5, 1887, *The Alarm*, July 7, 1888. See also Fischer's letter in *Freiheit*, October 9, 1886.
3. Lucy Parsons, "The Eleventh of November, 1887"; "Publisher's Note," Parsons, *Anarchism*.
4. *Two Letters of Albert R. Parsons*; *Life of Albert R. Parsons*, p. 236.
5. Parsons to Justus H. Schwab, August 30, 1887, *The Alarm*, June 30, 1888; *Freedom*, September 1887. The London *Anarchist* of August 1887 reported that the prisoners were "in good trim."
6. *The Alarm*, November 10, 1888.
7. August Spies to Robert Reitzel, September 11, 1886, *Der arme Teufel*, September 18, 1887; *Freiheit*, September 27, 1886.
8. Allan Nevins, *Grover Cleveland: A Study in Courage* (New York: Dodd, Mead & Co., 1932), p. 318.
9. *Freedom* (New York), November 1933.
10. Buchanan, *Story of a Labor Agitator*, pp. 373-74.
11. *Waco Day*, November 8, 1887.
12. Quoted in Chushichi Tsuzuki, *The Life of Eleanor Marx, 1855-1898* (Oxford: Clarendon Press, 1967), p. 138.
13. Edward and Eleanor Aveling, *The Working-Class Movement in America* (London: S. Sonnenschein, 1888), p. 170; Yvonne Kapp, *Eleanor Marx*, 2 vols. (New York: Pantheon, 1972-1976), II, 161.
14. Aveling, *Working-Class Movement*, pp. 201-203.
15. *Free Society*, November 6, 1898.
16. Aveling, *Working-Class Movement*, p. 200.
17. *Chicago Daily News*, September 23, 1886.

18. Aveling, *Working-Class Movement*, pp. 200-202.

19. William Holmes to H. H. Sparling, July 17, 1886, Socialist League Archive.

20. *Chicago Herald*, November 27, 1887; *Liberty*, July 16, 1887; *Freedom*, August 1898.

21. See Avrich, *An American Anarchist*, pp. 54ff.

22. *The Alarm*, December 3, 1887.

23. *Liberty*, April 15, 1893; David, *History of the Haymarket Affair*, p. 141.

24. In December 1885 Lum addressed a memorial meeting for John Brown in New York. *The Alarm*, December 26, 1885.

25. Dyer Lum to Voltairine de Cleyre, July 4, 1890, Ishill Papers, Harvard University.

26. *Free Society*, February 3, 1901.

27. Dyer D. Lum, "To Arms: An Appeal to the Wage Slaves of America," *The Alarm*, June 13, 1885, reprinted April 24, 1886, the last issue before the Haymarket incident; ibid., March 20, 1886.

28. Voltairine de Cleyre, *Selected Works of Voltairine de Cleyre*, ed. Alexander Berkman (New York: Mother Earth Publishing Association, 1914), p. 287; de Cleyre, "Dyer D. Lum," *Freedom*, June 1893; Lum to de Cleyre, April 1, 1890, Ishill Papers, University of Florida.

29. *Note to Our Readers*, October 8, 1886; *To the Readers of the Alarm*, Parsons Papers; *Liberty*, October 30, 1886; *Freedom*, June 1893.

30. *The Alarm*, November 5, 1887.

31. *Freedom*, June 1893.

32. *Liberty*, February 12, 1887; *The Alarm*, December 22, 1888.

33. H. F. Charles, "A Voice from America," *The Commonweal*, December 17, 1887; *Free Society*, November 6, 1898.

34. *Liberty*, February 12, 1887; *The Commonweal*, December 17, 1887.

35. *Free Society*, November 6, 1898; *Autobiographies of the Haymarket Martyrs*, p. 167.

36. Schaack, *Anarchy and Anarchists*, p. 169.

37. Albert R. Parsons to Peter Peterson, June 29, 1887; Ernst Schmidt to George Schilling, July 19, 1887, Schilling Papers.

38. Albert Parsons to Lucy Parsons, August 20, 1886, *Life of Albert R. Parsons*, pp. 234-35.

39. *Two Letters of Albert R. Parsons*; *Life of Albert R. Parsons*, pp. 235-36.

40. Parsons to Lum, December 25, 1886; Lizzie Holmes to Parsons, December 23, 1886, Parsons Papers.

41. *Liberty*, February 12, 1887.

42. Russell, *Shifting Scenes*, p. 100.

43. *The Knights of Labor*, November 6, 1886.

44. Ibid.; Nina Van Zandt, preface to Spies, *Auto-Biography*.

45. *The Alarm*, January 14, 1888.

46. Nina Van Zandt, preface to Spies, *Auto-Biography*.

47. William P. Black to George A Schilling, January 18, 1887; Hortensia M. Black to Schilling, January 17, 1887, Schilling Papers. Mrs. Black wrote also to Neebe (January 17, 1887), begging him to dissuade Spies from marrying Nina. Labadie Collection.

48. *The Labor Enquirer* (Chicago), February 26, 1887.

49. *Liberty*, June 8, 1889; *Workmen's Advocate*, December 17, 1887.

50. *Chicago Tribune*, January 19 and 20, 1887, quoted in Barnard, *Eagle Forgotten*, p. 116.

51. *The Alarm*, December 31, 1887.

52. August Spies to Canute R. Matson, February 23, 1887, Chicago Historical Society.

53. James K. Van Zandt to Matson, February 17, 1887, Chicago Historical Society.

54. In the sources on the case her name often appears, erroneously, as Ida Mueller, or Miller. Lingg wrote Elise letters brimming with affection, excerpts from which were published in *The Alarm*, December 17, 1887.

55. Schaack, *Anarchy and Anarchists*, p. 275.

56. Russell, *Shifting Scenes*, p. 99; Young, *Life and Times*, pp. 103-104. Young's sketches of the men are reproduced on p. 103.

57. *The Alarm*, November 10, 1888.

58. De Cleyre, *Haymarket Speeches*, p. 37.

59. *Free Society*, November 5, 1899; *The Alarm*, November 19, 1887; *Workmen's Advocate*, December 3, 1887.

60. *The Alarm*, August 11, 1888.

61. Parsons Papers.

62. *Liberty*, February 12, 1887; Adolph Fischer to Dyer Lum, August 30, 1887, Labadie Collection.

63. Parsons to Justus Schwab, September 21, 1887, *Life of Albert R. Parsons*, p. 240. See also Parsons to Schwab, August 30, 1887, *The Alarm*, June 30, 1888.

64. *The Alarm*, November 10, 1888; *Life of Albert R. Parsons*, pp. 240-41. The tickets, one of which is preserved in the Tamiment Library, read: "Grand Raffle. For a Boat. It Was Wittled [sic] by A. R. PARSONS, with a Small Knife. This Is for the Benefit of A. R. Parsons. Tickets 25 Cents."

65. Schaack, *Anarchy and Anarchists*, pp. 273-74; *The Alarm*, January 14, 1888.

66. *The Alarm*, November 10, 1888.

67. *Two Letters of Albert R. Parsons; Life of Albert R. Parsons*, pp. 235-36.

68. Ibid.

69. Seward Mitchell to Albert Parsons, January 4, 1887, Parsons Papers.

The envelope was addressed "To A. R. Parsons, The Brave, Heroic *Man*, Whose Presence *Honors* Cell 29, Chicago, Illinois."

70. August Spies to Robert Reitzel, September 11, 1886, *Der arme Teufel*, September 18, 1886.

71. *The Alarm*, June 16 and 23, 1888.

72. *Mother Earth*, November 1912. Cf. Lizzie Holmes, "The Memorable 11th of November," *Free Society*, November 9, 1902.

73. *The Alarm*, July 7, 1888; *Freiheit*, October 9, 1886.

74. Adolph Fischer to Henry D. Lloyd and William M. Salter, November 4, 1887, Lloyd, *Henry Demarest Lloyd*, I, 88-89.

75. *Die Autonomie*, October 8, 1887; *Liberty*, February 12, 1887. See also Lingg's attack on reformist socialism in *Freiheit*, November 27, 1886.

76. Parsons, *Anarchism*, p. 107.

77. Lum, *Concise History*, p. 192. See also the charter of the Anarchist Publishing Association, October 21, 1886, Chicago Historical Society.

78. See William H. Parsons, *Dawn of the Social Revolution* (Chicago: "Knights of Labor" Publishing Co., 1887), a twenty-four-page outline of the book, Executive Clemency Files, Illinois State Archives.

79. Parsons, "To the Reader," *Anarchism*, p. 9. See also *Life of Albert R. Parsons*, p. 241; *The Alarm*, December 3, 1887; and William Holmes, "Notes from Chicago," *Freedom*, January 1888.

80. *The Knights of Labor*, November 6, 1886; Ashbaugh, *Lucy Parsons*, pp. 98-99.

81. *The Alarm*, June 30, 1888.

82. Ibid., July 7, 1888.

Chapter 21: Governor Oglesby

1. Schaack, *Anarchy and Anarchists*, p. 618; Busch, "Haymarket Riot," p. 302.

2. August Spies to George Schilling, October 11, 1887, Schilling Papers.

3. Justus H. Schwab to Ernst Schmidt, September 3, 1887; Benjamin F. Butler to Johann Most, September 15, 1887; August Spies to George Schilling, September 18, 1887, Schilling Papers.

4. Roger A. Pryor to George Schilling, September 3, 1887, Schilling Papers.

5. Ernst Schmidt to George Schilling, September 18, 1887; William P. Black to George Schilling, October 7, 1887, Schilling Papers; William Dean Howells to William M. Salter, December 1, 1887, Salter Papers.

6. *United States Supreme Court Reports. . . . Cases Argued and Decided in the Supreme Court of the United States in the October Term, 1887*, pp. 85-91, in Bernard R. Kogan, ed., *The Chicago Haymarket Riot: Anarchy on Trial* (Boston: D. C. Heath & Co., 1959), pp. 88-90.

7. Ashbaugh, *Lucy Parsons*, p. 127.

8. Robert G. Ingersoll to George Schilling, November 3, 1887, Schilling Papers; *Letters of Robert G. Ingersoll*, p. 629; Larson, *American Infidel*, pp. 220-21.

9. Barnard, *Eagle Forgotten*, p. 110.

10. Robert G. Ingersoll to George Schilling, November 3, 1887, Schilling Papers.

11. Henry D. Lloyd to William M. Salter, December 21, 1887, Salter Papers; Lloyd, *Henry Demarest Lloyd*, I, 92.

12. William Holmes, "Reminiscences of November 11," *Free Society*, November 4, 1900.

13. *Freedom*, December 1887.

14. Ashbaugh, *Lucy Parsons*, p. 126.

15. *Free Society*, November 4, 1900.

16. Schaack, *Anarchy and Anarchists*, p. 623.

17. Schmidt, *He Chose*, p. 150.

18. Buchanan, *Story of a Labor Agitator*, p. 382; *Chicago Tribune*, November 9, 1887; McConnell, "The Chicago Bomb Case," p. 735.

19. Everett Carter, "The Haymarket Affair in Literature," *American Quarterly* 2 (Fall 1950), 272.

20. Gregory Weinstein, *The Ardent Eighties* (New York: International Press, 1928), pp. 153-55.

21. Howells, *Life in Letters*, I, 393.

22. William Dean Howells to William M. Salter, November 24, 1887, Salter Papers; Cady, *Realist at War*, p. 71; Albert Mordell, *Quaker Militant: John Greenleaf Whittier* (Boston: Houghton, 1933), pp. 261-63.

23. Howells, *Life in Letters*, I, 398-99.

24. William Dean Howells to Thomas S. Perry, April 14, 1888, ibid., I, 413.

25. Quoted in Cady, *Realist at War*, pp. 72-73.

26. Garlin, *William Dean Howells*, p. 37; Howells, *Life in Letters*, I, 403; Whitlock, *Forty Years of It*, p. 72.

27. *New York Evening Mail*, November 3, 1887.

28. Robert G. Ingersoll to George Schilling, November 7, 1887, Schilling Papers; *Letters of Robert G. Ingersoll*, p. 629; *Lucifer*, May 7 and 14, 1903; Larson, *American Infidel*, pp. 220-21.

29. *Liberty*, October 8, 1887; *The Word*, November 1887. On Train see Dennis B. Downey, "George Francis Train: The Great American Humbug," *Journal of Popular Culture* 14 (Fall 1980), 252-61.

30. August Spies to George Schilling, September 18, 1887, Schilling Papers; Russell, *Shifting Scenes*, p. 101.

31. *Chicago Daily News*, as quoted in *Liberty*, November 5, 1887. Train had published a poem, "Sounding Alarm," in *The Alarm* of September 19, 1885.

32. Albert R. Parsons to George F. Train, October 14, 1887, in Parsons,

Anarchism, p. 193. The *Daily Psycho-Anarchist* appeared briefly in Chicago in October 1887 before being suppressed. I have been unable to locate any copies.

33. *The Alarm*, January 14, 1888.
34. Ibid.; Louis Ruchames, ed., "John Brown, Jr., and the Haymarket Martyrs," *Massachusetts Review* 5 (Summer 1964), 765-68. See also *The Alarm*, December 17, 1887; and *Man!*, November 1937.
35. Ruchames, "John Brown, Jr.," p. 767.
36. *The Alarm*, November 28, 1885.
37. *The Standard*, October 8, 1887.
38. Ibid.
39. "Henry George and the Chicago Anarchists," *Freedom*, March 1889; *The Commonweal*, November 12, 1887.
40. Benjamin R. Tucker, "Henry George, Traitor," *Liberty*, November 1896; *The Road to Freedom*, November 1931. Cf. *Workmen's Advocate*, October 15, 1887.
41. Henry George to Mr. McGee, October 15, 1887, George Papers.
42. Henry George to Richard J. Oglesby, November 5, 1887, George Papers.
43. Ibid.
44. Note of Governor Oglesby, January 29, 1888, Oglesby Papers.
45. Oglesby Papers. Ironically, Lowell himself thought the anarchists "well hanged." Carter, "The Haymarket Affair," p. 271; Carter, *Howells and the Age of Realism*, pp. 181-82.
46. Clara Shuntz to Richard J. Oglesby, November 2, 1887, Oglesby Papers; John H. Keiser, *Building for the Centuries: Illinois, 1865-1898* (Urbana: University of Illinois Press, 1977), p. 100.
47. Federation of Trades Unions, *An das arbeitende Volk der Vereinigten Staaten von Nordamerika!*, Grinnell Papers.
48. *Report of the Proceedings of the Sixth National Convention*, pp. 16-17, in Quint, *Forging of American Socialism*, p. 34.
49. Gompers, *Seventy Years*, p. 273. See also Bernard Mandel, *Samuel Gompers* (Yellow Springs, Ohio: Antioch Press, 1963), p. 56; and Calmer, *Labor Agitator*, p. 150.
50. Samuel Gompers to James W. Smith, October 13, 1887, in Philip Taft, *The A.F. of L. in the Time of Gompers* (New York: Harper & Row, 1957), p. 67.
51. Ibid.; Gompers to Smith, November 15, 1887, ibid.
52. Samuel Gompers to Richard J. Oglesby, November 7, 1887, Executive Clemency Files, Illinois State Archives.
53. *The Labor Enquirer* (Denver), October 22, 1887; Mandel, *Samuel Gompers*, pp. 55-56.
54. *Workmen's Advocate*, October 8, 1887; L. Glen Seretan, *Daniel De*

Leon: The Odyssey of an American Marxist (Cambridge, Mass.: Harvard University Press, 1979), p. 30.

55. Parsons Papers; *Freedom*, November 1887.

56. Madison, *American Labor Leaders*, p. 63; Gerald A. Stearn, ed., *Gompers* (Englewood Cliffs, N.J.: Prentice-Hall, 1971), p. 35.

57. August Spies to George Schilling, October 11, 1887, Schilling Papers.

58. *The Knights of Labor*, October 8, 1887.

59. Powderly, *Thirty Years*, pp. 549-54; *The Commonweal*, October 29, 1887.

60. *The Advance and Labor Leaf*, November 19, 1887; Powderly, *Thirty Years*, pp. 549-54.

61. Terence V. Powderly, *The Path I Trod* (New York: Columbia University Press, 1940), p. 363.

62. *The Advance and Labor Leaf*, November 19, 1887; August Spies to George Schilling, October 17, 1887, Schilling Papers.

63. Charlotte Wilson, "The Condemned Anarchists," *The Commonweal*, November 12, 1887; Scrapbook SB40, Tamiment Library.

64. *The Anarchist*, November 1887; Henry Seymour to A. H. Simpson, November 24, 1886, Parsons Papers.

65. *Freedom*, October 1886, November 1887.

66. Tsuzuki, *Eleanor Marx*, pp. 153-54; Kapp, *Eleanor Marx*, II, 214-15.

67. Henry M. Hyndman, *The Chicago Riots and the Class War in the United States* (London: S. Sonnenschein, Lowery & Co., 1886), pp. 1-2; R. Laurence Moore, *European Socialists and the American Promised Land (1880-1917)* (New York: Oxford University Press, 1970), pp. 33-34.

68. *The Commonweal*, January 29 and September 24, 1887.

69. Ibid., October 22, 1887.

70. William Morris to Robert Browning, November 7, 1887, facsimile in Zeisler, *Reminiscences of the Anarchist Case*, following p. 36.

71. *The Commonweal*, October 15, 1887.

72. Ibid., October 22, 1887; R. Page Arnot, *William Morris: The Man and the Myth* (New York: Monthly Review Press, 1964), pp. 86-89.

73. *Freedom*, December 1887.

74. Ibid.; Executive Clemency Files, Illinois State Archives. See also George Bernard Shaw to Frank Harris, October 7, 1908, Shaw, *Collected Letters*, ed. Dan H. Laurence, 2 vols. (New York: Dodd, Mead, 1965-1972), I, 812-13.

75. See *The Commonweal*, October 29, 1887; *Freedom*, November 1887; *The Alarm*, December 17, 1887.

76. *The Commonweal*, December 4, 1886, April 28, 1888; *John Swinton's Paper*, December 5, 1886; Executive Clemency Files, Illinois State Archives. See also Paul Avrich, "J. W. Fleming," *Freedom*, July 23, 1977.

Chapter 22: Springfield

1. Lloyd, *Henry Demarest Lloyd*, I, 89. See also Destler, *Henry Demarest Lloyd*, pp. 162-63.
2. August Spies to William M. Salter, November 3, 1887, Salter Papers.
3. August Spies, Michael Schwab, and Samuel Fielden to Richard J. Oglesby, November 3, 1887, Executive Clemency Files, Illinois State Archives; *Chicago Inter Ocean*, November 6, 1887.
4. Samuel Fielden to Richard J. Oglesby, November 5, 1887, in McLean, *Rise and Fall of Anarchy*, pp. 219-21; Schaack, *Anarchy and Anarchists*, pp. 627-28.
5. Michael Schwab to Richard J. Oglesby, November 8, 1887, *Chicago Inter Ocean*, November 9, 1887; Schaack, *Anarchy and Anarchists*, p. 628.
6. August Spies to Richard J. Oglesby, November 6, 1887, Oglesby Papers; *Chicago Tribune*, November 10, 1887; McLean, *Rise and Fall of Anarchy*, pp. 221-23.
7. Buchanan, *Story of a Labor Agitator*, p. 391.
8. Executive Clemency Files, Illinois State Archives; *Vorbote*, November 9, 1887; *The Alarm*, November 5, 1887; McLean, *Rise and Fall of Anarchy*, pp. 214-19.
9. Adolph Fischer to Typographical Union No. 9, November 8, 1887, Chicago Historical Society; English translation in *Industrial Worker*, December 28, 1946, and *Freedom*, January 4, 1947.
10. Adolph Fischer to Paul Bulian, July 27, 1886, *Freiheit*, August 28, 1886.
11. *The Alarm*, January 14 and November 10, 1888.
12. *Free Society*, November 6, 1898.
13. Ibid., November 6, 1898, November 5, 1899; *Mother Earth*, November 1912.
14. *The Alarm*, January 28, 1888; *Free Society*, November 6, 1898.
15. *Liberty*, February 12, 1887.
16. *La Révolte*, October 15-21, 1887; *The Alarm*, December 17, 1887.
17. Parsons to Justus Schwab, August 30, 1887, *The Alarm*, June 30, 1888.
18. *The Alarm*, August 11, 1888.
19. Parsons, *Appeal*; Parsons, *Anarchism*, pp. 178-85.
20. Parsons, *Anarchism*, pp. 185-86. See also Parsons's letter of November 3, 1887, *The Alarm*, November 19, 1887.
21. *The Alarm*, December 3, 1887.
22. *Life of Albert R. Parsons*, p. 230. For a different version see Stone, *Fifty Years a Journalist*, pp. 175-76.
23. *Life of Albert R. Parsons*, pp. 183-86.
24. Ibid.
25. Ibid. See also Black in *Free Society*, November 6, 1898.

26. *Free Society*, November 4, 1900.
27. *Mother Earth*, November 1912.
28. Dyer Lum to George Schilling, June 24, 1887, Schilling Papers.
29. Voltairine de Cleyre to George Schilling, July 12, 1893, Schilling Papers; Dyer Lum, "Waldheim," in *In Memoriam, Chicago, November 11, 1887* (Berkeley Heights, N.J.: The Oriole Press, 1937).
30. *Freedom*, June 1893.
31. *Life of Albert R. Parsons*, p. 228.
32. Lum to de Cleyre, March 1, 1891, Ishill Papers, University of Florida.
33. Lum to de Cleyre, April 1, 1890, March 1, 1891, Ishill Papers, University of Florida; *Freedom*, June 1893.
34. Schilling to Lum, September 2, 1888, Schilling Papers, University of Chicago; *The Alarm*, September 8, 1888.
35. George White to Richard J. Oglesby, October 27, 1887; J. C. Smith to Oglesby, November 7, 1887, Oglesby Papers.
36. *The Nation*, October 27 and November 10, 1887; Sproat, *The Best Men*, pp. 204, 223.
37. Lloyd, *Henry Demarest Lloyd*, I, 89-91; Altgeld, *Reasons*, p. 57; George Schilling to John P. Altgeld, May 12, 1893, Executive Clemency Files, Illinois State Archives.
38. *Chicago Tribune*, November 10, 1887; Altgeld, *Reasons*, p. 56; Altgeld, *Live Questions* (Chicago: George S. Bower & Sons, 1899), pp. 390-91.
39. Altgeld, *Reasons*, p. 56.
40. George Schilling to Joseph Labadie, n.d. [November 1887], Labadie Collection.
41. *The Anarchist*, July 1888; *Free Society*, November 4, 1900.
42. *The Anarchist*, December 1887, July 1, 1888; *Chicago Herald*, November 8, 1887; *The Commonweal*, November 12, 1887.
43. *The Alarm*, November 10 and December 22, 1888.
44. Ibid., December 17, 1887; Lum to de Cleyre, September 2, 1890, Ishill Papers, University of Florida.
45. De Cleyre, *Haymarket Speeches*, p. 8; Harry de Cleyre to Agnes Inglis, December 29, 1947, Labadie Collection.
46. Dyer Lum to Joseph Labadie, November 6, 1887, Labadie Collection.
47. *The Alarm*, December 22, 1888.
48. *The Anarchist*, July 1, 1888.
49. William M. Salter to August Spies, November 7, 1887, Salter Papers.
50. August Spies to William M. Salter, November 7, 1887, Howells Papers.
51. Lum to de Cleyre, November 22, 1890, Ishill Papers, Harvard University.
52. Adolph Fischer to William M. Salter, November 7, 1887, Salter Papers.
53. Spies to Salter, November 7, 1887, Salter Papers.

54. *Chicago Tribune*, November 10, 1887; Schaack, *Anarchy and Anarchists*, pp. 628-29.
55. M. E. Stone to R. B. Peattie, November 6, 1887, Oglesby Papers.
56. Oglesby to Peattie, November 7, 1887, Oglesby Papers.
57. Gompers, *Seventy Years*, p. 238.
58. Lloyd, *Henry Demarest Lloyd*, I, 92-93. The Lloyds suffered the loss of a fortune estimated at more than five million dollars.
59. Gompers, *Seventy Years*, p. 238.
60. *Chicago Tribune*, November 10, 1887; *The Labor Enquirer* (Chicago), November 14, 1887; Buchanan, *Story of a Labor Agitator*, pp. 389-90; Calmer, *Labor Agitator*, p. 118. For Captain Black's appeal see *The Knights of Labor*, December 17, 1887.
61. *Chicago Tribune*, November, 11, 1887; Gompers, *Seventy Years*, p. 238; Mandel, *Samuel Gompers*, p. 57; Stearn, *Gompers*, pp. 25-26.
62. Buchanan, *Story of a Labor Agitator*, pp. 393-99.
63. Ibid.; Spies to Oglesby, November 6, 1887, Oglesby Papers. Oglesby's comment is written on the letter.
64. Parsons to Oglesby, November 8, 1887, Oglesby Papers; *The Alarm*, November 19, 1887; McConnell, "Chicago Bomb Case," pp. 735-36.
65. Lloyd Papers; *Chicago Tribune*, November 10, 1887.
66. McConnell, "The Chicago Bomb Case," p. 736.
67. Ibid.
68. *Chicago Tribune*, November 11, 1887; *The Commonweal*, December 24, 1887; *The Anarchist*, July 1, 1888. See Schaack, *Anarchy and Anarchists*, p. 635, for a facsimile of Lingg's last note. That he wrote in his blood "Long live anarchy!" as some writers assert, is a legend.
69. *The Anarchist*, December 1887.
70. Alexander Berkman to Emma Goldman, June 21, 1934, Berkman Archive.
71. "The Tragedy of Chicago," *Freedom*, December 1887.
72. *The Alarm*, December 17, 1887.
73. De Cleyre, *Haymarket Speeches*, p. 8; Harry de Cleyre to Agnes Inglis, December 29, 1947, Labadie Collection. See also Barnard, *Eagle Forgotten*, p. 113.
74. *The Alarm*, November 10, 1888.
75. William Dean Howells to Francis F. Browne, November 11, 1887, *Life in Letters*, I, 401-402.
76. *Chicago Times*, November 12, 1887; *The Alarm*, November 19, 1887; Adelman, *Haymarket Revisited*, p. 50.
77. *Mother Earth*, November 1912.
78. Goldman, *Living My Life*, pp. 42, 87.
79. Governor Oglesby's proclamation, November 10, 1887, Executive

Clemency Files, Illinois State Archives; Schaack, *Anarchy and Anarchists*, p. 638.

80. Schmidt, *He Chose*, pp. 158-59. Cf. Buchanan, *Story of a Labor Agitator*, p. 401: "a sadder group I have never seen, and I hope may never see the like again."

81. Lloyd, *Henry Demarest Lloyd*, I, 96. Edwin D. Mead wrote to Lloyd (November 21, 1887) that he and Salter had been "*Christians* enough through the whole ordeal." Lloyd Papers.

82. *Liberty*, November 1896; Keiser, *Building for the Centuries*, p. 100.

83. Buchanan, *Story of a Labor Agitator*, p. 401.

84. Black to Schilling, November 10, 1887, Schilling Papers.

85. Buchanan, *Story of a Labor Agitator*, pp. 404-11. See also *Free Society*, November 6, 1898.

Chapter 23: The Scaffold

1. *The Alarm*, November 19, 1887.
2. Ibid.
3. Ibid.; *Life of Albert R. Parsons*, pp. 242-43.
4. Schmidt, *He Chose*, p. 156.
5. Spies, *Reminiscenzen*, p. 166.
6. *The Alarm*, January 14, 1888.
7. Ibid., January 28, 1888.
8. Ibid.; *Acht Opfer des Klassenhasses: Leben und Sterben der verurtheilten Chicagoer Arbeitsführer* (New York: Labor News Co., 1890), pp. 23-24.
9. Russell, *Shifting Scenes*, pp. 103-104; Mother Jones, *Autobiography*, p. 22.
10. *The Labor Enquirer* (Denver), September 4, 1886; *Liberty*, September 24, 1887.
11. *The Alarm*, June 23, 1888.
12. Schaack, *Anarchy and Anarchists*, p. 640; Russell, *Shifting Scenes*, pp. 103-104; Young, *Life and Times*, p. 105.
13. *Freedom*, January 1888; Stone, *Fifty Years a Journalist*, p. 177.
14. *Free Society*, November 4, 1900. Cf. *Mother Earth*, November 1912.
15. Robert Reitzel, *Des armen Teufel: Gesammelte Schriften*, 3 vols. (Detroit: Reitzel Club, 1913), III, 97ff.; Adolf E. Zucker, "Robert Reitzel as a Poet," *German American Annals* 13 (1915), 61; Schmidt, *He Chose*, p. 151; *Freedom*, June 1898.
16. Dyer Lum to Voltairine de Cleyre, March 1, 1891, Ishill Papers, University of Florida; November 10, 1891, Ishill Papers, Harvard University.
17. Abe Isaak, Jr., "The Chicago Martyrdom," *Free Society*, November 8, 1903.

18. *Mother Earth*, November 1912; *Free Society*, November 6, 1898. See also *Freedom*, January 1888; *The Rebel*, November 20, 1895; and introduction to *Famous Speeches*, 1899 ed.
19. T. P. Quinn, "Some Recollections," *Free Society*, November 6, 1898.
20. *The Labor Enquirer* (Chicago), November 19, 1887.
21. *Chicago Herald*, November 13, 1887; Adelman, *Haymarket Revisited*, p. 55.
22. Lizzie M. Swank, "A Fiendish Act," *The Labor Enquirer* (Chicago), November 19, 1887.
23. Ibid.
24. Ibid. See also Lucy Parsons, "The Eleventh of November, 1887"; *The Firebrand*, November 15, 1896; and Buchanan, *Story of a Labor Agitator*, pp. 420-22.
25. *Life of Albert R. Parsons*, pp. 243-45.
26. Ibid., p. 245. A week earlier Parsons had written: "there is but one God—Humanity. Any other kind of religion is a mockery, a delusion, and a snare." *Chicago Tribune*, November 4, 1887.
27. *The Word*, December 1887; Buchanan, *Story of a Labor Agitator*, p. 420; *Life of Albert R. Parsons*, p. 241.
28. Chicago Historical Society; *Life of Albert R. Parsons*, p. 241.
29. *Life of Albert R. Parsons*, p. 246.
30. Parsons to Lum, November 11, 1887, *The Alarm*, November 19, 1887; Parsons, *Anarchism*, p. 200; *Life of Albert R. Parsons*, p. 248.
31. *The Alarm*, December 31, 1887; Spies, *Reminiscenzen*, p. 170.
32. Salter Papers; *Chicago Times*, November 12, 1887.
33. *The Alarm*, November 19, 1887.
34. Ibid., January 14, 1888.
35. Chicago Historical Society; *Industrial Worker*, December 28, 1946; *Freedom*, January 4, 1947.
36. Parsons, *Anarchism*, pp. 199-200; *Famous Speeches*, p. 122.
37. *Life of Albert R. Parsons*, p. 247.
38. Ibid.; Calmer, *Labor Agitator*, p. 123.
39. *Chicago Tribune*, November 12, 1887; *Acht Opfer des Klassenhasses*, p. 26; McLean, *Rise and Fall of Anarchy*, pp. 231-38.
40. *Chicago Tribune*, November 12, 1887.
41. Ibid.
42. Chicago Historical Society; Oglesby Papers.
43. *Workmen's Advocate*, November 19, 1887.
44. *Chicago Daily News* and *Chicago Tribune*, November 12, 1887. In New York Abraham Cahan "shared her agony as over and over again I read the details in the newspapers." *Education*, p. 329.
45. Quoted in Adamic, *Dynamite*, p. 82.
46. Lizzie Holmes, "The First Decade: November 11, 1887-1897," *Free*

Society, November 28, 1897; *The Rebel*, November 20, 1895; *The Fire-brand*, November 15, 1896. See also George Brown, "November Memories," *Mother Earth*, November 1912; Buchanan, *Story of a Labor Agitator*, p. 423; and Mother Jones, *Autobiography*, p. 23.

47. *Chicago Daily News*, November 14, 1887; *The Labor Enquirer* (Chicago), November 19, 1887; Ashbaugh, *Lucy Parsons*, pp. 139-40.
48. *Chicago Herald*, November 14, 1887; *The Alarm*, November 19, 1887.
49. *The Alarm*, November 19, 1887; *Acht Opfer des Klassenhasses*, pp. 36-38.
50. *The Alarm*, November 19, 1887; *Vorbote*, November 23, 1887; *Acht Opfer des Klassenhasses*, pp. 39-40.
51. *The Alarm*, December 31, 1887; Ashbaugh, *Lucy Parsons*, pp. 141-42.
52. William Dean Howells to William Cooper Howells (his father), November 13, 1887, *Life in Letters*, I, 402.

Chapter 24: Repercussions

1. C. E. Loomis to Richard J. Oglesby, November 11, 1887; Matson to Oglesby, November 12, 1887, Oglesby Papers.
2. Quoted in Carter, "The Haymarket Affair," p. 271; Carter, *Howells and the Age of Realism*, pp. 181-82.
3. Barnard, *Eagle Forgotten*, p. 115; Pierce, *History of Chicago*, III, 287.
4. *London Times*, November 12, 1887; Jack Lindsay, *William Morris: His Life and Work* (London: Constable, 1975), p. 324.
5. *Free Society*, November 9, 1902.
6. Pringle, *Theodore Roosevelt*, p. 111; Mary Herma Aikin in *The Commonweal*, May 4, 1889; Sandburg, *Always the Young Strangers*, pp. 133-34.
7. Lloyd, *Henry Demarest Lloyd*, I, 99; Destler, *Henry Demarest Lloyd*, p. 168; Herman Kogan, *The First Century: The Chicago Bar Association, 1874-1974* (Chicago: Rand-McNalley, 1974), p. 72.
8. *Chicago Herald*, January 3, 1888; Clarence S. Darrow to Henry D. Lloyd, January 4, 1888; William P. Black to Henry D. Lloyd, January 5, 1888, Lloyd Papers.
9. Henry D. Lloyd, "Voices of the Gallows," November 11, 1887, Lloyd Papers; Lloyd, *Henry Demarest Lloyd*, I, 98. Lloyd called the first draft "Hymn to the Gallows."
10. Howells, *Life in Letters*, I, 401-405. Cf. Howells to William M. Salter, November 14, 1887, Salter Papers.
11. Howells to Salter, November 20, November 24, and December 11, 1887, Salter Papers.
12. In Cady, *Realist at War*, pp. 73-77.
13. Ibid.

14. Howells to Salter, November 20, 1887, Salter Papers; Salter to Howells, November 27, 1887, Howells Papers.
15. *Liberty*, November 19, 1887; George Schilling to Joseph Labadie, November 6, 1887, Labadie Collection; Mandel, *Samuel Gompers*, p. 57.
16. Buchanan, *Story of a Labor Agitator*, p. 415; McConnell, "Chicago Bomb Case," p. 738; Black, preface to *Famous Speeches*, 1912 ed.; Benjamin F. Butler to Black, February 14, 1888; Black to Schilling, April 7, 1888, Schilling Papers; *The Alarm*, December 17, 1887.
17. Cahan, *Education*, p. 328; *Free Society*, November 28, 1897.
18. *The Anarchist*, December 1887.
19. Grinnell Papers; *Yidishes Tageblat*, November 10, 1888.
20. Oglesby Papers.
21. *The Commonweal*, August 11 and November 24, 1888; *The Alarm*, December 8, 1888.
22. J. William Lloyd, "Vengeance: An Open Letter to the Communist-Anarchists of Chicago," *Liberty*, January 14, 1888.
23. *Solidarity*, April 15, 1898.
24. Dyer Lum to Voltairine de Cleyre, March 1, 1891, Ishill Papers, University of Florida; Lum to de Cleyre, February 5, 1892, Ishill Papers, Harvard University. See also de Cleyre to Schilling, June 27, 1893, Schilling Papers.
25. *The Commonweal*, May 13, 1893.
26. De Cleyre, *Selected Works*, pp. 284-96.
27. *The Alarm*, February 11, 1888.
28. Art Young, *On My Way* (New York: Liveright, 1928), p. 123; M. M. Trumbull, *The Trial of the Judgment: A Review of the Anarchist Case* (Chicago: Heath & Howe Publishing Co., 1888), p. 4; Oglesby Papers.
29. *The Alarm*, February 25 and March 24, 1888.
30. *The Labor Enquirer* (Denver), November 14, 1887; *Workmen's Advocate*, November 19, 1887; *The People*, November 17, 1887.
31. *Liberty*, November 19, 1887.
32. *Freedom*, December 1887.
33. Lewis and Smith, *Chicago*, p. 165.
34. *Liberty*, November 10, 1888; *Lucifer*, November 18, 1887.
35. William Holmes, "The Order of the Gallows," *The Commonweal*, April 12, 1890; *Twentieth Century*, November 13, 1890.
36. *Freedom*, November 1888.
37. Facsimile in *Life of Albert R. Parsons*, p. 240.
38. Peter Kropotkin, "Before the Storm," *Freedom*, December 1888.
39. *Lucifer*, December 10, 1903.
40. *Liberty*, November 21 and 28, 1891; *Freedom*, December 1891; Walter Crane, *An Artist's Reminiscences* (New York: Macmillan, 1907), pp. 364-65; *Free Society*, November 23, 1902.

41. *The Firebrand*, November 24, 1895, November 26, 1896.

42. Ibid., December 15, 1895.

43. Goldman, *Living My Life*, p. 221.

44. *The Alarm*, December 17, 1887, June 23, 1888; *The Commonweal*, October 18, 1890; *Freedom* (Chicago), March 1892.

45. Irving S. Abrams, "The Haymarket Tragedy," *Freedom*, November 11, 1972.

46. Lewis and Smith, *Chicago*, p. 166.

47. Lang, *Tomorrow Is Beautiful*, pp. 27, 31, 291.

Chapter 25: The Pardon

1. Lloyd, *Henry Demarest Lloyd*, i, 103; Browne, *Altgeld*, p. 87.

2. *Chicago Times*, January 5, 1889; *The Alarm*, January 12, 1889; Adelman, *Haymarket Revisited*, p. 24.

3. *Chicago Times*, January 15, 1889; Adelman, *Haymarket Revisited*, p. 97; Ashbaugh, *Lucy Parsons*, pp. 165-67.

4. Zeisler, *Reminiscences of the Anarchist Case*, p. 15; John N. Hills to Oscar Neebe, June 28, 1893, Labadie Collection.

5. Schmidt, *He Chose*, p. 166; Browne, *Altgeld*, p. 87.

6. Altgeld, *Live Questions*, pp. 196-203.

7. Ibid.

8. Ibid.

9. Harvey Wish, "Governor Altgeld Pardons the Anarchists," *Journal of the Illinois State Historical Society* 31 (December 1938), 430.

10. Abbot, *Watching the World Go By*, p. 109; Schilling Papers.

11. *Liberty*, May 6, 1893.

12. Clarence S. Darrow, *The Story of My Life* (New York: Scribner's, 1932), pp. 100-101.

13. McConnell, "Chicago Bomb Case," p. 738; Barnard, *Eagle Forgotten*, pp. 185-86.

14. Gary, "Chicago Anarchists"; Barnard, *Eagle Forgotten*, p. 197.

15. *Liberty*, May 6, 1893; M. M. Trumbull, "Judge Gary and the Anarchists," *The Arena*, October 1893, pp. 544-61; Sarah E. Ames, *An Open Letter to Judge Joseph E. Gary* (Chicago: S. E. Ames, 1893); Clarence Darrow to George Schilling, April 28, 1893, Schilling Papers; Kogan, "William Perkins Black," p. 94.

16. Charles A. Madison, *Critics and Crusaders: A Century of American Protest*, 2d ed. (New York: Frederick Ungar, 1959), p. 373; Browne, *Altgeld*, pp. 72-73; Barnard, *Eagle Forgotten*, pp. 179-82.

17. Darrow, *Story of My Life*, p. 101.

18. *Boston Herald*, January 12, 1895, quoted in Browne, *Altgeld*, pp. 109-110.

19. McConnell, "Chicago Bomb Case," p. 738.
20. *Chicago Inter Ocean*, March 16, 1902, in Browne, *Altgeld*, pp. 90-91; William Dose To William Hinrichsen, June 26, 1893, Executive Clemency Files, Illinois State Archives.
21. Whitlock, *Forty Years of It*, pp. 73-74.
22. *Liberty*, November 1896; *Journal of the Illinois State Historical Society* 46 (Summer 1953), 246.
23. Altgeld, *Reasons*, pp. 49-50.
24. Ibid., pp. 36, 62-63.
25. Ibid., p. 35.
26. Whitlock, *Forty Years of It*, p. 75.
27. Browne, *Altgeld*, pp. 107-108; Wish, "Governor Altgeld Pardons the Anarchists," p. 441; Ginger, *Altgeld's America*, pp. 85-86.
28. *Journal of the Illinois State Historical Society* 46 (Summer 1953), 173; Symes and Clement, *Rebel America*, p. 176; Sproat, *Best Men*, p. 241.
29. Whitlock, *Forty Years of It*, pp. 74-75; Darrow, *Story of My Life*, p. 102; McConnell, "Chicago Bomb Case," p. 738. According to Jane Addams, *Twenty Years at Hull House* (New York: Macmillan, 1910), p. 207, "a magnanimous action was marred by personal rancor, betraying for the moment the infirmity of a noble mind."
30. *Chicago Tribune*, June 30, 1893; *New York Times*, June 28, 1893, in Wish, "Governor Altgeld Pardons the Anarchists," p. 444.
31. *Liberty*, July 1, 1893.
32. Schilling Papers; Altgeld Correspondence, Illinois State Archives.
33. Lloyd, *Henry Demarest Lloyd*, I, 103-104.
34. Emma F. Altgeld to Jessie B. Lloyd, July 14, 1893, Altgeld Papers.
35. Enclosed with Michael Schwab to George Schilling, July 5, 1893, Schilling Papers.
36. Wish, "Governor Altgeld Pardons the Anarchists," p. 448.
37. Darrow, *Story of My Life*, p. 104.
38. George Schilling to Johann Waage, October 15, 1913, Schilling Papers; *Chicago Inter Ocean*, March 16, 1902, in Wish, "Governor Altgeld Pardons the Anarchists," p. 444.
39. Ashbaugh, *Lucy Parsons*, p. 243; *Discontent*, November 7, 1900.

Chapter 26: The Legacy

1. Cesare Lombroso, "Illustrative Studies in Criminal Anthropology: The Physiognomy of the Anarchists," *The Monist*, January and April, 1891.
2. Michael Schwab, "A Convicted Anarchist's Reply to Professor Lombroso," ibid., July 1891; Yellen, *American Labor Struggles*, p. 69.
3. Avrich, *An American Anarchist*, p. 178; Ishill, *Reclus*, p. 61.
4. Whitlock, *Forty Years of It*, pp. 37-41.

5. *John Swinton's Paper*, May 16, 1886; Powderly, *Thirty Years*, p. 543; Gompers, *Seventy Years*, pp. 175, 237; Commons, *History of Labor*, II, 386.

6. Higham, *Strangers in the Land*, p. 55.

7. Leon Whipple, *The Story of Civil Liberty in the United States* (New York: Vanguard Press, 1927), pp. 301-303; E. P. Hutchinson, *Legislative History of American Immigration Policy, 1798-1965* (Philadelphia: University of Pennsylvania Press, 1981), p. 97.

8. Commons, *History of Labor*, II, 414.

9. Rayback, *History of American Labor*, pp. 168-69; Pierce, *History of Chicago*, III, 289; Wiebe, *Search for Order*, p. 79.

10. *The Commonweal*, June 29, 1889; Adelman, *Haymarket Revisited*, p. 39.

11. *Mother Earth*, November 1912; Adelman, *Haymarket Revisited*, p. 39.

12. Ironically, the restoration was paid for in part by the Chicago Teamsters' Union. *The International Teamster*, April 1971. I am grateful to Sally Genn for calling my attention to this item.

13. *New York Times*, October 8, 1969, October 6, 1970, February 12, 1972; Adelman, *Haymarket Revisited*, pp. 39-40.

14. E. B. McKenzie to A. H. Simpson, November 3, 1887, Parsons Papers.

15. *Liberty*, July 31, 1886.

16. *Autobiographies of the Haymarket Martyrs*, p. 91. Cf. *Famous Speeches*, p. 33; and Ross Winn, "A Voice from Texas," *The Rebel*, October 20, 1895: "Their death was the real beginning of the Anarchist propaganda in America."

17. *The Rebel*, November 20, 1895; Dr. Michael A. Cohn, *Free Society*, November 24, 1901.

18. Goldman, *Living My Life*, pp. 9-10, 508; Goldman to Samuel Klaus, February 7, 1930, Nettlau Archive.

19. Alexander Berkman to Hudson Hawley, June 12, 1932, Berkman Archive; *Mother Earth*, November 1912.

20. Emma Goldman, *Voltairine de Cleyre* (Berkeley Heights, N.J.: The Oriole Press, 1932), p. 41.

21. See Avrich, *An American Anarchist*, pp. 47-51; and de Cleyre, *Haymarket Speeches*.

22. William D. Haywood, *Bill Haywood's Book: The Autobiography of William D. Haywood* (New York: International Publishers, 1929), p. 31.

23. "The Chicago Anniversary," *Freedom*, December 1888.

24. In the United States, however, the A F of L had already been observing the first Monday of September as Labor Day and did not shift the date to conform to European practice. See Sidney Fine, "Is May Day American in Origin?" *The Historian* 16 (Spring 1954), 121-34.

25. *Freedom*, November 1889, November 1890.
26. Gompers, *Seventy Years*, p. 239.
27. Hippolyte Havel, "After Twenty-Five Years," *Mother Earth*, November 1912; *The Road to Freedom*, March 1928; Olga Lang, *Pa Chin and His Writings* (Cambridge, Mass.: Harvard University Press, 1967), pp. 126, 225, 254.
28. *Mother Earth*, November 1916.
29. Witter Bynner, *Journey with Genius* (New York: John Day & Co., 1951), p. 52.
30. O. William Neebe to Paul Avrich, June 8, 1981.
31. *Life of Albert R. Parsons*, p. xxxv.
32. *Freedom*, December 1888, December 1898.

Chapter 27: The Bombthrower

1. Altgeld, *Reasons*, p. 49.
2. *Workmen's Advocate*, May 14, 1887.
3. *Famous Speeches*, pp. 77, 93; Lloyd, *Henry Demarest Lloyd*, I, 106. Cf. William H. Parsons in *Life of Albert R. Parsons*, pp. 6-7.
4. *Famous Speeches*, p. 95; *Autobiographies of the Haymarket Martyrs*, p. 54.
5. *Die Autonomie*, April 7, 1887.
6. Schaack, *Anarchy and Anarchists*, pp. 174-75, 383-84. Cf. McLean, *Rise and Fall of Anarchy*, p. 19: "Rudolph Schnaubelt was the arch fiend who hurled the deadly bomb."
7. Agnes Inglis interview with George Schilling, June 22, 1933, Labadie Collection; Schmidt, *He Chose*, pp. 138-43.
8. Harris, *The Bomb*, p. 1. Harris, it would seem, borrowed this idea from Charles Edward Russell, who wrote in 1907 that Schnaubelt "made his way back to Germany, there to live and die in peace." *Shifting Scenes*, pp. 91-92, reprinted from *Appleton's Magazine*, September 1907.
9. *Mother Earth*, November 1914.
10. *Freedom* (New York), December 1933; Agnes Inglis interview with Lucy Parsons, June 21, 1933; Lucy Parsons to Carl Nold, January 17, 1933, Labadie Collection.
11. Franz Joseph Schnaubelt to Paul Avrich, March 20, 1981; Henry R. Schnaubelt to Paul Avrich, March 21, 1981; interview with Henry R. Schnaubelt, Stockton, Calif., September 24, 1981. A third brother, Henry, died of tuberculosis in San Diego at the age of thirty-five.
12. Franz Joseph Schnaubelt to Paul Avrich, March 8, 1981; interviews with Henry R. Schnaubelt, September 24, 1981; Dr. Milton W. Thorpe, Hayward, Calif., September 26, 1981; and Mary Schwab, Walnut Creek, Calif., September 26, 1981.

13. *The Commentator*, July 1937, pp. 79-80.
14. Fred Schnaubelt to Paul Avrich, March 12, 1980; Franz Joseph Schnaubelt to Paul Avrich, March 20, 1981.
15. *The Labor Enquirer* (Denver), May 15, 1886.
16. *Freiheit*, May 15, 1886; *Boston Herald*, May 16, 1886; *Mother Earth*, November 1912.
17. *Famous Speeches*, p. 12; *Autobiographies of the Haymarket Martyrs*, pp. 97-98.
18. Charles Doering, "The 11th of November," *The Firebrand*, November 7, 1896; T. P. Quinn, *Free Society*, November 6, 1898.
19. Nettlau, *Anarchisten und Sozialrevolutionäre*, p. 387. See also David, *History of the Haymarket Affair*, pp. 523-24.
20. Carl Nold to Agnes Inglis, January 12, 1933, Labadie Collection.
21. Lum, "August Spies," *Twentieth Century*, September 3, 1891. See also *The Alarm*, November 10, 1888.
22. *Lucifer*, May 21, 1886.
23. *The Alarm*, December 29, 1888.
24. *Chicago Herald*, November 27, 1887; de Cleyre, *Haymarket Speeches*, p. 5; Lum to de Cleyre, March 1, 1891, Ishill Papers, University of Florida.
25. De Cleyre, *Haymarket Speeches*, p. 12.
26. Jack McPhaul, "Who Hurled the Haymarket Bomb?" *Chicago Sun-Times*, May 5, 1957, based on an interview with Dr. Frank Heiner. See also David, *History of the Haymarket Affair*, p. ix.
27. *Chicago Tribune*, June 30, 1886.
28. *The Knights of Labor*, November 5, 1887; David, *History of the Haymarket Affair*, pp. 518-21.
29. Carl Nold to Agnes Inglis, January 12, 1933, Labadie Collection.
30. Nold to Inglis, March 1 and September 28, 1933, Labadie Collection.
31. Most, *Revolutionäre Kriegswissenschaft*, p. 61.
32. Nold to Inglis, September 28, 1933, Labadie Collection.

Chapter 28: Epilogue

1. Barnard, *Eagle Forgotten*, p. 237; *Free Society*, November 6, 1898.
2. Goldman, *Living My Life*, p. 221.
3. Adelman, *Haymarket Revisited*, pp. 107-108; interview with M. W. Thorpe.
4. *Abstract of Record*, I, 28-29; *Chicago Tribune*, July 3, 1893, July 5, 1894; Barnard, *Eagle Forgotten*, p. 238; Elizabeth Gurley Flynn, *The Rebel Girl: an Autobiography: My First Life (1906-1926)* (New York: International Publishers, 1973), p. 79; *Mother Earth*, May 1916; *The Alarm*, May 1916.

5. *The Rebel*, November 20, 1895; *Free Society*, November 6, 1898.

6. Lloyd, "A Visit to Sam. Fielden," *The Comrade*, February 1904; *Free Society*, November 27, 1898. See also Fielden's "Comments on the Trial," ibid., November 9, 1902.

7. Abbot, *Watching the World Go By*, p. 120; Keiser, *Building for the Centuries*, pp. 287-88.

8. *The Anarchist*, November 1887.

9. *I*, November 1898.

10. Zeisler, *Reminiscences of the Anarchist Case*, p. 18; Lloyd, *Henry Demarest Lloyd*, I, 105.

11. Kogan, "William Perkins Black," p. 94.

12. *Freedom* (Chicago), April 1, 1891.

13. *The Comrade*, February 1904.

14. Goldman, *Living My Life*, pp. 222-23.

15. Lizzie Holmes, "In Remembrance," *Free Society*, November 10, 1901; *The Road to Freedom*, September 1, 1926, February 1929.

16. Frank O. Beck, *Hobohemia* (Rindge, N.H.: Richard R. Smith, 1956), p. 62.

17. Irving S. Abrams in *Freespace*, December 5, 1978; Abrams to Agnes Inglis, February 1, 1949, Labadie Collection; Ralph Chaplin, *Wobbly: The Rough-and-Tumble Story of an American Radical* (Chicago: University of Chicago Press, 1948), pp. 364-65.

18. Ashbaugh, *Lucy Parsons*, pp. 259-60.

19. *Man!*, March 1936; Beck, *Hobohemia*, pp. 64-66; Chaplin, *Wobbly*, pp. 364-65.

20. *Free Society*, November 6, 1898.

21. *The Knights of Labor*, October 19, 1889; *The Commonweal*, November 16, 1889.

22. *The Commonweal*, August 11, 1888; Graham Taylor, *Pioneering on Social Frontiers* (Chicago: University of Chicago Press, 1930), pp. 131-32.

23. Ashbaugh, *Lucy Parsons*, pp. 207-208.

24. *Proceedings of the First Convention of the IWW*, pp. 56, 169.

25. Lucy E. Parsons, *The Principles of Anarchism* (Chicago: L. E. Parsons, n.d.), p. 3.

26. Chaplin, *Wobbly*, p. 168; Lang, *Tomorrow Is Beautiful*, p. 31; unidentified clipping, Parsons Papers.

27. See, for example, *The Alarm*, June 30, 1888.

28. *Lucifer*, September 29, 1900.

29. *Freedom*, May 1898; *Mother Earth*, May 1913; Whipple, *Story of Civil Liberty*, pp. 308-309.

30. "Rattler" to Lucy Parsons, January 28, 1889, Parsons Papers.

31. Lucy Parsons, introduction to Calmer, *Labor Agitator*, p. 5.

32. Lucy Parsons to Carl Nold, September 25, 1930, February 27, 1934, Labadie Collection. Emma Goldman complained to Alexander Berkman that Lucy "goes with every gang proclaiming itself revolutionary." *Nowhere at Home: Letters from Exile of Emma Goldman and Alexander Berkman*, ed. Richard and Anna Maria Drinnon (New York: Schocken Books, 1975), p. 170.
33. Lucy Parsons to George Schilling, September 19, 1935, Schilling Papers; Ashbaugh, *Lucy Parsons*, pp. 256-57.
34. Beck, *Hobohemia*, p. 57.
35. Unidentified clipping, Parsons Papers.
36. Ammon A. Hennacy, *The One-Man Revolution in America* (Salt Lake City: Hennacy Publications, 1970), p. 150.
37. George Schilling to Lucy Parsons, December 1, 1893, Schilling Papers. Cf. Philip Van Patten to Schilling, April 11, 1893, Schilling Papers.
38. William Holmes, "Methods of Propaganda," *Solidarity*, December 17, 1892.
39. Johann Most to Max Nettlau, October 24, 1890, Nettlau Archive.
40. Fischer to Oglesby, November 1, 1887, in McLean, *Rise and Fall of Anarchy*, p. 215.
41. Alexander Berkman, *Now and After: The ABC of Communist Anarchism* (New York: Vanguard Press, 1929), p. 60.
42. *Freedom*, November 1888.

BIBLIOGRAPHY

Although there has been only one previous full-length history of the Haymarket affair, the literature on the case is so voluminous that a comprehensive list of sources would fill a sizable volume in itself. What follows makes no attempt at being an exhaustive bibliography. It includes, rather, only the principal manuscript collections and periodicals, along with secondary works that are particularly useful and important. The full range of sources, both archival and printed, is cited in the reference notes to the text.

Archival Materials

The Chicago Historical Society houses a rich collection of Haymarket materials, including letters, photographs, leaflets, police reports, records of the Pioneer Aid and Support Association, and a complete transcript of the trial, of which the *Abstract of Record* is a two-volume abridgment.

The Newberry Library in Chicago has the papers of Carter H. Harrison (including letters from August Spies and John Peter Altgeld), two boxes of clippings on the case, and a number of relevant periodicals.

The Illinois State Historical Library at Springfield houses the papers of Governors Oglesby, Fifer, and Altgeld, as well as of George A. Schilling (augmented by further Schilling papers at the University of Chicago).

The Illinois State Archives, Springfield, contain the Executive Clemency Files, with extensive material reflecting the efforts to obtain a commutation of the sentences imposed on the anarchists, and additional papers of Governors Oglesby, Fifer, and Altgeld.

The State Historical Society of Wisconsin at Madison has the papers of Albert R. Parsons, Richard T. Ely, Henry Demarest Lloyd, and Cyrus H. McCormick, Jr., along with photographs and printed materials.

The Labadie Collection at the University of Michigan, Ann Arbor, contains letters of August Spies, Adolph Fischer, Lucy Parsons, Nina Van Zandt, William Holmes, Dyer Lum, George Schilling, and other important figures in the case, as well as a Haymarket scrapbook, photographs, leaflets, and an array of additional sources.

The Julius S. Grinnell Collection, held by H. P. Kraus Rare Books of New York, is an important source of printed and manuscript materials accumulated by the prosecutor in the case.

Other significant materials, including scrapbooks, correspondence, and photographs, are to be found in the Tamiment Library of New York University, the Special Collections Division of Columbia University, the International Institute of Social History at Amsterdam (especially the Socialist League Archive, Nettlau Archive, Peukert Archive, Berkman Archive, and letters of Johann Most and Michael Schwab), the University of Illinois at Urbana (The Baskette Collection and the Thomas J. Morgan Papers), the Houghton Library of Harvard University (the papers of William Dean Howells and the Joseph Ishill Collection), the University of Florida at Gainesville (further Ishill materials, including letters of Dyer Lum), Knox College in Galesburg, Illinois (the papers of William M. Salter), the University of California at Berkeley (the Haskell and International Workmen's Association Papers), and the New York Public Library (the papers of Henry George and miscellaneous printed sources).

Newspapers and Journals

In addition to the Chicago daily press, the following periodicals are the most significant:

The Alarm. Chicago, New York, 1884-1889. Edited by Albert R. Parsons and Dyer D. Lum.

The Alarm. Chicago, 1915-1916. Edited by Lucy E. Parsons.

Anarchist. Chicago, 1886. Edited by George Engel and Adolph Fischer.

Der Anarchist. St. Louis, New York, 1889-1895. Edited by Claus Timmermann.

The An-archist. Boston, 1881. Edited by Edward Nathan-Ganz.

Der arme Teufel. Detroit, 1884-1900. Edited by Robert Reitzel.

Die Autonomie. London, 1886-1893. Edited by Josef Peukert.

Die Brandfackel. New York, 1893-1894. Edited by Claus Timmermann.

Budoucnost. Chicago, 1883-1886. Edited by Norbert Zoula.

Chicagoer Arbeiter-Zeitung. Chicago, 1876ff. (with Saturday and Sunday editions, *Der Vorbote* and *Die Fackel*). Edited by August Spies, Michael Schwab et al.

The Commonweal. London, 1885-1894. Edited by William Morris.

Dělnické Listy. Chicago, 1887-1893. Edited by F. J. Hlaváček.

The Demonstrator. Home, Washington, 1903-1908. Edited by James F. Morton, Jr.

Discontent. Home, Washington, 1898-1902. Edited by Charles L. Govan et al.

The Firebrand. Portland, Oregon, 1895-1897. Edited by Abe Isaak et al.

Free Society. San Francisco, Chicago, New York, 1897-1904. Edited by Abe Isaak.

Freedom. London, 1886-1927. Edited by Peter Kropotkin et al.

Freedom. New York, Chicago, 1890-1892. Edited by Lucy E. Parsons.

Freiheit. New York, 1882-1910. Edited by Johann Most (published in England and Switzerland, 1879-1882).

The Individualist. Denver, 1889-1890. Edited by Frank Q. Stuart.

John Swinton's Paper. New York, 1883-1887. Edited by John Swinton.

Der Kämpfer. St. Louis, 1896. Edited by Otto Rinke.

The Knights of Labor. Chicago, 1880s. Edited by George E. Detwiler.

The Labor Enquirer. Denver, 1882-1888; Chicago, 1887-1888. Edited by Joseph R. Buchanan et al.

The Liberator. Chicago, 1905-1906. Edited by Lucy E. Parsons.

Liberty. Boston, New York, 1881-1908. Edited by Benjamin R. Tucker.

Lucifer. Valley Falls, Topeka, Chicago, 1883-1907. Edited by Moses Harman.

Mother Earth. New York, 1906-1917. Edited by Emma Goldman and Alexander Berkman.

Nemesis. Baltimore, 1884.

New England Anzeiger. New Haven, 1878-1885. Edited by Paul Gebhard.

New Jersey Arbeiter-Zeitung. Jersey City Heights, 1884.

Den Nye Tid. Chicago, 1880s. Edited by Peter Peterson.

Die Parole. St. Louis, 1884-1890. Edited by Joseph Reifgraber.

Práce. Chicago, 1887.

Proletář. New York, 1885ff.

The Rebel. Boston, 1895-1896. Edited by Harry Kelly et al.

The Socialist. Chicago, 1878-1879. Edited by Frank Hirth, assistant editor, Albert R. Parsons.

Solidarity. New York, 1892-1898. Edited by F. S. Merlino and John H. Edelmann.

Sturmvogel. New York, 1897-1899. Edited by Claus Timmermann.

Truth. San Francisco, 1882-1884. Edited by Burnette G. Haskell.

Twentieth Century. New York, 1888-1898. Edited by Hugh O. Pentecost.

The Word. Princeton, Massachusetts, 1872-1893. Edited by Ezra H. Heywood.

Workmen's Advocate. New Haven, 1885-1891.

Die Zukunft. Philadelphia, 1884-1885. Edited by Moritz A. Bachmann.

Books and Articles

The History of the Haymarket Affair by Henry David, published in 1936 by Farrar & Rinehart and reissued, with a new introduction, in 1958 by Russell & Russell, remains an informative work. Alan Calmer's *Labor Agitator: The Story of Albert R. Parsons* (New York: International Publishers, 1937), is a readable popular biography, though lacking in documentation. Carolyn Ashbaugh's *Lucy Parsons: American Revolutionary* (Chicago: Charles H. Kerr Publishing Company, 1976) contains much valuable material. William J. Adelman, *Haymarket Revisited* (Chicago: The Illinois Labor History Society, 1976) provides a helpful guide to Chicago, centering on the events of the case. And *The Chicago Haymarket Riot: Anarchy on Trial*, edited by Bernard R. Kogan (Boston: D. C. Heath, 1959) is a useful collection of primary sources.

Two works of fundamental importance are *The Autobiographies of the Haymarket Martyrs*, edited by Philip S. Foner (New York: Humanities Press, 1969), and *The Famous Speeches of the Eight Chicago Anarchists in Court* (2d ed., Chicago: Lucy E. Parsons, 1910), originally published in 1886 by the Socialistic Publishing Society and reissued in several editions. For further material in the same vein the reader should consult Lucy E. Parsons, ed., *Life of Albert R. Parsons* (2d ed., Chicago: Lucy E. Parsons, 1903), which first appeared in 1889; Albert Parsons, *Anarchism: Its Philosophy and Scientific Basis as Defined by Some of Its Apostles* (Chicago: Lucy E. Parsons, 1887); *August Spies' Auto-Biography* (Chicago: Nina Van Zandt, 1887); and *Reminiscenzen von August Spies*, edited by Albert Currlin (Chicago: Christine Spies, 1888).

The best biography of Johann Most remains Rudolf Rocker's *Johann Most: Das Leben eines Rebellen* (Berlin: "Der Syndikalist," 1924), while the best biography of Governor Altgeld is Harry Barnard's *"Eagle Forgotten": The Life of John Peter Altgeld* (Indianapolis: Bobbs-Merrill, 1938), both containing much information on the case. Other works of significance are Dyer D. Lum, *A Concise History of the Great Trial of the Chicago Anarchists in 1886* (Chicago: Socialistic Publishing Company, 1887); John D. Lawson, ed., *American State Trials*, XII (St. Louis: F. H. Thomas Law Book Co., 1919), containing an abbreviated record of the trial; Michael J. Schaack, *Anarchy and Anarchists* (Chicago: F. J. Schulte, 1889); and Max Nettlau, *Anarchisten und Sozialrevolutionäre* (Berlin: "Der Syndikalist," 1931). Finally, among the most important articles are the recollections of William and Lizzie Holmes cited in the reference notes, and Samuel P. McConnell, "The Chicago Bomb Case: Personal Recollections of an American Tragedy," *Harper's Magazine*, May 1934.

INDEX

Library of Congress Cataloging in Publication Data

Avrich, Paul.
The Haymarket tragedy.

Bibliography: p.   Includes index.
1. Chicago (Ill.)—Haymarket Square Riot, 1886.
2. Anarchism and anarchists—United States—
History—19th century. I. Title.
HX846.C4A97   1984   335'.83'0973   83-26924
ISBN 0-691-04711-1 (alk. paper)
ISBN 0-691-00600-8 (pbk.)

Paul Avrich is Distinguished Professor of History at
Queens College and the Graduate School, City University of New York.
He is the author of several books on Russian and American anarchists.